# Transformational Leadership Styles, Management Strategies, and Communication for Global Leaders

Darcia Ann Marie Roache
*University of Saskatchewan, Canada*

A volume in the Advances in Logistics, Operations, and Management Science (ALOMS) Book Series

IGI Global
PUBLISHER of TIMELY KNOWLEDGE

Published in the United States of America by
IGI Global
Business Science Reference (an imprint of IGI Global)
701 E. Chocolate Avenue
Hershey PA, USA 17033
Tel: 717-533-8845
Fax: 717-533-8661
E-mail: cust@igi-global.com
Web site: http://www.igi-global.com



Library of Congress Cataloging-in-Publication Data

Names: Roache, Darcia Ann-Marie, 1970- editor.
Title: Transformational leadership styles, management strategies, and communication for global leaders / edited by Darcia Ann-Marie Roache.
Description: Hershey, PA : Business Science Reference, [2023] | Includes bibliographical references and index. | Summary: "This book will aim to provide relevant theoretical, conceptual/procedural, frameworks, and the latest empirical research findings in the that critically examines area of leadership, leadership styles, management studies, and communication for leaders globally. It will be written for professionals, organizational leaders, and practitioners who want to improve their understanding of leadership roles, styles, management practices, principles, and communication strategies to bring about change, information, and knowledge to society"-- Provided by publisher.
Identifiers: LCCN 2023010027 (print) | LCCN 2023010028 (ebook) | ISBN 9781668488225 (hardcover) | ISBN 9781668488232 (paperback) | ISBN 9781668488249 (ebook)
Subjects: LCSH: Leadership. | Management--Technological innovations. | Employee motivation. | Interpersonal communication. | Communication in management. | Communication in organizations.
Classification: LCC HD57.7 .T7323 2023 (print) | LCC HD57.7 (ebook) | DDC 658.4/092--dc23/eng/20230302
LC record available at https://lccn.loc.gov/2023010027
LC ebook record available at https://lccn.loc.gov/2023010028

This book is published in the IGI Global book series Advances in Logistics, Operations, and Management Science (ALOMS) (ISSN: 2327-350X; eISSN: 2327-3518)

British Cataloguing in Publication Data
A Cataloguing in Publication record for this book is available from the British Library.

# Advances in Logistics, Operations, and Management Science (ALOMS) Book Series

John Wang
Montclair State University, USA

ISSN:2327-350X
EISSN:2327-3518

## Mission

Operations research and management science continue to influence business processes, administration, and management information systems, particularly in covering the application methods for decision-making processes. New case studies and applications on management science, operations management, social sciences, and other behavioral sciences have been incorporated into business and organizations real-world objectives.

The **Advances in Logistics, Operations, and Management Science** (ALOMS) Book Series provides a collection of reference publications on the current trends, applications, theories, and practices in the management science field. Providing relevant and current research, this series and its individual publications would be useful for academics, researchers, scholars, and practitioners interested in improving decision making models and business functions.

## Coverage

- Networks
- Risk management
- Computing and information technologies
- Operations Management
- Production Management
- Organizational Behavior
- Marketing engineering
- Decision analysis and decision support
- Information Management
- Finance

IGI Global is currently accepting manuscripts for publication within this series. To submit a proposal for a volume in this series, please contact our Acquisition Editors at Acquisitions@igi-global.com or visit: http://www.igi-global.com/publish/.

The Advances in Logistics, Operations, and Management Sciencc (ALOMS) Book Series (ISSN 2327-350X) is published by IGI Global, 701 E. Chocolate Avenue, Hershey, PA 17033-1240, USA, www.igi-global.com. This series is composed of titles available for purchase individually; each title is edited to be contextually exclusive from any other title within the series. For pricing and ordering information please visit http://www.igi-global.com/book-series/advances-logistics-operations-management-science/37170. Postmaster: Send all address changes to above address. 

## Titles in this Series

*For a list of additional titles in this series, please visit: www.igi-global.com/book-series*

***New Perspectives and Possibilities in Strategic Management in the 21st Century Between Tradition and Modernity***
Javier Martínez-Falcó (University of Alicante, Spain & Stellenbosch University, South Africa) Bartolomé Marco-Lajara (University of Alicante, Spain) Eduardo Sánchez-García (University of Alicante, Spain) and Luis A. Millan-Tudela (University of Alicante, Spain)
Business Science Reference • © 2023 • 514pp • H/C (ISBN: 9781668492611) • US $315.00

***Government Impact on Sustainable and Responsible Supply Chain Management***
Atour Taghipour (Normandy University, France)
Information Science Reference • © 2023 • 354pp • H/C (ISBN: 9781668490624) • US $240.00

***Transport and Logistics Planning and Optimization***
Jaouad Boukachour (University of Le Havre, France) and Abdelhamid Benaini (University of Le Havre, France)
Business Science Reference • © 2023 • 317pp • H/C (ISBN: 9781668484746) • US $250.00

***Black Women's Formal and Informal Ways of Leadership Actualizing the Vision of a More Equitable Workplace***
Audrey D. Bowser (Arkansas State University, USA) Kimberley M. Davis (University of Arkansas at Pine Bluff, USA) and Natalie A. Johnson-Leslie (Arkansas State University, USA)
Information Science Reference • © 2023 • 300pp • H/C (ISBN: 9781668438275) • US $215.00

***Considerations and Characteristics of the Millennial Leader in Today's Global Society***
Tymon M. Graham (TMGraham Consulting, LLC, USA)
Business Science Reference • © 2023 • 300pp • H/C (ISBN: 9781668447116) • US $240.00

***The Economics of Talent Management and Human Capital***
Sharif Uddin Ahmed Rana (Paris Graduate School and World Talent Economy Forum, Malaysia) and Adrian David Cheok (Imagineering Institute, Malaysia)
Business Science Reference • © 2023 • 300pp • H/C (ISBN: 9781668466414) • US $235.00

***Entrepreneurship Ecosystems and Their Opportunities and Challenges***
Mohammed El Amine Abdelli (University of Brest, France) Shajara Ul-Durar (University for Creative Arts, UK) and Hala Wasef Hattab (British University in Egypt, Egypt)
Business Science Reference • © 2023 • 300pp • H/C (ISBN: 9781668471401) • US $250.00

IGI Global
PUBLISHER of TIMELY KNOWLEDGE

701 East Chocolate Avenue, Hershey, PA 17033, USA
Tel: 717-533-8845 x100 • Fax: 717-533-8661
E-Mail: cust@igi-global.com • www.igi-global.com

*To empowerment, motivation, continuity, and transformational leadership for all those who mentor, lead, and guide others, globally. Knowledge, communication, and management strategies are assigned for your flourishing!*

# Table of Contents

# Detailed Table of Contents

discussion. The findings from the panel discussion identified the themes of mindfulness, radical candor, professionalism, relatability, resilience, and engagement. These themes provide the skills needed for aspiring school principals to lead schools toward a vision of academic excellence.



The purpose of this chapter was to determine the type of leadership of a high school principal in Kingston, Jamaica. The sample size was 74. The data collection methods were a questionnaire and an interview. The results showed that the students and teachers perceived their principal as displaying transformational and transactional leadership styles, while the principal saw himself as a situational leader. The results also showed changes in the school, namely the number of student passes in the Caribbean Secondary Education Certificate Examinations and the Caribbean Advanced Proficiency Examinations, infrastructural upgrades and developments, and an increase in the participation of students and teachers in sports and extracurricular activities.



In order for higher education institutions (HEIs) in Africa to sustain higher education (HE), it is critical to re-examine leadership style and knowledge in the post-COVID-19 pandemic, especially dissemination of knowledge. Due to the effects of the pandemic on HEIs and its trajectory, this chapter is motivated to explore leadership style and knowledge in Africa's HEIs. Specifically, this chapter explores types of leadership styles and open knowledge in transforming HEIs in Africa. This chapter uses a literature review approach and content analysis. One of the findings of this chapter is that there are varying dynamics and evolution in transforming HEIs in Africa particularly from an open knowledge approach. The implication is for HEI experts and stakeholders to instill HE for societal good in transforming HEIs in Africa that focuses on open knowledge approach particularly in the post-COVID-19 pandemic so that HEIs are not only providing HE but HE for good.



The chapter explored administrative communications from schools, divisions, and the province as perceived by special education teachers in Saskatchewan, Canada during school closures. Through one-on-one online interviews and a thematic analysis, the present study investigated how and how often school leaders communicated with school staff, and what they communicated about, as well as what special education teachers were concerned about regarding administrative communications across the board. Most staff meetings were held virtually on a weekly basis with one exception: meetings were held infrequently at one federal school. Teachers felt that these meetings helped facilitate the discussions among teachers and school leaders about online teaching and learning. Ineffective communications between administration at different levels was a concern for teachers because some communications were delayed and insensitive to the needs of students and their families as well as teachers. Finally, educational implications for crisis leadership were also discussed in this chapter.



Leadership is a concept applicable in all fields and beneficial to all. The benefits individuals receive from leaders heavily depend on the leadership styles that leaders use. Hackett stated that leadership is the most critical competency for any organization that aims to develop its people. School leadership is a salient part of students learning in all educational institutions, and as such, the type of leadership that is practiced in schools is crucial to the teaching, classroom procedures, and the school environment as these impact student performance. Bass states that transformational leadership is how leaders' behaviours impact their followers. Bass and Avolio stated that the transformational leadership style allows individuals to feel valued and gives them a sense of purpose, respect, and trust in their leaders. This chapter focuses on the impact of transformational leadership styles on educational stakeholders.



This chapter presents a secondary analysis of five case studies to explore leadership dynamics in the context of the "new normal." This analysis illuminates the essential role of transformational leadership in addressing emergent challenges. The chapter focuses on four primary facets: emotional intelligence; conflict management; diversity, equity, and inclusion; and fostering an environment of learning and development. Results reveal that successful leaders can navigate conflict effectively and encourage emotional intelligence; enhance diversity, equity, and inclusion; and promote an ecosystem for learning and development within their teams. Further, findings demonstrate that cultivating transformational leadership styles can significantly enhance these competencies. As such, transformational leadership emerges as a crucial strategy for organizations aiming to succeed in the new normal. The chapter concludes with recommendations for leaders and organizations based on the insights gleaned from the case studies.



Leadership has been widely studied and recognized as important over time. This chapter has two main objectives. The first one is to analyse the perceptions that individuals have about leadership, either as a trait or a process, and the extent to which such perceptions are influenced by age. Secondly, the chapter aims to understand the presence of authentic leaders and if a person's age defines the relevance of this type of leadership. To attain these purposes, the concept of leadership is analyzed, as the transactional

# Foreword

The world around us is going through a period of significant change. Whether the change is political, technological or societal leaders must rise to the challenge and guide their organizations amidst this turmoil. To find a successful pathway through requires a leadership approach that understands the impact of change thereby embracing change. One such approach is transformational leadership. This volume of academic endeavors dives into the influence of transformational leadership on organizations and employees. It accomplishes this by looking at various perspectives of transformational leadership, the significance of leadership, skills, knowledge and abilities required, and the effectiveness of it.

This volume is broken into four sections. The first section includes three chapters. These chapters form a holistic view of leadership and sets the reader up with a clearer picture of the context and definition of leadership. The editor, Dr. Darcia Roache starts it all off with a look at "Management and Communication Taxonomies of a Transformational Leadership Approach for Organizational Effectiveness." By doing so, she underpins the justification for the volume. The next chapter, as any wise academic will tell you to do, lays out the definition of leadership and various approaches. Dr. Benson's chapter provides the reader with a clear overview of leadership approaches. By doing so, he sets the stage for the remaining chapters to build on that understanding and provide the reader with the basis of comparison. The final chapter in the first section takes us past theory and into the realty of leadership. Dr. Natasha Johnson's chapter, "Leadership in Action: An Introspective Reflection," pulls the reader into the real world. Here we get a deeper understanding of the complexities faced by leaders in the dynamic environment we face today.

Through the media we see the focus of the ever-changing environment through the lens point of either political or business reactions. What is often neglected is the need to educate the future members of society that will either play the role of implementing change as employees or managers. But education also needs to develop leaders that can step forward and guides us through the transformation created by innovation and nature. This is the emphasis of the next section, "Transformational Leadership in Educational Institutions."

This section contains six chapters. The lead chapter, "Enabling Transformational Complexity Leadership in Education" by Dr. Beryl Peters and Timothy Shawn Beyak, serves to open our eyes and minds to the complexities in education today. The authors bring out the justification for the application of transformation leadership but do by guiding us through the factors needed to enable transformation. Veysel Altunel, Elizabeth Castro, Saleria Shaffer, Paula Thompson, and Dr. Carlos Lee follow this up with an investigation of what factors are required by Principals in elementary schools. Their chapter, "An Examination of Transformational School Leadership Qualities of Elementary Principals," brings to us a clear picture of what it takes to navigate this new environment from a human perspective.

The next chapter moves us forward from justifying the need and understanding the qualities needed by a transformational leader to getting a glimpse of the impact of transformational leadership. Prof. Cynthia Onyefulu and Dr. Tashieka Simone Burris-Melville in their chapter, "Assessing the Impact of Transformational Leadership Style at a Selected High School in Jamaica," illustrate the power and depth of change that a transformational leader can bring about. For the next chapter, "Leadership Style and Knowledge in Transforming Higher Education Institutions in Africa," Dr. Kezia Herman Mkwizu dives deeper into what it takes for a leader to undertake transforming an organization in the education environment. The ensuing chapter provides insight into yet another facet of the educational system, the special education sector. The chapter, "Administrative Communications Among School Leaders and Special Education Teachers During COVID-19" by Dr. Pei-Ying Lin, illustrates the impact of the pandemic on communication and how leaders dealt with it.

The final chapter of the section completes the picture of the impact of transformational leadership by exploring the perspectives of various stakeholders in the educational setting. Dr. Kareen Reid's, chapter on "The Impact of Transformational Leadership Style on Educational Stakeholders" is an insightful investigation on how leadership does not merely impact the followers but a wide range of people and organizations. We are reminded that we do not live and work in a bubble and thus must be aware of the ripple effect of our actions.

The next section, "Leadership, Skills, and Motivation," includes six chapters moves away from the educational environment and guides us through different factors of leadership. Dr. Suzzette Ann-Marie Harriott indicates that in a post pandemic world we will need transformational leaders who understand and utilize emotional intelligence to help followers make sense of the world around them. The chapter, "Leadership in the New Normal: Navigating Conflict, Empowering Emotional Intelligence Through Cultivating Transformational Leaders," exposes the growing complexity and the conflict arising from and within it that leaders need to deal with. As Dr. Harriott rightly points out, a transformational leadership approach fused with emotional intelligence presents a strong voice to carry us forward.

The next two chapters move away from transformational leadership to provide a more balanced and open view of leadership in these chaotic times. What is the impact of age as a factor in the perception of leadership is the focus of "Authentic Leadership: Does Age Influence How Leadership Is Perceived?" by Dr. Susana Bernardino and Dr. Beatriz Teixeira. This fascinating chapter is followed by an equally fascinating chapter on the influence of culture on leadership. "Inclusive Leadership in the Amish Community" by Dr. Charles Keim and Hannah Keim provides significant insight into not only a different leadership approach but also the impact of faith and culture on leadership. When we think of the Amish communities, we think of a community that turns away from the turmoil in our environment, but the authors open us up to how this group of people deal with change from an inclusive perspective. Dr. Ansar Abbas and co-authors' chapter, "The Path of an Independent Thinker to an Inclusive Leader: The Journey of Leadership Transformation," leads the reader on an insightful analysis of the journey of Imran Khan, the former Prime Minister of Pakistan. The work follows him along the path from cricketer to a transformative inclusive leader.

The next two chapters explore motivational skills required by leaders to create employee engagement to achieve organizational goals. The research setting moves from Pakistan to Albania in an exploration of the impact of a leader's ability to motivate followers in a for-profit organization. Alma Duklaska, Alessandro Ferrazza and Dr. Giuseppe Cantafio utilize a case study approach to reveal that motivational variables such as recognition and reward did have a positive influence on engagement and job satisfaction. However, it appeared to have no impact on turnover intentions. To gain a deeper understanding of motivation and the theories of it, Muhammad Junaid Ahsan, walks the reader through the evolution of the theories of motivation.

The last section of the book, "Approaches and Application of Leadership," tackles key components of leadership approaches. In the section, seven (7) chapters unlock the intricacies of the application of those approaches from different perspectives such as change management and sustainability. The section starts with Dr. Quisenberry and co-author's "Complexities of Change Management Strategy During Healthcare Mergers." Here we get first-hand perspective of the complexities of a merger within the healthcare sector. The authors use their experience and knowledge to walk the reader through the success and not so successful change management strategies used by leaders. The next chapter of the section revisits emotional intelligence but within small and medium enterprises. The Relationship Between Emotional Intelligence and Leadership Styles of Managers in Small and Medium Enterprises by Ashly Nyathi and Dr. Sadrag Panduleni Shihomeka provides insights from frontline managers on leaderships approaches the impact of emotional intelligence.

Christell Chesney, Dr. Simon Black, Shanna Challenger, and Arica Hill put forward the argument that leadership plays a key role in the longevity of sustainability programs. Their chapter, "Leadership for Longevity and Sustainability in Antigua and Barbuda, West Indies: The Offshore Islands Conservation Program," highlights the need to ensure leadership skills and careful recruitment to maintain organization drive and continued success. Dr. Pérez-Uribe and colleagues add happiness as a desired outcome for leaders. Their research presented in their chapter, "Happiness at Work in Colombian Companies: A Perspective Under the Rise Model," reasons that to generate a harmonious organizational culture leaders should strive to strengthen happiness in the workplace.

The last three (3) chapters explore what support do leaders need to achieve goals. "The Art of Team Science: Exploring Team Dynamics and Implications for Leadership Practice" by Dr. Ralph Gigliott, Alexis Rotondo, Dr. Daniel Horton, and Dr. Nancy Reichman investigates the need for leaders to encourage building relationships, processes and structures to facilitate team effectiveness. Dr. Kevin Richardson and Dr. Darrell Norman Burrell return to the concept of sustainability with "The Intersection of Social Entrepreneurship, Sustainability, and Environmental Public Health." They provide the reader with a deeper understanding of the connections between social entrepreneurship and its contributions of to sustainability within the field of environmental public health. The final chapter rounds it all off with a call for organizations to add a Chief Strategic Transformational Officer to their top management team. Dr. Simon Cleveland and Dr. Marisa Cleveland argument is a sign of the growing importance of the need to recognize the volatility of the environment we live in by organizations.

This volume moves from the holistic view to more detailed nuances regarding transformational leadership. More importantly it does so from multiple perspectives. We see it from the various levels of education, from public to private organizations, from theoretical to practical, from different leadership approaches, cultural lens, and with an international scope. This clearly indicates the complexity of the issues of transformational leadership, communication, and change management. The dedication of this volume is to those who empower, motivate, seek continuity by mentoring, leading, and guiding others through transformational leadership, globally. It is only through the combined efforts of us all that we open the opportunities to grow, learn and make this world a better place today and tomorrow.

I could continue on in further detail about the need for transformational leadership, the necessary skills and the transformative power that is needed today. However, I will not because the chapters in this volume do so with more knowledge and wisdom then I possess. So, I encourage you to read this volume if you are a leader, follower, educator, public servant or business person. The knowledge and insights you will gain from it will open doors of understanding and help clear the vision of tomorrow.

*S. Bruce Thomson*
*MacEwan University, Canada*

# Preface

As the editor of *Transformational Leadership Styles, Management Strategies, and Communication for Global Leaders,* I am thrilled to present this edited reference book that delves into the dynamic and influential world of leadership, management, and communication within organizations. The impact of transformational leadership styles and effective management strategies on organizational effectiveness and employee performance cannot be overstated, and this book aims to explore, discuss, and recommend perspectives and approaches to help leaders thrive in today's global landscape.

Over the years, the concept of leadership has evolved, adapting to various situations, practices, and change management approaches in organizations. Transformational leadership, in particular, plays a crucial role in motivating and inspiring others to collectively work towards achieving an organization's vision and mission. As we move forward, it is evident that leadership requires a paradigm shift to address the challenges and opportunities in organizational behavior, motivation, communication, and management functions. Thus, the need for a comprehensive and authoritative edited book on transformational leadership, management strategies, and communication for global leaders becomes increasingly apparent.

This book aspires to provide readers with relevant theoretical frameworks, conceptual insights, procedural guidelines, and the latest empirical research findings in the realm of leadership, leadership styles, management studies, and communication. Whether you are a seasoned professional, an aspiring organizational leader, or a practitioner seeking to enhance your understanding of leadership roles, styles, management practices, principles, and communication strategies, this book aims to equip you with valuable knowledge to drive positive change in your sphere of influence.

I have carefully curated a diverse range of topics that cover essential aspects of leadership, including the theories of leadership and communication, the impact of transformational leadership styles, leadership and relationship building, emotional intelligence, change management, sustainability, performance management, motivational theories, social justice, and much more. The content presented here is meant to inspire new ideas, challenge existing beliefs, and stimulate constructive discussions among readers from various sectors, such as business, education, and beyond.

## CHAPTER OVERVIEWS

Chapter 1 delves into a grounded theory approach to explore the relationship between transformational leadership, management practices, and communication strategies on organizational effectiveness and employee performance. The findings from interviews with participants from various countries contribute to the global understanding of leadership success factors.

A comprehensive overview of leadership definitions, historical evolution, and classification of leadership theories forms the foundation of Chapter 2. By providing this contextual understanding, the chapter sets the stage for exploring transformational leadership's distinctive features within the broader landscape of leadership theories.

The focus of Chapter 3 is on introspective leadership, emphasizing reflective practice as a crucial element for effective leadership. The chapter highlights the cyclical nature of introspection and its role in guiding leaders to analyze, personalize, and reinforce their actions, interactions, and outcomes.

Chapter 4 delves into Complexity Leadership Theory, exploring how it can be applied to address challenges in the education system. Through real-world examples, the authors showcase the potential of Complexity Leadership in facilitating transformative change within complex adaptive systems.

Examining the role of transformational leadership in school environments, Chapter 5 showcases how transformational leadership qualities in school principals contribute to developing sustainable and successful schools. The findings provide aspiring school leaders with essential skills for leading schools towards academic excellence.

Focusing on a high school principal's leadership style in Jamaica, Chapter 6 presents insights derived from a study involving questionnaires and interviews. The results shed light on the perceived leadership styles, changes in the school, and their impact on student performance and engagement.

Exploring the impact of leadership styles and open knowledge in Africa's Higher Education Institutions post-COVID-19, Chapter 7 employs a literature review and content analysis to highlight the dynamics and evolution of transforming HEIs in Africa.

Chapter 8 investigates how special education teachers in Canada perceived administrative communications during school closures. Through interviews and analysis, it examines the effectiveness of communications and the implications for crisis leadership in the education sector.

Chapter 9 investigates the influence of transformational leadership styles on educational stakeholders. It explores how transformational leadership behaviors impact followers and foster a sense of purpose, respect, and trust among individuals within an educational context.

Chapter 10 presents a secondary analysis of case studies, highlighting the role of transformational leadership in addressing challenges within the context of the "New Normal." It emphasizes emotional intelligence, conflict management, diversity, equity, inclusion, and fostering a culture of learning and development.

Chapter 11 delves into the perceptions of leadership and the relevance of authentic leadership, examining how age influences these perceptions. It explores the presence of authentic leaders and their impact on various generations within organizations.

Investigating the leadership dynamics within the Old Order Amish community, Chapter 12 explores how leaders cultivate a sense of belonging. It delves into leadership roles, selection processes, and responses to technological changes.

Focusing on the transformative journey of Imran Khan, Chapter 13 uses his story as an example of grit, persistence, and leadership. It aims to motivate readers by highlighting the story of an individual's rise to prominence through commitment and leadership.

Chapter 14 examines the influence of leadership on employee motivation and performance in the Albanian private sector. Through case study research, it uncovers the factors that contribute to high levels of motivation and job satisfaction among employees.

Exploring the connection between leadership theories and social work, Chapter 15 analyzes various motivational theories and their relevance to promoting effective leadership within social work organizations.

Chapter 16 delves into the complexities of change management and leadership in healthcare organizations. It highlights the challenges and opportunities for these organizations to adapt and thrive, especially in the face of unprecedented events like the COVID-19 pandemic.

Examining the relationship between emotional intelligence and leadership styles, Chapter 17 explores the impact on managers in small and medium enterprises. It showcases the positive correlation between emotional intelligence and different leadership styles.

Chapter 18 offers insights into the leadership and management of conservation efforts within island communities. By utilizing the Conservation Excellence Model, it provides practical lessons for maintaining high-performing organizations.

Focusing on happiness at work, Chapter 19 analyzes variables that contribute to harmonious organizational culture. By utilizing statistical analysis, it uncovers the factors that significantly impact employee happiness.

Chapter 20 delves into the intricacies of teamwork, team dynamics, and team collaboration within the context of effective leadership. It highlights the importance of effective leadership in fostering positive relationships, trust, and collaboration among team members.

Exploring the intersection of social entrepreneurship, sustainability, and leadership, Chapter 21 examines how leaders can drive positive change by addressing social problems, promoting sustainable practices, and fostering sustainable business models.

Chapter 22 proposes the establishment of a Chief Transformation Officer role at the C-Suit level. This role focuses on facilitating change initiatives, promoting learning culture, and guiding organizations through transformational changes.

We invite you to journey through these diverse and insightful chapters that collectively contribute to a deeper understanding of leadership's multifaceted impact on various spheres of life.

I extend my gratitude to the esteemed contributors who have generously shared their expertise and insights to enrich this book's content. Their valuable contributions have made this endeavor possible and have elevated the quality and depth of knowledge presented within these pages.

Ultimately, my hope is that this book serves as a valuable resource for CEOs, executive members, team leaders, human resource directors, and anyone passionate about fostering effective leadership, communication, and management practices in their respective organizations. Together, let us embark on this journey of exploring transformational leadership's strategic capabilities and fostering positive shifts in organizational paradigms to build a better future for organizations and society at large.

*Darcia Ann Marie Roache*
*University of Saskatchewan, Canada*

# Acknowledgment

The book on *Transformational Leadership Styles, Management Strategies, and Communication for Global Leaders* could not have completed without the collegiality and contributions of each of the authors of chapters. Thank you all for invaluable insights and stories that emphasized the importance of transformational leadership styles, management studies, and communication in different educational and business organizations to support the significance of the book. Non-authors, Professor Canute Thompson, Dr. Amalisha Sabie Aridi, and Dr. Ann-Marie Wilmot your feedback has improved the topics and helped identify areas than needed to be improved.

We don't always achieve success by ourselves, there are always others to give a helping hand. My efforts have been aided by my supporting family members: Remigijus, Dunstan, Rohan, Antoinette, Simone, Kelly-Ann, Adethe, Eulalee, Tanesha, Cory, Xaiver, Bruce, and Seymour. I know one of you will be next with your edited book.

My mother, Moran, you are the best!

Dr. S. Bruce Thomson, thanks for writing the foreword, Richard Muschette for constant motivation and encouragement, and my students for interest in the book. Thanks to the Lord Jesus Christ from whom all blessings, wisdom, and knowledge emulates. Without Him, we are insufficient!

Finally, I acknowledge the generous support and guidance from the IGI Global Publisher team members. Elizabeth Barrantes, Assistant Development Editor, Melissa Wagner, Vice President of Editorial IGI Global, and Mrs. Jocelynn Hessler, Senior Development Editor, IGI Global.

As editor, I am grateful for collegiality and contribution of each of the authors of chapters in the book on, Transformational Leadership Styles, Management Strategies, and Communication for Global Leaders.

# Section 1
# Introduction

# Chapter 1
# Transformational Leadership Style:
## Management and Communication Taxonomies for Organizational Effectiveness

**Darcia Ann Marie Roache**
*University of Saskatchewan, Canada & Capilano University, Canada & University Canada West, Canada*

## ABSTRACT

*The qualitative study used a grounded theory approach on interview using a standard set of questions about transformational leadership style, management, and communication strategies for organizational effectiveness and employees' performance. The study sample was 10 participants from organizations in America, Canada, and Jamaica. The NVivo 10 qualitative analysis software was used to assist in the development of codes, categories, and themes from the interviews, using data obtained and analysed from the constant comparison method. The findings contribute to the body of knowledge on how transformational leadership styles, management functions, and communication can create initiatives for organizational leaders' success globally. The conclusion indicated that organizational effectiveness is grounded in transformational leadership style, employees' motivation, empowerment, and emotional intelligence.*

## INTRODUCTION

Scholars have used a variety of words to describe leadership: Administration, power, control, authority, supervision, and management (Schafer, 2010; Northouse, 2013). The definition of leadership is a method of practice by which a person manipulates others by organizing and directing the progress of procedures in an organization or group (Kedsuda & Ogunlana, 2008; Schafer, 2010; Stogdill, 1950). Whether the subject of leadership is a shared influential process or a specialized role of one individual, leaders are

DOI: 10.4018/978-1-6684-8822-5.ch001

the individuals with the assignment to the specialized role (de Vries et al., 2010; Kedsuda & Ogunlana, 2008; Schafer, 2010; Stogdill, 1950).

Definitions of leadership include words such as *traits, styles, influence, interaction patterns, role relationships,* and *occupational administrative positions* (Northouse, 2013). Most definitions of leadership reflect a process whereby a leader exerts intentional influence over subordinates to guide, structure, and facilitate activities, and relationships in a group or organization (Yooyanyong & Muenjohn, 2010; Northouse, 2013). Some leaders are charismatic individuals who allow followers to express their ideas and to participate in organizational decision-making (Paulsen et al., 2009; Stid & Bradach, 2009). As challenging economic conditions force organizational leaders to make difficult budgetary decisions, the integration of equity into the organization's core mission and strategic process is essential for organizational sustainability (Hopen, 2010; Kotter, 1990). For a leader to build organizational capacity and long-term sustainability, the leader must use systematic actions including a diverse workforce composition, perpetual training and development of team members, and policy advocacy for open communication and transparency (Cordova, et al., 2010). It is imperative for leaders to synchronize all departments and employees so the employees meet the objectives, vision, and the mission statements of the organization (Verma, 2010). Mission statements and vision statements are guidelines that leaders in organizations must follow (Verma, 2010). The mission and vision statements measure outcomes of organizational performance and leaders should ensure that they are inspirational for followers (Richard et al., 2013).

Transformational leaders provide guidance and support for the development and growth of an organization (Antelo et al., 2010). To manage change, leaders must consider innovative approaches to implement and manage innovative ideas as the leaders allow organizational team members to participate in the change process (Clawson, 2009). Change quotient is the ability of leaders to lead the change in their organizations, have the ability to recognize the need for change, manage the change, and understand and master the change process so that employees can quickly adapt to the environment and the business of change (Clawson, 2009).

If leaders are effective, they will recognize the need for change in their organizations; leaders must communicate this need effectively to all individuals in their organizations. The future of organizations is dependent on leaders (a) demonstrating transformational leadership, (b) embracing diverse communication systems, (c) possessing the agility to foresee trends, (d) proactively defining innovative strategies, and taking full advantage of the power of the followers (Clawson, 2009). Leaders who can communicate effectively make strong contributions in the attainment of a competitive edge for the organization, in the attainment of continued growth for the organization, and in the attainment of long-term sustainability for the organization (Clawson, 2009). Leaders must deal proactively with the many internal and external challenges that have an effect on the organization (PricewaterhouseCoopers, 2008).

According to Yukl (2007), leaders influence and lead the organization through focused and concerted efforts. Leaders seek to understand their employees by seeking to learn their employees' assumptions, beliefs, conscious thoughts, expectations, and values (Yukl, 2007). An organization's leaders must maintain a consistent effort to influence their employees to maintain organizational effectiveness and for the leaders to enhance the employees' performance (Clawson, 2009). Emotional intelligence (EI) may be a skill that leaders employ in leading their employees to perform at their full potential (Goleman, 1995). As leaders begin to show an emotional concern and attachment to the individuals in the organization, employees can be more motivated to achieve individual and organizational goals (Goleman, 1995; Jogulu & Wood, 2008).

Effective leadership involves meta-cognition, social intelligence, and EI (Crowne, 2009). Meta-cognition is the knowledge of or control over the ability of an individual to process information (Crowne, 2009). When leaders understand their own cultural knowledge and information, the leaders are practicing meta-cognition (Crowne, 2009). Social intelligence is a tactical practice by which the leaders can interact effectively with their followers (Crowne, 2009). Leaders must be aware of their personal feelings and the feelings of followers (Crowne, 2009). There is a need for leaders to have the skills to incorporate consideration for the emotions and motivations of their followers to facilitate the process of cognitive development of the employees. Leaders can cognitively control emotions as well as cognitively control their thoughts (Yukl, 2007). Goleman (1995) supported the assumption that leaders who effectively employed their EI in leading the organization were likely to be more successful in achieving success for the organization than leaders who do not successfully develop and utilize their EI (Goleman, 1995).

Leaders are managers who are engaged in management practices, planning, organizing, controlling, and leading of material, human, and capital resources of organization for effectiveness and efficiency. According to Schermerhorn et al. (2020) "managers are people in organizations who directly support, supervise, and help activate the work efforts and performance accomplishments of others" (p. 9). In planning, leaders have to set the direction, lead to inspire the efforts of others, organize to create structures, and control to ensure results, and at the same time measure employees' performance and take corrective actions where necessary (Schermerhorn et al., 2020). Management is associate with effectiveness in organization as good management in their planning process, define objectives, determine where they stand with these objectives, develop premises for future conditions, analyze alternatives and make plans, and implement the plan and evaluate results (Schermerhorn et al., 2020). All the factors will transform the organization.

Many individuals who would be leaders lack the knowledge to lead others. These would-be-leaders who might take on leadership positions in an organization without exceling, believing they were not born to be leaders (Mililo, 2009). Leaders are flexible and knowledgeable. Every individual is capable of being an effective leader. Leaders supply the vision that is essential in all organizations (Rowley, 1997). A visionary leader (a) communicates challenges to the employees, (b) clarifies projects for the employees, (c) makes employee involvement desirable, (d) provides stability to the organization, espouses effective teamwork, and (f) has the ability to inspire followers to commit to the organization (Kantabutra & Avery, 2007).

Gabrielsson et al. (2009) argued that because of 21st century globalization, leadership is more than an organizational phenomenon; leadership is a cultural, political, social, and economic element of a successful organization. Successful leaders of organizations must bring together teams from diverse cultures to achieve a balanced and integrated organization in order for the leader to lead the organization to expand into the global marketplace (Shelton et al., 2002). In a study of the leadership styles of Anglo-Australian employees and Chinese-Australian employees, researchers discovered that the Chinese-Australian employees favored a leader who exhibited concern for the group's relationships (Casimir & Keats, 1996). The Anglo Australian employees favored joint problem solving and self-interests as the most important elements in a group dynamic (Casimir & Keats, 1996; Morris et al., 1998; Tinsley & Pillutla, 1998). Leaders must master the art of communication to achieve innovative benchmarks of organizational effectiveness and to improve employee performance (Froschheiser, 2008). Froschheiser (2008) postulated that the most important key to leaders in organizations is clear communication. For leaders to be effective, they must (a) be compelling communicators, (b) visualize their organization's success, and (c) master communication to reach innovative levels of leadership (Froschheiser, 2008). Researchers have proposed that leaders with EI are more apt to exhibit visionary leadership behaviors and display effectiveness at the individual, organizational, and team level (Froschheiser, 2008; Groves, 2006).

Bednarz (2011) found that principles, strength, and visualization are characteristic of visionary leaders. A visionary leader uses inspiration and a realistic perspective of the future, inviting team members to the vision for the future that the leader has chosen (Bednarz, 2011). Leaders with a realistic vision exude energy, optimism, and vitality while motivating followers (Bednarz, 2011). By using EI, visionary leaders move beyond the barriers of conventional thinking in an attempt to serve the good of the organization and its employees. Bandura (1994) described self-efficacy for leaders as the possession of individual viewpoints regarding their capacity to create a higher level of performance by the team members. Through their beliefs, individuals generate different meanings through emotional, rational, motivational, and choice practices (Bandura, 1994). Leaders must learn to value employees' insights and views and promote higher levels of employee performance toward organizational visions and goals (Antonakis et al., 2004).

Researchers accept creativity as practiced by leaders through contemporary ground- breaking techniques as the key to organizational effectiveness and performance (Dewhurst & Fitzpatrick, 2007). To be effective, a leader must identify the critical human resources needed to reach organizational objectives and provide leadership training and mentorship to the members of the organization (Dewhurst & Fitzpatrick, 2007). A leader must remove barriers that are prohibitive to employees openly expressing opinions or sharing ideas (Dewhurst & Fitzpatrick, 2007). According to Tyler and Erickson (2007), communication is a vital factor in organizational effectiveness. When communication breaks down, the results may range from lack of motivation among employees to employees not sharing innovative concepts and ideas (Tyler & Erickson, 2007). The leader must have strong communication skills when attempting to create a positive cultural environment for followers to function within organizations. A strong organizational culture is vital for (a) employees to pursue personal development, (b) employees to generate opportunities for higher levels of performance, (c) the promotion of openness, and (d) the leaders to show employees appreciation for their hard work (Tyler & Erickson, 2007). Leaders who communicate effectively can inspire and motivate employees by allowing individuals the freedom to engage in the organizational activities and to apply effective listening skills as they communicate a vision of development and progress (Kets de Vries & Florent-Treacy, 1999; Shaffer, 2008). Through recognition and praise for employee and team accomplishments, leaders energize employees to reach their peak performance. Effective leaders increase employee involvement in organizational decision-making (Gilley et al., 2009).

Thompson (2010) and Gilley et al. (2009) posited that employees must believe in the mission and vision of the organization in order for the leader and the employees to bring about organizational effectiveness and enhanced employee performance. Thompson (2010) found that transparency by leaders has been a critical contribution to the strategic development of the organization. Some forms of communication in organizations include employees' handbooks, in-house journals and magazines, memos, newsletters, posters, and suggestion boxes (Hackman & Johnson, 2009). The involvement of key stakeholders and departmental personnel in the strategic formulation and implementation of decisions made by organizational leaders has been an effective move by leaders to foster unity and dedication within organizations (Thompson et al., 2005). Through organizational structure and culture, leaders build communication, train personnel, and employees commit to the organizational vision (Thompson et al., 2005). Leaders are responsible for formulating the strategic goals of the organization. According to Ebert and Griffin (2011), and provide guidance to employees, allocate resources, define the organizational culture, and assess employee performance.

Thompson et al. (2005) have stated that strategic performance by the employees of an organization include a strategic vision in which the organization's leaders set the objectives, analyze the organization, and make critical adjustments to the organization. Leaders must monitor and take corrective actions to prepare the organization for the future by "developing a strategic vision, setting objectives, crafting a strategy to achieve the objectives and vision, implementing and executing the strategy, and monitoring developments, evaluating performance, and making corrective adjustments" (Thompson et al., 2005, p. 18). Organizational leaders must revise the organization's strategies when needed to enhance employees' performance (a) to adjust for changing conditions, (b) adapt to new opportunities, and (c) communicate ideas to stakeholders (Thompson et al., 2005).

Johnson et al. (2008) argued that leaders should be cognizant of the importance of effective communication for organizational effectiveness and success. Leaders who can communicate effectively improve the image of the organization, whereas leaders who are ineffective communicators produce inaccuracies and mistakes in the organization. Jones and George (2003) postulated that if leaders are ineffective in their communication, the performance of the organization is insufficient.

## STATEMENT OF THE PROBLEM

The general problem was the failure of organizations due to the lack of transformational leaders within organizations with effective communication skills to improve organizational effectiveness and employee performance (Behery, 2008). Handford and Coetsee (2003) found that 90% of organizations that lack transformational leaders were failures, and 89% of organizations lack transformational leaders who could communicate the organizational vision effectively to employees in order for the leader to create a motivating environment that fosters change. A plethora of literature exists on transformational leadership styles, and researchers have determined that this style of leadership is crucial for organizations to sustain a competitive advantage in the marketplace (Armstrong, 2001; "Leaders are Made Not Born," 2002).

Previous literature on transformational leadership had a focus on change, development, and organizational communication (Neuman, 2003; Pounder, 2001). Prior to the 1990s, the majority of employees in the workforce in traditional office settings used face-to-face communication (Neuman, 2003; Pounder, 2001). With e-mail, leaders have had the opportunity to communicate with internal and external stakeholders with speed and over distance; through email, the leaders prevent repetition and improve access to information (Neuman, 2003; Pounder, 2001). E-mails are a quick means of communication; emails improve internal information sharing and can be a means for knowledge creation within an organization (Neuman, 2003; Pounder, 2001). The email, intranets, video-conferencing, and instant messaging have become an integral part of workplace operations and activities (Neuman, 2003; Pounder, 2001). Scholars have shown that face-to-face communication in the workplace has decreased by 46% (O'Kane et al., 2007).

Since the 1990s, organizational stakeholders have been focusing on developing transformational leadership practices and effective communication strategies to improve organizational performance. The specific problem is that organizational leaders continue to fail in their strategies, and little is known about their communication and leadership styles, which are paramount in guiding committed and demotivated employees for organizational effectiveness (Abdolvand et al., 2008; Robbins, 2005, & Schein, 2004). Without this knowledge, leaders and their ability to implement these strategies for organization success may prove futile with their lived experiences. Research revealed that approximately 95% of organizational strategies were failures within the first five years of operation, and 60-80% of organizational procedures for restructuring initiatives have been failures because of leaders who have ineffective communication skills vital to decision-making in organizations (Abdolvand et al., 2008; Shore, 2005). Employees' resistance to change has been because of failures in communication from leaders who have been ineffective in communicating the right vision and mission to the employees (Abdolvand et al., 2008).

Some leaders fail to select the right kind of communication and the appropriate medium to communicate for solicitation of feedback from employees (Abdolvand et al., 2008; Shore, 2005). Some leaders lack communication skills or are hindered in their pursuit of positive reactions from employees as they attempt to build a collaborative and team-based organization (Clawson, 2009). Organizations devoid of transformational leadership and communication conduits may lack innovative leaders to motivate followers (McLaurin & Al Amri, 2008). This qualitative, grounded research study was an exploration of the manner in which transformational leaders are able to communicate effectively, in order to maximize their organizational effectiveness and elevate the performance of employees (McLaurin & Al Amri, 2008; Thompson et al., 2005). Transformational leaders communicate effectively, use the approach leadership style, and management principles with their employees for organizational effectiveness. Effective leadership will stimulate the right attitude and behavior among employees to enhance their performance in an organization. According to Berkowitz (2010), leadership style compared to the general definition of leadership explains the approaches that leaders will use to interact with others. Hoxha (2015) in support, postulated that, while leadership refers to persuading employees to accomplish their tasks and that of the organization, leadership style explains ways in which leader gets the task done. Hoxha (2015) further stated that leadership style refers to the skills that leaders used to accomplish the task.

## PURPOSE OF THE STUDY

The purpose of the qualitative, grounded study was an exploration of how transformational leadership styles, management strategies, and effective communication could enhance organizational effectiveness for leaders globally. The study used data obtained and analyzed from the constant comparison method.

## METHODOLOGY AND RESEARCH DESIGN

The grounded theory design was used to obtain the goals of the study. Glaser and Strauss (1967) stated that the purpose of the grounded theory design is to provide the consistency, clarity, scope, and integration needed to uncover the core understanding from the research. Glaser and Strauss (1967) posited that theory assists researchers to predict and explain behavior, advance knowledge, assist researchers in making decisions, and guide new research. Grounded theory as described by Goulding (2002) is a continuous interaction or relationship between data collection and analysis. The collection of data in the current qualitative grounded theory study was accomplished through participants' responses to the interview questions. According to Glaser and Strauss (1967), the grounded theory approach allows researchers to attain background information, current experience, and knowledge needed to assist in describing the research.

Glaser and Strauss (1967) stated that researchers using a grounded theory design have the freedom to generate new thoughts explaining human behavior because of their conversations. Creswell (1998) stated that interviews and conversations with participants are acceptable in grounded theory designs.

The study used structured interviews. The sample for the study consisted of 20 participants and was consistent with Thomson's (2010) suggested sample size for qualitative grounded theory studies from educational and business organizations. Glaser and Strauss (1967) stated that qualitative methods enable researchers to explore why and how something occurs. The grounded theory design achieved the accomplishment of the goals of the study.

There were 10 organizations in this study, and employees within these organizations ranged from 150 to 200. A purposeful sampling was used to select the participants for this study. Participants include senior leaders with at least 4 to 15 years of leadership experience in their respective organizations on transformational leadership style, management, and communication to enhance employee performance and improve organizational effectiveness. Effective communication is an essential element that organizational leaders must embrace to enhance organization profitability and employee performance (Locker & Findlay, 2009).

This information might be helpful to organizational leaders in achieving their goals and objectives as they seek to minimize the communication barriers encountered by employees, consumers, and stakeholders. This qualitative, grounded theory study revealed information about the relationship of transformational leadership style, management and communication in organization, organizational effectiveness, and employee performance (Hesselbein et al., 1996). Ozaralli (2003) argued that communication and team performance were significant improvements to organizational effectiveness.

## STUDY DATA ANALYSIS PROCESS

To develop the emerging themes and patterns data underwent coding and analysis. The data analysis started when the first research participant was interviewed. The data coding was based on the interview questions used to develop the themes (open coding), this connects the list of themes with each other, and categories related themes with different level concept (axial coding). In the initial coding phase, coding took place after each interview. At the end of this phase, concepts and themes were emerged.

In the second phase coding of the previous interviews underwent continuous analysis. This was useful to refine and re-examine the resurfacing of additional data from the continuous interviews with the participants. The constant comparative analysis of the data concentrated on further refinement on selective phrases that continued to develop common themes and concepts. The concepts were sorted by source as the reference count continued. Themes became significant when most of the research participants expressed the concepts during the interview.

During the data analysis, new categories, concepts surfaced, and new themes emerged, and a story surrounding the study phenomena began to emerge (selective coding). Relationship from various themes form different concepts and assisted with the interconnectivity of the story surrounding the phenomena of transformational leadership style, organizational effectiveness, emotional intelligence, effective communication, and motivation.

## RESEARCH QUESTIONS

The research study involved the investigation of one main research question, and two sub-questions. The main research question: What are the effects of transformational leadership style-management and communication on organizational effectiveness? One sub-questions existed in the main research:

RQ1: What leadership style(s) organizational leaders perceive as contributing to organizational effectiveness?

## SIGNIFICANCE OF THE STUDY TO LEADERSHIP

Stewart and Brown (2020) suggested that leaders who can communicate effectively could enhance quality working relationships in an organization, foster harmony among employees, improve trust between all stakeholders, and improve performance of employees in the organization. This study is significant to organizational leaders and their leadership style(s) and how they communicate. Communication cultivates a culture, enhances effectiveness, and promotes problem-solving and effective decision-making of organizational leaders (Stewart & Brown, 2020; Northouse, 2013). Powell (2007) postulated that organizational success is dependent on the employment of effective communication, management functions, and skills of leaders. Leaders must communicate the strategic direction of the organization to followers in a manner that initiates growth opportunities, organizational effectiveness within the organization or global.

## LITERATURE REVIEW

This chapter includes an overview of the relevant literature on how transformational leadership style, management, and communication can impact for organizational effectiveness. Figure 1 illustrated an infographic summary of the literature review for the chapter and briefly discussed each element.

*Figure 1. Infographic summary for chapter literature review*

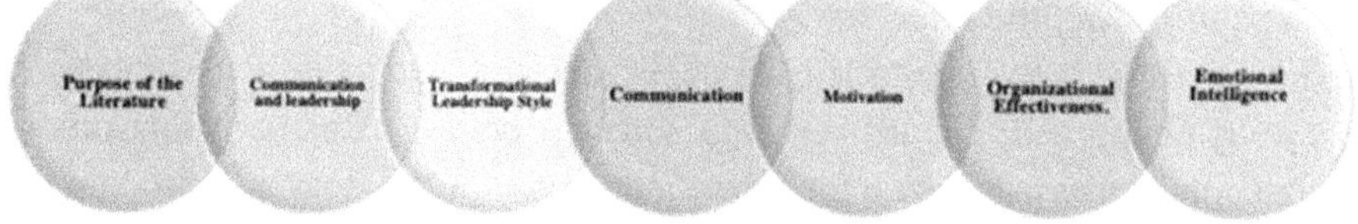


## PURPOSE OF THE LITERATURE

This section gives an overview of the purpose of the study leading to the overview and discussion on the relevant literature in relation to the chapter title, transformational leadership styles, management, and communication taxonomies for organizational effectiveness.

## COMMUNICATION AND LEADERSHIP

Communication is defined as process by which two or more persons transmit information, effectively (Locker & Findlay, 2009, McShane et al., 2021, Uhl-bien et al., 2023). Effective communication is vital to all organizations, leaders, managers, and "no organization or company could exist without it" (McShane et al., 2021, p. 233). According to McShane et al. (2021):

*in the age of knowledge, ideas are the foundation of success in almost every field. You can have the greatest idea in the world, but if you can't persuade anyone else to follow your vision, your influence and impact will be greatly diminished. (p. 233)*

Communication is important for leaders in organization to aid in effective decision-making, information sharing between external and internal stakeholders, for problem solving, discover opportunities, to change behaviour, and to support employee well-being (McShane et al., 2021).

For a leader to improve organizational effectiveness and employee performance, effective communication skills should correlate with a leader's ability to lead, direct, plan, and organize (Guo (2009; Schermerhorn et al., 2020). Transformational leaders must communicate a message in a clear manner, so that they foster a better understanding among employees; a leader minimizes conflicts, and influences attitudes and behavior, in order to maintain positive workplace interaction (Guo, 2009). Communication is a two-way process, shared and transferred by the leader, and includes a communication of goals and objectives to the stakeholders for strategic development (Findlay & Locker, 2009, Guo, 2009).

Guo and Sanchez (2009) postulated that, through effective communication, leaders create an exchange of thoughts, ideas, emotions, and understanding between the sender of the message and the intended receiver. Communication cannot be effective without an understanding of the meaning (Guo & Sanchez, 2009). If leaders who are transformational, transactional, and charismatic can adopt the two-way communication process of exchanging information, the results will be effective communication and a transparency of organizational needs (Guo, 2009). The authenticity and accuracy of the message from a leader may, at times, lead to employee assumptions that are a distortion of the truth (Guo, 2009; Locker & Findlay, 2009; Stewart & Brown 2020).

Leaders should pursue the appropriateness of a communication method that fits the culture of their organization (Guo & Sanchez, 2009). Guo (2009) posited that any communication method has its audience. Face-to-face meetings and video conferences have the highest information carrying capacity, because the sender can use verbal and nonverbal communication cues, and the receiver can provide instant feedback (Guo, 2009; Guo & Sanchez, 2009). Written communication is more appropriate for business organizations, as written communication involves detailed information (Guo, 2009). The traditional method of communication is slower than electronic mail (emails) and other computer-aided communication (Guo, 2009; Guo & Sanchez, 2009).

Emails and faxed messages are relatively rich in information. "Letters, radio, television, newspapers, magazines, bulletins, and newsletters tend to be low in information richness" (Guo, 2009, p. 5). The communication method is adhesive to the culture of the organization (Guo, 2009; Laudon & Laudon, 2000). Technology has changed the way leaders communicate, and some leaders are at the introductory stage of the product life cycle, learning the advancement and dynamism of computer technology (McShane et al. 2021). Email has become a major communication medium, as it allows the sender of an email to transmit information between leaders or a large group of dispersed employees, with a corresponding reduction in cost and time in the deliverance of messages (Guo, 2009).

Guo (2009) acknowledged that leaders with technological experience use email and instant messaging to change, save, and send communications to many individuals at the same time, providing clear and concrete instructions, rather than abstract words. Negativity associated with email usage corresponds to the possibility of information overload, computer viruses, ineffectiveness of communicating emotions, misinterpreted tones of messages, and misunderstandings between sender and receiver (Guo, 2009).

All elements of communication require cohesive organization to be effective (Daft, 2010). Daft (1997) described organizational communication as the process of exchanging and understanding information, with the intent of the leader's ability to influence and motivate behavior. Locker & Findlay, (2009) stated that the basic communication models are information sources, encoders, message, channels, information receivers, decoders, and noises. The sender of a message is an information source, with a purpose to communicate a message (Daft, 2010). The encoder communicates the message using symbolic forms (Kotler & Armstrong, 2006). A code using gestures, language, or written words translates the purpose of the message. The carriers of the message are the channels, which can be verbal (e.g., oral), nonverbal (e.g., a smile), electronic (e.g., email message), or written (e.g., a memo) requests (Locker & Findlay, 2009).

Kotler and Armstrong (2006) described the receiver as one who decodes the message using contextual factors and perceptual filters. The noise source can be a disruption to the messages received by the receiver. Shannon (1994) stated the importance of the communication process, which begins with the source of the information, and is then followed by the transmitter, the receiver of the message, and the destination. The transmission of the message creates noise as a source of feedback that distorts the communication process. Guo (2009) found that leaders must select the appropriate channel of communication and understand the symbolic meanings and richness of messages. To improve organizational effectiveness and employee performance, leaders must improve on communications that reflect the culture and preferred style of communication, both internal and external to the organization (Guo, 2009; Kotler & Armstrong, 2006). Vested leaders take on the responsibility of communicating effectively with internal and external consumers (Guo, 2009; Kotler & Armstrong, 2006).

Effective communication with these stakeholders can be a part of the organization once managers have developed successful communication skills. Thus, skilled managers must focus on ways to improve their communication, in order to foster a better understanding among employees, minimize conflicts, and influence the attitudes and behaviors that contribute to maintaining a positive workplace environment (Guo, 2009). Kotler and Armstrong (2010) and Guo (2009) stated that when leaders understand the elements of the communication process, in relation to the communicated message, they assist the organization in achieving its intended purpose. The communication process, which consists of sender, encoder, media, decoder, receiver, response, feedback, and noise elements, is imperative for the organization to achieve effectiveness, high levels of employee performance, and organizational goals and objectives.

## TRANSFORMATIONAL LEADERSHIP STYLE

Leadership is the "process of influencing people so that their efforts are oriented towards achieving the goals of the organisation" (Muzondiwa et al. 2022). Leaders are needed in organizations to ensure that mission, vision, and goals of organizations are achieved and requires management strategies. Leadership in organisations is a "management approach in which leaders help set strategic goals for the organisation whilst motivating individuals within the group to successfully carry out assignments in service to those goals" (Tokar, 2020 as cited by Muzondiwa et al., 2022, p.3). "Leadership implies the capability to extract the utmost potential in others (van Dongen, 2014; Muzondiwa et al., 2022, p. 3). Leaders with these characteristics can be classified as transformational. Greeshman (2020) said these leaders extend beyond interaction and have the ability to influence and inspire employees to look past their own interests, generate awareness of and alignment with the organisation's purpose, mission.

Transformational leadership theory was first coined by Downton (1973). Downton further mentioned leadership as having tendencies such as transactional, charismatic, and inspirational Downton (1973). Avolio et al. (1991), Bass and Avolio (1990) mentioned the four Is of transformational leadership, idealised influence (model ethical behaviour, exhibit enthusiasm about company strategy), inspirational motivation (to impart a vision that is appealing and worthy), intellectual stimulation (empowerment of employees to learn) and individualised consideration (giving employees a feeling of ownership in company goals and independence). Bass and Avolio (1990) work were used as part of measuring transformational leadership (Avolio et al., 1991; Bass & Avolio, 1990; Muzondiwa et al., 2022). Transformational leadership is a process whereby a person engages, motivates, and creates connection with others (Northouse, 2013). Transformational leaders inspire and motivate followers to achieve organizational effectiveness. Bass (1995) contended that transformation leaders change:

*"Subordinates to disciples and pioneers" and give them reasons "around which they can rally."*

## MOTIVATION

According to Katzell and Thompson, (1990) motivation is the "conditions and processes that account for the arousal, direction, magnitude, and maintenance of effort" (p. 144). While motivation moves the individual to action, transformational leadership is the impetus to drive the action into the strategic directions to achieve goals and objective. To facilitate organizational goals a motivated workforce is an eminent component. However, it should be based on efficacy, power, and relationality. Schein (2010) put forth a strong argument for the analytical outcomes that relationship and intimacy can achieve for the leadership of an organization. According to Schein (2010) organizations are ultimately the result of people collaborating for a common purpose, and the basic relationship between the employees and the organization can, therefore, be thought of as the most fundamental cultural dimensions to build a typology as it provides critical categories for analyzing assumptions about authority and intimacy.

Saraswathi et al. (2011) as cited by Olurorimi (2015) defined motivation as the:

*Wiliness to exert high levels of effort, towards organizational goals, conditioned by the effort's ability to satisfy some individual needs. Motivation is the force that causes people to behave the way they do. It could be further seen on the strength of person's motives. Motives are needs, wants, drives or impulses within an individual. (p. 1)*

Schermerhorn et al. (2008) postulated that the content theories of motivation focus on individual behaviors and needs. For example, Maslow's hierarchy of needs theory,

Alderfer's existence, relatedness, and growth (ERG) theory, McClelland's acquired needs theory, Herzberg's two-factor theory, and the process theories of motivation, are examinations of the thought process that individuals engage in when seeking motivation such as equity, expectancy, and goal achievement (Schermerhorn et al., 2008).

Herzberg's two-factor theory focused on "outcomes that can lead to high levels of motivation and job satisfaction, and outcomes that can prevent people from being dissatisfied" (Jones et al., 2000, p. 436). Accordingly, individuals have two sets of needs or factors - motivator and hygiene. Hygiene factors are "sources of job dissatisfaction, and are associated with job context or work setting, while the motivator factors are sources of job satisfaction and are related to job content" (Schermerhorn et al., 2008, p. 115). Motivator factors relate to the nature and challenges of the "work itself, outcomes, such as interesting work, autonomy, responsibility, being able to grow and develop on-the-job, and a sense of accomplishment and achievement help to satisfy motivator needs" (Jones et al., 2000, p. 436). The hygiene factors "relate to the physical and psychological context in which the work is performed" (Jones et al., 2000, p.436). Outcomes that satisfy the hygiene factors are: Pleasant and comfortable working conditions, pay, job security and status, good relationships with co-workers, and effective supervision (Ghazi et al., 2013; Herzberg, 1959; Jones et al., 2000). The absence of these hygiene factors can create dissatisfaction for workers and if these factors are sufficiently met, they will bring satisfaction and motivation to workers (Dartey-Baah & Amoako, 2011).

Motivational theories have an impact on how workers can contribute to the success of the organization. Abraham Maslow's needs theory of motivation classified human needs on a hierarchy, from the lower-order physiological, safety, and social needs, to the higher order needs of esteem and self-actualization (Schermerhorn et al., 2008). Leaders should have mechanisms in place to motivate followers when their level of need ceases to be a motivation to them (Schermerhorn et al., 2008). Transformational leadership involves various activities, including motivating employees, meeting their individualized needs, and challenging the way they work (Bass & Avolio, 1994; Northouse, 2013). Transformational leadership involves a leader who cultivates employees' acceptance of the mission of the organization (Northouse, 2013). Daily communication would be better if listeners stopped trying to evaluate what individuals say, before they understand what is being said (Wood, 2009). The content of communication is comprised of 7% verbal communication, 38% hearing communication, and 55% visual communication (Wood, 2009). For any message communicated and received, these figures relate to the relative component of what is said, heard, and seen (Wood, 2009). Transformational leaders must use the best approach to motivate employees' performance for organizational effectiveness. The use of emotional intelligence in communication adds value to organizational effective.

## EMOTIONAL INTELLIGENCE

The importance of leaders' empathy and the ability of leaders to exercise control over self, stress, and employees, were significant attributes for organizational success. EI is:

*The ability to perceive accurately, appraise, and express emotion; the ability to access and/or generate feelings when they facilitate thought; the ability to understand emotion and emotional knowledge; and the ability to regulate emotions to promote emotional and intellectual growth. (McEnrue & Groves, 2006, p. 5)*

Cherniss and Goleman (2001) argued that the imperativeness of leaders possessing EI is relevant to employee stability and growth in the organization.

Leaders must possess the ability to deal with stressful and difficult situations in organizations, without losing control. Leaders need to maintain their composure when dealing with employees who are experiencing tremendous emotional pressure; this composure will motivate and stimulate employees in their performance, and employees will emulate their leaders (Cherniss & Goleman, 2001). Solan (2008) argued that EI means, "knowing one's feelings and others, determining emotions and feelings controlling them and sympathizing with other people" (p. 1). The findings have clear indications that EI is vital to leaders in organizations for the recognition, use, understanding, and management of one's own and others' emotional state, and the ability to use those feelings to motivate, plan, and achieve developmental strategies for organizations (Solan, 2008).

## FINDINGS

The emergent themes from the data were the common leadership styles and communication methods used by leaders to communicate with employees, consumers, and stakeholders. The participants' responses to various questions provided documentation for the themes identified. Themes were derived from the participants' patterns, experiences, and responses. Group themes defined the emerging patterns based on the participants' experiences. Themes emerged from experiences demonstrated patterns that were identified for leaders in general.

*Table 1. Emergent themes*

| *Emergent Themes* |
|---|
| Theme 1: Leadership Styles |
| Theme 2: Organizational Effectiveness |
| Theme 3: Employees' Empowerment |
| Theme 4: Emotional intelligence |
| Theme 5: Effective communication |
| Theme 6: Motivation |

## Theme 1: Leadership Styles

Participants shared that various leadership styles can be used by leaders, including authoritative, charismatic, democratic, participatory, transactional, and transformational and comment on advantages and weakness. Participants stated that leaders who demonstrate transformational leadership style are "encouraging and understanding of their needs and motivation in the organizations" are supportive and provide opportunities for their professional growth and development in the organization" (Participants 1-5).

While several participants remarked that leaders were authoritative, Participant 7 observed, "The charismatic leadership style helps to maintain a balance in terms of accountability. The charismatic aspects facilitate empowerment of individuals, which helps them to develop commitment to organization and activities/ tasks assigned" (Participant 7). By contrast, Participant 9 mentioned that "lack of employees' involvement in decision making, some employees could see the authoritative approach as selfish leadership style" (Participant 1)

Other participants noted negative issues related to leadership styles: "Delays in feedback for assistance because of the processes to be undertaken" (Participant 7).

"Suggestions may not be accepted, which allows persons to feel rejected" (Participant 3).

There were positive comments regarding leadership style as well. "Strengths are the development of additional leaders who can serve the organization at a later date; people are able to demonstrate their abilities and talent" (Participant 08). "My leadership style is charismatic. I allow the other team members to assist with the management of the department" (Participant WB 08). Participant 4 observed, Open-door participatory policy style of leadership will encourage effective communication; Information should be clear and easily understood with no room for ambiguity; Information should be sent through the appropriate channels to:

"Meet the relevant situation, e.g., an email or telephone call would be most appropriate for calling an urgent meeting instead of a letter "(Participant 6).

"Provide growth for employees in the organization" (Participant 9).

Research participants indicated that leadership styles had an importance relationship with organizational performance and regardless of the style(s) used, the impact could be negative or positive. Some leaders indicated that they displayed both the transformational and transactional leadership styles at the same time, depending on the situation. If a leader has too much of one style and less of the other, the duties to be performed will not be accomplished in the organization. The findings support the literature that leadership styles positively affect organizational performance at difference levels of effectiveness (Antonakis et al., 2004). With charisma, leaders instill faith, pride, and respect, which is a gift for transmitting a sense of mission and vision, and seeing what is important. Individual consideration of leaders assisted with delegation of projects, coaching, educating, stimulating learning experiences, and treating people as worthwhile human beings (Bass, 1990). Intellectual stimulation involves providing followers with a flow of challenging ideas that stimulate a rethinking of old ways of doing things.

The findings revealed that leadership styles were critical for organizational effectiveness. Based on the findings different leadership styles were needed for leaders to function, such as, transformational, transactional, instructional, democratic, decision-making, participative, and communicative. Effective leadership was needed in organizations to communicate the policy directives. The literature from Owings and Kaplan (2012) highlighted that organizational leadership had relevance to grow the organization and to ensure that policies and administrative practices are accomplished.

Leaders who stimulate followers intellectually arouse an awareness of problems and of followers' own thoughts and responses, creating a cognitive-emotional milieu for them to explore and experiment with increasingly challenging goals (Luthans, 2011; Northouse, 2013; Xirasagar, 2008). Transformational leadership theory has been significantly influential leadership model on education (Berkovich, 2016; Owings & Kaplan, 2012). The transformational leadership style has been characterized as the most utilized leadership style wherein leaders change, inspire, and engage followers (Hassan, 2008). Transformational leadership recognise the importance of inspiring and motivating others to achieve shared vision (Kouzes & Posner, 2017; Northouse, 2013). Transformational leaders convert their followers into leaders and encourage their effectiveness within the organization.

## Theme 2: Organizational Effectiveness

The finding revealed that organizational effectiveness and efficiency encourage employee effectiveness by allowing leaders and employees to contribute to the mission, implement transformational leadership style, motivate employees, provide effective communication, training, and provide effective leadership. One participant explained, "When targets are met, and employees are empowered, customers are satisfied and organizational goals are met" (Participant 3). Participant 5 commented, "A good leader leads from the front and by example. "Do not ask of your employees something which you are not willing to do yourself" (Participant 6). Willing to offer advice and to garner support for the organization in various ways" (Participant 4). Participant 10 revealed, "I motivate and empower both managers and workers."

Participant 9 revealed the importance of "allowing employees to contribute to the mission and the vision of the organization via interaction, meetings, constructive feedback" are ways leaders could demonstrate effectiveness in the organization,

Participant 10 explained how to implement transformational leadership by being hands on with members of the organization at all levels. For example, serving coffee at staff meetings. Frequently standing at the door and personally greeting all staff and recognizing all personal achievements of all staff including personal birthdays, births, marriages, and other personal issues via human resource department. Always looking for ways to improve personal relationship with all employees (Participant 2).

The findings revealed the need for effective leadership to motivate and empower employees' action and ability, integral for employee and organizations' effectiveness. Transformational leaders is needed to motivate and empower employees toward job satisfaction. The findings support the literature as according to Smoak-Mancheno et al. (2009), transformational leaders motivate and empower employees to work collectively to achieve organizational and personal goals. This type of leadership offers employees' job satisfaction, positive attitudes, trust, commitment, and enhanced job performance. Empowered and motivated employees are extremely committed to the organization, to achieve short term and long-term objectives (Avolio et al., 2004; Northouse, 2013).

Participants in the study stated that organizational effectiveness contributes to an organization achieving its goals, missions, and objectives. Effectiveness differs in organizations, but the common elements are how organizational leaders use inputs to achieve outputs, obtain qualified human resource elements to capitalize on human capital, and implement training programs to develop employees. Transformational leaders are responsible for crafting and executing strategies that create organizational effectiveness and employees' empowerment.

## Theme 3: Employees' Empowerment (EE)

Employees who are empowered experience job satisfaction, shared vision, trust, and recognition. "Employee empowerment is claimed to be a technique which both encourages the necessary level of commitment to organizational goals and provides the necessary discretion and autonomy to generate the level of customer service required" (Lashley, 1998, p. 4). Empowerment is an essential management issue for leaders, as they seek to transform business operations (Dessler, 2012; Robbins, 2011; Robbins & Judge, 2011). Employee empowerment consists of four components: shared vision, organizational support, knowledge and learning, and institutional recognition.

Shared vision is a helpful factor as leaders of organizations communicate the strategic directions of the organization to all stakeholders. Organizational support is a focus on team members receiving guidance from the executive level. A dynamic of organizational support for employees can lead to knowledge acquisition and learning where individuals learn to share knowledge, make decisions based on a common consensus, and engage in brainstorming. Through institutional recognition of employees, leaders demonstrate respect and recognition for all team members, regardless of their positions in the organization (Robbins & Judge, 2011, Northouse, 2013). Empowerment is the function of leaders delegating authority hierarchically in organizations and sharing information to all levels, from management to junior employees. Empowerment for lower-level employees is the ability to participate in decision-making and to commit to the goals and objectives of the organization (Dessler, 2012; Robbins, 2005). Empowered employees are motivated to perform any task or take on any additional assigned duties given to them by their superiors.

For organizational leaders and employees' empowerment, communication should be effective and readily available to employees and stakeholders to achieve strategic goals and execute strategies for the organization. This information is vital for leaders to evaluate the level of employee performance and make corrections to foster future performance achievement and improvement (Dessler, 2012; Owings & Kaplan, 2012; Robbins, 2011). Emotional intelligence assists leaders to understand their emotions so that they understand that of others and be able to demonstrate that social intelligence to their followers.

## Theme 4: Emotional Intelligence (EI)

The findings revealed that leaders in organizations use emotional intelligence as a developmental strategy to balance the interests of individuals with those of the organization. Nearly all participants related to the concept of *emotional intelligence*. Participant 1 expressed that it "Allows employees to confide in you as you are sympathetic to employees needs/feelings". Participant 2 revealed that "It depends on the situation, and objectivity of the decisions, as each situation is different, and would require more emotional intelligence". Another participant indicated the need to "assess ability to manage employees, use logical reasoning, assertiveness, and empathy is vital" (Participant 4).

One participant noted,

*Emotional intelligence most definitely affects my leadership style because of the vast diversity of employees which I have to work and associate with. The level of intellect, skills and especially the varied backgrounds require a high level of emotional intelligence to operate efficiently on a daily basis. (Participant 3)*

Participant 6 responded, "Positively, when employees say that their supervisors empathize with them, they are better motivated to performance. When you can feel the employee's pain, and work with them the end result will positively affect the organizations" (Participant 7).

One participant indicated,

*Emotional intelligence affects my leadership style in a positive manner. Display empathy and apathy towards employees, staff feel comfortable to relate personal issues that may affect performance. It enables the possibility of solving performance issues and motivates staff as they feel comfortable in an organization with open door policy is always effective. (Participant 9)*

Another responded,

*It helps a lot because it enables me to understand and analyze the environment that I work in and also the culture of the organization, and so I am able to design strategies to get the most out of my workers. (Participant 10)*

The findings were supported of the literature on emotional intelligence. Respondents indicated that EI would enable leaders in their ability to manage, and to detect emotional clues in employees' performance; however, leaders must first be aware of their own emotions before they can be aware of others. When organizational leaders use EI as a developmental strategy, the outcome can be rewarding. EI balances the interests of individuals with the organization. Cherniss and Goleman (2001) stated that EI encourages leaders think creatively and innovatively, while demonstrating characteristics of empathy assertiveness and responsibility. Organizations need leaders who are equipped with these characteristics advance competitiveness and logical reasoning.

## Theme 5: Effective Communication (EC)

Effective communication is the lifeblood of any organization. Communication includes individuals sending messages, listening, and providing feedback to one another. Communication effectiveness has been a guide for leaders as they have planned, organized, controlled, and led the organization. For organizational activities to be fully employed, effective communication should be transmitted from the leaders involved in designing strategic decisions to the lower-level hierarchical structure of the organization.

Participants stated that supervisors should try to communicate with their employees continuously, disseminate information in a timely manner, and utilize the management by objective techniques. For communication to be effective in some organizations, the provision of additional equipment was needed to provide staff with easy access to communication. Participants noted, as their recommendations for more effective communication, more observation of leaders by followers, more frequent staff intervention in decision-making, and open and timely communication. Some participants noted that good communication was essential to organizational effectiveness and supervisors and employees need to strive to be more accepting of each other's views and ideas. Leaders stressed that when goals differ, clear communication is more essential for individuals to work out organizational solutions that are acceptable and possible for all persons involved.

Fernandez (2009) argued that effective communication is possible when leaders use a method that communicates accepted behavior, express emotions, and appropriate leadership styles. Leaders should use communication methods that are easily understood when communicating with employees, as the ability of leaders to communicate effectively will affect employee performance. If leaders lack the ability to communicate effectively, employees will perform poorly (Kotler & Armstrong, 2010; Owings & Kaplan, 2012).

Leaders in the study recommend strategies for effective communications to include proper training and adequate equipment to foster learning and growth. Leaders should hold employees accountable and implement strategies to correct deficiencies when there is non-adherence. Participants in the study stated that methods used for communication must be accessible and relevant to persons; these persons must be able to use and understand the mode of communication, and there should be a medium for feedback. Study participants also noted that the training of staff members on how to communicate effectively with each other was a good recommendation, and that effective communication should be part of the strategic policy in organizations.

Leaders used various models to communicate how their respective organization's impact message effectively, and to enhance the communication process. The media or medium that works best to enhance effective communication should be encouraged by leaders of an organization. Kikoski (1993) stated, "effective communication truly begins not with the sender sending but with the receiver but the receiver receiving the message. The communication is complete only when the message has been "mutually and accurately understood" (p. 5). Guo and Sanchez (2009) stated leaders should master the art of effective communication, which begins with a clear understanding of the receiver's ideas and thoughts, and the meaning of the sender's message.

Participants in the study used various communication methods, such as meetings, e-mail, facebook, and documents such as ads, letters, surveys, brochures, and memorandums. Participants indicated that leaders who use these communication methods add value to the effectiveness and efficiency of organizational operations. Participants added that regardless of the methods used, there should be simplicity and clarity of message from the sender to the receiver.

## Theme 6: Motivation of Employees (ME)

According to Manolopoulos (2007), employees in any organization have motivation factors such as reward and satisfaction. Employees in organizations have varied needs, depending on their powers, positions, and status; therefore, the factors of motivation for each employee would be different. Ownings and Kaplan, (2012) defined motivation as derived from the Latin word "movere," which means to move. Motivation acts as an interest by which a person performs beyond expectations. Motivation represents those psychological processes within an individual, whereby they experience arousal, direction, and persistence of activities that are goal oriented. Individuals must be sufficiently stimulated and energetic, have a clear focus on what is to be achieved, and must be willing to commit their energy to realize their goals (Ownings & Kaplan, 2012). According to the responses from participants, the most effective motivating factors were high wages, good working conditions, promotions, job security, appreciation by supervisors, commendations for an excellent job performed, and extrinsic rewards. In the private sector, organizational employees were motivated within the culture of the organization. Incentives from this type of organization might include a weekend vacations, blackberry phones, non-cash, and cash payments. When employees were motivated, productivity was high; therefore, managers were responsible to ensure that organizational growth was a prerequisite for employees' motivation. A strong relationship existed among employees who were motivated in the organization; participants in the research stated that when employees were motivated, they performed better.

Employees were motivated by several factors, including job satisfaction, job enlargement, excellent performance evaluations, recreation, training, socialization with team members, teamwork, and respect (Gibson et al., 2003; Robbins, 2005, Robbins & Judge, 2011). Stakeholders should practice and pursue the goals of the organization with those who have an interest in its success. Leaders were responsible for chartering the buy-in and support of the organization by employees, through consultation, motivation, and effective communication. Leaders must use their communication skills to include employees in all communication efforts, regardless of the level of the employee within the organization. Leaders must listen to the needs of the employees and communicate them to organizational department heads. Bowditch and Buono (2005) argued that leaders of firms should communicate the organizational directions in a logical manner to employees, as a failure to do so could result in uncertainty among employees in the work environment. Employees, who obtained recognition from their employers, felt appreciated, felt a sense of advancement, had a positive attitude, experienced a decline in absenteeism, and experienced an increase in productivity (Bowditch & Buono, 2005). Leaders can optimize approaches in the work environment to motivate employees, such as open communication, benefits, appropriate tools, participative management, and clear feedback (Locker & Findlay, 2009; Robbins, 2005).

## RESULTANT THEORY

The major theory that emanates from the study is *Inspirational Leadership Motivation Theory*. This theory focuses on how the goals of the organization can be achieved when employees are motivated. Leaders and their leadership styles are integral in the process, as they have a responsibility to communicate the goals or strategies to the employees. Inspirational motivation is achieved when the organizational structure and culture synchronizes with the established objectives of the organization. Inspirational motivation theory concretizes the fact that when employees are empowered, when leaders expressed their emotional intelligence towards employees, when they used a communication style that is appropriate to the situation, when information technology is used to improve the effectiveness and efficiencies of the operations of the organization, regardless of the communication barriers, organizational objectives will be met. Motivation is the result of leaders interacting with employees and their situations in order to achieve individual and organizational goals.

Leaders and their leadership styles are integral in the process, as they have a responsibility to communicate the goals/strategies to the employees. Inspirational motivation is achieved when the organizational structure, and culture is synchronized with the established objectives of the organizations. Inspirational motivation theory concretizes that when employees are empowered, when leaders expressed their emotional intelligence towards employees, when they used a communication style that is appropriate to the situation, when information technology is used to improve the effectiveness and efficiencies of the operations of the organization, regardless of the communication barriers, organizational objectives will be met. Motivation is the result of leaders interacting with employees and their situations in order to achieve individual and organizational goals.

*Inspirational Leadership Motivation Theory* puts in perspectives that effective communication has to be constant, regardless of the communication barriers in organization, therefore leaders should find a strategy to link communication with the organizational activities. Tyler and Erickson (2007), when communication breaks down, the results may range from lack of motivation among employees to employees not sharing innovative concepts and ideas. Leaders who communicate effectively can inspire and motivate employees by allowing them the freedom to engage in the organizational activities (Kets de Vries & Florent-Treacy, 1999; Shaffer, 2008).

## LIMITATIONS AND IMPLICATIONS

Leaders in the study responded to face-to-face interviews and answered research questions based on their perceived reflections of their leadership style and communication methods. Participants revealed the need for leaders to effectively communicate with employees to enhance organizational effectiveness.

Leaders who motivated, inspired, and built successful relationships with employees resulted in excellent customer service and profit maximization. As leaders guide organizational transformation in a changing global business environment, there exist the need to meet and fulfill employees' needs (Bass et al., 2003). The study's limitations affected the interpretation of the results with leaders from certain geographic regions and population. Hence, the interpretation was limited to experiences and perceptions of leaders from those regions. Most of the themes emergent from the study corresponded with other research studies on transformational leadership characteristics, including: (a) idealized influence, (b) inspirational motivation, (c) intellectual stimulation, and (d) individualized consideration (Bass et al., 2003). Various transformational leadership researchers highlighted the existence of relationships and their effect on organizational productivity through the inspiration of employees (Bass et al., 2003). Leaders must empower followers by responding to their needs, as well as the goals and objectives of the organization.

The findings related to the stated purpose and significance of the study that transformational leadership styles and effective communication were important aspects to organizational effectiveness in any organization. Transformational leaders provided motivation and embraced the organizational culture, structure, and policies. For change, innovations, and strategic directions leaders need to accomplish the strategic vision, mission, and objectives of the organization. This is possible with effective communication and shared vision. The results of the study correspond with the current literature as participants based on their lived experiences indicated that transformational leaders create the direction, vision, encouragement, trust, and commitment that followers need to increase organizational effectiveness and employees' performance. Transformational leaders foster constant interaction and communication among employees, which improves the employees' cohesion, interdependence, and support for the organization. When leaders lacked the ability to communicate effectively poor employee performance exists (Bass, 1995; Locker & Findlay, 2009).

## IMPLICATIONS

Implications of the findings may be encouraging for current and future leaders in organizations, as they assess and re-assess the leadership styles, organizational effectiveness, and communication strategies in their management of employees and organizational success. The study participants indicated that they used transformational leadership styles; however, noted that there were times in certain situations when other leadership approaches were needed. Leaders demonstrated different leadership styles depending on the situation of the organizations. The participants stated that leadership training could be used to change how leaders communicate within organizations and mentioned that training is investment in the human resources and human capital for organizations. Trained employees were more equipped to add value and enhance the goodwill of the organization. According to Chaudhry and Roomi (2010), "training is an investment in human resources, and an investment in human resources is an investment in organization" (p. 2). Organizational leaders who invest more in training and development of employees achieve higher productivity levels for the organization. Trained employees with proper skills, knowledge, and attitude give the organization a competitive advantage.

Pineda (2010) stated that "training is a key strategy for generating skills in people, since it enables them to both learn and unlearn skills - in other words, to acquire new skills and change inappropriate skills" (p. 2). Trained employees will transfer their knowledge to an organizational process that enables problem-solving (Robbins, 2011). Evaluation should be conducted prior to training, in order to analyze the value to the organization, and the ease of measurement of training outcomes (Dessler, 2011). The results measure the effect of training on the achievement of organizational objectives, such as productivity, turnover, time, quality, and objectives (Mathis & Jackson, 2000). The training evaluation should be linked directly with quality systems of the organization for effectiveness and efficiency. Also, the information provided should identify results of the training, deficiencies encountered, and improvements needed to maximize the function and outcome of training (Mathis & Jackson, 2000; Dessler 2011).

## SUMMARY

The current qualitative, grounded theory developed a theory about the exploration of transformational leadership style as a management and communication taxonomies *for organizational effectiveness*. The participants were from organizations in United States of America, Canada, and Jamaica. The researcher used data obtained and analyzed from the constant comparison method. Organizations and employees are critical components of organizational success, effectiveness, and efficiency. Several reasons are included in the literature for the lack of effectiveness in organizations; these may be seen as factors affecting the environment, according to ecologists in organizations. Conversely, the upper echelon linked lack of effectiveness to leadership and the leadership style of leaders in organizations. Participants in this study indicated the need for effective communication and transformational leadership styles in organizations, so that leaders can demonstrate how businesses and organizations could be transformed.

The study included information regarding transformational leadership styles and communication for organizational effectiveness with a desire to succeed in organizations. Leaders, regardless of their leadership style, should possess technical, human, and conceptual skills (Ebert & Griffin, 2011). Technical skills are helpful to leaders and employees in handling work-related problems, informing individuals how to communicate, interacting and working effectively, and providing conceptual skills for recognizing opportunities such as long-range plans and threats of the organization (Ebert & Griffin, 2011; Northouse, 2013). A lack of these skills results in the downfall of leaders (Newstrom & Davis, 2002).

All leaders should be familiar with elements of how to lead or follow in any given situation, as organizational culture dictates that the role of leaders' changes depending on the organizational situation. Factors such as leadership styles, organizational effectiveness, employee empowerment, emotional intelligence, effective communication, and motivation were the core themes that emanated from the study. Leaders, regardless of their communication challenge(s) focus on organizational effectiveness to meet the highly challenging expectations of organizations globally should pay attention to these variables. According to Kandlousi et al. (2010), "if the formal process of communication, which is an important figure of an organization, does not provide adequate information to their employees, employees will turn to the informal form of communication" (p. 3). Both formal and informal communication have an inevitable role in an organizational life (Crampton et al., 1998). According to Locker and Findlay (2009), the existence of informal communication systems in an organization is unavoidable; employees resist being treated by their superiors as a means to an end and interact as an entity, bringing with them their own problems and purposes that give rise to spontaneous behavior. Transformational leadership style calls for management and communication for organizational effectiveness.

## RECOMMENDATIONS AND CONCLUSIONS

Leadership responsibility lies in the effectiveness of organization; the management strategies used, the communication channel used by a leader to invoke an atmosphere of trust, respect, and shared goals for the organization and its employees. Leadership is important to any organizational culture and structure. Leadership styles include assertiveness and responsiveness, improving behaviors, enhancing communication, and minimizing conflicting issues (Darling & Leffel, 2010). Transformational leadership according to Bass and Avolio (1996) is characterized by: Idealized influence, inspirational motivation, intellectual stimulation, and individualized consideration. Bass et al. (2003) postulated that transformational leadership style is vital in organizations to inspire, motivate employees, and build relationships with internal and external consumers; this accomplishes organizational transparency and transformation in times of immense changes in the business environment. The research may provide additional knowledge to the existing body of research on organizational effectiveness, leadership styles, communication, and how transformational leader could use management functions effectively in their operations. Yukl (2008) reported that organizational effectiveness has been the main focus of organizations. The recommendations provided could help leaders to become more successful in their management and leadership ability.

Leaders are invested with the bases of power and the capacity to make strategic decisions, develop organizational capacity, and assure moral conduct for internal and external consumers (Guo, 2009). Effective communication in any organization is composed of various factors. Barriers to communication include noise, communication channels, basic communication models, the source of information, how the encoder encodes messages, and how the message is decoded (Daft, 2010; Dessler, 2011).

Effectiveness is the hallmarks of organizational operations. Four of the participants indicated that effective communication is important for the motivation and empowerment of employees. Three study participants said that, in an organization with EE, leaders need to lead by example. Three study participants stated that employee empowerment is their priority in an organization with employee empowerment. Study participants indicated that training for employees was the hallmark of an organization to empower their employee and that the implementation of new technologies was essential for training to be conducted. Employee empowerment is associated with personal recognition for work effectively conducted was evidence of an organization with EE. The participants indicated that the factors necessary for an organization to have EE include, effective communication, leading by example, training and motivation of employees. Participants saw the imperativeness of effective communication by leaders as the major attribution of any successful organization. Antonakis et al. (2004) and Schein (2004) posited that, when organizational leaders communicate accurately and effectively with internal and external consumers, other organizational factors will resolve overtime.

Motivated and empowered employees appear to be the most highly valued competency. The participants indicated that motivation and empowerment could cause an increase in organizational efficiency and effectiveness. Motivation is the result of leaders interacting with employees and their situations to achieve individual and organizational goals. Through empowerment, leaders allow employees to assume responsibility for their work; thus, empowerment increases motivation (Robbins, 2011).

## REFERENCES

Abdolvand, N., Albadvi, A., & Ferdowsi, Z. (2008). Assessing readiness for business process reengineering. *Business Process Management Journal, 14*(4), 497–511. doi:10.1108/14637150810888046

Antonakis, J., Cianciolo, A. T., & Sternberg, R. J. (2004). *The nature of leadership*. Sage.

Avolio, B. J., Zhu, W., Koh, W., & Bhatia, P. (2004). Transformational leadership and organizational commitment: Mediating the role of psychological empowerment role and moderating role of structural distance. *Journal of Organizational Behavior, 25*(8), 951–968. doi:10.1002/job.283

Bass, B. M. (1985). *Leadership and performance beyond expectations*. Free Press.

Bass, B. M. (1990). From transactional to transformational leadership: Learning to share the vision. *Organizational Dynamics, 18*(3), 19–31. doi:10.1016/0090-2616(90)90061-S

Bass, B. M., & Avolio, B. J. (1994). *Improving organizational effectiveness through transformational leadership*. SAGE.

Bass, B. M., & Avolio, B. J. (2004). *Transformational leadership development: Manual for the multifactor leadership questionnaire*. Consulting.

Bass, B. M., Jung, D., Avolio, B., & Berson, Y. (2003). Predicting unit performance by assessing transformational and transactional leadership. *The Journal of Applied Psychology, 88*(2), 207–218. doi:10.1037/0021-9010.88.2.207 PMID:12731705

Bowditch, J. L., & Buono, A. F. (2005). *A primer on organizational behaviour* (6th ed.). John Wiley & Sons.

Berkowitz, B. (2010). Orienting Ideas in Leadership. *The Community Tool Box*. Retrieved from: www.ctb.ku.edu/en/

Burns, J. M. (1978). *Leadership*. Harper & Row.

Burns, J. (1978). *Leadership. Harper and Row: New York*. Lexington Books.

Charmaz, K. (2006). *Constructing grounded theory: A practical guide through qualitative analysis*. SAGE.

Chaudhry, N. I., & Roomi, M. A. (2010). Accounting for the development of human capital in manufacturing organizations: A study of the Pakistani textile sector. *Journal of Human Resource Costing & Accounting, 14*(3), 178–195. doi:10.1108/14013381011095463

Crampton, S. M., Hodge, J. W., & Mishra, J. M. (1998). The informal communication network: Factors influencing grapevine activity. *Public Personnel Management, 27*(4), 569–584. doi:10.1177/009102609802700410

Cherniss, C., & Goleman, D. (Eds.). (2001). *The emotionally intelligent workplace: How to select for, measure and improve emotional intelligence in individuals, groups, and organizations*. Jossey-Bass.

Creswell, J. W. (1998). *Qualitative inquiry and research design: Choosing among five traditions*. Sage.

Crowne, K. A. (2009). The relationships among social intelligence, emotional intelligence and cultural intelligence. *Organizational Management Journal*, *6*(3), 148–163. doi:10.1057/omj.2009.20

Daft, R. L. (2010). *Management* (9th ed.). South-Western Cengage Learning.

Darling, J., & Leffel, A. (2010). Developing the leadership team in an entrepreneurial venture: A case focusing on the importance of styles. *Journal of Small Business and Entrepreneurship*, *23*(3), 355–371. doi:10.1080/08276331.2010.10593490

Dessler, G. (2011). *Human resource management* (12th ed.). Prentice-Hall.

de Vries, R. E., Bakker-Pieper, A., & Oostenveld, W. (2010). Leadership=communication? Relations of leaders' communication styles, knowledge sharing and leadership outcomes. *Journal of Business and Psychology*, *25*, 367–380. doi:10.100710869-009-9140-2 PMID:20700375

Dewhurst, S., & Fitzpatrick, L. (2007). Bringing out the excellent communicator in managers. How to help your leaders fulfill their communication responsibilities. *Strategic Communication Management*, *11*(5), 20–23.

Downton, J. V. (1973). *Rebel leadership: Commitment and charisma in the revolutionary process*. Free Press.

Ebert, R. J., & Griffin, R. W. (2011). *Business essentials* (8th ed.). Prentice Hall.

Fernandez, S. (2009). Peter Drucker's leap to faith: Examining the origin of his purpose driven life and its impact on his views of management. *Journal of Management History*, *15*(4), 404–419. doi:10.1108/17511340910987329

Gallo, C. (2022). How Great Leaders Communicate. *Business Communication: Harvard Business Review*. https://hbr.org/2022/11/how-great-leaders-communicate

Gibson, J., Ivancevich, J., Donnelly, J. Jr, & Konopaske, R. (2003). *Organizations: Behavior, structure, processes* (11th ed.). McGraw-Hill/Irwin.

Glaser, B. G., & Strauss, A. (1967). *The discovery of grounded theory: Strategies for qualitative research*. Aldine.

Guo, K. L. (2009). Effective communication in health care: Strategies to improve communication skills for managers. *Business Review (Federal Reserve Bank of Philadelphia)*, *12*(2), 8–19.

Guo, K. L., & Sanchez, Y. (2009). *Workplace communication*. Retrieved from http:// healthadmin.jbpub.com/Borkowski/chapter4.pdf

Greeshma, G. (2020). *Multinational corporation: Meaning, definitions, concept, characteristics, types, strategic approach, rationale and regulations*. Retrieved from https://www. businessmanagementideas.Com

Herzberg, F. (1959). *The motivation to work*. John Wiley & Sons.

Hesselbein, F., Goldsmith, M., & Beckhard, R. (1996). *The leader of the future: The Drucker foundation*. Jossey-Bass.

Hopen, D. (2010). Leadership and change. *Journal for Quality and Participation*, *32*(4), 3–4.

Hoxha, A. (2015). Empowerment and trust as mediators of the relationship between transformational leadership and organizational effectiveness. *European Journal of Economic and Political Studies*, *8*, 43–60.

Jogulu, U. D., & Wood, G. J. (2008). A cross-cultural study into peer evaluations of women's leadership effectiveness. *Leadership and Organization Development Journal*, *29*(7), 600–616. doi:10.1108/01437730810906344

Jones, G. R., George, J. M., & Hill, C. W. L. (2000). *Contemporary management* (2nd ed.). Irwin McGraw-Hill.

Kandlousi, N. S., Ali, A. J., & Abdollahi, A. (2010). Organizational citizenship behavior in concern of communication satisfaction: The role of the formal and informal communication. *International Journal of Business and Management*, *5*(10), 51–61. doi:10.5539/ijbm.v5n10p51

Katzell, R. A., & Thompson, D. E. (1990). Work motivation: Theory and practice. *The American Psychologist*, *45*(2), 144–153. doi:10.1037/0003-066X.45.2.144

Kedsuda, L., & Ogunlana, S. O. (2008). Performance and leadership outcome correlates of leadership styles and subordinate commitment. *Engineering, Construction, and Architectural Management*, *15*(2), 164–184. doi:10.1108/09699980810852682

Kets de Vries, M. F. R., & Florent-Treacy, E. (1999). *The new global leaders*. Jossey-Bass.

Kotler, P., & Armstrong, G. (2006). *Principles of marketing* (11th ed.). Prentice Hall.

Kikoski, J. (1993). Effective communication in the International workplace: Models for public sector managers and theorists. *Public Administration Quarterly*, *17*(1), 84.

Kotler, P., & Armstrong, G. (2010). *Principles of marketing* (13th ed.). Prentice Hall.

Kouzes, J. M., & Posner, B. Z. (2017). *The leadership challenge: How to keep getting extraordinary things done in organizations*. Jossey-Bass.

Lashley, C. (1998). Towards an understanding of employee empowerment in hostitality services. *International Journal of Contemporary Hospitality Management*, *7*(1), 27–32. doi:10.1108/09596119510078207

Locker, K. O., & Findlay, M. (2009). *Business communication now* (Canadian Edition). McGraw-Hill, Ryerson.

Luthans, F. (2011). *Organizational behavior* (11th ed.). McGraw-Hill Irwin.

Manolopoulos, D. (2007). An evaluation of employee motivation in the extended public sector in Greece. *Employee Relations*, *30*(1), 63–85. doi:10.1108/01425450810835428

Mathis, R. L., & Jackson, J. H. (2000). *Human resource management* (9th ed.). South-Western College Publishing.

McEnrue, M. P., & Groves, K. (2006). Choosing among tests of emotional intelligence: What is the evidence? *Human Resource Development Quarterly*, *17*(1), 9–42. doi:10.1002/hrdq.1159

McLaurin, J. R., & Al Amri, M. B. (2008). Developing an understanding of charismatic and transformational leadership. *Proceeding of the Allies Academies, 15*(2), 333-337.

McShane, S. L., Tasa, K., & Steen, S. L. (2021). *Canadian organizational behaviour* (11th ed.). SAGE.

Muzondiwa, Y. T., Swarts, I., & Schultz, C. M. (2022). The relationship between transformational leadership, perceived organisational effectiveness and organisational culture in a selected multinational corporation in Africa. *SA Journal of Human Resource Management, 20*(1), 1–11. doi:10.4102ajhrm.v20i0.1888

Neuman, W. L. (2003). *Social research methods: Qualitative and quantitative approaches* (5th ed.). Allyn & Bacon.

Newstrom, J. W., & Davis, K. (2002). *Organizational behavior: Human behavior at work* (11th ed.). McGraw-Hill, Irwin.

Northouse, P. G. (2013). Leadership: Theory and practice (6th ed.). Sage.

O'Kane, P., Palmer, M., & Hargie, O. (2007). Workplace interactions and the polymorphic role of e-mail. *Leadership and Organization Development Journal, 28*(4), 308–324. doi:10.1108/01437730710752193

Owings, W. A., & Kaplan, L. S. (2010). *Leadership and organizational behaviour in education: Theory into Practice*. Pearson.

Paulsen, N., Maldonado, D., Callan, V. J., & Ayoko, O. (2009). Charismatic leadership, change, and innovation in an R&D organization. *Journal of Organizational Change Management, 22*(5), 511–523. doi:10.1108/09534810910983479

Pounder, J. S. (2001). New leadership and university organizational effectiveness: Exploring the relationship. *Leadership and Organization Development Journal, 22*(5/6), 281–291. doi:10.1108/EUM0000000005827

Richard, A. (2013). *Theory Building in Applied Disciplines*. Berrett-Koehler Publishers.

Robbins, S. P., & Judge, T. A. (2010). *Essentials of organizational behavior* (10th ed.). Prentice Hall.

Robbins, S. P., & Judge, T. A. (2011). *Organizational behavior* (14th ed.). Academic Press. doi:10.1108/13639511011085060

Schafer, J. (2010). Effective leaders and leadership in policing: Traits, assessment, development, and expansion. *Policing: An International Journal of Police Strategies & Management, 33,* 644-663. https://www.doi:10.1108/13639511011085060

Schein, E. H. (2004). *Organizational culture and leadership* (3rd ed.). Harper and Row.

Schermerhorn, J. R., Bachrach, D. G., & Wright, W. (2020). *Management* (5th ed.). Wiley.

Schermerhorn, J. R., Hunt, J. G., & Osborn, R. N. (2008). *Organizational behavior* (10th ed.). John Wiley & Sons.

Shaffer, J. (2008). Creating a leadership engine to power performance. *Strategic Communication Management, 12*(6), 28–32.

Smoak-Mancheno, L., Endres, G. M., Potak, R., & Athanasaw, Y. (2009). The individual cultural values and job satisfaction of the transformational leader. *Organization Development Journal*, *27*(3), 9–22.

Solan, A. M. (2008). The relationships between emotional intelligence, visionary leadership, and organizational citizenship behavior in continuing higher education. *Dissertation Abstracts International*, *69*(8), B. (UMI No. 3325538)

Stewart, G. L., & Brown, K. G. (2020). *Human resource management: Linking strategy to practice* (4th ed.). Wiley.

Stogdill, R. M. (1948). Personal factors associated with leadership: A survey of the literature. *The Journal of Psychology*, *25*(1), 35–71. doi:10.1080/00223980.1948.9917362 PMID:18901913

Thomas, K. W., & Velthouse, B. A. (1990). Cognitive elements of empowerment. An "interpretative" model of intrinsic task motivation. *Academy of Management Review*, *15*(4), 666–681.

Thompson, A. A., Strickland, A. J., & Gamble, J. E. (2005). *Crafting and executing strategy: Text and reading* (14th ed.). McGraw-Hill.

Tyler, C. F., & Erickson, A. (2007). Have you got the business to become a leaders? *Strategic Communication Management*, *11*(4), 15.

Wood, G. (2009). *Body language myth: The 7%-38%-55% rule.* Retrieved from https://psycentral.wordpress.com/2009/03/03/body-language-myth-7-38-55-ruledr-gary-wood-psycholog/

Wood, J. (1999). Establishing internal communication channels that work. *Journal of Higher Education Policy and Management*, *21*(2), 135–149. doi:10.1080/1360080990210202

Xirasagar, S. (2008). Transformational, transactional and laissez-faire leadership among physician executives. *Journal of Health Organization and Management*, *22*(6), 599–613. doi:10.1108/14777260810916579 PMID:19579573

Yooyanyong, P., & Muenjohn, N. (2010). Leadership styles of expatriate managers: A comparison between American and Japanese expatriates. *The Journal of American Academy of Business, Cambridge*, *15*(2), 161–168.

Yukl, G. (2008). How leaders influence organizational effectiveness. *The Leadership Quarterly*, *19*(6), 708–722. doi:10.1016/j.leaqua.2008.09.008

# Chapter 2
# Leadership:
## Definitions, Historical Evolution, and Classifications of Leadership Theory

**Lyle Benson**
*MacEwan University, Canada*

## ABSTRACT

*As Bass has stated, leadership is a universal phenomenon. It is important for each person to create their own definition of leadership and then try to demonstrate personal actions that are consistent with their leadership definition, especially in a constantly changing business environment. To create a foundation of understanding of leadership, this chapter provides an overview of the definitions of leadership, the historical evolution of leadership, and the classification of leadership theories. Although the focus of the book is on transformational leadership and change, it is necessary to provide an easy-to-use reference for leadership styles because it places the specific leadership approaches in their appropriate context.*

## INTRODUCTION

One must ask, "Does leadership training improve a person's leadership abilities?" The unequivocal answer is, "Yes!" People who take leadership training will improve their leadership effectiveness. In his review of over 3,000 leadership studies, Stogdill (1974, p, 180) stated, "Results of research support that direct training in techniques of leadership result in improved effectiveness as a leader." Bass (2008, p.3), who carried on Stogdill's work and reviewed over 7,000 leadership studies, also concluded that studies have shown that direct training in leadership techniques tends to improve trainees' leadership and effectiveness in groups. The research evidence has also found that generally, leadership is transferable; a leader in one situation will tend to emerge as a leader in another situation and the more similar the situations are the greater the likelihood that leadership transference will occur.

DOI: 10.4018/978-1-6684-8822-5.ch002

The second question is, "Does leadership training improve youths' leadership abilities when they become adults?" Again, the answer is, "Yes!" Huckaby and Sperling (1981, pp.20-21) asked, "Do we have any empirical data that suggests a relationship between leadership among adults and leadership training among children and youth?" in summarizing the research on transfer of leadership from situation to situation and from adolescence to adulthood Bass (1981, p.479) noted that both Cowley (1928,1931) and Bogardus (1928, 1929,1931) observed that great leaders obtained their leadership first in one situation and then transferred that leadership to other similar situations and finally gained sufficient esteem and experience to succeed as leaders in almost any situation they entered. Bass (1981, p.479) also provided several examples of research (Clem & Dodge, 1933; Courtney, 1938; Levi, 1930; Page, 1935; & Shannon, 1929) that determined that leadership in school and college was a predictor of leadership later in life, business activities, and social interactions. It was found that academic achievement was not as predictive of later leadership as leadership involvement in extracurricular activities. The research evidence suggested that leadership in high school and college generally was a moderate predictor of leadership in adulthood; thus, to some extent, leadership transferred from adolescence to adulthood. The focus on developing youth's leadership knowledge, skills, and abilities is crucial for the development of society. The earlier educators and businesses can provide leadership opportunities for youth, the sooner youth can impact the world.

These two questions are essential for practitioners to appreciate because practitioners are on the frontlines of applying leadership theories and developing leaders.

1. Definitions of Leadership

The oldest quoted leadership definition is by the Chinese philosopher Lao Tzu.

The best leaders are those whose existence is merely known by the people.
The next best are those who are loved and praised.
The next are those who are feared.
The next are those who are despised.
It is only when one does not have enough faith in others that others will have no faith in him.
The great leaders value their words highly.
They accomplish their task; complete their work.
And when they are done the people say, "We did this ourselves!"

Through over 100 years of Western leadership research, there has yet to be an agreement about a single definition of leadership or the approach to studying leadership. In 1974 Stogdill (p.259) stated, "There are almost as many definitions of leadership as there are persons who have attempted to define the concept." In 1978 McGregor Burns (as cited in Bass, 1981, p.5) also quipped, "Leadership is the most studied and least understood phenomenon of our times." Bennis and Nanus (1985, p.4) are often quoted as having found over 350 definitions of leadership. One of the main problems in trying to have a single definition of leadership is that "leadership is a dynamic process." Leadership is influenced by the goal to be achieved by the leader, the followers, the task to be done, internal and external environmental influences, and the time frame. Bass and Bass (2008, pp. 15-23) synthesized over 7,000 leadership research studies and provided representative definitions of leadership through each decade of the $20^{th}$ century (see Table 1).

*Table 1. Representative definitions of leadership in the 20th century (Bass & Bass, 2008, p. 15)*

| Decade | Representative Definitions of Leadership Through the 20th Century |
|---|---|
| 1920s | Impressing the will of the leader on those lead and inducing obedience, respect, loyalty, and cooperation. |
| 1930s | A process through which the many were organized to move in a specific direction by the leader. |
| 1940s | The ability to persuade and direct beyond the effects of power, position, or circumstances. |
| 1950s | What leaders do in groups and the authority accorded to leaders by the group members. |
| 1960s | The influence to move others in a shared direction. |
| 1970s | The leader's influence is discretionary and varies from one member to another. |
| 1980s | Inspiring others to take some decisive action. |
| 1990s | The influence of the leaders and the followers who intended to make fundamental changes that reflected the common purpose. |
| 21st Century | The leader is seen as most responsible and accountable for the organization's actions. |

Bass and Bass (2008, pp. 15-23) declared there were three broad perspectives of leadership definitions and 20 sub-categories (see Table 2).

*Table 2. Leadership definitions (Bass & Bass, 2008, p. 15)*

| Broad Leadership Definitions | Sub-Category Leadership Definitions |
|---|---|
| 1. Leadercentric | Leader as a Personality |
| | Leadership as an Attribution |
| | Leaders as the Foci of Group Process |
| | Leader as a Symbol |
| | Leadership as the Making of Meaning |
| | Leadership of Thought |
| | Leadership as Purposive Behavior |
| | Leadership as Persuasive Behavior |
| | Leadership as the Initiation of Structure |
| | Leadership as the Exercise of Influence |
| | Leadership as Discretionary Influence |
| | Leadership as the Art of Inducing Compliance |
| 2. Leadership as an Effect | Leaders as an Instrument of Goal Achievement |
| | Leadership as an Effect of Interaction |
| 3. Interaction between the Leader and the Led | Leadership as a Process |
| | Leadership as a Power Relationship |
| | Leadership as a Differentiated Role |
| | Recognition of the Leader by the Led |
| | Identification with the Leader |
| | Leadership as a Combination of Elements |

Several definitions of leadership from the 1950s through to the 1980s are provided to allow one to reflect and create one's personal leadership definition. Stogdill's (1974, p.411) definition of leadership was initiating structure in expectation and interaction. Lassey and Saskin (1983, p.110) reviewed Stogdill and Bass's (1974) 11 different perspectives on the definitions of leadership. They summed up their findings by saying, "Any or all of the meanings noted by Stogdill might apply to any particular circumstance, but no single definition is universally applicable." They noted that leadership clearly leads towards goal achievement, involves interaction and influence, and universally results in some form of change structure of behavior or groups, organizations, or communities (p.110). Lassey and Saskin's comment points to the observable actions of leaders: goal achievement, methods of interaction and influence, and results.

In 1957 Hemphill and Coons (as cited in Bass, 1981, p.10 & Yukl, 2013, p.7) defined leadership as the behavior of an individual when he is directing the activities of a group towards a goal. At about this same time, Junda (1960, p.358) thought leadership was a type of power relationship characterized by a group member's perception that another group member had the right to prescribe behavior patterns for the former regarding his activity as a group member. Tannenbaum, Weshler, and Massarik (1961, p.24) combined both aspects when they defined leadership as interpersonal influence exercised in a situation and directed through the communication process toward attaining a specified goal or goals. Later Jacobs (1976, p.232) tried a more economical approach when he defined leadership as an interaction between persons in which one presents information of a sort in such a manner that the other becomes convinced that his outcomes (benefits/costs) will be improved if he behaves in the way suggested or desired. Kochan, Schmidt, and deCotis b (1975, p.285) became even more mathematical when they defined leadership as an influence process whereby P's actions change O's behavior, and P views the influence attempt as legitimate, and the change is consistent with P's goals. Katz and Khan (1978, p.528), whose three-skill set typology (technical, human relations, and conceptual) categorized the skills a leader needs, provided a broader definition of leadership as the influential increment over and above mechanical compliance with the routine directive of the organization. Cribbion (1981, pp.12-13) also acknowledged that there were as many different definitions of leadership as people were trying to define it. His definition was the ability to gain consensus and commitment to common objectives beyond organizational requirements, which are attained with the experience of contribution and satisfaction on the art of the workgroup (pp.12-13). Sessoms and Stevenson's (1981, p.50) definition required the act of commanding and directing the actions of leaders and the process by which groups achieve their goals. If leadership is the act of moving people toward goal achievement, there must be followers, group goals, and a leader to achieve such a goal. Leadership, then, is the interaction of all three. Hersey and Blanchard (1977, p.3) of Situational Leadership fame noted that leadership occurs anytime one attempts to influence the behavior of an individual or group regardless of the reason. In studying the philosophy of leadership, Hodgkinson (1983, p.196) believed leadership could be understood as the effecting of policy and values through collective organizational action. However, it was Gordon's (1980, p.160) definition which pointed out the need for leadership development when he stated: "Being the leader does not make you one, because leaders don't automatically get the respect and acceptance of their group members; so to earn the leadership of their group and have a positive influence on the group members, leaders must learn specific skills and methods."

Last, Wholistic Leadership (Benson, 1991, p.51) occurs when an individual, a group, or an organization intentionally influences the behaviors, attitudes, and values of another individual, group, or organization in the areas of work skills, people skills, or self-skills to improve performance to achieve individual goals, group goals, or organization goals. This definition synthesizes many of Stogdill's perspectives on defining leadership. Benson's definition states:

1. who is influencing – individuals, groups, or organizations.
2. who is being influenced - individuals, groups, or organizations.
3. what areas are being influenced – behaviors, attitudes, or values.
4. how are they being influenced – work skills, people skills, or self-skills.
5. why are they being influenced – to improve performance.
6. desired outcomes – to achieve individual, group, or organizational goals.

The most important concept to be aware of is how a person defines and understands leadership because this will determine how the person leads and the actions the person will and will not do. Based upon the other internal and external environmental factors, a person's actions will either make them an effective or ineffective leader.

## 2. HISTORICAL EVOLUTION OF LEADERSHIP

In the opening of The Bass Handbook of Leadership, Bass and Bass (2008, p.3) state: "Leadership is a universal phenomenon." Smith and Kruger (as cited in Bass, 2008, p.3) concluded that leadership occurs universally among all people regardless of culture, whether they are isolated Indian villages, Eurasian steppe nomads, or Polynesian fisherfolk. Bass (1981, p.7) also provided a historical background to the word "leader," noting that the 1933 Oxford dictionary designated the word "leader" as coming into use in 1300. As an early example, on June 15, 1381, Richard II, King of England, said to the rebels at Smithfield after the death of Wat Tyler, "I, myself, will be your King; I will be your captain and your leader" (Palmer & Palmer, 1985, p. 223). Before this time, other words were used to separate and distinguish leaders from followers. Some of these words were head of state, ruler, military commander, prince, proconsul, chief, and king.

To understand the historical evolution perspective of leadership, one must understand who the leaders in the past were and their roles in their societies. As a generalization, the leaders of the past were responsible for the well-being and protection of their people. This meant that the leader's role often included the knowledge and conduct of war. This is evidenced by the words used to describe leaders, including general, captain, commander, officer, and chief. These descriptors are still part of our leadership terminology today. This is also evidenced by how many world leaders have had a military background or were successful in military actions. Some include the ancient Biblical Kings and Prophets, the Roman Caesars, the Middle Eastern Sultans, and the Asian Khans. Historically in Europe, there were all the Kings and Queens and the generals Napoleon Bonaparte and the Duke of Wellington; in the United States, George Washington, Abraham Lincoln, Ulysses S. Grant, and Robert E. Lee; and Russia, the Czars. More recently, there were Adolf Hitler, Sir Winston Churchill, Dwight D. Eisenhower, Charles DeGaulle, and Joseph Stalin during WWII. And in its aftermath, there was Mao Tse Tung. This does not mean that all the world leaders were graduates of military colleges. Still, it does tell that the historical military role of leaders has significantly impacted our understanding of leadership and how we define and think about it today.

A second historical evolution perspective one must understand about leadership is the influence of the dominant culture on the evolution of leadership. One such recent Western influence is the United Kingdom. The British used the word Prime Minister to describe their leaders, which is still used internationally by many countries England colonized. Another influence is the United States. Their word to represent their country's top leader is President. President is prevalent internationally to describe world leaders, business leaders, community club leaders, and sports leaders. However, it must be noted that the French used President at about the same time as the Americans.

The third historical evolution perspective is that the role of leaders has evolved from the tribe and the clan to the principality and nation-state to business and mega-multinational corporate conglomerates. Business has introduced new roles that are not military but include some nomenclature from them. Two such words are administrative officers and chief executive officers. Today, some business words that describe leaders include foreman, supervisor, manager, director, section head, and president. The critical point is that each part of society will establish a language to define leader and leadership and what these words mean to it. It may create new words or incorporate words from the past or present within its society or from another society. For example, in Canada, military, government, business, education, and sport all have overlapping words to define leaders in these organizations (see Table 3).

*Table 3. Leadership positions in organizations*

| Military | Government | Business | Education | Sport |
|---|---|---|---|---|
| | | | Principal | |
| Officer Ranks | | Chief Executive Officer | | Chief Executive Officer |
| | President | President | | Club President |
| | | Superintendent | Superintendent | |
| | Administrative Officer | Administrative Officer | | Administrative Officer |
| | Manager | Manager | | Manager |
| | Supervisor | Supervisor | | |
| | Trainer | Trainer | | Trainer |
| | | Coach | Coach | Coach |
| Captain | | | Team Captain | Captain |

## 3. CLASSIFICATIONS OF LEADERSHIP THEORIES

In 1995, Graen and Uhl-Bien (p.220) noted that classifying leadership theories into general studies approaches had become more difficult. This is because leadership is complex, and the research question one asks naturally limits the perspective one can take to study leadership. Through decades of leadership research, there has yet to be an agreement about a single definition of leadership or the approach to the study of leadership. This is a good thing.

When studying leadership, a person must understand the various broad categories of leadership theories. Yukl (1981, pp. 7-9) suggested that almost all leadership research studies could be classified into one of four approaches. These approaches are trait, behavior, situational, and power and influence.

These approaches explained most of the research up to the 1980s. Three other approaches to update leadership theories were added by van Wart (2003 p.213) transformational, servant leadership, and wholistic- multifaceted. Different approaches are emerging, focusing on teams, systems, and context, but these six areas by Yukl (1981 & 2013) and van Wart (2003) cover most leadership theories and research.

## 3A. Great Man Approach

In this approach, great men or women influenced society. As previously mentioned, these people were often military leaders. However, they could also be Kings and Queens, Czars or Czarinas, religious leaders, or people who altered what society believed or thought or how it acted. Some of these people include Sir Isaac Newton (science, math, and physics), Martin Luther (religion), and Charles Darwin (science and biology).

*Table 4. Great man leadership theories*

| Year | Author | Concept |
|---|---|---|
| 1841 | Thomas Carlyle | Heroes and hero worship. |
| 1869 | Galton | Hereditary genius. |

## 3B. Trait Approach

The trait approach evolved from the great man approach. It emphasized the leader's personal qualities and skills. From the 1920s to late 1940, most leadership studies tried to discover traits that distinguished leaders from followers. The assumption underlying the trait approach was "leaders are born." It was assumed that leaders were different from followers. Traits studies included physical, intellectual, emotional, and attitudinal attributes and characteristics. If these traits could be identified, finding leaders would be easy. The problem was that each new study added a unique trait. The result was that there were not enough common traits across situations to be practically helpful for leader identification and development. Stogdill's 1948 review of leadership training studies indicated no significant difference in personal qualities between leaders and followers. Stogdill (1948, p.64) stated, "A person does not become a leader by possessing some combination of traits." Because of Stogdill's review, leadership trait research almost ended.

However, Kirkpatrick and Locke (1991, p.49) revised trait research noting that "Recent research, using a variety of methods, has made it clear that successful leaders are not like other people. The evidence indicates that certain core traits significantly contribute to business leaders' success." They also noted that traits alone were a necessary but insufficient condition for successful leadership – traits were only a precondition. Leaders must take specific actions to be successful. Kirkpatrick and Locke's (1991, p.49) leadership literature review identified six traits that differentiated leaders from non-leaders. These traits from Kirkpatrick and Locke (1991, pp.49-56) are summarized in Table 4.

*Table 5. Trait leadership theories*

| Year | Author | Concept |
|---|---|---|
| 1940 | Bird | Traits |
| 1947 | Jenkins | Traits |
| 1955<br>1965<br>1978 | Katz, Mann, Khan | Three Skill Typology<br>Technical, human relations, and conceptual skills. |
| 1964 | Ewing | Managerial Mind |
| 1975 | McClelland, Atkinson | Need for Achievement, Power, and Affiliation |
| 1991 | Kirkpatrick, Locke | Six Major Traits<br>Drive, leadership motivation, honesty and integrity, self-confidence, cognitive ability, and specific business knowledge. |

*Table 6. Six major leader traits (Kirkpatrick & Locke, 1991, pp. 49-56)*

| Major Trait | Sub Trait | Explanation |
|---|---|---|
| **Drive** | **Achievement** | High desire for achievement, obtain satisfaction from successfully competing challenging tasks, attaining standards of excellence, and developing better ways of doing things. |
| | **Ambition** | Desire to get ahead, demonstrate drive and determination, and set hard, challenging goals for themselves and their organization. |
| | **Energy** | Has physical, mental, and emotional vitality and stamina. |
| | **Tenacity** | Able to overcome obstacles with their will and perseverance, and persistence in their activities and follow through. |
| | **Initiative** | Make choices and take actions that lead to change. |
| **Leadership Motivation** | | Have a strong desire to lead, gain the power to influence others, to be in a leadership role rather than a subordinate role. |
| **Honesty & Integrity** | | Honesty refers to being truthful, ethical, and principled. Integrity refers to having congruence in speech and actions. This results in trust between the leader and followers. |
| **Self Confidence** | **Emotional Stability** | Remain composed and even-tempered. Able to handle pressure and not prone to moodiness, anger, and inconsistent behavior. |
| **Cognitive Ability** | | Able to reason inductively and deductively to solve problems, make correct decisions, and formulate strategies. |
| **Specific Business knowledge** | | A high degree of knowledge about their organization, industry, and technical matters. |

## 3C. Behavior Approach

The behavior approach evolved from the trait approach. The behavior approach, which began in the 1930s, focused on the actions and behaviors leaders did and not on their personal qualities. The behavior approach assumes that "leaders can be made." That is, what a leader does determines their effectiveness or ineffectiveness. Therefore, leadership can be taught, and people can be trained to become more effective leaders.

*Table 7. Behavioral leadership theories*

| Year | Author | Concept |
|---|---|---|
| 1939 | Lewin, Lippet, White | Leadership Styles<br>Autocratic, Democratic, and Laisses-faire. |
| 1940's-<br>1950's | Katz, Khan, Morse, Guin, Floor | University of Michigan Studies<br>Employee-centered and task-centered. |
| 1940's | Hemphill, Fleishman, Harris, Burtt, Stogdill, Coons, Bass | Ohio State University Studies<br>Consideration and initiation of structure. |
| 1948<br>1953<br>1969<br>1976<br>1977 | Bennes, Sheats<br>Bales<br>Schein<br>Bradford<br>Lord, Johnson, Johnson | Task and Maintenance Functions<br>23 communication behaviors. |
| 1960's | Blake, Mouton | Managerial Grid<br>Concern for production and concern for people. |
| 1965 | Miner | Managerial Motivation<br>Support for higher-level actions, competitive element, active and supportive behavior, exercise power, direct subordinate behavior, assume a position of visibility, and administrative duties. |
| 1966 | Bowers, Seashore | Four Factors in Leaders' Behavior<br>Supportiveness, interaction facilitation, goal emphasis, and work facilitation. |
| 1967 | Likert | Systems Four<br>Leadership determines organizational climate, communication patterns, and goal-setting activities. |
| 1973 | Mintzberg | Managerial Roles<br>Interpersonal, informational, and decisional. |
| 1979 | Yukl, Nemeroff | Managerial Behavior Survey<br>19 behaviors |

## 3D. Situational Adaptive Approach

The Situational Adaptive approach evolved from the behavior approach. This approach began in the early 1950's till the 1980s. The first notion was that situational variables affected and determined a leader's behavior, affecting a leader's effectiveness. This advanced into the contingency approach, which sought to determine which specific situational variables were present. This would determine which leader behaviors would be most effective when those contingency variables were present. Then a person could be trained to identify the variables and adjust their behavior to suit the situation, increasing their leadership effectiveness. Like the trait approach, researchers found that often there were too many situational variables to specifically train people to identify to enable them to be effective.

## 3E. Power and Influence Approach

This approach began in the late 1950s. It attempted to explain leadership about the leader's source and amount of power, how the leader used power to influence individuals and groups, how power is gained or lost, and the consequences of power.

*Table 8. Situational leadership theories*

| Year | Author | Concept |
|---|---|---|
| 1950's<br>1967 | Fiedler, Chemers, Meyer | LPC Contingency Model<br>Least preferred co-worker (LPC), leader-member relations, position power, and task situation. |
| 1958 | Tannebaum, Schmidt | Decision-Making Model<br>Vary leadership styles, from task-directed behavior to relationship-directed behavior. |
| 1969-<br>1980's | Hersey, Blanchard | Situational Leadership<br>Vary leader behaviors, from directive to supportive behaviors, are based on followers' ability, willingness, and self-confidence. |
| 1971 | House, Dessler, Mitchell | Path-Goal Theory<br>Vary leaders' behaviors from supportive, directive, participative, and achievement-oriented based on workers' expectations and role clarification, |
| 1972 | Reddin | Three D Theory<br>Appropriate and inappropriate task and relationship behaviors. |
| 1973 | Vroom, Yetton | Normative Decision Making<br>Rules to protect the quality of the decision and the acceptance of the decision. |
| 1973 | Kerr, Jermier | Leader Substitutes theory<br>Situation task-oriented behavior or relationship-oriented behavior makes the leader redundant or ineffective. |
| 1975 | Osborn, Hunt | Adaptive-Reactive Theory<br>Macro variables are the same for all people in the organization. |
| 1981<br>2013 | Yukl | Multiple-linkage model<br>Subordinate effort and commitment, subordinate ability and role clarity, organization of work and task assignments, cooperation and teamwork, resources needed to do the work, and external coordination. |
| 1986<br>1987 | Fiedler, Garcia | Cognitive Resources Theory<br>Describe conditions in which intelligence and experience are related to group performance. |

*Table 9. Power and influence leadership theories*

| Year | Author | Concept |
|---|---|---|
| 1958 | Kelman | Types of Influence Processes<br>Instrumental compliance, internalization, and personal identification. |
| 1959 | French, Raven | Power Sources and Influence<br>Reward, coercive, legitimate, expert, and referent. |
| 1965 | Cartwright | Situational Engineering or Ecological Control Power<br>Control over the physical environment, technology, and organization of the work. |
| 1970<br>1979 | Jacobs<br>Hollander | Social Exchange Theory<br>Leader depends on members' loyalty, demonstrated competence, and contribution to shared objectives. |
| 1971 | Hicks et al. | Strategic Contingencies Theory<br>Explains how organizational subunits gain or lose power to influence important decisions. |
| 1975 | Graen, Dansereau, Haga, Cashman | Vertical Dyad Linkage Model or<br>Leader-Member Exchange Theory<br>Relationship between leader and subordinate, in-group and out-group. |
| 1977<br>1981 | Salancik, Pfeffer | Institutionalization of Power<br>Subunits maintain a dominant position within the organization even after their expertise is no longer critical to the organization. |

## 3F. Transformational Approach

Weber first described charismatic leaders in 1921 (as cited in Bass & Bass, 2008, p. 30). This approach re-emerged in the late 1970s, emphasizing the changing nature of an organization's internal and external environments and that leaders must create change through visioning activities, changing organizational structures and culture, and inspiring followers. Charisma is a Greek word meaning "divinely inspired gift. (as cited in Yukl, 2013, p.309). Followers believe their leader has exceptional qualities. Several charismatic leaders from the 20th century include Adolf Hitler, Sir Winston Churchill, Mahatma Gandhi, J.F. Kennedy, and Martin Luther King, Jr.

*Table 10. Transformational leadership theories*

| Year | Author | Concept |
|---|---|---|
| 1921<br>1947 | Weber | Charismatic Leader<br>Charisma occurs during a social crisis when a leader emerges with a radical vision that offers a solution to the crisis and attracts followers who believe in the vision. |
| 1977<br>1987<br>1990<br>1995 | House<br>Conger, Kanungo<br>Meindl<br>Shamir | Charismatic Leader<br>Close contact with the leader. |
| 1978<br>1985<br>1985<br>1986 | McGregor Burns<br>Bass<br>Bennis, Nanus<br>Tichy, Devanna | Transformational Leadership vs. Transactional Leadership<br>Appeal to followers' moral values about ethical issues vs. appealing to followers' self-interests to transform organizations. |
| 1993 | Hammeer, Champy | Reengineering Corporations |
| 1995 | Champy | Reengineering Management |
| 1995 | Peters, Austin | Passion for Excellence |

## 3G. Ethical, Servant, Spiritual, and Authentic Leadership Approach

This approach started in the late 1970s, dealing with leaders' ethical dilemmas in fulfilling their responsibilities to followers, stakeholders, and society. It focuses on the values, morals, and personal integrity of leaders.

## 3H. Multifaceted Wholistic Approach

This approach started in the 1970s by trying to integrate all of the previous approaches into a wholistic perspective merging transactional (manager - trait and behavior) and transformational (leader – vision, values, and change) approaches. Bass and Avillo (1990, p.xi) reflected that the recent study of leadership had more studies on executives instead of managers and small groups and more inclusion from other schools of thought.

*Table 11. Ethical, servant, spiritual, and authentic leadership theories*

| Year | Author | Concept |
|---|---|---|
| 1977 | Greenleaf | Servant Leadership<br>Service to followers is the primary responsibility of leaders and the essence of ethical leadership. |
| 1978 | McGregor Burns | Transformational Leadership vs. Transactional Leadership<br>Appeal to followers' moral values about ethical issues vs. appealing to followers' self-interests to transform organizations. |
| 1984 | Kohlberg | Six sequential stages of moral development. |
| 1989 | Depree | Art of Leadership |
| 1990 | Rost | 21st Century Leadership |
| 1993<br>1997 | Chappel<br>Fairholm | Spiritual Leadership<br>Creating conditions that increase followers' sense of spiritual meaning in their work. |
| 1994 | Bennis, Parikh, Lessem | Beyond Leadership: Balancing Economics, Ethics, and Ecology |
| 1997 | Zand | Leadership Triad: Knowledge, Trust, and Power. |
| 1998 | Becker | Integrity<br>Emphasizes honesty and consistency between a person's espoused values and behaviors. |
| 2003 | Trevino, Brown, Hartman | Ethical Leadership<br>Leaders' efforts to influence the ethical behaviors of others. |
| 2004 | Avolio, Gardner, Walumbwa, Luthans, Mayo | Authentic Leadership<br>Consistency in a leader's words, actions, and values. |

*Table 12. Multifaceted wholistic leadership theories*

| Year | Author | Concept |
|---|---|---|
| 1971<br>1998 | Yukl | Leadership In Organizations |
| 1979 | Winter | Convergence among leadership and management competencies. |
| 1981-1991 | Benson | Wholisitic Leadership Development Model<br>Work, people, and self-skills. |
| 1990 | Bass, Avillo | Transactional and transformational leadership for individual, team, and organizational development. |
| 1996 | Hunt | Leadership: A New Synthesis and<br>Out-of-the-Box leadership |
| 1997 | Chemers | Integrative Theory of Leadership |
| 2013 | Yukl | Strategic leadership in organizations. |
| 2013 | Yukl | Cross-cultural leadership and diversity. |

## CONCLUSION

Leadership research has come a long way since 1978 when McGregor Burns (as cited in Bass, 1981, p.5) quipped, "Leadership is the most studied and least understood phenomenon of our times." We now know specific details about what leaders do and do not do, making them more effective or ineffective. Also, many new areas of theory around ethical, spiritual, and authentic leadership are emerging. Our task is to integrate this knowledge to make us better leaders. For practitioners, each person needs to create their definition of leadership and then try to demonstrate personal actions consistent with their leadership definition. Benson (n.d., personal communication, 2000) declared, "Managers make you believe they can do anything! Leaders make you believe you can do anything!"

## REFERENCES

Bass, B. M. (1981). *Stogdill's Handbook of Leadership*. The Free Press.

Bass, B. M., & Bass, R. (2008). *The Bass Handbook of Leadership* (4th ed.). Free Press.

Bennis, W., & Nanus, B. (1985). *Leaders: Strategies for taking charge*. Harper and Row.

Benson, L. E. (1991). *A youth leadership case study* [Doctoral dissertation]. The University of Alberta.

Bird, C. (1940). *Social psychology*. Appleton-century.

Bogardus, E. S. (1928). World leadership types. *Social Sociology Resources*, *12*, 573–599.

Bogardus, E. S. (1929). Leadership and attitudes. *Social Sociology Resources*, *13*, 377–387.

Bogardus, E. S. (1931). Leadership and social situations. *Social Sociology Resources*, *16*, 164–170.

Carlyle, T. (1907). Heroes and hero worship. Boston: Adams. (Original publication 1841)

Clem, O. M., & Dodge, S. B. (1933). The relation of high school leadership and scholarship to post-school success. *Peabody Journal of Education*, *10*(6), 321–329. doi:10.1080/01619563309535159

Courtney, M. E. (1938). Persistence of leadership. *The School Review*, *46*(2), 97–107. doi:10.1086/440187

Cowley, W. H. (1928). Three distinctions in the study of leaders. *Journal of Abnormal and Social Psychology*, *23*(2), 144–157. doi:10.1037/h0073661

Cowley, W. H. (1931). Traits of face-to-face leader. *Journal of Abnormal and Social Psychology*, *26*(3), 304–313. doi:10.1037/h0074766

Cribbion, J. I. (1981). *Leadership: Strategies for organizational effectiveness*. AMACOM.

Fayol, H. (1949). *General and industrial management*. Pitman.

Galton, F. (1869). Hereditary genius. New York: Appleton. doi:10.1037/13474-000

Graen, G., & Uhl-Bien, M. (1995). Relationship-based approach to leadership: Development of leader-member exchange (LMX) theory over 25 years: Applying a multi-level multi-domain perspective. *The Leadership Quarterly*, *6*(2), 219–247. doi:10.1016/1048-9843(95)90036-5

Hemphill, J. K. & Coons, A.E. (1981). Development of the Leader Behavior Description Questionnaire. In *Stogdill's Handbook of Leadership*. New York: The Free Press.

Hersey, P., & Blanchard, K. H. (1977). *The management of organizational behavior* (3rd ed.). Prentice Hall.

Huckaby, W. O., & Sperling, H. B. (1981). Leadership giftedness: An idea whose time has not yet come. *Roeper Review*, *3*(3), 19–22. doi:10.1080/02783198109552528

Jacobs, H. L. (1976). A critical evaluation of Fiedler's contingency model of leadership effectiveness in its application to interdisciplinary task groups in public school settings. *Dissertation Abstracts International*, 4912.

Katz, D., & Khan, R. L. (1978). *The social psychology of organization* (2nd ed.). John Wiley.

Katz, R. L. (1955, Jan.). Skills of an effective supervisor. *Harvard Business Review*, 33–42.

Kirkpatrick, S. H., & Locke, E. A. (1991). Leadership: Do traits matter? *Academy of Management Education*, *5*(2), 48–60.

Kochan, T. A., Schmidt, S. M., & deCotis, T. A. (1975). Supervisor-subordinate relations: Leadership and headship. *Human Relations*, *28*(3), 279–294. doi:10.1177/001872677502800306

Lewin, K., Lippet, R., & White, R. K. (1939). Patterns of aggressive behavior in experimentally created social climates. *The Journal of Social Psychology*, *10*(2), 271–301. doi:10.1080/00224545.1939.9713366

McGregor Burns, J. (1978). *Leadership*. Harper and Row.

Page, D. P. (1935). Measurement and prediction of leadership. *American Journal of Sociology*, *41*(1), 31–43. doi:10.1086/217003

Sessoms, D. H., & Stevenson, J. L. (1981). *Leadership and group dynamics in recreation services*. Allyn Bacon.

Shannon, J. R. (1929). The post-school careers of high school leaders and high school scholars. *The School Review*, *37*(9), 656–665. doi:10.1086/438921

Smith, H. L., & Krueger, L. M. (1933). *A brief summary of the literature on leadership*. Indiana University, School of Education Bulletin.

Stogdill, R. M. (1974). *Handbook of leadership: A survey of the literature*. Free Press.

Tannenbaum, R., & Schmidt, W. H. (1958). How to choose a leadership pattern. *Harvard Business Review*, *36*, 95–101.

Tannenbaum, R., Weschler, I. R., & Massarik, F. (1961). *Leadership and Organizations*. McGraw-Hill.

van Wart, M. (2003). Public-Sector leadership theory. *Public Administration Review*, *63*(2), 214–228. doi:10.1111/1540-6210.00281

Yukl, G. (1981). *Leadership in Organizations*. Prentice Hall.

Yukl, G. (2013). *Leadership in Organizations* (5th ed.). Pearson Education: Prentice Hall.

# Chapter 3
# Leadership in Action:
## An Introspective Reflection

**Natasha N. Johnson**
https://orcid.org/0000-0001-8145-2153
*Georgia State University, USA*

## ABSTRACT

*This chapter highlights reflective practice as the core element of the ongoing art of introspective leadership. Firstly, while there is no one without the other, what does exist here is a dependent and independent variable. The independent variable, reflective practice, undeniably begins with self. Any person committed to a life of professional development must realize that one's personal development comes first. The introspection and assiduous work required is prodigious, to say the least. A practitioner understands that this work is cyclical in nature. As underlined in this chapter, it is essential to recognize the role of introspection in leadership. This work is a recurrent process; all actions, reactions, and interactions are interconnected, and it is imperative that leaders spend sufficient time analyzing, personalizing, and reinforcing these constructs.*

## INTRODUCTION

Leadership is the ability to inspire, motivate and guide a group of people toward a common goal or purpose (Heiss, 2023). To be an effective leader, one must possess certain qualities such as vision, empathy, communication, adaptability, and resilience (Tang, 2019). Good leaders must also have self-awareness and the ability to reflect on their own actions and decisions (Gill, 2002). Moreover, self-reflection is a process by which one examines one's thoughts, feelings, and behaviors to gain insight into oneself and improve personal and professional growth (Amanchukwu et al., 2015). By way of this process, influential leaders – and people – are able to understand their strengths and weaknesses, identify areas for improvement, and make necessary changes going (and growing) forward (Rahmani et al., 2018; Sohmen, 2013).

DOI: 10.4018/978-1-6684-8822-5.ch003

Combining leadership and reflection is essential for personal and organizational success (Hamilton, 2021; Nesbit, 2012). Introspective leaders possess the ability to look inward and reflect on their thoughts, feelings, and behaviors. They are self-aware and understand the impact of their actions on others (Moldenhauer, 2019), and they use this self-awareness to guide their decisions and interactions with others (Pounder, 2001). As such, here are six defining traits and practices of a reflective leader:

1. Self-awareness: Introspective leaders are aware of their own strengths, weaknesses, values, and beliefs. They understand how their biases and perspectives shape their thoughts, decisions, and interactions (Showry & Manasa, 2014; Watts, 2012).
2. Emotional intelligence: Introspective leaders are emotionally intelligent and can recognize and regulate their own emotions as well as the emotions of others. They use this understanding to build positive relationships with their team (Anand & UdayaSuriyan, 2010; Panait, 2017; Vitello-Cicciu, 2003).
3. Reflection: Introspective leaders regularly reflect on their own thoughts, feelings, and behaviors. They use this reflection to identify areas in need of improvement and to make better decisions in the future (Daudelin, 1996; Mitchell, 2019).
4. Humility: Introspective leaders are humble, willing to admit their mistakes, and take responsibility for their actions. They use their mistakes as opportunities for growth and learning (Maldonado et al., 2022; Mohan, 2022).
5. Active listening: Introspective leaders are good listeners and are open to feedback from others. They use this feedback to improve themselves and their leadership style (Gustafson et al., 2022; Yue et al., 2021).
6. Empathy: Introspective leaders have compassion for others and can see situations from their perspective. They use this understanding to build trust and respect with their team (Frei & Morriss, 2020; Hagman, 2021).

Underscored here, an introspective leader is self-aware, emotionally intelligent, reflective, humble, a good listener, and empathetic. These traits and practices allow influential leaders to build strong relationships with their teams and make better decisions for the betterment of their respective organizations.

## LEADERSHIP IN ACTION

Leadership in action refers to applying leadership principles and behaviors practically in real-life situations. It involves leaders taking specific steps and demonstrating efficient leadership qualities to achieve desired outcomes. In an ever-emerging, post-pandemic environment, successful leaders recognize the need to move away from the status quo and embrace necessary transformation. They understand the expectations and nuances of their constituencies, working to lead in affirming, effective, authentic, and compassionate ways. Thus, leaders must adapt their approaches and implement strategies for success in this capacity.

Traditional command and control leadership paradigms are becoming outdated, and leaders must adapt to the current socioeconomic, technological, and cultural changes and climates. Conscious leadership, which emphasizes mindfulness, empathy, and collaboration, is gaining prominence. It involves adopting new mindsets, models, and methods to thrive in the evolving leadership landscape. Leading by example is a decisive and intentional action pertinent to effective leadership. When those in headship demonstrate the behaviors and values they expect from their team members, it fosters trust, accountability, and a positive workplace culture. Leaders inspire and motivate their teams to perform at peak efficiency by embodying the qualities they want to see in others.

Influential, effective leaders exhibit certain behaviors that align with their team's goals and boost morale. These behaviors include effective communication, transparency, empathy, decision-making, accountability, and fostering a positive work environment. Leaders who demonstrate these behaviors create an atmosphere of trust, motivation, and efficiency. Good leadership encompasses achieving results and actively listening, being proactive, and supporting individual and company goals. Successful leaders create strategies to advance business goals, delegate responsibilities, and inspire and train their team members. Leadership in action, then, involves intentionality and setting examples that inspire and gain the trust of others.

Leaders prioritize others, have a clear vision or goal, practice gratitude, show up and actively engage with their team, provide feedback, foster collaboration, and lead with integrity. As such, leadership in action entails adapting to changing circumstances and embracing new leadership paradigms. This work involves leading by example, prioritizing individual and organizational development, exhibiting effective leadership behaviors, and achieving results while supporting and empowering others. By implementing these principles and taking appropriate actions, the effective leader continually works to create positive and impactful leadership experiences.

## A LOOK AT THREE INTROSPECTIVE LEADERSHIP THEORIES

Introspective leadership theories are based on the idea that effective leadership requires a deep understanding of one's own personality, values, beliefs, and motivations. These theories suggest that introspective leaders are better equipped to make decisions, motivate and inspire their team, and create a positive organizational culture. One example of an introspective leadership theory is Transformational Leadership Theory (see Sashkin, 2004). It suggests that efficacious leaders inspire and motivate their followers by being positive role models and creating a vision for the future. Transformational leaders are self-aware, authentic, and emotionally intelligent, using these qualities to build strong relationships with their constituents (Bass & Riggio, 2006).

A second example of introspective leadership-in-action is Authentic Leadership Theory (see Avolio & Gardner, 2005), emphasizing the importance of leaders being true to themselves and their values. Authentic leaders are introspective, transparent, and ethical, inspiring trust and respect from their followers by demonstrating integrity and consistency (Avolio & Walumbwa, 2014). Servant Leadership Theory is a third introspective approach that underlines the importance of putting the needs of others first. Servant leaders are reflective, empathetic, and compassionate, prioritizing their people's well-being and development over their own personal interests (Cooper et al., 2005).

Thirdly, action-centered leadership (John Adair) focuses on balancing three primary responsibilities: (1) achieving the task, (2) developing the team as a whole, and (3) nurturing constituents on an individual level. This leadership model helps streamline the management and governance processes, enabling leaders to handle different individuals, teams, and tasks simultaneously. It is especially beneficial relative to complex organizational environments. Organizational leadership in action involves prioritizing individual development, implementing professional development programs, and leveraging coaching to enhance skills and competitiveness. By investing in their employees' growth, leaders build stronger teams, identify internal talent, and create a continuous learning and improvement culture.

Together, these and other introspective leadership theories point to the significance of self-reflection and the need for self-awareness in efficacious leadership. In this way, effective leaders are keen on understanding themselves, their limits, and their own biases, values, and motivations. From there, they can create a vision for the future, build strong relationships with their community members, and create positive organizational cultures promoting growth, collaboration, and success. In the sections below, I underscore the necessity of reflective leadership, as highlighted via the journeys of two action-centered school principals.

## HIGHLIGHTING THREE REFLECTIVE LEADERSHIP JOURNEYS

### Participant Selection

In addition to my own educational leadership journey, working on an undertaking of this nature gave me a unique opportunity to connect with, observe, evaluate, and learn from two very different Principals in two varying school systems. The first Principal, referred to hereafter as Principal A, is a middle-aged white woman who took headship over an elementary school in the Southeast region of the United States roughly ten years ago. Since then, she has worked relentlessly and tirelessly to positively change this school's culture. My relationship with her stemmed from my time serving as a community member on this school's Leadership Team. Then, I worked with this Principal to analyze the School Intervention Plan (based on school data dating from 2013-14 to present) and conduct a Readiness for Change analysis using this same institution as a prototype.

The second Principal I collaborated with – Principal B – is a younger African American woman. Her career path began as a teacher turned assistant Principal before working her way up to her current role as Principal. She is a founding Principal; the elementary school she runs is located in the Northeast region of the United States. I met her while we were both in graduate school back in 2005. Since then, we have remained friends, peers, and active educators in our respective fields. For the purpose of this piece, I had a chance to interview Principal B via Skype. In addition, I analyzed the effectiveness of her school based on the ten most commonly agreed-upon characteristics of effective schools (Hoyle, 1985; Hoyle et al., 2005; Langely & Jacobs, 2014).

### Data Collection

My involvement with both of these leaders-in-practice allowed me to see school management not simply through the lens of an administrator but explicitly through the lens of the commander-in-charge. In this way, I collected first-hand data via interviews, using this information as an applicable platform to reinforce and strengthen my capabilities as a teacher-counselor-practitioner-reflective leader. This paper highlights two perspectives: Principal A's path as she took over an existing institution and worked to promote change, and Principal B, as she moved up through the ranks at her current location and launched her own school when the opportunity presented itself.

While both stories differ, this remains the same: a leader's interchangeable role as decision maker, effective communicator, authority figure, manager of conflict, executor of vision, and agent of change is never *truly* done. I have acquired much knowledge through this process, and in the sections below, I merged our accounts, experiences, insights, and notes for continued progress moving forward. As such, what follows is an account of our primary takeaways from this impactful and rewarding experience.

## LEADERSHIP IN ACTION: FIVE PRIMARY TAKEAWAYS

In alignment with my own growth, development, and reflection as a leader, in the following sections, I highlight the following five primary takeaways, gathered from both Principals' vast and varying experiences: (1) the role of the leader as an effective decision-maker, (2) the importance of being a good communicator, (3) the ability to successfully balance and implement one's authority, power, and influence, (4) the leader as a capable and consistent manager of conflict, and (5) the responsibility of the leader as creator and advancer of a tangible vision.

### Key Theme #1: Decision Making

During her tenure as an assistant Principal, Principal B was assigned the unique task of creating a program in which struggling students' test scores, at one time in the 20th percentile, would be raised to at least the 50th percentile. Given only three years to implement this undertaking efficaciously, the average person would easily have buckled under the magnitude alone. Being the leader that she is, Principal B not only embraced the challenge head-on, but she succeeded with flying colors. At that time, she was the assistant Principal, and everyone knew that her future goal of leading her own school depended on how she would carry out this charge. At the onset, Principal B gathered her team of associates and began to break things down. According to Gorton and Alston (2012), "the initial question that an administrator must ask is, 'To what extent do I possess the competency, resources, personal influence, or power necessary to implement this alternative'?" (p. 43). Given this situation, the only real alternative was taking on a system that obviously was not working and figuring out how to make it work.

I have had ample practice making decisions as a referent leader. As a referent leader, my ability to draw conclusions, make assessments, and render verdicts did not necessarily impact a large number of people. As a "titled" leader, however, managing my constituency quickly became top priority. The Principal's role as decision maker is magnified simply because of the great responsibility that lies therein. Yet, as I reflect on the responsibility of an administrator as decision-maker through these collective experiences, I have come to understand that "experience in making decisions is not, in itself, a sufficient basis for improvement without reflection upon and assessment of that experience" (Gorton & Alston, 2012, p. 64). With that said, I am more aware now than ever before of the enormity of the leader's role as the ultimate decision-maker. There is no getting around it; the effective leader can logically make consistently good decisions that positively influence an entire school culture (Leithwood & Jantzi, 1990).

### Key Theme #2: Communication

At Principal A's school, the consensus is this: keep the lines of communication open so that even when there is discord, it is not covert. There are few things worse in a school culture than negative, ineffective communication. Gorton and Alston (2012) shine a light on the extreme importance of effective communication:

*More frequently than not, failures in communication lie at the heart of problems in organization, goal setting, productivity, and evaluation...No one can manage a modern organization who is not knowledgeable in communication principles and techniques and skilled in their use. (p. 101)*

My time spent at this school brought me back to a period in which I received my first taste of leadership. Then, it was the 2004-2005 school year, I was a 4th-year teacher, and I was tasked with coordinating, managing, and overseeing events, meetings, and activities within the grade I was teaching at the time. My official title was "9th-grade team leader." In addition, I was a member of the School Leadership Team, and it was also the year I began working on my M.S.Ed in School Counseling. As busy as I was, I always made myself available to and for my students, and it was something I was very proud of. The problem I created was that I made no time for my colleagues; I did not communicate with them as I should have. This behavior affected our meetings, cross-curricular planning time, and overall interactions. Something certainly had to give.

Scheffer et al. (2012) make it unequivocally clear that communication is much more than one party interacting with another. Instead, it depends "as much on what leaders believe or don't believe about their employees as it does on what they say or don't say. It depends as much on values, beliefs, and attitudes as it does on structures, systems and approaches" (pp. 100-101). As a reflective leader in this context, I am paying attention; I see where I went wrong in the past, and I relish the opportunity to be the effective communicator I know I should and must continue to be.

## Key Theme #3: Authority, Power, and Influence

Principal A is all of five feet, three inches tall, weighing roughly 100 pounds on her heaviest day. However, her constituents refer to her as "the ninja." I chuckled when I first heard a teacher refer to her in this manner. It was immediately evident that despite her petite physical stature, she is absolutely a force to be reckoned with. As I mentioned earlier, she became the head of this school roughly ten years ago. Since then, she has earned the respect of all staff members under her guidance and leadership. When I inquired about what it was, specifically, that made Principal A a "ninja," the response was overwhelmingly the same: she pulls no punches and plays no games. As an insider, I learned that several leaders passed through this particular school within a short amount of time. The culture became one in which employees learned not to stay too committed to any specific leader because, in one teacher's words, "they were bound to leave anyway." I have had some experience entering a school mid-year; how does an administrator take the reins and demand the required respect? Gorton and Alston (2012) make it quite evident that "the use of authority is an inescapable part of an administrator's job. The important question, then, is not *whether* authority should be exercised, but *how* and *in what circumstances*" (p. 82).

Under extenuating circumstances, as with this case, Principal A, by her own account, "did what she had to do." She continues to receive high marks among her staff, which is clearly because she understands that "authority is what makes individuals leaders, but reflection – ongoing, honest, and objective reflection – is what makes them effective leaders" (Scheffer et al., 2012, p. 5). As a practitioner-turned-specialist-turned-leader, I fully appreciated what I witnessed – a manager who entered under less than stellar circumstances and quickly and efficiently used her authority, power, and influence to positively impact the school's culture.

## Key Theme #4: Conflict Management

Conflict management has long been an area of weakness for me, both personally and professionally. In the past, I believe the one barrier to reaching the other side of the "glass ceiling" has been my inefficiency in handling and managing conflict. Thankfully, as I continued to rise through the ranks as an individual and an educator, I learned – oftentimes the hard way – that conflict does not simply dissipate into thin air; left unaddressed, it does not automatically resolve itself.

I am Caribbean-American and have encountered more than my share of instances in which I assumed "cultural differences" was the culprit. While this may be true, it is not an excuse for not comprehensively addressing areas of conflict. Gorton and Alston (2012) note…"conflict is often inevitable in an educational organization, and to some extent, it may indicate that important changes are being proposed, considered, or implemented" (p.150). On several occasions, I had the opportunity to witness Principal A as an effective manager of conflict. I watched while numerous teachers, on the brink of disaster, were soothed entirely by the sound of her voice alone. Each instance concluded with the same twofold result: investigate the root of the problem and actively work to seek resolutions.

Even in my earlier years as a teacher, I found that if I could squelch the minor problems, they never festered and grew into big problems. I quickly learned then that "an important first step in conflict resolution is to identify potential or minor problems at an early stage before they further deteriorate and become unmanageable" (Gorton & Alston, 2012, p. 144). This rule continues to ring true today and permeates my personal and professional lives. The general rule of thumb is that one must address situations while they are still minuscule, and they will not end up becoming unmanageable, thorn-in-the-side problems down the line.

## Key Theme #5: Vision

A "leader's understanding of the need for power and the approach to its use is essential to progress. The leader must also have the organizational vision necessary to direct the organization into the future and the ability to articulate this vision" (Gorton & Alston, 2012, p. 8). I have long admired Principal B's tenacity and commitment to her vision. Very early in her years as an educator, she knew she would one day be the person in charge. By the time we met in 2005, she was already working on her licensure in school leadership. I began working on my advanced certificate in school administration in 2008, and one month later, I met my husband on a cruise. Five months later, I moved from my home state to his, and the idea of earning my advanced certificate fell by the wayside.

Everything truly happens as it should because then, I did not have the vision I have now. As a matter of fact, the primary reason I decided to become a school administrator at the time was because of the exponential pay increase. That alone is never a reason to become a school leader, and I acknowledge that. How would things have been different had I continued through the program then? Scheffer et al. (2012) note, "A vibrant and meaningful vision starts with leadership, but vision is effective only to the extent that it is communicated and collectively owned throughout an organization" (p. 63). At that time, I possessed a plan; while it was a good plan, it was in no way a meaningful, longitudinal, culture-impacting vision.

It goes without saying that I am in a different place now than I was at that time. As a leader, I now know that the "vision tends to set [our] horizons. Once we recognize [this], we can take [it] into account as we make decisions and manage the everyday routine… It (the vision) becomes crucially important as we seek to implement change" (Whitaker, 2010, p. 33). My scope is different now than it was then.

After making that (first of many) major move in 2008, I spent ample time prioritizing my own personal development. Much time has transpired since then; I have grown tremendously in many ways. Now, I no longer have a "plan;" I am proud to say that I possess a real, tangible, and executable vision for reform.

## REFLECTIVE LEADERSHIP, REFLECTIVE PRACTICE, REFLECTIVE LIFE

Reflective practice is the core element comprising the ongoing art of thoughtful leadership. Firstly, while there is no one without the other, what does exist here is a dependent and independent variable. The independent variable, reflective practice, undeniably begins with self. Any person committed to a life of professional development must realize that one's personal development comes first. The introspection and assiduous work required is, at minimum, prodigious. A practitioner understands that this work is cyclical, for "reflection tends to focus interactively on the outcomes of action, the action itself, and the intuitive knowing implicit in the action" (Schön, 1983, p. 56). This work is recurrent in nature; all actions, reactions, and interactions are interconnected, and sufficient time must be spent analyzing and personalizing these constructs. If this system is not adhered to, there will be failure because "when a practitioner does not reflect on his own inquiry, he keeps his intuitive understandings tacit and is inattentive to the limits of his scope of reflective attention" (Schön, 1983, p. 282).

### My Own Reflection: Moving the Needle Forward

Reflective leadership can only be implemented once a person can honestly face self, understanding that "reflective leadership is a process of taking stock of ourselves, of objectively looking at our actions, our beliefs, and our espoused theories and theories-in-use. Knowledge, choice, and perception, taken collectively, constitute the mirror by which this takes place" (Scheffer et al., 2012, p. 42). Through my own leadership journey, I have come to understand that a reflective leader is constantly growing, building, and inquiring. "When someone reflects-in-action, he becomes a researcher in the practice context… because his experimenting is a kind of action, implementation is built into his inquiry" (Schön, 1983, p. 68). While the job of the truly contemplative practitioner is never complete, the remuneration is the emergence of a holistic person, one whose reward is the fulfillment of a contemplative life.

### The Reflective Practitioner

Schön, throughout his text, offers the reader a broad scope of what it means to be a reflective practitioner, highlighting the importance of continual questioning, revisiting, and managing on a sizeable organizational scale. Schön (1983) provides us with much of the "what" reflective conversations look like, what effective top-to-bottom structures look like, and what limitations and implications exist for practitioners in the field. He tells us that "it is our capacity to see unfamiliar situations as familiar ones, and to do in the former as we have done in the latter, which enables us to bring our past experience to bear on the unique case" (p. 140). It is inevitable - we bring ourselves, our past experiences, and our beliefs into every current and future situation we encounter. Elaborating even further, he adds that "it is our capacity to *see-as* and *do-as* that allows us to have a feel for problems that do not fit existing rules" (1983, p. 140). This aptitude we possess serves as a precursor to our effective handling of subsequent circumstances that are bound to arise. The reflective practitioner, then, is one who, over time, continually builds a repertoire, one in which a variety of tools are amassed for productive, diligent, operational use.

Regarding conflict, "the expectation is that 'legitimate conflicts' will surface...a manager's task is to ensure that such conflicts are neither suppressed nor circumvented. Organizational learning...depends on the 'working out' of such conflicts" (Schön, 1983, p. 254). This journey leads to the debunking of numerous implications, and there are no Band-Aid fixes to managing conflict. The contemplative leader and practitioner knows that early identification is imperative, for "clearly an important first step in conflict resolution is to identify potential or minor problems at an early stage before they further deteriorate and become unmanageable" (Gorton & Alston, 2012, p. 144). Conflict is unavoidable; nevertheless, it presents ample opportunity for reflective practitioners to bring unity to their constituency as leaders; to build competency and credibility to their craft.

## Hanging the Mirror

Inasmuch as Schön provides us with the "what," Scheffer et al. provide us with the "whom." The tone in *Hanging the Mirror* is consistently one in which all related elements of reflective, effective leadership are directly connected to one's employees. Communication, recognition, involvement, and capturing the human spirit are just an iota of the many responsibilities and accountabilities underscored in the role of the reflective leader. The "who," of course, is the commander-in-charge, tasked with building a culture that directly connects to one's personnel. These are the people who, ultimately, are directly impacted by their leader's vision or the lack thereof.

It is a well-known fact that communication is a fundamental aspect of building a well-run organization, but do we realize how significant this notion truly is? One of the many roles of the reflective practitioner and leader is to create a communication-rich culture. Scheffer et al. (2012) make it clear that communication is much more than one party interacting with another. In fact, it depends "as much on what leaders believe or don't believe about their employees as it does on what they say or don't say. It depends as much on values, beliefs, and attitudes as it does on structures, systems and approaches" (pp. 100-101). Productive, industrious personnel can only exist when they are aligned with a motivational, reflective, communicative leader who executes a clear and consistent vision (Gorton & Alston, 2012).

## Leadership: Title vs. Practice

I initially began working on my advanced certificate in school leadership and administration in March of 2008. At that time, I was educated, experienced, knowledgeable, and zealous and held referent, informal leadership among my coworkers and peers. Yet, what I know now, unbeknownst to me then, is that I was far from ready for a life of formal headship. While I possessed many formidable qualities at the time, I was not genuinely committed to ongoing, reflective practice. I was a leader by title, but there was a missing element – "authority is what makes individuals leaders, but reflection – ongoing, honest, and objective reflection – is what makes them effective leaders" (Scheffer et al., 2012, p. 5). Despite my zeal as a teacher and guidance counselor, I lacked effectiveness because I tended to be emotionally turbulent, did not open the lines of communication with my coworkers, and was reluctant to share newfound knowledge with others. My espoused theories conflicted with my theories-in-use; I knew, theoretically, that "only by a searching reexamination of ongoing patterns of behavior can we begin assembling a picture of the values, paradigms, and assumptions that give impetus to our actions and form to our decisions"

(Scheffer et al., 2012, p. 28). However, I did not put what I believed I knew into my own daily practice. I was not nearly as trusting as I should have been. I was mildly interested in the input of others, and I made little effort to recognize work that I believed to be "part of the job."

## Change

I, myself, am no stranger to change. I have lived in two countries, three states, and more cities than I can count; I know from my own experience how taxing and overwhelming the prospect of change can be. Change allows for setting a system of perpetual alterations, adjustments, and variations in motion. Simply put, change can be challenging, particularly for the unaccustomed. It is human nature to seek comfort and, with that, a residual state of homeostasis. The problem in most instances is that comfort quickly turns into complacency, which can eventually turn into entitlement. When people reach this state, expecting them to actively and willingly support a climate of change is seemingly impossible. According to Whitaker (2010), "One essential component of leading change is to support and reinforce any attempts to move in the right direction – and to do so promptly, as they occur" (p. 101).

Managerial support for attempts of this nature is significant. When people see that their efforts are supported, they will be more inclined to continue to seek change. The role of the leader, then, is "trying to develop an understanding of the [system change] and people's concerns about it. To accomplish these objectives, the administrator needs to create a climate or atmosphere conducive to objectivity, trust, and confidence" (Gorton & Alston, 2012, pp. 198-199). The truly reflective leader understands the significance of cultivating a culture of respect; in doing so, one's constituency can "buy-in" to change, simply because they trust their leader's ability to impart this change.

What changed for me between then and now? After meeting my husband on a cruise and relocating my home city and state to his, three months thereafter, we were wed. We spent the next fifteen years to date traveling, collectively living in two countries, three states, and more cities than I can count; throughout this time, we continue expanding our scopes, visions, and levels of communication. We challenge each other daily in our pursuit of more. There is no more significant motivator than regular, ongoing accountability in one's quest to improve. Just as iron sharpens iron, so "knowing-in-practice consists of a self-reinforcing system in which role frame, strategies of action, relevant facts, and interpersonal theories of action are bound up together" (Schon, 1983, p. 234). I also became an educator in another country for some time, an experience that indelibly proliferated my worldview.

Today, I finally understand that "if determination is critical to a reflective discipline, patience, and perseverance are its twin sisters. Reflective leadership – indeed a reflective practice of any kind – is less about growing by leaps and bounds than pursuing a steady process of little-by-little, day-by-day" (Scheffer et al., 2012, p. 158). Now, through my daily commitment to being better, do I fully understand that "the work of reflection is largely internal, but not until it becomes manifested in our daily choices does it impact those around us" (Scheffer et al., 2012, p. 128). This work never ends, and yet, while my achievements still matter a great deal to me, my legacy now matters even more.

# THE MIRROR WITHIN

Gorton and Alston (2012) revealingly note, "Most individuals not only lack awareness of their values, attitudes, and how they are affected by them but also lack criteria and standards for evaluation" (p. 50).

While the reflective leader's job is to impact and impart change, how can this be done without first having an authentic sense of self? The more I looked within, the uglier things became. I was a master teacher but a not-so-nice person. I hoarded information, was minimally willing to communicate with my colleagues, and was known for setting expectations – for both parents and students – that were too high. I needed a change, which would only come once I admitted it had to start with me.

Whitaker (2010) articulated it best: "Change is inevitable; growth is optional… In a rapidly changing world, [educational] leaders must choose growth – for themselves personally and for the organizations they serve – and determine how to achieve that growth" (p. 1). I needed to learn, and I have, that I am not managing organizations, structures, and institutions. I am leading people, and this concept alone is what makes all the difference. People are not robots programmed to do whatever they are told to do. Instead, people require interaction, communication, feedback, reinforcement, and consistency. I was proud to have acquired many of these elements as a master educator, but I had not quite mastered them all.

When I became a college counselor and instructor in the Fall of 2008, I knew that being a leader in higher academia was where I belonged. It allowed me to evolve as a frontrunner, a leader of children and adults, and a coordinator of various services. From there, I earned my Ed.S. in Instructional Leadership (2015) and my Ed.D. in Educational Leadership (2019). I continue to relish the opportunity I now have to serve as a leader in higher education. I have been granted a chance to face myself in the mirror and to realize that "the work of reflection is largely internal, but not until it becomes manifested in our daily choices does it impact those around us" (Scheffer et al., 2012, p. 128). This is what separates true leaders from the fold and what I continually strive for, the ability to serve unremittingly as a reflective leader-practitioner in life first and subsequently in practice (Patterson, 2015).

This piece highlights that combining leadership and self-reflection is essential for personal and organizational success (Nesbit, 2012). Introspective leaders are able to look inward and reflect on their own thoughts, feelings, and behaviors. They are self-aware and understand the impact of their actions on others (Moldenhauer, 2019), and they use this self-awareness to guide their decisions and interactions with others (Pounder, 2001). In tandem with the five primary takeaways outlined above, the reflective leader is a strong communicator and effective decision-maker, able to balance and implement authority, power, and influence, a capable conflict manager, and a palpable vision advancer (Day et al., 2020; Hallinger & Heck, 1999; Huguet, 2017).

## CONCLUSION

To move this needle forward, I conclude this chapter by emphasizing the following five essential practices of the effective leader, one who understands the relevance and importance of ongoing introspection:

1. Setting aside time for reflection: Creating a space to reflect on one's thoughts and actions without distractions is necessary. This space could be a quiet room, a journal, or a daily meditation practice (Johns, 2009; Mitchell, 2019). Regardless of the method, consistency is key.
2. Asking for (and accepting) feedback: Seeking feedback from one's peers, subordinates, or mentors shows inclusivity. Doing so can help leaders gain different perspectives and identify blind spots (McCauley, 2001; Moldenhauer, 2019).
3. Challenging one's assumptions: Examining one's beliefs and assumptions about oneself and others exhibits transparency. Are one's opinions based on facts or perceptions? Challenging preconceived

notions allows one to better understand one's organizational culture and climate (Hamilton, 2021; Raber Hedberg, 2009).

4. Celebrating successes and failures: Dually acknowledging one's successes and failures and learning from them is essential for the visible leader. Using one's successes to build confidence and failures to identify improvement areas allows one's team to move and grow as a collective (Maldonado et al., 2018; Pittman, 2020).
5. Practicing empathy: Attempting to see situations from other people's perspectives undoubtedly goes a long way. Exhibiting compassion allows the leader to build stronger relationships with one's team and make better, more informed decisions (Arnold, 2005; Hagman, 2021).

In sum, it is necessary to remember that leadership and introspective reflection are ongoing processes (Branson, 2007; Nesbit, 2012). An efficacious and contemplative leader is committed to learning, reflecting, and continuously striving to improve while executing a mission-minded vision that all constituency members can believe in (Bolman & Deal, 2008; Johnson, 2016, 2017).

## REFERENCES

Amanchukwu, R. N., Stanley, G. J., & Ololube, N. P. (2015). A review of leadership theories, principles and styles and their relevance to educational management. *Management*, *5*(1), 6–14.

Anand, R., & UdayaSuriyan, G. (2010). Emotional intelligence and its relationship with leadership practices. *International Journal of Business and Management*, *5*(2), 65.

Arnold, R. (2005). *Empathic intelligence: Teaching, learning, relating*. UNSW Press.

Avolio, B. J., & Gardner, W. L. (2005). Authentic leadership development: Getting to the root of positive forms of leadership. *The Leadership Quarterly*, *16*(3), 315–338. doi:10.1016/j.leaqua.2005.03.001

Avolio, B. J., & Walumbwa, F. O. (2014). *Authentic leadership theory, research and practice: Steps taken and steps that remain*. Academic Press.

Bass, B. M., & Riggio, R. E. (2006). *Transformational leadership*. Academic Press.

Bolman, L. G., & Deal, T. E. (2008). *Reframing organizations: Artistry, choice, and leadership* (4th ed.). Jossey-Bass.

Branson, C. M. (2007). Improving leadership by nurturing moral consciousness through structured self-reflection. *Journal of Educational Administration*, *45*(4), 471–495. doi:10.1108/09578230710762463

Cooper, C. D., Scandura, T. A., & Schriesheim, C. A. (2005). Looking forward but learning from our past: Potential challenges to developing authentic leadership theory and authentic leaders. *The Leadership Quarterly*, *16*(3), 475–493. doi:10.1016/j.leaqua.2005.03.008

Daudelin, M. W. (1996). Learning from experience through reflection. *Organizational Dynamics*, *24*(3), 36–48. doi:10.1016/S0090-2616(96)90004-2

Day, C., Sammons, P., & Gorgen, K. (2020). *Successful School Leadership*. Education Development Trust.

Frei, F. X., & Morriss, A. (2020). Begin with trust. *Harvard Business Review*, *98*(3), 112–121.

Gill, R. (2002). Change management—Or change leadership? *Journal of Change Management*, *3*(4), 307–318. doi:10.1080/714023845

Gorton, R. A., & Alston, J. A. (2012). *School leadership and administration: Important concepts, case studies, & simulations* (9th ed.). McGraw-Hill.

Gustafson, L. P., Short, A. K., & Hamilton, N. W. (2022). Teaching and Assessing Active Listening as a Foundational Skill for Lawyers as Leaders, Counselors, Negotiators, and Advocates. *Santa Clara Law Review*, *62*, 1.

Hagman, G. (2021). Empathy: Expanding the Capacity for Humanness and Freedom. *Psychoanalytic Review*, *108*(2), 155–168. doi:10.1521/prev.2021.108.2.155 PMID:33999701

Hallinger, P., & Heck, R. (1999). Can leadership enhance school effectiveness. *Educational management: Redefining theory, policy and practice, 178*, 190.

Hamilton, M. K. (2021). Introspective faculty assessment of self leadership. *SAGE Open*, *11*(3). doi:10.1177/21582440211031902

Heiss, K. (2023). *Introduction to leadership*. Kenneth Heiss.

Hoyle, J. R. (1985). *Skills for successful school leaders*. Academic Press.

Hoyle, J. R., English, F., & Steffy, B. (2005). *Skills for successful 21st century school leaders*. R&L Education.

Huguet, B. C. S. (2017). Effective leadership can positively impact school performance. *On the Horizon*, *25*(2), 96–102. doi:10.1108/OTH-07-2016-0044

Johns, C. (2009). *Becoming a reflective practitioner*. John Wiley & Sons.

Johnson, N. N. (2016). *10 Skills for Successful School Leaders* [Conference session]. 2016 American Association of School Personnel Administrators Annual Conference, Orlando, FL. 10.13140/RG.2.2.15691.80169

Johnson, N. N. (2017). *Bolman & Deal's Four-Frame Model of Successful Organizational Leadership* [Conference session]. 2017 American Association of School Personnel Administrators Annual Conference, Chandler, AZ. 10.13140/RG.2.2.31126.45121

Langely, N., & Jacobs, M. M. (2014). *5 Essential Skills for Successful School Leaders: Moving from Good to Great*. Rowman & Littlefield.

Leithwood, K., & Jantzi, D. (1990). Transformational leadership: How principals can help reform school cultures. *School Effectiveness and School Improvement*, *1*(4), 249–280. doi:10.1080/0924345900010402

Maldonado, T., Vera, D., & Ramos, N. (2018). How humble is your company culture? And, why does it matter? *Business Horizons*, *61*(5), 745–753. doi:10.1016/j.bushor.2018.05.005

Maldonado, T., Vera, D., & Spangler, W. D. (2022). Unpacking humility: Leader humility, leader personality, and why they matter. *Business Horizons*, *65*(2), 125–137. doi:10.1016/j.bushor.2021.02.032

McCauley, C. D. (2001). Leader training and development. *The nature of organizational leadership: Understanding the performance imperatives confronting today's leaders*, 347-383.

Mitchell, K. (2019). Reflection on Leadership. *AASA Journal of Scholarship & Practice*, *16*(2), 4–6.

Mohan, S. (2022). The hidden powers of vulnerability and humility. *Leader to Leader*, *2022*(105), 40–45. doi:10.1002/ltl.20649

Moldenhauer, E. (2019). Leadership Development: Introspective Foundations. *Leadership As We Know It*, 119.

Nesbit, P. L. (2012). The role of self-reflection, emotional management of feedback, and self-regulation processes in self-directed leadership development. *Human Resource Development Review*, *11*(2), 203–226. doi:10.1177/1534484312439196

Panait, C. (2017). Emotional intelligence in leadership. *Sci. Res. Educ. Air Force*, *19*(2), 133–138.

Patterson, E. (2015). 'What are leaders' experiences of reflection?' What leaders and leadership developers need to know from the findings of an exploratory research study. *Reflective Practice*, *16*(5), 636–651. doi:10.1080/14623943.2015.1064386

Pittman, A. (2020). Leadership rebooted: Cultivating trust with the brain in mind. *Human Service Organizations, Management, Leadership & Governance*, *44*(2), 127–143. doi:10.1080/23303131.2019.1696910

Pounder, J. S. (2001). "New leadership" and university organisational effectiveness: Exploring the relationship. *Leadership and Organization Development Journal*, *22*(6), 281–290. doi:10.1108/EUM0000000005827

Raber Hedberg, P. (2009). Learning through reflective classroom practice: Applications to educate the reflective manager. *Journal of Management Education*, *33*(1), 10–36. doi:10.1177/1052562908316714

Rahmani, M., Roels, G., & Karmarkar, U. S. (2018). Team leadership and performance: Combining the roles of direction and contribution. *Management Science*, *64*(11), 5234–5249. doi:10.1287/mnsc.2017.2911

Sashkin, M. (2004). Transformational leadership approaches. *Revue de Synthese*.

Scheffer, A., Braun, N., & Scheffer, M. (2012). *Hanging the mirror: The discipline of reflective leadership*. Wasteland Press.

Schön, D. A. (1983). *The reflective practitioner: How professionals think in action*. Basic Books, Inc.

Showry, M., & Manasa, K. V. L. (2014). Self-Awareness-Key to Effective Leadership. *The IUP Journal of Soft Skills*, *8*(1).

Sohmen, V. S. (2013). Leadership and teamwork: Two sides of the same coin. *Journal of IT and Economic Development*, *4*(2), 1–18.

Tang, K. N. (2019). *Leadership and Change management*. Springer Singapore. doi:10.1007/978-981-13-8902-3

Vitello-Cicciu, J. M. (2003). Innovative leadership through emotional intelligence. *Nursing Management*, *34*(10), 28–32. doi:10.1097/00006247-200310000-00010 PMID:14557778

Watts, G. W. (2012). The power of introspection for executive development. *The Psychologist Manager Journal, 15*(3), 149–157. doi:10.1080/10887156.2012.701136

Whitaker, T. (2010). *Leading school change: 9 strategies to bring everybody on board.* Eye on Education, Inc.

Yue, C. A., Men, L. R., & Berger, B. K. (2021). Leaders as communication agents. *Current trends and issues in internal communication. Theory into Practice*, 19–38.

## KEY TERMS AND DEFINITIONS

**Authentic Leadership:** Is a management style that emphasizes leaders' alignment with their personal core values and beliefs. It involves leading in a genuine, ethical, and transparent way. Authentic leaders are true to themselves and act in a manner that reflects their internal values and beliefs. They are characterized by qualities such as humility, transparency, vulnerability, purposefulness, self-awareness, and a focus on building relationships.

**Effective Leadership:** Is the ability to guide, inspire, and manage a group of people in a way that achieves desired goals and outcomes. Various leadership styles and characteristics contribute to and underscore effective leadership.

**Introspective Leadership:** Refers to a leadership approach that involves looking inward and examining one's own thoughts, emotions, judgments, and perceptions to enhance self-awareness and personal growth as a leader. By engaging in introspection, leaders gain a deeper understanding of themselves, their values, strengths, weaknesses, and motivations, which can then inform their decision-making, interactions with others, and overall leadership style.

**Leadership:** Is a crucial aspect of management and the success of an organization. It involves guiding and influencing a group to work together to achieve common goals. Effective leadership skills are essential for individuals in influential roles to direct and complete tasks, support initiatives, create a sense of unity within a team, and empower others.

**Leadership-in-Action:** Refers to the practical application of leadership principles and behaviors in real-world situations. It involves taking specific actions and demonstrating leadership qualities to effectively guide and influence others toward achieving common goals. Leadership-in-action encompasses various aspects and strategies leaders can employ to drive organizational success, inspire their teams, and address societal challenges.

**Reflective Leadership:** Is a practice that involves self-reflection, contemplation, and learning in the context of leadership development. It emphasizes thinking about oneself as a leader, gaining self-awareness, and aligning one's values, goals, and ambitions. Reflective leadership is recognized as a critical part of learning from experience and professional development.

**Transformational Leadership:** This leadership style focuses on inspiring and motivating individuals to achieve positive changes and accomplish common goals. It involves leaders who are energetic, enthusiastic, and passionate about their work, and they can convey a clear vision to their team members. Transformational leaders aim to bring about meaningful transformations in their organizations and create a positive impact on their constituencies and society as a whole.

# Section 2
# Transformational Leadership in Educational Institutions

# Chapter 4
# Enabling Transformational Complexity Leadership in Education

**Beryl Peters**
*University of Manitoba, Canada*

**Timothy Shawn Beyak**
https://orcid.org/0000-0002-6963-2634
*J.H. Bruns Collegiate, Canada*

## ABSTRACT

*This chapter answers calls for a transformational, distributed, action-centered approach to leadership to engage with, problematize, and take action to address complexities and challenges facing education. Complexity leadership theory is informed by complexity theory, grounded in complex adaptive systems, and characterized by multi-level, dynamic interactions, and emergence. The authors describe ways that their formal and informal leadership roles as consultant, administrator, academic, and teacher-leader, illustrate and illuminate the potential of complexity leadership for the education system. They explore this potential as embedded in the context of an action research project enacted across all levels of the education system. These leadership practices may motivate and encourage formal and informal leaders to consider purposeful, planned ways to enable transformative change within complex adaptive systems.*

## INTRODUCTION

The authors are two educators situated in both formal and informal leadership roles, grappling with the many unprecedented, complex, and evolving challenges facing today's public education system. Within the education system, they have supported government, academia, in-service and pre-service teachers, and Kindergarten -- Grade 12 students, as they explore and address pressing issues affecting education. The authors find inspiration in the work of many colleagues who are also striving to empower learn-

DOI: 10.4018/978-1-6684-8822-5.ch004

ers to confront global, local, and educational complexities, and have witnessed abundant examples of transformational formal and informal leadership within the context of their provincial education system.

However, these leadership practices are not networked and often occur within localized, islanded communities. The potential for networked transformation, innovation, and adaptability within the education system is untapped. The authors see the need for leadership in education to be reconceptualized to address urgent issues affecting education systems, including human rights issues, social and economic inequities, global pandemics, democratic erosion, political instability and turmoil, climate change and sustainability, artificial intelligence, and growing technological demands as shown in Figure 1. They join the call for a transformational, distributed, action-centered approach to leadership (Harris, 2020) to engage with, problematize, and take action to address the complexities and challenges facing education. They propose that Complexity Leadership (Uhl-Bien, 2021a; Uhl-Bien & Arena, 2018; Uhl-Bien & Marion, 2007), informed by complexity theory, grounded in complex adaptive systems, and characterized by multi-level formal and informal interactions, flexibility, and adaptability, can equip educators with actionable strategies for responding to contemporary challenges in education.

The authors begin by placing themselves within the context of their provincial education system and by defining their roles as formal and informal education leaders. They then probe past and current definitions of leadership, as well as understandings of networked and distributed leadership models, that lead to their current understandings of Complexity Leadership in education. They describe the theoretical basis and qualities of Complexity Leadership, and through their lived experiences and leadership roles, they illustrate the potential for Complexity Leadership in the education system.

The authors use the lens of a collaborative, participatory action research study and draw on their experiences and the development of the resources underpinning the study, to illustrate how creativity, innovation, adaptability, and emergence of ideas can be prompted and enabled through Complexity Leadership at all connected levels of the education system. They conclude the chapter with a discussion of the challenges for implementing a Complexity Leadership approach, suggestions and strategies for implementing Complexity Leadership in education, and implications for a Complexity Leadership approach to education and other complex adaptive systems.

*Figure 1. Urgent issues affecting education systems*

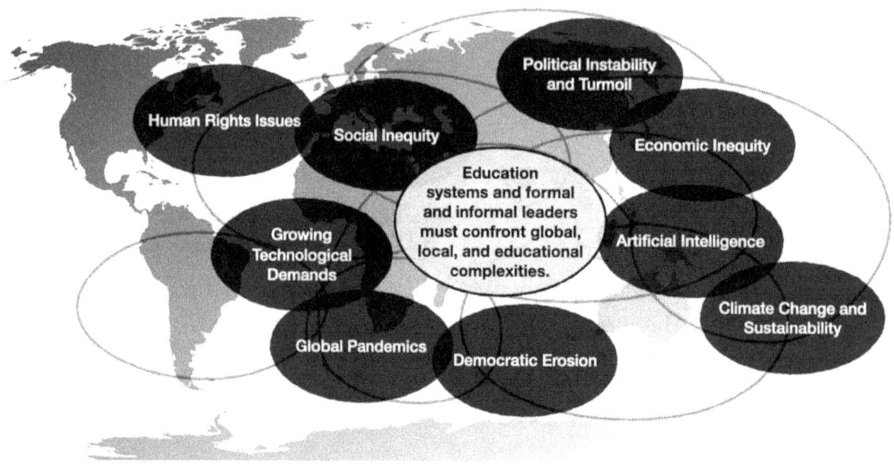

## LEADERSHIP OVERVIEW

Theories and concepts about formal leadership are wide ranging, divergent, contentious, and have significantly shifted and evolved over the last 100 years. Fennell (2021) traces the evolution of leadership theories and approaches in the health and human-service workforce, beginning with the "Great Man Theory" of the 1840s and leading to distributed leadership approaches and complexity theory applications in the 2000s. Recent approaches to leadership have included adaptive, authentic, ethical, spiritual, inclusive, servant leadership, transactional, transformational, distributive leadership, and complexity leadership, as well as many other diverse paradigms (Lundqvist et al., 2023; Northouse, 2022).

Although the nature of leadership has been debated for millennia, there is no current consensus for a definition of leadership (Bolden et al., 2023; Northouse, 2022). However, despite the multitude of ways to conceptualize and categorize leadership and the hundreds of definitions, Northouse (2022) identifies common properties central to diverse characterizations of leadership: "(a) leadership is a process, (b) leadership involves influence, (c) leadership occurs in groups, and (d) leadership involves common goals" (p. 6).

In education systems, conceptualizations of school leadership have centered around traditional and narrow definitions of leadership describing hierarchical, assigned governance positions such as the role of school principal (Fairman & Mackenzie, 2015; Harris, 2020). The mainstream educational leadership research focuses largely on these formal leadership roles (Evans, 2022), supported by a long history of educational leadership practice defined as "influence to achieve organisational goals" (James et al., 2020, p. 618). Transformational Leadership, a term introduced by Burns (1978) and further developed and popularized by Bass (1985) is one of the most enduring leader-follower models in education leadership, in which followers are empowered, intellectually stimulated, influenced, and inspired by the role model of a charismatic leader (Bass, 1985; Bass & Steidlmeier, 1999). Transformational Leadership is among the most studied model of leadership in education (Gumus et. al., 2018), along with distributed leadership, instructional leadership, and teacher leadership (Gumus et. al., 2018).

Research studying formal leadership in which individual leaders influence others dominates the traditional scholarly literature (Kruse, 2021; Liu et al., 2022) and most leadership models up to the 21st century and ongoing perpetuate the notion of an individual leader with power to influence followers (Bolden et al., 2023; Western, 2019). However, the disruptive effects of the COVID-19 pandemic on global education systems have sparked growing calls for more collaborative and networked approaches to leadership (Harris, 2020). Such calls add to existing literature advocating for a definition of leadership as distributed across multiple system levels, undertaken by any member of the system, and not dependent on a formal assigned leadership role (Bligh, 2016; Hammond et al., 2017; Kegan & Lahey, 2016; Liu et al., 2022).

Recent networked, distributed approaches to educational leadership counter the hierarchical model of individual leader as locus of power and expand on the definition of distributed leadership originally proposed by Gronn (2002). Gronn claimed that conventional leadership models focusing on stand-alone leaders and prescribed division of labor weren't appropriate for systems like schools that featured changing divisions of labor and adaptive team-based approaches. Gronn proposed a distributed leadership model based on the criterion of conjoint agency, distinguished by interpersonal synergy and reciprocal influence. He highlighted two main types of synergies: formal and informal. Gronn described formal synergies as "based on role incumbency while informal synergies are anchored on personal relations" (2002, p. 437). Gronn's model influenced current models of distributed leadership, widely applied to education, that focus on the networked interactions between individuals within the organization rather than on the individual leader's actions (James et al., 2020).

Mifsud (2023), in a systematic review of distributed leadership in education (2010-2022), points out the diverse definitions and conceptualizations of distributed leadership as applied to school leadership. Distributed leadership is conceptualized variously as a framework for both formal and informal leaders working together as co-leaders (Harris, 2013; Mifsud, 2023) and as informal leadership which might be described as the "antithesis of top-down, hierarchical leadership" (Mifsud, 2023, p. 3).

## LEADERSHIP AS FORMAL AND INFORMAL

Complexity Leadership Theory (CLT) builds on the informal leadership processes of distributed, shared leadership and views leadership as "occurring in both formal *and* informal processes, and as emerging in and interacting with complex interactive dynamics" (Uhl-Bien & Marion, 2011, p. 468). Complexity Leadership Theory is a recent evolution in leadership models, introduced into the leadership literature by Uhl-Bien, Marion, and McKelvey (2007) in an article titled "Complexity Leadership Theory: Shifting leadership from the industrial age to the knowledge era" and reconceptualized over the years (Hazy & Uhl-Bien, 2014; Uhl-Bien, 2021a; Uhl-Bien & Arena, 2018).

The authors have served as informal leaders within the education system by: working with teacher partners and teacher teams; mentoring pre-service and in-service teachers; presenting at conferences and professional development workshops; serving on advisory boards, executive and working committees; guest lecturing; disseminating research; and through their writing. As formal leaders, one author led provincial arts education curriculum development and currently holds a position as Director of Practicum at the largest University in their home province, and the second author is a teacher-leader in the local and national education community.

The authors locate their entwined formal and informal leadership and practice within the bureaucratic structures of the education system and have experienced the bottom-up, multi-way, recursive, emergent, non-linear, complexity dynamic described by Marion and Uhl-Bien (2002) "that is generated through interactive bonding among interdependent, need-seeking individuals, each of which are driven by their local (bounded) assessments of social and organizational events" (pp. 5-6).

Although the formal/informal interactive dynamics characterized by CLT are located within bureaucratic structures, they are not grounded in them or in the managerial practices and rationalized control associated with such structures. The dynamics of leadership are distinguished from the individual leaders who act upon and influence the phenomenon of complex interactive, interdependent leadership dynamics (Uhl-Bien et al., 2007). These dynamics are what distinguish CLT from other similar shared leadership models. CLT is consistent with principles of distributed leadership and other models of decentralized leadership, but unlike those models, CLT is grounded in complexity theory and understandings of complex adaptive systems. CLT also has similarities to transformational leadership theory (Bass, 1985; Burns, 1978). However, Marion and Uhl-Bien (2002) emphasize that "while both models address processes for creating transformation to stimulate organizational effectiveness, they do so from very different perspectives" (p. 3). The authors describe differing constructs and consequential differences, for example control vs decentralized control and interdependent interaction vs. direct leadership emulated by individuals. Different to transformational leadership theory and distributive leadership, complexity leadership theory offers "a framework for describing how leadership in organizations can enable complexity dynamics that allow the organization to operate as *adaptive*, rather than *bureaucratic*, systems" (Hazy & Uhl-Bien, 2014, p. 718). A conceptual framework for leadership premised on the "dynamic relationship between the bureaucratic, administrative functions of the organization and the emergent, informal dynamics of complex adaptive systems (CAS)" (Uhl-Bien et al., 2007, p. 298) is unique to leadership models. The complex adaptive system is a key characteristic of all iterations of Complex Leadership Theory not previously recognized in the leadership literature (Hazy & Uhl-Bien, 2014).

Complex adaptive systems are described variously in the literature as complex dynamic systems (Koopmans, 2020; Larsen–Freeman, 2019) and as complex adaptive systems (Fidanboy, 2022; Stacey, 1996). Regardless of terminology, understandings of dynamic, adaptive complex systems draw from theorizations about complexity (Byrne, 1998; Byrne & Callaghan, 2023; Cilliers, 1998) also discussed in the literature as complexity science (Richardson & Cilliers, 2001), complexity thinking (Davis & Sumara, 2006; Hager & Beckett, 2019), dynamic systems theory (Fogel et al., 1997), and as a theory of emergence (Goldstein, 2000). The present authors draw from this diverse body of research and choose the terminology of complexity theory underpinning complex adaptive systems. The term complexity thinking is also used in this chapter to refer to "a way of thinking and acting" (Davis & Sumara, 2006, p. 25). The following discussion endeavors to define complexity theory and complex adaptive systems to support sense-making of Complexity Leadership Theory.

## COMPLEXITY THEORY

Given the increasing intricacies and challenges of our world, there are growing calls for a complexity theory approach to systems analysis; one with tools, language, and conceptual understandings that can meaningfully analyze, interpret, and respond to the many complex, diverse, pressing, and evolving issues and challenges for systems (Turner & Baker, 2019). Complexity theory has been conceptualized in a variety of ways: as an empirical theory (Byrne, 1998), as a metaphor (Newell, 2008), as a descriptive theory (Morrison, 2008), and as a way to conceptualize the real world (Mason, 2008a). The present authors characterize complexity theory as an "an ontologically founded framework of understanding" (Byrne & Callaghan, 2023, p. 14) and as descriptive theory. A descriptive theory names and characterizes a phenomenon (Varpio et al., 2020), and when also construed as a pragmatic, complexity theory can offer insights "to prompt the emergence and affect the character" (Davis, 2008, p. 54) of complex phenomena.

Complexity theory originated in the natural sciences during the last century (Guile & Wilde, 2022; Hager & Beckett, 2019) and has been applied to complex systems such as education, health care, economics, and other areas of the social sciences (Hager & Beckett, 2019). Complexity theory has been used in the social sciences as a conceptual framework to describe and analyze the behaviors and changes over time of dynamic, non-linear complex systems made up of many interacting, interconnected parts (Knight, 2022; Semetsky, 2008). In education, complexity theory has been used for nearly three decades to analyze curriculum, educational research and philosophy, educational change, and other related areas (Knight, 2022).

Complexity theory has been defined as "a theory of change, evolution, adaptation and development" (Morrison, 2008, p. 16). In contrast to linear, explanatory, predictable, reductionist, or causal theories for understanding phenomena, complexity theory recognizes no such efforts and makes no such claims. Instead, complexity theory is concerned with systems that change and adapt, and with the dynamic interactions within the systems that have the potential to create new properties and behaviours (Mason,

2008b). When interactions between multiple, non-linear relations generate new structures, behaviours, and qualities, this phenomenon is known as emergence. Emergence, together with relations, are defining features of complex systems (Hager & Beckett, 2019) as elaborated by Mason (2008b):

*One of the most important insights of complexity theory is this notion of emergence which implies that, given a sufficient degree of complexity in a particular environment, new (and to some extent unexpected) properties and behaviours emerge in that environment. The whole becomes, in a very real sense, more than the sum of its parts in that the emergent properties and behaviours are not contained in or able to be predicted from the essence of the constituent elements or agents. A central concern of complexity theory is thus with the relationships among the elements or agents that constitute a particular and sufficiently complex environment or system. (p. 33)*

## COMPLEX ADAPTIVE SYSTEMS

Complexity thinking and theory are not new to the authors' roles as formal and informal leaders and to their teaching, learning, and research. They have explored complexity thinking and related theories for over a decade, and their graduate research was grounded in complexity theory (Peters, 2011) and complexity as rhizomatic (Beyak, 2021). For decades they have worked within the complex adaptive system of education. A complex system such as education or healthcare can be described as a group of diverse, non-linear parts or agents "that form a unified whole in their interactions, relationships, or dependencies" (Alonso-Yanez et al., 2021, p. 65). Agents in a complex system are unified by common purpose and perspective (Uhl-Bien et al., 2007), and when the properties of these systems—for example, education—prompt them to change and adapt, they are known as complex adaptive systems (CAS).

Despite decades of theorizing, there is no single, unifying definition or conceptualization of complex adaptive systems (Knight, 2022). However, Knight (2022) concludes that common properties of CAS in education are well-captured by Davis and Sumara (2006). Enduring respect for Davis and Sumara's characterizations of complex phenomena is reassuring, since one of the present authors has been drawing from this conceptualization of complex phenomena for many years (Peters, 2011). Davis and Sumara (2006) emphasize that while there are disagreements about complexity research, taxonomy, and approaches, there is reasonable consensus for the meaning of complexity and what constitutes complex phenomena. A phenomenon is complex when it is: self-organizing (emergent), bottom-up, scale-free, nested, ambiguously bounded but organizationally closed, structure-determined, located far from equilibrium, and made up of short-range behaviours (Davis & Sumara, 2006) as shown in Figure 2.

Uhl-Bien and Arena (2018) caution that most organizations are not designed as complex adaptive systems, but instead as bureaucratic systems structured for efficiency and control rather than for adaptability and emergence. Uhl-Bien and Marion (2014) argue that because organizations are not naturally complex adaptive systems, complexity leadership is needed so that leaders can create the conditions for organizations to function as complex adaptive systems and thus enable dynamic interactions and emergence.

Traditional approaches to leadership are not effective in enabling the dynamic interactions between non-linear relations that can occasion emergence, change, and learning in complex adaptive systems, and such leadership models can even inhibit the effective functioning of complex adaptive systems (Uhl-

Bien et al., 2007). Complex adaptive systems need a different kind of leadership than the traditional, hierarchical, linear leadership models of the past.

Groups of people assigned to meet top-down, leader-set, and pre-defined goals and visions are not enabled to their full potential to produce innovative change or emergent complexity. A different kind of leadership is required that can appropriately occasion interactive, interdependent social networks to produce emergence. Complexity Leadership Theory provides a framework to enable and foster emergence, learning, and creativity in complex adaptive systems (Uhl-Bien et al., 2007).

*Figure 2. Complex systems*

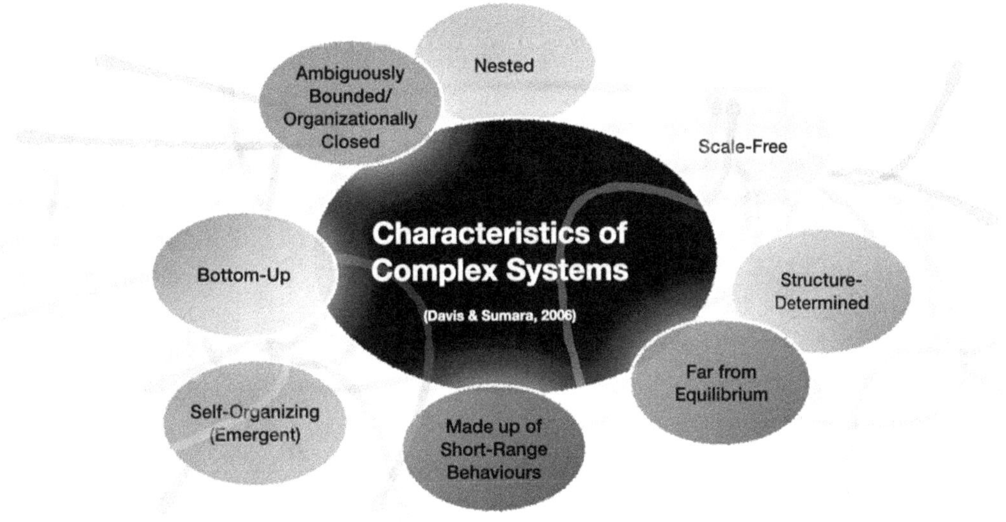


## COMPLEXITY LEADERSHIP

As both formal and informal leaders working in the CAS of education, the authors have observed the need for a leadership model with the potential to enable the education system to react, adapt, and innovate more flexibly and effectively in response to existing and evolving complex challenges. They believe that traditional understandings of the heroic individual leader (Uhl-Bien & Marion, 2011), situated within a prescriptive, controlled, static, hierarchical bureaucracy, are insufficient to generate creative solutions to current volatile world challenges and urgent societal needs. Leadership models premised on command, control, stability, avoidance of uncertainty, rationality and efficiency, are not designed for or capable of addressing complexity (Fennell, 2021; Uhl-Bien & Arena, 2018). However, models that shift away from top-down leader-led stable structures to more relational, human-centered, and flexible models such those grounded in distributed, decentralized leadership models (Gronn, 2002) are also insufficient to enable emergence of ideas and interactions across and within a complex adaptive system. For those enabling processes and for a theoretical framework appropriate for interactive, decentralized leadership in complex adaptive systems (Lichtenstein et al., 2006) we turn to Complexity Leadership Theory (Uhl-Bien et al., 2007).

As appropriate for a theory defined by interactions and emergence, Complexity Leadership Theory has evolved over the years. Complexity Leadership Theory as proposed by Uhl-Bien, Marion, and McKelvey (2007) was conceptualized around three leadership functions: Administrative Leadership, Enabling Leadership, and Adaptive Leadership, as shown in Figure 3. These functions have been retitled and repositioned over the years (Hazy & Uhl-Bien, 2014; Uhl-Bien & Arena, 2018) and re-conceptualized with the integration of new concepts and theories (Uhl-Bien, 2021a; 2021b; Uhl-Bien & Arena, 2018). Reconceptualization of this theory to introduce the concept of entrepreneurial leadership (Uhl-Bien & Arena, 2018) does not align well with an education system not purposed for entrepreneurship, so for our purposes we use terminology drawn from the seminal description of Complexity Leadership Theory (Uhl-Bien et al., 2007).

*Figure 3. Complexity leadership theory*
*Source: Uhl-Bien et al. (2007)*

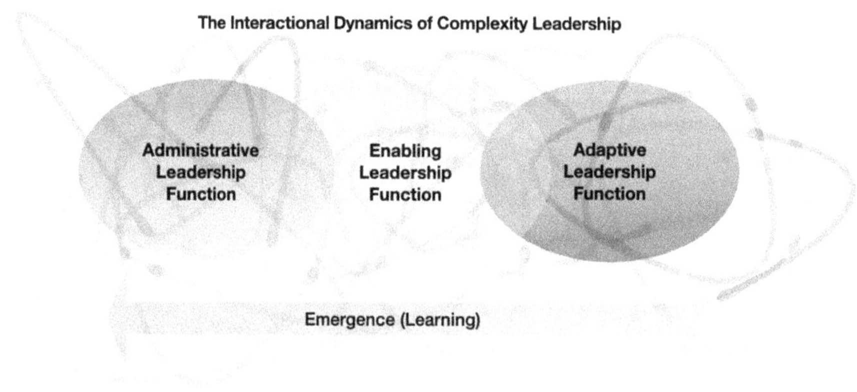


Key understandings common to the diverse interpretations and evolutions of Complexity Leadership Theory include:

- Leadership is understood to be a "complex, interactive dynamic" (Uhl-Bien et al., 2007, p. 298);
- Leadership is understood in its context of practice (Uhl-Bien, 2021a);
- Systems (Uhl-Bien & Arena, 2018) and spaces (Uhl-Bien 2021a; 2021b) conceived as "adaptive" have the potential to adapt, innovate, and learn;
- Complex adaptive systems and spaces feature rich, distributed connectivity driven by complexity rather than by bureaucracy (Uhl-Bien & Arena, 2018);
- Complex adaptive spaces and systems can be enabled by the interactions of formal and informal leaders (Uhl-Bien et al., 2007);
- Paradigms for Complexity Leadership are grounded in complexity theory (Hazy & Uhl-Bien, 2014); and,
- Emergence is a key feature of complexity theory and of complex adaptive systems and spaces (Uhl-Bien & Marion, 2011).

## ADMINISTRATIVE LEADERSHIP, ENABLING LEADERSHIP, AND ADAPTIVE LEADERSHIP FUNCTIONS

*Administrative leadership* is grounded in the system's organizing bureaucracy but is understood to be more than leadership undertaken by people in administrator roles (Uhl-Bien & Arena, 2018). Administrative leadership is "leadership in the formal systems, structures and processes" (p. 98) that, from a Complexity Leadership perspective, builds vision, provides organizational strategies and resources, and grounds decisions and actions in consideration for how they will impact creativity, learning, and adaptability (Uhl-Bien et al., 2007).

*Adaptive leadership* "refers to adaptive, creative, and learning actions that emerge from the interactions of CAS as they strive to adjust to tension (e.g., constraints or perturbations)" (Uhl-Bien et al., 2007, p. 305). Adaptive leadership is conceptualized as an informal dynamic emerging from the agents interacting within the CAS that produces "new ideas, innovation, adaptability, and change" (Uhl-Bien and Marion, 2011, p. 474).

*Enabling leadership* describes the ways that both formal and informal leaders catalyze the conditions for emergence in a complex adaptive system. Leaders can enable adaptive spaces and processes, new forms, and the emergence of knowledge flow, creativity, and innovation (Uhl-Bien & Arena, 2018; Uhl-Bien et al., 2007) by creating the conditions for complex emergence. Uhl-Bien, Marion, and McKelvey (2007) describe conditions for "emergent change behaviours" (p. 309) as "interaction, interdependence, asymmetrical information, complex network dynamics, and tension" (p. 309).

Administrative and enabling leadership, purposefully intended to interact for emergence, are entangled leadership functions in which no role is viewed as more important than another and roles are "entangled within and across people and actions" (Uhl-Bien et al., 2007, p. 306).

## COMPLEXITY LEADERSHIP THEORY IN PRACTICE

Although Complexity Theory Leadership is a recent contribution to the Leadership literature, examples and case studies from the literature illustrate the potential for CLT in education and other complex adaptive systems. Complexity Leadership has been predominantly taken up in Healthcare (Belrhiti et al., 2018; Porter-O'Grady, 2020; Uhl-Bien et al., 2020); however, there are few empirical studies; the research literature is predominantly explorative or explanatory, and it does not evaluate the effectiveness or viability of this leadership approach (Belrhiti et al., 2018; Fennell, 2021). For example, CLT has been used as a practical framework for nursing leadership (Crowell & Boynton, 2020), the supporting leadership framework for a nursing simulation center (Bryant & Murillo (Graham), 2023), and a way to frame a theory of practice for complex leadership competency in health care (Ford, 2009). In a survey study of managers working in Serbian health care organizations that examined the differences in maturity within the three CLT leadership functions, researchers concluded that these leadership functions had practical applications for policy and for improvement of quality of service and outcomes for Serbian healthcare organizations (Horvat & Filipovic, 2018).

CLT has been widely applied as a theoretical means of understanding and enhancing the operation of various complex systems around the world, from broadly promoting learning and innovation in organizations (Mendes et al., 2016) to potential applications for state-owned enterprises in Ghana (Donkor & Zhou, 2019). CLT has been studied in the world of agile software development. A case study concluded that agile coaches at Spotify were able to practice enabling leadership that positively affected the quality of interactions among employees (Bäcklander, 2019). CLT was used as the theoretical framework in two Dutch case studies that examined a regional agricultural development and an urban redevelopment. In both case studies, research findings uncovered different and contextual enabling and adaptive leadership strategies for creating favorable conditions to enable emergence of complex innovations (Nooteboom & Termeer, 2013).

In education, Complexity Leadership Theory has been applied as a theoretical framework for understanding the complex dynamics of education in a range of contexts. CLT has been used as a theoretical framework to envision ways to support the preparation and development of Early Childhood Education (ECE) leadership in Australia (Gibbs et al., 2019; Gibbs, 2022) by mapping CLT onto ECE settings and demonstrating its potential useful application for ECE. CLT was then proposed as a framework to cultivate leadership and opportunities for leadership development in Early Childhood Education and Care (Gibbs, 2021).

CLT was used as a leadership lens in case study research to understand education leadership practices to diffuse an education innovation in six Singapore primary schools (Ho et al., 2021). The Administrative, Enabling, and Adaptive leadership functions were analyzed at different levels of the case study and researchers concluded that the "three entangled CLT leadership roles provide a useful framework for practitioners to make sense of the different kinds of leadership required to support innovation, learning and adaptability, how stakeholders in various positions can enact such leadership, and how such leadership practices interact and reinforce one another across ecological levels" (Ho et al., 2021, p. 20).

The potential for CLT in education in Canada is illustrated by a three-year Canadian mixed methods study to explore a Design-based Professional Learning Intervention (Alonso-Yanez et al., 2021). Education leadership practices informed by CLT and investigated through a complexity thinking lens discovered "emergent sites of leadership that enabled pedagogical practices to foster student success" (Alonso-Yanez et al., 2021, p. 72). Using a complexity thinking lens, researchers identified processes and actions for systemic change across the school system that "support learning, well-being, and safety" (p. 78).

A recent but growing body of literature suggests the potential for CLT for complex adaptive systems and the need for further empirical research. The authors next add their voices to those advocating for the need for contemporary leadership models to account for "diversity and continuous change in complex, interactive dynamic environments from which emergent, unexpected outcomes result" (Alonso-Yanez, 2021, p. 65).

## COMPLEXITY LEADERSHIP IN THE LOCAL CONTEXT

Approaches to leadership must be examined within the context of practice (Hallinger, 2018). Formal and informal leadership practices in Canadian education are diverse, since provinces and territories have legislative authority for education. Each province or territory determines the curriculum, policy, organization, and legislation for all levels of education for each specific provincial or territorial context. In Manitoba, Kindergarten -- Grade 12 public schools are governed by thirty-seven different school divisions and while provincial curriculum is common across schools, curriculum implementation and teaching approaches vary across school divisions and between schools. Manitoba is home to five public universities and one private university; three universities have Bachelor of Education programs, and one university offers graduate studies in education.

In education, the individual learner is nested in the collective classroom, which is nested within the school, within a larger school division or district, within the curricular structures, mandates, organization, and teacher certification process of a provincial education body, located in the global education system as shown in Figure 4. Functions of administrative and enabling

leadership occasion conditions for emergence within and across the nested interconnected levels of the complex adaptive education system in Manitoba. The authors illustrate these leadership functions within and across levels through their lived experiences working within the complex adaptive system of education in Manitoba. This system is understood to be dynamic, non-linear, interdependent, adaptive, emergent (Kaplan & Garner, 2020), and nested (Davis & Sumara, 2006). Using the lens of a participatory action research project and the development of resources that support the project, the authors begin at the outermost level of the nested system and share leadership examples at subsequent levels to illustrate the decentralized nature of Complexity Leadership as levels interact with each other in dynamic, non-linear ways, with resulting creativity, adaptability, and emergence.

*Figure 4. Complex adaptive system of education*

## THE ACTION RESEARCH PROJECT

In a review of UNESCO's 2021 book *Reimagining our futures together: A new social contract for education*, Carney (2022) describes the book's foundational principles as "the right not only to education throughout life but one imbued with meaning and value" (p. 568). Carney reports that the new social contract calls out for education to be "reimagined as a public endeavour, judged by its capacity to create shared purposes amongst individuals and communities. Curricula must change. Teachers must become facilitators of change processes. Universities must co-create and disseminate their work in new networks aimed at the [sic] strengthening the common good" (p. 568). The action research project described in this chapter is one attempt to address that call and in doing so, illustrate the potential for CLT to enable the change across all levels required to meet this challenge and mandate for the global education system. The action research project illustrates how agents in the education system at every level collaborate to ensure that all learners in the local system have access to education imbued with meaning and value. It begins with curriculum change and shared purpose; it supports teachers to become facilitators of change processes through co-creation and collaboration with school administration, universities and government. This action research project is both an example of the potential for and a practical application of CLT in the education system and illustrates a potential strategy for implementing CLT in education to enable learning and innovation at all interconnected levels of the education system.

The critical participatory action research study the authors are currently participating in, is grounded in and designed around the recently updated Manitoba Dance, Dramatic Arts, Music, and Visual Arts curriculum frameworks, considered to be innovative and progressive (Barton, 2021). The action research study is titled "Design and transform K to 12 learning spaces with the arts: A pedagogy of multiliteracies." The project goals are to identify and analyze current approaches and promising practices for designing quality learning spaces with the Arts and multiliteracies in K–12 schools in Manitoba and to then develop, evaluate, and implement a conceptual model or models for this design.

Participatory Action Research (PAR) methodology is highly congruent to Complexity Leadership Theory since both approaches strive to give agents voice and empower them to transform practice. Like Complexity Leadership, PAR is collaborative, contextual, and grounded in interactive, interdependent, and entangled relationships. PAR relies on different leadership functions, including administrative leadership for planning and coordination of the research project, enabling leadership to foster the conditions for emergence, and an embedded, adaptive leadership dynamic to generate action, innovation, and change. The goal of PAR to enable and empower emergence and innovation "may bring about significant changes to important education domains, such as school policies, curricular reform, and education in general" (Morales, 2019, p. 323).

Approaches to Complexity Leadership are "multi-level, processual, contextual, and interactive" (Uhl-Bien & Marion, 2009, p. 631). The action research study illustrates the overlapping, entangled roles of administrative, enabling, and adaptive leadership functions in Complexity Leadership across all levels of the nested education system to occasion and trigger emergence. The bilingual Manitoba research study was enacted across multiple levels of government and associated legislation, two Manitoba Universities (one English and one French), community artists/consultants, three school divisions, six schools, nine teachers, and their classroom learners in English, French, and French Immersion programs. We trace the functions of Complexity Leadership beginning at the outer government ring of the nested education system.

## CURRICULUM DEVELOPMENT FROM A COMPLEXITY LEADERSHIP PERSPECTIVE

The action research project is underpinned by the Manitoba Dance, Dramatic Arts, Music, and Visual Arts curriculum frameworks, for which the first author served as writer and project leader in her role as provincial arts education curriculum consultant. The curriculum development project illustrated the entangled leadership functions theorized by Uhl-Bien and Marion (2007). In Manitoba, subject-area curriculum frameworks are mandated for use in the Kindergarten -- Grade 12 public schools and for B. Ed programs. Manitoba develops curriculum frameworks unique to its local context and provides recommended subject-area time allotments for each subject area.

As provincial Arts Education consultant for the English program (2009–2019), Dr. Peters was given a mandate to collaborate with the Arts consultant for the French and French Immersion programs to develop and implement new provincial Arts curriculum frameworks and implementation resources for the province of Manitoba. Manitoba took a collaborative, consultative approach to curriculum development and implementation. Divisional superintendents were directed to nominate experienced teachers to provincial development and implementation teams, and a local lead writer was hired for each Kindergarten to Grade 8 and Grades 9–12 Drama, Dance, Music, and Visual Arts curriculum framework (Manitoba Education and Advanced Learning, 2015). Together with the Arts consultant for the French and French Immersion programs, Dr. Peters collaborated with four development teams of experienced local teachers and writers to draft, review, refine, pilot, and implement the arts curriculum frameworks. Following the development of draft curriculum frameworks, new teacher teams then reviewed, developed, and piloted the frameworks and supporting implementation resources. Although they did not define it as such at the time, the collaborators' process was a function of Complexity Leadership approaches in that "leadership is a process in which leaders and teams interact, exchange knowledge and learn from each other in order to collectively generate novel and useful output" (Alblooshi et al., 2021, p. 351).

The curriculum development project illustrated the entangled leadership functions theorized by Uhl-Bien and Marion (2007). Senior administration of the Department of Education provided the necessary structures and processes that Davis and Sumara (2006) might describe as "enabling constraints" (p. 147). Education legislation supported the task of curriculum renewal, a project with proscribed and not prescribed constraints that orientated the collaborators' actions while allowing for "flexible and varied response" (p. 148). Administrative leadership processes such as assigning Dr. Peters to the project of Arts curriculum development and implementation, allocating stable financial and human resources to support the project, and providing direction for structuring the overall framework for the project, created coherence while enabling space and possibility for emergence.

As enabling leaders, the two Arts consultants managed the entanglement between the bureaucratic and emergent functions of the organization (Uhl-Bien & Marion, 2007). Managing entanglement involves creating the enabling conditions for innovation and adaptability and "facilitating the flow of knowledge and creativity from adaptive structures into administrative structures" (Uhl-Bien & Marion, 2007, p. 305).

Over a years-long process, the consultant team leaders, writers, and teacher-teams exchanged knowledge and learned from each other to generate innovative curriculum frameworks relevant to their provincial context. They worked to provide an environment conducive to enabling dynamic interactions by "asking questions, providing feedback, testing ideas, discussing results and evaluating outcomes" (Alblooshi et al., 2021, p. 351), thus creating the conditions for prompting complex emergence.

As formal project leader, Dr. Peters had the flexibility to adjust and adapt to the team's shared problems, challenges, and activities, because she was not working in isolation or apart from the writers and development teams. She was empowered to create enabling processes because the institution for which she worked also empowered and fostered the autonomy of its consultants to increase complexity rather than seek to reduce it. That autonomy included a mandate to create and coordinate one development team and one implementation/pilot team for each of the Dance, Dramatic arts, Music, and Visual Arts curriculum frameworks. However, such administrative and enabling leadership processes that allowed the consultants to select and bring diverse groups of people together do not guarantee complex adaptive behaviours that result in innovative change (Marks et al., 2001; Uhl-Bien & Marion, 2009). Uhl-Bien & Marion (2009) claim that "if interdependence is not felt, complex adaptive behavior will likely not occur because individuals will not be motivated to engage" (p. 642). Interdependence is a condition for complex adaptive behaviours and if the formal leader does not intentionally foster interdependencies among participants, then complex adaptive behaviours are less likely to occur (Uhl-Bien & Marion,

2009). In Dr. Peters' context, she was fortunate that interdependencies were an inherent part of the process. Teachers were nominated to curriculum and implementation teams based on their experience, expertise, and interest in a particular Arts speciality. She did not have to work to motivate participants, to create engagement with the project or subject area, or to create a sense of connectedness with the project and its goal. All writers and teacher participants declared and provided compelling evidence for a committed, strong, shared goal of creating and renewing Arts curricula for their province, and all were passionate about their specific Arts subject area.

Emergence is not necessarily generated whenever a system has multiple interconnected and interdependent parts interacting with each other. The emergence of complex phenomena must be triggered or occasioned (Davis & Sumara, 2012) to generate innovation, change, learning, and new and unanticipated behaviours, solutions, and outcomes. Davis and Sumara (2006) describe certain conditions necessary for complex emergence. They identify complementary dyads of diversity/redundancy, neighbor interactions/decentralized control, and coherence/randomness and point out that these are by no means the only conditions for complex emergence (Davis & Sumara, 2006). However, these are meaningful conditions for an education context and the ones that can be occasioned by leaders to create sites of "emergence" (Osberg & Biesta, 2007) in complex adaptive systems.

Davis and Sumara (2006) describe internal diversity and redundancy as essential conditions for emergence. Redundancy is not understood in mechanistic terms as surplus or unnecessary qualities, but rather as the deep commonalities of the group, a key distinguishing feature of complex systems (Davis & Sumara, 2006). In the Manitoba curriculum project, redundancies took the form of a shared project and goal to develop new Arts curricula, common Arts language, shared social and community structures as Arts educators, shared contexts as public school educators, and shared passions about the importance of Arts Education.

Internal diversity was present in the make-up of teacher teams. The two Manitoba Arts consultants were enabled by their administrative structures and processes to gather teacher teams who were united in their passion for Arts Education and their desire to ensure quality Arts Education for learners in their province, but who were also highly diverse groups with multiple perspectives about Arts Education that were shared during discussions. The tension between redundancy and diversity, often expressed through heated exchanges and debates arising from their multiple perspectives, prompted emergent thinking and curricular possibilities. The initial drafts which the team workshopped, emerged over time to take completely new forms as a result of the enabling processes that fostered new ideas and encouraged critical reflection, re-thinking, and revision.

The curriculum teams' meetings, discussions, and assigned readings supported conditions for emergence that Davis and Sumara (2006) characterize as "enabling neighbor interactions through decentralized control" (p. 136). Davis and Sumara describe neighbors not as the people in the group, but as the interacting ideas and questions of the people in the group. Rich, complex, and creative ideas do not emerge just because teacher teams are brought together around a table for discussion. Instigators were needed to prompt further conditions for complex emergence. The Arts consultants provided a variety of materials which their teams could engage and respond to, along with the necessary extensive time for all team members to meet together to exchange ideas. Teachers were given release time and funding for substitute teachers so that they could attend regular day-long meetings.

Participating teachers were provided opportunities to engage with each other and the lead writers to propose and debate new ideas and to allow those ideas to "bump against one another" (Davis & Sumara, 2006, p. 143). The Arts consultants provided a sufficient density of ideas and resources to disrupt previously held thinking about Arts Education and curriculum, and create the disequilibrium needed to stimulate creative thinking. They met regularly with government project-management teams to share the ideas, challenges, and questions of teacher development teams, and received feedback to take back to the writers and teacher teams, thus facilitating a flow of knowledge and creative ideas. Members of the process at all levels were enabled and empowered to think with and learn from each other and to make recommendations and contribute to decision-making through meetings, workshops, writing, consultations, reviews, and piloting processes over a years-long period.

Because neither senior administration or the arts consultants prescribed or dictated the outcomes of the curriculum project, the development process resulted in a decentralization of control (Davis & Sumara, 2006) as the Arts consultants shared control for curriculum development with the project writers and teacher development teams. Davis and Sumara view shared control as another way of conceptualizing decentralized control. Since the goal of this curriculum project was to develop innovative curriculum, the consultants were required to explore the literature and various new curriculum models, be open and give space to new ideas, and adjust and find new solutions to emergent learning and questions, all triggers for emergence. They provided examples of curriculum for discussion, but no prescribed template for curricula. No singular view was imposed; instead, responsibilities for problematizing existing curriculum and for innovating new Arts curriculum frameworks were shared with the teams. If the consultants had directed their teacher teams to create outcomes-based curricula following models used in the Department of Education and around the world at that time, they would never have produced the complexity-informed Arts curriculum frameworks that resulted.

The Arts consultants provided the necessary "enabling constraints" (Davis & Sumara, 2006, p. 136) for complex emergence by setting the conditions for what Davis and Sumara term "randomness, and coherence" (pp. 135-136). Their shared goal to create new guiding curricula and their focus on discourses around Arts Education created the necessary coherence, while multiple opportunities were provided for the conditions of randomness, or what the teacher teams referred to as "plussing" and Kelly (2016) refers to as "in collaborative idea generation, the idea of accepting any act and adding to it" (p. 220). The invitation and openness to consider other possibilities, ideas, and perspectives enabled emergence. The resulting curriculum frameworks required new patterns of behaviour on the part of the development teams as well as from Arts educators in the field, as they moved from formerly skills- and outcomes-based curriculum models to process-based and recursive learning models, grounded in complexity thinking, creative processes, and critical reflection.

The two Arts consultants had the flexibility to practice enabling leadership for complex emergence because the administrative leadership created structures and processes that allowed them to do so. They were enabled to gather teacher teams who were united in their passion for Arts Education and their desire to ensure quality Arts Education for learners in their province, but who were also highly diverse groups with multiple perspectives about Arts Education. Teacher teams were then enabled by the complementary combinations of diversity and redundancy, neighbour interactions and decentralized control, and coherence and randomness (Davis & Sumara, 2006) to give rise to complex emergence resulting in new and innovative Arts curriculum frameworks. The generative dynamics and emergent change activities embedded in the specific context of their complex adaptive education system (Uhl-Bien et al., 2007) are key components of Complexity Leadership where formal and informal leaders "act in ways that influence this dynamic and the outcomes" (Uhl-Bien et al., 2007, p. 299). It was the interactive social network of formal and informal leaders, including writers, teachers, consultants, and project management team leaders, rather than one individual, that drove the process and created innovative change.

## COMPLEXITY LEADERSHIP IN AN ACTION RESEARCH STUDY IN THE EDUCATION SYSTEM

The four Manitoba arts education curriculum frameworks were the sources of planning for the action research project and were also the lenses through which arts-based multiliteracy, multimodal student learning was analyzed. The administrative leadership functions provided the curricular structures in the form of the arts curriculum frameworks as well as the ethics protocols required by the two participating universities. The bureaucratic constraints were sufficient to provide coherence and redundancy while allowing spaces for the co-researchers to design an action research plan and planning resources that enabled emergence at the school and classroom levels. Dynamic interactions occurred between and within each level of the study. Interdependent behaviours, critical to the success of dynamic change in complex adaptive systems (Uhl-Bien & Marion, 2009), occurred at each level.

One of this chapter's authors served as university-based co-researcher, in partnership with Julie Mongeon-Ferré, the French and French Immersion Arts consultant for the Department of Education, and the other author served as teacher participant in the study. While the researcher provided administrative structure for the project through the goals of the study, the allotted time frame and length of study, and the ethics protocols guiding recruitment and participation, the researcher did not prescribe the learning goals, the inclusion of particular arts and multiliteracies, individual classroom projects and inquiries, pedagogy, or teaching practices. Each classroom teacher was enabled to design their own projects to include their choice of arts and multiliteracies, in collaboration with the researchers. In some classrooms, the researchers functioned as informal leaders on the side, offering resources, suggestions, and sometimes planning and co-teaching with classroom teachers; in other classrooms, they engaged in interactions by questioning and offering comments about observations. Classroom teachers in turn enabled conditions for emergence in their individual classroom contexts and for their unique learners as illustrated next in this chapter.

### Enabling Leadership to Prompt Complex Emergence

To support teachers participating in the action research study, the researchers developed an Arts and multiliteracies design tool based on the Manitoba Arts curriculum frameworks (Manitoba Education and Advanced Learning, 2015) as a planning framework for teachers as they designed for Arts and multiliteracies learning, teaching, and assessment. The design tool was framed around nine questions intended to prompt and enable emergence of creative ideas for designing with Arts and multiliteracies. This design tool was taken up in various ways by participating teachers. In some instances, the classrooms were already highly complex units where teachers were functioning as enabling leaders occasioning complex emergence and adaptive responses from students, and the design tool was not needed as a prompt. Second author Tim Beyak, whose experiences are described in the following section, was one such teacher; his previous research, writing, and work with students and colleagues had already deeply explored the potential of complex adaptive, rhizomatic systems for innovation, creativity, and student agency. Rhizomatic systems are non-linear, decentered, interconnected, and non-hierarchical and flourish within CASs that enable emergence. Exploration of these systems was central to Tim's graduate work and rhizomatic thinking was foundational to the pedagogy and practices of his classroom. As an informal leader, Tim interacted at multiple levels in the education system as a teacher, a graduate student, and a practitioner and enabled adaptive responses and prompted complex emergence in various nested areas.

His enabling leadership in the classroom supported the conditions for rich interconnectivity within this site of complex emergence. His enabling leadership occasioned interactive, interdependent teaching and learning that was entangled, non-linear, and rhizomatic, and where practices involved interactions within a complex adaptive system for innovation, creativity, and student agency. Transformational, distributed, and action-centered approaches to complexity leadership (Harris, 2020) have been integral to Tim's work as a teacher, graduate student and practitioner, and formal, informal, and enabling leader in the education system.

As interconnected agents (Knight, 2022; Semetsky, 2008), Tim and his students were nested in the collective classroom and engaged in the functions of a complex adaptive system. Together they engaged in practices and processes of teaching and learning characterized by dynamic complex interactions that gave way to the emergence of new structures, behaviours, and qualities not found in isolation. For example, as part of the action research project to "Design and transform K to 12 learning spaces with the arts," Tim designed a superhero and supervillain inquiry project for his *Grade 12 Global Issues: Citizenship and Sustainability* (GICS) course (Manitoba Education and Training, 2017). The interconnected agents involved in this process included the teacher, students in the GICS course, a researcher from the academy and second author of this chapter, other students and teachers in the school, school administration, and members of the public. This superhero and supervillain project was positioned as the capstone inquiry and action project for the GICS course—a culminating inquiry project—where Tim's students explored issues of interest in global studies through a process deeply rooted in the GICS curriculum and enabled in a complex system of theories and practices of inquiry, discourse, discourse analysis multiliteracy, multimodality, and transliteracy.

The superhero project was divided into two parts. The first part of the project was more rooted in the more traditional and expected inquiry process where students engaged with a global issue and produced a written essay in APA format. The second part of the project was situated within an unusual context of multiliteracy, multimodality, and the Arts, where students created heroes, villains, origin narratives, tales, adventures, journeys, costumes, artifacts, videos, drawings, paintings, songs, voices, and so forth. In part two of the project, students used their inquiry findings from the first part of the project and cast them into the multimodal elements of design as they created and instantiated the creation of superhero and supervillain characters, origin stories, and narratives, spawned from their formal inquiry work.

Students opened their processes and immersed in their topics of choice. They searched the Internet for information and accessed electronic databases and books. They engaged with primary and secondary sources, expository and narrative texts, images, videos, music, artworks, speeches, message boards, and graffiti. They made annotations from many communicative forms, which they engaged by applying their learning about discourse analysis that involved elements of multisensory, multimodality, and multiliteracy.

Subsequently, Tim's students interrogated their annotations and conferenced with him and one another. They considered ideas, contemplated values, beliefs, and worldviews, and developed many questions. In some instances, students drew from their emergent flows of queries and further engaged in the turnings of their inquiry processes. Often, peers provided one another with new questions and the generative nature of these neighbours, members of a knowledge-producing community were moved beyond their physical bodies or social groupings and engaged in a process where their work became more significant than the single enquiring mind alone. As a result, Tim noted greater levels of complex emergent learning and complex emergent leadership in his students, guiding one another in processes that strengthened their neighbouring community.

Through the oscillations between cycles of work and processes of conferencing, students worked on their projects and with each passing day, their immersion into their work developed depth and insights. In many cases, students continued to find deeply impactful questions about their topics, further stimulating understanding and promoting the development of a culture of critical discourse analysis. In some instances, certain students were enabling leaders for one another as they discussed the turns of their inquiry with one another and shared with friends and family members. Many students interacted with their peers and engaged in practically critically examining one another's topics, questions, and approaches to the inquiry work.

In the context of a complex adaptive system, emergence was characteristic of the teaching and learning in Tim's classroom. His behaviours and choices as an enabling leader guided pedagogy in relation to the implementation of the curriculum, but as important to curricular understanding was how the classroom was enabled in non-traditional and self-organizing ways. In this classroom a great deal of time was used to carefully explore, and scaffold content and context related to foundational information and theories for the course. As the learning continued over time, students came to share language, common understandings, foundational knowledge, enduring understandings, and in-depth case-studies tied to global studies.

When it was time for students to carry out their superhero and supervillain projects, emergence and powerful innovation took place. Students moved through inquiry cycles that explored topics, they set questions to enable their research, they adapted with each encounter of new material, ideas, and learning. They moved into more complex ways of exploring, interpreting, and analyzing as they engaged in learning and meaning making. The nature of Tim's enabling leadership encouraged an environment that was self-organizing, ambiguous, and moved in ways that were not limited to top-down instruction—but laterally between students and from the bottom up too as each student mastered areas of interest and inquiry through their work. The time afforded to students was generous, but the generous amount of time was balanced with accountability and milestones, regular dialogue with peers and conferencing with the teacher to problem-solve, question, share, speak to individual's growth, and to strategize for roadblocks. Each reciprocal turn of inquiry, dialogue, conferencing, and questioning prompted deeper and more complex understandings that informed deeper and more complex research and learning.

As an enabling leader in the classroom and by position students as enabling leaders too, an exciting innovation took place where emergence re-cultured the classroom in a profound way that informed students in their learning, informed Tim in relation to his pedagogy and practice, and informed the researcher from the academy in her work too. The opportunities for students to engage their inquiry learning through a process governed by choice and interest that enabled cycles of critical questioning by individuals of their own work, and by peers who shared their work with one another. Tim provided an abundance of materials and multimodal sources of quality information. Tim's invited students to engage within the complexity of knowledge sources and provided an opportunity for students to immerse within unique areas of personal interest related to global studies. And while the context of their inquires varied between each student, they were highly connected to one another in a rich culture of learning and practice as table groups shared in learning, engaged one another in questions, problem-solved, co-researched, positioned their opinions, and shared their concerns. In the midst of this CAS of classroom, the teaching and learning was non-linear, distributed, self- organizing, adaptive, and connected.

Additionally, Tim's students transformed their work into profoundly artful and powerful multimodal forms of transliteracy that included text, illustration, music, forms of visual art, and multimedia. In culmination, the students' superheroes and supervillains and were exhibited in the public spaces of the school where interactions with other students, school staff, administrators, and members of the public occurred. These artistic, creative, and complex artifacts installations

In this educative context Tim demonstrated enabling leadership having structured the practices of teaching and learning to enable conditions for emergence. This emergence involved the learning of his students, the positioning of the students' inquiry work in the public spaces where others could interact.

Tim situated the curriculum, his pedagogy, and opportunities for teaching and learning within contexts that were complex, rhizomatic, discursive, and entangled. system the formal and informal interactions between Tim and his students engaged Students in the GICS course learned about global studies through recursive processes of teaching, learning, and inquiry, where they examined issues related to discourses, power, and discourse communities and individuals of those communities that shape realities, global issues, and lived experiences of human and nonhuman entities in our lifeworlds.

## LIMITATIONS

Because Complexity Leadership Theory has not been extensively studied and there is little empirical research for a CLT approach to leadership (Belrhiti et al., 2018), practical applications of CLT are limited. CLT is defined and conceptualized differently in the literature, which further challenges the utility of this leadership approach. Consensus on when and how CLT is appropriate for use is also limited (Belrhiti et al., 2018) and arguments for its use are mainly as an analytical tool, conceptual metaphor (Ho et al., 2021) or as a philosophical lens for observing leadership (Fennell, 2021). CLT may support learning, creativity, innovation, and emergence in organizations considered to be complex adaptive systems, but there are no causal indicators to support this thinking. Morrison's (2010) questions about the direct application of complexity theory to school leadership practice are still relevant today. Morrison acknowledges the descriptive power of complexity theory but offers cautions regarding its utility for predictive purposes.

In systems with a long-standing history of top-down bureaucracy, efforts to implement a CLT informed approach would likely be met with resistance. Any efforts to implement a CLT would also require a commitment of funds and resources to support the necessary education and understanding needed to support a shift to CLT. Education and training would be needed not just for key individuals but for entire teams across the nested education or other complex adaptive system, an expensive proposition. Without adequate supports and education, understandings of CLT could be misapplied, resulting in negative, rather than positive effects for the organization. CLT was elaborated with the authors' local contexts but these contexts and others described in the literature, could not be generalized to other complex adaptive systems.

However, despite limitations, the authors believe that leadership of complex adaptive systems characterized by uncertainty, unpredictability, and diversity, can no longer rely on traditional leadership models designed for stable, non-complex, centrally controlled organizations. Complexity Leadership Theory has the potential to help organizations in understanding their complex systems and how to foster formal and informal leadership roles, new structures, behaviours, practices, interactions, and dynamics that can help them innovate and flourish.

## CONCLUSION

We live in an emergent, complex world characterized by unpredictability and volatility. Traditional forms of leadership focused on control, stability, and on reducing complexity are ill-adapted to understand and respond to such a world. Complexity Leadership, with its focus on complex interactive dynamics and ways to condition emergence, is an approach to leadership with the potential to overcome bureaucratic limitations associated with hierarchically governed organizations (Uhl-Bien & Marion, 2014) with (Uhl-Bien et al., 2007). In the education context of this chapter's authors, Complexity Leadership offers considerations for exciting, productive possibilities for the education system. The goals of the education system are to improve access and learning for all students and to imbue education with meaning and value (Carney, 2022). Through the CLT leadership functions, efforts to meet those goals were undertaken at all levels of the scale-independent education system through the action research project. The provincial Department of Education supported learning with guiding policy, curriculum, and standards for teacher certification; Universities provided professional learning to pre-service and in-service teachers and collaborative research opportunities to improve practice; teachers worked to support meaningful learning for all students in their classrooms; and students co-constructed knowledge with teachers and researchers for meaningful, deep learning.

Learning in education has been historically conceived as a context-free, replicable, stable commodity (Hager & Beckett, 2019) "encapsulated in curriculum, libraries and textbooks" (p. 88) and evaluated by standardized tests. The language frequently used by members of this system captures that commodification (Hager & Beckett, 2019): course loads, course delivery, outcomes, timetables, and quantifiable descriptors for quality control. Such language then permeates and affects approaches to pedagogy and practice, and how people within the context of the education system view themselves and each other. Complexity Leadership approaches can disrupt thinking about the education system as a commodity-producing bureaucracy, shifting to a view of education as a complex adaptive system where interactive dynamics generate rich emergence of ideas and learning, and empower educators to act as informal enabling leaders.

A shift in education leadership practices is also necessary to ensure the flexibility, adaptability, and creativity needed to prepare for the "known unknowns" (Byrne & Callaghan, 2023, p. 2), and to confront and respond to current and pressing knowns facing education systems: social inequalities, social injustices, the need for decolonization of education (Battiste, 2017; Smith et al., 2019) accessibility, sustainability, and more. This shift can only happen in education and in other complex adaptive systems if all formal and informal leaders are knowledgeable about the conditions needed to produce emergence, and how they can catalyze those conditions throughout the nested system. The enabling and enacting of those conditions cannot occur discontinuously or merely at one point at a time in the nested system, but must occur simultaneously, as in the "vital simultaneities" of Davis and Sumara (2006, p. 153).

As a complex adaptive system, education has sufficient coherence to provide orienting, guiding structures and processes while simultaneously allowing openness to change and conditions for emergence. Using a Complexity Leadership approach, the provincial education institution mandate to set strategic and operational policy direction, standards, funding, and accountability requirements for Kindergarten -- Grade 12 education (Manitoba Education and Early Childhood Learning, 2023) is not set against the goals of the individuals in the system who are designing curriculum, creating positive school environments, designing and assessing learning, and more. Instead, formal and informal leaders interact in such a way that control is decentralized and individuals at all levels of the system share and trigger rich ideas and interactions for emergence.

A Complexity Leadership approach ensures internal redundancies such as common language, shared pedagogy and practices, shared resources, shared technology, shared responsibilities, shared spaces, and more, so that interactions and idea exchanges are purposely enabled between individuals. Using such an approach, Department of Education formal leaders would not focus on controlling all aspects of the system and designing for efficiencies, but rather on creating spaces to encourage educational dialogue and on ways to create feedback loops between all nested levels of the system.

Spaces for exchanges and debate of ideas could be intentionally created across all nested levels of the system. Rather than one-time professional development (PD) in-services typical of school PD days, sustained conversations of "neighbor interactions" across all nested levels of the system (Davis & Sumara, 2006) would promote innovation and new thinking. In Manitoba, the *Manitoba Education Research Network* and its research collaborations across the nested system and resulting publications, have been defunded. Such collaborations are important sources of emergence and innovation and deserve priority funding.

The cultural patterning created by one of the chapter authors for dyadic recursive dialogue and thinking could be extended to become part of the school culture. Teachers would be enabled to connect the islands of innovative practice described at the outset of this chapter through regular release time to meet with colleagues in their school environments and beyond, and to regularly share and debate ideas and practices beyond the infrequent single PD days allocated for teachers throughout the yearly school calendar. Structures could be set up to facilitate regular knowledge exchanges and debates on pressing issues between the Department of Education, the local Teachers' Society, Faculties of Education, school and divisional leaders, teachers, and the learners within the system. Pockets of innovation such as: B.Ed teacher education classes held in school classrooms; M.Ed cohorts learning together within schools and divisions; researchers collaborating with teachers and their learners in the classrooms; school, community, university, and Department of Education partnerships and inquiries; and other possibilities for encouraging dynamic interactions could become established practice rather than isolated occurrences.

Sites of learning that connect K-12 classrooms and learners, pre-service and in-service teachers, universities and the Department of Education could be created in the form of professional teaching development schools. In that way, previously held thinking might be disrupted and challenged, leading to new, meaningful, and productive practices and pedagogies. As the entanglement of leadership practices becomes more rhizomatic and complex over time, the conditions for emergence become more robust and sustained, and the potential to generate emergence increases.

From a Complexity Leadership perspective, formal and informal leaders would work to ensure enabling constraints critical for complex emergence and for learning to flourish. Ensuring a balance of coherence and randomness allows the system "to maintain a focus of purpose/identity and sources of disruption and randomness that compel the collective to constantly adjust and adapt" (Davis & Sumara, 2006, p. 147). In the education system this might mean, as Uhl-Bien and Arena (2018) suggest, that enabling leaders consciously work to build trust, relationships, and shared goals across the nested education system. They must plan ways to connect individuals and diverse ideas, and to intentionally create spaces so that tensions occur, and equilibrium is disrupted.

Emergence is fundamental to all life and learning, and central to policymaking and implementation (Byrne & Callaghan, 2023). Leadership for now and the future must be broadened from previous traditional, hierarchical, linear approaches so that we may understand our complex systems and worlds and learn together to continuously adapt to changes and challenges—the known unknowns. Complexity Leadership describes the conditions to prompt and occasion emergence for education and for all complex adaptive systems.

Our learning does not end with this chapter. Our explorations of Complexity Leadership have led to us next consider how Complexity Leadership might be occasioned in other contexts. Research is needed to explore the processes for re-conceptualizing education leadership and leadership for other complex adaptive systems as Complexity Leadership, and how those leadership processes can best be implemented. Complexity Leadership has potential to encourage formal and informal leaders to cast pebbles, the ripples from which then cross, collide, and combine to generate ever-expanding conditions for emergence. Complexity Leadership has the exciting promise to realize the untapped potential for networked transformation, innovation, and adaptability within the education system.

## REFERENCES

Alblooshi, M., Shamsuzzaman, M., & Haridy, S. (2021). The relationship between leadership styles and organisational innovation: A systematic literature review and narrative synthesis. *European Journal of Innovation Management*, *24*(2), 338–370. doi:10.1108/EJIM-11-2019-0339

Alonso-Yanez, G., Preciado-Babb, A., Brown, B., & Friesen, S. (2021). Emergence in school systems: Lessons from complexity and pedagogical leadership. *Canadian Journal of Educational Administration and Policy / Revue Canadienne en administration et politique de l'éducation*, (196), 65–82. https://doi.org/ doi:10.7202/1078518ar

Bäcklander, G. (2019). Doing complexity leadership theory: How agile coaches at Spotify practise enabling leadership. *Creativity and Innovation Management*, *28*(1), 42–60. doi:10.1111/caim.12303

Barton, G. (2021). *Developing literacy and the arts in schools*. Routledge.

Bass, B. M. (1985). *Leadership and performance beyond expectations*. Harper & Row.

Bass, B. M., & Steidlmeier, P. (1999). Ethics, character, and authentic transformational leadership behavior. *The Leadership Quarterly*, *10*(2), 181–217. doi:10.1016/S1048-9843(99)00016-8

Battiste, M. (2017). *Decolonizing education: Nourishing the learning spirit*. University of British Columbia Press.

Belrhiti, Z., Giralt, A. N., & Marchal, B. (2018). Complex leadership in healthcare: A scoping review. *International Journal of Health Policy and Management*, *7*(12), 1073–1084. doi:10.15171/ijhpm.2018.75 PMID:30709082

Beyak, T. S. (2021). *Entangled agencies: A rhizomatic exploration of assemblages from a global studies classroom* [Master's Thesis]. University of Manitoba. https://mspace.lib.umanitoba.ca/xmlui/handle/1993/35192?show=full

Beyak, T. S. (2022). "Thing-power": Art, assemblage, and entanglement as practitioner action research. *Canadian Journal of Action Research*, *22*(3), 45–68. https://journals.nipissingu.ca/index.php/cjar/article/view/579

Bligh, M. C. (2016). Introduction: Exploring compelling contexts through paradox, tension, and new approaches to leadership. In C. Peus, S. Braun, & B. Schyns (Eds.), *Leadership lessons from compelling contexts* (pp. 1–27). Emerald Group. doi:10.1108/S1479-357120160000008001

Bolden, R., Gosling, J., & Hawkins, B. (2023). *Exploring leadership: Individual, organizational, and societal perspectives* (2nd ed.). Oxford University Press.

Bryant, K., & Murillo (Graham), C. L. (2023). Leadership skills and attributes needed to run a simulation center. In P. R. Jeffries (Ed.), *Clinical simulations in nursing education: Advanced concepts, trends, and opportunities* (2nd ed., pp. 1-15). Lippincott Williams & Wilkins.

Burns, J. M. (1978). *Leadership*. Harper & Row.

Byrne, D. (1998). *Complexity theory and the social sciences*. Routledge.

Byrne, D., & Callaghan, G. (2023). *Complexity theory and the social sciences: The state of the art* (2nd ed.). Routledge. doi:10.4324/9781003213574

Carney, S. (2022). Reimagining our futures together: A new social contract for education. *Comparative Education*, *58*(4), 568–569. doi:10.1080/03050068.2022.2102326

Cilliers, P. (1998). *Complexity and postmodernism: Understanding complex systems*. Routledge.

Crowell, D. M., & Boynton, B. (2020). *Complexity leadership: Nursing's role in health care delivery* (3rd ed.). FA Davis.

Davis, B. (2008). Complexity and education: Vital simultaneities. In M. Mason (Ed.), *Complexity theory and the philosophy of education* (pp. 46–61). Wiley-Blackwell. doi:10.1002/9781444307351.ch4

Davis, B., & Sumara, D. (2006). *Complexity and education: Inquiries into learning, teaching, and research*. Lawrence Erlbaum.

Davis, B., & Sumara, D. (2012). Fitting teacher education in/to/for an increasingly complex world. *Complicity: An International Journal of Complexity and Education*, *9*(1), 30–40. doi:10.29173/cmplct16531

Donkor, F., & Zhou, D. (2019). Complexity leadership theory: A perspective for state-owned enterprises in Ghana. *International Journal of Educational Leadership and Management*, *7*(2), 139–170. doi:10.17583/ijelm.2019.3647

Evans, L. (2022). Is leadership a myth? A 'new wave' critical leadership-focused research agenda for recontouring the landscape of educational leadership. *Educational Management Administration & Leadership*, *50*(3), 413–435. doi:10.1177/17411432211066274

Fairman, J. C., & Mackenzie, S. V. (2015). How teacher leaders influence others and understand their leadership. *International Journal of Leadership in Education*, *18*(1), 61–87. doi:10.1080/13603124.2014.904002

Fennell, K. (2021). Conceptualisations of leadership and relevance to health and human service workforce development: A scoping review. *Journal of Multidisciplinary Healthcare*, *14*, 3035–3051. doi:10.2147/JMDH.S329628 PMID:34737575

Fidanboy, M. (2022). *Organizations and complex adaptive systems*. Routledge. doi:10.4324/9781003182764

Fogel, A., Lyra, M., & Valsiner, J. (Eds.) (1997). *Dynamics and indeterminism in developmental and social processes*. Lawrence Erlbaum.

Ford, R. (2009). Complex leadership competency in health care: Towards framing a theory of practice. *Health Services Management Research*, *22*(3), 101–114. doi:10.1258/hsmr.2008.008016 PMID:19633178

Gibbs, L. (2021). Leading through complexity in early childhood education and care. *Australasian Journal of Early Childhood*, *46*(4), 335–341. doi:10.1177/18369391211050139

Gibbs, L. (2022). Leadership emergence and development: Organizations shaping leading in early childhood education. *Educational Management Administration & Leadership*, *50*(4), 672–693. doi:10.1177/1741143220940324

Gibbs, L., Press, F., & Wong, S. (2019). Complexity leadership theory: A framework for leading in Australian early childhood education settings. In P. Strehmel, J. Heikka, E. Hujala, J. Rodd, & M. Waniganayake (Eds.), *Leadership in early education in times of change: Research from five continents* (pp. 173–186). Verlag Barbara Budrich. doi:10.2307/j.ctvmd84fc.16

Goldstein, J. (2000). Emergence: A construct amid a thicket of conceptual snares. *Emergence*, *2*(1), 5–22. doi:10.1207/S15327000EM0201_02

Gronn, P. (2002). Distributed leadership as a unit of analysis. *The Leadership Quarterly*, *13*(4), 423–451. doi:10.1016/S1048-9843(02)00120-0

Guile, D., & Wilde, R. J. (2022). Complexity theory and learning: Less radical than it seems? *Educational Philosophy and Theory*, 1–9. doi:10.1080/00131857.2022.2132934

Gumus, S., Bellibas, M. S., Esen, M., & Gumus, E. (2018). A systematic review of studies on leadership models in educational research from 1980 to 2014. *Educational Management Administration & Leadership*, *46*(1), 25–48. doi:10.1177/1741143216659296

Hager, P., & Beckett, D. (2019). *The emergence of complexity: Rethinking education as a social science*. Springer. doi:10.1007/978-3-030-31839-0

Hallinger, P. (2018). Bringing context out of the shadows of leadership. *Educational Management Administration & Leadership*, *46*(1), 5–24. doi:10.1177/1741143216670652

Hammond, M., Clapp-Smith, R., & Palanski, M. (2017). Beyond (just) the workplace: A theory of leader development across multiple domains. *Academy of Management Review*, *42*(3), 481–498. doi:10.5465/amr.2014.0431

Harris, A. (2013). *Distributed leadership matters: Perspectives, practicalities, and potential*. Corwin Press. doi:10.4324/9780203607909

Harris, A. (2020). COVID-19–school leadership in crisis? *Journal of Professional Capital and Community*, *5*(3/4), 321–326. doi:10.1108/JPCC-06-2020-0045

Hazy, J. K., & Uhl-Bien, M. (2014). Changing the rules: The implications of complexity science for leadership research and practice. In D. V. Day (Ed.), *The Oxford handbook of leadership and organizations* (pp. 709–732). Oxford University Press.

Ho, J., Foo Seong Ng, D., Chua, P. H., & Binte Munir, N. (2021). Leadership across schools to diffuse an education innovation: Applying complexity leadership theory with ecological leadership. *International Journal of Leadership in Education*, 1 23. doi:10.1080/13603124.2021.2010283

Horvat, A., & Filipovic, J. (2018). Service quality and maturity of health care organizations through the lens of Complexity Leadership Theory. *Journal of Evaluation in Clinical Practice*, *24*(1), 301–307. doi:10.1111/jep.12789 PMID:28714561

James, C., Connolly, M., & Hawkins, M. (2020). Reconceptualising and redefining educational leadership practice. *International Journal of Leadership in Education*, *23*(5), 618–635. doi:10.1080/13603124.2019.1591520

Kaplan, A., & Garner, J. K. (2020). Steps for applying the complex dynamical systems approach in educational research: A guide for the perplexed scholar. *Journal of Experimental Education*, *88*(3), 486–502. doi:10.1080/00220973.2020.1745738

Kegan, R., & Lahey, L. L. (2016). *An everyone culture: Becoming a deliberately developmental organization*. Harvard Business Review Press.

Kelly, R. (2016). *Creative development: Transforming education through design thinking, innovation, and invention*. Brush Education.

Knight, B. (2022). The classroom as a complex adaptive system (CAS): Credible framing, useful metaphor or mis-designation? *International Journal of Complexity in Education*, *3*(1), 33–59.

Koopmans, M. (2020). Education is a complex dynamical system: Challenges for research. *Journal of Experimental Education*, *88*(3), 358–374. doi:10.1080/00220973.2019.1566199

Kruse, S. D. (2021). Hiding in plain sight: Systems thinking and school organization. *Journal of Educational Administration*, *59*(1), 43–58. doi:10.1108/JEA-01-2020-0011

Larsen–Freeman, D. (2019). On language learner agency: A complex dynamic systems theory perspective. *Modern Language Journal*, *103*, 61–79. doi:10.1111/modl.12536

Lichtenstein, B. B., Uhl-Bien, M., Marion, R., Seers, A., Orton, J. D., & Schreiber, C. (2006). Complexity leadership theory: An interactive perspective on leading in complex adaptive systems. *Emergence*, *8*(4), 2–12.

Liu, Z., Riggio, R. E., Reichard, R. J., & Walker, D. O. (2022). Everyday leadership: The construct, its validation, and developmental antecedents. *International Leadership Journal*, *14*(1), 3–35.

Lundqvist, D., Wallo, A., Coetzer, A., & Kock, H. (2023). Leadership and learning at work: A systematic literature review of learning-oriented leadership. *Journal of Leadership & Organizational Studies*, *30*(2), 205–238. doi:10.1177/15480518221133970

Manitoba Education and Advanced Learning. (2015). *Grades 9 to 12 visual arts: Manitoba curriculum framework*. The Government of Manitoba. https://www.edu.gov.mb.ca/k12/cur/arts/visual/framework_9-12.html

Manitoba Education and Early Childhood Learning. (2023, April 10). *Mandate*. Manitoba Education and Early Childhood Learning. https://www.edu.gov.mb.ca/aboutus.html

Manitoba Education and Training. (2017). *Global issues: Citizenship and sustainability*. https://www.edu.gov.mb.ca/k12/cur/socstud/global_issues/full_doc.pdf

Marion, R., & Uhl-Bien, M. (2002, December). *Complexity v. transformation: The new leadership revisited* [Paper presentation]. Managing the Complex IV-Conference on Complex Systems and the Management of Organizations, Ft. Meyers, FL.

Marks, M. A., Mathieu, J. E., & Zaccaro, S. J. (2001). A temporally based framework and taxonomy of team processes. *Academy of Management Review*, *26*(3), 356–376. doi:10.2307/259182

Mason, M. (2008a). Complexity theory and the philosophy of education. In M. Mason (Ed.), *Complexity theory and the philosophy of education* (pp. 1–15). Wiley Blackwell. doi:10.1002/9781444307351.ch1

Mason, M. (2008b). What is complexity theory and what are its implications for educational change? In M. Mason (Ed.), *Complexity theory and the philosophy of education* (pp. 32–45). Wiley Blackwell.

Mendes, M., Gomes, C., Marques-Quinteiro, P., Lind, P., & Curral, L. (2016). Promoting learning and innovation in organizations through complexity leadership theory. *Team Performance Management*, *22*(5/6), 301–309. doi:10.1108/TPM-02-2016-0004

Mifsud, D. (2023). A systematic review of school distributed leadership: Exploring research purposes, concepts and approaches in the field between 2010 and 2022. *Journal of Educational Administration and History*, 1–26. Advance online publication. doi:10.1080/00220620.2022.2158181

Morales, M. P. (2019). Participatory action research (PAR) in education. In C. A. Mertler (Ed.), *The Wiley handbook of action research in education* (pp. 317–341). Wiley Blackwell. doi:10.1002/9781119399490.ch15

Morrison, K. (2008). Educational philosophy and the challenge of complexity theory. In M. Mason (Ed.), *Complexity theory and the philosophy of education* (pp. 16–31). Wiley-Blackwell. doi:10.1002/9781444307351.ch2

Morrison, K. (2010). Complexity theory, school leadership and management: Questions for theory and practice. *Educational Management Administration & Leadership*, *38*(3), 374–393. doi:10.1177/1741143209359711

Newell, C. (2008). The class as a learning entity (complex adaptive system): An idea from complexity science and educational research. *SFU Educational Review*, *2*(1), 5–17. doi:10.21810fuer.v2i.335

Nooteboom, S. G., & Termeer, C. J. A. M. (2013). Strategies of complexity leadership in governance systems. *International Review of Public Administration*, *18*(1), 25–40. doi:10.1080/12294659.2013.10805238

Northouse, P. (2022). *Leadership: Theory and practice* (9th ed.). Sage.

Osberg, D., & Biesta, G. J. (2007). Beyond presence: Epistemological and pedagogical implications of 'strong' emergence. *Interchange, 38*(1), 31–51. doi:10.100710780-007-9014-3

Peters, B. (2011). *A formative study of rhythm and pattern: Semiotic potential of multimodal experiences for early years readers* [Doctoral dissertation]. University of Manitoba. https://mspace.lib.umanitoba.ca/handle/1993/4855

Porter-O'Grady, T. (2020). Complexity leadership: Constructing 21st-century health care. *Nursing Administration Quarterly*, *44*(2), 92–100. doi:10.1097/NAQ.0000000000000405 PMID:32134867

Richardson, K., & Cilliers, P. (2001). What is Complexity Science? A view from different directions. *Emergence*, *3*(1), 5–23. doi:10.1207/S15327000EM0301_02

Semetsky, I. (2008). Re-reading Dewey through the lens of complexity science, or: On the creative logic of education. In M. Mason (Ed.), *Complexity theory and the philosophy of education* (pp. 79–90). Wiley-Blackwell. doi:10.1002/9781444307351.ch6

Smith, L. T., Tuck, E., & Yang, K. W. (Eds.) (2019). *Indigenous and decolonising studies in education: Mapping the long view*. Routledge.

Stacey, R. D. (1996). *Complexity and creativity in organizations*. Berrett-Koehler Publishers.

Turner, J. R., & Baker, R. M. (2019). Complexity theory: An overview with potential applications for the social sciences. *Systems*, *7*(1), 4. doi:10.3390ystems7010004

Uhl-Bien, M. (2021a). Complexity and COVID-19: Leadership and followership in a complex world. *Journal of Management Studies*, *58*(5), 1400–1404. doi:10.1111/joms.12696

Uhl-Bien, M. (2021b). Complexity leadership and followership: Changed leadership in a changed world. *Journal of Change Management*, *21*(2), 144–162. doi:10.1080/14697017.2021.1917490

Uhl-Bien, M., & Arena, M. (2018). Leadership for organizational adaptability: A theoretical synthesis and integrative framework. *The Leadership Quarterly*, *29*(1), 89–104. doi:10.1016/j.leaqua.2017.12.009

Uhl-Bien, M., & Marion, R. (Eds.). (2007). *Complexity leadership: Part 1: Conceptual foundations*. IAP.

Uhl-Bien, M., & Marion, R. (2009). Complexity leadership in bureaucratic forms of organizing: A meso model. *The Leadership Quarterly*, *20*(4), 631–650. doi:10.1016/j.leaqua.2009.04.007

Uhl-Bien, M., & Marion, R. (2011). Complexity leadership theory. In A. Bryman, D. Collinson, K. Grint, B. Jackson & M. Uhl-Bien (Eds.), The SAGE handbook of leadership (pp. 468-482). SAGE Publications.

Uhl-Bien, M., Marion, R., & McKelvey, B. (2007). Complexity leadership theory: Shifting leadership from the industrial age to the knowledge era. *The Leadership Quarterly*, *18*(4), 298–318. doi:10.1016/j.leaqua.2007.04.002

Uhl-Bien, M., Meyer, D., & Smith, J. (2020). Complexity leadership in the nursing context. *Nursing Administration Quarterly*, *44*(2), 109–116. doi:10.1097/NAQ.0000000000000407 PMID:32134869

Varpio, L., Paradis, E., Uijtdehaage, S., & Young, M. (2020). The distinctions between theory, theoretical framework, and conceptual framework. *Academic Medicine*, *95*(7), 989–994. doi:10.1097/ACM.0000000000003075 PMID:31725464

Western, S. (2019). *Leadership: A critical text* (3rd ed.). SAGE.

## KEY TERMS AND DEFINITIONS

**Agents:** Agents in a complex adaptive system may be individuals, teams, schools, departments, or parts of the system.

**Complex Adaptive Systems:** Open, non-linear, unpredictable, distributed systems whose dynamic interactions and properties allow them to adapt to change, be self-organizing, emergent, adaptive, and connected.

**Complexity Leadership Theory:** A leadership theory (Uhl-Bien et al., 2007) grounded in complexity theory and about ways to enable interactive dynamics and emergence (learning, creativity, and adaptation) through informal and formal leadership functions and processes in complex adaptive systems.

**Complexity Theory:** Complexity theory is defined in many different ways. It has been defined as a theory of change and learning and can be used to describe ways that agents interacting in dynamic ways can change, adapt, learn, and create new properties and behaviours.

**Emergence:** When agents in a complex adaptive system interact with one another to produce new structures, behaviours, and qualities that are not found in the individual parts alone, this phenomenon is known as emergence.

**Formal and Informal Leaders:** Formal leaders have official status as a leaders and assigned leadership roles and responsibilities. Informal leaders have no official status as leader but they have influence within the system to enable dynamic interactions and emergence.

**System:** A whole structure, organization, or organism consisting of many nested parts interacting together to meet the common goals.

# Chapter 5
# An Examination of Transformational School Leadership Qualities of Elementary Principals

**Henderson Lewis Jr.**
https://orcid.org/0000-0002-5640-3189
*Louisiana State University, USA*

**Veysel Altunel**
https://orcid.org/0000-0002-4562-1594
*Louisiana State University, USA*

**Elizabeth P. Castro**
*Louisiana State University, USA*

**Saleria Shaffer**
*Louisiana State University, USA*

**Paula A. Thompson**
*Louisiana State University, USA*

**Carlos G. Lee**
*Louisiana State University, USA*

## ABSTRACT

*School leadership is an integral part of fostering a positive culture and climate in schools. The art of leading schools establishes a mission and vision that yields positive student learning outcomes. The leadership style that cultivates a school environment of community, excellence, and collegiality is transformational leadership. Transformational leadership qualities in school principals aid in developing sustainable and successful schools. Using a qualitative framework, three elementary school principals share their experiences of leading teams in the midst of a global pandemic while serving on a panel discussion. The findings from the panel discussion identified the themes of mindfulness, radical candor, professionalism, relatability, resilience, and engagement. These themes provide the skills needed for aspiring school principals to lead schools toward a vision of academic excellence.*

DOI: 10.4018/978-1-6684-8822-5.ch005

## INTRODUCTION

School leaders have the primary responsibility of ensuring the successful operations of their school and the academic success of the students in their building. There is significant weight placed on the decisions that are made by school leaders on behalf of the school's stakeholders, especially during times of crisis. As such, school leaders, more specifically principals, must tap into leadership qualities when making decisions during crises. Historically, transformational leadership has been studied as the primary leadership style of school principals (Berkovich, 2016). Hai, Van, and Thi (2021) explain transformational leadership as a leadership style that focuses on inspiring and motivating followers to work together toward achieving a shared vision while cultivating their individual potential. Transformational leadership focuses on creating robust connections, establishing high standards, and providing tailored assistance and guidance to assist in the growth and progress of others. This leadership style lends itself to five areas of leadership styles: charismatic leadership, visionary leadership, individualized consideration, positive organizational outcomes, and ethical leadership. School leaders typically rely on the use of transformational leadership as a method of leading the organization. This chapter will discuss how transformational leadership theory has been used by school principals during times of crisis to support igniting change in the school building both culturally and academically.

### Purpose

The purpose of this qualitative study is to investigate the skills principals need to be effective in a crisis. For this study, the qualitative research design was used to answer the research question from the perspective of the participants. This chapter will examine how school principals lead during and after a global pandemic using the attributes of transformational leadership and the principals' ability to incorporate the identified qualities as a school leader to lead transformational change in schools both culturally and academically, as well as leverage the qualities to engage with staff, students, and families. Through this study, the researcher sought to identify key characteristics and behaviors of transformational leaders and their impact on the organization. This study used a phenomenological focus group approach to gain insight and understanding of principals' leadership during and after a global pandemic as well as explore the qualities of a transformational leader. This chapter also discusses the ability to incorporate the identified qualities as a school principal to lead transformational change in schools both culturally and academically and leverage them to engage with staff, students, and families.

In the research on the leadership theories that influence principalship, the transformational leadership theory is explored. For this study, the transformational leadership theory served as the theoretical framework which aided in the study design, data collection, and data analysis processes which led to finding answers to the research question.

### Study Design

Some questions that researchers seek to answer require a research methodology that goes beyond the analytical structure of quantitative research. For those research questions seeking to understand the perspective, experiences, and opinions of a person or group of people, quantitative research methodology is not always substantiated. Researchers use the qualitative research methodology when they are looking to inquire about the whys and hows of human behavior (Guest et al, 2013). Finding answers to questions that require a deeper look into the personal experiences, feelings, and expressed values of the participants calls for qualitative research to be conducted. According to Guest et al (2013), qualitative research is research using methods such as participant observation or case studies that result in a narrative, descriptive account of a setting or practice. In other words, the practices to collect data for qualitative research studies are formed around using storytelling and other methods to understand the lived experiences of participants. The discussion and results of qualitative research methods steer from the analytical practices of quantitative research, to focus on forming answers to the research question directly from the perspectives of the participants.

### Research Questions

The overarching question for this research was: How does transformational leadership guide your decisions, school culture, student achievement, and employee satisfaction within your school? This research study focused on understanding the lived experiences of school leaders when transformational leadership is their leadership style.

## LITERATURE REVIEW

Many leadership styles are often used to describe leaders. In the field of education, two styles of leadership have been commonly discussed, transactional and transformational leadership. Hallinger (2003) describes transformational leadership as the ability of an organization to develop the capacity to innovate. Burns (1978) notes that transactional leadership exchanges one thing for another. For example, rewards are offered for productivity or denied for the lack of productivity. Nevertheless, leaders who follow transformational leadership "stimulate and inspire followers to both achieve extraordinary outcomes and, in the process, develop their leadership capacity" (p.9). With transformational leadership, individual followers' needs are responded to by the leaders, individuals gain growth and development, and the objectives and goals of individual followers, the leader, the group, and the larger organization are aligned. Jacobsen et al (2021) explain transactional leadership as an organization that offers rewards for completing tasks and following the vision of the organization.

For this study, a clear understanding of transformational leadership and how it is utilized by school leaders before, during, and after a crisis. Transformational leaders rely on stakeholders to provide input versus commanding direct control of curriculum and overall school development. Transformational leadership develops relationships with all involved in supporting the vision of the school and gives opportunities for the staff to work towards and contribute to the development of shared goals. Transformational leadership is characterized by key qualities which drive the success and growth of school communities. These qualities include but are not limited to being charismatic, visionary, inspirational, and empathetic. According to Ghasabeh and Provitera (2017), a strong component of an effective transformational leader is the ability to be a charismatic leader. Charismatic leaders inspire and motivate others through their magnetism. In addition to being charismatic, another quality that defines a transformational leader is being a visionary. Odumeru and Ifeanyi (2013) discuss that the leader has a vision that is appealing and inspiring to the stakeholders with optimism for future goals. Another key quality is having the ability to inspire others to go beyond their interest and work towards a common goal. The leaders promote organizational commitment. Odumeru and Ifeanyi (2013) point out that this type of leadership motivates the staff to put the group's interests first. Basham (2012) states that effective leaders can be empathetic and place themselves in another's place and cultivate and utilize listening skills. The culmination of these characteristics presented by transformational leaders leads to the implementation and success of a school vision.

Transformational leadership has been proven to be robust in various sectors, such as military and business settings. In this study, we focus on educational settings, which is a crucial social sector, to investigate how transformational leadership may have a potential impact on the development and performance of different educational stakeholders. Challenging and complex situations are inevitable in education. Challenging situations require intellectual stimulation from the leader. Transformational leadership in challenging situations expresses the vision and communicates expectations and confidence in the team. They communicate with confidence, optimism, and the ability to maintain a positive focus during challenging situations. Transformational leaders value creativity and autonomy among each team member thus creating team comments and high performance. Team members are included in the decision-making process to creatively problem-solve. Transformational leaders mold how their followers think about and frame problems and obstacles. Chaotic events can become mere opportunities for decisive actions. Transformational leaders do not react to the energy of the group, but they find subtle ways to foster transformation and trust in the group.

In addition to transformational and transactional leaders, schools are being led by authentic and culturally responsive leaders. Authentic and culturally responsive leaders build trust by fostering a community that utilizes teachers, students and families, and local businesses. According to Kilic and Yavus (2021), authentic leaders are focused and self-confident people who know how their behaviors and thoughts are understood by their followers, know their strengths and weaknesses and those of their followers, know their moral beliefs, are aware of their environment in which they work, can overcome obstacles, and have positive and ethical values. Authentic leaders prioritize the well-being of their students, staff, and community and create a positive, collaborative, and inclusive environment that encourages growth and learning for all.

A similar leadership style found in education is culturally responsive leadership which like authentic leadership prioritizes building strong relationships, promoting equity, and creating inclusive environments. Culturally responsive leaders are competent in the cultural makeup of all stakeholders. The National Center for Education Statistics (NCES) reports that in 2014, students of color represented slightly more than half (50.5%) of all public school students, an increase from 38.8% in 2000 (McFarland et al., 2018). Meanwhile, teacher demographics have remained stagnant. NCES data list 81.9% of public school teachers in 2012 as White (the latest year available), a small decrease from 84.3% in 2000 (Musu-Gillette et al., 2016, US ED, 2016). They are not just White; they are predominantly White, female, and middle-class. Why is this important? Research shows that student's race, ethnicity, and cultural background significantly influence their achievement (Aceves & Orosco, 2014). Yet many teachers are inadequately prepared to address the needs of their culturally and linguistically diverse learners (Skiba, et al., 2011; Darling-Hammond, 2010; Miller, 2009). Culturally responsive leadership nurtures inclusive environments and improved learning for students and families with culturally and linguistically diverse backgrounds. It involves developing leadership pedagogies, practices, and policies that create inclusive schooling environments. Culturally responsive leaders work to understand their own biases as well as patterns of discrimination. They remedy crises, identify negative effects on student achievement, and have the personal courage and commitment to persist.

Culturally responsive leaders support teachers' reflection and refinement of their instructional approaches to be more inclusive of the cultural factors of students. Educational leaders must consider ways to support staff's development of culturally relevant pedagogy practices within the classroom to foster a supportive learning environment (Aasebo et al., 2017; Grill, 2010; Miranda & Cherng, 2018). Culturally responsive leadership fosters awareness and movement towards greater cultural awareness and the balance of power in the classroom between teachers and students. The pandemic years have taken a dramatic toll on the nation's public schools, according to data from the Institute of Educational Sciences, affecting staffing, students' behavior, attendance, nutrition, and mental health. A May 2022 survey found more than 80% of public schools reported "stunted behavioral and socioemotional development" in their students because of the COVID-19 pandemic," a 56% increase in "classroom disruptions from student misconduct," and a 49% increase in "rowdiness outside of the classroom." All schools surveyed reported a 55% increase in "student tardiness." The use of cell phones, computers, or other electronics when not permitted for all schools increased by 42%. (De Leon, J, 2022). Culturally responsive leaders advocated making changes to their daily or yearly academic calendar to mitigate potential mental health issues for students and staff. California, New Jersey, New York, and Massachusetts lawmakers supported efforts to make high school and middle school classes start no earlier than 8:30 am. Culturally responsive Louisiana leaders pursued a range of interventions, from intensive tutoring to summer learning opportunities. They ensured that students' daily classroom instruction was built on high-quality, standards-based instructional materials and teaching techniques that were the core component of the work. (Leader B, personal communication, October 11, 2022)

Although authentic and culturally responsive leadership are different in their ways from transformational leadership, this style of leadership can be a key component of being a transformational leader. Authentic and culturally responsive leaders are better able to build trust and rapport with their stakeholders, which can enhance their ability to inspire and motivate. Inspiring and motivating followers is essential to being an effective transformational leader. Rizvi (2022) states that transformation is seen in many instances as the more effective leadership style over authentic leadership especially in this rapidly changing and competitive world. He also points out that transformational leadership is adept at change management. Transformational leaders are ideal for leading during times of transition because they can inspire stakeholders to embrace new ideas and ways of completing tasks (Rizvi, 2022) This can be seen as necessary in times of unprecedented changes needed such as was seen when the pandemic impacted the world.

Diverse practices and benefits of transformational leadership have been well documented in the body of scholarship. Leithwood (1994) advocates the training of transformational leadership for school leaders through principal preparation programs as it may enhance school leaders' ability to facilitate change in school restructuring initiatives and meet the demands of schools in the 21st century. In the same vein, Simsek (2013) suggests that transformational leadership is capable of preparing all school participants to gain new knowledge, establishing new organizational norms and meaning, and transforming school culture in general.

Different school participants on various occasions have performed the practice of transformational leadership. From a global perspective, transformational leadership has also been applied in assorted cultures. For instance, Shields and Hesbol (2020) found that transforming a school to meet the changing needs of students is a complex and challenging task that requires courage and flexibility from school leaders. It is essential for leaders to tackle persistent prejudice and discrimination and to change negative assumptions, mindsets, and cultures to promote inclusion, equity, and excellence for all students. Also, this study highlights the importance of dispositional preparation for school leaders to address the evolving, culturally distinct needs of students and their families. Comparably, Alger (2008) used data from teacher leaders and their principals to investigate perceptions of teacher leaders' leadership practices, discrepancies in perceptions, and the impact of demographic factors on teacher leaders' leadership behaviors. His study found teacher leaders to be effective in engaging in transformational leadership behaviors, such as challenging the status quo and being involved in school improvement efforts. In a study conducted in the UAE, Litz and Scott (2017) aimed to examine the practice of transformational leadership by school principals and compare the perceptions of principals and teachers to those in Western countries. The study adopted a mixed methodology and revealed variations in perceptions related to transformational leadership, which may be due to cultural differences. As a result, a Modified Transformational Model is proposed, based on a paradigm more suitable for Middle Eastern/Islamic contexts, which may be useful for leaders who wish to adopt transformational leadership with cultural accommodations.

The utilization of transformational leadership by school principals during the COVID-19 pandemic is expected to positively influence teachers, improve learning processes and resources, and ultimately enhance the quality of schools. Savitri and Sudaryah (2021) examined the impact of transformational leadership on teacher performance during the Covid-19 pandemic. The study found that transformational leadership had a positive effect on teacher performance, improving it by 44%, by motivating teachers to exceed their expected performance, leading to greater effort, commitment, and satisfaction, and highlighting the importance of capacity building for improving teacher performance and achieving educational goals effectively and efficiently. Similarly, Antonopoulou et al. (2021) assessed that passive leadership has a negative correlation with digital leadership implementation. Leaders equipped with appropriate digital skills and practicing transformational leadership will be more effective in managing their responsibilities and contributing to the optimal development of academic institutions.

The recent global pandemic impacted schools around the globe and school systems around the world had to assess the immediate needs and the impacts of COVID-19 on learners and educators. Schools had to allocate resources to purchase technology and train teachers to improve their instructional practices to transition to virtual teaching effectively. The change in education also impacted how school leaders not only led their schools but the new skills that school leaders needed globally to lead schools not only through a global pandemic but moving forward. Today there are skills that principals around the globe may not have considered to be a part of the skills necessary to be an educational leader. Moving forward it is going to be imperative for educational leaders to understand the skills and behavior that are necessary to lead schools in the world today.

During this trying time of the COVID-19 pandemic, businesses along with school systems were also facing similar challenges of engaging employees and achieving high levels of productivity. Chanana and Sangeeta (2021) point out that a key to an organization's success is to have high employee engagement. To achieve engagement, Chanana and Sangeeta (2021) state that an organization needs commitment, job satisfaction, and organizational citizenship. For businesses to achieve employee engagement, many organizations implemented strategies during COVID-19. Jones and Kober (2019) suggested the following strategies to achieve superior engagement among employees. These strategies include: 1. Focus on your core values. 2. Support your employees to stay motivated during tough times. 3. Ask for employee feedback. 4. Be upfront with communication with employees by being honest and upfront. 5. Commit to your employee's employment. Similar strategies being implemented can be seen in businesses and schools across America during these unprecedented times. Leadership in the workplace had to step up and ensure employee engagement and satisfaction with their employees.

## Theoretical Framework

Many leadership theories exist to explain the behaviors of leaders in organizations and provide guidelines for leaders to follow when making decisions for their organizations. Innately, leaders will oftentimes possess qualities from multiple leadership theories at a time, in any given circumstances. These qualities come together to support the leader in making decisions that positively benefit the outcomes that the organization is tasked to produce. Principals, and other school leaders, have to make decisions in their building that ultimately impact the outcomes for their students. With the futures of students at stake, principals need to lead in ways that will result in the best possible outcome for those students. Transformational leadership, unlike other leadership theories, relies on external and internal transformations which lead to greater impact on stakeholders. According to Foon (2016), Transformational leadership is a process in which "leaders and followers raise one another to higher levels of motivation and morality" (pg. 590). Within transformational leadership, the process of increasing motivation and morality within key stakeholders results in people achieving their goals and ambitions. One key feature of transformational leadership is the leaders' ability to create a sense of belonging amongst stakeholders within the organization, which aids in the motivation to work toward the best outcomes. Performance is positively impacted by the utilization of transformational leadership skills to encourage goal achievement amongst key players.

Berkovich (2016) asserts that transformational leadership has been one of the most widely used leadership styles among school leaders during the last two decades. The popularity of the use of the theory comes from the focus on engaging stakeholders in the process of leadership. In education, the principal must rely heavily on teachers to deliver instruction, coaches to coach teachers toward instruction, support employees to provide additional support throughout the building, and others to handle the daily operational needs. Because of this dependency on stakeholders at all levels, the use of a leadership theory that focuses on motivating others to enhance performance and increase their sense of belongingness in the organization makes sense (Sparks, 2021).

"Transformational leadership has traditionally emphasized vision and inspiration, focusing upon establishing structures and cultures which enhance the quality of teaching and learning, setting directions, developing people and (re)designing the organization" (Day et al., 2016). In times of crisis, leaders who employ transformational leadership practices must utilize those established structures and cultures to increase the level of belongingness amongst staff and inspire them to make an impact. Building and maintaining the team culture is as important to the outcome as the decisions that the principal makes during the crisis. One example of the crisis was the shift from in-person learning to virtual learning which happened during the Covid-19 pandemic. To effectively navigate that crisis, especially from a virtual landscape, principals had to employ transformational leadership practices which motivated staff members to remain vigilant in educating students, while navigating other impacts of the pandemic. By understanding the core values and beliefs, and philosophy of education of transformational leaders, common leadership qualities are revealed that are associated with the information the literature provides about transformational leadership.

## Participants

The principals for this study all were previous names State Principals of the Year for their respective years. Three participants were examined in this study. These participants were selected based on the criteria of their current active status as a school principal and their willingness to participate in data collection activities such as the panel interview. There were over forty years of experience in the education profession amongst the three participants and diverse experience in their roles throughout their careers. In this section, a portrait of each participant will be provided before exploring the theoretical framework which guided this qualitative study.

**Participant 1.** At the time of the study, leader A served in her position as the founding School Leader of an elementary school. In 2014, she and a team of 10 dedicated educators, went door to door to recruit 100 founding kindergartener students and their families. Under her leadership, the team has grown to a staff of 80, and the school now serves approximately 560 students in PreK through 4th grade. The school of Leader A has been recognized as a top-performing high-poverty school, meaning the school scored in the top 20 percent of the schools in the state that serve a population of greater than 75 percent economically disadvantaged students. Before her principal role, Leader A served as the Assistant Principal. Leader A has over 15 years of experience in education and has a passion to ensure students surpass their threshold of success. As a result of her dedication to serving her students. In 2020, leader A was named the State Principal of the Year. The table below provides describe leader A.

**Participant 2.** Leader B serves as a principal of an elementary school. He started his journey as a substitute teacher in 2003. In 2010, leader B became a certified teacher and went on to become a principal in 2017. Two years into his role, leader B was able to take this poverty and crime-stricken neighborhood school, from a state academically failing school to being a school ranked #1 of the top 10 high-performing schools for 3$^{rd}$-grade literacy and the highest in Progress and growth. He was awarded the Louisiana State Principal of the Year award in 2021. The table below describes leader B.

**Participant 3.** Leader C is the principal of an elementary school. He has achieved many accomplishments from School Teacher of the Year in 2009 and the State Middle School Association Outstanding Teacher of the Year in 2011. He was awarded the State Principal of the Year award in 2022. Leader C is a compassionate leader that has led staff to ensure that all students experience success, which has driven his dedication and commitment to the students and families in his school community. The table below describes leader C.

Understanding the lived experiences of these three principles as they navigated crises through the use of transformational leadership qualities was necessary to answer the research question. Through their unique experiences as school leaders, the principals shared their stories about crises that impacted their school buildings. In sharing those stories, they talked about the skills and tools needed to work with their staff to find solutions and implement structures that would support their schools in moving toward achieving outcomes.

## Data Collection

The data were collected using a phenomenological approach in moderating a one-hour panel discussion. The panel featured three highly experienced principals in Louisiana. Data collection for this study involved the careful and detailed transcription of an online panel discussion session that was held via Zoom at Louisiana State University. The panel discussion was immediately transcribed using Otter.ai®

transcription software by trained personnel. Following the transcription using Otter.ai®, trained personnel reviewed the data and check for accuracy. To maintain the anonymity of the participants, participants' data were identified by participant identities as assigned before the panel discussion (Participant 1, Participant 2, and Participant 3).

The panel discussion was attended by a diverse audience, including master's and doctoral students, teachers, and education professionals who had the opportunity to learn about the experiences and expertise of the principals of the year in Louisiana. The panelists shared their experiences and discussed the skills they acquired during their administration. The topics covered in the discussion included strategies for effective leadership, challenges faced by school administrators especially during and after the COVID pandemic, ways to promote student success and achievement, shifts in education, and community involvement in schools.

## Data Analysis

As a qualitative data analysis method, thematic analysis is used to identify, analyze, and report patterns (themes) within data (Marriam, 2009). Creswell's (2013) model of data analysis is employed in the current study, which involves a spiral process that includes four distinct procedures. The first procedure involves managing the files by transcribing the data, organizing the text files, and reflecting on how they relate to the research questions to gain a sense of the issue at hand. The second procedure entails forming a tentative list of codes that expand as the data are reviewed and re-reviewed. The third procedure focuses on reducing the codes to categories through the process of categorical aggregation. Finally, the fourth procedure involves interpreting the data to abstract beyond the categories and discover the larger meaning of the data by linking the raw data with the existing research literature. Once these four procedures have been completed, a detailed picture of the analyzed data can be presented. In this study, we employed thematic analysis to identify the most commonly discussed transformational leadership qualities among the State Principals of the Year during the panel discussion.

After carefully reviewing the transcript of the panel discussion and identifying segments of the data related to transformational leadership qualities, we engaged in an iterative process of open coding, where we identified all relevant segments of the data, and then organized these code categories with common phrases and words with similar meanings. We then reviewed these phrases and words and then merged them into themes that were relevant to the data as a whole. From this analysis, five themes were revealed that captured the most salient aspects of data from the panel discussion. During the thematic analysis process, it became clear that the panelists spoke extensively about the importance of having a clear and inspiring vision for the school, the need to inspire and motivate staff, students, and families, and the importance of empathy and a deep understanding of stakeholders' needs and concerns. Once we identified the themes, we reviewed them in relation to the research questions and the broader context of the study. This allowed us to identify the most important themes and their relationship to our research questions, which in turn allowed us to conclude the importance of transformational leadership qualities for leading effectively during and after a global pandemic.

## Results

Thematic analysis is a flexible and powerful method for analyzing qualitative data and allows us to identify and report on key themes related to transformational leadership qualities in this study. The themes we identified provide insights into the most important leadership qualities needed for leading during times of crisis and can inform future research and practice in educational leadership. The five themes included mindfulness, professionalism, relatability, resilience, and engagement. In the following section, these five themes and the sub-themes are explained in detail with quotes from the participants.

## Mindfulness

Being mindful as a school leader is one of the most critical qualities that all three leaders agreed upon. Based on their discussion, having good listening skills, being able to optimize human capital, and applying radical candor are three important components that contribute to mindfulness.

*Listening Skills.* In this panel discussion about transformational leadership in education, one principal shares their experience of improving their listening skills through what they call a "listening tour." The principal recognized that they had previously been a poor listener, often listening only to respond or defend their ideas. Through the listening tour, the principal met with every single person on their faculty, taking notes and actively listening without any preconceived notions or biases. This experience gave them valuable insight into what they needed to do as a leader moving forward, highlighting the importance of developing good listening skills in effective leadership.

Another participant shared their experiences with becoming an active listener. This participant expressed that as a result of becoming an active listener, they allowed themselves to allow others to take part in the vision, mission, and goals. This aided in helping the organization execute the vision and mission of the organization. This act allowed the participant to understand that they are not an anomaly and that others should be heard. Hearing other members of the organization helps the organization move forward. Moreover, it aids in achieving the goals set forth by the leadership.

It can be seen in the speaker's deliberate efforts to become good listeners and to approach conversations with an open and non-judgmental attitude. By acknowledging their previous shortcomings and actively working to improve their listening skills, the speakers demonstrate the importance of being mindful and present in interactions with others, particularly in a leadership role.

*Optimization.* Optimizing human capital is an essential component of effective leadership in educational settings. The panel discussion highlighted several strategies for capitalizing on human capital, including recognizing and utilizing individual strengths, delegating responsibilities, and leveraging the expertise of the school community. One leader emphasized the importance of recognizing and utilizing individual strengths, stating, "let them operate where they're strongest." This approach acknowledges that each member of the school community possesses unique talents and abilities that can be harnessed to improve outcomes for students. By recognizing and leveraging individual strengths, leaders can create a school culture that values diversity and promotes collaboration.

Delegating responsibilities was also highlighted as a key strategy for optimizing human capital. One leader noted that delegation "comes along with your shared vision," and emphasized the importance of allowing others to take part in executing the shared vision, mission, and goals of the school community. By delegating responsibilities, leaders can distribute the workload and empower individuals to take ownership of their roles within the school community.

Finally, the panel discussion emphasized the importance of surrounding oneself with individuals who possess complementary skills and expertise. One leader noted, "I'm not the smartest in the room, but I make sure I have the smartest around me." This approach recognizes that effective leadership is not about possessing all the answers but rather about leveraging the collective knowledge and skills of the school community to achieve common goals.

Taken together, these vignettes illustrate the importance of optimizing human capital through delegation, recognizing and utilizing individual strengths, and leveraging the expertise of the school community. Through effective leadership that optimizes human capital, school communities can work together to achieve their shared goals.

*Radical Candor.* Radical candor was another key concept in the leaders' discussion of transformational leadership in educational settings that can demonstrate one's mindfulness. They defined radical candor as providing direct feedback while also demonstrating care and empathy towards the individual. The leaders believed that providing direct feedback with high expectations for growth and development was essential for promoting growth among teachers and leaders. They acknowledged that providing feedback can be challenging but emphasized that it is crucial for success. In addition, the leaders stressed the importance of demonstrating care and empathy towards teachers and leaders to create a positive work environment. Overall, the leaders' discussion highlighted the importance of radical candor as a critical component of transformational leadership in educational settings.

## Professionalism

Besides being mindful as school leaders, demonstrating professionalism in various situations is another important factor for effective transformational leadership. The three leaders on the panel underlined the importance of clarity in communication with team members and establishing a positive and nurturing school culture.

*Clarity.* Clarity has emerged as a crucial transformational skill for educators, particularly in the context of educational leadership. Leaders, in particular, need to have absolute clarity when it comes to setting goals, making plans, and communicating priorities to their team members. According to a panelist, "the big thing that really helped me start to kind of get some success at the school was like absolute clarity, clarity on goals, the precision of our plans, having very specific priorities and letting people know". To achieve success, educational leaders need to maintain a "laser focus" and ensure that everyone on the team is aware of what is expected of them. Clarity also helps in creating a shared understanding of what needs to be done to make the school a great place for kids. As the panelist mentioned, "what we all need to do to be a great place for kids" should be communicated clearly to all team members. In essence, clarity is a foundational aspect of educational leadership that enables leaders to set direction, build consensus, and achieve goals in a coordinated and effective manner. Therefore, leaders must prioritize clarity in their communication and decision-making processes to foster success in their educational setting.

*Culture.* Culture has emerged as a critical aspect of transformational leadership in educational settings, with leaders playing a vital role in fostering a positive and impactful culture. According to a panelist, "we're supposed to be in this seat to grow leaders, to grow others, to come and take our place after we leave". Leaders, therefore, need to create a culture that is focused on developing and nurturing leaders at all levels of the organization. This requires them to be actively involved in coaching, listening, and observing, while also communicating their vision to their team members. As the panelist mentioned, "your vision is still going forth", even if you were to leave the organization, due to the people that you have surrounded yourself with. This indicates the importance of building a culture that is centered on shared values and goals, rather than relying solely on the presence of a single leader. To achieve this, leaders must foster an environment of collaboration, trust, and respect, where everyone feels valued and empowered to contribute to the organization's vision. This involves creating opportunities for professional development, providing regular feedback, recognizing achievements, and promoting a growth mindset. In essence, culture plays a crucial role in the success of educational organizations, and leaders have a key responsibility in shaping and cultivating this culture to create a positive and impactful environment that promotes growth and development.

## Relatability

Being Relatable encompasses various personality traits such as humor, empathy, and the ability to connect with others. According to one panelist, "it is humor" that helps to create an enjoyable atmosphere in the workplace. Finding joy and humor in the micro-moments of the day can have a positive impact on one's mindset and overall job satisfaction. Another panelist emphasized the importance of personal experiences, stating that becoming a parent while growing up in a school had a significant impact on the way they viewed families. The participant stated they understood some of the difficulties of life but reminded us that you still show up for those you have been entrusted to. Building relationships and having fun with colleagues and students also adds to the Relatable aspect of being a leader. As one panelist expressed, "why not make it the best 8 hours, 10 hours, or 12 hours of the day?"

Empathy is also a crucial component of being relatable. Practicing empathy towards students, parents, and colleagues is essential in creating a welcoming and inclusive environment. As one panelist reflected, "it really made us stand back and take the time for us and to practice empathy for the kids as well as the people in the building with you." Thus, being Relatable in educational settings is essential for leaders in building positive relationships with students, parents, and colleagues, fostering a culture of inclusivity, and promoting job satisfaction.

## Resilience

The COVID-19 pandemic has had a significant impact on the education sector, particularly for leaders who have had to navigate unprecedented challenges. Resilience has emerged as a crucial transformational aspect for educators in dealing with these challenges. The pandemic has exposed deficits and deficiencies in technology that educators had to learn to operate, pushing them to catch up with the 21st century in education, as one leader noted, "they jumped in and tried to learn it. They learned to try and they did learn it." This has provided an opportunity for educators to think outside the box and find new ways to reach and teach their students, particularly through technology, which is a crucial avenue for student success in the 21st century. The pandemic has also forced educators to rethink school operations, schedules, and classroom activities, leading to new and improved practices. This has created a new sense of urgency and belief in what can be achieved, as one leader noted, "if we can keep it that way and can continue to feel that same sense of urgency, we'll really move mountains with our kiddos." Therefore, resilience is essential for leaders to navigate these challenges and ensure that students receive the best education possible.

## Engagement

Engagement beyond school is an important aspect for leaders to connect with the community of their schools. This engagement can manifest itself in various forms, such as personal relationships with families, partnerships with parents, and visible access to the community. As described by Marco French, the new principal of Queensboro, connecting with the community can be as simple as going door-to-door and asking if there is anything the school can do for them. This approach builds trust and fosters a sense of community, which can translate into support for the school. Building personal relationships with families is also crucial, as noted by Margot, who believes that this relationship between teachers and families is everything. Margot also stresses the importance of visible accessibility, which can take the form of an open-door policy or providing personal cell phone numbers. Finally, according to the panel discussion, communicating with the community in engaging ways and going where the people are is vital. As stated by one of the panelists, "when they know you, you're going to get the benefit of the doubt," and this can make the leader's job easier. In summary, engagement beyond school is a crucial aspect for leaders to connect with their schools' communities, build trust, and garner support.

The five themes come together to express a logical progression of skills that move the school leader from more personal to external transformation as they navigate through crises. The scope increases from mindfulness to engagement. Mindfulness and professionalism are personal in that it is modeled both internally and externally by the school leader. During these phases of transformational leadership, the leader is focused more on the internal process of preparing themselves to transform their team in meaningful ways. The leader then moves to a relatability phase where connecting to the personal life, family dynamics, and values of their stakeholders becomes most important. Digging deep into how their personal experiences are similar to those that they are leading leads the principal to the more external phases. Resilience is the first external phase and includes practical considerations of the crisis. The leader is focused more on persevering through the crisis and successfully transforming the impact that the crisis may have on the work. The final stage, engagement, embodies all of the phases by creating a space for bigger community involvement.

## Implications for Practice

Research on transformational leadership practices that have supported school leaders through crisis and decision-making processes exists. For decades, transformational leadership theory has been the theoretical framework most widely used to study the experiences of school leaders (Berkovich, 2016). In this study, the experience of three principals led to the discovery of the skills needed for principals to navigate through crises from a transformational leadership lens. Participants agreed transformational leadership improved student outcomes, increased teacher motivation and job satisfaction, encouraged collaboration and teamwork, and allowed staff members to be heard to create a culture of shared vision, mission, and goals. Transformational leaders are leaders that create environments where staff members are active participants in meeting the goals of the organizations (Chen et al, 2020). Five themes were uncovered: mindfulness, professionalism, relatability, resilience, and engagement. Each of these five themes was supported by skill sets that have proven beneficial to navigate larger crises such as the Covid-19 pandemic.

Within the theory of transformational leadership, reflection is an essential part of the theory in practice (Aasebo, 2017). The first implication is for school leaders to reflect on their practices in decision-making to ensure that their process aligns with the scope of moving from the more personal phase (mindfulness) to the more external phase (engagement) during a crisis. In reflecting on their decision-making processes, whether connected specifically to the pandemic or other school-level crises that they have faced, school leaders would benefit from comparing their actions to the scope of transformational leadership practices discussed in this study. Beyond reflection, intentionality in using the scope as a guide for school leaders to model effective leadership for the stakeholders in their building as an everyday practice may be beneficial.

The results of this study are not exclusive to crises. School leaders may be more equipped to navigate crises if they use these skills for team building, relationship building, and coaching. The next implication for school leaders as they navigate the crises that come with the profession is in designing coaching models based on the transformational leadership scope of practices that developed from this study. For example, implementing the radical candor skill that has been studied to be effective during the mindfulness stage in having routine coaching conversations with staff members, will lay a foundation for feedback to be a natural part of the school culture. Therefore, during times of crisis, when feedback is given from the leader to staff members, there has been an established practice of constructive feedback which will be more easily accepted by staff members during crises.

Finally, the results of this study should be examined to support in designing a framework for school leaders to navigate through the decision-making process in schools. Every school is different, the staff at each school come with diverse sets of skills and experiences, and the needs of the students in each school building vary drastically. Developing a universal framework for transformational leadership best practices during the time of crisis or crucial decision-making may provide practitioners with a standard of leadership that may be applicable in all situations. This framework can become an essential component of school leadership programs, supporting practitioners in reflecting on their personal experiences and using the framework to anticipate crisis events that may impact their school.

## Implications for Future Research

This chapter purposely focuses on one crisis that has universally impacted elementary school principals, the Covid-19 pandemic. During the data collection process, three principals provided the researcher with their perspectives of their lived experiences as leaders during a worldwide crisis. While things rapidly changed in the school building, there was a consecutive rapid change across the world. These changes were felt around the world in many schools, many classrooms, and by many educational stakeholders, therefore the first implication for research is to expand this study to include the perspectives of more school leaders in different geographic areas, grade levels, and other crises. Beyond the pandemic, other circumstances may fall under the category of crisis that can be studied to understand if these results are transferable to other situations. For example, studying the transformational leadership practices of school leaders after natural disasters resulting in short-term school closures may be helpful in uncovering skills necessary to navigate those situations.

Additional research could extend beyond the scope of transformational leadership practices discovered through the data analysis process in this study. Each of the five themes, which essentially were developed into phases during the transformation process, could be studied independently as both necessary steps during the process and beneficial practices during the career of the school leader. Researching each theme separately may uncover more specific skills and practices which support building stronger culture, more effective coaching practices, and better decision-making among school leaders. Finally, much has been studied around the lens of transformational leadership. Transactional leadership has been compared to transformational leadership in some of the research on school leadership (Foon, 2016). Future research which includes a comparison of principals' practices through crisis under different theoretical frameworks such as servant leadership, democratic leadership, and coaching leadership, may uncover additional qualities which may support school leaders in their profession.

## CONCLUSION

Sparks (2021) states that "researchers have developed leadership models in education that are generally characterized by a set of unique leadership qualities that are articulated and can be applied to different educational contexts" (pg. 13). The transformational leadership theory has been used to explore the experiences of school leaders in the educational context of crisis. During the Covid-19 pandemic, the elementary school leaders that participated in this study had to tap into their transformational leadership skills to influence change and ensure the successful transition of their school from a traditional model to a remote learning environment. Through their perspectives, we learned that five themes guided the practices of these school leaders and supported their implementation of change in their school buildings. Moving from personal (mindfulness) to external (engagement) was an essential process for transforming the school culture during such a drastic time.

## REFERENCES

Aasebo, T. S., Midtsundstad, J. H., & Willbergh, I. (2017). Teaching in the age of accountability: Restrained by school culture? *Journal of Curriculum Studies*, *49*(3), 273–290. doi:10.1080/00220272.2015.1072249

Aceves, T. C., & Orosco, M. J. (2014). *Culturally responsive teaching*. University of Florida: Collaboration for Effective Educators. Retrieved May 25, 2020 from https://ceedar.education.ufl.edu/tools/innovationconfigurations/

Aspers, P., & Corte, U. (2019, February 27). What is qualitative in qualitative research? *Qualitative Sociology*, *42*(2), 139–160. doi:10.100711133-019-9413-7 PMID:31105362

Basham, L. M. (2012). Transformational leadership characteristics necessary for todays leaders in higher education. *Journal of International Education Research*, *8*(4), 343–348. doi:10.19030/jier.v8i4.7280

Berkovich, I. (2016). School leaders and transformational leadership theory: Time to part ways? *Journal of Educational Administration*, *54*(5), 609–622. doi:10.1108/JEA-11-2015-0100

Braun, V., & Clarke, V. (2006). Using thematic analysis in psychology. *Qualitative Research in Psychology*, *3*(2), 77–101. doi:10.1191/1478088706qp063oa

Chanana, N., & Sangeeta. (2020, October 1). Employee engagement practices during COVID-19 lockdown. *Journal of Public Affairs*, *21*(4). Advance online publication. doi:10.1002/pa.2508 PMID:33041656

Chen, H., Wang, X., Liu, X., & Li, X. (2020). Transformational leadership, teacher job satisfaction, and student academic achievement: A moderated mediation model. *Frontiers in Psychology*, *11*, 1181.

Chenail, R. (2011). Learning to appraise the quality of qualitative research articles: A contextualized learning object for constructing knowledge. *Qualitative Report*, *1*(16), 236–248. doi:10.46743/2160-3715/2011.1049

Creswell, J. W. (2013). *Qualitative inquiry and research design: Choosing among five approaches* (3rd ed.). Sage Publications.

Day, C., Gu, Q., & Sammons, P. (2016) The impact of leadership on student outcomes: how successful school leaders use transformational and instructional strategies to make a difference. *Educational Administration Quarterly, 52*(2), 221-258.

Day, C., Gu, Q., & Sammons, P. (2016). The impact of leadership on student outcomes: How successful school leaders use transformational and instructional strategies to make a difference. *Educational Administration Quarterly*, *52*(2), 221–258. doi:10.1177/0013161X15616863

De Leon, J. (2022). 7 things we learned about COVID's impact on education from a survey of 800 schools. *The 74*. Retrieved May 25, 2020, from https://www.the74million.org/article/7-things-we-learned-about-covids-impact-on-education-from-survey-of-800-schools/

Foon, M. (2016) The theoretical framework of transformational and transactional leadership styles in enhancing job satisfaction of Nurse educators in Malaysia. *International Journal of Social Science and Humanities Research, 4*(1), 590-595.

Ghasabeh, M. S., & Provitera, M. J. (2017). Transformational leadership: Building an effective culture to manage organisational knowledge. *The Journal of Values Based Leadership*, *10*(2), 1–19. doi:10.22543/0733.102.1187

Gillet, N., & Vandenberghe, C. (2014). Transformational Leadership and Organizational Commitment: The Mediating Role of Job Characteristics. *Human Resource Development Quarterly*, *25*(3), 321–347. doi:10.1002/hrdq.21192

Guest, G., Namey, E., & Mitchell, M. (2013). *Qualitative research: Defining and designing*. SAGE Publications, Ltd. doi:10.4135/9781506374680

Hai, T. N., Van, T. T., & Thi, H. N. (2021). Relationship between transformational leadership style and leadership thinking of provincial administration leaders. *Emerging Science Journal, 5*(5). https://ijournalse.org/index.php/ESJ/article/view/610

Hallinger, P. (2003). Leading educational change: Reflections on the practice of instructional and transformational leadership. *Cambridge Journal of Education*, *33*(3), 329–352. doi:10.1080/0305764032000122005

Jacobsen, C. B., Anderson, L. B., Bollingtoft, A., & Eriksen, T. L. M. (2021, January 28). Can leadership training improve organizational effectiveness? Evidence from a randomized field experiment on transformational and transactional leadership. *Public Administration Review*, *82*(1), 117–131. doi:10.1111/puar.13356

Jones, M. D., & Kober, J. J. (2019). Employee engagement in difficult times. *World Class Benchmarking*. http://worldclassbenchmarking.com/ employee-engagement-in-difficult-times/

Kiliç, M. Y., & Yavuz, M. (2021). The evaluation of authentic leadership in terms of trust in managers and schools' levels of openness to change. *Cukurova University Faculty of Education Journal*, *50*(2), 1033–1068. doi:10.14812/cuefd.863251

McFarland, J., Hussar, B., Wang, X., Zhang, J., Wang, K., Rathbun, A., Barmer, A., Forrest Cataldi, E., & Bullock Mann, F. (2018). *The condition of education 2018.* U.S. Department of Education. Washington, DC: National Center for Education Statistics. Retrieved May 25, 2018 from https://nces.ed.gov/pubsearch/pubsinfo. asp?pubid=2018144

Merriam, S. B. (2009). *Qualitative research: A guide to design and implementation*. Jossey-Bass.

Musu-Gillette, L., Robinson, J., McFarland, J., KewalRamani, A., Zhang, A., & Wilkinson-Flicker, S. (2016). *Status and trends in the education of racial and ethnic groups 2016.* National Center for Education Statistics. Retrieved May 25, 2021 from https://nces.ed.gov/pubs2016/2016007.pdf

Rizvi, H. (2022, September 21). *Authentic leadership vs transformational leadership, difference, pros and cons*. Hidayat Rizvi. https://hidayatrizvi.com/authentic-leadership-vs-transformational-leadership/

Skiba, R. J., Honer, R. H., Chung, C.-G., Rausch, M. K., May, S. L., & Tobin, T. (2011). Race is not neutral: A national investigation of African American and Latino disproportionality in school discipline. *School Psychology Review*, *40*(1), 85–107. doi:10.1080/02796015.2011.12087730

Sparks, J. (2021). Understanding Transformational Leadership during a Time of Uncertainty. *Alabama Journal of Educational Leadership.*, *8*, 10–15.

# Chapter 6
# Assessing the Impact of Transformational Leadership Style at a Selected High School in Jamaica

**Tashieka Simone Burris-Melville**
https://orcid.org/0000-0002-5321-8877
*University of Technology, Jamaica*

**Cynthia Onyefulu**
*University of Technology, Jamaica*

## ABSTRACT

*The purpose of this chapter was to determine the type of leadership of a high school principal in Kingston, Jamaica. The sample size was 74. The data collection methods were a questionnaire and an interview. The results showed that the students and teachers perceived their principal as displaying transformational and transactional leadership styles, while the principal saw himself as a situational leader. The results also showed changes in the school, namely the number of student passes in the Caribbean Secondary Education Certificate Examinations and the Caribbean Advanced Proficiency Examinations, infrastructural upgrades and developments, and an increase in the participation of students and teachers in sports and extracurricular activities.*

## INTRODUCTION

A learning institution is headed by an educational or school leader who leads, manages and influences behaviours and the mindsets of those working under the people leadership. As pointed out by Anastasiou (2021) and Cohen et al. (2009), school leaders are the most influential factor in school improvement (as cited in Kaleem et al., 2021).

DOI: 10.4018/978-1-6684-8822-5.ch006

According to Othman et al. (2012), the terms leadership and management are not interchangeable; rather, a leader develops and communicates a vision while a manager plans, organises, and implements the leader's vision and helps the leader to achieve the vision and goals. Several scholars have studied leadership, and this is why leadership is said to be the "most studied and least understood topic" (Benmira & Agboola, 2021, p. 3).

There is no consensus on the definitions of the terms leadership and management. However, leadership was defined as the "process whereby an individual influences a group of individuals to achieve a common goal" (Northouse, 2016, p. 6), while Kaehler and Grundei (2019) explained that management can be seen from two perspectives, namely, functional and institutional ways. The functional way means "the act of managing," while the institutional way sees managers as "those people assigned to management positions" (p. 14). For the term school or educational leadership, Jovanovic and Ciric (2018) described it as "a process of influencing employees to achieve organisational goals and organisational excellence" (p. 497). Jovanovic and Ciric added that an educational leader should have a vision and the ability to predict the future. They added that the concept of leadership within the educational context is that the leader should be able to, among other things, account for the institution's achievements, and develop new teaching and learning programmes, while considering the school dynamics.

School leadership is integral in shaping educational environments and achieving successful outcomes for all stakeholders. Transformational leadership has gained significant attention in the field of education. In fact, effective school leadership is inextricably linked to transformational leadership practices. Numerous studies have confirmed that transformational leadership is one of the most impactful leadership models that drive change and foster a positive school climate (Berkovich, 2016; Leithwood & Sun, 2012; Lin Tengi et al., 2017).

Within the Jamaican education context, school leaders must contend with the changing landscape coupled with the complex challenges their schools face. Several educational institutions are underperforming as they consistently fail to meet the standards of academic achievements and student outcomes (Thompson, 2020). Consequently, school leaders are engaging in transformational leadership practices as a primary strategy to achieve a turnaround in their overall school performance. Hutton (2011) highlighted nine factors that define high-performing principals in Jamaica. These included having a philosophy of school and self, stressing the importance of personal characteristics and tendencies, engaging in transformational and situational leadership practices, having a system that supports students' growth and development, focusing on students' academic achievement and performance, a programme that supports strong staff development and involvement, developing an effective school plant, having a strong community presence, and having a cordial, although sometimes fractious relationship with the Ministry of Education (MoE).

The literature suggests that transformational leadership practices have a positive impact on various aspects of Jamaican schools, including student achievement, teacher job satisfaction, organizational commitment, professional development, and teacher efficacy (Hutton, 2016; Palmer et al., 2014; Smith et al., 2015).

For school leaders to be effective, and influential in improving their schools, they should have leadership styles and methodological approaches that enable them to implement their strategic vision in their institutions (Leithwood et al., 2004, as cited in Jovanovic & Ciric, 2018). Therefore, principals' leadership styles are virtual in their ability to lead and manage their institutions since they have to use one that will align with their "followers' needs" (Vilhauer, 2018, p. 7). However, this is not always the case because leadership style has been known to be influenced by several factors, such as the person's personality type, the personalities of the followers, the nature of the tasks to be done, and the nature of the environment (D'Souza, 2003). In contrast, Othman et al. (2012) were of the view that top management leadership styles are influenced by transformational, transactional, and social demographic factors.

## School Context

The study to be used is located in St. Andrew. It is a government-owned institution and was established in 1979 with 600 students. This non-traditional high school currently has 1,460 students from first to sixth form, Grades 7-13. The sixth form programme began in 2014 with 51 students. The student population is 1,600 (720 males & 880 females), with 76 teaching staff (Student Handbook, n. d.).

The current principal is aimed at making the school a model high school in Jamaica. Prior to this principal, there were three others, dating back to when the school began in the 1970s. The school has an active Board of Management, which supports the functioning of the school through a set of guidelines (Student Handbook, n. d.).

Apart from the board of management, which is expected for all schools in Jamaica, the principal is assisted by a senior management team of two vice principals, a bursar, a plant manager, and a senior secretary. At the time of this study, there are 23 senior teachers with key portfolios, appointed to assist the principal (Student Handbook, n. d.). The daily operations of the school and the seven departments, namely, (1) Business Education, (2) Human Ecology and Hospitality Services, (3) Humanities, (4) Language and Literature, (5) Mathematics, (6) Technical Education and Performing Arts, and (7) Sports and Science. Each department is led by a head, are under the leadership of the principal and the two vice principals. The head's role is "to assist teachers in planning the curriculum and supervising instructional delivery" (Student Handbook, n. d., p. 6).

The school's vision statement is "To provide an exemplary education for every student in a globally competitive 21st-century environment" (Student Handbook, n. d., p. 2). According to the principal's message in the handbook, this vision is "to provide an exemplary education for every student while partnering with parents and the community at large, to create a positive and inclusive environment for high-quality learning and teaching, where everyone is valued and respected" (Student Handbook, n. d., p. 2).

The mission statement is "... to develop competent graduates with a positive self-esteem and a desire for lifelong learning through a nurturing, motivated, competent staff; a relevant, rigorous curriculum and a safe, orderly, positive environment" (Student Handbook, n. d., p. 2). The school motto is "To learn, To love, To serve" (Student Handbook, n. d., p. 2). The motto is embedded in the school crest.

## Statement of the Problem

The high school studied has had different principals who have led with different leadership styles since its inception. During the tenure of these principals, there have been developments. However, with the leadership of the current principal, there has been a remarkable transformation in several aspects of the school. This includes an improvement in the appearance of the school's physical facilities, students' passes in the Caribbean Advanced Proficiency Examination (CAPE), and the number of students getting up to five subjects in the Caribbean Secondary Education Certificate (CSEC). The principal has also promoted and motivated students in the football club (Jane Doe, personal communication, April 9, 2023).

Despite these achievements, there is no empirical study on the school, except for a few citing online and by news media. It is against this background that the researchers investigated the transformation of the school by capturing the views of the different stakeholders of the school through a questionnaire and interview.

## Purpose of the Study

The purpose of this study is twofold. First, to determine the type of leadership a principal is using in a selected high school in Kingston, Jamaica. Second, to describe how the principal and the senior management staff of the high school influenced transformation in some aspects of the institution.

## Research Questions

The following questions guided the research study:

1. How does the principal define his/her leadership style?
2. What impact has the principal's transformational leadership style made on the school?
3. To what extent are there differences in students' and teachers' perceptions of their principal's leadership behaviours?

## Delimitations of the Study

The study focused on the transformational leadership of the current principal of a high school and the changes that occurred under his leadership, as well as the management team, through the perceptions of some senior students and teachers. Therefore, the perceptions of the previous leaders and the auxiliary and technical staff of the school were not captured.

## Limitations of the Study

Some students and teachers were not willing to respond to the questionnaire despite the repeated efforts of the researchers, and the sample size was small. Therefore, the results do not represent the perceptions of the students and staff of the school. Furthermore, the researchers were unable to collect data on teacher performance, which would have enhanced the results of the principal's transformational leadership style.

## Significance of the Study

There is much research on leadership in general and school leadership in particular in Jamaica. However, this study contributes to the academic literature on transformational leadership and responses to the call for more studies on the topic. Furthermore, most of the studies were done through the qualitative approach. This study showcased how a school principal with a transformational leadership style changed a non-traditional high school using the quantitative approach to capture more stakeholder views. The principal, teachers, students, and the Ministry of Education may find this study useful in providing empirical evidence on transformation leadership practices. It can also be useful for others to use in future studies while filling the gap in the literature.

## Theoretical Framework

In this study, the focus is on modern or recent theories, namely, transformational and transactional leadership, which is seen "as belonging on a continuum" instead of two separate leadership styles (Vilhauer, 2018, p. 19). These theories were chosen due to the multi-factor leadership questionnaire (MLQ) by Avolio and Bass (1995), which measures transformational and transactional leadership behaviours, including passive avoidant.

According to Bass and Avolio (1995), "transformational leadership is a conscious, moral and spiritual process that provides development patterns for an organisation through a reliable equal power leadership" (as cited in Korejan & Shahbazi, 2016, p. 454). Avolio and Bass (2002) stated that leaders under this type of leadership are those "who motivate others to do more than originally intended and often more than they thought possible" (p. 1). On the other hand, transactional leaders reward followers' efforts as well as punish those who fail to accomplish their set goals (Benmira & Agboola, 2021). Hence, Bass (1997) saw this type of leader as those that use three components in their leadership. These components are (a) *contingent reward* (i.e., the use of award and punishment with the followers in order to achieve its vision/goals within the organisation), and (b) *management by exception (active)*.

The rest of the chapter is organised under the following main headings, namely, literature review, methods, results, discussion, and conclusion.

## LITERATURE REVIEW

### Theoretical Foundations

As mentioned earlier, transformational and transactional leadership theories guided this study because of the multifactor leadership questionnaire, which was used to assess the principal's transformational leadership style in order to provide empirical evidence to support the impact of this style on the school. Both theories are described below.

### Transformational Leadership

In this theory, "leaders encourage, inspire and motivate followers" (Benmira & Agboola, 2021, p. 4). Korejan and Shahbazi (2016) described this type of leader as one who is "inspiring and creative and leads people in a way that they try more than their abilities in the organisation and also invent and innovate in their work area" (p. 453). Korejan and Shahbazi defined it as a leader "who seeks to create ideas and new perspectives to create a new path of growth and prosperity in front of the organisation" (p. 454). Olson (2006) described a transformational leader as someone who is "able to communicate a vision for the organisation that staff members adopt as their own, and to instil pride, motivation, and direction for them while moving them toward shared organisational goals" (p. 2). Although these definitions are different, there are some similarities. For example, they motivate, inspire, innovate, and create an environment that will facilitate them to lead and achieve their vision.

Furthermore, Kouzes and Posner (2023), in exploring the concept of transformational leadership, identified five key practices that exemplary leaders demonstrate. Table 1 presents their model of exemplary transformational leadership practices.

*Table 1. Model of exemplary transformational leadership practices*

| Dimension | Transformational Leaders | Model |
|---|---|---|
| Model the Way | Set an example through their actions and behaviours | They clarify values, establish standards, and align their actions with the shared vision. |
| Inspire a Shared Vision | Inspire and motivate others by creating a compelling vision of the future. | They communicate this vision effectively and engage others in its pursuit. |
| Challenge the Process | Encourage innovation, risk-taking, and continuous improvement. | They actively seek opportunities to challenge the status quo and foster a culture of innovation. |
| Enable Others to Act | Empower their followers by building trust, promoting collaboration, and providing support and resources. | They create an environment where individuals feel valued and capable of making a meaningful contribution. |
| Encourage the Heart | Recognise and celebrate the achievements of individuals and teams. | They provide encouragement, support, and appreciation, fostering a positive and inclusive climate. |

Source: Kouzes and Posner (2023)

## Transactional Leadership

In this type of leadership, the leader is said to rely on "authority to motivate employers" (Benmira & Agboola, 2021, p. 4). These are leaders who are actively involved in the implementation of the policies that will lead to the achievement of vision/goals by observing their followers within an organisation and taking necessary actions based on their performance or outputs before the situation worsens. (c) Management by exception (passive), these leaders play a passive role by not taking action even when problems occur until the situation worsens (Bass, 1997, as cited in Mustofa et al., 2022).

Even though the components or dimensions of transformational and transactional leadership seem to be separate, Bass and Avolio (1994) and Avolio and Bass (2004), later developed the full range of leadership by seeing the two as a continuum. In this nine-factor model or the full range of leadership, Bass and Avolio identified leadership behaviours that were grouped into the following components, namely, (1) idealised attributes or idealised influence (attributes), (2) idealised behaviours or idealised influence (behaviours), (3) inspirational motivation, (4) intellectual stimulation, (5) individual consideration, (6) contingent reward, (7) management by exception (active), (8) management by exception (passive), and (9) laissez-faire. The focus of this study is on transformational leadership and how the principal was able to change the school.

## Characteristics of Transformational Leaders

Transformational leaders generally tend to show four main characteristics, namely, (1) being *charismatic* by appealing to the followers to understand the vision of the organisation and working together to achieve it, (2) using *inspirational leadership* by raising each other's level of motivation, (3) *intellectual stimulation*, and (4) the consideration of the *needs of followers* by acknowledging and addressing them (Dubinsky et al., 1995; as cited in Alessa, 2021). Other authors suggested similar characteristics, such as (1) influencing and interacting with followers and adapting their behaviours to meet challenges within the organisation, and (2) participating in the process of organisational change by working together to achieve the vision (Tengi et al., 2017, as cited in Alessa, 2021). Yammarino et al. (1993) added that transformational leaders endeavour to elevate the needs of followers and encourage changes in followers either as individuals or groups within the organisations (as cited in Alessa, 2021). Furthermore, the characteristic of transformational leaders involves influencing their followers by motivating them to develop moral values needed to bring about self and organisational (Burns, 1978; Tengi et al., 2017, as cited in Alessa, 2021).

## The Effects of Transformational Leadership

Alessa (2021) noted a positive correlation between transformational leadership and organisational outcomes. This is because transformational leaders are said to make significant contributions to the performance of the organisations, such as academic performance in the case of educational institutions. For instance, in Saudi Arabia, Al Madhahaji (2017, as cited in Alessa, 2021), found that public educational institutions with transformational leadership had higher academic performance because the leadership promoted best practices such as being creative in developing ideas and facilitating and empowering knowledge sharing among staff, which enhanced staff commitment with the institutions.

Furthermore, a study by Buil et al. (2019) on the effect of transformational leadership on employee performance in Spain revealed a connection between transformational leadership and job performance because this type of leadership motivated followers which in turn increased their engagement levels. A similar result on the impact of transformational leadership was noted by Mathende and Yousefi (2021), who found that this type of leadership style made significant contributions to how employees in beverage manufacturing companies listed in the Zimbabwe stock exchange performed and grew. Furthermore, Savovic (2017) found a positive effect transformational leadership style had on employees in a company in the Republic of Serbia. According to Savovic, the employees had a positive assessment of the leadership on two dimensions, namely, inspirational motivation and idealised influence, but found less positive on intellectual stimulation and individualised consideration.

## Traits of a Successful Leader

There are several theories of leadership and different perspectives (trait & personality) of what qualities a leader should have to make them successful. Bass (1985) stated that successful leaders have the following traits "self-confidence, ambitious, dependable and decisive, stability, internal locus of control, sensitivity to others, integrity, energetic, and dominant and persistent" (as cited in Othman et al., 2012, p. 384). Bass and Stogdill (1990) believed that for leaders to be effective, their behaviours matters. According to Bass and Stogdill, the two dimensions of effective leaders are "orientation to task and orientation to people" (as cited in Othman et al., 2012, p. 384). Othman et al. (2012) explained that people with task-oriented leadership styles focus on "improving competency and performance of followers" (p. 384), through clarification of expectations for attaining the goals of the organisations. On the other hand, leaders who are oriented to people, are those who focus on building relationships while empowering the flowers. These two dimensions of effective leaders fit with transformational and transactional leadership, which differentiate between orientation to task (tasks-oriented) leaders and orientation to people (relationship-oriented) leaders (Othman et al., 2012). Lok and Crawford (2001) concluded that transformational and transactional leadership styles "contribute to organisational success" (as cited in Othman et al., 2012, p. 385). Vilhauer (2018), citing the definition of Northouse (2016), defined transformational leadership as "a leadership style that focuses on the links between leaders and followers" (p. 12). To create this link, these types of leaders "motivate followers to achieve their full potential so that leaders and followers can achieve their goals" (p. 12). On the other hand, transactional leadership was defined as "a leadership style that encompasses many other leadership models" (p. 12). These leaders focus "on the exchange between the leader and the follower" (Northouse, 2016, as cited in Vilhauer, 2018, p. 12).

# METHODS

## Research Design

The descriptive research design was used in this study to capture participants' perceptions about the transformational leadership practices at their selected high school in Jamaica. Citing Calderon (2006), Rillo and Alieto (2018) defined this design as "a purposive process of gathering, analysing, classifying, and tabulating data about prevailing conditions, practices, processes, trends, and cause-effect relationships and then making adequate and accurate interpretation about such data with or without or sometimes minimal aid of statistical methods" (p. 169). This design was used because the researchers wanted to capture the transformation that has taken place in the school among the students and the teachers.

## Population and Sample

The high school used for this study has 76 teachers, including the principal, vice principals, and teachers. The student population is 1,600 (720 males & 880 females). The technical and auxiliary staff were not considered in this study. The principal was invited to participate in the study; therefore, no sampling was done; however, 50 senior students and 50 teachers were purposefully selected based on their responsibilities in the school. It should be noted that the senior students were those in Grades 11 to 13, who were at least 15 years and over at the time of this study.

## Data Collection

The revised version of the multi-factor leadership questionnaire (MLQ) by Avolio and Bass (1995) was used to collect data from senior students and teachers. This questionnaire was used because it was designed to assess mainly transformational and transactional leadership styles. Pahi et al. (2015) described it as one of the top-ranked scales for measuring leadership. The researchers applied for permission and paid for the license from the company Mind Garden, Inc., which had the authorisation to reproduce the instrument before the researchers were able to use this questionnaire.

This revised version of the questionnaire measures two main components, namely, the transformational, and transactional characteristics of a leader. It has 45 descriptive statements with a six-point response format ranging from "Not at all" to "Frequently, if not always." Since this questionnaire does not have demographic items, an extra page was added to capture this missing part. The extra items to the teacher questionnaire included gender, age range, qualification, teaching experience, number of years in the school, and position held. For the students' questionnaire, gender, age, grade, and number of years in the school were added. The questionnaire was administered in person from March 14 to April 5, 2023. This length of time was given to enable the participants time to complete and return the questionnaire. Furthermore, an interview was conducted with the principal on April 6, 2023.

## Data Analysis

The data collected from the questionnaire were analysed using descriptive statistics for the demographic data or profile items and the mean scores of the nine dimensions, while independent samples *t*-test was used for one research question to determine differences in the teachers' and students' views on the transformational qualities of their principal.

The interview responses were transcribed and analysed using the six-step thematic analysis by Braun and Clake (2012, as cited in Maguire & Delahunt, 2017). Among other things, this involved coding, searching for themes, reviewing the themes, defining the themes, and writing up the findings in a narrative format.

## Reliability and Validity

The psychometric properties of the MLQ are described in this section. The first to be discussed is reliability and followed by validity.

Although the MQL has 45 items, 36 that measured the nine factors or dimensions were used for the reliability analysis. Each factor or dimension has four items. The nine remaining items (extra effort, effectiveness, & satisfaction) measure outcomes separately from the leadership style and behaviour. The Cronbach Alpha method was used in estimating the reliability coefficients. The overall reliability coefficients were 0.93 for the students' questionnaire and 0.94 for the teachers' questionnaire. According to a study by Bajcar and Babiak (2022), the multifactor leadership questionnaire has shown different reliability coefficients across different studies. A similar view was expressed by Avolio et al. (1999), Casimer et al. (2006), Oshagbemi and Gill (2004), and Stordeur et al. (2001), who found a reliability coefficient ranging from 0.64 to 0.92. The coefficients obtained in this study were interpreted as good (above 0.70) based on the rule of thumb provided by George and Mallery (2016). As shown in Table 2, the reliability coefficients of five of the nine dimensions were below 0.70, while four were above 0.70. The *individualised consideration* dimension had the highest coefficient of 0.78, while the *laissez-faire* dimension had the lowest reliability coefficient. The variations are similar to the results obtained originally by Avolio and Bass (2004) and by Vilhauer (2018). This may be attributed to the sample size used in the current study, as well as other contextual factors.

Content validity was used to ensure that the items provided answers to the research questions. To assess the factor structure of the MLQ, the researchers relied on the different validation studies conducted by Antonakis et al. (2003), Avolio and Bass (1997), Avolio, Bass, and Jung (1995), Boehnke et al. (2003), Hasim and Mahmood (2012), and more recently by Pahi et al. (2015), since the number of participants in this study was too small for factor analysis. Although the results of these studies varied, the variations may be due to the analysis methods used and contextual factors (environmental risks, gender, & leader hierarchy) from the study settings (Antonakis et al., 2003). In the study by Antonakis et al. (2003), they concluded that the MLQ is "a valid and reliable instrument that can adequately measure the nine components comprising the full-range theory of leadership" (p. 286). A similar view was expressed by Northouse (2016), who concurred that the Avolio and Bass model was one of the validated leadership models of the 21st century.

*Table 2. The reliability of the nine dimensions of the MQL*

| Construct | Number of Items | Alpha Obtained | Alpha MQL Sample* |
|---|---|---|---|
| **Transformation Leadership** | | | |
| Idealised Influence (Attributes) | 4 | 0.77 | 0.70 |
| Idealised Influence (Behaviours) | 4 | 0.68 | 0.64 |
| Inspirational Motivation | 4 | 0.68 | 0.76 |
| Intellectual Stimulation | 4 | 0.75 | 0.64 |
| Individualised Consideration | 4 | 0.78 | 0.62 |
| **Transactional Leadership** | | | |
| Contingent Reward | 4 | 0.65 | 0.60 |
| Management by Exception (Active) | 4 | 0.68 | 0.75 |
| **Passive/Avoidant Leadership** | | | |
| Management by Exception (Passive) | 4 | 0.71 | 0.64 |
| Laissez-Faire | 4 | 0.49 | 0.60 |

*Note: Alpha MQL Sample provided by Avolio & Bass, 2004, as cited in Vilhauer, 2018, p. 58

## Ethical Issues

The researchers applied to the Research Ethics Committee of the Faculty and were granted ethical clearance to conduct the study. A letter was written to the principal asking permission to conduct the study in the school. Among other things, the purpose of the study, the participants' roles, confidentiality, benefits and harm were explained in a letter. The students were given a copy of the assent form, while the teachers signed an informed consent form before data were collected. One of the vice-principals granted the permission on behalf of the students since it was difficult to access the parents/guardians of these students.

# RESULTS

One hundred questionnaires were distributed to 50 students and 50 teachers. The overall response rate was 74%. For the students, the response rate was 84% and for teachers was 64%. The response rates were considered good, given the number of distributed questionnaires among the students and teachers. According to Babbie (2020), a good survey response rate is 70 and above. Effects were made several times to encourage more to respond to the questionnaire; however, this did not increase the participation rate.

## Respondents' Characteristics

Of the 74 participants who responded to the questionnaire, 20 were males, and 54 were females. For the students' group, 13 (31%) were males, 26 (61.9%) were females, and three preferred not to declare their gender. The students' age ranged from 15 years to 19 years, with an average age of 17 years. Students are in different grades from 10 to 12; however, a majority of them were in Grades 11 and 12. The average number of years the students have been in the school is five years. Some have been in the school for up to seven years since they are in the sixth form, doing the CAPE programme.

As shown in Table 3, more female teachers participated in the study compared to males. The highest qualification among those who responded was a master's degree. For the profile section of the questionnaire, a teacher did not respond; however, 31 responded. See Table 3 for the teachers' demographics.

*Table 3. Teachers' demographics*

| Variable | | Frequency | Percentage |
|---|---|---|---|
| Gender | Male | 7 | 22.6 |
| | Female | 21 | 67.7 |
| | Prefer not to declare | 3 | 9.7 |
| Age Range | 35 years & Below | 16 | 51.6 |
| | 36 – 45 years | 7 | 22.6 |
| | 46 - & Above | 8 | 25.8 |
| Qualification | Bachelor's Degree | 24 | 77.4 |
| | Master's Degree | 7 | 22.6 |
| Teaching Experience | 5 years & Below | 12 | 38.7 |
| | 6 – 10 years | 8 | 25.8 |
| | 11 – 20 years | 5 | 16.1 |
| | Above 20 years | 6 | 19.4 |
| Years in the School | 5 years & Below | 16 | 51.6 |
| | 6 – 10 years | 11 | 35.5 |
| | Above 10 years | 4 | 12.9 |

*Research Question 1:* How does the principal define his/her leadership style?

To address the first research question, an interview was conducted with the principal on April 6, 2023. When asked about his leadership style, the principal asserted *I never once saw myself as a transformational leader. I see myself as a situational leader. I tend to adapt based on the circumstances or situations to meet the needs of my team.* Although the principal saw his style as more of a situational leader, the students and teachers rated him as a transformational leader on the five dimensions. See Figure 1 for the words used by the principal in defining his leadership approach. These were summarised under four dimensions, namely, inspirational motivation, intellectual stimulation, individualised influence, and individualised consideration.

The principal noted that from the onset, he created a vision to help bring about the changes he wanted, as well as strategies for achieving that vision. He said he told the Board of Management even before getting the job that:

*Figure 1. Elements of transformational leadership in the school studied*

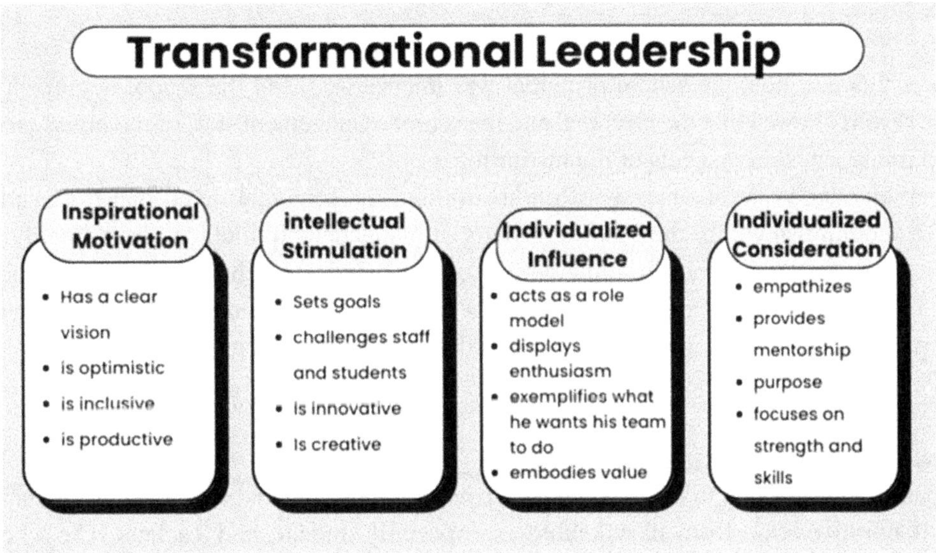


*I can guarantee you that people will start speaking differently about this school after three years. I was asked why are you so confident, and I responded I believe in my ability to get things done if not get rid of me (Principal, Male).*

Therefore, during the first couple of weeks as the principal, he used informal one-on-one talks, small group, and large group meetings to communicate the vision.

*When I came in, I started going around and talking to people. I just had a normal conversation. So, I'm feeling out people as the saying goes in Jamaica. I wanted to know what was their thought process on the vision. I met with the VPs, and I had a meeting with them and documented everything. I communicated with them my expectations. The second thing was to have a meeting with the senior teachers, with the managers, and in that middle management meeting, I had some points on my agenda, and I told them that I'm on a mission to change things. (Principal, Male).*

The principal strategically engaged his team in an inclusive effort to create the vision as well as inspire and motivate them to commit to the shared vision of the organisation. Thus, during the meeting with the staff,

*I remember we crafted a new vision and mission statement. The vision and the mission were written on every agenda for every meeting held at the school. And after a time, it started permeating the entire school. So the vice principals, when they have meetings, must have the vision and mission on it. Heads of Departments must have it on their agenda, the year coordinators, form teachers, and even the prefect body must have the mission and vision statements on their meeting agendas. This also applied to me as a principal. Yes, up to this day, even my principal's report to the Board, you will see the vision and the mission, and everybody is aware of the vision and the mission (Principal, Male).*

***Research Question 2:*** What impact has the principal's transformational leadership style made on the school?

To answer this question, the school principal was interviewed, and the school documents were reviewed. The results showed that the principal and the senior management staff of the high school worked as a team to transform some aspects of the institution.

Having conducted a SWOT analysis of the institution, the principal noted that the major changes he wanted to accomplish within the first three years of his leadership included branding the school as a school of choice, improving the academic performance of students, rehabilitating the school plant by conducting infrastructural upgrades, and providing a variety of sports and extra-curricular activities for students to participate in. Consequently, the results discussed below focus on those areas.

## Student Performance

The principal highlighted that to bring about positive change in students' academic performance, it had to take a collaborative effort from all stakeholders, especially students and teachers. The school leadership provided a record of student performance in two secondary examinations, namely, the Caribbean Secondary Education Certificate (CSEC) Examinations and the Caribbean Advanced Proficiency Examination (CAPE). The CSEC examinations are used to assess and certify eligible students after five years of their secondary school education, while the CAPE provides certification to eligible students who have attained a minimum of five years of secondary education. See Tables 4 and 5 for students' performance in CSEC and CAPE.

*Table 4. Students' pass rate in CSEC examinations: 2017 to 2022*

| Subject | 2017 | 2018 | 2019 | 2020 | 2021 | 2022 |
|---|---|---|---|---|---|---|
| English A | 82% | 86% | 85% | 87% | 75% | 84% |
| Mathematics | 44% | 64% | 38% | 71% | 36% | 34% |
| Integrated Science | 77% | 53% | 40% | 92% | 78% | 57% |
| Social Studies | 55% | 65% | 80% | 82% | 43% | 66% |
| Physical Education & Sports | 100% | 100% | 100% | 100% | 100% | 100% |
| Information Technology | 82% | 94% | 95% | 100% | 84% | 94% |

As shown in Table 4, for the CSEC examinations, the pass rate for students was consistently high over the 6-year period in English A, Physical Education and Sports, and Information Technology. These subjects were selected because they are regarded as core subjects. However, there are non-core subjects where the students have done very well. These include Food, Nutrition and Health Technical, Family and Resource Management Technical, music, Theatre Arts, and Office Administration. It should also be noted that from 2020 to 2022, there was a dip in pass rates due to the coronavirus period.

*Table 5. Students' pass rate in CAPE examinations: 2017 to 2022*

| Subject | 2017 | 2018 | 2019 | 2020 | 2021 | 2022 |
|---|---|---|---|---|---|---|
| Biology (Unit 2) | 100% | 100% | 100% | 100% | 88% | 60% |
| Caribbean Studies | 100% | 100% | 98% | 98% | 87% | 89% |
| Communication Studies | 97% | 92% | 90% | 96% | 85% | 79% |
| Entrepreneurship (Unit 2) | 100% | 100% | 100% | 100% | 100% | 100% |
| Information Technology (Unit 2) | 100% | 100% | 95% | - | 100% | 91% |
| Physical Education (Unit 1) | 100% | 100% | 100% | 100% | 100% | - |

As shown in Table 5, for the CAPE examinations, the pass rate for students was consistently high over the 6-year period in the following CAPE subjects Biology (Unit 2), Entrepreneurship (Unit 2), Information Technology (Unit 2), and Physical Education. Other subjects with high pass rates are Management of Business (Unit 2), Sociology (Unit 2), and Tourism (Unit 2).

Regarding the students, the school principal stated:

*It's all about consistency and holding the students accountable. We created a lot of opportunities for students to grow and develop their leadership skills. We established the Sixth Form Association. They have a president, vice president, public relations officer, secretary, and Treasurer. This was also encouraged among the lower grades. Thus, we have a first-form association, second-form association, third-form association, and so on (Principal, Male).*

## Student Leadership

Essentially, we are instilling a culture of leadership in the students rather than just waiting until they reach fifth form or higher.

*Also, my staff meetings are like workshops and seminars. When teachers come to staff meetings, we operate as a community of learners, and they are expected to come and contribute to strategic planning. Therefore, I motivate them intellectually to try new things to see things in a different way, and that's what they must also do at their departmental meeting. At each meeting, different teachers are assigned to come and do a presentation on different areas like holistic learning, how boys learn, how to improve test scores, or how to manage behavioural challenges in the classroom (Principal, Male).*

These activities, according to the principal, set the tone for the academic performance of students to improve. *What you find is that people started learning, and teachers started accepting the possibility that boys learn differently than girls. We then had to make adjustments to the classroom environment. All first, second, and third-form classes were arranged as all boys and all grades* (Principal, Male).

## Infrastructural Upgrades and Developments

Over the years, a number of upgrades were done by the school leadership to provide better accommodation for both students and teachers. These include offices for the vice-principals, six new classrooms, a teacher centre, offices for the work experience coordinator and the plant supervisor, a behaviour modification room, conference rooms, an examination coordinator room, technical vocational labs, and a lecture room.

The principal stated that:

*Well, if you are going to provide an environment conducive to teaching, then we must start with rehabilitating the school plant. There were wires hanging out of the classrooms, buildings leaking, a lot of students marking on the walls, and the bathrooms were dirty and smelly. So immediately, we started tiling. We pulled out all the windows and replaced them with new ones. We wanted to create a five-star hotel effect with the rehabilitation of the school plant. We painted everywhere in one colour for uniformity. We got millions of dollars and renovated the netball court. We renovated the girls, boys, and staff bathrooms. We have smart TVs in about 10 classrooms. We renovated the EDPM Lab. We took the computers out and turned it into a conference room with an interactive whiteboard. We renovated the library and did several other things. (Principal, Male)*

## Sports and Extracurricular Activities

The principal underscored the importance of establishing extracurricular and sporting activities to supplement the academic programmes at the schools. *Even though we started doing very well academically, we know that being involved in sports helps to build the profile of the school. Thus, I carefully examined which of these sports I was going to target* (Principal, Male).

*Research Question 3:* To what extent are there differences in students' and teachers' perceptions of their principal's leadership behaviours?

The students and teachers were asked to rate their principal's leadership behaviours under nine sub-scales or dimensions measured by the MQL. On the MQL questionnaire, the first five dimensions, namely, *Idealised Influence (Attributed), Idealised Influence (Behaviour), Inspirational Motivation, Intellectual Stimulation,* and *Individual Consideration,* measure *transformational leadership*, while *Contingent Reward* and *Management by Exception (Active)* dimensions measure *transactional leadership*. The last two dimensions (Management by Exception (Passive) & Laissez-Faire) measure *passive avoidant* leadership style. As shown in Table 6, the transformational leadership dimensions were rated high between the two groups.

Students and teachers appeared to perceive their principal's leadership style as transformational, although the principal views his leadership style as situational. The students' ratings of their principal's leadership behaviour were slightly higher than their teachers on the following dimensions: Idealised Influence (Attributed), Intellectual Stimulation, and Individual Consideration, while the teachers' ratings were higher on Idealised Influence (behaviour), and Inspirational Motivation. However, when it comes to the transactional leadership aspect of the questionnaire, students and teachers also gave high ratings. This was not the case for the Passive Avoidant aspect of the questionnaire when both groups' ratings were slightly lower. It is safe to conclude from the results that the students and teachers perceived their principal as a transformational leader.

*Table 6. The nine dimensions of leadership*

| Dimension | Students ($n$ = 42) | | Teachers ($n$ = 32) | |
|---|---|---|---|---|
| | Mean | SD | Mean | SD |
| Idealised Influence (Attributed) | 8.52 | 4.44 | 7.81 | 4.37 |
| Idealised Influence (Behaviour) | 10.5 | 3.57 | 11.5 | 3.14 |
| Inspirational Motivation | 11.9 | 3.44 | 12.1 | 3.07 |
| Intellectual Stimulation | 8.88 | 3.52 | 6.69 | 4.37 |
| Individual Consideration | 6.74 | 4.27 | 6.44 | 4.84 |
| Contingent Reward | 9.38 | 3.69 | 9.16 | 3.31 |
| Management by Exception (Active) | 10.5 | 3.51 | 9.06 | 4.05 |
| Management by Exception (Passive) | 7.83 | 4.28 | 5.78 | 4.19 |
| Laissez-Faire | 5.52 | 3.56 | 6.25 | 3.43 |

An independent $t$-test was performed to determine if there was a significant difference between the students and the teachers' perceptions. As shown in Table 7, there was a significant difference in students' and teachers' perceptions of dimensions of Intellectual Stimulation, $t(72) = 2.390, p = 0.010$; Management by Exception (Active), $t(72) = 1.688, p = 0.048$; and Management by Exception (Passive), $t(72) = 2.060, p = 0.021$.

For the *Intellectual Stimulation* dimension, the students perceived their principal as a leader that re-examines assumptions in order to question if they are appropriate, and seeks different perspectives when solving problems when compared to the teachers' perceptions. For the *Management by Exception (Active)* dimensions, the students believed that their principal focuses attention on mistakes and deviations from standards and gives attention when dealing with mistakes and complaints when compared to the teachers' perceptions. For *Management by Exception (Passive),* the students felt that their principal displays behaviour that suggests that he is a firm believer in not fixing something when it is not broken.

*Table 7. Independence samples t-test for the nine dimensions of leadership*

| Dimension | $t$ | $df$ | $P$-Value |
|---|---|---|---|
| Idealised Influence (Attributed) | 0.687 | 72 | 0.247 |
| Idealised Influence (Behaviour) | -1.277 | 72 | 0.103 |
| Inspirational Motivation | -0.112 | 72 | 0.456 |
| Intellectual Stimulation | 2.390 | 72 | 0.010 |
| Individual Consideration | 0.283 | 72 | 0.389 |
| Contingent Reward | 0.262 | 72 | 0.397 |
| Management by Exception (Active) | 1.688 | 72 | 0.048 |
| Management by Exception (Passive) | 2.060 | 72 | 0.021 |
| Laissez-Faire | -0.882 | 72 | 0.190 |

When the ratings of the students and teachers were examined in all nine dimensions, the two groups rated their principal's leadership behaviour higher on *Inspirational Motivation, Management by Exception (Active),* while their scores were between average and slightly above average for *Idealised Influence (Attributed), Idealised Influence (Behaviour), Intellectual Stimulation,* and *Contingent Reward.* The principal's ratings for *Individual Consideration, Management by Exception (Passive),* and *Laissez-Faire* dimensions were below average.

## DISCUSSION

### Leadership Style

Regarding the results of research question one, the results showed that the principal's leadership style was more aligned with transformational leadership, although he described his approach as situational leadership. This is because of the activities he (the principal) was engaged in, which brought about successful changes in students, teachers, and infrastructure at the institution. Hence, it was safe to conclude that the principal's leadership approach is consistent with the descriptions of transformational leadership expressed by Bass and Avolio (1990; 1994), Kouzes and Posner (2023), and Northouse (2016), to name a few. For instance, the principal made a lot of changes in the school, and Bass and Avolio (1990) indicated that transformational leaders are change agents dedicated to improving the performance of their followers. Furthermore, the principal's leadership approach was also consistent with the views of Kouzes and Posner (2023), who stated that transformational leadership's core tenets, include setting a clear vision, inspiring others, empowering individuals, fostering innovation, and creating a positive organisational culture. It emphasises the importance of building strong relationships, trust, and collaboration within teams and organisations (see Figure 1). While Northouse (2016) saw people with transformational leadership as those, who connect leaders and followers.

It is worth noting that in being a transformational leader, the principal made deliberate attempts to meet with the different stakeholders about his vision and plan for the school. These meetings, to a large extent, allowed the principal to implement his plan as a new school leader when he started. One of the primary reasons organisational change initiatives fail is because of resistance to change (Gerwing, 2016). Moreover, individuals often resist change because it is hard, disruptive, and awakens fear about the unknown (Gerwing, 2016). The principal was fully aware of this, thereby, met and had some support to implement his vision.

### Leadership Impact

Regarding research question two, which focused on the impact of the principal's transformational leadership style made on the school, the results showed improvements in the academic performance of students in CSEC and CAPE examinations (Student Handbook, n. d.). For example, in the CSEC examination, the number of students obtaining five or more passes has increased (School Magazine, 2019). According to the School Magazine (2019), in CSEC subjects such as Mathematics and English, student performance moved from "41.3% in 2014 to 59.7% in 2017", and in 2018, "Mathematics increased from 44% to 64%" and in English, it "moved from 82% to 86%" (School Magazine, 2019). These increases in Mathematics and English were consistent with the overall student performance in the two subjects in Jamaica, which was announced by the then Minister of Education, Mr. Reid, who stated that "there were increases of 4.5 and 2.9 percentage points for Mathematics and English Language, respectively" (Morris, 2018, n. p.). Tedla and Kilango (2022), in a descriptive research study of secondary schools in China, noted that principals' roles and behaviours could lead to higher student performance. This view was also expressed by Woods and Martin (2016), who conducted a narrative case study in Missouri, America, and also noted that the principal's behaviours lead to an increase in academic achievement.

Concerning the infrastructures, the results showed improvements. This is because the principal rehabilitated the school buildings, by upgrading classrooms, staff rooms, laboratories, and sports facilities for students and teachers, and added new classrooms, a teacher centre, offices for the work experience coordinator and the plant supervisor, a behaviour modification room, conference rooms, an examination coordinator room, and a lecture room. Other developments include establishing several Wi-Fi Zones for students and staff and fencing the school compound with security guards and Closed Circuit Television (CCTV) cameras. To better manage the school premises, the principal, in 2015, employed a plan supervisor (Student Handbook, n. d.; School Magazine, 2019). Barrett et al. (2019) noted that a better physical learning environment is associated with student performance and better school attendance by students and teachers. Barrett et al. (2019) stated that many building-related factors influence the well-being of its occupants" (p. 14). A similar view was expressed by Kai and Zimmer (2016), who concluded that investing in school infrastructure has positive effects on student aptitude.

Concerning sports and extracurricular activities, the results showed that students and staff are encouraged to participate. According to the Student Handbook (n. d.), the school has 24 functional clubs and societies; this was also highlighted in the interview. The students also participate actively in "Inter-Secondary School Sports Association (ISSA) games, including Boys and Girls Champs, Manning Cup Football, Cricket, Netball, and Hockey" (Student Handbook, n. d.).

Two notable performances of the students in sports were documented in the School Magazine (2019), namely, the male and female under 19 and under 16 competitions in 2017, and in 2018, the students performed very well during the Manning Cup Football. In a study done by Broh (2002), it showed that participation in some extra curriculum activities promoted student development and had a positive effect on student achievement. A similar finding was revealed by Cornelißen and Pfeifer (2007), who also believed that student participation had positive effects on educational achievement. Dou et al. (2016) concluded that school leaders influence student achievement in several ways, namely, by establishing goals, setting high expectations, allocating resources, improving the learning environment, and communicating with stakeholders.

## Perceptions of Principal's Leadership Behaviours

Regarding research question three, the results showed that the students' ratings of their principal's leadership behaviours were slightly higher than their teachers on the following dimensions: *Idealised Influence (Attributed), Intellectual Stimulation*, and *Individual Consideration*, while the teachers' ratings were higher on *Idealised Influence (behaviour),* and I*nspirational Motivation*. Furthermore, the *t*-test result showed a significant difference in students' and teachers' perceptions of dimensions of *Intellectual Stimulation*, *Management by Exception (Active)*, and *Management by Exception (Passive)*. These ratings by students and teachers are consistent with the results of a study by Savovic (2017), which showed that some dimensions of transformational leadership were rated high and impacted employees' performance in Serbia. A similar result was revealed by Mathende and Yousefi (2021), which also reported higher ratings on some dimensions of transformational leadership in the Zimbabwe study. No study on student performance was located to support the current study.

Regarding the transactional leadership aspect of the questionnaire, students and teachers gave high ratings to their principal's leadership behaviours. This was not the case for the Passive Avoidant aspect of the questionnaire, where both groups' ratings were slightly lower. It is safe to conclude from the results that the students and teachers perceived their principal as a transformational leader. These results showed mixed. For instance, the results, while showing some aspects of transformational leadership, also showed that the principal was also perceived as a transactional leader and passive/avoidant leadership. This is consistent with the works of Bass and Avolio (1994), which stated that every leader would use different leadership styles to an extent. Furthermore, Avolio (2011) stated that leaders who use different dimensions and styles in the right situations are said to be more effective. A study by Vilhauer (2018), showed that transformational leaders, among other things, encouraged intellectual stimulation, while transactional leaders displayed management by exception (active) and management by exception (passive). This is consistent with the current results.

## CONCLUSION

The purpose of this study was to determine the type of leadership a principal is using in a selected high school in Kingston, Jamaica, and to describe how the principal and the senior management staff of the high school changed some aspects of the institution. The results showed that the principal described himself as a situational leader. However, the results of this study showed that the principal, while leading the school, displayed mostly transformational leadership style and, to an extent, transactional leadership style. The principal and his senior management staff have made a lot of changes in the school in three key areas, namely, the rate of students' passes in some subjects at the CSEC and CAPE examinations. There was also remarkable improvement in infrastructural developments to make the school environment more comfortable and safe for the students and teachers. In sports and extracurricular activities, the students and teachers have been encouraged to participate, and the students are competing in several sporting activities. It is hoped that this chapter will contribute to the literature on transformational leadership in Jamaica and will showcase the changes made in the school over the few years the principal and his team have led the school.

## ACKNOWLEDGMENT

We want to acknowledge the efforts of the principal, who participated in the interview. We also acknowledge the two vice principals, who assisted the researchers during the data collection phase, as well as the students and teachers who completed the questionnaire.

## REFERENCES

Alessa, G. S. (2012). The dimensions of transformational leadership and its organizational effects in public universities in Saudi Arabia: A systematic review. *Frontiers in Psychology*, *12*, 1–16. doi:10.3389/fpsyg.2021.682092 PMID:34867578

Antonakis, J., Avolio, B. J., & Sivasubramaniam, N. (2003). Context and leadership: An examination of the nine-factor full-range leadership theory using the multifactor leadership questionnaire. *The Leadership Quarterly*, *14*(3), 261–295. doi:10.1016/S1048-9843(03)00030-4

Avolio, B. J. (2011). Full range leadership development. *Sage (Atlanta, Ga.)*.

Avolio, B. J., & Bass, B. M. (1997). *Full range leadership development: Manual for the MLQ multifactor leadership questionnaire*. Mindgarden.

Avolio, B. J., & Bass, B. M. (2004). *Multifactor leadership questionnaire: Manual and sample set* (3rd ed.). Mind Garden.

Avolio, B. J., Bass, B. M., & Jung, D. I. (1995). *MLQ multifactor leadership questionnaire: Technical report*. Mindgarden.

Avolio, B. J., Bass, B. M., & Jung, D. I. (1999). Re-examining the components of transformational and transactional leadership using the multifactor leadership questionnaire. *Journal of Occupational and Organizational Psychology*, *72*(4), 441–462. doi:10.1348/096317999166789

Babbie, E. R. (2020). *The practice of social research* (15th ed.). Cengage.

Bajcar, B., & Babiak, J. (2022). Transformational and transactional leadership in the Polish organizational context: Validation of the full and short forms of the multifactor leadership questionnaire. *Frontiers in Psychology*, *13*, 1–18. doi:10.3389/fpsyg.2022.908594 PMID:35645888

Barrett, P., Treves, A., Shmis, T., Amasz, D., & Ustinova, M. (2019). *The impact of school infrastructure on learning: A synthesis of the evidence*. Word Bank Group. doi:10.1596/978-1-4648-1378-8

Bass, B. M., & Avolio, B. J. (1990). Developing transformational leadership: 1992 and beyond. *Journal of European Industrial Training*, *14*(5), 21–27. doi:10.1108/03090599010135122

Bass, B. M., & Avolio, B. J. (Eds.). (1994). *Improving organizational effectiveness through transformational leadership*. Sage.

Bass, B. M., & Avolio, B. J. (1995). *MLQ multifactor leadership questionnaire, leader form, rater form, and scoring*. Mind Garden.

Benmira, S., & Agboola, M. (2021). Evolution of leadership theory. *BMJ Leader*, *5*, 3–5. doi:10.1136/leader-2020-000296

Berkovich, I. (2016). School leaders and transformational leadership theory: Time to part ways? *Journal of Educational Administration*, *54*(5), 609–622. doi:10.1108/JEA-11-2015-0100

Boehnke, K., Bontis, N., DiStefano, J. J., & DiStefano, A. C. (2003). Transformational leadership: An examination of cross-national differences and similarities. *Leadership and Organization Development Journal, 24*(1), 5–15. doi:10.1108/01437730310457285

Broh, B. A. (2002). Linking extracurricular programming to academic achievement: Who benefits and why? *Sociology of Education, 75*(1), 69–95. doi:10.2307/3090254

Buil, I., Martinez, E., & Matute, J. (2019). Transformational leadership and employee performance: The role of identification, engagement and proactive personality. *International Journal of Hospitality Management, 77*, 64–75. doi:10.1016/j.ijhm.2018.06.014

Casimer, G., Waldman, D. A., Bartram, T., & Yang, S. (2006). Trust and the relationship between leadership and follower performance: Opening the black box in Australia and China. *Journal of Leadership & Organizational Studies, 12*(3), 68–84. doi:10.1177/107179190601200305

Corneließen, T., & Pfeifer, C. (2007). The impact of participation in sports on educational Attainment: New evidence from Germany. *Economics of Education Review, 29*(1), 94–103. doi:10.1016/j.econedurev.2009.04.002

D'Souza, A. A. (2003). *Leadership: A trilogy on leadership and effective management.* Paulines Publications.

Dou, D., Devos, G., & Valcke, M. (2016). The effects of autonomy gap in personnel policy, principal leadership and teachers' self-efficacy on their organizational commitment. *Asia Pacific Education Review, 17*(2), 339–353. doi:10.100712564-016-9428-7

George, D., & Mallery, P. (2016). *IBM SPSS statistics 23 step by step: A simple guide and reference* (14th ed.). Routledge. doi:10.4324/9781315545899

Gerwing, C. (2016). Meaning of change agents within organizational change. *Journal of Applied Leadership and Management, 4*, 21–40.

Hasim, R. A., & Mahmood, R. (2012). How do Malaysian academic staff perceive their leaders' leadership styles in relation to their commitment to service quality? *The International Journal of the Arts in Society, 5*(3), 231–242.

Hutton, D. (2011). Revealing the essential characteristics, qualities and behaviours of the high performing principal: Experiences of the Jamaican school system. *The International Journal of Educational Leadership Preparation, 5*(3), 1–15.

Hutton, D. M. (2016). The rating of high-performing principals' performance on their leadership dimensions by senior administrators, middle managers and classroom teachers. *Research in Comparative and International Education, 11*(2), 194–207. doi:10.1177/1745499916632423

Jovanovic, D., & Ciric, M. (2018). Benefits of transformational leadership in the context of education. *The European Proceedings of Social & Behavioural Sciences*, 496–503. doi:10.15405/epsbs.2016.09.64

Kaehler, B., & Grundei, J. (2019). *HR governance: A theoretical introduction.* Springer. doi:10.1007/978-3-319-94526-2

Kai, H., & Zimmer, R. (2016). Does investing in school capital infrastructure improve student achievement? *Economics of Education Review*, *53*, 143–158. doi:10.1016/j.econedurev.2016.05.007

Kaleem, S., Din, M. U., & Rehman, A. (2021). Impact of principals' leadership style on schools climate, teachers' performance and academic achievement of the students in South Districts of Khyber Pakhtunkhwa. *Elementary Education Online*, *20*(6), 518–527. doi:10.17051/ilkonline.2021.06.055

Khan, Z. A., Nawaz, A., & Khan, I. (2016). Leadership theories and styles: A literature review. *Journal of Resources Development and Management*, *16*, 1–7.

Korejan, M., & Shahbazi, H. (2016). An analysis of the transformational leadership theory. *Revue des Sciences Fondamentales et Appliquées*, *8*(3), 452. doi:10.4314/jfas.v8i3s.192

Kouzes, J. M., & Posner, B. Z. (2023). *The leadership challenge: How to make extraordinary things happen in organizations*. John Wiley & Sons.

Leithwood, K., & Sun, J. (2012). The nature and effects of transformational school leadership: A meta-analytic review of unpublished research. *Educational Administration Quarterly*, *48*(3), 387–423. doi:10.1177/0013161X11436268

Lin Tengi, M., Mansor, M., & Hashim, Z. (2017). A review theory of transformational leadership for school. *International Journal of Academic Research in Business & Social Sciences*, *7*(3), 792–799.

Maguire, M., & Delahunt, B. (2017). Doing a thematic analysis: A practical step-by-step learning and teaching scholars. *All Ireland Journal of Higher Education, 9*(2), 3351. https://ojs.aishe.org/index.php/aishe-j/article/view/335

Mathende, T., & Yousefi, M. (2021). Transformational leadership role and means efficacy on work performance under volatile uncertain complex and ambiguous environment. *Open Journal of Leadership*, *10*(4), 277–299. doi:10.4236/ojl.2021.104018

Mona High School. (2019). *Fortieth Anniversary: 1979 – 2019*. Publishing House Ltd.

Mona High School. (n.d.). *Student Handbook*. monahighschool.org

Moradi Korejan, M. M., & Shahbazi, H. (2016). An analysis of the transformational leadership theory. *Revue des Sciences Fondamentales et Appliquées*, *8*(3, 3S), 452–461. doi:10.4314/jfas.v8i3s.192

Morris, A. (2018). *Increase in CSEC passes*. Jamaica Information Service. https://jis.gov.jm/increase-in-csec-passes/

Mustofa, M. U. A., Gulton, R. Z., Bayuny, A. F. R., & Mustofa, M. A. H A. (2022). Transactional and transformational leadership in Islamic perspectives. *Indonesian Journal of Development Studies*, 13 – 19.

Northouse, P. G. (2016). *Leadership: Theory and practice* (7th ed.). Sage.

Olson, M. S. (2006). *A model for transformational nurse leadership and intrapreneurism: The nursing leadership cycle of integrity* [Master's Thesis]. Washington State University, Vancouver Campus. https://rex.libraries.wsu.edu/esploro/outputs/graduate/A-Model-for-Transformational-Nurse-Leadership/99900590537001842

Oshagbemi, T., & Gill, R. (2004). Differences in leadership styles and behaviour across hierarchical levels in UK organisations. *Leadership and Organization Development Journal*, *25*(1), 93–106. doi:10.1108/01437730410512796

Othman, J., Lawrence, J., & Mohammed, K. A. (2012). Review of factors that influence leadership styles among top management in small and medium-size enterprises. *International Business Management*, *6*(3), 384–389. doi:10.3923/ibm.2012.384.389

Pahi, M. H., Umrani, W. H., Hamid, K. A., & Ahmed, U. (2015). Examining multifactor leadership questionnaire construct: A validation study in the public hospitals of Sindh, Pakistan context. *IPBJ*, *7*(2), 27–39.

Palmer, D., Hermond, D., & Gardiner, C. (2014). Principals' leadership practices and mathematics pass rate in Jamaican high schools. *Administrative Issues Journal: Connecting Education, Practice, and Research*, *4*(2), 35–47. doi:10.5929/2014.4.2.1

Rillo, R. M., & Alieto, E. O. (2018). Indirect markers in Korean and Persian English essays: Implications for teaching writing to EFL learners. *The Journal of English as an International Language, 13*(2.2), 165 – 184. doi:10.2139/ssrn.3588006

Savovic, S. (2017). The impact of the dimensions of transformational leadership on the post-acquistion performance of the acquired company. *Economic Horizons*, *19*(2), 97–109. doi:10.5937/ekonhor1702095S

Smith, P., Francis, D., & Harper, A. (2015). Reframing transformational leadership for education and nation building in the Caribbean. *Caribbean Educational Research Journal*, *3*(2), 76–89.

Stordeur, S., D'Hoore, W., & Vandenberghe, C. (2001). Leadership, organizational stress, and emotional exhaustion among hospital nursing staff. *Journal of Advanced Nursing*, *35*(4), 533–542. doi:10.1046/j.1365-2648.2001.01885.x PMID:11529953

Sultana, U. S., Darun, M. R., & Yao, L. (2015). Transactional or transformational leadership: Which works best for now? *International Journal of Industrial Management*. https://ijim.ump.edu.my/images/pdf/4.pdf

Tedla, B. A., & Kilango, N. C. (2022). The role of school leadership toward improving student's achievement: A case study of secondary schools in Changchun, China. *Journal of Positive School Psychology*, *6*(4), 6744–6755.

Thompson, C. S. (2020). Theories and applications of transformational school leadership. *Journal of Thought*, *54*(3/4), 55–72.

Vilhauer, H. (2018). *An investigation into full-range leadership and leadership development methods in public parks and recreation organizations in California* [Doctoral Dissertation]. The University of San Francisco. https://repository.usfca.edu/cgi/viewcontent.cgi?article=1423&context=diss

Woods, E. H., & Martin, B. N. (2016). What leadership behaviours were demonstrated by the principal in a high poverty, high achieving elementary school? *Cogent Education*, *3*(1), 1172935. doi:10.1080/2331186X.2016.1172935

WorkandJam. (n.d.). *Mona High*. https://www.workandjam.com/bl/education/schools/mona-high.htm

# Chapter 7
# Leadership Style and Knowledge in Transforming Higher Education Institutions in Africa

**Kezia Herman Mkwizu**
https://orcid.org/0000-0003-4436-9603
*The Open University of Tanzania, Tanzania*

## ABSTRACT

*In order for higher education institutions (HEIs) in Africa to sustain higher education (HE), it is critical to re-examine leadership style and knowledge in the post-COVID-19 pandemic, especially dissemination of knowledge. Due to the effects of the pandemic on HEIs and its trajectory, this chapter is motivated to explore leadership style and knowledge in Africa's HEIs. Specifically, this chapter explores types of leadership styles and open knowledge in transforming HEIs in Africa. This chapter uses a literature review approach and content analysis. One of the findings of this chapter is that there are varying dynamics and evolution in transforming HEIs in Africa particularly from an open knowledge approach. The implication is for HEI experts and stakeholders to instill HE for societal good in transforming HEIs in Africa that focuses on open knowledge approach particularly in the post-COVID-19 pandemic so that HEIs are not only providing HE but HE for good.*

## INTRODUCTION

The role played by Higher Education Institutions (HEIs) in the provision of Higher Education (HE) to individuals such as researchers, economists, farmers, presidents, lawyers, editors, business executives, doctors, educators and ambassadors in society is very important. Indeed, HE has enabled the society to enjoy the services of professionals and thus contributing to the advancement of socio-economic development globally. However, the disruption of HEIs can bear negative consequences as evident in the Coronavirus disease 2019 (COVID-19) global pandemic declared by the World Health Organization (2020) on 11 March 2020. Various individuals in the society attaining their primary, secondary and higher education could not physically continue with education due to closures as a measure to combat

DOI: 10.4018/978-1-6684-8822-5.ch007

the pandemic (African Development Bank Group, 2020; African Union, 2021; Bozkurt & Sharma, 2020; Debbarma & Durai, 2021; Donnelly & Patrinos, 2022; Garcia-Morales et al., 2021; Huang et al., 2020; Kagoya & Mkwizu, 2023; Mkwizu, 2022a, 2022b; Pokhrel & Chhetri, 2021; Stock et al., 2021; United Nations Children's Fund, 2021; United Nations Educational, Scientific and Cultural Organization, 2020).

In addition, the United Nations mentioned that closing of schools and learning institutions worldwide affected the majority of the student population (94%) worldwide (United Nations, 2020). With such disruptions due to the pandemic, transformation of education is inevitable. In fact, Garcia-Morales et al. (2021) highlighted that HEIs are undergoing radical transformation in terms of digitalizing education and training processes while academics lack technological capabilities for online teaching. Furthermore, the act of alternative digital measures used by HEIs to provide online teaching and learning (Kagoya & Mkwizu, 2023; Seetal et al., 2021) so that individuals in society continue to receive education is rather a gesture of leadership style. On the other hand, various scholars and reports such as Daniel (2022) and World Economic Forum (2021) commented that education has changed forever due to the COVID-19 pandemic. Seetal et al. (2021) also opined that there were challenges whereby most academics did not have the adequate training in using technologies to teach.

Other scholars and reports cited more challenges for HE including Africa that is related to online teaching and learning in the pandemic like lack of academic social interaction, Information Communication Technologies (ICT), students learning difficulties, the infrastructure and facilities for the use of technologies such as "Go to webinar", "Liveto" and "Zoom" (Coman et al., 2020; Ivanec, 2022). In Africa, transforming the HEIs which was disrupted by the COVID-19 has caught the attention of many African scholars stating the need for curriculum changes to improve teaching and learning along with upgrading skills and women leadership in HE as noted in studies by Batinoluho (2022a, 2022b), Kidere and Mkwizu (2022), Migumi (2021), Mkwizu and Kimeto (2022a), Mohamed (2023), and Urio et al. (2021). Furthermore, Mohamed (2023) stated that majority of the HEIs lack formal curriculum plans in the context of Somalia. Curriculum change challenge is also noted in Mozambique as indicated by Ndaipa et al. (2023) noting that there is a need for integration of local languages and ethnoscience in the internalization of university curriculum.

Due to the effects of the pandemic on HEIs and its trajectory as well as adding literature in the field of education, the main purpose of this chapter is to explore leadership style and knowledge in transforming HEIs in Africa. Specifically, this chapter explores types of leadership styles and open knowledge in transforming HEIs in Africa. This chapter's question is;

*"What are the leadership styles and open knowledge needed in transforming HEIs in Africa?"*

The outcome of this chapter is significant because it provides implications and recommendations to be considered by education practitioners, researchers, academicians and the society at large on the issue of leadership style and open knowledge in transforming HEIs in Africa in the post-COVID-19. Furthermore, the findings of this chapter support the global efforts towards the Education 2030 Agenda indicated in United Nations Educational, Scientific and Cultural Organization (2022) that puts emphasis on embracing HEIs through open institutions while Wilson et al. (2020) advocates for open knowledge institutions.

## Leadership Style

Leadership in general is defined as the process which facilitates the individual and the use of collective efforts to achieve a shared objective (Harshitha et al., 2018). In addition, Harshitha et al. (2018) also defined leadership style as the actions of a leader such as visionary, coaching, collaborative, and consensus. Previously, the study by Nazim and Mahmood (2016) defined leadership style as a general way a leader behaves towards his subordinates in attaining objectives. Equally, the study by Al-Thawabiya et al. (2023) define leadership style as a vital element needed to increase the healthcare organizational productivity. This chapter defines leadership style as the act of a leader in embracing transformational skills which considers ideas and knowledge of team members in shaping HEIs.

However, various scholars have mentioned different types of leadership styles with majority stating the four key leadership styles which are autocratic, democratic, transactional and transformational as compiled in Table 1.

*Table 1. Major types of leadership styles*

| Major Types of Leadership Styles | Source |
|---|---|
| Autocratic leadership style | Chukwusa (2018) |
| Democratic leadership style | Harshitha et al. (2018) Khan et al. (2016) |
| Transactional leadership style | Harshitha et al. (2018) Khan et al. (2016) |
| Transformational leadership style | Al-Husseini et al. (2021)<br>Choi et al. (2017)<br>Harshitha et al. (2018)<br>Khan et al. (2016, 2020) |

Leadership has various styles and studies such as Chukwusa (2018) mentioned about autocratic leadership style while Khan et al. (2016) and Harshitha et al. (2018) highlighted on transformational, democratic and transactional leadership styles. The *autocratic leadership style* is considered to work better when high-directive decisions are taken (Chukwusa, 2018). Therefore, this suggests that leaders of HEIs may consider adopting autocratic leadership style during high-directives in decision making situations.

*Democratic leadership style* termed as participative or shared leadership whereby the inputs from team members and peers are considered and valued (Harshitha et al., 2018). Valuing and considering team members are crucial aspects in transforming HEIs, and according to Matama and Mkwizu (2021), the team member traits can assist in the efficiency of managing public HEIs particularly at public university level in terms of sense-of-urgency and timeliness.

The *transactional leadership* style is considered to have specific tasks and are performance-based results (Harshitha et al., 2018). Due to transactional leadership being performance-based then this suggest that the HEIs leaders who are seeking performance-based tasks to accomplish goals may adopt this approach of leadership style. According to Nita (2023) transformational leadership style when put in practise in the context of stable environment is capable of predicting performance. In the study by Nita (2023), the findings from a quantitative survey indicate an increase role of transactional leadership style within the highly digitalized HEI framework compared to transformational leadership style.

*Transformational leadership* is defined by Choi et al. (2017) as the role model among the team members through sharing ideas and knowledge in order to facilitate working cooperatively and efficiently. This implies that transformational leadership style focuses on the leader being a role model. Khan et al. (2020) summarized transformational leadership style by commenting that it is a type of leadership which maximizes the level of professional performance of work. But transformational leadership style also creates positive and valuable change in the followers (Nazim & Mahmood, 2016). Also, Al-Husseini et al. (2021) noted that transformational leadership is an influencing factor in knowledge management including in higher education. The HEIs leaders that wish to create positive and valuable change within their universities can ideally apply the transformational leadership style.

## Open Knowledge

Labate (2020) termed knowledge as an asset of economic worth. In this chapter, knowledge simply refers to the production and distribution of knowledge by higher education learning institutions. Subsequently, the concept of knowledge is broad and has various definitions depending on the nature of its use or perception. For example, (Guerriero, 2017, p.3) described knowledge from the perspective of teacher knowledge which has components of teacher professionalism and professional competence. Further literature shows that knowledge has been described with more components and these are declarative knowledge and procedural knowledge as indicated by past scholars such as Mayer (1987) and Mark and Greer (1995). In fact, Mayer (1987) opined that the two components of sematic knowledge and factual knowledge define declarative knowledge.

Declarative knowledge refers to any subject matter of education and teaching-learning with facts, dates, events, theories, concepts or rules while procedural knowledge is any subject matter of education and teaching or the "how" of doing things or basically putting practicing declarative knowledge (Mayer, 1987; McGraw & Harbison-Briggs, 1989) cited in Rwanamiza (2009). On the other hand, Rwanamiza (2009) defines knowledge as any subject matter in the form of processes of education in general and of teaching and learning. Besides the types of knowledge such as declarative knowledge, procedural knowledge and conditional knowledge as cited in Rwanamiza (2009), the concept of knowledge still has other definitions including in the field of education.

In education, the concept of knowledge has further been connected to other concepts. For instance, the concepts of content, pedagogical, assessment and curriculum thus contributing to terms like common content knowledge, pedagogical knowledge, pedagogical content knowledge, knowledge of assessment and curriculum knowledge which can be noted in studies namely Amador et al. (2022), Andrews et al. (2022), Annala (2022), Hale et al. (2016), Love and Hughes (2022), and Widodo (2017). The study by Rycroft-Smith (2022) mentioned knowledge brokering which is considered as knowledge mobilization. According to Levin (2011, p.15), knowledge mobilization is defined as the multiple ways in which stronger connections are made in research, policy and practice. Santos-Hermosa and Atenas (2022) as scholars have done studies in the disciplines of education and economic by highlighting open knowledge.

Open knowledge from an openness view is considered as access to knowledge developed through public funds (Santos-Hermosa & Atenas, 2022). According to Molloy (2011), open knowledge is defined as the freedom to use, re-use and re-distribute a published article or item with no restrictions beyond a requirement for attribution and share-alike. In this chapter, open knowledge simply refers to distribution of knowledge on open access basis by HEIs.

## Higher Education Institutions (HEIs)

Education in general is not a knew terminology. Chazan (2022) stated that it is important to have a clear understanding of the definition of education. The concept of education has also caught the attention of earlier studies like Ning-xue (2019) who noted that there are different definitions of education. Previous scholars like Xiao and Hu (2010) defined education as an activity of cultivating people and promoting the development of the human body and mind at all times worldwide. But Ruyter et al. (2019) have defined education as teaching, learning and evaluation. Furthermore, education at higher level which is termed as higher education has been explained as education received at a university (Mukhtar et al., 2015). Kanwar and Sanjeeva (2022) added that HEIs are governed by norms that are set by the affiliating university. According to the United Nations Educational, Scientific and Cultural Organization, the HEIs are considered as essential actors that engage in promoting lifelong learning (United Nations Educational, Scientific and Cultural Organization, 2023). In this chapter, HEIs refers to education that simply focuses on the teaching, learning and research activities in higher institutions mainly universities.

## Evolutionary Economic Geography Theory

This chapter adopts the evolutionary economic geography theory in the education field with relevance in guiding the specific objective of exploring the types of leadership styles and open knowledge in transforming HEIs in Africa. The evolutionary economic geography is hinged on the concepts of path creation and path dependency which are ideal in investigating types of leadership styles and open knowledge in HEIs. Therefore, in this chapter, the path dependency and path creation concepts guide in exploring the types of leadership styles that display a path or evolution of dependency or creation in connection with open knowledge in transforming HEIs which are geographically located in the region of Africa. Hence, this chapter poses the question; "*What are the leadership styles and open knowledge needed in transforming HEIs in Africa*?"

The evolutionary economic geography theory was developed and improved by Storper along with Boschma and Frenken as indicated in Boschma and Frenken (2006) and Henning (2019). The work of Boschma and Frenken positioned evolutionary economic geography theory towards institutional and neoclassical economic geography (Boschma & Frenken, 2006). The assumption of evolutionary economic geography theory is also embedded in acknowledging the concepts of time and history to comprehend regional development (Henning, 2019). Various studies have applied evolutionary economic geography theory to understand regional development and these include Eadson and Veelen (2023) and He et al. (2022). Additionally, the concept of path creation in evolutionary economic geography theory is defined by Njos et al. (2020) as purposive experimentation, technology development, and competition between agents leading to the emergence of a new path. But then Mackinnon et al. (2018) has already commented that there is scant literature on path creation in economic geography studies both theoretically and empirically. This is an indication that more studies are needed to integrate evolutionary economic geography theory in various developments of the society such as transformation in HEIs in reference to leadership styles and open knowledge.

Whilst, most studies by Asadi and Samimi (2023), Boschma (2022a), Boschma and Frenken (2006), Breul and Prub (2021), He et al. (2022), and Storper (1997) concentrated on economic, diversification, local development, policy and environmental change through time and history, this chapter views the change in terms of education through time and the global pandemic history hence the education change in the light of leadership styles and knowledge in transforming HEIs in Africa. In fact, Boschma (2022b) extended the use of evolutionary economic geography theory to explore research agenda in education but the focus was on Global Value Chain (GVC), Global Production Network (GPN), Global Innovation Systems (GIS) and Global Innovation Networks (GIN) with one of the principles being path dependency. The concept of path dependency is defined by Boschma (2014) and Storper (1997) as how history matters in places, and how cities and regions follow specific trajectories and develop new growth paths. However, Boschma (2022b) did not link leadership style and knowledge particularly in the context of Africa which this chapter addresses.

The evolutionary economic geography theory has developed further in explaining developments in tourism as a sector. For instance, in tourism, the evolutionary economic geography theory can assist in examining and explaining tourism from an economic geography perspective (Brouder, 2014; Brouder & Eriksson, 2013; Brouder et al., 2020; Ioannides et al., 2014). Although Martin and Sunley (2022) mentioned of evolutionary economic geography theory in historical social sciences, there is additional literature on evolutionary economic geography theory in tourism evident in studies such as Henning (2019), Mkwizu (2022a), and Zhao et al. (2022). The study by Mkwizu (2022a) also applied evolutionary economic geography theory to guide in conceptualizing and exploring dynamics in advertising induced by natural forces such as the pandemic. Mkwizu (2022a) found that advertising dynamics can have path dependency or path creation in tourism promotion for destinations. Furthermore, some African countries like Kenya and Tanzania displayed both path dependency and path creation as advertising dynamics as the destinations for these countries were evolving in the COVID-19 pandemic to promote tourism (Mkwizu, 2022a). The study in this chapter follows a similar approach since HEIs were also affected by the pandemic.

The pandemic changed HEIs and more studies are needed to further understand these institutions in the post-COVID-19. The HEIs operate in many countries including Africa and therefore, the assumption of this chapter is that, the transformation of these institutions can also be viewed as dynamic and evolution in education. Hassink and Ma (2017) opined that most economic geography theories explain more of spatial patterns for the manufacturing sector compared to the service sector like tourism. This chapter is of the opinion that education is a service.

## Leadership Style and Knowledge in Transforming Higher Education Institutions in Africa

At a global level, the study by Montgomery et al. (2021) hinted that some universities and research organizations have chosen a leadership position on openness of knowledge citing that openness demonstrates an increase in the Return on Investment (ROI) on research or a pathway to lowering the overall costs of scholarly communications. Labate (2020) noted that the trends that affect circulation and distribution of knowledge include the need for interdisciplinary, exam-driven emphasis, and restraining of technical knowledge through paywalls, patents and copyrights. Whilst distribution of knowledge can be affected by issues connected to interdisciplinary or paywalls, it is clear that some universities through their leadership are beginning to see the positive aspects of open knowledge such as ROI on research. Equally, Wilson et al. (2022) through the Curtis Open Knowledge Initiative encourage open knowledge by HEIs. However, there are still few studies connecting the concepts of leadership style and knowledge in transforming HEIs. In fact, Montgomery et al. (2021) advocate for universities to become open knowledge institutions.

In Africa, the study by Rwanamiza (2009) in Rwanda stated that knowledge encompasses cognition, affectivity and psycho-motivity. By cognition, it refers to facts, dates, events, theories, concepts, rules, formulas and algorithms while affectivity is the state of mind, feelings and attitudes (Rwanamiza, 2009). Furthermore, Rwanamiza (2009) elaborated the psycho-motivity which is described as skills, competence and behaviours. Africa is home to one of the oldest HEIs as centres of knowledge such as Ez-Zitouna University in Tunisia, the University of Qarawlyln in Morocco and Sankore University in Timbuktu (Adams et al., 2010; Alemu, 2018; Arbaoui, 2012; Assie-Lumumba, 2005; erudera, 2021; Zeleza, 2006). Subsequently, the production of knowledge in the form of theses, dissertations and conference papers in the context of Open and Distance Learning (ODL) as a HEI are shared through institutional repository (Mkwizu & Ngaruko, 2020). Other African scholars namely Mkwizu and Kimeto (2022b) mentioned about knowledge dissemination challenges including in Africa and encouraged establishing of local journals, and opined further by stating that;

*It is important that emerging journals co-exist with reputable journals so that young researchers can gain easy entry into the publication world at an early stage. Inclusiveness will assist the exchange of knowledge in a fair manner. (Mkwizu, K.H)*

*Let us always focus on research quality and not quantity. (Kimeto, J.C)*

South African institutions show good progress on the path to openness through promotion and clarification of institutional open knowledge policies (Wilson et al., 2019). However, there are less studies connecting knowledge in transforming HEIs with the concept of leadership styles.

Leadership styles in literature has been mentioned by Asrar-ul-Haq and Anwar (2018), Pizzolitto et al. (2022), Jaroliya and Gyanchandani (2022), Thanh and Quang (2022), and Dehghanan et al. (2021). For instance, Pizzolitto et al. (2022) conducted a systematic literature review which showed that there are four leadership styles and these are authoritarian, autocratic, directive and paternalistic. Karakitapoğlu-Aygün et al. (2021, p. 475) stated that the authoritarian leadership style exercises discipline, authority, and control over followers while Li et al. (2019, p. 931) referred to autocratic and direct leadership styles as the act of limiting the autonomy and self-determination through impersonal procedures and rules.

On the other hand, the paternalistic leadership style is described as having a genuine interest in subordinate's well- being and their private and professional lives (Hiller et al., 2019). Apart from the four leadership styles, Pizzolitto et al. (2022) also mentioned about destructive leadership styles. Destructive leadership style has been studied alongside Laissez-faire leadership style. For instance, laissez-faire leadership style refers to the absence of leadership by avoiding to make decisions or responding to requests (Bass & Stogdill, 1990; Klasmeier et al., 2022; Skogstad et al., 2007).

Africa's literature on leadership style in relation to HE is evident in few studies. These studies include Dorasamy and Rampersad (2014), and Frantz et al. (2020). The leadership study using qualitative approach focused on students' leadership development in South Africa with findings indicating that students attending leadership initiatives expressed dealing better with complex issues and use leadership practices to benefit stakeholders (Dorasanny & Rampersad, 2014). Equally, Frantz et al. (2020) acknowledged that universities in South Africa are experiencing a period of change. Therefore, Frantz et al. (2020) conducted a qualitative study on academics and professionals in leadership of HEIs within South Africa and the findings showed leadership programme did impact on how the academics and professionals reflect leadership styles. The leadership style that was appreciated was the ethical leadership style due to fairness and consistency in building others as opposed to ruling (Frantz et al., 2020). Another study by Sebola (2021) used research documentary method to examine HEIs and indicated that the universities in South Africa particularly public universities in the past 15 years have not made noticeable inputs to the national human capital development in reference to research output performance, academic staffing profile and knowledge contribution. Whereas Sebola (2021) did study HEIs but the aspect of leadership is less covered and therefore, this chapter addresses leadership style in relation to open knowledge in transforming HEIs.

In summary, most studies on leadership styles for HEIs as indicated by (Asrar-ul-Haq & Anwar, 2018; Bass & Stogdill, 1990; Dehghanan et al., 2021; Hiller et al., 2019; Jaroliya & Gyanchandani, 2022; Klasmeier et al., 2022; Karakitapoğlu-Aygün et al., 2021, p. 475; Li et al., 2019, p. 931; Pizzolitto et al., 2022; Skogstad et al., 2007; Thanh & Quang, 2022) have not specifically connected leadership styles and open knowledge. The few studies that have mentioned leadership styles in Africa such as Dorasamy and Rampersad (2014), and Frantz et al. (2020) concentrated on leadership styles in relation to leadership programmes and development and not open knowledge. To contribute to the body of knowledge on transforming HEIs, this chapter's main objective is exploring leadership style and knowledge in transforming HEIs in Africa.

## METHOD

This chapter uses a literature review approach, descriptive analysis and content analysis. The literature review approach and in particular the integrative literature review is utilized in capturing relevant information on HEIs in Africa and open knowledge while content analysis avails emerging themes from the reviewed literature.

### Integrative Literature

This chapter uses a literature review approach as a research methodology to extend its application as a research method in the education discipline to study leadership style and knowledge in transforming HEIs in Africa given the fact that other disciplines in the fields of business, ICT, and tourism have used this approach as evidenced from studies such as Eliana (2015), Kagoya and Mkwizu (2023), and Mkwizu (2020). The use of literature review as a research methodology is further evidenced in the publication by Snyder (2019) emphasizing that literature review as a research method is more relevant than ever. Snyder (2019) further mentioned that there are different types of reviews when conducting a literature review as a research method and this includes the use of review type called integrative literature review. The integrative literature review is considered by Torraco (2005) as a distinctive form of research which basically generates new knowledge about the topic that is being reviewed.

In Toronto and Remington (2020), an integrative literature review method is defined as synthesizing research and drawing conclusions from diverse sources on a topic, thus availing the ability to provide a holistic understanding of a specific phenomenon. Moreover, incorporating a literature review approach with integrative literature review, Mkwizu (2020) found that in the field of tourism, and particularly for Africa, there was a need to intensify the use of digital marketing to harness tourism opportunities. Equally, Eliana (2015) applied integrative literature review to study digital natives and found that there were three core common terms used, including digital natives. Hence, in bringing the awareness on the state of knowledge in education in relation to the concept of digital native, Eliana's application of integrative literature review recommends for the focus to shift to learners in the digital era.

Given the popularity of the use of a literature review approach, including the integrative review by other disciplines and scholars, this chapter selects the integrative literature review approach which allows for synthesis of existing literature to draw findings, conclusions and recommendations on the issue of leadership styles and open knowledge in transforming HEIs in the context of Africa. In addition to the application of literature review methodology with integrative review approach, this chapter also utilizes content analysis on the reviewed literature related to leadership styles and open knowledge in the pre and post pandemic period with the inclusion criteria of relevant literature in the pre to post-COVID-19 for the years 2019, 2020, 2021 and 2022.

This chapter adopts Mkwizu and Ngaruko (2019) approach in selecting relevant literature by using words of interest according to the study topic. Hence, the search on google (mainly journals such as those from SAGE, Taylor and Francis Online, book chapters as well as conference papers that are peer-reviewed as indicated in Table 2 focused on keywords "leadership style", "knowledge" "open knowledge" "Africa", "transformation in higher education institutions", "higher education institutions" and "higher education" for purposes of exploring leadership styles and knowledge in transforming HEIs in Africa. The literature that did not have these search words or were not between the period of 2019, 2020, 2021 to 2022 were excluded. Relevant literature that was reviewed is a total of 11 papers (7 journal articles, 2 book chapters and 2 conference papers) as per Table 2 from Addow (2022), Engelbrecht (2022), Frantz et al. (2020), Gebretsadik (2022), Migumi (2021), Mkwizu (2019), Mkwizu and Ngaruko (2020), Msila (2022), Sebola (2021), Mwambari et al. (2022), and Wilson et al. (2020).

*Table 2. Summary of reviewed papers including database*

| No | Source/Type | Country in Africa | Study Title | Method | Findings |
|---|---|---|---|---|---|
| 1 | Mkwizu (2019) Conference Paper- *At the 1st Doctoral Research Conference* | Tanzania | Community and Research in Higher Education: Any Repository opportunities for Thesis? | Literature review | Exposure of PhD theses through the institution repository system in order to share research output. |
| 2 | Frantz et al. (2020) Journal Article- *Journal of Human Resource Management* | South Africa | Reflection of academic and professional leaders on leadership in a higher education institution. | qualitative | Academics and professionals in HEIs prefer ethical leadership style. |
| 3 | Sebola (2021) Journal article- *Human Resource Development International* | South Africa | South Africa's public education institutions, university research outputs, and contribution to national human capital. | Research documentary | HEIs in South Africa have not made noticeable inputs to the national human capital development. |
| 4 | Mkwizu and Ngaruko (2020) Journal article- *Global and Lokal Distance Education-GLOKALde* | Tanzania | Implied benefits of Open and Distance Learning in Tanzania. A qualitative approach on its benefits in Tanzania. | qualitative | Provision of services even during the COVID-19 pandemic. |

continues on following page

*Table 2. Continued*

| No | Source/Type | Country in Africa | Study Title | Method | Findings |
|---|---|---|---|---|---|
| 5 | Msila (2022) Journal article- *International Journal of Information and Education Technology* | South Africa | Higher Education Leadership in a Time of Digital Technologies: A South African Case Study | qualitative | Varied skills in technologies and emotional intelligence can assist digital leaders to support their teams whilst enhancing their institutions' performance. Effective digital leaders depend on a strong vision and creating an atmosphere of sharing and support. |
| 6 | Engelbrecht (2022) Book chapter- *IntechOpen* | South Africa | Consistency in Leadership during a Pandemic: Managing Academics at a Private Higher Education Institution in South Africa | qualitative | Consistency in leadership. Minor adjustments to leadership approaches are required to work in a remote online environment. A combination of various leadership approaches enhances a leader's efficiency. |
| 7 | Gebretsadik (2022) Journal article- *SAGE Open* | Ethiopia | An Exploration of Change Leadership at Public Higher Education Institutions in Ethiopia | quantitative | Change readiness in the university is low and met usually with resistance from the academic staff of the university. Significant relationship between change leadership and change readiness of the academic staff of the university |
| 8 | Mwambari et al. (2022) Journal article- *The World Quarterly* | Kenya | The impact of open access on knowledge production, consumption and dissemination in Kenya's higher education system | Qualitative and exploratory | Open access (OA) to access knowledge is mostly appreciated by the interviewed students. |
| 9 | Migumi (2021) Book chapter- *IntechOpen* | Uganda | Higher Education Institutions (HEIs) in Africa embracing the "New Normal" for knowledge production and innovation: Barriers, realities and possibilities. | quantitative survey | The demand for new knowledge and educational opportunities will continue to grow. Blended learning in higher education in Africa will become the order of the day. |

*continues on following page*

*Table 2. Continued*

| No | Source/Type | Country in Africa | Study Title | Method | Findings |
|---|---|---|---|---|---|
| 10 | Addow (2022) Journal article- *Journal of Environmental Economics, Commerce and Educational Management* | Somalia | The influence of leadership styles on employee performance in higher education-case study from the University of Somalia (UNISO). | quantitative | Transactional and transformational leadership styles are strongly correlated with employee performance. While the laissez-faire leadership style is relatively strong with employee performance. |
| 11 | Wilson et al. (2020) Conference Paper- *ELPUB 2020: 24th edition of the International Conference on Electronic Publishing* | Ghana Rwanda South Africa Uganda | Open access and research dissemination in Africa | Literature review | Open knowledge landscape shows the rate of Gold open access publication is growing in Ghana, South Africa and Uganda. Locally published journals avail OA opportunities. Open knowledge Challenges due to reasons such as a lack of OA platforms, lack of awareness and readiness of some researchers to publish in OA outlets. |

**Source**: Author's Compilation

## Literature Analysis

### Descriptive Analysis

This chapter uses descriptive analysis to profile the reviewed literature in terms of authorship, year, country and method used. The descriptive analysis is assisted by the Statistical Package for Social Sciences (SPSS) version 25. Descriptive analysis is used extensively in research to describe demographics and characteristics of the study samples such as participants background information or profile of reviewed articles as the case for studies and reports such as Atuzarirwe et al. (2020), Kagoya and Mkwizu (2019, 2020, 2023), Kara and Mkwizu (2020), Kilic-Cakmak et al. (2013), Mkwizu and Kagoya (2019), Mkwizu et al. (2020), Pizzolitto et al. (2022), United Nations Children's Fund (2021), and World Economic Forum (2021).

## Content Analysis

The content analysis avails emerging themes from the reviewed literature. Content analysis in terms of summarizing reviewed literature and identifying themes has been deployed in a number of past studies to provide insights on investigated issues in research, for example, Goktas et al. 2012 applied content analysis and found that quantitative and descriptive analysis methods were popular in the sampled scholarly articles subjected for review to explore educational research in Turkey. Similarly, Kilic-Cakmak et al. (2013) applied content analysis to investigate educational technology research in published articles with findings showing that the most used methods are quantitative, questionnaires and convenience sampling. This chapter also employs content analysis for purposes of summarizing the integrating literature review as well as coding to identify emerging themes relevant to address the specific objective of leadership styles and open knowledge in transforming HEIs in Africa.

## RESULTS

The reviewed papers had more single authors than co-authors as summarized in Table 3.

*Table 3. Distribution of authors*

| Authors | Percentage (%) |
|---|---|
| Authors:<br>Single Author<br>Co-Authors | <br>63.3<br>36.4 |

Country distribution for the reviewed papers in Table 4 shows most of the studies are from South Africa (36.4%) followed by Tanzania (18.2%). Interestingly, there is one paper that covers four countries namely Ghana, Rwanda, South Africa and Uganda in a single study. This implies that from the reviewed papers

*Table 4. Distribution of countries*

| Countries | Percentage (%) |
|---|---|
| Countries: | |
| Tanzania | 18.2 |
| Ethiopia | 9.1 |
| Kenya | 9.1 |
| Somalia | 9.1 |
| South Africa | 36.4 |
| Uganda | 9.1 |
| Ghana, Rwanda, South Africa, Uganda | 9.1 |

after South Africa, this is followed by Tanzania and Uganda then Ethiopia, Kenya, Ghana and Somalia.

Qualitative method (36.4%) is mostly used in the reviewed papers followed by quantitative methods (27.3%) and then literature review (18.2%) as indicated in Table 5.

The content analysis based on Table 1 revealed sub-themes coding for leadership styles and open knowledge as per Table 6.

*Table 5. Distribution of methods*

| Methods | Percentage (%) |
|---|---|
| Methods: | |
| Literature review | 18.2 |
| Quantitative | 27.3 |
| Qualitative | 36.4 |
| Research documentary | 9.1 |
| Qualitative and exploratory | 9.1 |

*Table 6. Subthemes for leadership styles and open knowledge in HEIs in Africa*

| Theme | Subthemes/Code |
|---|---|
| Leadership style | Transactional (LS 1)<br>Transformational (LS2)<br>Laissez-faire (LS3)<br>Resistance (LS4)<br>Ethical (LS5)<br>Consistent (LS6)<br>Visionary and sharing (LS7)<br>Online (LS8) |
| Open knowledge | Institutional Repository (OK1)<br>Local journals (OK2)<br>Open Access (OK3) |

## DISCUSSION

The profile of the reviewed papers implies that most studies on leadership styles and open knowledge in HEIs are done by single authors as opposed to co-authors hence the need for more collaborative research as indicated in the study by Mkwizu and Ngaruko (2019). Equally, the country distribution shows that there are more studies in South Africa on the topic of leadership styles and open knowledge in HEIs compared to other countries such as Ethiopia, Kenya, Rwanda, Somalia, Tanzania and Uganda. Even the method that is most used in the reviewed literature is qualitative implying that qualitative approaches are favoured by the single authors when investigating leadership. In addressing this chapter's question, the findings reveal that there are a number of leadership styles used in HEIs in Africa as outlined in the integrative studies by (Addow, 2022; Engelbrecht, 2022; Frantz et al., 2020; Gebretsadik, 2022; Msila, 2022) which are summarized and coded in Table 6. Although the study by Pizzolitto et al. (2022) indicated four major leadership styles, this chapter's findings in Table 6 show that in the context of transforming HEIs in Africa, there are 9 key leadership styles that are being adopted and promoted in connection to activities such as open access for knowledge dissemination and these are;

1) Transactional
2) Transformational
3) Laissez-faire
4) Resistance
5) Ethical
6) Consistent

7) Visionary and sharing
8) Online
9) Resilient

Leadership styles of transactional and transformational are noted for Somalia which proved to be strongly connected with staff performance compared with the laissez-faire leadership style while resistance leadership style is highlighted for Ethiopia particularly for academic staff implying a challenge in transforming HEIs in that country. The ethical and consistent leadership styles are indicated for South Africa while visionary and sharing leadership style is mostly in Tanzania. On the other hand, the online leadership style is evident in terms of managing online and remote along with open access publication for Kenya, Ghana, Rwanda, South Africa and Uganda when transforming HEIs. This implies that the education leaders in Africa's HEIs exercise leadership styles that can promote transformation in HEIs within Africa which can be categorized as transactional leadership style; transformational leadership style; laissez-faire leadership style; resistance leadership style; ethical leadership style; consistent leadership style; visionary and sharing leadership style; and online leadership style. However, the leadership styles vary with the country and activity related to knowledge. For instance, online leadership style in managing remote online environments in South Africa.

Interestingly, for the study by Mkwizu and Ngaruko (2020) conducted in Tanzania where knowledge is shared through the university repository implies an open knowledge approach to disseminate research output. This corroborates with Mkwizu and Kimeto (2022b) and Wilson et al. (2020) in encouraging accessibility to knowledge via openness. Also, the comment by some of the participants that receiving services even during the pandemic (Mkwizu & Ngaruko, 2020) implies that there is resilience in leadership style. Therefore, this chapter findings that there is "resilient leadership style" as a path creation that was adopted in transforming The Open University of Tanzania as a HEI when experiencing changes induced by the global pandemic.

Additionally, the "online leadership style" implies that this type of leadership style can be applied in remote online environments but also activities involving managing and supervising online aspects of HEIs. Whereas most studies in the literature (Choi et al., 2017; Harshitha et al., 2018; Khan et al., 2016, 2020; Pizzolitto et al., 2022; et al., 2018) have commonly indicated leadership styles (authoritarian, autocratic, democratic, directive, laissez-faire, paternalistic, transactional, and transformational), this study has added resilient leadership style, ethical leadership style, consistent leadership style and online leadership style in connection to knowledge to transform HEIs in the context of Africa.

Furthermore, open knowledge in transforming HEIs in Africa hinges on institutional repository (OK1), local journals (OK2) and open access (OK3). From an evolutionary economic geography theory in terms of path dependence and path creation, the findings of this study on open knowledge implies that the transformation of HEIs based on the identified leadership styles have knowledge path dependence on institutional repository. In addition, there is also knowledge path creation by creating local journals as well as knowledge path appreciation through appreciating open access as indicated in the study by Mwambari et al. (2022) that Kenyan students appreciate open access to retrieve knowledge.

## CONCLUSION

Therefore, this chapter can conclude that in exploring leadership styles and open knowledge in transforming HEIs in Africa, the leadership styles are transactional, transformational, Laissez-faire, resistance, ethical, consistent, visionary and sharing, online, and resilient in relation to open knowledge in terms of institutional repository, local journals and open access displaying the evolution of knowledge path dependence, knowledge path creation, and knowledge path appreciation. This chapter's conclusion has theoretical, and practical implications.

### Implications

The theoretical implication in the use of evolutionary economic geography theory in guiding the study on leadership style and open knowledge in transforming HEIs should not be limited to the concepts of path dependence and path creation. This study has shown that when exploring leadership style in connection with open knowledge in transforming HEIs then the concept of "path appreciation" in the context of Africa can be added rather than depending solely on path dependency and path creation.

Moreover, the practical implication but also in support of the Education 2030 Agenda, it is imperative that HEIs experts and stakeholders instil HE for societal good in transforming HEIs in Africa. This can be achieved via institutional repository, local journals and open access publishing appreciation particularly in the post-COVID-19 pandemic. The HEIs are not only providing HE but HE for good by incorporating various leadership styles like "resilient leadership style", "online leadership style" and "consistent leadership style" in the provision of open knowledge in HEIs operating within the continent of Africa.

### Recommendations

This chapter recommends that education practitioners, researchers, academicians and the society to consider the 9 leadership styles and open knowledge paths in transforming HEIs in Africa in the post-COVID. Other countries can emulate leadership styles particularly resilient, consistent and online to successfully transform HEIs in Africa. However, a resistant leadership style is noted as a challenge for the transformation of HEIs. Therefore, the education sector should opt for training programs on how HEIs can apply other leadership styles to mitigate resistance.

### Limitations of This Chapter

Application of integrative literature review, descriptive analysis and content analysis are the methodology limitations of this study on leadership styles and open knowledge in the context of transforming HEIs within Africa.

### Direction for Further Studies

The use of mixed methods may also be useful for further studies. Future research may apply quantitative studies based on the emerged sub-themes to further understand the patterns of leadership styles and open knowledge in transforming HEIs within and outside the continent of Africa.

## REFERENCES


Adams, J., King, C., & Hook, D. (2010). *Global research report Africa*. https://hedbib.iau-aiu.net/pdf/ThompsonReuters_globalresearchreport-africa.pdf

Addow, A. A. (2022). The influence of leadership styles on employee performance in higher education-case study from the University of Somalia (UNISO). *EPRA International Journal of Environmental Economics, Commerce and Educational Management*, *9*(7), 743.

African Development Bank Group. (2020). *Impact of COVID-19 on Africa's education: Reflection on promising interventions and challenges, towards a new normal*. https://www.afdb.org/en/news-and-events/events/impact-covid-19-africas-education-reflecting-promising-interventions-and-challenges-towards-new-normal-36810

African Union. (2021). *Policy brief on school reopening in Africa during the COVID-19 pandemic*. https://cieffa.au.int/en/documents/2021-10-18/policy-brief-school-reopening-africa

Al-Husseini, S., El Beltagi, I., & Moizer, J. (2021). Transformational leadership and innovation: The mediating role of knowledge sharing amongst higher education faculty. *International Journal of Leadership in Education*, *24*(5), 670–693. doi:10.1080/13603124.2019.1588381

Al-Thawabiya, A., Singh, K., Al-Lenjawi, B. A., & Alomari, A. (2023). Leadership styles and transformational leadership skills among nurse leaders in Qatar, a cross-sectional study. *Nursing Open*, *10*(6), 3440–3446. doi:10.1002/nop2.1636 PMID:36760040

Alemu, S. K. (2018). The meaning, idea and history of University/Higher education in Africa: A brief literature review. *FIRE: Forum for International Research in Education*, *4*(3), 210–227.

Amador, J. M., Rogers, M. A. P., Hudson, R., Phillips, A., Carter, I., Galindo, E., & Akerson, V. L. (2022). Novice teachers' pedagogical content knowledge for planning and implementing mathematics and science. *Teaching and Teacher Education*, *115*, 103736. doi:10.1016/j.tate.2022.103736

Andrews, T. C., Speer, N. M., & Shultz, G. V. (2022). Building bridges: A review and synthesis of research on teaching knowledge for undergraduate instruction in science, engineering, and mathematics. *International Journal of STEM Education*, *9*(66), 66. Advance online publication. doi:10.118640594-022-00380-w

Annala, J. (2022). What knowledge counts-boundaries of knowledge in cross-institutional curricula in higher education. *Higher Education*. Advance online publication. doi:10.100710734-022-00891-z

Arbaoui, L. (2012, October 2). *World News*. http://www.moroccoworldnews.com

Asadi, S. P., & Samimi, A. J. (2023). Local development challenge in lagging-behind areas: Insights from new and evolutionary economic geography. *GeoJournal*, *88*(1), 397–407. doi:10.100710708-022-10612-9 PMID:35261430

Asrar-ul-Haq, M., & Anwar, S. (2018). The many faces of leadership: Proposing research agenda through a review of literature. *Future Business Journal*, *4*(2), 179–188. doi:10.1016/j.fbj.2018.06.002

Assie-Lumumba, N. (2005). Higher education in Africa: Crises, reforms and transformation. Senegal: Council for the Development of Social Science Research in Africa (CODSERIA).

Atuzarirwe, C., Mkwizu, K. H., & Matama, R. (2020). Standardization and internationalization of tourism small businesses: A study of Hotels in Kampala, Uganda. *ATLAS Tourism and Leisure Review*, *2020*(1), 11–22.

Bass, B. M., & Stogdill, R. M. (1990). *Bass & Stogdill's handbook of leadership: Theory, research, and managerial applications* (3rd ed.). Free Pr.

Batinoluho, L. (2022a). Training needs assessment for tourism businesses in Tanzania. *Journal of Tourism, Culinary and Entrepreneurship*, *2*(2), 200–225. Advance online publication. doi:10.37715/jtce.v2i2.2671

Batinoluho, L. (2022b). Tourism business clusters: A tool for transforming MSEMs in the tourism industry in Tanzania. *Journal of Tourism, Culinary and Entrepreneurship, 2*(20). doi:10.37715/jtce.v2i2.2660

Boschma, R. (2022a). *Evolutionary Economic Geography and Policy. Papers in Evolutionary Economic Geography (PEEG) 2220.* Utrecht University, Department of Human Geography and Spatial Planning, Group Economic Geography. https://ideas.repec.org/p/egu/wpaper/2220.html

Boschma, R. (2022b). Global value chains from an evolutionary economic geography perspective: A research agenda. *Area Development and Policy*, *7*(2), 123–146. doi:10.1080/23792949.2022.2040371

Boschma, R. A., & Frenken, K. (2006). Why is economic geography not an evolutionary science? Towards an evolutionary economic geography. *Journal of Economic Geography*, *6*(3), 273–302. doi:10.1093/jeg/lbi022

Bozkurt, A., & Sharma, R. C. (2020). Education in normal, new normal, and next normal: Observations from the past, insights from the present and projections for the future. *Asian Journal of Distance Education*, *15*(2), i–x.

Breul, M., & Prub, F. (2021). Applying evolutionary economic geography beyond case studies in the global north: Regional diversification in Vietnam. *Singapore Journal of Tropical Geography*, *43*(1), 26–42. doi:10.1111jtg.12412

Brouder, P. (2014). Evolutionary economic geography: A new path for tourism studies? *Tourism Geographies*, *16*(1), 2–7. doi:10.1080/14616688.2013.864323

Brouder, P., Clave, S. A., Gill, A., & Ioannides, D. (2020). *Tourism Destination Evolution.* Routledge. https://www.routledge.com/Tourism-DestinationEvolution/Brouder-Clave-Gill-Ioannides/p/book/9780367668259

Brouder, P., & Eriksson, R. H. (2013). Tourism evolution: On the synergies of tourism studies and evolutionary economic geography. *Annals of Tourism Research*, *43*, 370–389. doi:10.1016/j.annals.2013.07.001

Chazan, B. (2022). What is education? *Principles and Pedagogies in Jewish Education*, 5-12. https://link.springer.com/chapter/10.1007/978-3-030-83925-3_2#DOI

Choi, S. B., Kim, K., & Kang, S. W. (2017). Effects of transformational and shared leadership styles on employees' perception of team effectiveness. *Social Behavior and Personality*, *45*(3), 377–386. doi:10.2224bp.5805

Chukwusa, J. (2018). Autocratic leadership style: Obstacle to success in academic libraries. *Library Philosophy and Practice*, *1*, 1–11.

Coman, C., Tiru, L. G., Mesesan-Schmitz, L., Stanciu, C., & Bularca, M. C. (2020). Online teaching and learning in higher education during the Coronavirus pandemic: Students' perspective. *Sustainability (Basel)*, *12*(24), 10367. doi:10.3390u122410367

Daniel, J. (2022). Open Schooling: New era, new relevance, new methods. *International Journal of Open Schooling*, *1*(1), 1–8. https://www.nios.ac.in/media/documents/IJOS/articles/IJOS_Ch-17.pdf

Debbarma, I., & Durai, T. (2021). Education disruption: Impact of COVID-19 on students from the Northeast states of India. *Elsevier Public Health Emergency Collection, 120*, 105769. https://www.ncbi.nlm.nih.gov/pmc/articles/PMC7708175/

Dehghanan, H., Gheltarani, F., Rahimi, S., & Nawaser, K. (2021). A systematic review of leadership organization: Introducing the concept of a task-relationship-change leadership network. *International Journal on Management of Innovation & Technology*, *18*(7), 2130007. doi:10.1142/S021987702130007X

Donnelly, R., & Patrinos, H. A. (2022). Learning loss during COVID-19: An early systematic review. *Prospects*, *51*(4), 601–609. doi:10.100711125-021-09582-6 PMID:34785823

Dorasanny, N., & Rampersad, R. (2014). Perceptions on a student leadership development initiative. *Corporate Ownership and Control*, *12*(1), 9.

Eadson, W., & Veelen, B. (2023). Green and just regional path development. *Regional Studies, Regional Science*, *10*(1), 218–233. doi:10.1080/21681376.2023.2174043

Eliana, G. E. (2015). An integrative review of literature on learners in the digital era. *Studia Paedagogica*, 161-184.

Engelbrecht, W. H. (2022). *Consistency in leadership during a pandemic: Managing academics at a private higher education institution in South Africa*. https://www.intechopen.com/online-first/80578

erudera. (2021). *The oldest university in the world*. https://erudera.com/resources/oldest-universities/

Frantz, J., Lawack, V., & Rhoda, A. (2020). Reflection of academic and professional leaders on leadership in a higher education institution. *SA Journal of Human Resource Management*, *18*. doi:10.4102ajhrm.v18i0.1373

Garcia-Morales, V. J., Garrido-Moreno, A., & Martin-Rojas, R. (2021). The transformation of higher education after the COVID disruption: Emerging challenges in an online learning scenario. *Frontiers in Psychology*, *12*, 616059. doi:10.3389/fpsyg.2021.616059 PMID:33643144

Gebretsadik, D. M. (2022). An exploration of change leadership at public higher education institutions in Ethiopia. *SAGE Open*, *12*(2), 1–11. doi:10.1177/21582440221091256

Goktas, Y., Hasancebi, F., Varisoglu, B., Akcay, A., Bayrak, N., Baran, M., & Sozbilir, M. (2012). Trends in educational research in Turkey: A content analysis. *Educational Sciences: Theory & Practice*, *12*(1), 455–459.

Guerriero, S. (2017). *Teachers' pedagogical knowledge and the teaching profession*. https://www.oecd.org/education/ceri/Background_document_to_Symposium_ITEL-FINAL.pdf

Hale, L. V. A., Lutter, J. C., & Shultz, G. V. (2016). The development of a tool for measuring graduate students' topic specific pedagogical content knowledge of thin layer chromatography. *Chemistry Education Research and Practice*, *17*(4), 700–710. doi:10.1039/C5RP00190K

Harshitha, G., Raj, S., Jake, S., & Nihal, J. (2018). Impact of Leadership on Team's Performance. *Engineering and Technology Management Student Projects*, 1912.

Hassink, R., & Ma, M. (2017). Tourism area research and economic geography theories: Investigating the notions of co-evolution and regional innovation systems. In P. Brouder, S, Anton Clave, A. Gill., & D. Ioannides (Eds.), Tourism destination evolution. Routledge.

He, C., He, S., Mu, E., & Peng, J. (2022). Environmental economic geography: Recent advances and innovative development. *Geography and Sustainability*, *3*(2), 152–163. doi:10.1016/j.geosus.2022.05.002

Henning, M. (2019). Time should tell (more): Evolutionary economic geography and the challenge of history. *Regional Studies*, *53*(4), 602–613. doi:10.1080/00343404.2018.1515481

Hiller, N. J., Sin, H. P., Ponnapalli, A. R., & Ozgen, S. (2019). Benevolence and authority as weirdly unfamiliar: A multi-language meta-analysis of paternalistic leadership behaviors from 152 studies. *The Leadership Quarterly*, *30*(1), 165–184. doi:10.1016/j.leaqua.2018.11.003

Huang, R., Tlili, A., Chang, T. W., Zhang, X., Nascimbeni, F., & Burgos, D. (2020). Disrupted classes, undisrupted learning during COVID-19 outbreak in China: Application of open educational practices and resources. *Smart Learning Environments*, *7*(19), 1–15. doi:10.118640561-020-00125-8

Ioannides, D., Halkier, H., & Lew, A. A. (2014). Evolutionary economic geography and the economies of tourism destinations. *Tourism Geographies*, *16*(4), 535–539. doi:10.1080/14616688.2014.947315

Ivanec, T. P. (2022). The lack of academic social interactions and student's learning difficulties during COVID-19 Faculty lockdowns in Croatia: The mediating role of the perceived sense of life disruption caused by the pandemic and the adjustment to online studying. *Social Sciences (Basel, Switzerland)*, *11*(2), 42. doi:10.3390ocsci11020042

Jaroliya, D., & Gyanchandani, R. (2022). Transformational leadership style: A boost or hindrance to team performance in IT sector. *Vilakshan - XIMB Journal of Management*, *19*(1), 87–105. doi:10.1108/XJM-10-2020-0167

Kagoya, M. S., & Mkwizu, K. H. (2019). Factors influencing African Youths at Higher Education Institutions to Shop Online: A Study of Uganda. *International Journal of Research Methodology in Social Science*, *5*(2), 70–77. https://zenodo.org/record/3354104#.XZtpk9IzbZs

Kagoya, S., & Mkwizu, K. H. (2023). Digital Transformation and Mental Health in Higher Learning Institutions. In *Proceedings of the 2nd International Conference on Finance, Information Technology and Management – ICFITM*. SciTePress. 10.5220/0011601400003581

Kagoya, S. M., & Mkwizu, K. H. (2020). ICT in Panelist Sessions to Enhance Completion of PhD Studies in Public Universities: Study of Uganda and Tanzania. *ATLAS Tourism and Leisure Review, 2020*(1), 63–73.

Kanwar, A., & Sanjeeva, M. (2022). Student satisfaction survey: A key for quality improvement in the higher education institution. *Journal of Innovation and Entrepreneurship, 11*(1), 27. doi:10.118613731-022-00196-6

Kara, S. N., & Mkwizu, K. H. (2020). Demographic factors and travel motivation among leisure tourists in Tanzania. *International Hospitality Review, 34*(1), 81–103. doi:10.1108/IHR-01-2020-0002

Karakitapoğlu-Aygün, Z., Gumusluoglu, L., Erturk, A., & Scandura, T. A. (2021). Two to Tango? A cross-cultural investigation of the leader-follower agreement on authoritarian leadership. *Journal of Business Research, 128*, 473–485. doi:10.1016/j.jbusres.2021.02.034

Khan, H., Rehmat, M., Butt, T. H., Farooqi, S., & Asim, J. (2020). Impact of transformational leadership on work performance, burnout and social loafing: A mediation model. *Future Business Journal, 6*(40). https://fbj.springeropen.com/articles/10.1186/s43093-020-00043-8

Khan, Z. A., Nawaz, A., Khan, I., & Khan, D. I. (2016). Leadership theories and styles: A literature review. *Journal of Resources Development and Management, 16*. https://core.ac.uk/download/pdf/234696192.pdf

Kidere, F., & Mkwizu, K. H. (2022). Sustainability Tourism Education in Developing Countries: A Case of Selected Universities in the East African Communities. *Proceedings of the International Conference on Innovation and Education for Sustainable Human Resources Development*. https://drive.google.com/file/d/126m9AFUwCQ9BuhGW7lv7P-AlRUZO8-jV/view

Kilic-Cakmak, E., Cebi, A., Mihci, P., Gunbatar, M. S., & Akcayir, M. (2013). A content analysis of educational technology research in 2011. *Procedia: Social and Behavioral Sciences, 106*, 74–83. doi:10.1016/j.sbspro.2013.12.010

Klasmeier, K. N., Schleu, J. E., Millhoff, C., Poethke, U., & Bormann, K. C. (2022). On the destructiveness of laissez-faire versus abusive supervision: A comparative, multilevel investigation of destructive forms of leadership. *European Journal of Work and Organizational Psychology, 31*(3), 406–420. doi:10.1080/1359432X.2021.1968375

Labate, H. (2020). *Knowledge access and distribution: The future(s) of what we used to call 'curriculum'*. https://unesdoc.unesco.org/ark:/48223/pf0000374153

Levin, B. (2011). Mobilizing research knowledge in education. *London Review of Education, 9*(1), 15–26. doi:10.1080/14748460.2011.550431

Li, R., Chen, Z., Zhang, H., & Luo, J. (2019). How do authoritarian leadership and abusive supervision jointly thwart follower proactivity? a social control perspective. *Journal of Management, 47*(4), 930–956. doi:10.1177/0149206319878261

Love, T. S., & Hughes, A. I. (2022). Engineering pedagogical content knowledge: Examining correlations with formal and informal preparation experiences. *International Journal of STEM Education*, *9*(1), 29. doi:10.118640594-022-00345-z

Mackinnon, D., Dawley, S., Pike, A., & Cumbers, A. (2018). *Rethinking Path Creation: A Geographical Political Economy Approach*. Papers in Evolutionary Economic Geography (PEEG) 1825, Utrecht University, Department of Human Geography and Spatial Planning, Group Economic Geography,

Mark, M. A., & Greer, J. E. (1995). The VCR Tutor: Effective instruction for device operation. *Journal of the Learning Sciences*, *4*(2), 209–246. doi:10.120715327809jls0402_3

Martin, R., & Sunley, P. (2022). Making history matter more in evolutionary economic geography. *Advances in Economic Geography*, *66*(2), 65–80. doi:10.1515/zfw-2022-0014

Matama, R., & Mkwizu, K. H. (2021). Sense-of- Urgency and Timeliness in Higher Education efficiency: Study of Uganda. *International Journal of Arts. Management and Humanities*, *10*(1&2), 6–17.

Mayer, R. E. (1987). *Educational Psychology: A Cognitive Approach*. Little, Brown.

McGraw, K. L., & Harbison-Briggs, K. (1989). *Knowledge Acquisition: Principles and Guidelines*. Prentice-Hall.

Mkwizu, K. H. (2019). *Community and Research in Higher Education: Any Repository opportunities for Thesis?* In 1st Doctoral Research Conference, Dar es Salaam, Tanzania.

Mkwizu, K. H. (2020). Digital marketing and tourism opportunities for Africa. *International Hospitality Review*, *34*(1), 5–12. doi:10.1108/IHR-09-2019-0015

Mkwizu, K. H. (2022a). Advertising Dynamics and Destination Evolution in Tourism Promotion for Africa. *African Journal of Hospitality, Tourism and Leisure*, *11*(SE2), 1698–1706.

Mkwizu, K. H. (2022b). Virtual Reality and Open Schooling: Challenges and Opportunities. *International Journal of Open Schooling*, *1*(1), 97–108. https://www.nios.ac.in/media/documents/IJOS/articles/IJOS_Ch-19.pdf

Mkwizu, K. H., & Kagoya, M. S. (2019). Panelist Sessions and PhD Studies: UTAUT Approach. *International Journal of Research Methodology in Social Science*, *5*(2), 49–57. https://zenodo.org/record/3334935#.XS5DJD9KjZs

Mkwizu, K. H., & Kimeto, J. C. (2022a). Challenges and Strategies for managing Customer Services Education and Tourism in the Post-COVID-19 pandemic: A Comparative Study of Tanzania and Kenya. *Education@ETMA, 1*(3), 13–26.

Mkwizu, K. H., & Kimeto, J. C. (2022b). *Perspectives: How are citation metrics marginalizing knowledge in developing countries?* Emerald Publishing. https://www.emeraldgrouppublishing.com/opinion-and-blog/how-are-citation-metrics-marginalising-knowledge-developing-countries?fbclid=IwAR3Iby6tVKwCj2XXU7y1PySCxstZuO8yDc9UWq9dvQp1Sh1ti-HDgk3haZg

Mkwizu, K. H., Mtae, G. H., Schultz, J. L., Gardner, B., Otieno, B., Charles, R. P., Belete, B., Koroma, W., & Udoh, A. (2020). Technology Usage in Tourism: Comparative Study of Tanzania and USA. *ATLAS Tourism and Leisure Review*, *2020*(1), 74–88.

Mkwizu, K. H., & Ngaruko, D. D. (2020). Implied benefits of Open and Distance Learning in Tanzania. A qualitative approach on its benefits in Tanzania. *Global and Lokal Distance Education-GLOKALde*, *6*(2), 80–89.

Mkwizu, K. H., & Ngaruko, D. P. (2019). Authorship and collaborative research among scholars in Open and Distance Learning Institutions in Africa. *Asian Journal of Distance Education*, *14*(2), 47–57.

Mohamed, A. A. (2023). A review of curriculum change and innovation for higher education in Somalia. *European Journal of Education Studies*, *10*(5), 135–144. doi:10.46827/ejes.v10i5.4785

Molloy, J. C. (2011). The Open Knowledge Foundation: Open data means better science. *PLoS Biology*, *9*(12), e1001195. doi:10.1371/journal.pbio.1001195 PMID:22162946

Montgomery, L., Hartley, J., Neylon, C., Gillies, M., Gray, E., Herrmann-Pillath, C., Huang, C. K., Leach, J., Potts, J., Ren, X., Skinner, K., Sugimoto, C. R., & Wilson, K. (2021). *Open knowledge institutions: Reinventing Universities*. https://mobile.eduq.info/xmlui/bitstream/handle/11515/38307/montgomery-et-al-open-knowledge-institutions-mit-press-2021.pdf?sequence=2&isAllowed=y

Msila, V. (2022). Higher education leadership in a time of digital technologies: A South African case study. *International Journal of Information and Education Technology (IJIET)*, *12*(10), 1110–1117. doi:10.18178/ijiet.2022.12.10.1728

Mugimu, C. B. (2021). *Higher Education Institutions (HEIs) in Africa embracing the "New Normal" for knowledge production and innovation: Barriers, realities and possibilities*. https://www.intechopen.com/chapters/79255

Mukhtar, U., Anwar, S., Ahmed, U., & Baloch, M. A. (2015). Factors effecting the service quality of public and private sector universities comparatively: An empirical investigation. *Research World*, *6*(3), 132.

Mwambari, D., Ali, F. A., & Barak, C. (2022). The impact of open access on knowledge production, consumption and dissemination in Kenya's higher education system. *Third World Quarterly*, *43*(2), 1408–1424. doi:10.1080/01436597.2022.2056010

Nazim, F., & Mahmood, A. (2016). Transformational and transactional leadership style and job satisfaction of college teachers. *Journal of Education and Practice*, *7*(34), 18–22.

Ndaipa, C. J., Edstrom, K., Langa, P., & Geschwind, L. (2023). Internationalization of the curriculum in higher education: A case from Mozambican university. *Cogent Education*, *10*(1), 2188773. doi:10.1080/2331186X.2023.2188773

Ning-xue, F. (2019). Persistence and change: Evolution of the definitions of education in the past 40 years after the China's reform and opening-up. *US-China Education Review B*, *9*(2), 53–68. doi:10.17265/2161-6248/2019.02.003

Nita, V., & Guțu, I. (2023). The role of leadership and digital transformation in higher education students' work engagement. *International Journal of Environmental Research and Public Health*, *20*(6), 5124. doi:10.3390/ijerph20065124 PMID:36982029

Njos, R., Sjotun, S. G., Jakobsen, S., & Floysand, A. (2020). Expanding analyses of path creation: Interconnections between territory and technology. *Economic Geography*, *96*(3), 266–288. doi:10.1080/00130095.2020.1756768

Pizzolitto, E., Verna, I., & Venditti, M. (2022). Authoritarian leadership styles and performance: A systematic literature review and research agenda. *Management Review Quarterly*. https://link.springer.com/article/10.1007/s11301-022-00263-y

Pokhrel, S., & Chhetri, R. (2021). A Literature review on impact of COVID-19 Pandemic on teaching and learning. *Higher Education for the Future*, *8*(1), 133–141. doi:10.1177/2347631120983481

Ruyter, D., Oades, L., & Waghid, Y. (2019). *Meaning(s) of human flourishing and education: A research brief by the International Science and Evidence Based Education Assessment: An initiative by UNESCO MGIEP*. https://en.unesco.org/futuresofeducation/sites/default/files/2021-03/Flourishing%20and%20Education_ISEEA%20Research%20Brief.pdf

Rwanamiza, E. (2009). Knowledge, education, learning and teaching: Meanings and relationships. *Journal of the American Association for the Advancement of Curriculum Studies, 5.*

Rycroft-Smith, L. (2022). Knowledge brokering to bridge the research-practice gap in education: Where are we now? *Review of Education*, *10*(1), e3341. doi:10.1002/rev3.3341

Santos-Hermosa, G., & Atenas, J. (2022). Building capacities in open knowledge: Recommendations for library and information science professionals and schools. *Frontiers in Education*, *7*, 866049. doi:10.3389/feduc.2022.866049

Sebola, M. (2021). South Africa's public education institutions, university research outputs, and contribution to national human capital. *Human Resource Development International*. https://www.tandfonline.com/doi/full/10.1080/13678868.2022.2047147

Seetal, I., Gunness, S., & Teeroovengadum, V. (2021). Educational disruption during the COVID-19 crisis in Small Island Developing States: Preparedness and efficacy of academics for online teaching. *International Review of Education*, *67*(1-2), 185–217. doi:10.100711159-021-09902-0 PMID:34024933

Skogstad, A., Einarsen, S., Torsheim, T., Aasland, M. S., & Hetland, H. (2007). The destructiveness of laissez-faire leadership behavior. *Journal of Occupational Health Psychology*, *12*(1), 80–92. doi:10.1037/1076-8998.12.1.80 PMID:17257068

Snyder, H. (2019). Literature review as a research methodology: An overview and guidelines. *Journal of Business Research*, *104*, 333–339. doi:10.1016/j.jbusres.2019.07.039

Stock, C., Helmer, S. M., & Heinrichs, K. (2021). COVID-19 related disruption in higher education students' health and wellbeing: Implications for university action. *Frontiers in Public Health*, *10*. https://www.frontiersin.org/articles/10.3389/fpubh.2022.1015352/full PMID:36187608

Storper, M. (1997). *The regional world: Territorial development in a global economy*. Guilford Press.

Thanh, N. H., & Quang, N. V. (2022). Transformational, transactional, Laissez-faire leadership styles and employee engagement: Evidence from Vietnam's Public Sector. *SAGE Open*, *12*(2), 1–18. doi:10.1177/21582440221094606

Toronto, C. E., & Remington, R. (2020). *A step-by-step guide to conducting an integrative review*. https://dl.uswr.ac.ir/bitstream/Hannan/141158/1/9783030375034.pdf

Torraco, R. J. (2005). Writing Integrative Literature Reviews: Guidelines and Examples. *Human Resource Development Review*, *4*(3), 356–367. doi:10.1177/1534484305278283

doi:10.1177/1534484305278283

United Nations. (2020). *Policy Brief: Education during COVID-19 and beyond*. https://www.un.org/development/desa/dspd/wp-content/uploads/sites/22/2020/08/sg_policy_brief_covid-19_and_education_august_2020.pdf

United Nations Children's Fund. (2021). *Education disrupted: The second year of the COVID-19 pandemic and school closures*. https://data.unicef.org/resources/education-disrupted/

United Nations Educational, Scientific and Cultural Organization. (2020). *COVID-19 impact on education*. https://en.unesco.org/COVID-1919/educationresponse

United Nations Educational, Scientific and Cultural Organization. (2022). *Knowledge-driven actions: Transforming higher education for global sustainability*. https://unesdoc.unesco.org/ark:/48223/pf0000380519

United Nations Educational, Scientific and Cultural Organization. (2023). *The role of higher education institutions for lifelong learning*. https://www.uil.unesco.org/en/role-higher-education-institutions-lifelong-learning

Urio, P., Murphy, S. P., Moses, I., Chua, C., & Darkwa, I. (2021). Exploring the gendered effects of the COVID-19 pandemic on academic staff in Tanzania. *Alliance for Africa Partnership Perspectives, 1*. https://muse.jhu.edu/article/837365

Widodo, A. (2017). Teacher Pedagogical Content Knowledge (PCK) and students' reasoning and wellbeing. *Journal of Physics: Conference Series*, *812*, 012119. doi:10.1088/1742-6596/812/1/012119

Wilson, K., Brookes-Kenworthy, C., Hosking, R., Huang, C. K., Montgomery, L., Neylon, C., & Ozaygen, A. (2019). *Open knowledge profile of South Africa higher education and research institutions*. https://openknowledge.community/wp-content/uploads/2020/11/South-Africa-Institutional-open-knowledge-report-2019.pdf

Wilson, K., Kiuna, A., Lamptey, R., Veldsman, S., Montgomery, L., Neylon, C., Hosking, R., Huang, C. K., & Ozaygen, A. (2020). Open access and research dissemination in Africa. *ELPUB 2020: 24th edition of the International Conference on Electronic Publishing*. 10.4000/proceedings.elpub.2020.20

Wilson, K., Montgomery, L., Neylon, C., Huang, C. K., & Handcock, R. N. (2022). The Curtin Open Knowledge Initiative: Sharing data on scholarly research performance. *LIBER Quarterly*, *32*(1), 1–22. doi:10.53377/lq.11544

World Economic Forum. (2021). *The COVID-19 pandemic has changed education forever. This is how.* https://www.weforum.org/agenda/2020/04/coronavirus-education-global-covid19-online-digital-learning/

World Health Organization. (2020). *WHO Director-General's opening remarks at the media briefing on COVID-19 – 11 March 2020.* https://www.who.int/director-general/speeches/detail/who-director-general-s-opening-remarks-at-the-media-briefing-on-covid-19---11-march-2020

Xiao, C., & Hu, L. (2010). Etymological archeology and modern research of the concept of education. *University Education Science, 121*(3).

Zeleza, P. (2006, November 11). *Beyond Afro Pessimism: Historical Accounting of African universities.* Pambazuka News. http://www.pambazuka.net/en/category.php/features

Zhao, S., Huang, T., & Xi, J. (2022). Understanding the evolution of regional tourism efficiency: Through the lens of evolutionary economic geography. *Sustainability (Basel), 14*(7), 11042. doi:10.3390u141711042

# Chapter 8
# Administrative Communications Among School Leaders and Special Education Teachers During COVID-19

**Pei-Ying Lin**
https://orcid.org/0000-0002-3845-0635
*University of Saskatchewan, Canada*

## ABSTRACT

*The chapter explored administrative communications from schools, divisions, and the province as perceived by special education teachers in Saskatchewan, Canada during school closures. Through one-on-one online interviews and a thematic analysis, the present study investigated how and how often school leaders communicated with school staff, and what they communicated about, as well as what special education teachers were concerned about regarding administrative communications across the board. Most staff meetings were held virtually on a weekly basis with one exception: meetings were held infrequently at one federal school. Teachers felt that these meetings helped facilitate the discussions among teachers and school leaders about online teaching and learning. Ineffective communications between administration at different levels was a concern for teachers because some communications were delayed and insensitive to the needs of students and their families as well as teachers. Finally, educational implications for crisis leadership were also discussed in this chapter.*

## INTRODUCTION

During the coronavirus (COVID-19) outbreak, in the US, students with special needs in preK to Grade 12 comprised 14% of the public-school student body, meaning that COVID school closures and shifts to online learning left about 6.93 million students in limbo, without their usual educational support (National Center for Education Statistics, n.d.; Young & Donovan, 2020). In Canada—with its smaller population—a national survey reported that 202,350 students under aged 15 have been identified as hav-

DOI: 10.4018/978-1-6684-8822-5.ch008

ing mild, moderate, or profound disabilities (3.7%) (Human Resources and Skills Development Canada, 2011). Despite being considerably smaller, that figure is still a serious reminder of the necessity for special education in Canada. Concerning these students' online learning, this qualitative study explores administrative strategies and school leadership to grapple with their implications, particularly in relation to administrative communications and learning outcomes.

Since there are abundant studies on the challenging aspects of students' learning during lockdowns (e.g., Álvarez-Guerrero et al., 2021; Berasategi et al., 2021; Dhiman et al., 2020), but relatively fewer studies conducted on the administrative aspects, we can certainly learn from the voices of special education teachers who possess first-hand experience with—and witnessed the experiences of—school administrators, teachers themselves, families and students with special needs.

It is widely acknowledged that home-to-school communication is the key to the success of children before and during the COVID-19 pandemic (e.g., Asri et al, 2021; Bromley & Yazdanpanah, 2021; Broomhead, 2018; Dias et al., 2020; Forkosh-Baruch & Hershkovitz, 2019; Merello, 2021; Parmigiani et al., 2020; Yazcayir & Gurgur, 2021). As previous research on crisis leadership have emphasizes the important role of administrative communications and support during the turbulent times (Fernandez & Shaw, 2020; Gainey, 2009; Grissom & Condon, 2021; Smith & Riley, 2012; Stone-Johnson et al., 2023), it is imperative to carry out the present study.

## LITERATURE REVIEW

Within the framework of crisis leadership, it emphasises on the two-way communications among leaders and stakeholders. Of the nine key attributes identified by Smith and Riley (2012), a strong and successful school crisis manager should possess the leadership qualities that make them a communicator. When implementing the crisis management plans, effective school leaders should make decisions and information accessible, clear, and transparent to the stakeholders, and thus, misinformation or miscommunication can be minimized or avoided (Gainey, 2009; Grissom & Condon, 2021). As Fernandez and Shaw (2020) suggest, establishing and maintaining effective and transparent communications is critical for building trust both within and outside school communities. In addition, to minimize the confusion, school leaders should also employ quick and decisive decision-making processes and actions to optimise the response strategies based on the assessments of crises (Weick, 1993).

School leaders are required to acquire a range of crisis management skills that enable them to accurately assess varied risks, make decisive decisions, assign roles, responsibilities, and resources to school personnel, establish and maintain the lines of communications with stakeholders, resort to short-term solutions to problems, as well as reflect on their responses to the crisis and lessons learned during the crisis (Gainey, 2009; Harris & Jones, 2020; Pearson & Mitroff, 1993; Stern, 2013). Such reflections would be useful for organizations to build crisis management plans that make good use of valuable lessons learned throughout the crisis management stages (e.g., three response phases: prevention, responding, and recovery [Gronn, 2003]), and use them as a guide for planning and programming for long-term solutions as well as future crises. These crisis management plans reflect the needs of organizations and stakeholders in the school communities as well as should prepare school leaders and staff to be ready for responding to the crises and also to build a better capacity for recovery from crises (Brock, 2006; Kennedy-Paine et al., 2013; Stern, 2013).

Crisis leadership highlights the importance of school leaders demonstrating effective communication skills with stakeholders in the school community. For instance, Brelsford et al. (2020) delved into the experiences of teachers from five school districts in Texas during periods of school closure. They found that communication, along with accountability and interpersonal relations, stood out as critical factors in performing their job duties. Proactiveness, frequency, collaboration, flexibility, accuracy, and transparency; along with a variety of methods (e.g., hosting weekly online meetings for individual department and staff meetings across departments, collaborating with teachers to solve problems and meet the needs of students and their families) used to deliver information in a timely, clear, and accurate fashion; were all imperative in achieving effective communications.

Harris and Jones (2020) explored school leadership and challenges at a global scale, at the beginning of lockdown. Smith (2020) illuminated that every school administrator was caught in an unforeseeable storm when the school closure policy was enacted on such short notice. Their leadership has been continuously challenged by the increasing changes of regulations and restrictions throughout the outbreak. In this position, no head of department or institute could ensure that their own judgement, considerations, and decisions regarding the imposed rules would result in a favourable outcome. No sufficiently relevant preparation or training existed prior to the outbreak. Most of the skills needed for the adaption were lacking, or inconsistently possessed by the schoolteachers and staff, such as outdated or non-existing technological knowledge and skills. Aside from that, this study also suggests that communication, a key component in upholding leadership, became broken or tenuous when virtual communication suddenly became the norm, especially since this mode relies on digital capability. With those limitations, distributed leadership became the adaptation. In many cases, dispatching responsibility and accountability to the teachers themselves was the only practical option. Teachers' resourcefulness then became necessary for their survival as an educator, protector, and caretaker all at once (Harris & Jones, 2020).

## METHODS

The present study was undertaken to understanding the experiences of a group of special education teachers who worked with students with special needs and their families during the school lockdowns. This qualitative study involved in-depth semi-structured interviews with participating teachers to understand the essence of their shared lived and unique experience during the school closures (e.g., Malterud et al., 2016; Russell & Aquino-Russell, 2011; Sanders, 1982; Shorey & Ng, 2022). This study did not aim to describe, examine, or predict the statistical relationships among a set of variables, to test a hypothesis for an untested or inconclusive theory, or to validate an existing set of variables within a theoretical model or theory (e.g., Habib et al., 2023; Wolfe et al., 2023). Take together, the qualitative approach fits better than a quantitative one due to the purpose of the present study.

### Participants

After obtaining ethical approval from the Research Ethics Board at the University of Saskatchewan, we recruited participants at local schools in the Prairie Province of Saskatchewan. Participants who expressed interest to participate were informed verbally and oral consent was obtained. Only these participants received the email invitation for one-on-one online interview. These interviews were conducted in a private that were not accessible by individuals outside the research team during the interview. Participants were recommended to do likewise. All data were kept strictly confidential and were identified only by pseudonyms on a password protected computer. Having said that, no guarantee of privacy of data can be made with use of a videoconferencing platform.

Twelve elementary and secondary teachers who have worked with students with special needs agreed to participate in the one-on-one confidential online interviews between January and March 021 (see Table 1). The number of years that participating teachers taught at school ranged from 2 to 26. Nearly half of the participants ($n = 5$) have taught at rural or remote schools, where seven participants have taught at urban schools. Two-thirds of participants have obtained a Master's degree ($n = 8$). The size of schools that participants served varied: a majority of schools served fewer than 600 students ($n = 10$), while two schools had larger cohorts. The number of students with special needs each participating teacher served also varied, ranging from 10 to 50 students.

*Table 1. Participating teacher characteristics and backgrounds (school year 2021–2021)*

| Pseudonym | Years Taught | | Grade Level Taught | The Highest Level of Education | School Type | School Size | Number of Students With Special Needs Each Teacher Served |
|---|---|---|---|---|---|---|---|
| Lauren | 8 | | Elementary | Master's | Urban | 1–300 students | 21–30[a] |
| Diana | 2 | | Pre-K & Elementary | Master's | Urban | 301–600 students | 40–50 |
| Kaylee | 13 | | Pre-K & Elementary | Bachelor's | Rural or remote | 1–300 students | 12 |
| Kimberly | 10 | | Pre-K & Elementary | Bachelor's | Rural or remote | 301–600 students | 10 |
| Scarlett | 10 | | Pre-K & Elementary | Bachelor's | Rural or remote | 1–300 students | 12 |
| Grace | 9 | | Secondary | Master's | Urban | 301–600 students | 10-20 |
| Abigail | 7 | | Pre-K & Elementary & Secondary | Master's | Rural or remote | 1–300 students | 35 |
| Catalina | 9 | | Secondary | Master's | Urban | 601–900 students | 16 |
| Liliana | 26 | | Elementary & Secondary | Bachelor's | Urban | 301 –600 students | 23 |
| Charlotte | 16 | | Secondary | Master's | Urban | more than 1200 students | 24 plus 6 online students |
| Isabelle | 9.5 | | Elementary & Secondary | Master's | Urban | 1–300 students | 10 |
| Natalie | 15 | | Pre-K & Elementary & Secondary | Master's | Rural or remote | 301–600 students | 15 |

*Note.* [a] The teacher currently works at three different schools, and so the number of students with special needs she serves varies from school to school.

## Context of the Study

In the province of Saskatchewan, school administrators and school system leaders should provide leadership to schools in general, and more specifically, work with special education teachers and support staff such as educational assistants to support the special education programs and services to those who are considered most vulnerable in both physical and remote learning settings. At the onset of the COVID-19 pandemic, a supplementary education plan was put in place across the province and school buildings were forced to close in mid-March 2020. Students with and without special needs could choose to attend or not to attend online classes - attendance was not mandatory. Schools in the province re-opened in September 2020. To address the research questions, our data analysis and discussion focus on special education teachers' perceptions of school leadership during school closures from March to September 2020.

## DATA ANALYSIS

All interview data was audiotaped and transcribed. Thematic analysis was performed to analyze the rich descriptions from twelve participating teachers to identify the observable patterns in rich detail. The themes that emerged have helped us better understand the positive experiences, challenges and concerns with respect to administrative support to special education teachers and the families of students with special needs. More specifically, the author followed the six phases of thematic data analysis suggested by Braun and Clarke (2006) and Rennie (2012) to analyze the interview data. Trained personnel first transcribed the data and the transcriptions were then read, re-read and systematically coded by the author. The codes were reviewed and categorized into possible themes and were also mapped with the interview data. The identified themes were reviewed again to ensure each of the themes represented the parts and entire set of data. Finally, the themes were named and linked back to the purpose of the present study and existing literature for further discussion. The interview data provided thick descriptions of special education teachers' perceptions of administrative communications and support. The thick descriptions authentically portrayed the topic in rich detail, and thus, the trustworthiness of interpretations and inferences drawn from the interview data were established through the lens of readers who read the rich descriptions.

## RESULTS

The purpose of the current study was to better understand the communications exchanged among school leaders and special education teachers during the period of school closures due to the COVID-19 pandemic. The following section described the relevant and significant data with respect to how and how often school leaders communicated with school staff, and what they communicated about, as well as what teachers were concerned about regarding administrative communications across the board.

## Weekly Administrative Communications

Many participating teachers indicated that staff meetings were held on a weekly basis through video-conferencing technologies such as Zoom or Microsoft Teams. Given that the norm was school leaders meeting with staff once a week, two participating teachers shared that there were two staff meetings each week, one formal and the other casual (e.g., chats at the online staff room, virtual lunches) to focus on the wellness and well-being of staff. In particular, Liliana commented that:

*We had a staff meeting every Thursday morning at 9 am. We connected with all of our EAs and teachers. There's about 40 of us and it was very supportive.... The other thing that our staff did is we had – we called it the 8 o'clock staff room and our vice principal would start a Zoom meeting and everybody had the link and if they wanted to join and just sit and talk about what we usually talk about when we're visiting in the staff room... it was done very thoughtfully so that they could kind of look us in the eye and say 'how is my staff member doing?' Are they falling apart or being okay? (Elementary & Secondary, Teacher)*

Kaylee (Pre-K & Elementary Teacher), also shared that "We're very wellness focussed at our school. ...'How are you doing' ... What's working, what's not, what do you need help with....". Further, she also noted that "We also had a weekly get together for lunch... we didn't talk about school. That was the goal....you got your lunch... you just visited....we had weekly staff meetings, plus we had our lunch date together, too". Besides the weekly staff meetings, Diana (Pre-K & Elementary Teacher) also pointed out that their principal touched base daily with the staff to "make sure that everyone was doing what they needed to be doing and had the support that they needed to be successful".

A majority of special education teachers indicated that they spent time at staff meetings to discuss online teaching and learning as a result of the unanticipated switch to online teaching. For example, Diana pointed out that "Most things that we talked about were unprecedented. ...we had never once talked about Zoom before COVID. ...We had started dabbling in things like Google Classroom and Seesaw...it became very much at the forefront of our professional discussion" (Pre-K & Elementary Teacher). One teacher shared more details about the conversations at staff meetings. Natalie noted that:

*We talked a lot about how to get computers out to people, how to get internet, how to check in on kids that we were really worried about, where kids went and fell off the radar, having a parade...so everyone could wave at everybody. We met ... to figure out as many things - what kind of technology we're going to use? Can we get paper packages out to people? How are we gonna assess like the gaps that are resulting?...It's all unprecedented.*

One teacher, Scarlett (Pre-K & Elementary Teacher), was worried about her students who did not attend online classes and how to continue engaging them in the virtual learning environments. She shared that "Usually it was which kids aren't coming online, whom are we seeing, who are we not seeing, how can we get those kids back online? .... lots of our conversations were about how to get kids online and how to get them to stay there. How to get them to keep coming". (Pre-K & Elementary Teacher)

One special education teacher, Kimberly (Pre-K & Elementary Teacher), who was also the vice-principal at a rural Saskatchewan school shared how they communicated with families to set up the work boundaries. She commented that:

*We set it as five o'clock PM, if you sent an email or a call after that then you'd be contacted the next morning. We also had to set parameters on when teachers would send out information. Some parents wanted us to be sending it on Sunday, ...teachers felt like... not Sunday's a work day too....we sent out a communication letter to our parents and said, "Information will not be posted until Monday morning... teachers will not respond to you on Saturday and Sunday.*

It is worth noting that three teachers felt that the ineffective communications between administration at different levels was a major concern. Charlotte (Secondary Teacher) She commented that:

*[O]urs [school leader] has been really supportive, our principal was amazing... the Ministry needed to communicate better with the school divisions. Because when stuff was happening, sometimes it was a day's notice. ... they didn't talk to the school divisions, they didn't talk with our Federation President ... It was just the Ministry talking "Okay this is what we're gonna do." Then all of the sudden it's like a half an hour before it's going to happen, our Director of Education got a phone call... that's my biggest concern is not with our school division, our principals, our superintendents.... They were really quite supportive but it's the Ministry and the lack of information that we got in a timely manner.*

Another teacher, Abigail who worked at one federal school said that "We've talked a little bit about the packages [paper-and-pencil learning packages for students], but nothing that's really...no major decisions are made...it's kind of just left in limbo". She explained the decision-making process for her school: "what is said in our meetings has to then all be taken back to the director ... for approvals and stuff like that when we're changing policies". The other teacher, Grace noted that:

*[O]ur administration, everyone was doing the best they could, but nobody had answers and nobody knew what to do and decisions were changed daily.... to be an administrator at the time would have been a challenge, but when nobody knows what they are doing, it can just become really muddy.*

She continued to explain how leaders at different administration levels communicated. She described that:

*[E]verybody just kept waiting for the level above them to make decisions...our division would wait for the Minister of Education, and the Minister of Education would wait for ... Saskatchewan health authority, and Saskatchewan Health Authority would wait for federal government, right? Nobody was really comfortable making decisions because nobody knew what to do, and nobody...wanted to be the one to make a wrong decision.*

## DISCUSSION

This study set out to explore special education teachers' perceptions of administrative communications and support in remote teaching environments during school closures due to the COVID-19 pandemic. The thematic analysis of teacher interview data produced three main themes: a) weekly administrative communications, b) mixed feelings about administrative support, and c) supplementary education plans and their impacts on the learning progress.

Teacher interview data reveals that school administrators hosted staff meetings on a weekly basis, mostly one meeting per week. Often, these staff meetings provided opportunities for school administrators to discuss and resolve issues and concerns derived from online teaching and learning such as the delivery of paper-and-pencil learning packages to doorways when school buildings closed as well as provided updates and decisions obtained from the administration at the upper levels, such as the school division and provincial planning committee. This finding is consistent with school principals' work at local schools in Manitoba, principals who needed to engage with staff consistently and transparently as well as promoted team collaboration meaningfully (Hauseman et al., 2020). That is, maintaining ongoing communications with members of their school communities had become an essential aspect of a school leader's duties during the unprecedented times. Given that hosting weekly staff meetings was a common practice for public schools in Saskatchewan, one teacher at a rural federal school raised a concern that few staff meetings were available – at that school- during school closures and school leaders did not "really see that there's a problem" regarding online teaching and learning. Although school leaders felt that they were held accountable for supporting students and staff (Hauseman et al., 2020), this finding suggests that there was a variation in school leaders' ways of doing and responding to the needs of students and teachers during COVID-19.

Building technological capacities of school personnel had come very much to the forefront of the professional conversations among school administrators, teachers, and support staff. Results of the present study echo the two-pronged approach of school leadership that principals extended their role and developed "extensive digital leadership" skills as a results of school closures (Pollock, 2020; Robertson, 2020; Sider, 2020). Hosting regular online staff meetings at local Saskatchewan schools echoes recent studies that highlight the importance of using a variety of virtual communication venues (e.g., Zoom, Google Meet, & Microsoft Team) to maintain two-way communications among school leaders and staff on a daily basis (Brelsford et al., 2020; Oyeniran & Oyeniran, 2020). In addition, the present findings seem to be consistent with other research conducted in different provincial and international contexts. For example, when in-person schooling was suddenly moved to online, Ontario parents of children with special needs spoke of their terrifying experiences with online learning and their children's responses to it (Bayrani, 2022). This study illuminates one aspect of educational policy—mode of delivery—that can and has significantly affected learners with special needs. In the context of Nigeria's school lockdowns (Oyeniran & Oyeniran, 2020), school leadership required effective communications using various channels such as online office hours, texting groups via mobile phone applications, and school media. In addition, establishing a digital space and community where teachers could ask questions and be addressed not only by fellow teachers but also by school principals and administrators was found to be critical. In another recent study, Sholikhati et al. (2021) explored online learning from elementary school teachers' and advisors' perspectives in Indonesia. Despite the numerous obstacles surrounding distance learning, one element had been identified as affecting learning outcomes most significantly: The choice of media. Different media pose different access issues, and beyond that, different media possess different strengths and weaknesses for the purpose of education. Understandably, it is educators or administrators—as well as access limitations—that control what media are utilized, leaving learners and parents to work with the given media as well as they are able. Sholikhati et al. reported that teachers continued to strive to improve the effectiveness of their virtual teaching with the available media, through collaboration with the families of students with special needs.

## CONCLUSIONS AND RECOMMENDATIONS

Through one-on-one online interviews with twelve special education teachers in Saskatchewan, Canada, the present study identified a main theme through a thematic analysis. Most staff meetings were held virtually on a weekly basis with one exception- meetings were held infrequently at one federal school. Teachers felt that the weekly staff meetings helped facilitate the discussions among teachers and school leaders about issues surrounding online teaching and learning (e.g., technology access and support for families, professional development on technologies, & paper-and-pencil packages to be sent to homes).

As with crisis leadership, effective communication is at the core of the successful school leadership in the chaotic times (Ho & Tay, 2020; Kafa & Pashiardis, 2020; O'connell & Clarke, 2020). Given that it is acknowledged crises such the COVID-19 pandemic has placed extra demand on administrative leaders and increase the uncertainty and complexity of their work (Marshall et al., 2020; Pollock, 2020; Sider, 2020), it is recommended that administrative leaders at different levels continue to make a concert effort to make sure the communications with all school community members are clear, transparent and consistent, and so everyone in the community are informed of announcements, updates, and response action plans in the capricious times (Grissom & Condon, 2021; Hauseman et al., 2020; O'connell & Clarke, 2020). In particular, a group of American elementary and secondary teachers pointed out that communications that were "proactive, frequent, collaborative, flexible, accurate, and transparent" worked for the teachers and parents (Brelsford et al., p. 13). In contrast, communications that were "reactive, delayed, contradictory, and insensitive" did not work for stakeholders in the school community (p. 13). A variety of communication channels have been used to facilitate the communications, such as regular staff meetings, emails, newsletters, virtual platforms, and social media (Hauseman et al., 2020; Ho & Tay, 2020; Kafa & Pashiardis, 2020; Tremmel et al. 2020). According to these studies, it would be beneficial for the province and school divisions to use different communication venues to effectively inform stakeholders across the board as well as to promote "proactive, frequent, collaborative, flexible, accurate, and transparent" communications among stakeholders in the school community.

## REFERENCES

Álvarez-Guerrero, G., de Aguileta, A. L., Racionero-Plaza, S., & Flores-Moncada, L. G. (2021). Beyond the school walls: Keeping interactive learning environments alive in confinement for students in Special Education. *Frontiers in Psychology*, *12*, 662646. Advance online publication. doi:10.3389/fpsyg.2021.662646 PMID:33897572

Asri, D. N., Cahyono, B. E. H., & Trisnani, R. P. (2021). Early reading learning for special needs students: Challenges on inclusive primary school during COVID-19 pandemic. *Linguistics and Culture Review*, *5*(S1), 1062–1074. doi:10.21744/lingcure.v5nS1.1489

Bayrami, L. (2022). *The implications of virtual teaching and learning in Ontario's publicly funded schools, K-12*. Ontario Teachers' Federation. https://www.otffeo.on.ca/en/wp-content/uploads/sites/2/2022/05/The-Implications-of-Virtual-Teaching-and-Learning-Lisa-Bayrami-FULL-VERSION.pdf

Bayrami, L. (2022). *The implications of virtual teaching and learning in Ontario's publicly funded schools, K-12*. Ontario Teachers' Federation.

Berasategi Santxo, N., Idoiaga Mondragon, N., Ozamiz-Etxebarria, N., & Dosil-Santamaria, M. (2021). Well-being of adolescents in de-escalation situation: Physical, emotional, social, and academic impact. *Frontiers in Psychology*, *12*, 646027. doi:10.3389/fpsyg.2021.646027 PMID:34512431

Braun, V., & Clarke, V. (2006). Using thematic analysis in psychology. *Qualitative Research in Psychology*, *3*(2), 77–101. doi:10.1191/1478088706qp063oa

Brelsford, S. N., Camarillo, E. E., Garcia, A. S., Garcia, G., Lopez, V. R., Montoya, C. P., ... Merchant, B. (2020). Keeping the bus moving while maintaining social distance in a COVID-19 world. *International Studies in Educational Administration*, *48*(2), 12–20. doi:10.3390oc5010136

Bromley, J., & Yazdanpanah, L. K. (2021). Teachers' views of parental involvement in the schooling of low literacy refugee and migrant children: An Australian study. *Teaching English as a Second Language for Foreign Language, Electronic Journal, 25*(2), 1 15. https://eric.ed.gov/?id=EJ1314733

Broomhead, K. E. (2018). Perceived responsibility for developing and maintaining home-school partnerships: The experiences of parents and practitioners. *British Journal of Special Education*, *45*(4), 435–453. doi:10.1111/1467-8578.12242

Dhiman, S., Sahu, P. K., Reed, W. R., Ganesh, G. S., Goyal, R. K., & Jain, S. (2020). Impact of COVID-19 outbreak on mental health and perceived strain among caregivers tending children with special needs. *Research in Developmental Disabilities*, *107*, 103790. doi:10.1016/j.ridd.2020.103790 PMID:33091712

Dias, M. J., Almodóvar, M., Atiles, J. T., Vargas, A. C., & Zúñiga León, I. M. (2020). Rising to the Challenge: Innovative early childhood teachers adapt to the COVID-19 era. *Childhood Education*, *96*(6), 38–45. doi:10.1080/00094056.2020.1846385

Eacott, S., MacDonald, K., Keddie, A., Wilkinson, J., Niesche, R., Gobby, B., & Fernandez, I. (2020). COVID-19 and inequities in Australian Education–Insights on federalism, autonomy, and access. *International Studies in Educational Administration*, *48*(2), 6–14. doi:10.3390oc5010136

Egbo, B. (2009). *Teaching for diversity in Canadian schools*. Pearson.

Erchick, D. J., George, A. S., Umeh, C., & Wonodi, C. (2017). Understanding internal accountability in Nigeria's routine immunization system: Perspectives from government officials at the national, state, and local levels. *International Journal of Health Policy and Management*, *6*(7), 403–412. doi:10.15171/ijhpm.2016.150 PMID:28812836

Fernandez, A. A., & Shaw, G. P. (2020). Academic leadership in a time of crisis: The coronavirus and COVID-19. *Journal of Leadership Studies*, *14*(1), 39–45. doi:10.1002/jls.21684

Forkosh-Baruch, A., & Hershkovitz, A. (2019). Knowing me, knowing you: Teachers' perceptions of communication with their students on Facebook. *Interdisciplinary Journal of E-Learning & Learning Objects*, *15*, 59–80. doi:10.28945/4256

Gainey, B. S. (2009). Crisis management's new role in educational settings. *The Clearing House: A Journal of Educational Strategies, Issues and Ideas*, *82*(6), 267–274. doi:10.3200/TCHS.82.6.267-274

Grissom, J. A., & Condon, L. (2021). Leading schools and districts in times of crisis. *Educational Researcher*, *50*(5), 315–324. doi:10.3102/0013189X211023112

Habib, U. E. H., Nasir, A. R., Ullah, F., Qayyum, S., & Thaheem, M. J. (2022). BIM roles and responsibilities in developing countries: A dedicated matrix for design-bid-build projects. *Buildings*, *12*(10), 1752. doi:10.3390/buildings12101752

Harris, A., & Jones, M. (2020). COVID 19–school leadership in disruptive times. *School Leadership & Management*, *40*(4), 243–247. doi:10.1080/13632434.2020.1811479

Hauseman, C., Darazsi, S., & Kent, S. (2020). Collaboration, communication and wellness: Response to the COVID-19 pandemic in Manitoba schools. *International Studies in Educational Administration*, *48*(2), 70–77. doi:10.3390oc5010136

Ho, J. M. P. Y., & Tay, L. Y. (2020). Ensuring learning continues during a pandemic. *International Studies in Educational Administration*, *48*(2), 49–55. doi:10.3390oc5010136

Human Resources and Skills Development Canada (HRSDC). (2011). *Disability in Canada: A 2006 profile.* Cat. No.: HS64-11/2010.

Jameson, J. M., Stegenga, S. M., Ryan, J., & Green, A. (2020). Free appropriate public education in the time of COVID-19. *Rural Special Education Quarterly*, *39*(4), 181–192. doi:10.1177/8756870520959659

Karasel Ayda, N., Bastas, M., Altinay, F., Altinay, Z., & Dagli, G. (2020). Distance education for students with special needs in primary schools in the period of COVID-19 epidemic. *Propósitos y Representaciones*, *8*(3), 587. doi:10.20511/pyr2020.v8n3.587

Kidson, P., Lipscombe, K., & Tindall-Ford, S. K. (2020). Co-designing educational policy: Professional voice and policy making post-COVID. *International Studies in Educational Administration*, *48*(2), 15–22. doi:10.3390oc5010136

Kong, M., & Thompson, L. A. (2020). Considerations for young children and those with special needs as COVID-19 continues. *JAMA Pediatrics*, *174*(10), 1012–1012. doi:10.1001/jamapediatrics.2020.2478 PMID:32870247

LaBonte, R., Barbour, M. K., & Nagle, J. (2021). *Pandemic pedagogy in Canada: Lessons from the first 18 months*. Canadian eLearning Network.

Lochmiller, C. R. (2021). Rural superintendents' responses to COVID-19: Navigating local control during a public health crisis. *Frontiers in Education*, *6*(617058), 1–14. doi:10.3389/feduc.2021.617058

Malterud, K., Siersma, V. D., & Guassora, A. D. (2015). Sample size in qualitative interview studies: Guided by information power. *Qualitative Health Research*, *26*(13), 1753–1760. doi:10.1177/1049732315617444 PMID:26613970

Maria, O., & Ilias, K. (2020). The effect of administrative actions on satisfaction of primary and secondary public school principals. *Journal of Contemporary Education Theory & Research*, *4*(1), 21–27. doi:10.5281/zenodo.3769323

Merello, Á. (2021). *Barriers and facilitators for children with special educational needs education during the COVID-19 pandemic: A systematic literature review in 2020* [Unpublished Master's thesis]. Jönköping University. http://www.diva-portal.org/smash/get/diva2:1552898/FULLTEXT01.pdf

Metcalfe, L. S., & Perez, I. (2020). Blinded by the unknown: A school's leader's actions to support teachers and students during COVID-19 school closures. *Journal of School Administration Research and Development*, *5*(S1), 49–54. doi:10.32674/jsard.v5iS1.2746

National Center for Education Statistics. (n.d.). *Fast facts: Back-to-school statistics.* https://nces.ed.gov/fastfacts/display.asp?id=372

Nelson, M., & Murakami, E. (2020). Special education students in public high schools during COVID-19 in the USA. *International Studies in Educational Administration*, *48*(3), 109–115. doi:10.3390oc5010136

O'Connell, A., & Clarke, S. (2020). A school in the grip of COVID-19: Musings from the principal's office. *International Studies in Educational Administration*, *48*(2), 4–11. doi:10.3390oc5010136

Oyeniran, S., & Oyeniran, F. M. (2020). A descriptive analysis of educational services in Nigeria during COVID-19 lockdown. *International Studies in Educational Administration*, *48*(2), 21–27. doi:10.3390oc5010136

Parmigiani, D., Benigno, V., Giusto, M., Silvaggio, C., & Sperandio, S. (2020). E-inclusion: Online special education in Italy during the Covid-19 pandemic. *Technology, Pedagogy and Education*, *30*(1), 111–124. doi:10.1080/1475939X.2020.1856714

Pollock, K. (2020). School leaders' work during the COVID-19 pandemic: A two-pronged approach. *International Studies in Educational Administration*, *48*(3), 38–44. doi:10.3390oc5010136

Pollock, K., & Hauseman, D. C. (2015). Principal Leadership in Canada. In H. Arlestig, C. Day, & O. Johansson (Eds.), *A decade of research on school principals: Cases from 24 countries* (pp. 211–244). Springer International Publishing. doi:10.1007/978-3-319-23027-6

Reed, L. C., & Swaminathan, R. (2014). An urban school leader's approach to school improvement: Toward contextually responsive leadership. *Urban Education*, *51*(9), 1096–1125. doi:10.1177/0042085914553675

Rennie, D. L. (2012). Qualitative research as methodical hermeneutics. *Psychological Methods*, *17*(3), 385–398. doi:10.1037/a0029250 PMID:22823104

Robertson, S. (2020). Going hard and early: Tertiary teaching under lockdown in New Zealand. *International Studies in Educational Administration*, *48*(2), 107–113. doi:10.3390oc5010136

Rosenstein, A. H., & Naylor, B. (2012). Incidence and impact of physician and nurse disruptive behaviors in the emergency department. *The Journal of Emergency Medicine*, *43*(1), 139–148. doi:10.1016/j.jemermed.2011.01.019 PMID:21421291

Russell, R. C., & Aquino-Russell, C. E. (2011). Living and working between two worlds: Using qualitative phenomenological findings to enhance understanding of lived experiences. In *The role of expatriates in MNCs knowledge mobilization* (pp. 177–192). Emerald Group Publishing Limited. doi:10.1108/S1876-066X(2011)0000027012

Sanders, P. (1982). Phenomenology: A new way of viewing organizational research. *Academy of Management Review*, *7*(3), 353–360. doi:10.2307/257327

Saskatchewan Ministry of Education. (2015). *Actualizing a needs-based model.* https://publications.saskatchewan.ca/#/products/33546

Saskatchewan Ministry of Education. (2017). *The adaptive dimension for K-12 students.* https://publications.saskatchewan.ca/#/products/86567

Sharp, C., Nelson, J., Lucas, M., Julius, J., McCrone, T., & Sims, D. (2020). *Schools' responses to COVID-19: The challenges facing schools and pupils in September 2020.* National Foundation for Educational Research.

Sholikhati, N. I., Prayogo, M. M., & Santoso, J. (2021). The Effect of Distance Learning on Learning Outcomes of Children with Special Needs in Inclusive Schools in the New Normal. *Indonesian Journal of Disability Studies*, *8*(1), 145–154. doi:10.21776/ub.ijds.2021.008.01.11

Sider, S. R. (2020). School principals and students with special education needs in a pandemic: Emerging insights from Ontario, Canada. *International Studies in Educational Administration*, *48*(2), 78–84. doi:10.3390oc5010136

Smith, C. (2020). Challenges and opportunities for teaching students with disabilities during the COVID-19 pandemic. *International Journal of Multidisciplinary Perspectives in Higher Education*, *5*(1), 167–173. doi:10.32674/jimphe.v5i1.2619

Stone-Johnson, C., Hubbard, L., Resultan, B., & Steilen, K. (2023). Responsible School Leadership: Exploring Role Expansion in Crisis and Beyond. *Journal of School Leadership*, *0*(0), 472–490. Advance online publication. doi:10.1177/10526846231174149

Svalina, V., & Ivic, V. (2020). Case study of a student with disabilities in a vocational school during the period of online virtual classes due to COVID-19. *World Journal of Education*, *10*(4), 115–123. doi:10.5430/wje.v10n4p115

Yazcayir, G., & Gurgur, H. (2021). Students with special needs in digital classrooms during the COVID-19 pandemic in Turkey. *Pedagogical Research*, *6*(1), em0088. Advance online publication. doi:10.29333/pr/9356

Young, J., & Donovan, W. (2020). Shifting to online learning in the COVID-19 Spring. Policy brief. Pioneer Institute for Public Policy Research.

# Chapter 9
# The Impact of Transformational Leadership Style on Educational Stakeholders

**Kareen Reid**
https://orcid.org/0009-0000-3161-074X
*University of Saskatchewan, Canada*

## ABSTRACT

*Leadership is a concept applicable in all fields and beneficial to all. The benefits individuals receive from leaders heavily depend on the leadership styles that leaders use. Hackett stated that leadership is the most critical competency for any organization that aims to develop its people. School leadership is a salient part of students learning in all educational institutions, and as such, the type of leadership that is practiced in schools is crucial to the teaching, classroom procedures, and the school environment as these impact student performance. Bass states that transformational leadership is how leaders' behaviours impact their followers. Bass and Avolio stated that the transformational leadership style allows individuals to feel valued and gives them a sense of purpose, respect, and trust in their leaders. This chapter focuses on the impact of transformational leadership styles on educational stakeholders.*

## INTRODUCTION

Leadership is an applicable concept in all fields and beneficial to all. The benefits individuals receive from leaders heavily depend on their applied leadership styles. Fu and Yukl (2000) noted that leadership is a process that aims at influencing others to accomplish organizational goals. School leadership is a salient part of students learning, and as such, the type of leadership practiced in schools is crucial to the teaching, classroom procedures and the school environment as these impact students' performance (Day et al., 2016; Leithwood & Sun 2020). According to Hall (2020), leadership within educational organizations must aim to create relationships among staff, and these relationships are critical to successful schools. Leaders are the most influential persons in schools; as such, whatever they do significantly impact

DOI: 10.4018/978-1-6684-8822-5.ch009

the learning community. Moreover, studies have shown that school leadership significantly influences student outcomes and school success (Leithwood & Sun, 2020)). Leadership sets the tone of schools, how effective the teaching and learning process is, and the level of professionalism among teachers and students' learning outcomes.

Not all school leaders lead in the same way. There are different leadership styles, one of which is transformational leadership. Bass (1998) believed transformational leadership involved how leaders' behaviours impact their followers. Further, Bass (1998), and Avolio (1999), stated that the transformational leadership style allows individuals to feel valued and gives them a sense of purpose, respect, and trust in their leaders. Leaders who practice transformational leadership raise the awareness and consciousness of their followers about the importance of outcomes and accomplishments. Through this approach, followers understand how to work towards the greater good for their team, organization, and the wider society; as such, everyone benefits. In addition, Mwesigwa, et al. (2020) see transformational leaders as individuals who seek new ways to effect change and are less likely to stick within the status quo as they aim to shape the environment in which they operate as they encourage employees to collaborate for the benefit of the institution. Previous studies have suggested that transformational leaders work proactively toward transforming schools' culture, promoting reforms and professional work practices that will enhance schools' initiatives (Kadiyono et al., 2020; Lusiani et al., 2020). School leaders who practice transformational leadership significantly influence teachers, school climates, students, families, and other educational stakeholders. The chapter will highlight how transformational leadership can create change and how leaders display their management strategies and communication to enhance areas of the education system. The effect of transformational leaders on educational also impacts educational organizations' climate, culture and diversity. Ultimately, this book chapter focuses on the impact of transformational leadership on educational stakeholders.

## Transformational Leadership

Transformational leaders in education are agents of change, and they encourage their followers to perform at their best, set high expectations and seek to achieve them (Avolio & Bass, 2004; Bass & Avolio, 1993; Bass et al., 2003; Masi & Cook, 2000; Northouse, 2021). According to Northouse (2021), transformational leaders are "concerned with emotions, values, ethics, standards and long-term goals" (p. 171). Transformational leaders take the time to see their followers as people, not just employees. Antonakis et al. (2003) agreed that transformational leaders motivate the individuals they lead to realize their dreams. In the education system, this should be one of the main goals of school leaders, as they should have their followers' interests at heart.

In transformational leadership, according to Liu et al. (2010), leaders and followers work together to achieve common goals and shared values and create opportunities to build strong relationships within the learning community. Based on the input of these authors, transformational leadership is incumbent upon school leaders to engage in such practice as this can enhance their ability to grow and become more effective in their role as leaders. Despite the positive outcomes of transformational leadership, some researchers argue that this practice has some drawbacks. Khalil et al. (2022) noted that there is no notable influence on subordinates' motivation, attitudes or behaviours that stem from transformational leadership. Eaton (2022), however, argued that in transformational leadership control rather than positively impact the organization for change. Woudtra (2021) also argued that transformational leadership tends to benefit individuals at the top of an organization while ignoring those at the bottom. Transformational leadership is also viewed by Ahmed et al. (2022), Chen (2022) and Lustick (2021) as allowing a single person to be a leader rather than a group; they believe that this practice can lead to an undermining of collegiality and shared leadership.

## Transformational Leadership and the Impact on Teachers

Burns (1978) viewed transformational leadership as a process through which leaders and followers support each other toward a desired goal. When transformational leaders positively influence their followers, they foster trust, admiration, loyalty, and respect because they see the work of their followers and give them purpose, vision, and identity.

The transformational leadership approach may be effective in educational organizations. According to Ardianto et al. (2020), Bass and Bass (2008), Geijsel et al. (2003, 2009), Leithwood and Jantzi (2006), and Moolenaar et al. (2010), transformational school leaders may operate on the four main elements geared towards supporting the teaching and learning process. These four elements include individualized consideration, intellectual stimulation, inspirational motivation, and idealized influence. Individualized consideration is when the leader acts as a mentor or coach and considers that two persons are alike. In this case, the transformational leader demonstrates empathy, provides support and creates opportunities for open communication. When teachers are supported, they are motivated to perform. Intellectual stimulation is another element that transformational leaders use to obtain ideas from their followers. This strategy is used to help individuals think independently, which ultimately benefits the institution. Inspirational motivation is the third element of transformational leadership. This element includes leaders articulating and communicating their vision effectively. Thus, followers understand and see the need to invest in their tasks and work effortlessly to achieve the desired goal.

The last element is idealized influence. During this aspect, the transformational leader becomes the role model by demonstrating ethical behaviour, displaying a high sense of pride, and earning the respect and trust of the individuals they lead. Once leaders display this behaviour in the learning environment, it creates unity and more significant opportunities to transform all individuals within the learning community.

Transformational leaders can obtain performance beyond expectations and expand boundaries by setting challenges or goals to steer and motivate themselves and other members of the group to higher levels of performance (Avolio & Bass, 2004; Bass & Avolio, 1993; Bass et al. (2003); Masi & Cook, 2000; Northouse, 2021). Although transformational leadership significantly impacts the education system, these leaders do not operate in a vacuum. Rather, it takes a level of commitment from all stakeholders. Novitasari and Asbari (2021) noted that leadership or leaders' behaviours could impact the performance of teachers in any learning institution as leaders or leadership can influence, motivate, direct, or control an individual, and this will determine if they complete a given task effectively or efficiently to achieve the desired goal.

Based on Novitasari and Asbari's statement, teachers are critical to institutional activities, which involves having direct and daily contact with students. Teachers who teach effectively demonstrate social and emotional stability and a sense of caring by showing interest in students and their intellectual ability, and these teachers can bring out the best in their students (Onyekuru & Ibegbunam, 2013). These teachers are also agents of change and commit themselves to maintaining and practicing change. MacDonald and Sanchez (2010) noted that teachers' qualities and the nature of their commitment to change are driving forces that determine the quality of work in the teaching and learning environment. Leithwood et al.

(2004) also stated that once teachers are committed to change, they desire to become involved and make extra effort to implement those changes that will impact classroom structures and processes.

Transformational leadership in schools contributes to effective teaching and helps to boost teachers' motivation, skills, the learning community, and the school atmosphere (Ibrahim et al., 2014). Andriani et al. (2018) noted that if teachers are not motivated, it can affect their teaching performance, and their performance level will only increase when they are motivated. Sun and Leithwood (2017) agreed with Andriani et al. (2018) and noted that transformational leaders influence teachers' competencies, trust, efficacy, and level of commitment, and these attributes positively relate to student learning.

## Transformational Leadership and Students' Engagement

According to Hess and Kelly (2007), school leaders are critical to school improvement and are seen as frontline managers who lead their teams to high levels of effectiveness. Educational leaders who practice transformational leadership are better able to achieve these levels of efficacy. In the learning community, transformational leaders work with teachers through continuous evaluation, which allows teachers to enhance their competence and work better with students to improve their academic performance (Mehrad et al., 2020). Schools rely heavily on school leaders' ability to influence change and transformation. According to Hui et al. (2018), transformational leaders are able to achieve and exceed performance in their schools. Arokiasamy et. al. (2016) noted that transformational leadership influences school conditions and the quality of the curriculum, encourages continuous learning among staff, and builds relationships that extend to the broader community to enhance organizational goals.

As Leithwood et al. (2008) noted, four main elements are infused into the teaching and learning process that impact students learning. These are organizational structure, management and leadership process, the teaching and learning process, and the curriculum. Leithwood et al. (2008) believed much attention is not given to these areas; hence, educational leaders must ensure interaction with these elements to positively impact teaching and learning outcomes. Therefore, a transformational leader's role is to empower the school community, build new visions, establish goals, model best practices, and enforce high-performance expectations. Transformational leader is also expected to endorse school culture and create a sense of belonging that is conducive to learning for all students (Novita & Sulaiman., 2022).

Although transformational leaders may indirectly impact students' learning outcomes, Kruger et al. (2007) contended that the primary role of such leaders' is to foster a sense of effectiveness that will empower teachers and enhance student success. Leaders who practice transformational leadership have meaningful relationships with students, which can impact their achievement, social interaction, and relationship-building capabilities (Apriwandi et al., 2019). Therefore, transformational leadership must be practiced in the learning community as an effective change strategy.

Transformational leaders who demonstrate outstanding leadership skills influence teachers' confidence and consequently lead to higher student performance in schools (Karadag et al., 2015; Mason et al., 2014). Although various factors can impact students' performance, they may vary according to the school and location. However, transformational leaders can alleviate the problem of low academic achievement by finding ways to motivate their learners, providing encouragement and by being an idealised example to the students they lead (Waithiegeni., 2013). Therefore, once transformational leaders lead followers to change, good performance in school achievement could be attributed to good administration.

Leithwood and Sun (2012) and Leithwood et al. (2020) explained the eight dimensions of transformational leadership.

*The first dimension of developing a widely shared vision means identifying, developing and articulating a shared vision or general purpose for their schools that is appealing and inspiring to staff. The second dimension is building consensus about school goals and priorities; the third is providing individual support by listening to staff members' opinions and attending to their needs. The fourth dimension is exhibiting modelling behaviour by being ethical, respecting, and trusting the staff. The fifth dimension is demonstrating high-performance expectations, so teachers hold high expectations for students and become influential innovators. The sixth dimension, strengthening school culture, means promoting an atmosphere of caring and trust by building a set of shared values and thus bringing forth the seventh dimension of building a collaborative culture. The last dimension is to provide intellectual stimulation by encouraging employee creativity and evaluating and refining practices. (p. 400)*

These eight dimensions of transformational leadership if practiced by school leaders would influence followers to maintain a successful school.

## The Effects of Transformational Leadership and Parental Partnership

Families play a crucial role in their children's education and life. Therefore, building relationships with students and their families is necessary at all stages of the teaching and learning process. Jeynes (2018) and Sheldon (2020) maintained that building relationships with the families of a learning community is crucial to student success. These relationships contributes to significant learning outcomes and enhances school attendance, reduces behaviour and disciplinary problems, and narrows achievement gaps. Garbacz et al. (2017) noted that if parents are not connected to their children's learning, it may increase disengagement and negatively influence their psychological and academic adjustments. Parental involvement also allows good schools to become better.

Building connections with families takes the effort of teachers and school leaders. Teachers are strategically positioned to interact with families and make connections through the creation of opportunities for families to participate in their children's learning, whether at school or home (Epstein et al., 2018). Teachers can also build these relationships through parent-teacher conferences and home visits (Jung & Sheldon., 2018, 2020; Wright et al., 2018). On the other hand, school leaders should take the initiative to create the right school conditions to support and sustain family partnerships (Epstein et al., 2018). Epstein continued by imploring school leaders to create a positive culture, provide parents with the tools necessary to support their children and find ways to encourage parents to use those tools to assist their children.

Transformational leaders are responsible for embracing inclusive and supportive practices that motivate teachers to continue giving their best in welcoming and empowering families and building and maintaining positive partnerships. For these familial partnerships to be effective, transformational leaders must maintain more substantial commitment and collaboration with teachers and the school community to endorse shared values and goals (Yulianti et al., 2019). In the learning community, transformational school leaders also prioritize values, self-respect, equality, and integrity, creating an environment where parents can feel comfortable, welcomed and supportive (Heinrichs, 2018)). According to Heinrichs 2018, school leaders who practice these attributes work and build better relationships with all stakeholders who are connected to the learning community. Leithwood et al. (2020) contended that transformational leaders help contribute to higher pedagogical quality. Once transformational leaders can elicit high commitment from teachers to work with students and their families. Once teachers can understand students' families and see them without harsh judgement, it will enhance relationships and the institution will perform at its highest level (Heinrichs, 2018).

## Transformational Leadership and School Climate

The school climate plays a significant part in students' learning and is connected to how students develop emotionally in the learning community (DeWitt, 2018; DeWitt & Slide, 2014). Pinkas and Bulic (2017) defined school climate as "the invisible dimension of school life" (p. 38). According to McCarley et al. (2016) and Smith and Scouppe (2018), different factors influence the feeling one may have about the learning community. These factors include safety, relationship, and a sense of belonging, which can impact the success of schools. McCarley et al. (2016) further stated that transformational school leaders have the potential to create a shared vision that will positively influence school climate; as such, it is incumbent upon school leaders to enact practices that are aimed at making this initiative possible in the schools they lead.

School climate is crucial to teacher retention and resilience, and it motivates students to actualize their true potential, creates a feeling of safety, encourages positive relationships, and allows students to develop a sense of belonging (Hooper & Bernhardt, 2016; Smith & Shouppe, 2018). Transformational leaders are seen as agents of change; therefore, they believe these attributes are essential to school development. As such, they encourage stakeholders within the learning community to work towards building positive relationships with students and their families. Transformational school leaders must take the initiative to build a school climate that will motivate families to invest in their children's education and engage in the learning community (Barr & Saltmarsh, 2014). A good school climate facilitates a just climate where students and teachers are treated fairly regardless of their socioeconomic status, mental health issues, or physical challenges, and this can be possible if everyone is treated with the same level of equity. All in all, the school climate should be free from discrimination (Wang, 2019).

School climate comprises five dimensions: safety, relationship, teaching and learning, environment, and school improvement processes (Capp et al., 2020; Garcia-Moya et al., 2019; Gage et al., 2016). These authors further stated that achievement, mental health, and physical health are directly related to school climate. It is, therefore, necessary to maintain these practices as they will result in teacher retention and increase the graduation rate and student success. An effective school climate can be attributed to self-efficacy and collective efficacy.According to Rudassil et al. (2018), there are other dimensions of school climate, such as community, equity leadership and shared beliefs; however, they vary and overlap in scope (Thapa et al., 2013).

Transformational school leaders can enhance teacher self-efficacy by creating opportunities for professional development, the opportunity to share best practices, collaborate on achieving a shared vision, ensuring that they have the resources needed for teachers to be effective and provide feedback that will help to be more productive. remove barriers that prevent teachers from focusing solely on instruction (Vos et al., 2012). These authors further expressed that stakeholders could develop strategies to manage and improve students' performance once the school climate is discovered. School climate significantly affects staff job satisfaction and can be a strategy used to maintain positive work performance (Vos et al.,

2012). A positive school climate within schools encourages learning and development, which is crucial to students becoming responsible global citizens (Vos et al., 2012).

Leaders who lead with a transformational approach work with their team to achieve common goals. They also see the need to honour cultural responsiveness and inclusivity of all students regardless of their cultural background so that teaching and learning can be effective (Hooper & Bernhardt, 2016). Once leaders take the transformational approach to school climate, these leadership practices can help to alleviate the challenge of students who struggle with underperformance as they put measures in place to improve their academic outcomes (Herman et al., 2017; Hitt & Meyers, 2018). Griffith (2004) noted that transformational leaders would create a supportive school climate that facilitates school-family partnerships that empower families to become genuine partners. Research has shown that once families are connected to the learning community, students learning is positively impacted.

According to Kellar and Slayton (2016), the beliefs and mindset of school leaders can influence school climate; as such, schools must practice good leadership that will influence stakeholders positively. Transformational leaders can foster an effective school climate that creates trusting relationships with teachers and the wider school community, leading to more effective learning outcomes (McCarley et al., 2016). Yu et al. (2002) also noted that an essential function of transformational leaders is to shape school climates that create an organizational culture that promotes care, respect, and cooperation. Ultimately, students will also become encouraged to believe they can inspire their school's vision.

Transformational leaders are responsible for creating a school climate conducive to change (Engels et al., 2008). Early researchers Halpin and Croft (1962) saw school climate as the personality of a school that could be seen as open or close. These researchers further stated that an open climate creates the opportunity for relationships among teachers and administrators where teachers can make decisions, given their school leaders' direction, support, structure, and consideration. On the other hand, if schools operate in a closed climate, it encourages insecure relationships, a lack of trust among colleagues, and low teacher morale.

A close climate also highlights communication barriers that can hamper the flow and success of schools (McCarley et al., 2016). Buchhloz (2001) further argued that these barriers might include personal feelings of inadequacy, withholding information which may expose practitioners to criticism, and individuals may find it challenging to assert themselves, share their opinion, assume leadership roles, or perform their duties effectively. A closed school climate also limits the level of interaction between teachers and students, which leads to academic performance not being valued or rewarded, as such levels of expectation can become low (Tableman, 2004). Transformational leaders always push for an open climate that builds and improves stakeholder relationships. When transformational school leaders are supportive, teachers are more willing to invest in change and are more enthused to utilize new knowledge about instructional practices to maximize the teaching and learning process (Moolenaar et al., 2010). Building a positive school climate relies heavily on the relationship created in the learning community, and for that to be possible, teachers and leaders must lead by example.

## Transformational Leadership and School Culture

Culture may be described as a set of customs, beliefs, values, philosophies, perspectives, expectations, attitudes, myths, and norms that emerge from individuals within an organization (Hoy & Miskel., 2010). In a learning community, culture is formed through constant interactions with teachers, students, and the wider community, it shapes school identity and represents unwritten feelings within the learning environment (Hoy & Miskel, 2013). Hoy and Miskel further stated that every school has a culture whether it is acknowledged or not, and this culture can create a purpose or cause discord. According to Barth (2002), school culture impacts life and learning. Deal and Peterson (2016) supported this statement by noting that it "sharpens the focus of daily behaviour and increases attention to what is important and valued" (p. 11). School leaders must interact with students, teachers, and members of the school community to be sensitive to their needs and build relationships. These practices establish close ties and create positive school cultures (Marzano et al., 2005).

For schools to be successful, it takes a collaborative culture. Lucas and Valentine (1998) and Gruenert and Whitaker (2015) noted that successful schools have norms and values that focus on teaching, enhancing students' learning, providing opportunities for open dialogue, and encouraging strong collaboration among all. These authors identified six school cultural practices. These are (a) collaborative leadership, where school leaders aim to foster collaborative relationships among staff, (b) teacher collaboration, where teachers aim to have constructive dialogue that is geared towards enhancing the school's vision, (c) professional development, where teachers are allowed to enhance their practices to perform their task more effectively, (d) unity of purpose, teachers are encouraged to share best practices, working together to accomplish the common goal, (e) teachers are encouraged to maintain collegial support becoming more willing to work together as a team and finally, and (f) learning partnerships creating those partnerships with parents, teachers, students and the broader community that will enhance schools achievements.

Building a school culture geared towards supporting and maintaining educational programs that will lead students to success can be challenging for school leaders. However, having a good teaching staff and gaining the trust of parents and students are factors that significantly influence students' academic achievement. School leadership styles influence school culture (Kalkan et al., 2020). According to Ciftgul & Cetinkanat (2021), influential school leaders develop school cultures that encourage shared values and beliefs, influence teachers' organizational cultures and promote care and trust among all individuals connected to the learning community.

Transformational school leaders are seen as change agents; however, Leithwood et al. (2004) expressed that school leaders must aim to understand a school's culture before they try to change it. Bulach (2001) supported this statement by stating that leaders must identify an organization's existing culture before trying to change it. The goal of school leaders is to transform teaching and learning and the culture of schools (Fullan, 2001). If school leaders are to lead effectively, they must make an extra effort to understand the institution's purpose, why it exists, and the population they serve; then, the culture will be clearly defined. A clearly defined culture will contribute to the institution's smooth running and the school's success (Kylte & Bogotch, 2000). Leaders who practice transformational leadership see the need to move beyond individual self-interest and focus on the good of the school by accessing what is suitable and essential to move the school forward (Ngang, 2011).

The attributes and practices of a transformational leader are crucial to school culture, as depicted in the diagram below. The conceptual framework was adapted from the works of Leithwood and Jantzi (2005) and Lucas and Valentine (2002) to illustrate the relationship between transformational leadership practices and school culture. See Figure 1.

As shown in Figure 1, influential school culture depends on school leaders taking the initiative to create a positive school culture. This can be done by fostering a community that supports collaboration among teachers. Those teachers who spend time enhancing the curriculum, instruction and assessment methods while focusing on the individuals they work for and what they can contribute to the school's culture are a positive move in the right direction.

*Figure 1. Conceptual framework (Leithwood & Jantzi, 2005; Lucas & Valentine, 2002)*

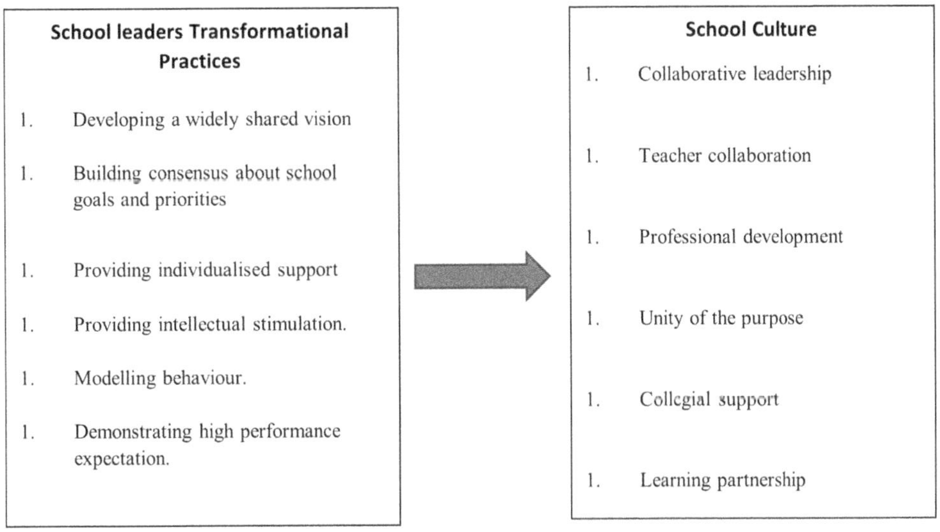


## Transformational Leadership's Impact on Cultural Diversity and Inclusion in Schools

Diversity represents a social system of people with different sexuality, class, religion, ethnicity, gender, and culture (Fiske & Lee, 2008). Diversity in schools can be seen as students' background, teachers and leaders' family structure, language, or social and cultural identity (Villegas & Lucas, 2002). While Corbett and Slee (2000) noted that inclusion is:

*About providing a framework within which all children- regardless of ability, gender, language, ethnic or cultural origin- can be valued equally, treated with respect, and provided with equal opportunities at school… is an unabashed announcement, a public and political declaration and celebration of difference which requires continual proactive responsiveness to foster an inclusive educational culture. (p. 134)*

Schools are becoming increasingly diverse due to immigration, contributing to the demographic shift in schools. School leaders are crucial in administering educational goals and practices that facilitate all students regardless of their cultural background. According to Timmons and Wagner (2008), stakeholders within the learning community should address the learning needs of students and contribute to an inclusive learning environment where students can feel equally valued. Fullan (2004) argued that progressing towards an effective inclusive school culture would rely on practitioners within the school system who are willing to promote diversity and play an active role in the lives of their students. It would mean that parents, teachers, students, school leaders and the wider society all have a role in building such a community where inclusion and diversity are accepted and practiced.

Transformational school leaders in multicultural institutions should aim to work effectively with students, teachers, and families from different cultural backgrounds. According to (Kozikoglu, & Tosun, 2020), leaders in educational organizations must initiate change so that individuals whose traits such as language, religion, ethnic roots, cultural values, and beliefs are different from their own can feel a sense of belonging. Akman et al. (2017) noted that multiculturalism is grounded in inclusion and empathy in a multicultural institution, which is crucial to harmoniously managing cultural differences. Some researchers may highlight some negative impacts of multiculturalism, such as Fleras and Elliot (1992), who stated that "multiculturalism separates and intensifies misunderstanding and hostility and puts one group against another in the competition for power and resources" (p. 132). They believe multiculturalism suppresses the fight for equity; however, a transformational leader must move beyond this view and implement measures to create a learning environment that reflects equality for all students.

Transformational leaders should see the need to recruit and retain teachers who will work with students from diverse backgrounds (Branch & Kritsonis, 2006). Johnson & Lambert (2020) noted that school leaders who support diversity and inclusion create learning environments that will accommodate teachers working with families with diverse backgrounds; once this is done, students will see the connection between their families and school, positively impacting their learning. This connection with families also creates home and school partnerships and strengthens family engagement (Epstein, 2018). In a diverse learning community, transformational leaders allow students to focus on their strengths and encourage them to maximize their abilities (Sun & Leithwood, 2012). Diversity in schools may attract prejudice and discriminatory behaviours, which can impact the learning outcomes of all students. (Levett et., al, 2003) noted that discrimination could affect students' educational attainment and performance. Therefore, transformational leaders must work assiduously with stakeholders to implement and enforce measures that will alleviate or tackle such behaviour if they occur.

Transformational leaders must engage in strategies to enforce the need for change, respect, and tolerance while informing students about the benefits of respecting the cultures of others (Avolio et al., 2009; Bogotch, 2014). Once this is done, the teaching and learning process becomes more effective, and learning outcomes will be more meaningful. Lopez (2014) suggested that school leaders who work with diverse groups should engage in practices that challenge approaches that exclude diverse students' voices and experiences. Transformational leaders who are seen as agents of change must find ways to alleviate these challenges by taking a shared vision approach that guides all members in achieving the institution's goals. Although transformational leaders allow individuals to do the work, they also find ways to motivate individuals not only to share in the vision but work to achieve the vision and goal of the institution (Sheilds, 2010). According to Galbraith (2004), inclusive schools constantly undergo changes, which could mean students' attitudes may change due to external factors. Therefore, it is incumbent on transformational leaders to motivate their teachers to inspire students despite the changes that may occur.

An inclusive and diverse learning community creates an environment where all students have a sense of belonging; and respect is shown to all, regardless of their cultural background. Teachers and school leaders should work with students to develop a culture of tolerance and apply different ways of thinking. Once this is created and practiced, students will bemotivated to work together to achieve high levels of productivity; thus, school leaders who take on the transformational leadership style work assiduously to make the dream of diversity and inclusion a reality in their schools through shared vision and motivation.

## CONCLUSION

The conclusion that may be drawn from this chapter is that transformational leaders positively impact education. The chapter looked at what is transformational leadership, the impact of transformational leadership on teachers, transformational leadership and student's engagement, transformational leadership and parental partnership, transformational leadership and school climate, transformational leadership and school culture and transformational leadership, the impact on cultural diversity and inclusion in schools.

Transformational leaders are agents of change; they lead by example and have the necessary skills to enact practices to create change in all areas of a learning community. Once transformational leaders enact practices that will positively impact the lives of all stakeholders, individuals will be motivated to become a part of the vision and work towards accomplishing the common goal of the educational organization. For goals to become actualized in any learning institution, strong leaders can empower their teams. Although some researchers may negatively view transformational leadership, I believe that leaders who practice the transformational leadership approach are taking a step in the right direction: to effect change within the institution they lead, positively impacting the lives of students who will become contributing citizens of society.

## REFERENCES


Ahmed, S., Khalil, M. I., Chowdhury, B., & Haque, R., bin S Senathirajah, A. R., & bin Omar Din, F. M. (2022). Motivators and barriers of artificial intelligent (AI) based teaching. *Eurasian Journal of Educational Research, 100*(100), 74–89.

Akman, Y., & Imamoglu Akman, G. (2017). Ogretmenlerin cok kulturlu egitim tutumunun sosyal zeka algisina gore incelenmesi [Examination of multicultural education attitude of teachers according to social intelligence perception]. *Sakarya University Journal of Education, 7*(1), 34–48. doi:10.19126uje.306954

Andriani, S., Kesumawati, N., & Kristiawan, M. (2018). The influence of the transformational leadership and work motivation on teachers' performance. *International Journal of Scientific & Technology Research, 7*(7), 19–29.

Antonakis, J., Avolio, B. J., & Sivasubramaniam, N. (2003). Context and leadership: An examination of the nine-factor full-range leadership theory using the Multifactor Leadership Questionnaire. *The Leadership Quarterly, 14*(3), 261–295. doi:10.1016/S1048-9843(03)00030-4

Apriwandi, A., Asrin, A., & Sudirman, S. (2019). Implementation of character education management in junior high school 1 Praya. *International Journal of Multicultural and Multireligious Understanding, 6*(6), 381–389.

Ardianto, H., Sunaryo, W., & Sumardi. (2020). increasing learning organization through transformational leadership and self-efficacy of Buddhist private junior high school teachers throughout Banten Province. *Journal of Education Management, 8*(1), 1–6.

Arokiasamy, A. R. A., Abdullah, A. G. K., Ahmad, M. Z., & Ismail, A. (2016). Transformational leadership of school principals and organizational health of primary school teachers in Malaysia. *Procedia: Social and Behavioral Sciences, 229*, 151–157. doi:10.1016/j.sbspro.2016.07.124

Avolio, B. J., & Bass, B. M. (2004). *Multifactor leadership questionnaire* (TM). Mind Garden, Inc. Menlo Park, CA.

Avolio, B. J., Bass, B. M., & Jung, D. I. (1999). Re-examining the components of transformational and transactional leadership using the multifactor leadership. *Journal of Occupational and Organizational Psychology*, *72*(4), 441–462. doi:10.1348/096317999166789

Barr, J., & Saltmarsh, S. (2014). "It all comes down to the leadership" the role of the school principal in fostering parent-school engagement. *Educational Management Administration & Leadership*, *42*(4), 491–505. doi:10.1177/1741143213502189

Barth, R. S. (2002). The culture builder. *Educational Leadership*, *59*(8), 6–11.

Bass, B. M. (1998). *Transformational Leadership: Industrial.* Military, and Educational Impact.

Bass, B. M., & Avolio, B. J. (1993). Transformational leadership and organizational culture. *Public Administration Quarterly*, 112–121.

Bass, B. M., Avolio, B. J., Jung, D. I., & Berson, Y. (2003). Predicting unit performance by assessing transformational and transactional leadership. *The Journal of Applied Psychology*, *88*(2), 207–218. doi:10.1037/0021-9010.88.2.207 PMID:12731705

Bass, B. M., & Bass, R. (2008). *Handbook of leadership: Theory, research, and application.* Free Press.

Bogotch, I. (2014). Educational theory: The specific case of social justice as an educational leadership construct. International Handbook of Educational Leadership and Social (In) Justice, 51-65.

Branch, R. M., & Kritsonis, W. A. (2006). National Agenda: Minority Teacher Recruitment, Development, and Retention. *Online Submission, 3*(1).

Buchholz, W. (2001). Open communication climate. Bentley College.

Bulach, C. R. (2001). A 4-step process for identifying and reshaping school culture. *Principal Leadership*, *1*(8), 48–51.

Burns, J. M. (1978). Leadership. New York: Harper and Row. *The Leadership Quarterly*, *2*(1).

Capp, G., Astor, R. A., & Gilreath, T. D. (2020). Advancing a conceptual and empirical model of school climate for school staff in California. *Journal of School Violence*, *19*(2), 107–121. doi:10.1080/15388220.2018.1532298

Cashin, J., Crewe, P., Desai, J., Desrosiers, L., Prince, J., Shallow, G., & Slaney, S. (2000). Transformational leadership.

Chen, J. (2022). Understanding teacher leaders' behaviours: Development and validation of the Teacher Leadership Inventory. *Educational Management Administration & Leadership*, *50*(4), 630–648. doi:10.1177/1741143220945704

Ciftgul, R., & Cetinkanat, A. C. (2021). The impact of school principals on teachers' organisational culture perceptions and organisational citizenship behaviors. *Revista de Cercetare si Interventie Sociala*, *72*, 93–108. doi:10.33788/rcis.72.6

Corbett, J., & Slee, R. (2000). An international conversation on inclusive education. In Inclusive Education. Policy, context, and comparative perspectives (pp. 133-146). Academic Press.

Day, C., Gu, Q., & Sammons, P. (2016). The impact of leadership on student outcomes: How successful school leaders use transformational and instructional strategies to make a difference. *Educational Administration Quarterly*, *52*(2), 221–258. doi:10.1177/0013161X15616863

Deal, T., & Peterson, K. (2016). *The shaping school culture field book*. John Wiley & Sons. doi:10.1002/9781119210214

DeWitt, P., & Slade, S. (2014). *School climate change: How do I build a positive environment for learning?* ASCD.

DeWitt, P. M. (2018). *School climate: Leading with collective efficacy*. Corwin Press. doi:10.4135/9781071873229

Eaton, L. (2022). *Transformational leadership: A political science theory transformed by management studies. How did this happen, and why does it matter?* [Doctoral dissertation]. Victoria University of Wellington.

Engels, N., Hotton, G., Devos, G., Bouckenooghe, D., & Aelterman, A. (2008). Principals in schools with a positive school culture. *Educational Studies*, *34*(3), 159–174. doi:10.1080/03055690701811263

Epstein, J. L. (2018). School, family, and community partnerships in teachers' professional work. *Journal of Education for Teaching*, *44*(3), 397–406. doi:10.1080/02607476.2018.1465669

Fiske, S. T., & Lee, T. L. (2008). Stereotypes and prejudice create workplace discrimination. *Diversity at Work,* 13-52.

Fleras, A., & Elliott, J. L. (1992). The" nations within": aboriginal-state relations in Canada, the United States, and New Zealand. Oxford University Press.

Fu, P. P., & Yukl, G. (2000). Perceived effectiveness of influence tactics in the United States and China. *The Leadership Quarterly*, *11*(2), 251–266. doi:10.1016/S1048-9843(00)00039-4

Fullan, M. (2001). *Leading in a Culture of Change*. Jossey Bass.

Fullan, M. (2004). *Leadership and sustainability: System thinkers in action*. Corwin Press.

Gage, N. A., Larson, A., & Chafouleas, S. M. (2016). The meriden school climate survey–student version: Preliminary evidence of reliability and validity. *Assessment for Effective Intervention*, *41*(2), 67–78. doi:10.1177/1534508415596960

Galbraith, P. (2004). Organisational leadership and chaos theory: Let's be careful. *Journal of Educational Administration*, *42*(1), 9–28. doi:10.1108/09578230410517440

Garbacz, S. A., Herman, K. C., Thompson, A. M., & Reinke, W. M. (2017). Family engagement in education and intervention: Implementation and evaluation to maximize family, school, and student outcomes. *Journal of School Psychology*, *62*, 1–10. doi:10.1016/j.jsp.2017.04.002 PMID:28646971

García-Moya, I., Bunn, F., Jiménez-Iglesias, A., Paniagua, C., & Brooks, F. M. (2019). The conceptualisation of school and teacher connectedness in adolescent research: A scoping review of literature. *Educational Review*, *71*(4), 423–444. doi:10.1080/00131911.2018.1424117

Geijsel, F., Sleegers, P., Leithwood, K., & Jantzi, D. (2003). Transformational leadership effects on teachers' commitment and effort toward school reform. *Journal of Educational Administration*, *41*(3), 228–256. doi:10.1108/09578230310474403

Geijsel, F., Sleegers, P., Stoel, R., & Kruger, M. (2009). The effect of teacher psychological and school organizational and leadership factors on teachers' professional learning in Dutch schools. *The Elementary School Journal*, *109*(4), 406–427. doi:10.1086/593940

Griffith, J. (2004). Relation of principal transformational leadership to school staff job satisfaction, staff turnover, and school performance. *Journal of Educational Administration*, *42*(3), 333–356. doi:10.1108/09578230410534667

Gruenert, S., & Whitaker, T. (2015). *School culture rewired: How to define, assess, an transform it*. ASCD.

Hall, S. (2020). *The work of representation*. Routledge. doi:10.4324/9780429355363-15

Halpin, A., & Croft, D. (1962). The Organizational Climate of Schools (Vol. 11, No. 7). Midwest Administration Center, University of Chicago.

Heinrichs, J. (2018). School leadership based in a philosophy and pedagogy of parent engagement. *School Leadership & Management*, *38*(2), 187–201. doi:10.1080/13632434.2017.1406905

Herman, R., Gates, S. M., Arifkhanova, A., Bega, A., Chavez-Herrerias, E. R., Han, E., ... Wrabel, S. L. (2017). *School leadership interventions under the every student succeeds act: Evidence review*. Academic Press.

Hess, F. M., & Kelly, A. P. (2007). Learning to lead: What gets taught in principal-preparation programs 1. *Teachers College Record*, *109*(1), 244–274. doi:10.1177/016146810710900105

Hitt, D. H., Woodruff, D., Meyers, C. V., & Zhu, G. (2018). Principal competencies that make a difference: Identifying a model for leaders of school turnaround. *Journal of School Leadership*, *28*(1), 56–81. doi:10.1177/105268461802800103

Hooper, M. A., & Bernhardt, V. L. (2016). *Creating capacity for leading and equity in schools*. Routledge. doi:10.4324/9781315668697

Hoy, W. K., & Miskel, C. G. (2013). *Educational administration: Theory, research, and practice* (9th ed.). McGraw-Hill.

Hoy, W. K., Miskel, C. G., & Turan, S. (2010). *Educational administration: eğitim yönetimi; teori, araştırma ve uygulama; theory, research, and practice*. Nobel.

Hui, L., Phouvong, S., & Phong, L. B. (2018). Transformational leadership facilitates innovation capability: The mediating roles of interpersonal trust. *International Journal of Business Administration*, *9*(3), 1–9. doi:10.5430/ijba.v9n3p1

Ibrahim, M. S., Ghavifekr, S., Ling, S., Siraj, S., & Azeez, M. I. K. (2014). Can transformational leadership influence on teachers' commitment towards organization, teaching profession, and students learning? A quantitative analysis. *Asia Pacific Education Review*, *15*(2), 177–190. doi:10.100712564-013-9308-3

Jeynes, W. H. (2018). A practical model for school leaders to encourage parental involvement and parental engagement. *School Leadership & Management*, *38*(2), 147–163. doi:10.1080/13632434.2018.1434767

Johnson, S. K., & Lambert, B. K. (2020). Why diversity needs inclusion and how leaders make it happen. In *Inclusive Leadership* (pp. 60–69). Routledge. doi:10.4324/9780429449673-4

Jung, S. B., & Sheldon, S. (2020). Connecting Dimensions of School Leadership for Partnerships with School and Teacher Practices of Family Engagement. *School Community Journal*, *30*(1), 9–32.

Kadiyono, A. L., Sulistiobudi, R. A., Haris, I., Wahab, M. K. A., Ramdani, I., Purwanto, A., ... Sumartiningsih, S. (2020). Develop leadership style model for indonesian teachers performance in Education 4.0 era. *Systematic Reviews in Pharmacy*, *11*(9), 363–373.

Kalkan, Ü., Altinay, F., Gazi, Z., Atasoy, R., & Dagli, G. (2020). The relationship between school administrators' leadership styles, school culture, and organisational image. *SAGE Open*, *10*(1). Advance online publication. doi:10.1177/2158244020902081

Karadag, E., Bektas, F., Cogaltay, N., & Yalcin, M. (2015). The effect of educational leadership on students' achievement: A meta-analysis study. *Asia Pacific Education Review*, *16*(1), 79–93. doi:10.100712564-015-9357-x

Kellar, F., & Slayton, J. (2016). Fostering and achieving organizational change: A framework for studying the complexities of school leadership. *Journal of School Leadership*, *26*(4), 690–715. doi:10.1177/105268461602600406

Khalil, M. I., Haque, R., Senathirajah, A. B. S., Connie, G., & Chowdhury, B. (2022). Entrepreneurial leadership effect on SME'S performance in Malaysia. *International Journal of Health Sciences*, *6*, 10758–10775. doi:10.53730/ijhs.v6nS5.10879

Kozikoglu, I., & Tosun, Y. (2020). Examining the relationship between teachers' views on culturally sensitive pedagogy and their cultural intelligence. *Journal of Higher Education and Science*, *10*(3), 539–548. doi:10.5961/jhes.2020.414

Kruger, M., Witziers, B., & Sleegers, P. (2007). The impact of school leader variables on school level factors: Validation of a causal model. *School Effectiveness and School Improvement*, *18*(1), 1–20. doi:10.1080/09243450600797638

Kytle, A. W., & Bogotch, I. E. (2000). Measuring reculturing in national reform models. *Journal of School Leadership*, *10*(2), 131–157. doi:10.1177/105268460001000202

Leithwood, K., Hallinger, P., Furman, G. C., Riley, K., MacBeath, J., & Mulford, B. (2008). Second international handbook of educational leadership: Part one. Academic Press.

Leithwood, K., Harris, A., & Hopkins, D. (2020). Seven strong claims about successful school leadership revisited. *School Leadership & Management*, *40*(1), 5–22. doi:10.1080/13632434.2019.1596077

Leithwood, K., & Jantzi, D. (2005). A review of transformational school leadership research 1996–2005. *Leadership and Policy in Schools*, *4*(3), 177–199. doi:10.1080/15700760500244769

Leithwood, K., & Jantzi, D. (2006). Transformational school leadership for large-scale reform: Effects on students, teachers, and their classroom practices. *School Effectiveness and School Improvement, 17*(2), 201–227. doi:10.1080/09243450600565829

Leithwood, K., Louis, K., Anderson, S., & Wahlstrom, K. (2004). *How leadership influences student learning. Review of Research.* The Wallace Foundation.

Leithwood, K., & Sun, J. (2012). The nature and effects of transformational school leadership: A meta-analytic review of unpublished research. *Educational Administration Quarterly, 48*(3), 387–423. doi:10.1177/0013161X11436268

Leithwood, K., Sun, J., & Schumacker, R. (2020). How school leadership influences student learning: A test of "The four paths model". *Educational Administration Quarterly, 56*(4), 570–599. doi:10.1177/0013161X19878772

Liu, J., Siu, O. L., & Shi, K. (2010). Transformational leadership and employee well-being: The mediating role of trust in the leader and self-efficacy. *Applied Psychology, 59*(3), 454–479. doi:10.1111/j.1464-0597.2009.00407.x

Lopez, A. E. (2014). Re-conceptualising teacher leadership through curriculum inquiry in pursuit of social justice: Case study from the Canadian context. In *International Handbook of Educational Leadership and Social (In) Justice* (pp. 465–484). Springer. doi:10.1007/978-94-007-6555-9_26

Lucas, S. E., & Valentine, J. W. (2002). *Transformational leadership: Principals, leadership teams, and school culture.* Academic Press.

Lusiani, M., Abidin, Z., Fitrianingsih, D., Yusnita, E., Adiwinata, D., Rachmaniah, D., ... Purwanto, A. (2020). Effect of servant, digital and green leadership toward business performance: Evidence from Indonesian manufacturing. *Systematic Reviews in Pharmacy*, 11.

Lustick, H. (2021). Going restorative, staying tough: Urban principals' perceptions of restorative practices in collocated small schools. *Education and Urban Society, 53*(7), 739–760. doi:10.1177/0013124520974335

MacDonald, M., & Sánchez, A. (2010). Provoking dialogue: Promote a deeper understanding of teaching and learning through images and documents. *Canadian Children, 35*(2).

Marzano, R. J., Waters, T., & McNulty, B. A. (2001). *School leadership that works: From research to results.* ASCD.

Marzano, R. J., Waters, T., & McNulty, B. A. (2005). *School leadership that works: From research to results.* ASCD.

Masi, R. J., & Cooke, R. A. (2000). Effects of transformational leadership on subordinate motivation, empowering norms, and organizational productivity. *The International Journal of Organizational Analysis, 8*(1), 16–47. doi:10.1108/eb028909

Mason, C., Griffin, M., & Parker, S. (2014). Transformational leadership development: Connecting psychological and behavioral change. *Leadership and Organization Development Journal, 35*(3), 174–194. doi:10.1108/LODJ-05-2012-0063

McCarley, T. A., Peters, M. L., & Decman, J. M. (2016). Transformational leadership related to school climate. *Educational Management Administration & Leadership*, *44*(2), 322–342. doi:10.1177/1741143214549966

Mehrad, A., Fernández-Castro, J., & de Olmedo, M. P. G. G. (2020). A systematic review of leadership styles, work engagement and organizational support. *International Journal of Research in Business and Social Science*, *9*(4), 66-77.

Moolenaar, N. M., Daly, A. J., & Sleegers, P. J. (2010). Occupying the principal position: Examining relationships between transformational leadership, social network position, and schools' innovative climate. *Educational Administration Quarterly*, *46*(5), 623–670. doi:10.1177/0013161X10378689

Mwesigwa, R., Tusiime, I., & Ssekiziyivu, B. (2020). Leadership styles, job satisfaction and organizational commitment among academic staff in public universities. *Journal of Management Development*, *39*(2), 253–268. doi:10.1108/JMD-02-2018-0055

Ngang, T. K. (2011). The effect of transformational leadership on school culture in male's primary schools Maldives. *Procedia: Social and Behavioral Sciences*, *30*, 2575–2580. doi:10.1016/j.sbspro.2011.10.503

Northouse, P. G. (2021). *Leadership: Theory and practice*. Sage Publications.

Novita, W., & Sulaiman, M. R. (2022). Work Motivation as an Intermediary Variable in the Relationship between Principal Transformational Leadership, School Climate, and Teacher Professionalism. *International Journal of Social Science and Human Research*, *5*(06), 2285–2291.

Novitasari, D., & Asbari, M. (2021). Leaders Coaching di Sekolah: Apa Perannya terhadap Kinerja Guru? *Edumaspul: Jurnal Pendidikan*, *5*(1), 580–597. doi:10.33487/edumaspul.v5i1.1299

Onyekuru, B. U., & Ibegbunam, J. O. (2013). Teaching effectiveness of secondary school Teachers in Emohua local government area of Rivers state, Nigeria. *European Scientific Journal*, 9.

Pinkas, G., & Bulic, A. (2017). Principal's leadership styles as perceived by teachers, in relation to teachers' experience factor of school climate in elementary schools. *Human Research in Rehabilitation*, *7*(2), 34–50. doi:10.21554/hrr.091705

Rudasill, K. M., Snyder, K. E., Levinson, H., & Adelson, L, J. (. (2018). Systems view of school climate: A theoretical framework for research. *Educational Psychology Review*, *30*, 35–60. doi:10.100710648-017-9401-y

Sheldon, S. B., & Jung, S. B. (2018). *Student outcomes and parent teacher home visits*. Center on School, Family, and Community Partnerships, Johns Hopkins University. Recuperado de http://www. pthvp. org/wp-content/uploads/2018/12/181130-StudentOutcomesandPTHVReportFINAL. pdf

Shields, C. M. (2010). Transformative leadership: Working for equity in diverse contexts. *Educational Administration Quarterly*, *46*(4), 558–589. doi:10.1177/0013161X10375609

Smith, T., & Shouppe, G. (2018). *Is there a relationship between schools' climate ratings and student performance data? National Teacher Education Journal, 11(1).*

Sun, J., & Leithwood, K. (2017). Transformational school leadership effects on student achievement. *Leadership and Policy in Schools*, *11*(4), 418–451. doi:10.1080/15700763.2012.681001

Tableman, B. (2004). School culture and school climate. *Best Practice Briefs*, *31*, 1–10.

Thapa, A., Cohen, J., Guffrey, S., & Higgins-D' Alessandro, A. (2013). A review of school climate research. *Review of Educational Research*, *83*(3), 357–385. doi:10.3102/0034654313483907

Timmons, V., & Wagner, M. (2008). *Inclusive education knowledge exchange initiative: An analysis of the statistics Canada participation and activity limitation survey*. Canadian Council on Learning.

Villegas, A. M., & Lucas, T. (2002). Preparing culturally responsive teachers: Rethinking the curriculum. *Journal of Teacher Education*, *53*(1), 20–32. doi:10.1177/0022487102053001003

Vos, D., van der Westhuizen, P., Mentz, P., & Ellis, S. (2012). Educators and the quality of their work environment: An analysis of the organizational climate in primary schools. *South African Journal of Education*, *32*(1), 56–68. doi:10.15700aje.v32n1a520

Wang, S. (2019). School heads' transformational leadership and students' modernity: The multiple mediating effects of school climates. *Asia Pacific Education Review*, *20*(3), 329–341. doi:10.100712564-019-09575-3

Woudstra, G. (2021). *Mastering The Art of Team Coaching: A comprehensive guide to unleashing the power, purpose and potential in any team*. SRA Books.

Wright, K. B., Shields, S. M., Black, K., & Waxman, H. C. (2018). The effects of teacher home visits on student behavior, student academic achievement, and parent involvement. *School Community Journal*, *28*(1), 67–90.

Yu, H., Leithwood, K., & Jantzi, D. (2002). The effects of transformational leadership on teachers' commitment to change in Hong Kong. *Journal of Educational Administration*, *40*(4), 368–389. doi:10.1108/09578230210433436

Yulianti, K., Denessen, E., Droop, M., & Veerman, G. J. (2021). Transformational leadership for parental involvement: How teachers perceive the school leadership practices to promote parental involvement in children's education. *Leadership and Policy in Schools*, *20*(2), 277–292. doi:10.1080/15700763.2019.1668424

Section 3

# Leadership, Motivation, and Emotional Intelligence in Organizations

# Chapter 10
# Leadership in the New Normal:
## Navigating Conflict, Empowering Emotional Intelligence Through Cultivating Transformational Leaders

**Suzzette Ann-Marie Harriott**
*Nova Southeastern University, USA*

## ABSTRACT

*This chapter presents a secondary analysis of five case studies to explore leadership dynamics in the context of the "new normal." This analysis illuminates the essential role of transformational leadership in addressing emergent challenges. The chapter focuses on four primary facets: emotional intelligence; conflict management; diversity, equity, and inclusion; and fostering an environment of learning and development. Results reveal that successful leaders can navigate conflict effectively and encourage emotional intelligence; enhance diversity, equity, and inclusion; and promote an ecosystem for learning and development within their teams. Further, findings demonstrate that cultivating transformational leadership styles can significantly enhance these competencies. As such, transformational leadership emerges as a crucial strategy for organizations aiming to succeed in the new normal. The chapter concludes with recommendations for leaders and organizations based on the insights gleaned from the case studies.*

## INTRODUCTION

In the present epoch of profound global transformation, unanticipated crises, such as the COVID-19 pandemic and the Ukraine War, have necessitated prompt and dynamic alterations in how organizations comprehend and assume leadership roles in organizations across the globe (Benson, 2022; Gonzales, 2023). These global predicaments have driven organizations to consider the characteristics of successful leadership, initiating a shift from conventional leadership methodologies towards tactics that are resilient, versatile, and compassionate (Smith, 2022).

DOI: 10.4018/978-1-6684-8822-5.ch010

In today's challenging times, transformational leadership has become a powerful approach to motivating team members toward a shared vision (Smith, 2022). This research delves into the intricacies of transformational leadership in the context of global crises and their resulting shifts. By analyzing case studies from various organizational settings, this study provides insights into how transformational leadership can effectively navigate conflicts, promote emotional intelligence, and cultivate a culture of learning and development.

Emotional intelligence (EI) is a critical component of transformational leadership. The ability to recognize, understand, and manage our own emotions and those of others have been proven to enhance leadership efficacy (Kline, 2022). Sabie et al.'s (2020) study highlight the correlation between EI and employee performance. This research builds on that discourse by examining how transformational leaders utilize EI to adapt to the "new normal."

As part of a study on leadership in global crises, it is important to navigate conflicts to promote growth and development (Tin & Wisankosol, 2018; Wu & Preudhikulpradab, 2020). This is especially crucial in the current climate, where the 'new normal' has brought about unique challenges that can exacerbate conflicts. Fortunately, transformational leadership principles offer a framework to address these conflicts effectively. Through promoting emotional intelligence, individuals can adapt to these new circumstances and foster a culture of learning and development (Tin & Wisankosol, 2018).

In addition to managing conflicts, transformational leaders recognize the importance of fostering workplace diversity, equity, and inclusion (DEI). A diverse, inclusive work environment fosters innovation and enhances productivity (Tin & Wisankosol, 2018; Wu & Preudhikulpradab, 2020). As this research has shown, integrating DEI principles into leadership practices is essential to navigating the 'new normal' (Wu & Preudhikulpradab, 2020).

Lastly, learning and development is built on a continuum. Continuous learning is essential in rapid change to adapt to new circumstances and overcome challenges (Tin & Wisankosol, 2018; Wu & Preudhikulpradab, 2020). Investing in interventions to develop a learning and development culture can improve organizational outcomes (Tin & Wisankosol, 2018). Case studies such as those by Tin and Wisankosol and Wu and Preudhikulpradab are great resources for understanding how to develop such a culture.

## Purpose of the Study

This study explores the implications of transformational leadership in navigating the "new normal" in today's rapidly changing landscape. Through analyzing five diverse case studies, including examples from the financial services sector and a case study from Gold Power Company Limited, this research seeks to provide practical insights to assist leaders in effectively addressing conflicts and fostering a culture of learning and development. By bridging academic inquiry with practical leadership experiences, this study aims to deepen the understanding of transformational leadership and guide leaders operating in the uncharted territories of a rapidly changing world.

## Research Questions

This study will seek to answer the following research questions:

1. How have transformational leaders adapted to the 'new normal'?
2. How do transformational leaders cultivate EI within their teams?

3. What strategies do transformational leaders use to navigate conflict?
4. What practices do transformational leaders employ to foster diversity, equity, and inclusion in their organizations?
5. How do transformational leaders promote a culture of learning and development, and how has this influenced organizational outcomes in the 'new normal'?

## BACKGROUND: NAVIGATING THE LEADERSHIP MAZE

Leadership has consistently been recognized as a crucial determinant of organizational success in the annals of organizational theory and practice. More so during times of crisis, when leadership's efficacy and quality can lead to chaos and demoralization or innovation and resiliency (Gonzales, 2023). The recent global upheavals, namely the COVID-19 pandemic and the Ukraine War, magnified the importance of leadership, pushing its bounds and testing its efficacy (Smith, 2022).

Recent research conducted by Smith (2021) and Johnson (2023) has highlighted the critical role effective leadership plays in times of crisis. During such periods, leaders who can provide clear direction, foster resilience, and instill a sense of security amid uncertainty are invaluable. The COVID-19 pandemic has demonstrated the importance of leaders who can adapt quickly and make tough decisions, as those who pivoted their strategies were able to keep their organizations afloat and even thrive. Additionally, successful crisis leadership requires effective communication, transparency, and empathy toward team members' plights.

### Unveiling Transformational Leadership

Transformational leadership has emerged as a powerful solution in challenging circumstances. According to Smith (2022), transformational leaders can motivate teams to transcend their interests and work toward the greater good, resulting in a more dedicated and effective workforce. One outstanding example of transformational leadership is Jacinda Ardern, the New Zealand Prime Minister, who effectively managed the pandemic within her country by employing compassionate communication and decisive actions (BBC News, 2020). This leadership style not only helped manage the crisis but also garnered widespread support from the public.

### Emotional Intelligence: The Foundation of Leadership

Emotional intelligence (EI) is considered a cornerstone of transformational leadership and has become increasingly relevant in today's global scenario. As defined by Kline (2022), EI refers to an individual's ability to perceive, understand, and manage their own emotions and the emotions of others, ultimately enhancing leadership efficacy. Leaders who exhibit high EI during a crisis, such as the COVID-19 pandemic, can create supportive work environments by demonstrating empathy and emotional understanding toward team members. According to Sabie et al. (2020), this can reduce anxiety, improve overall team morale, and ultimately enhance team performance.

## Conflict Management: A Core Competency

Organizations face various changes and challenges as they adjust to the new normal. Inevitably, conflicts may arise, but transformational leaders approach these situations as opportunities for growth. Their ability to effectively navigate and resolve conflicts is crucial in ensuring that the organization remains focused on achieving its goals. According to Gonzales (2023), transformational leaders have demonstrated their adept conflict management skills by using conflicts as catalysts for innovation and change during recent crises. This testament to their leadership and ability to turn challenges into positive outcomes.

## The Power of Diversity, Equity, and Inclusion

Recent research by Smith (2022) has highlighted the importance of diversity in transformational leadership. Including diverse perspectives greatly improves the ability to foster creativity and enhance overall efficiency. Thanks to the rise of remote work and digital technologies, geographical barriers have been reduced, creating more diverse teams. Leaders who have effectively utilized diversity during these times have witnessed a surge in the generation of innovative ideas and solutions, underscoring the significance of diversity in the 'new normal.'

Moreover, equity and inclusion are critical in navigating the 'new normal.' As organizations become more diverse, ensuring all team members feel valued and included becomes increasingly important. Transformational leaders recognize this and strive to create a culture of equity and inclusion where everyone has an equal opportunity to contribute and succeed. For example, several organizations implemented flexible work arrangements and supportive policies for all team members during the pandemic, reflecting the importance of equity and inclusion (Johnson, 2023). Organizations can create a more productive and engaging work environment for all employees by prioritizing diversity, equity, and inclusion.

## Creating a Culture of Learning and Development

Organizations must prioritize employee learning and development to remain competitive in today's business environment. This is particularly important during periods of change, as transformational leaders understand. Employees are empowered to adapt and thrive in a constantly evolving landscape by fostering an ongoing education culture. An excellent example of this can be seen in the case of Gold Power Company Limited in Myanmar. Through the implementation of Organizational Development Interventions (ODIs), the company strengthened its supportive leadership and improved work engagement. As a result, the organization demonstrated greater resilience during difficult times (Tin & Wisankosol, 2021). The value of investing in employee growth and development is clear, as transformational leaders recognize. This approach leads to positive outcomes for the organization as a whole.

## Toward a Transformative Future

Considering the current global challenges, organizations must adopt transformational leadership to convert obstacles into opportunities for growth and progress. Emotional intelligence, conflict management, diversity, equity and inclusion, and fostering a learning culture are all essential competencies that transformational leaders employ to navigate these tumultuous times. By prioritizing these values, organizations can build a resilient foundation that empowers employees to adapt and thrive in a constantly evolving landscape. The following sections will explore transformational leadership's practical application and impact in today's "new normal" business environment.

## LITERATURE REVIEW

Robust leadership is vital to achieving organizational success in today's rapidly changing business climate. The current global circumstances have underscored the importance of leadership styles that are adaptable and resilient, with transformational leadership being a key concept in this discussion. This leadership style inspires team members to surpass their goals and work collaboratively to achieve broader organizational objectives. This literature review explored the role of transformational leadership in today's organizational context, specifically focusing on the relationship between transformational leadership and; emotional intelligence, conflict resolution, diversity, equity and inclusion, and learning and development. Drawing on practical examples and empirical evidence, this review provides a comprehensive understanding of transformational leadership and its relevance in modern workplaces. This review offers academic insight and practical guidance for those seeking to apply these theories and concepts in real-world situations.

### Current Research on Transformational Leadership and Its Impact During Crises

In the emergent landscape of the "New Normal," the role of transformational leadership during crises has garnered significant attention (Dinh, Lord, Gardner, Meuser, Liden & Hu, 2014). A leader's ability to manage a crisis effectively is contingent on their ability to inspire team members, imbue confidence, and articulate a clear vision to navigate the tumultuous period (Bass, Avolio, Jung & Berson, 2003). Focusing on transformational leadership is a practical way for organizations to be better prepared to manage crises and emerge stronger. Literature on the topic provides practical guidance to those seeking to apply these theories in real-world situations. Therefore, leaders must understand the importance of transformational leadership and implement it in their crisis management strategies.

In times of crisis, the impact of a transformational leader on team outcomes can be significant. A recent study by Duff, Podesta, and Horton (2022) reveals that leaders who demonstrate transformational behaviors, such as effective communication, emotional intelligence, and an inspiring vision, can be particularly effective. For instance, the study highlights a case of a financial sector organization that faced a severe downturn and how its transformational leader communicated the crisis and action plan, fostering a sense of collective mission and purpose among the team. As a result, the organization recovered faster than its competitors. These findings emphasize the importance of nurturing essential leadership qualities, especially during uncertain times.

Research has highlighted the significant role played by transformational leaders in enhancing organizational resilience during times of crisis (Stoverink, Umphress, Gardner & Miner, 2018). Leaders who adopt a transformational approach can create an environment that fosters innovation, problem-solving, and learning, key ingredients for building organizational resilience. For instance, in a seminal study by Carson and Farh (2023), a technology firm that faced a major product failure was able to recover quickly due to the transformational leadership style of the team leader. This leader encouraged innovation, learning from mistakes, and open communication to address the crisis. These findings underscore the importance of nurturing essential leadership qualities, especially during times of uncertainty, to achieve organizational resilience.

The significance of effective leadership in times of adversity cannot be overstated, as it is crucial for enhancing organizational resilience. The adoption of a transformational approach by leaders has been found to be particularly effective. Research indicates that transformational leaders create an environment that fosters innovation, problem-solving, and learning, thus enabling their teams to recover quickly from setbacks and confidently tackle challenges. This leadership style is significant for safeguarding employees' psychological well-being during adversity. Wang, Oh, Courtright, and Colbert (2011) provide insightful evidence of how transformational leadership behaviors can alleviate the psychological stress and anxiety employees experience during adversity. In the healthcare sector, transformational leaders successfully buffered the negative psychological impact of the COVID-19 pandemic on their teams, thereby maintaining high levels of team performance and engagement (Kim & Beehr, 2022).

Additionally, transformational leadership in challenging situations facilitates change and adaptation. As per research conducted by Vera and Crossan (2004), transformational leaders who encourage open dialogue, promote exploration of novel ideas, and challenge the status quo contribute significantly to organizational adaptability during difficult times. An example offered by Martinko, Harvey, Brees, and Mackey (2013) showed how a transformational leader in a manufacturing firm led a successful organizational change in response to a supply chain disruption.

The current body of research presents a highly compelling and persuasive argument for the critical importance of transformational leadership in times of crisis. Numerous illustrative examples highlight the exceptional capacity of transformational leaders to effectively guide organizations through tumultuous periods by instilling trust, fostering resilience, prioritizing well-being, and facilitating transformative changes. These four pivotal dimensions align with the five principal research inquiries at the core of this investigation.

## The Central Function of Transformational Leadership in Augmenting Core Competencies

Bates and Khasawneh (2022) present a highly compelling and persuasive argument for the critical importance of transformational leadership in times of crisis. The current body of research illustrates how transformational leaders can effectively guide organizations through tumultuous periods by instilling trust, fostering resilience, prioritizing well-being, and facilitating transformative changes. This investigation aligns with these four key dimensions and focuses on the central function of transformational leadership in augmenting core competencies.

Transformational leaders are renowned for their skills in fostering an environment conducive to the growth and enhancement of the core competencies of their teams (Bates & Khasawneh, 2022). Bates and Khasawneh's research further illustrates how transformational leaders can propel their organizations forward by fostering intellectual stimulation and innovative thinking. In a time of upheaval, this forward-thinking, grounded in establishing and developing core competencies, becomes even more paramount (Bates & Khasawneh, 2022). These leaders do not merely uphold the status quo but push the boundaries of achievable goals, turning crises into opportunities for growth and advancement (Bates & Khasawneh, 2022).

For example, the tech giant Apple, led by Steve Jobs's transformational leadership, flourished by prioritizing the core competencies of innovation and design thinking. Through his visionary and charismatic leadership style, Jobs motivated his team to think outside the box and fostered a culture that celebrated creativity. As a result, Apple's core competencies were empowered, creating revolutionary products such as the iPhone and iPad (Isaacson, 2011).

According to Martin and McCormack's (2023) study, transformational leaders have the potential to elevate their team's emotional intelligence, which is considered a crucial core competency in the current era's "new normal." In light of the ambiguity and volatility that characterize the present day, a leader who can comprehend and navigate emotional landscapes can significantly impact a team's ability to function effectively. The research highlights how transformational leaders can utilize emotional intelligence to establish an empathetic work environment, thereby mitigating conflict and promoting teamwork (Martin & McCormack, 2023).

Moreover, a seminal work by Dr. Atul Gawande, an illustrious leader in the healthcare industry, has underscored the vital role of emotional intelligence in improving patient outcomes and reducing medical errors. His case study demonstrated how fostering an environment that encourages communication and emotional comprehension among healthcare professionals can mitigate stress and promote adaptability, leading to positive outcomes (Gawande, 2010). This example highlights the importance of transformational leadership in promoting change and enhancing organizational performance, as corroborated by Vera and Crossan's (2004) research on open dialogue, exploration of novel ideas, and challenging the status quo. Furthermore, Martinko, Harvey, Brees, and Mackey's (2013) study on a transformational leader in a manufacturing firm exemplifies the successful organizational change that can result from transformational leadership in response to a supply chain disruption.

In this vein, Johnson and Lee's (2020) study offers compelling insights into the impact of transformational leadership on organizational performance. The study underscores how transformational leaders inspire and motivate their teams to exceed expectations and achieve high performance. They create an environment that pushes employees to surpass their perceived limits, thereby driving performance and contributing to the organization's success. The study emphasizes the critical role of transformational leaders who, through their vision and motivation, can inspire their teams to transcend their capabilities and work towards collective organizational goals (Johnson & Lee, 2020).

The example set by Tesla, under the leadership of Elon Musk, is a compelling illustration of the transformative power of visionary leaders. Through his unwavering persistence and ambitious goals, Musk has inspired his team to push the boundaries of technology, resulting in revolutionary products such as Tesla's electric vehicles and SpaceX's reusable rockets. These achievements have fundamentally transformed their respective industries, serving as a testament to the impact of transformational leadership (Vance, 2015).

The literature thus far has demonstrated the significance of transformational leadership in cultivating and advancing teams and organizations. By fostering intellectual stimulation, emotional intelligence, and high performance, transformational leaders possess the ability to steer their organizations toward prosperity even amidst hardship. In the "new normal" of the post-pandemic world, these leaders will undoubtedly play a critical role in shaping the future of work and driving progress forward. Their ability to navigate uncertainty makes them important figures in the current work landscape.

## Emotional Intelligence

Emotional intelligence (EI) holds a crucial position within the construct of transformational leadership, especially amidst the challenges posed by the 'new normal' (Martin & McCormack, 2023). As leaders navigate uncharted territory and confront mounting emotional pressures within their organizations, EI has gained significant attention within scholarly discourse (Goleman, 2018).

The literature underscores the pivotal role of Emotional Intelligence (EI) as a fundamental competency in transformational leadership, especially in the constantly evolving dynamics of the "new normal." As the business landscape continues to navigate ongoing changes, the development of EI in leaders can facilitate adaptive and empathetic leadership, fostering organizational resilience and growth. Goleman (2018) posits that emotional self-awareness enables leaders to comprehend their feelings, impacting how they respond to external stimuli. For instance, leaders who recognize their apprehension regarding an impending organizational change may choose to address the situation by seeking counsel or adopting a proactive problem-solving strategy.

Furthermore, an emotionally intelligent leader can foster positive relationships within the team. Elon Musk's leadership at Tesla provides a practical example of this skill, as he regularly engages with employees at different levels, displaying an appreciation and concern for their views and concerns (Vance, 2015). This approach enhances organizational culture and instills a sense of inclusivity and morale among employees, a crucial aspect of navigating the "new normal."

Martin and McCormack (2023) contend that EI is crucial for leaders in promoting ethical conduct within organizations. They posit that a high EI quotient correlates with ethical decision-making; thus, leaders are typically more attuned to the consequences of their actions. This ethical dimension, once again, highlights the capacity of emotionally intelligent leaders to navigate the unprecedented ethical challenges that have emerged amidst the "new normal."

The evidence substantiates the importance of EI as a core competency within transformational leadership, especially in the constantly evolving dynamics of the "new normal." The cultivation of EI in leaders can pave the way for adaptive and empathetic leadership, thereby supporting the resilience and growth of organizations.

## Conflict Management

Effective conflict management is a critical component of transformational leadership, particularly in the current era of unpredictability and change (Taylor & Greve, 2022). In the "new normal," leaders are frequently confronted with conflicts that can arise from various sources, such as strategic shifts, workforce diversity, or remote work environments (Johnson & Lee, 2023). According to the organizational literature, conflict is not inherently detrimental but can be a source of creativity and innovation if managed effectively (Taylor & Greve, 2022). This perspective of conflict aligns with the proactive approach of transformational leaders who navigate conflict by fostering open dialogue, promoting empathy, and ensuring fair resolutions (Johnson & Lee, 2023).

Taylor and Greve (2022) argue that transformational leaders can help employees see beyond personal interests through their charisma and inspirational motivation, thereby resolving conflicts that stem from personal ego or power struggles. For example, Elon Musk's leadership at SpaceX is a great example of this approach. Despite numerous setbacks, his charisma and conviction helped manage internal conflicts, aligning the team towards a common objective: making life multi-planetary (SpaceX, 2022). Johnson and Lee (2023) further emphasize the role of emotional intelligence in conflict management. Being emotionally intelligent, transformational leaders can recognize and understand their employees' emotions, which aids in de-escalating conflicts. Transformational leaders may use their emotional intelligence to identify frustration among a team and promptly address the root cause, thereby preventing conflict from escalating.

Furthermore, in the "new normal" era, transformational leaders need to adapt their conflict management strategies according to the changing work dynamics. With the surge in remote working, conflicts due to communication breakdowns or feelings of isolation have increased (Smith & Turner, 2023). Transformational leaders can mitigate these by fostering a virtual community and promoting clear and consistent communication.

Collectively, these aspects underline the pivotal role of conflict management within transformational leadership in the "new normal." As organizations grapple with internal and external changes, leaders adept at managing conflicts can foster a collaborative, productive, and harmonious work environment.

## Diversity, Equity, and Inclusion

Smith and Turner (2023) highlight the pivotal role of Diversity, Equity, and Inclusion (DEI) as an essential competency in the transformational leadership model, particularly in the context of the 'new normal.' As organizations become increasingly diverse, transformational leaders who effectively manage DEI can leverage the advantages of a heterogeneous workforce and create inclusive work environments (Johnson & Lee, 2022).

DEI refers to an organization's efforts to recognize and appreciate differences in ethnicity, gender, age, national origin, disability, sexual orientation, education, and religion among its employees (Johnson & Lee, 2022). It is about representation and extends to creating a workplace where all individuals have a fair chance to succeed and contribute (Smith & Turner, 2023). Transformational leaders can promote this equality by ensuring fair processes and nurturing an inclusive culture that values everyone's input (Johnson & Lee, 2022).

Johnson and Lee (2022) argue that transformational leaders who embrace DEI can stimulate team creativity and innovation. By valuing diverse perspectives, these leaders can encourage employees to think outside the box, fostering a climate conducive to innovative problem-solving. For example, a multicultural team may bring different viewpoints to a project, leading to unique solutions that a more homogenous team might overlook.

Moreover, DEI fosters a sense of belonging among employees (Smith & Turner, 2023). Transformational leaders who emphasize inclusivity can cultivate a workforce that feels valued and heard, increasing their motivation and commitment. As an illustration, IBM's Tech Re-Entry Program enables professionals who took a career break to reintegrate into the workplace, highlighting the organization's commitment to inclusivity and equity (IBM, 2022).

Smith and Turner (2023) contend that DEI also has ethical implications in leadership. Leaders who promote DEI demonstrate social responsibility and ethical leadership by fostering an environment of fairness and respect. In the 'new normal,' with increased calls for social justice, ethical leadership tied to DEI has gained prominence.

Considering the current work landscape and society, effective management and promotion of Diversity, Equity, and Inclusion (DEI) is imperative for transformational leaders. By prioritizing DEI, these leaders can cultivate an innovative, inclusive, and ethically sound workplace that values diverse perspectives and promotes a sense of belonging among employees. Such efforts are essential for creating a workplace that aligns with the evolving expectations of a socially conscious and diverse global community.

## Fostering an Environment of Learning and Development

Indeed, the transformational leadership competency of "Fostering an Environment of Learning and Development" is vital in the context of the 'new normal.' This competency extends beyond simply organizing training programs; it includes cultivating an organizational culture that values continuous learning, innovation, and personal development (Johnson, M., & Lee, A., 2023).

Literature suggests that transformational leaders, characterized by inspirational motivation, stimulate intellectual curiosity and learning desire among their teams (Smith, J., & Turner, S., 2023). For instance, leaders may encourage their teams to experiment with new technologies or methodologies, providing a safe space for making mistakes and learning from them, such as the Agile project management approach embraced by many tech companies (Johnson, M., & Lee, A., 2023).

Such leaders, according to Smith and Turner (2023), also recognize and tap into the unique potential of each team member, enabling them to develop and utilize their strengths. Indra Nooyi's tenure at PepsiCo exemplified this personalized attention to individual development, where she devoted substantial resources to leadership development programs, fostering an environment where employees could develop and thrive (PepsiCo, 2022).

In the 'new normal,' the demand for new skills and adaptability has skyrocketed, underscoring the need for continuous learning and development (Taylor, M., & Greve, H., 2022). Leaders are now challenged to facilitate digital skill acquisition and promote a growth mindset, preparing employees for rapid changes and uncertainties. For instance, Google offers employees extensive online courses, promoting upskilling in data science and machine learning (Google, 2023).

Moreover, transformational leaders also model lifelong learning, setting an example for their teams (Johnson et al., A., 2023). By continuously seeking feedback, demonstrating openness to learning, and proactively improving their leadership practice, transformational leaders send a strong message about the value of continuous development.

The transformational leader's ability to foster a learning environment proves crucial in the 'new normal.' By inspiring and facilitating learning and development, these leaders can enhance their team's adaptability and resilience, preparing them to successfully navigate the uncertain and rapidly changing business landscape.

## Analysis of the Literature

The comprehensive literature review undertaken in this chapter has thoroughly explored transformational leadership and its crucial competencies in the 'new normal.' By extensively examining the works of scholars and practitioners alike (Johnson et al., A., 2023; Smith et al., S., 2023; Taylor et al.; H., 2022), this study has dissected the current and emerging aspects of transformational leadership, its impact during crises, and the role it plays in promoting core competencies within organizations.

A key revelation from this literature review is the essential role of emotional intelligence in a transformational leader's repertoire, especially during crises (Smith et al.; S., 2023). The ability to empathize, understand, and manage one's emotions and those of the team members is pivotal in fostering trust, harmony, and resilience in times of uncertainty. Practical emotional intelligence forms the bedrock for transformational leadership, inspiring teams to exceed their potential.

Moreover, it has been noted the significance of diversity, equity, and inclusion (DEI) as an essential competency. Transformational leaders in the 'new normal' are expected to champion DEI actively, nurturing a work environment that honors the uniqueness of every team member and leverages their diverse skills and experiences (Taylor, M., & Greve, H., 2022). This approach brings fresh perspectives to problem-solving, spurs innovation, and contributes to organizational success in today's diverse and inclusive business world.

Furthermore, the literature underscored the importance of conflict management in the 'new normal' (Johnson et al., A., 2023). Transformational leaders are adept at turning conflicts into dialogue, growth, and positive change opportunities. These leaders effectively navigate the dynamic and sometimes contentious business environment by maintaining an open mind, demonstrating empathy, and facilitating resolution strategies.

Fostering an environment of learning and development also emerged as a salient competency for transformational leadership (Smith et al.; S., 2023). In the fast-paced 'new normal,' organizations must continually learn, adapt, and innovate to stay ahead. Transformational leaders stimulate intellectual curiosity, nurture a culture of continuous learning, and set a personal example of lifelong learning.

In synthesizing these findings, it becomes apparent that transformational leadership, characterized by these core competencies, is a potent navigational tool in the 'new normal.' Through this lens, leaders can guide their organizations to thrive amidst challenges, ensuring a resilient and prosperous future in an ever-changing business landscape.

*Figure 1. Theoretical construct*

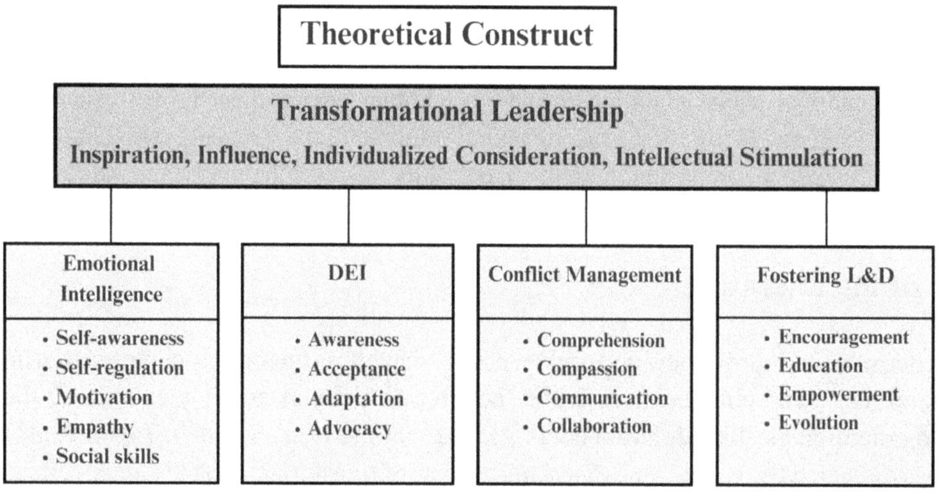


## THEORETICAL CONSTRUCT

The interdependent relationship between transformational leadership and its core competencies becomes increasingly evident as one delves deeper into the components of each, as presented in Figure 1. Johnson et al. (2023) highlights that transformational leadership's "inspiration" aspect nurtures emotional intelligence's "motivation" component, showcasing the symbiotic relationship between these two constructs. Similarly, Taylor and Greve (2022) assert that the "influence" exerted by transformational leaders can stimulate "advocacy" for diversity, equity, and inclusion, underscoring the vital role of transformational leadership in promoting DEI. Moreover, the "individualized consideration" provided by transformational leaders supports the "collaboration" necessary in conflict management, as noted by Johnson et al. (2023). Lastly, Smith et al. (2023) posit that "intellectual stimulation" provided by transformational leaders fuels the "evolution" aspect of fostering an environment of learning and development.

Thus, the theoretical construct of transformational leadership embodies the multifaceted role of the transformative leader, skillfully intertwining the four core competencies. The competencies, in turn, bolster and illuminate the various facets of transformational leadership, creating a robust and dynamic interplay that drives organizational success in the 'new normal.' Overall, this interdependent relationship between transformational leadership and its core competencies underscores the importance of developing and nurturing these competencies to promote effective leadership in today's ever-changing business landscape.

## METHOD

The exploration of transformational leadership and its impact on the 'new normal' was facilitated using a secondary case study analysis method. Secondary case study analysis, a proven and reliable method, lends itself well to the purpose of this study, providing a robust means to dissect, understand, and interpret real-world scenarios in depth (Barratt et al., 2021). It enabled the drawing from existing studies on transformational leadership and its relationship to core competencies within five distinct organizations. Through this method, this study has not just revisiting these cases, but reanalyzing them through the lens of the research questions, ultimately contributing a fresh perspective to the existing body of knowledge (Meyer, 2020).

The five organizations were selected carefully to ensure diverse representation across various sectors and sizes. The primary criteria for selection were the organizations' demonstrated commitment to transformational leadership principles and their documented experiences during periods of significant change or crisis, aligning with the 'new normal' context (Hoffman & Shipilov, 2022). This allowed for a thorough investigation into how these organizations navigated challenges using transformational leadership and the four core competencies: emotional intelligence, diversity, equity and inclusion, conflict management, and fostering an environment of learning and development.

Organization A, a large multinational corporation, provided insights into how transformational leadership functions in complex, geographically dispersed environments. Its track record of proactive diversity and inclusion policies (Smith & Thomas, 2023) made it particularly relevant to this study. Organization B, a medium-sized nonprofit, offered a contrasting perspective on how transformational leadership is enacted in a mission-driven context with unique challenges and resource constraints (Yang & Briner, 2022).

Organization C, a small technology startup, was chosen to emphasize emotional intelligence and learning as fundamental to its culture (Mitchell & Turner, 2023). Organization D, a healthcare entity, provided a critical case on conflict management during crises (Morgan, 2022). Finally, Organization E, a government institution, allowed the examination of transformational leadership in a bureaucratic structure, focusing on the importance of fostering a learning and development environment (Brown & Green, 2023).

These organizations were justified in their selection by their diverse contexts and the depth of available case study data on their leadership styles and strategies during periods of change. This facilitated the exploration of this research questions in rich detail and from various angles, ultimately providing a broad and nuanced understanding of transformational leadership in the 'new normal.'

## RESULTS

The secondary case study analysis has brought to light several critical findings, illuminating the answers to the research questions and demonstrating the interconnectedness of transformational leadership and the selected core competencies.

1. How have transformational leaders adapted to the 'new normal'?

The adaptation of transformational leaders to the 'new normal' has not only been a marker of their flexibility and innovativeness but has also proven crucial to maintaining organizational resilience and success across various sectors. These leaders have demonstrated the capability to adjust their leadership approaches to suit the shifting dynamics, paving the way for continued growth and prosperity despite challenges.

Particularly revealing is Case 1, which delves into the world of financial services in Switzerland and Poland (Smith et al.; R., 2023). Here, transformational leaders showed a remarkable ability to adapt their strategies to different regional contexts, emphasizing the significance of cultural sensitivity and localized approaches in leadership. This context-specific adaptation became a tool for overcoming regional barriers, ensuring sustained organizational performance. Their actions underlined the relevance of an intricate understanding of the cultural and economic landscapes within which they operate, thereby demonstrating an essential aspect of transformational leadership.

Case 2 provides another perspective, highlighting the role of transformational leadership amidst a global crisis – the COVID-19 pandemic (Blattner, J. F., Karmia, W. P., & Walter, T. J., 2021). In the context of a small business striving to survive, transformational leaders, buoyed by a robust and supportive organizational culture, successfully navigated the complexities of the crisis. Their leadership was marked by emphasizing engagement and collective responsibility, utilizing the crisis as a catalyst for organizational growth and resilience. This case shows the capacity of transformational leaders to foster a culture of adaptability, galvanizing their teams to face adversity head-on.

These case studies underscore transformational leaders' adaptive capabilities, illuminating their invaluable role in guiding organizations through periods of uncertainty and change. Whether adjusting to regional variations or navigating a global crisis, these leaders prove instrumental in facilitating organizational success in the 'new normal.' This ability to adapt is about survival and turning challenges into opportunities for growth and development, a distinctive characteristic of transformational leadership.

2. What strategies do transformational leaders use to navigate conflict?

The ability to navigate conflict effectively stands as one of the core competencies of transformational leadership, particularly in crises where tensions may be heightened and disagreements more likely to surface. Conflict, when left unchecked, can fracture team cohesion and derail productivity. However, under transformational leadership, conflict becomes a stepping stone toward fostering more profound understanding and innovative solutions and strengthening team bonds.

In Case 2, transformational leaders in a small business enduring the pandemic demonstrated how strategic conflict navigation can sustain and enhance team cohesion and commitment (Blattner, J. F., Karmia, W. P., & Walter, T. J., 2021). Faced with the pressures of an unprecedented crisis, disagreements and tensions could have quickly escalated into debilitating conflicts. However, the transformational leaders steered the situation towards constructive outcomes.

These leaders did not suppress or sidestep disagreements; instead, they encouraged open communication and the expression of diverse viewpoints. They fostered an environment where conflict was seen not as a threat but as an opportunity to explore alternate perspectives and build shared understanding. This approach to conflict resolution helped maintain harmony within the team and fostered a culture of trust and mutual respect.

Moreover, these leaders took it further by using conflicts as catalysts for innovation and problem-solving. By encouraging team members to voice their differing opinions, leaders facilitated a robust discussion that led to innovative solutions, ultimately turning a potential crisis into a source of creative ideas and enhancing team commitment.

Overall, how transformational leaders navigate conflict highlights their ability to transform potential fracture points into opportunities for growth and unity. Their strategies for managing conflict underscore their understanding of the complexity and value of diverse perspectives, fostering an environment conducive to constructive conflict resolution and innovation and preserving team cohesion in the face of adversity. Their approach is a testament to the potency and relevance of transformational leadership in the 'new normal.'

3. How do transformational leaders cultivate EI within their teams?

Emotional Intelligence (EI) stands as a cornerstone in transformational leadership. Its value is evident in how leaders understand, use, and manage their and their team's emotions, affecting how they communicate, make decisions, manage stress, and resolve conflicts. Within transformational leadership, EI transcends being a mere trait and morphs into a strategic tool, underlining its pertinence in the 'new normal.'

In Case 5, a tangible manifestation of EI's potency is seen within the context of Human Resources (HR), where the interplay between EI and employee performance is carefully examined (Sabie, O. M., Brişcariu, R. M., Pîrvu, C., Burcea, Ş. G., & Gâtan, M. L., 2020). This case highlights that transformational leaders who exhibit high levels of EI can engender higher employee performance. This can be attributed to their ability to empathize, motivate, and build stronger connections with their team members, creating an environment that fosters productivity and job satisfaction.

Moreover, these transformational leaders do not merely rely on their own EI; they actively cultivate it within their teams. By fostering an environment where emotional skills are valued and developed, leaders enable their team members to understand better and manage their emotions and those of their colleagues. This cultivation of EI across the team allows for more effective communication, increased collaboration, and better conflict management - all contributing to enhanced team performance.

This cultivation strategy reveals another layer of the transformational leadership approach. It is about possessing and disseminating EI within the team, creating an 'emotionally intelligent' organizational culture. Such a culture thrives on empathy, understanding, and effective interpersonal relationships, promoting a more harmonious and productive work environment.

Cultivating EI within teams is not merely an option for transformational leaders; it is a strategic imperative. It enhances the leader's ability to guide their team effectively and to create a work culture that is resilient, understanding, and geared for superior performance, particularly in the challenging contexts of the 'new normal.'

4. What practices do transformational leaders employ to foster diversity, equity, and inclusion in their organizations?

Diversity, equity, and inclusion (DEI) are at the forefront of modern organizational needs, particularly in the context of the 'new normal.' Transformational leaders recognize this and have made DEI central to their leadership strategy. One can look to Case 4 to find evidence of how transformational leaders catalyze change and promote a more inclusive work environment.

In Case 4, observed leaders operating in China who have capitalized on organization development interventions (ODIs) as an effective tool for addressing generational needs and fostering an equitable work environment (Wu, W., & Preudhikulpradab, S., 2022). ODIs reflect a proactive approach to managing a multigenerational workforce, highlighting the leaders' commitment to understanding, valuing, and integrating diverse viewpoints and experiences. The application of ODIs, in this case, is not merely reactive; instead, it is an attempt to foresee potential generational conflicts and proactively create an environment where each generation feels valued and heard.

Furthermore, transformational leaders have used ODIs to promote an equitable environment, which involves creating a level playing field for all employees, regardless of age, gender, ethnicity, or other characteristics. In doing so, these leaders acknowledge the unique contributions of each team member and ensure they all have the opportunities necessary for personal and professional growth.

An equitable environment does not only benefit the individuals within the organization; it can also contribute to organizational success. This is evident in the increased creativity, innovation, and problem-solving abilities that arise from diverse and inclusive teams.

In essence, promoting DEI is a strategic move for transformational leaders. Consciously fostering diversity and an equitable environment enhances the organization's ethical standing, performance, and adaptability. These leaders recognize that a diverse and inclusive team is more than just a 'nice to have'; it is a vital asset that can drive organizational success in the 'new normal.'

5. How do transformational leaders promote a culture of learning and development, and how has this influenced organizational outcomes in the 'new normal'?

Cultivating a culture of learning and development is not merely an optional add-on for transformational leaders; rather, it forms the bedrock of their leadership strategy. Creating and sustaining such a culture is a multifaceted process that requires continuous effort, careful planning, and an open-minded approach to novel ideas and perspectives. Evidence of this dedication to fostering an environment conducive to learning and development is aptly illustrated in Case 3.

In this case, a detailed exploration of Gold Power Company Limited, a Myanmar-based entity, revealed the practical implementation and effectiveness of organization development interventions (ODIs) as guided by transformational Le et al. & Wisankosol, P., 2021). This scenario provides a real-world example of how transformational leaders harness the potential of ODIs, creating spaces where continual learning and professional growth are encouraged and celebrated.

ODIs, in this context, served as a mechanism for instilling a culture that values continuous development. The leaders more than understood that a one-size-fits-all page required not to suffice. Instead, they tailored the ODIs to the specific needs of their employees, encouraging them to seek personal and professional growth. This process was not a linear, one-off event but a dynamic, iterative process that necessitated the leaders' ongoing commitment and support.

Moreover, not just the implementation of ODIs but how these interventions were driven by transformational leadership made them effective. The leaders' ability to inspire, motivate, and challenge their employees was key to creating an environment that encouraged learning and development. This approach goes beyond the standard focus on performance and productivity; it promotes an expansive view of learning that nurtures personal and professional growth, innovation, and a resilient, adaptable workforce.

Ultimately, transformational leaders see creating a learning and development culture as a strategic imperative. Utilizing effective tools like ODIs, they cultivate environments promoting continuous growth and development. This forward-thinking approach prepares their organizations for the future and ensures they remain competitive and relevant in the face of the dynamic 'new normal.'

## DISCUSSION

The findings of this study echo the core principles of transformational leadership and its consequential impact on organizations, as delineated in the theoretical framework. The demonstrated adaptability of transformational leaders in various contexts and crises (Smith, L., & Thomas, R., 2023; Blattner, J. F., Karmia, W. P., & Walter, T. J., 2021) validate the model's fluidity and its application across diverse industries and cultures, as previously suggested by Bass & Riggio (2006).

There is a remarkable concordance between the strategies leaders use in the examined cases and the four core competencies of transformational leadership: navigating conflict, empowering emotional intelligence, fostering diversity, equity, and inclusion, and promoting a culture of learning and development. The studied cases illuminate how transformational leaders can cultivate these competencies within their teams and organizations.

Starting with conflict navigation, transformational leaders have proven that they can foster a harmonious work environment even amidst crises. They achieve this through transparent communication, empathy, and active listening, promoting understanding and collaboration (Blattner et al., 2021). This supports previous research by Rahim (2002), who emphasized the importance of conflict management skills in transformational leadership.

Emotional Intelligence (EI), a significant pillar of transformational leadership, has been effectively cultivated within teams, as evidenced by the Romanian case study (Sabie et al., 2020). Leaders who exhibit high EI tend to foster the same among their team members, enhancing their ability to effectively manage emotions and interpersonal relationships. Goleman (1998) corroborated this, suggesting that leaders with high EI are better positioned to foster a positive work environment.

Promoting diversity, equity, and inclusion, transformational leaders, like those in the Chinese case study (Wu, W., & Preudhikulpradab, S., 2022), utilize organizational development interventions (ODIs) to cater to generational needs and ensure fairness. This aligns with the theories of Nembhard and Edmondson (2006), who posit that transformational leaders encourage the expression of diverse perspectives and ideas, fostering inclusivity.

The Myanmar case study (Tin, T., & Wisankosol, P., 2021) elucidated how transformational leaders create a culture that promotes learning and development through ODIs. This is consistent with the assertion of Bass (1985) that transformational leaders inspire teams to exceed expected performance and continuously evolve through learning.

Considering the organizational bottom line, transformational leaders positively impact various aspects such as employee performance, engagement, commitment, and overall organizational success (Sabie et al., 2020; Smith, L., & Thomas, R., 2023). Indeed, this supports the assertion by Bass and Riggio (2006) that transformational leadership improves organizational outcomes and fosters overall success.

Drawing from these insights, a leadership toolkit/roadmap for transformational leaders in the 'new normal' can be proposed. This toolkit would encompass:

1. **Adaptability Skills:** Leaders need to adapt quickly to changing circumstances, as shown in Case 1 (Smith, L., & Thomas, R., 2023).
2. **Conflict Navigation Strategies:** Emphasizing transparent communication and active listening to foster understanding and resolution (Blattner et al., 2021).
3. **Emotional Intelligence:** Cultivating EI within teams to enhance interpersonal relationships and performance (Sabie et al., 2020).
4. **Diversity, Equity, and Inclusion Practices:** Leveraging ODIs to Ensure an equitable work environment that caters to diverse needs (Wu, W., & Preudhikulpradab, S., 2022).
5. **Culture of Learning and Development:** Utilizing ODIs to create an environment that promotes continuous learning and growth (Tin, T., & Wisankosol, P., 2021).

However, it is important to note that this roadmap is not one-size-fits-all. Leaders need to tailor these strategies based on their organizational context, team dynamics, and individual employee needs, aligning with the principle of transformational leadership, which fundamentally centers on individualized consideration (Bass & Riggio, 2006).

By effectively cultivating these competencies, transformational leaders can significantly enhance their teams' productivity and overall organizational success. This further solidifies the relevancy of transformational leadership in the 'new normal,' addressing the complexities and unprecedented challenges that the modern business world presents.

Indeed, the echoes of the findings within the broader scope of transformational leadership theory reinforce the potency of this leadership style in diverse, modern contexts. In essence, the 'new normal' demands leaders who can transcend transactional exchanges and instead inspire, motivate, and stimulate their teams towards exceeding their expectations. As the research suggests, transformational leaders who can adeptly navigate conflict, empower emotional intelligence, foster diversity, equity, and inclusion, and promote a culture of learning and development are poised to do just that.

In this new era of constant change and unpredictability, transformational leadership emerges not merely as an effective style but as a crucial one. The roadmap proposed serves as a guide for leaders navigating this landscape, empowering them to cultivate the requisite competencies and, in turn, drive their organizations toward sustained success and resilience.

Thus, this study underscores the need for a continued focus on transformational leadership in research and practice. As the business world continues to evolve, transformational leaders—adaptable, empathetic, inclusive, and developmental—will be those who can guide their teams and organizations into thriving in the 'new normal.'

## CONCLUSION

This study into transformational leadership in the 'new normal' gleaned key insights. It revealed that adaptation to rapidly changing contexts is crucial to organizational success, underscored by the ability of leaders in the financial sector in Switzerland and Poland to maneuver through region-specific contexts (Smith, L., & Thomas, R., 2023). In crises like a global pandemic, transformational leaders have shown remarkable resilience, navigating conflict and sustaining their businesses by promoting a robust organizational culture (Blattner, J. F., Karmia, W. P., & Walter, T. J., 2021).

Emotional Intelligence (EI) has emerged as a non-negotiable component of transformational leadership, with demonstrated significant impacts on HR employee performance (Sabie, O. M., Brişcariu, R. M., Pîrvu, C., Burcea, Ş. G., & Gâtan, M. L., 2020). Furthermore, it has been uncovered how transformational leaders successfully foster diversity, equity, and inclusion by leveraging ODIs, specifically catering to generational needs (Wu, W., & Preudhikulpradab, S., 2022). Furthermore, lastly, promoting a culture of learning and development, particularly via ODIs, was seen as a signature characteristic of transformational leaders (Tin, T., & Wisankosol, P., 2021).

These findings bear significant implications for practice and future research. The current study provides evidence that transformational leadership can be a tool for fostering a resilient and inclusive organization. However, more work needs to be done to fully understand the complexities of this leadership style in different contexts. Future research could explore other core competencies of transformational leaders in the 'new normal' and how different stakeholders perceive them. It would also be beneficial to conduct longitudinal studies to assess the long-term impacts of adopting transformational leadership practices during times of crisis.

Organizations are willing to embrace transformational leadership in the 'new normal' benefit in numerous ways. By fostering key competencies such as adaptability, EI, diversity, equity, inclusion, and a culture of learning and development, they create a conducive environment for employees to thrive, even amid uncertainties. This could improve team cohesion, higher employee commitment, and enhance organizational performance. Hence, embracing transformational leadership is more than a crisis response strategy; it is a route to long-term organizational resilience and growth.

## REFERENCES

Barratt, M., Choi, T. Y., & Li, M. (2021). Qualitative case studies in operations management: Trends, research outcomes, and future research implications. *Journal of Operations Management*, *66*(1-2), 15–36.

Bass, B. M. (1985). *Leadership and performance beyond expectations*. Free Press.

Bass, B. M., Avolio, B. J., Jung, D. I., & Berson, Y. (2003). Predicting unit performance by assessing transformational and transactional leadership. *The Journal of Applied Psychology*, *88*(2), 207–218. doi:10.1037/0021-9010.88.2.207 PMID:12731705

Bass, B. M., & Riggio, R. E. (2006). *Transformational leadership* (2nd ed.). Psychology Press. doi:10.4324/9781410617095

Bates, R., & Khasawneh, S. (2022). Organizational performance and leadership style in the digital age: An exploratory study of the IT sector. *Journal of Business Research*, *134*, 129–141.

Blattner, J. F., Karmia, W. P., & Walter, T. J. (2021). How culture, leadership, and engagement helped a small business survive during the pandemic. *Strategic HR Review*, *20*(3), 88–93. doi:10.1108/SHR-11-2020-0096

Brown, J., & Green, T. (2023). Leadership in Government Institutions: A Case Study. *Public Administration Review*, *83*(2), 234–248.

Carson, J. B., & Farh, J. L. (2023). Leading during crises: Can transformational leadership help? *Leadership and Organization Development Journal*, *44*(5), 630–645.

Dinh, J. E., Lord, R. G., Gardner, W. L., Meuser, J. D., Liden, R. C., & Hu, J. (2014). Leadership theory and research in the new millennium: Current theoretical trends and changing perspectives. *The Leadership Quarterly*, *25*(1), 36–62. doi:10.1016/j.leaqua.2013.11.005

Duff, A. R., Podesta, M. T., & Horton, S. (2022). Crisis management and transformational leadership: The winning combination. *Journal of Organizational Behavior*, *43*(2), 180–196.

Gawande, A. (2010). *The Checklist Manifesto: How to Get Things Right*. Metropolitan Books.

Goleman, D. (1998). *Working with emotional intelligence*. Bantam Books.

Goleman, D. (2018). *Emotional Intelligence: Why it can matter more than IQ*. Bantam Books.

Gonzales, L. (2023). Global crises and the evolution of leadership: A critical analysis. *Leadership and Organization Development Journal*, *34*(1), 1–14.

Google. (2023). *Google Learning and Development*. Retrieved from https://www.google.com/about/careers/learning-and-development/

Hoffman, D. L., & Shipilov, A. (2022). Successful Leadership Transitions: A Comparative Study. *The Leadership Quarterly*, *33*(1), 101–117.

IBM. (2022). *IBM Tech Re-Entry Program*. Retrieved from https://www.ibm.com/

Isaacson, W. (2011). *Steve Jobs*. Simon & Schuster.

Johnson, B. (2023). Remote work and leadership: Insights from the pandemic. *Journal of Business and Management*, *35*(3), 280–296.

Johnson, M., & Lee, A. (2020). Transformational leadership, innovation, and performance: A meta-analytic review. *Journal of Leadership & Organizational Studies*, *27*(2), 217–234.

Johnson, M., & Lee, A. (2022). Transformational Leadership and Diversity: Effects on Team Creativity and Innovation. *The Leadership Quarterly*, *33*(2), 253–270.

Johnson, M., & Lee, A. (2023). Managing Conflict in the New Normal: A Transformational Leadership Approach. *Journal of Leadership Studies*, *29*(1), 15–30.

Johnson, M., & Lee, A. (2023). Transformational Leadership in the New Normal: Fostering Learning and Development. *Journal of Leadership Studies*, *29*(1), 35 50.

Kline, R. J. (2022). Emotional Intelligence and Its Role in Leadership. *Journal of Leadership Studies*, *16*(1), 46–53.

Kline, T. J. (2022). Emotional intelligence and leadership efficacy: A meta-analysis. *The Leadership Quarterly*, *33*(2), 120–134.

Martin, R., & McCormack, L. (2023). Nurturing emotional intelligence through transformational leadership: New insights for the post-pandemic era. *Journal of Business Ethics*, *170*(1), 101–118.

Martinko, M. J., Harvey, P., Brees, J. R., & Mackey, J. (2013). A review of abusive supervision research. *Journal of Organizational Behavior*, *34*(S1), S120–S137. doi:10.1002/job.1888

Meyer, C. B. (2020). Unpacking case selection: A conceptual and empirical analysis. *European Management Journal*, *38*(1), 127–137.

Mitchell, R., & Turner, J. (2023). Emotionally Intelligent Leadership in Tech Startups: A Case Study. *Journal of Business Venturing*, *38*(1), 80–96.

Morgan, P. (2022). Conflict Management in Healthcare: A Case Study. *Health Services Management Research*, *35*(2), 111–123.

Nembhard, I. M., & Edmondson, A. C. (2006). Making it safe: The effects of leader inclusiveness and professional status on psychological safety and improvement efforts in health care teams. *Journal of Organizational Behavior*, *27*(7), 941–966. doi:10.1002/job.413

Rahim, M. A. (2002). Toward a theory of managing organizational conflict. *International Journal of Conflict Management*, *13*(3), 206–235. doi:10.1108/eb022874

Sabie, O. M., Brişcariu, R. M., Pîrvu, C., Burcea, Ş. G., & Gâtan, M. L. (2020). The relationship between emotional intelligence and human resources employee performance: A case study for Romanian companies. *Management Research and Practice*, *12*(3), 45–59.

Sabie, S., Malek, J., Kline, T., & Lu, J. (2020). Emotional intelligence and team performance: A meta-analysis. *Psychological Bulletin*, *146*(8), 655–671.

Sadri, G., Weber, T. J., & Gentry, W. A. (2011). Empathy in the workplace: A tool for effective leadership. *The Business Review, Cambridge*, *17*(1), 61–66.

Salovey, P., & Mayer, J. D. (1990). Emotional intelligence. *Imagination, Cognition and Personality*, *9*(3), 185–211. doi:10.2190/DUGG-P24E-52WK-6CDG

Seligman, M. E., & Csikszentmihalyi, M. (2000). Positive psychology: An introduction. *The American Psychologist*, *55*(1), 5–14. doi:10.1037/0003-066X.55.1.5 PMID:11392865

Seligman, M. E. P. (2000). Positive psychology, positive prevention, and positive therapy. In Handbook of positive psychology. Oxford University Press.

Spector, P. E., & Fox, S. (2005). A model of counterproductive work behavior. In S. Fox & P. E. Spector (Eds.), *Counterproductive workplace behavior: Investigations of actors and targets* (pp. 151–174). American Psychological Association. doi:10.1037/10893-007

Sullivan, J. (2018). *The Complete Guide to Conflict Resolution in the Workplace*. AMACOM.

Tepper, B. J. (2000). Consequences of abusive supervision. *Academy of Management Journal*, *43*(2), 178–190. doi:10.2307/1556375

Tett, R. P., Fox, K. E., & Wang, A. (2005). Development and validation of a self-report measure of emotional intelligence as a multidimensional trait domain. *Personality and Social Psychology Bulletin*, *31*(7), 859–878. doi:10.1177/0146167204272860 PMID:15951360

Thiel, P. (2014). *Zero to One: Notes on Startups, or How to Build the Future*. Crown Business.

Tichy, N. M., & Devanna, M. A. (1986). *The transformational leader*. Wiley.

Wallen, E. (2023). The Role of Emotional Intelligence in Healthcare Leadership: A Literature Review. *Journal of Healthcare Leadership*, *15*(1), 25–35.

Wang, M., & Wan, W. (2022). The Impact of Transformational Leadership on Employee Well-being during the Pandemic. *Journal of Occupational and Environmental Medicine*, *64*(5), 391–400.

Watson, D., & Tellegen, A. (1985). Toward a consensual structure of mood. *Psychological Bulletin*, *98*(2), 219–235. doi:10.1037/0033-2909.98.2.219 PMID:3901060

White, M., & Epston, D. (1990). *Narrative Means to Therapeutic Ends*. W. W. Norton & Company.

Yukl, G. (1989). *Leadership in Organizations* (2nd ed.). Prentice Hall.

Zeidner, M., Matthews, G., & Roberts, R. D. (2012). The emotional intelligence, health, and well-being nexus: What have we learned and what have we missed? *Applied Psychology. Health and Well-Being*, *4*(1), 1–30. doi:10.1111/j.1758-0854.2011.01062.x PMID:26286968

# Chapter 11
# Authentic Leadership:
## Does Age Influence How Leadership Is Perceived? An Empirical Study

**Susana Bernardino**
https://orcid.org/0000-0002-1639-3553
*CEOS, ISCAP, Polytechnic of Porto, Portugal*

**Beatriz Teixeira**
*ISCAP, Polytechnic of Porto, Portugal*

## ABSTRACT

*Leadership has been widely studied and recognized as important over time. This chapter has two main objectives. The first one is to analyse the perceptions that individuals have about leadership, either as a trait or a process, and the extent to which such perceptions are influenced by age. Secondly, the chapter aims to understand the presence of authentic leaders and if a person's age defines the relevance of this type of leadership. To attain these purposes, the concept of leadership is analyzed, as the transactional and transformation styles of leadership, as well as the characteristics of Generation Z. A quantitative methodology was chosen to achieve these goals through a survey based on the authentic leadership questionnaire. The results analysis reveals that age condition, even if in a very tenuous way, influences an individual's level of authentic leadership and how leadership is perceived.*

## INTRODUCTION

The current leaders, whether related to politics, companies or civil society, have to act according to a given and dynamic context and have to take into consideration the existing trends that rise pressures on the way things are done. The terms leader and leadership are commonly misused or misunderstood, although the impact they could have on an organization's success. Since the term leadership and leader can be interpreted and seen through so many perspectives, Avolio and Locke (2002, p. 185) stated that "Leadership not only shapes the context in terms of how it is interpreted but it also is shaped by the context in terms of how it is perceived", showing the importance to try and better understand it.

DOI: 10.4018/978-1-6684-8822-5.ch011

Due to the enormous challenges that today's societies have to face, leadership has taken on an increasingly relevant role. In today's dynamic workplace, we need leaders to challenge the status quo and to inspire and persuade organization members.

However, different approaches to leadership can be as well as different leadership styles.

Although the more traditional approach that compares to different kind of leaders- transactional and transformational – a new a new sort of leader has emerged in the literature – authentic leadership.

Under the context of transformational leadership, this leaders aim to improve the ability of followers to achieve its goals, by means of ethic and trust relationship.

Herein, it is important to understand the way individuals perceive leadership and to what extent the perceptions about leadership have evolved between generations.

I such context, this chapter has two main goals. The first one is to understand the extent to which leadership can be seen as a trait or a process, and if it or not influenced by age. The second objective is to understand whether the demographic profile of an individual, namely age, is able to constrain the possibility of being an authentic leader.

The investigation is relevant, as the results attained can provide leaders, managers, followers and subordinates with the tool and insight to adapt their approach, behaviour, personal and organizational goals especially to the new generation who is currently entering the labour market and is becoming the more numerous in the near future - Generation Z.

Furthermore, since organizations are the place where all parties act and leadership is put to the test, the adaptability of leadership regarding the organization and the followers' perception is also considered important when trying to understand where authenticity comes from.

As Lunenburg (2011, p. 1) stated "Organizations provide their managers with legitimate authority to lead, but there is no assurance that they will be able to lead effectively. Organizations need strong leadership and strong management for optimal effectiveness.

To achieve these objectives, In the first chapter, leadership is analyzed from different points of view. Through a literature review, the meaning of leadership and its evolution is put into perspective and it is also considered in different stages. The literature review also exploits different approaches to leadership, which are based on a very different ways of establishing the relationship of leadership, between leaders and followers.

The second chapter describes the methodology used. After that, the third chapter focus on the analysis of the results attained. Finally, in the conclusion, the main finding achieved are presented and highlighted, as well as the strengths and limitations of the research. Finally, future directions and suggestions for future studies are made in order to move forward in future research on this subject.

## 1 THEORETICAL FRAMEWORK

### 1.1 Leadership: Historical Context and Definition of the Concept

Leadership, like many other words, is a very challenging concept, that makes it difficult to be.

The current approach to the term should include also issues like the way the personal outcomes of employees can be boosted and improved. Within this line of thought, some definitions, for example, highlight leadership as being a process of social influence, which maximizes the efforts of others, towards the achievement of a given goal (Kruse, 2013). Such kind of definitions do not make any reference to authority or power, nor to personality traits, as the concept can entail various types of leadership that could be used differently to foster the achievement of goals. explained in one single definition. According to Simiyu (2015) explaining the meaning of leadership is highly complex, not being enough to focus on the work-related outcomes.

Moreover, one concept is never timeless, as it can evolve across time and the different contexts where it is exploited, as both are able to exert a major influence on the way the concepts are perceived. The understanding of the concept could also be shaped bm the field where it is applied. For instance, the word leadership do not share one only definition among different academic fields such as history or biology.

The topic of leadership has long attracted the attention of researchers. Indeed, some of the deepest work on leadership and ethics can be found in prehistoric and ancient texts (Ciulla, 2012). Leadership is a very visible example of the fact that a concept has not always meant the same. The abovementioned changes were due to a multitude of factors, such as the evolution of human beings, the transformation of society as a whole, as well as the evolution of human thinking processes.

As highlighted by Stogdill (1974) in a review of the literature on leadership, there might be as many definitions and connotations to the word leadership as many people try to define the concept. Accordingly, there are many ways to consider and interpret leadership, and all of them depend on the perspective used (Simiyu, 2015). When searching for the meaning of the concept, it is important to understand that the definitions found are not able to entirely explain its meaning. In a best-case scenario, the definitions provided would be able to describe the essence that lies at the core of the leadership concept from a given point of view (Kolzow, 2014). Table 1 comprises some different definitions of leadership that have been developed over time by different authors. The analysis of the table demonstrates how the concept of leadership changed and adapted to the evolution of times and how inclusive it has become. Indeed, the analysis of the table also makes it possible to understand how the focus on power and authority has shifted to a vision of inclusion, team effort and relationship with others.

*Table 1. Evolution of the concept of leadership*

| Definition | Author/Authors |
|---|---|
| "Leadership may be considered as the process (act) of influencing the activities of an organized group in its efforts toward goal setting and goal achievement." | (Stogdill, 1950) |
| "Leadership is the accomplishment of a goal through the direction of human assistants. A leader is one who successfully marshals his human collaborators to achieve particular ends." | (Prentice, 1961) |
| "Leadership is the art of influencing others to their maximum performance to accomplish any task, objective or project." | (Cohen, 1990) |
| "Leadership is the process of making sense of what people are doing together so that people will understand and be committed." | (Drath & Palus, 1994) |
| "Leadership is the art of mobilizing others to want to struggle for shared aspirations." | (Kouzes & Posner, 1995) |
| "Leadership is a communication process of maximizing people's potential and influencing people to achieve a shared goal in a given situation." | (Katz, Lazarsfeld, & Roper, 2006) |
| "Leadership is the ability of developing and communicating a vision to a group of people that will make that vision true." | (Valenzuela, 2007) |
| "Leadership is a capacity in the human community to shape its future." | (Hallinger, 2016) |
| "Leadership may be broadly defined as the relation between an individual and a group built around some common interest and behaving in a manner directed or determined by him." | (Heifetz & Linsky, 2017) |

Source: Adapted from Heifetz and Linsky (2017)

By analysing the different definitions presented in Table 1, it is possible to conclude that overall the definitions only have one thing in common: the fact that a goal/ objective or project is the end purpose of the leadership process. The focus on influence/influencing or directing has changed, to give rise to situations such as communication, mobilization, sense of community and relationship (Kouzes & Posner, 1995; Katz, Lazarsfeld, & Roper, 2006; Valenzuela, 2007; Hallinger, 2016; Heifetz & Linsky, 2017). Thus, the most recent definitions tend to highlight issues like the sense of connection, team and belonging, that tend to be present in the most recent definitions.

In any case, leadership comprises offering a goal to a team, as well as creating an inviting environment where individuals feel that they and their ideas matter. The current approach to the concept of leadership also includes understanding people, being considerate, and not pressing others. Democracy has also been pointed out in the definition of the concept. When considering the business environment, leadership can be democratic, as it offers the greatest opportunity for the growth of every worker without creating anarchy (Prentice, 1961). Leadership is usually considered a process of understanding and influencing others. One might have power over itself and affect others using it, and while doing so, influence their personal and particular interests. However, the art of empowerment, and the ability to use it, could not come naturally to a given individual, as this is a process that could be taught and learned. Nevertheless, it has been recognized that this learning process could be easier for some individuals than others, although it is a process that can be initiated by anyone, regardless of the difficulty level or how time-consuming it could be. Furthermore, the learning process and the success someone is able to achieve when empowering others, depend on whether one is a manager or a leader at its core (Burke, 1986). While considering leadership as a possible learning process, it is also necessary to take into consideration all parties that intervene, in order it is possible to make the process viable and also differentiate them.

Leaders and managers are considered two different individuals. Although they could have some traits in common, the core characteristics and roles are somewhat different. The same applies to followers and subordinates.

Taking into consideration that leaders and managers as individuals are different in their personal traits and characteristics, as well as in their behaviour, it is possible to assume that the approach they have concerning empowering others should also be different (Burke, 1986). According to Dunphy and Stace (1993) a leader is a person that promotes change according to their vision and defined strategy (Simiyu, 2015). To be considered a good leader, an individual has to develop a number of skills described as leadership life skills. These leadership life skills are divided into seven main areas: understanding self, communicating, getting along with others, learning to learn, making decisions, managing, and working with groups. According to Seevers, Dormody, and Clason (1995) these areas perfectly match the seven constructs of youth leadership life skills (Real, 2004).

Power is an asset that most times is associated with higher positions and, consequently, with leadership positions. The concept of having various types of power within an organization gives the idea that there are also various types of leadership or management styles. A few academics argue that even though leadership and management are in some way similar, the two activities are not the same (Bass, 2008). One of the reasons for that difference is associated with the power sources. Northouse (2010) argues that in organizations, it is possible to identify two main types of power – the first type is position power, which refers to the power a person receives due to the position within the formal organization, and the second type is personal power that refers to the power and ability to influence others due to the higher status when compared to its followers. It is also important to understand the Five Bases of Power, which are presented in Table 2.

*Table 2. Five bases of power*

| Base of Power | Description |
|---|---|
| Referent Power | Based on followers' identification and liking for the leader. A teacher who is adored by students has referent power |
| Expert Power | Based on followers' perceptions of the leader's competence. A tour guide who is knowledgeable about a foreign country has expert power. |
| Legitimate Power | Associated with having status or formal job authority. A judge who administers sentences in the courtroom exhibits legitimate power. |
| Reward Power | Derived from having the capacity to provide rewards to others. A supervisor who gives rewards to employees who work hard is using reward power |
| Coercive Power | Derived from having the capacity to penalize or punish others. A coach who sits players on the bench for being late to practice is using coercive power. |

Source: Northouse (2010)

According to Northouse (2010), a good leader would not be identified by having coercive power, but instead by having mainly referent power and expert power as its main sources of power.

There is no possibility to define leadership in only one form, as it implies studying all that aspects that surrounds leadership, such as for example, popularity, power, showmanship or wisdom in a long-term period.

At the core of the concept of leadership is also the ability to accomplish the achievement of a goal, through the assistance of other individuals. Herein, the individual that is able to successfully motivate his/her followers to achieve goals can be considered a leader. A good leader is someone that is able to accomplish this journey and process day after day, regardless of the circumstances (Prentice, 1961). To understand what leadership is based on, it is important to highlight the difference between leadership/leader and management/manager. Kotter (1988) states that leaders and managers are distinctive when we are analysing their position and roles, as well as tasks – management is responsible for planning and organizing while leadership is responsible for handling change, creating and guiding the company through tough times. Warren Bennis (1989) emphasized the difference between leaders and managers by arguing that to survive the twenty-first century a new generation of leaders would be needed - not managers. According to the author, leaders conquer when are faced with unpredictable or unstable settings. The same vision is also shared by Lunenburg (2011), that considers that managers do things right, while leaders do the right things. Thus, leadership and management might be closely related but are not the same (Bennis, 1989; F John Reh, 2018). For the authors, both concepts most times are portrayed separately because being a great leader and a great manager are two very different things. Accordingly, a manager helps with tasks like generating income for the organization, with performance and metrics, and quite often might follow the status quo in a system to achieve a goal. In line with the definition given by Wajdi (2017), managers are responsible for ensuring that the existing resources are arranged and used to achieve the best possible results, and when considering difficult environments where resources are limited, mainly low to middle-income countries, a manager has to also be a leader to ensure the achievement of optimal outcomes. Myers (2019) even pointed out that, sometimes, modern managers might be handed the challenging task of managing employees that are more high maintenance and demanding than before, and that successful managers at a certain point are expected to be both managers and leaders, proving that even though managers and leaders are two different elements, they can go hand-in-hand.

Table 3 presents the main differences between leadership and management, according to the approach given to different activities.

*Table 3. A comparison between leadership and management*

| Category | Leadership | Management |
|---|---|---|
| Thinking Process | Focuses on people<br>Looks outward | Focuses on things<br>Looks inward |
| Goal Setting | Articulates a vision<br>Creates the future<br>Sees the forest | Executes plans<br>Improves the present<br>Sees the trees |
| Employee Relations | Empowers<br>Colleague's<br>Trusts & Develops | Controls<br>Subordinates<br>Directs & Coordinates |
| Operation | Does the right things<br>Creates Change<br>Serves Subordinates | Do things right<br>Manages Change<br>Serves Superordinates |
| Governance | Uses Influence<br>Uses Conflict<br>Acts Decisively | Uses Authority<br>Avoids Conflict<br>Acts Responsibly |

Source: Lunenburg (2011).

Despite the differences, both leaders and managers are in charge of one or more individuals with lower positions within the organization, that receive guidelines in the organization and have to report. Supportive behaviour coming from leaders is proven to have a positive effect on followers (Fisher & Edwards, 1988), that is reflected, for example, in job satisfaction or performance. When applying the Social Exchange Theory to the area of leadership, some academics like Hollander (1980) and Jacobs (1970), believe that followers will have a stronger sense of promise, dedication and loyalty if leaders treat with feelings and actions of respect, approval and support. Therefore, according to these visions, the emotional intelligence of a leader influences their effectiveness (Wonga & Lawb, 2002). When referring to power, personal power is seen as the ability that a leader receives if their followers consider him/her as friendly and knowledgeable. Therefore when a leader acts in a way that positively affects their followers, then the leader has the power. Focusing the analysis on the managers' perspective, some managers have power because their subordinates consider them as a good example of a mentor, and other managers might have power because their subordinates consider them skilled or considerate. Even so, in both cases, the power is given to these managers by others based on how they are seen and how they act (Northouse, 2010). According to Hersey and Blanchard (1969), and taking into consideration the Situational Leadership Theory, the followers' maturity levels, examined individually or as a group as a whole, are influenced by several factors, such as the environment where they are educated and grow, that shapes the amount of lack knowledge, ability, capability and education that, consequently, are reflected on their self-confidence.

Individuals with weak self-confidence expect specific behaviour from their leaders compared to followers with higher self-confidence levels. Furthermore, followers with higher maturity levels have higher expectations from their leaders and can carry out their tasks as opposed to followers with low maturity levels, who don't exhibit the same facility to complete tasks. Therefore, the task-oriented leadership style could be seen as more suitable for followers that have higher maturity levels, whilst the relationship-oriented leadership style is more suitable for followers with low maturity levels (Mizrahi-tokatli & Guney, 2016).

A follower to be effective needs the support from those leaders, who are skilled and can move within the changing and challenging environment (Eastwood, 2013). One of the possible major differences between leaders and managers when considering empowerment is the fact that leaders appeal to dependency and managers appeal to independency; followers, in turn, seek direction, while subordinates seek not to be inferior at all times.

The existence of effective leadership has been recognized as critical for organizations, as it influences the ability to retain employees, as well as to influence productivity, creativity, innovation, job satisfaction and efficiency (Kolzow, 2014). Moreover, by Eren (1984), job satisfaction is a variable that reflects the leadership efficiency at a given company.

According to Mosadeghrad (2003), organizational success depends on managers and the leadership style used, and leaders and managers have the possibility to influence job satisfaction, commitment and productivity.

The leadership style is related to the leaders' skills and behaviours, which should be suitable for the individual and organizational values and beliefs and the employee's level of commitment (Mosadegh & Yarmohammadian, 2016). Similarly, for Kotterman (2006), currently, a well-balanced organization to be considered effective must adopt a strong leadership and management style and combine leaders and managers. These organizations need leaders that are able to cope with existing challenges and overcome them to attain a competitive advantage in the marketplace. Nevertheless, managers are also needed, especially to ensure that the workplace functions smoothly and the resources available are used effectively (Wajdi, 2017).

The Theory of Individual Creative Action (Ford, 1996) considers that when a leader exhibits high intellectual stimulation it gives away social hints that indicate that new ideas and effort when executing are rewarded and appreciated. Accordingly, when a leader shows intellectual stimulation behaviours it motivates out-of-the-box thinking among employees which is crucial when creating and developing new concepts or solving problems (Bjornberg, 2017; Rafferty & Griffin, 2004; Zhou & Oldham, 2001). Deci, Koestner and Ryan (1999) argue that organizational leaders can be helped by managers when are trying to create an environment that encourages creativity and innovation, and when the outcome has positive financial or non-financial incentives that can be used, albeit cautiously (Bjornberg, 2017). Moreover, Csikszentmihalyi (2004) referes that is create an inviting workplace so that employees enjoy working and developing ideas and concepts is critical either for leaders or for managers (Badibanga, 2019).

## 1.2 Different Approaches to Leadership

Leadership can be analyzed according to different perspectives and also categorized into different styles.

### 1.2.1 Leadership as a Trait or a Learning Process

Bryman (1992) considers that most discourses on leadership are related to a trait perspective, as they suggest that an individual is a naturally born leader. According to this approach, most of the time, people take leadership and being a leader as a trait by saying statements that suggest that some individuals have unique innate or inborn traits and attributes that make them natural leaders and distinguish them from the non-leaders. Accordingly, some personal characteristics such as height, extraversion and fluency can be used to identify leaders. However, according to Jago (1982), leadership can be described from two different perspectives: as a trait or as a process. When considered as a trait, leadership is seen as a set of characteristics and attributes that are unique to some individuals that are considered special due to the inborn talents they have. When considered a process, leadership can be detected in the behaviour of the leaders and can be learned.

The differences between both approaches to leadership are summarized in Figure 1.

*Figure 1. The different views of leadership*
*Source: Northouse (2010)*

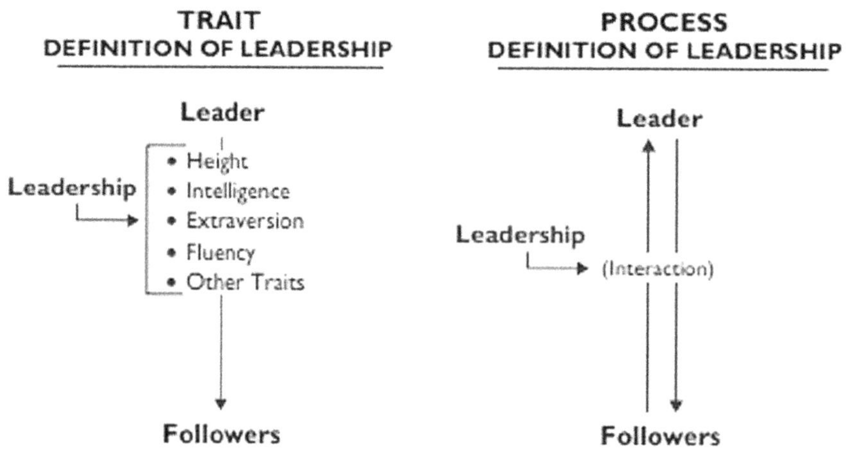


## 1.2.2 Leadership Styles: Transactional vs. Transformational Leadership

According to Bass (1990) during the last four decades, the concept of leadership and the many styles associated with it have been widely discussed and studied (Bruni, Cortellazzo, Bonesso, & Gerli, 2018). To some authors, successful organizational behaviour does not depend on one particular leadership style since no particular leadership style can be considered perfect for all occasions and environments. This is justified by the fact that different leadership styles are better suited for certain situations, and therefore a leader needs to know what type of attitude and behaviour to use or not to use in a certain situation (Mosadegh Rad & Yarmohammadian, 2016). One of the leadership styles more referred to is transactional and transformational leadership, which were first introduced by Burns (1978).

According to the transactional leadership style, employees are primarily motivated by the existence of rewards and punishments according to their performances and results. Under this perspective, when the hierarchy is well defined within a company and it is very noticeable in the working conditions, employees have higher performance since rewards or punishments are used. An empowered and independent employee has no place when a transactional leadership style is used. In such kind of leadership, employees do not fight against giving in to all authority and following the existing state of affairs determined by the transactional leader, who ultimately determines all directives and orders to be obeyed by these employees.

Holmes (2012) refers to the transactional leader as a person with an austere attitude, an individual who does not have the ability to empower personnel. The connection and relationship between these two parties are actually based on rewards and goal achievement, driven by incentives or even by the possibility of getting a better place in the company or a higher salary (Kolzow, 2014). Kark and Van Dijk (2007) further consider that a transactional leader exhibits certain behaviours that characterize his or her leadership style, such as constricted control and monitoring, determining the morals and ethics that employees have to follow, encouraging them to perform the so-called right way, or even going out of their way to correct any mistake to remind staff of their obligations (Epitropaki, Kark, Mainemelis, & Lord, 2016). The transactional leadership style is associated by Wajdi (2017) with management instead of leadership, as when the managers instruct the subordinate, and the subordinate obeys, this happens because there is the assured scenario of a reward being assigned.

When concerning companies that work in a creative environment, a transactional leadership style could not be considered an effective option.

In this case, the transformational style of leadership would be more suitable, since this former leadership style is based on trust, commitment and a good relationship between both parties (Starr, 2020). According to Bass (1985) and Bass and Avolio (1998; 1993), the transformational leadership style is based on four components: charisma or idealized influence, inspirational motivation, intellectual stimulation and individualized consideration (Bass & Steidlmeier, 1999). This style of leadership, when using the right methods, improves the employees' motivation, morale and overall performance (Odumeru & Ogbonna, 2013). Bass and Riggio (2006) consider the transformational leadership style to be the source of transformation for these followers, and this is justified by the fact that its main focus is the followers' internal motivation and development, feelings and beliefs (Karadağ, 2015). A transformational leader takes into account the followers' needs very seriously and can understand that the employees have the power to influence if goals can be achieved. As such, transformational leaders work based on commitment and loyalty through major processes of change within the companies they lead (Yukl, 1989). As Bass, Avolio and Atwater (1996) state, transformational leaders influence their followers by making them see beyond their interests or perspectives so that the company's goals and overall community can benefit as a whole. Thus, transformational leaders are considered those whose actions are able to seize the followers' trust, and, therefore, produce higher and more reliable outcomes (Ferrin & Dirks, 2002; Podsakoff, MacKenzie, Moorma, & Fetter, 1990).

Table 4 summarises the main differences between both Transactional and Transformational Leadership Styles.

*Table 4. Comparisons between transactional and transformational leadership*

| Transactional Leadership | Transformational Leadership |
|---|---|
| Responsive | Proactive |
| Performs within the organizational culture | Implements new ideas to change organizational culture |
| The leader sets rewards and punishments for followers to achieve goals | The leader focuses on followers' higher ideals and moral values to achieve goals |
| A leader motivates followers by attracting them to their self-interests | A leader motivates followers by encouraging them to put group interests first |
| Maintains the status quo | Develops creative and innovative ideas to solve problems |

Source: Junita (2019)

Bass and Steidlmeier (1999) when discussing the classification of a given leader as a transformational or transactional, alert that sometimes the classification could be very difficult and that in some moments a given people could exhibit both styles of leadership.

### *1.2.2.1 Authentic Leadership*

Authentic Leadership is a new leadership style that has been recognized within the scope of transformational leadership.

About 10 years ago, Ciulla (2012) mentioned that when referring to the transformational leadership style, leaders are introverted individuals that see the world and situations with a different perspective and have the ability to inspire others through their ideals and goals, and can be considered captivating and charismatic individuals (Burke, 1986).

According to the behaviours or attitudes followed by a leader, he/she could be associated with an ethical dimension. As a result of this, they could be categorised into authentic or inauthentic leadership. Transformational leaders and authentic leaders share some common characteristics such as self-confidence, hopefulness and resilience (Banks et al., 2016). Nevertheless, there is a major difference between them – transformational leaders are driven to make major changes and transformations within the organization to become change leaders, while authentic leaders strive for change as role models and to work as an example (Yavuz, 2019).

The term that connects authentic and transformational leaders is referred to as authentic transformational leadership. Authentic transformational leaders bring change to the followers' beliefs at the leaders' expense for the benefit of the followers' enjoyment and appreciation (Bass & Steidlmeier, 1999). In 2008, Walumbwa et al. (2008) brought to light the theory that authentic leadership is to be considered a pattern of leader behaviour. Later, Avolio et al. (2009), added that the theory that Authentic Leadership could be based on four individual but co-related components: (i) self-awareness, (ii) internalized moral perspective, (iii) balanced processing, and (iv) relational transparency. These four components would turn out to be the four categories used to evaluate Authentic Leadership in a further constructed questionnaire Authentic Leadership Questionnaire (Walumbwa, Avolio, Gardner, Wernsing, & Peterson, 2008). As far as the previous research carried out within the scope of the Authentic Leadership Questionnaire the authentic leader is an optimistic person, altruistic and kind (Avolio & Gardner, 2005). According to Cervo, Mónico, Santos Hutz and Pais (2016), in turn, the authentic leader is a self-effective individual, always ready to help, persistent and positive.

The Authentic Leadership Questionnaire consists of sixteen questions that fall into the four categories previously presented - self-awareness, internalized moral perspective, balanced processing, and relational transparency. To assess the level of authentic leadership of a given individual, the questionnaire makes use of 5 point Likert scale, which indicates the level of agreement with different sentences, ranging from strongly disagree (1) to strongly agree.

The sentences/ questions are placed in a specific order so that the person who answers the questionnaire is not aware of the four categories before the final evaluation. The scoring process is based on the sum-up of the scoring given to each category. After the scores are added and compared, the intensity of the authentic leadership level can be determined. Scores in the higher range (scores of sixteen and above points) indicate stronger authentic leadership, whereas scores in the lower range (fifteen or fewer points) indicate weaker authentic leadership (Northouse, 2010).

## 1.3 Leadership and the iGen/GenZ Generation

Different generations of individuals are found in our society. Generation Z is made up of individuals that were born between the years 1995 and the present time, therefore ranging between the ages of 1 and 28 years old. This generation is now reaching the opportunity to take their position in the workplace and enter the business world. According to Cabrera (2017), Generation Z can be considered the second wave of Generation Y because both generations have shared experiences over the years. However, despite sharing important events, both generations face different stages of devolvement, and this influences how both behave and perceive the external world. Generation Z has experienced numerous events that were able influenced them. Some examples include the 9/11, the Great Recession, China hosting the Olympics and even the beginning of the Mac versus Microsoft dispute for the top brand. This generation can be seen as individuals that think with their minds on the future and that they have no difficulty sharing their interest to pursue a college degree or even to plan a change for the future (McGaha, 2018). The HEAD Foundation and MIT (2017) consider that individuals from Generation Z were born in a very hectic period and because of this they value their education, feel helpless in a world with digital influence, fear the future of the planet, and worry about their carries. The same authors that Gen Z has a more prominent expectation that their leaders have motivating behaviour than Gen X managers. Gen X likes to think it offers strong personal ethics, but only a percent of Gen Z (12%) expect such values from their higher-ups" (Bresman & Rao, 2017, p. 1). This information is illustrative of the fact that each generation exhibits a different profile and thinks differently about others. According to Gomez, Mawhinney and Betts (2019), if employers want to attract Generation Z as future workers they must be ready to adapt to the speed of evolution within the company to keep up with the GenZ's world, and this evolution need to be focused on factors such as diversity, leadership and inclusivity since these factors are of high importance to GenZ's when looking for a job. For these reasons, it is possible to understand that each generation behaves and expects different qualities when referring to their leaders.

# 2 METHODOLOGY

This investigation aims to understand whether age is a key factor in an individual's level of authentic leadership and also can influence the perceptions individuals have about the concept of leadership. Thus, through an exploratory study, we aim to understand if there is or not a different perception or behaviour on leadership regarding two different age groups.

To attain these research objectives, a quantitative methodology was used. This approach was used due to its objectivity, the ability to compare the results attained between both age groups and the capacity to generalise the results attained. The information was collected through an online survey. The questionnaire used was divided into three parts. The first part aimed to gather some information to characterize the sample, namely age and gender. The second part aimed to assess the individuals' level of authentic leadership, based on the Authentic Leadership Questionnaire (ALQ) developed by Northouse (2010) and aimed to answer the research question "Is age a key factor in an individual's level of authentic leadership?". The third part was composed of three statements to assess the perceptions the respondents have about the concept of leadership and were built by the authors, according to the literature review.

The Authentic Leadership Questionnaire (ALQ) was translated from the English original version to Portuguese by the authors, to better fit the Portuguese audience.

The survey was developed on the online platform Google Forms, and made available through different social groups.

The evaluation scale used was the 5-point scale already implemented by the Authentic Leadership Questionnaire. In order to maintain the same standard of evaluation on the second part of the questionnaire presented to the public, the same 5-point scale was used (1-Strongly Disagree; 2-Disagree; 3-Neutral; 4-Agree; 5-Strongly Agree), since it is considered to be a better fit when the respondents are considered general public (Weijters, Cabooter, & Schillewaert, 2010; Revilla, Saris, & Krosnick, 2013).

The information was collected between the 7th of May 2020 and the 31st of May 2020. After that, in order to analyse the data, the software SPSS - Statistical Package for Social Sciences was used. The sample consisted of 125 respondents, all of them considered eligible for analysis.

## 3 RESULTS ANALYSIS

### 3.1 Sample Description

The characteristics of the sample are presented in Table 5.

*Table 5. Sample characteristics*

| | Frequency | Percentage |
|---|---|---|
| Gender | | |
| Female | 85 | 68 |
| Male | 40 | 32 |
| Age | | |
| 25 years old or younger | 57 | 45,6 |
| Older than 25 years old | 68 | 54,4 |

Source: Authors' own elaboration

Of the 125 individuals that participated in the study, 85 were female (68%) and 40 were male (32%). From the sample, 57 answers were provided by individuals 25 years old or younger (45,6%) and 68 by individuals older than 25 years old (54,4%).

### 3.2 Perceptions About the Concept of Leadership

The analysis of Table 6 reveals the perceptions of the respondents about the concept of leadership.

The majority of the respondents strongly agree that leadership is something that could be improved over time; in addition, 34,9% agree with this sentence. No respondents have mentioned not agreeing with the possibility of leadership is capable of being improved.

Most of the respondents also have reported sharing the vision that leadership could be taught, as 48% agree with this possibility and 20.8% strongly agree.

*Table 6. Perceptions about the concept of leadership: Descriptive statistics*

| | 1 | | 2 | | 3 | | 4 | | 5 | |
|---|---|---|---|---|---|---|---|---|---|---|
| | N | % | N | % | N | % | N | % | N | % |
| Leadership is an innate trait, born with the individual. | 8 | 6.4 | 34 | 27.2 | 30 | 24 | 33 | 26.4 | 20 | 16.0 |
| Leadership is something that can be taught. | 4 | 3.2 | 12 | 9.6 | 23 | 18.4 | 60 | 48.0 | 26 | 20.8 |
| Leadership is something that can be improved/ worked overtime | 0 | 0 | 0 | 0 | 10 | 8 | 38 | 30.4 | 77 | 61.6 |

Source: Authors' own elaboration

The assertion that considers that leadership is an innate trait, born with the individual, is one that only has the agreement or strong agreement of 42,4% of the respondents. It should also be mentioned that 27,2% of the respondents disagree with this possibility and 6,4% strongly disagree with it.

After that, we proceed to the analysis of the perceptions about the concept of leadership, according to age.

The results attained (Table 7), show that the youngest respondents, aged below 25 years old, consider slightly more that leadership can be improved over time, compared to respondents aged over 25 (mean value of 4,85 and 4,5, respectively). The same pattern is also found concerning the possibility of leadership could be taught (mean value of 3,82 on the younger respondents; and the mean value of 3,66 on the respondents older than 25). On the other hand, the fact that leadership is something innate, welcomes a slightly higher level of agreement in the case of older respondents compared to younger ones (mean value of 3,32 and 3,02, respectively).

*Table 7. Perceptions about the concept of leadership, by age*

| | Total | | 25 Years Old or Younger | | Over 25 Years Old | |
|---|---|---|---|---|---|---|
| | Mean | Std. Deviation | Mean | Std. Deviation | Mean | Std. Deviation |
| Leadership is an innate trait, born with the individual. | 3.18 | 1.187 | 3.02 | 1.246 | 3.32 | 1.126 |
| Leadership is something that can be taught. | 3.74 | 1.001 | 3.82 | 1.002 | 3.66 | 1.002 |
| Leadership is something that can be improved/worked overtime | 4.54 | 0.642 | 4.58 | 0.596 | 4.5 | 0.68 |

Source: Authors' own elaboration

However, when analysing the correlations among the different variables and the respondents' age, we observe that no statistically significant is found between them (Table 8). This result suggests that the people's understanding of leadership and the fact that it may be innate is not influenced according to the age profile of the respondents.

*Table 8. Correlation analysis between perceptions about the concept of leadership and age*

| | Correlation |
|---|---|
| Leadership is an innate trait, born with the individual. | 0,117 |
| Leadership is something that can be taught. | -0,089 |
| Leadership is something that can be improved/worked overtime | -0,046 |

Source: Authors' own elaboration

## 3.3 Authentic Leadership

Through the investigation, we intended to assess the presence of authentic leadership and the extent to which the presence of a such type of personality could be conditioned by age.

The analysis of descriptive statistics (Table 9), on the variables comprised in the ALQ shows that the variable that receives a higher percentage of agreement from the respondents is "my actions reflect my core values", as 84,8% of the respondents agree or strongly agree with it.

After that, it follows "I listen closely to the ideas of those who disagree with me" (that receives 80% of positive answers), "My morals guide what I do as a leader" (79,2% of positive answers between the respondents), "I admit my mistakes to others" (77,6% of positive answers) or "I listen very carefully to the ideas of others before making decisions" (with which 74,4% agree or strongly agree).

On the other side, the variables to which the respondents agree the least are "I openly share my feelings with others" (agreed by only 48% of the respondents), "I do not allow group pressure to control me" (49.6% of positive answers) and "I do not emphasize my own point of view at the expense of others" (with which 53% of the respondents agree).

*Table 9. ALQ descriptive statistics*

| | 1 | | 2 | | 3 | | 4 | | 5 | |
|---|---|---|---|---|---|---|---|---|---|---|
| | N | % | N | % | N | % | N | % | N | % |
| I can list my three greatest weaknesses. | 2 | 1.6 | 9 | 7.2 | 27 | 21.6 | 62 | 49.6 | 25 | 20.0 |
| My actions reflect my core values | 1 | 0.8 | 7 | 5.6 | 11 | 8.8 | 61 | 48,8 | 45 | 36,0 |
| I seek others' opinions before making up my own mind. | 4 | 3.2 | 14 | 11.2 | 20 | 16.0 | 54 | 43,2 | 33 | 26,4 |
| I openly share my feelings with others | 8 | 6.4 | 26 | 20.8 | 31 | 24.8 | 43 | 34,4 | 17 | 13,6 |
| I can list my three greatest strengths | 2 | 1.6 | 9 | 7.2 | 35 | 28.0 | 55 | 44.0 | 24 | 19,2 |
| I do not allow group pressure to control me | 3 | 2.4 | 15 | 12.0 | 45 | 36.0 | 50 | 40.0 | 12 | 9.6 |
| I listen closely to the ideas of those who disagree with me | 1 | 0.8 | 5 | 4.0 | 19 | 15.2 | 59 | 47.2 | 41 | 32.8 |
| I let others know who I truly am as a person | 5 | 4.0 | 13 | 10.4 | 27 | 19.2 | 51 | 40.8 | 32 | 25.6 |
| I seek feedback as a way of understanding who I really am as a person | 4 | 3.2 | 14 | 11.2 | 21 | 16.8 | 57 | 45.6 | 29 | 23.2 |
| Other people know where I stand on controversial issues | 3 | 2.4 | 9 | 7.2 | 31 | 24.8 | 59 | 47.2 | 23 | 18.4 |

*continues on following page*

*Table 9. Continued*

| | 1 | | 2 | | 3 | | 4 | | 5 | |
|---|---|---|---|---|---|---|---|---|---|---|
| | N | % | N | % | N | % | N | % | N | % |
| I do not emphasize my own point of view at the expense of others | 7 | 5.6 | 17 | 13.6 | 34 | 27.2 | 47 | 37.6 | 20 | 16.0 |
| I rarely present a "false" front to others | 10 | 8.0 | 8 | 6.4 | 15 | 12.0 | 47 | 37.6 | 45 | 36.0 |
| I accept the feelings I have about myself | 1 | 0. | 6 | 4.8 | 32 | 25.6 | 54 | 43.2 | 32 | 25.6 |
| My morals guide what I do as a leader | 1 | 0.8 | 7 | 5.6 | 18 | 14.4 | 51 | 40.8 | 48 | 38.4 |
| I listen very carefully to the ideas of others before making decisions | 1 | 0.8 | 9 | 7.2 | 22 | 17.6 | 56 | 44.8 | 37 | 29.6 |
| I admit my mistakes to others | 3 | 2.4 | 3 | 2.4 | 22 | 17.6 | 55 | 44.0 | 42 | 33.6 |

Source: Authors' own elaboration

When analysing the valuation attached to different authentic leadership characteristics (Table 10), the main difference in the assessment made by respondents according to age is found in the assertion "I do not allow group pressure to control me" which has a higher mean value in respondents aged more than 25 (mean of 3,6) rather than the younger ones (average of 3,21). On the other hand, younger respondents, when compared with the older ones, on average valorise more "feedback as a way of understanding who I really am as a person", "seek others' opinions before making up my own mind" or "do not emphasize my own point of view at the expense of others".

*Table 10. ALQ, by age*

| | Total | | 25 Years Old or Younger | | Over 25 Years Old | |
|---|---|---|---|---|---|---|
| | Mean | Std. Deviation | Mean | Std. Deviation | Mean | Std. Deviation |
| I can list my three greatest weaknesses. | 3.79 | 0,901 | 3.89 | 0.748 | 3.71 | 1.008 |
| My actions reflect my core values | 4.14 | 0.855 | 4.16 | 0.702 | 4.12 | 0.97 |
| I seek others' opinions before making up my own mind. | 3.78 | 1.059 | 3.96 | 0.865 | 3.63 | 1.183 |
| I openly share my feelings with others | 3.28 | 1.133 | 3.3 | 1.117 | 3.26 | 1.154 |
| I can list my three greatest strengths | 3.72 | 0,912 | 3.72 | 0.881 | 3.72 | 0.944 |
| I do not allow group pressure to control me | 3.42 | 0.909 | 3.21 | 0.84 | 3.6 | 0,933 |
| I listen closely to the ideas of those who disagree with me | 4.07 | 0,844 | 4.11 | 0,772 | 4.04 | 0,905 |
| I let others know who I truly am as a person | 3,74 | 1,079 | 3.77 | 0.945 | 3,71 | 1.185 |
| I seek feedback as a way of understanding who I really am as a person | 3,74 | 1,039 | 3,95 | 0,99 | 3,57 | 1,055 |
| Other people know where I stand on controversial issues | 3,72 | 0,903 | 3,72 | 0,901 | 3,72 | 0,96 |
| I do not emphasize my own point of view at the expense of others | 3,45 | 1,088 | 3,61 | 0,921 | 3.31 | 1,2 |
| I rarely present a "false" front to others | 3.87 | 1.205 | 3,91 | 1,123 | 3,84 | 1,277 |
| I accept the feelings I have about myself | 3,88 | 0,876 | 3,88 | 0,803 | 3,88 | 0,939 |
| My morals guide what I do as a leader | 4,10 | 0,905 | 3,98 | 0,803 | 3,88 | 0,939 |

*continues on following page*

*Table 10. Continued*

| | Total | | 25 Years Old or Younger | | Over 25 Years Old | |
|---|---|---|---|---|---|---|
| | **Mean** | **Std. Deviation** | **Mean** | **Std. Deviation** | **Mean** | **Std. Deviation** |
| I listen very carefully to the ideas of others before making decisions | 3,95 | 0,915 | 4,05 | 0,811 | 3,87 | 0,991 |
| I admit my mistakes to others | 4,04 | 0,911 | 4,02 | 0,767 | 4,06 | 1,02 |

Source: Authors' own elaboration

In order to have a more comprehensive approach to the influence of age on the level of authentic leadership, correlation analysis was performed, using Spearman's Rho. The use of this non-parametric statistic was justified by the size of the sample gathered and the type of variables in the analysis.

The analysis of the correlation coefficients (Table 11) shows that a statistically significant association exist concerning two variables: "I do not allow group pressures to control me" (r=-0,230, α=0,01) and "I seek feedback as a way of understanding who I really am as a person" (r=0,189, α=0,05).

*Table 11. ALQ: Correlation analysis*

| | **Mean** |
|---|---|
| I can list my three greatest weaknesses. | 0.07 |
| My actions reflect my core values | -0,041 |
| I seek others' opinions before making up my own mind. | 0,125 |
| I openly share my feelings with others | -0,007 |
| I can list my three greatest strengths | -0,018 |
| I do not allow group pressure to control me | -0,230** |
| I listen closely to the ideas of those who disagree with me | 0,014 |
| I let others know who I truly am as a person | -0,008 |
| I seek feedback as a way of understanding who I really am as a person | 0,189* |
| Other people know where I stand on controversial issues | -0,026 |
| I do not emphasize my own point of view at the expense of others | 0,126 |
| I rarely present a "false" front to others | 0,003 |
| I accept the feelings I have about myself | -0,025 |
| My morals guide what I do as a leader | -0,155 |
| I listen very carefully to the ideas of others before making decisions | 0,082 |
| I admit my mistakes to others | -0,0706 |

Source: Authors own elaboration

Thus, the analysis of the results shows that the individuals' behaviour towards leadership does not vary significantly according to age, with the exciton of two variables, that are related to internalized moral perspective (that is more present in younger respondents) and other related to self-awareness, is more pronounced in respondents with more than 25 years old.

## 4. CONCLUSION

The current times are characterised by enormous transformations, increasingly requiring the involvement of all employees, in a bottom up approach, in the design of disruptive responses to the new challenges of everyday life. As such, the role that management and leadership assumes has been changing over time, increasingly rcquiring thc nccd to improve employees' ability to pursue objectives. Leading employees in an organisation can be done by using different styles, either of a transactional or transformational nature.

Taking into account the requirements imposed upon the leader, the debate about whether leadership can be considered as a process or as something imminently innate is intensified.

Considering that understanding leadership has been changing over the years and the fact that different generations display very different characteristics. In such context, this chapter brings new insights into the behaviours, expectations and beliefs on leadership held by different generations.

Based on the results attained in the empirical study, we can observe that age has some kind of influence on the way leadership is perceived. The investigation shows that age impact the internalized moral perspective, that is more relevant for individuals aged of 25 years old or lower. This finding suggest that gen Z is somewhat more comfortable with being authentic, considering others' opinions when making decisions, and letting their moral standards and values guide their conduct without letting outside pressure influence them. On the other hand, individuals aged more than 25 Years Old" are more characterized by a higher level of self-awareness.

As the investigation shows that age has a very limited impact on the perceptions of leadership and the authentic leadership score, in the future it would be positive to exploit the possible impact of other kinds of personal characteristics and also the kind of professional activity performed and that involves different levels of creativity. It would also be positive to enlarge the study to different types of economies, in order to assess if these perceptions are culturally or economically dependent.

## REFERENCES

Avolio, B., & Gardner, W. (2005). Authentic leadership development: Getting to the root of positive forms of leadership. *The Leadership Quarterly*, *16*(3), 315–338. doi:10.1016/j.leaqua.2005.03.001

Avolio, B. J., & Locke, E. E. (2002). Contrasting different philosophies of leader motivation: Altruism versus egoism. *The Leadership Quarterly*, *13*(2), 169–191. doi:10.1016/S1048-9843(02)00094-2

Avolio, B. J., Walumbwa, F. O., & Weber, T. J. (2009). Leadership: Current theories, research, and future directions. *Annual Review of Psychology*, *60*(1), 421–449. doi:10.1146/annurev.psych.60.110707.163621 PMID:18651820

Badibanga, J. (2019). *Promoting Flow and Generating Profifit: A Study of Millennial Managers Through Gamification* [Doctoral Dissertation]. College of Education and Human Services.

Banks, G., McCauley, K., Gardner, W., & Williams, C. (2016). A meta-analytic review of authentic and transformational leadership: A test for redundancy. *The Leadership Quarterly*, *27*(4), 634–652. doi:10.1016/j.leaqua.2016.02.006

Bass, B. M. (1985). *Leadership and performance beyond expectations*. Free Press.

Bass, B. M. (1990). From Transactional to Transformational Leadership: Learning to Share the Vision. *Organizational Dynamics*, *18*(3), 19–31. doi:10.1016/0090-2616(90)90061-S

Bass, B. M. (2008). *The Bass Handbook of Leadership: Theory, Research, and Managerial Applications*. Free Press.

Bass, B. M., & Avolio, B. J. (1993). Transformational leadership: A response to critiques. In M. M. Chemers & R. Ayman (Eds.), *Leadership theory and research: Perspectives and directions*. Free Press.

Bass, B. M., & Avolio, B. J. (1998). *Platoon readiness as a function of transformational/transactional leadership, squad mores and platoon cultures. Second Interim Report*. U.S. Army Research Institute in the Behavioral Sciences.

Bass, B. M., Avolio, B. J., & Atwater, L. E. (1996). The transformational and transactional leadership of men and women. *Applied Psychology*, *45*(1), 5–34. doi:10.1111/j.1464-0597.1996.tb00847.x

Bass, B. M., & Riggio, R. E. (2006). *Transformational leadership* (2nd ed.). Psychology Press. doi:10.4324/9781410617095

Bass, B. M., & Steidlmeier, P. (1999). *Ethics, Character, and Authentic Transformational Leadership Behavior*. Elsevier Science Inc. doi:10.1016/S1048-9843(99)00016-8

Bennis, W. G. (1989). Managing the Dream: Leadership in the 21st Century. *Journal of Organizational Change Management*, *2*(1), 6–10. doi:10.1108/09534818910134040

BjornbergN. H. (2017). *Creativity and Innovation Through the Job Demands-Resources Model* [PhD Dissertation]. Old Dominion University. https://digitalcommons.odu.edu/psychology_etds/63 doi:10.25777/rrhz-sz03

Bresman, H., & Rao, V. D. (2017). *What Generations X, Y and Z Want From Leadership*. Retrieved from https://knowledge.insead.edu/: knowledge.insead.edu/leadershiporganisations/what-generations-x-y-and-z-want-from-leadership-5716

Bruni, E., Cortellazzo, L., Bonesso, S., & Gerli, F. (2018). *Leadership style scale: conceptualization and initial validation*. Università Ca'Foscari Venezia, Department of Management: Working Paper Series.

Bryman, A. (1992). *Charisma and Leadership in Organizations*. SAGE.

Burke, W. (1986). Leadership as empowering others. In S. Srivastva (Ed.), *Executive Power* (pp. 51–77). Jossey-Bass.

Burns, J. M. (1978). *Leadership*. Harper & Row.

Cabrera, J. (2017). *Millennials, Generation Z and the US Army recruiting efforts: Innovative approaches to reach the newest generations yet*. Savannah College of Art and Design. http://ecollections.scad.edu/iii/cpro/DigitalItemViewPage.external?sp=1003864

Cervo, C. S., Mónico, L., Santos, N. R., Hutz, C. S., & Pais, L. (2016). Authentic Leadership Questionnaire: Invariance between samples of Brazilian and Portuguese employees. *Psicologia: Reflexão e Crítica, 29*(1), 40. Advance online publication. doi:10.118641155-016-0046-4

Ciulla, J. B. (2012). *Ethics Effectiveness: The Nature of Good Leadership." The Nature of Leadership* (2nd ed.). SAGE.

Cohen, W. (1990). *The Art of the Leader*. Prentice Hall.

Csikszentmihalyi, M. (2004). *Good business: Leadership, flow, and the making of meaning*. Penguin Group.

Deci, E. L., Koestner, R., & Ryan, R. M. (1999). A meta-analytic review of experiments examining the effects of extrinsic rewards on intrinsic motivation. *Psychological Bulletin, 125*(6), 627–700. doi:10.1037/0033-2909.125.6.627 PMID:10589297

Drath, W., & Palus, C. (1994). *Making Common Sense: Leadership as Meaning-Making in a Community of Practice*. Center for Creative Leadership. doi:10.35613/ccl.1994.2004

Dunphy, D., & Stace, D. (1993). The Strategic Management of Corporate Change. *Human Relations, 46*(8), 905–920. doi:10.1177/001872679304600801

Eastwood, G. (2013). Moral Choices and Leadership. *The International Journal of Ethical*, 2. Available at: https://scholarlycommons.law.case.edu/ijel/vol2/iss1/14

Epitropaki, O., Kark, R., Mainemelis, C., & Lord, R. (2016). Leadership and followership identity processes: A multilevel review. *The Leadership Quarterly Yearly Review, 28*, 104–129.

Eren, E. (1984). *Yonetim psikolojisi*. Istanbul Universites.

Ferrin, D. L., & Dirks, K. T. (2002). Trust in Leadership: Meta-Analytic Findings and Implications for Research and Practice. *The Journal of Applied Psychology, 87*(4), 611–628. doi:10.1037/0021-9010.87.4.611 PMID:12184567

Fisher, B. M., & Edwards, J. E. (1988). Consideration and initiating structure and their relationships with leader effectiveness: a meta-analysis. *Proceedings of the Academy of Management*, 201-205. 10.5465/ambpp.1988.4980535

Ford, C. M. (1996). A Theory of Individual Creative Action in Multiple Social Domains. *Academy of Management Review, 21*(4), 1112–1142. doi:10.2307/259166

Gomez, K., Mawhinney, T., & Betts, K. (2019). *Welcome to generation Z*. Available at: https://www2.deloitte.com/content/dam/Deloitte/us/Documents/consumer-business/welcome-to-gen-z.pdf

Hallinger, P. (2016). Bringing context out of the shadows of leadership. *Educational Management Administration & Leadership, 46*(1), 5–24. Advance online publication. doi:10.1177/1741143216670652

Heifetz, R. A., & Linsky, M. (2017). *Leadership on the Line, With a New Preface: Staying Alive Through the Dangers of Change*. Harvard Business Review Press.

Hersey, P., & Blanchard, K. (1969). Life Cycle Theory of Leadership. *Training and Development Journal*, *23*(5), 26–34.

Hollander, E. P. (1980). Leadership and Social Exchange Processes. In K. J. Gergen, M. S. Greenberg, & R. H. Willis (Eds.), *Social Exchange*. Springer. doi:10.1007/978-1-4613-3087-5_5

Holmes, J. (2012). *Transformational Leadership: Do Great Leaders Share the Same Traits?* Retrieved from Integrating Woman Leaders Foundation: http://integratingwomanleaders.com/transformational-leadership-do-greatleaders-share-the-same-traits/?goback=%2Egde_1022597_member_131169946

Jacobs, T. O. (1970). *Human ResourcesResearch Organization*. Leadership and Exchange in Formal Organizations.

Jago, A. G. (1982). Leadership: Perspectives in Theory and Research. *Management Science*, *28*(3), 315–336. doi:10.1287/mnsc.28.3.315

Junita, I. (2019). Transformational Leadership in Digital Era: Analysis of Nadiem Makarim (Founder of GO-JEK Indonesia) Leadership Figure. *MPRA Paper*, *91575*(1), 80–92. doi:10.33019/ijbe.v3i1.106

Karadağ, E. (2015). *Leadership and Organizational Outcomes: Meta-Analysis of Empirical Studies*. Springer. doi:10.1007/978-3-319-14908-0

Kark, R., & Van Dijk, D. (2007). Motivation to lead, motivation to follow: The role of the self regulatory focus in leadership processes. *Academy of Management Review*, *32*(2), 500–528. doi:10.5465/amr.2007.24351846

Katz, E., Lazarsfeld, P. F., & Roper, E. (2006). *Personal Influence - The Part Played by People in the Flow of Mass Communications*. Routledge.

Kolzow, D. R. (2014). *Leading from Within: Building Organizational Leadership Capacity*. Available at: https://www.iedconline.org/clientuploads/Downloads/edrp/Leading_from_Within.pdf

Kotter, J. P. (1988). *The Leadership Factor*. Free Press.

Kotterman, J. (2006). Leadership vs Management: What's the difference? *Journal for Quality and Participation*, *29*(2), 13–17.

Kouzes, J. M., & Posner, B. Z. (1995). *The Leadership Challenge*. JoeyBass.

Kruse, K. (2013). *What is Leadership?* Retrieved from Forbes: https://www.forbes.com/sites/kevinkruse/2013/04/09/what-isleadership/#305ccc45b90c

Lunenburg, F. C. (2011). Leadership versus Management: A Key Distinction - At Least in Theory. *International Journal of Management, Business Administration (London)*, *14*(1), 15–18. doi:10.24234/miopap.v3i3.15

McGaha, K. (2018). *An Interpretive Phenomenological Study Of America's Emerging Workforce: Exploring Generation Z's Leadership Preferences* [Dissertation]. University of Phoenix.

Mizrahitokatli, N., & Guney, S. (2016). Ideal Leadership Perception of Undergraduate and Graduate Students: An Application. *Business Management Dynamics*, *6*(6), 17–34.

Mosadegh Rad, A. M., & Yarmohammadian, M. H. (2016). *A Study of Relationship Between Managers' Leadership Style and Employees' Job Satisfaction*. Retrieved from https://www.researchgate.net/publication/263656844_A_survey_of_relationship_between_managers%27_leadership_style_and_employees%27_job_satisfaction

Mosadeghrad, A. M. (2003). *Principles of Health Care Administration*. Dibagran Tehran.

Myers, P. J. (2019). *Leadership, Empowerment, and Motivation: An Analysis of Modern Management*. CMC Senior Theses.

Northousc, P. G. (2010). *Leadership: Theory and practice* (6th ed.). Sage Publications.

Odumeru, J. A., & Ogbonna, I. G. (2013). Transformational vs. Transactional Leadership Theories: Evidence in Literature. *International Review of Management and Business Research*, *2*(2), 335–361.

Podsakoff, P., MacKenzie, S., Moorma, R., & Fetter, R. (1990). In Transformational leader behaviors and their effects on followers' trust in leader, satisfaction, and organizational citizenship behaviors. *The Leadership Quarterly*, *1*(2), 107–142. doi:10.1016/1048-9843(90)90009-7

Prentice, W. (1961). Understanding Leadership. *Harvard Business Review*. PMID:14723181

Rafferty, A. E., & Griffin, M. A. (2004). Dimensions of Transformational Leadership: Conceptual and Empirical Extensions. *The Leadership Quarterly*, *15*(3), 329–354. doi:10.1016/j.leaqua.2004.02.009

Real, L. (2004). *Development of youth leadership life skills of Texas youth as San Antonio Livestock Exposition school tour guides* [Master's thesis]. Texas A&M University. Available electronically from https: / /hdl .handle .net /1969 .1 /1332

Reh, F. J. (2018). *The role and responsibilities of today's manager*. Available at: https://www.thebalancecareers.com/what-is-a-manager-2276096

Revilla, M. A., Saris, W. E., & Krosnick, J. A. (2013). Choosing the Number of Categories in Agree-Disagree Scales. *Sociological Methods & Research*, *43*(1), 73–97. doi:10.1177/0049124113509605

Seevers, B., Dormody, T., & Clason, D. (1995). Developing A Scaled To Research And Evaluate Youth Leadership Like Skills Development. *Journal of Agricultural Education*, *28*(36), 28–34. doi:10.5032/jae.1995.02028

Simiyu, A. (2015). *Role of Leadership In Organizational Development*. Available at: https://www.researchgate.net/publication/273766248_ROLE_OF_LEADERSHIP_IN_ORGANIZATIONAL_DEVELOPMENT

StarrL. M. (2020). *Leadership Definitions and Themes*. doi:10.13140/RG.2.2.13471.79527

Stogdill, R. M. (1950). Leadership, membership and organization. *Psychological Bulletin*, *47*(1), 1–14. doi:10.1037/h0053857

Stogdill, R. M. (1974). *Handbook of leadership: A survey of theory and research*. Free Press.

Stogdill, R. M. (1974). *Handbook of leadership: A survey of theory and research.* Free Press.

Valenzuela, K. (2007). *I Want To Be A Leader.* https://ezinearticles.com/expert/Ken_Valenzuela/107414

Vecchio, R. P. (1988). *Organizational Behavior.* The Dryden Press.

Wajdi, B. N. (2017). The Differences Between Management And Leadership. *Sinergi: Jurnal Ilmiah Ilmu Manajemen, 7*(2), 75–84.

Walumbwa, F., Avolio, B., Gardner, W., Wernsing, T., & Peterson, S. (2008). Authentic leadership: Development and validation of a theory-based measure. *Journal of Management, 34*(1), 89–126. doi:10.1177/0149206307308913

Weijters, B., Cabooter, E., & Schillewaert, N. (2010). The effect of rating scale format on response styles: The number of response categories and response category labels. *International Journal of Research in Marketing, 27*(3), 236–247. doi:10.1016/j.ijresmar.2010.02.004

Wonga, C.-S., & Lawb, K. S. (2002). The effects of leader and follower emotional intelligence on performance and attitude: An exploratory study. *The Leadership Quarterly, 13*(3), 243–274. doi:10.1016/S1048-9843(02)00099-1

Yavuz, M. (2019). *Transformational Leadership and Authentic Leadership as Practical Implications of Positive Organizational Psychology.* Academic Press.

Yavuz, M. (2019). Transformational leadership and authentic leadership as practical implications of positive organizational psychology. In Handbook of Research on Positive Organizational Behavior for Improved Workplace Performance (pp. 122–139). IGI Global. ISBN 13.

Yukl, G. (1989). Managerial Leadership: A Review of Theory and Research. *Journal of Management, 15*(2), 251–289. doi:10.1177/014920638901500207

Zhou, J., & Oldham, G. R. (2001). Enhancing Creative Performance: Effects of Expected Developmental Assessment Strategies and Creative Personality. *The Journal of Creative Behavior, 35*(3), 151–167. doi:10.1002/j.2162-6057.2001.tb01044.x

## ADDITIONAL READING

Albadawi, B. I. (2023). Leadership Change for the Development Policy of Inclusive Education: Leadership Theories and Models. In Z. Khlaif, M. Sanmugam, & J. Itmazi (Eds.), *Comparative Research on Diversity in Virtual Learning: Eastern vs. Western Perspectives* (pp. 201–214). IGI Global. doi:10.4018/978-1-6684-3595-3.ch010

Baker, N. (2020). Authentic Leadership, Leader Optimism, and Follower Affective Commitment: An Experimental Study. In Ç. Doğru (Ed.), *Leadership Styles, Innovation, and Social Entrepreneurship in the Era of Digitalization* (pp. 329–344). IGI Global. doi:10.4018/978-1-7998-1108-4.ch013

Baykal, E. (2019). Transparency in Financial Communication: Effect of Authentic Leadership. In H. Dinçer & S. Yüksel (Eds.), *Handbook of Research on Global Issues in Financial Communication and Investment Decision Making* (pp. 110–126). IGI Global. doi:10.4018/978-1-5225-9265-5.ch006

Cui, Z. A., Knox, M. W., Rowlands, J., DeJesus, L., & Campbell, T. (2021). Authentic Leadership Competencies: Antecedents to Entrepreneurial Emergence. In D. Harper (Ed.), *Integration and Application of Business Graduate and Business Leader Competency-Models* (pp. 71–88). IGI Global. doi:10.4018/978-1-7998-6537-7.ch005

Figueiredo, P. C., Leal, S. E., Lopes, I., Cascão, A. F., & Gomes, P. (2022). Transformational and Authentic Leadership in Telework. In P. Figueiredo, E. Tomé, & J. Rouco (Eds.), *Handbook of Research on Challenges for Human Resource Management in the COVID-19 Era* (pp. 243–268). IGI Global. doi:10.4018/978 1 7998 9840 5.ch013

Kişi, N. (2019). Theoretical Perspective on Contemporary Leadership Styles: Transformational and Relational Leadership. In Ç. Doğru (Ed.), *Handbook of Research on Contemporary Approaches in Management and Organizational Strategy* (pp. 248–272). IGI Global. doi:10.4018/978-1-5225-6301-3.ch013

Rischard, M. W., Goodman Hayward, P., Chaudhuri, M., Brunnquell, C., Chattopadhyay, C., & Mello, A. C. (2022). Authentic Leadership Being Shared as a Collective. In V. Wang (Ed.), *Handbook of Research on Educational Leadership and Research Methodology* (pp. 130–150). IGI Global. doi:10.4018/978-1-6684-4144-2.ch008

Singh, A., Sengupta, S., & Sharma, S. (2016). Empathy and Mindfulness: Potential Antecedents to Authentic Leadership. *International Journal of Human Capital and Information Technology Professionals*, *7*(4), 1–14. doi:10.4018/IJHCITP.2016100101

Ünal, Z. M. (2022). Need for Leadership in Times of Crises: Integration of Modern and Post-Modern Leadership Approaches. In T. Connolly & S. Farrier (Eds.), *Leadership and Management Strategies for Creating Agile Universities* (pp. 45–64). IGI Global. doi:10.4018/978-1-7998-8213-8.ch004

## KEY TERMS AND DEFINITIONS

**Authentic Leadership:** Leadership style based on trust and relationship with others, with emphasis on ethical aspects.

**Generation:** Group of people who share a similar age and were born and lived around the same time.

**Leader:** Person who leads the leadership process, and who exerts influence on the followers.

**Leadership:** The process of influencing an individual or group of individuals in a given direction, defined by the leader.

**Management:** Process of coordinating resources in an effective and efficient manner.

**Personal Trait:** Stable characteristics of individuals that influence their behaviour and actions.

**Transactional Leadership:** Leadership style based on the rewards and punishments of the followers.

**Transformational Leadership:** Leadership style that emphasizes the leader's capacity to inspire the collaborators and create conditions for development as a way of pursuing objectives.

# Chapter 12
# Inclusive Leadership in the Amish Community

**Charles Keim**
*MacEwan University, Canada*

**Hannah Keim**
*McGill University, Canada*

## ABSTRACT

*This chapter examines the leadership practiced by the Old Order Amish located in the Holmes and Wayne counties of Ohio, USA. Contrary to popular stereotypes, this community is vibrant and growing, and it is notable for the strong sense of belonging among members. The leadership of the Amish is investigated to see how this sense of belonging is cultivated. The chapter outlines the role of leadership, how leaders are chosen, and leadership's response to the encroachment of technology. Leaders play a critical role in creating a sense of belonging within the community, and the way in which they do this holds practical lessons for how leaders can create a sense of belonging in their secular organizations.*

## INTRODUCTION

This chapter examines transformational leadership by looking at how leadership is practiced within the Old Order Amish. The Amish trace their roots to the Protestant Reformation in sixteen-century Europe and the teachings of Jakob Amman, an Anabaptist leader who sought to revitalize the anabaptist movement in 1693. Like many Anabaptist groups (anabaptist means re-baptizer), the Amish baptized adults who had been previously baptized as infants in state churches (Catholic or Protestant). Contemporary Amish are notable for their simple living, conservative dress, humility, and the shunning of modern technology. The Amish have demonstrated remarkable resilience and business acumen, and the role Amish leadership has played in creating strong, inclusive communities is highlighted. How leaders are chosen, and how decisions are made are unconventional and reveal critical elements for the creation and sustaining of a vibrant community in which people feel a strong sense of belonging. The chapter

DOI: 10.4018/978-1-6684-8822-5.ch012

opens with an overview of the Amish, including a couple who recently left the Amish community, before outlining the research context and methodology. It then provides context by asking who the Amish are, defining Amish leadership, and describing the process for selecting leaders. Leadership is further analyzed by exploring how the Amish have responded to the challenges of technology while striving to preserve their unique tradition and the harmony of their community. The wider implications Amish leadership holds for leaders in modern, secular organizations is then discussed.

## A Brief Overview of the Amish

In speaking with a couple who, approximately ten years ago, made the difficult decision to leave the Amish church, they were asked what they missed most about being Amish. Without hesitation, they responded, "the sense of belonging." To be a member of an Amish congregation, is to belong to a group of believers that surpasses typical religious claims of living in community. For the Amish, every facet of their life is bound up in their local congregation. A distinctive and symbolic feature of the Amish are their barn-raisings, in which hundreds of Amish gather to construct a member's barn. The barn is raised in a single day and the coordination and efficiency of the feat is impressive. Despite the absence of blueprints and the assigning of explicit roles, everyone appears to know what to do, and work progresses quickly. Notable, too, is the strong feeling of solidarity, with Amish (and occasionally non-Amish) from different churches and orders joining together. In many ways, the barn-raising represents the core of Amish society: people bound together by similar beliefs, selflessly giving of themselves for their neighbor, and working together in harmony. Barn-raisings are also remarkably inclusive, involving the efforts of everyone in the community. Elderly male members will standby and provide encouragement and direction where necessary. Female members will provide the midday meal and refreshments. Even children are encouraged to contribute what they can to the enterprise.

Barns dot the landscape, standing as silent but powerful symbols of the Amish community. Not only are barns raised by the community, but later, they may serve as a place of worship, with the local congregation holding church (typically in the hay loft) inside the barn where they pray, sing hymns together, and listen to the sermons; afterwards the congregants share a meal together. Services are held every second Sunday and there is no Sunday School for the children. The Amish are immediately recognizable for the conservative clothing they wear, the Pennsylvania Dutch they speak, and the horse and buggies they drive. Their faith includes adherence to a plain lifestyle that distinguishes them from the secular world. As such, they do not own automobiles and they shun modern conveniences like electricity, television, radios and computers. Unlike some religious groups, like the Hutterites, the Amish do not live in communes; they own their own properties, often run their own businesses, and have their own bank accounts. But the level of cohesion within the community is astonishing. Everyone seems to know and care for each other. If a member is sick, others will spring to their aid, providing them with food, money, company, or anything else that they require. For instance, when Eli Miller (not his real name) suffered a fall during harvest which required hospitalization, he returned home to find his crops harvested, his animals fed and watered, his family taken care of. If a house burns down, members contribute what they can to replace it; they do not have insurance—the community is their insurance.

While stories like this are common, more common is the pervasive sense of belonging within the Amish. Weekly rituals, like attending church, visiting with neighbors, softball games, potlucks and going to auctions, help to locate and solidify people within the larger web of their community. The couple who had left the Amish discussed how alone they now felt, and how much they missed the activities that had bound them to others, even though they now belong to a more progressive non-Amish congregation. While the couple followed their religious convictions, they were acutely aware of the high social price they had paid.

To gain a better understanding of how the Amish community creates this strong sense of belonging, the role of Amish leadership is examined and differentiated from modern, secular leadership models. The study is grounded by looking at how inclusion is cultivated within the Amish through their response to the encroachment of technology and reverence for tradition. The Amish are remarkable for their adaptation and innovation, yet technology is modified to preserve the core tenets of their beliefs and to ensure the integrity of their social coherence—adoption of new technology and practices are always made within the long shadow of the past. The decisions made by the congregation demonstrate an almost sacred regard for the decisions made by previous generations. The Amish example of leadership holds valuable lessons for how modern secular leaders can cultivate a stronger sense of belonging within their own organizations.

## Research Context and Methodology

The study focuses on the Old Order Amish located in the Holmes and Wayne counties of Ohio, U.S.A. The authors are closely connected with the Amish: their immediate family was raised Amish and their relatives still belong to the Old Order Amish. It was those relatives who provided key data and access to the larger Amish community. The primary data collection for this article was drawn from the lead author's six-month ethnographic investigation during which he lived with the Amish, attending church services, weddings, barn-raisings, and working alongside them. During this six-month period, multiple discussions were held with members whose ages spanned children to seniors and whose positions included bishops, song-leaders, deacons, ministers, and laity. The standard protocols of ethnographic research were followed by regular note taking regarding the details of the observations and conversations in the Amish community (Cunliffe, 2010; Gobo, 2008; Van Maanen, 1988). Additionally, since the relatives belonged to different congregations, data was drawn from several congregations. Follow-up discussions continue to this day.

A large set of archival data was also consulted, including books, census data, biographies, magazine features, and academic publications, some of which are cited below. This helped to locate the data within the larger context of Amish society. The data was analyzed using a thematic analysis approach (Terry, Hayfield, Clarke, & Braun, 2017) so that the central features of Amish leadership could be uncovered and recorded. Accordingly, the process of data analysis was comprised of coding the leadership references and aggregating the codes into broad themes followed by several iterations of going back to the field notes and archival data until reaching saturation (Guest, MacQueen, & Namey, 2012).

It is important to note that the Amish are not a single homogenous group (Kraybill et al., 2013; Nolt and Meyers, 2007); rather "the Amish" are comprised of at least four different groups that identify themselves as Amish: Beachy Amish, Amish Mennonites, New Order Amish, and Old Order Amish. While all these groups are "Amish" and trace their roots to Jakob Amman, significant differences exist between them. The chapter focuses on the Old Order Amish not only because of the authors' intimate knowledge of this group, but also because it is this order that is commonly meant when people speak of "The Amish." For most people, "Amish" calls to mind a stereotype that is most suitably expressed by the Old Order Amish. This order is the most visible and it has distinguished itself with its entrepreneurial spirit and ability to retain its spiritual identity while capitalizing on technological advances. For the remainder of the chapter, Amish is used when referring to the Old Order Amish.

## Who Are the Amish?

In the 1950s, Gertrude Edners Huntington, a PhD student at Yale University, decided that her dissertation would focus on an Ohio Amish community. Her professors urged her to complete the interviews as quickly as possible before the Amish died out. They felt that although this community was interesting, its resistance to technology and adherence to outdated customs would soon be overwhelmed by mainstream America. Her professors' concerns were misguided. In 1900, the Amish population numbered 6,000; in 2012, 275,000; and the most recent estimates place their number at 350,000. In Holmes County, Ohio, the population is 40.71% Amish, the largest concentration of Amish relative to non-Amish of any U.S. County (Donnermeyer, Anderson, and Cooksey 2013, p.100). Over the last few decades, Amish communities have grown significantly, which is remarkable given that they are not evangelical; they do not seek to convert others. In 1951, there were 200 church districts, which have grown to approximately 2,539 in 2019 ("Population Growth," *Amish Studies*, 2020). Currently, there are about 500 settlements spread across 31 states and 3 Canadian provinces. Donnermeyer (2015) reports that the Amish population doubles at a rate of every 20.5 years, which is striking, given the doubling time of 75.44 years for the American population. Given the austerity of the Amish lifestyle, it is surprising to note that between 85-95% of Amish youth eventually join the church ("Population Growth" *Amish Studies*, 2019).

The Amish share a plain and conservative clothing style. The women wear simple long dresses fastened with pins along with "kapps" or prayer coverings on their head, which are supposed to cover most of their hair. Their hair is put in a bun on the back of their head and is covered by the kapp. Depending on the occasion, one may often find these kapps covered by a larger black bonnet. The men wear trousers (without zippers) with plain suspenders and typically wear a distinctive Amish-style hat on their head. Though some Amish may use public transportation or hire a non-Amish person (referred to as "the English") to drive them, they typically prefer to travel using a horse and buggy. The horse and buggy has caused significant troubles for motorists travelling through Amish country. Typically, the Amish stick to the shoulders of the road so as not to impede motorists, but many of the county roads are narrow—without shoulders—causing traffic to back up behind the buggies, especially on hills where the horses slow to a walk.

The Amish belong to their local church, which is a small congregation that meets on a bi-weekly basis for several hours (it feels much longer!). Each church is led by a bishop and several preachers and deacons. There is no central agency or body that oversees the congregations or sets and enforces rules and regulations. Thus, one may find significant differences between churches that are but a few miles apart. As well, the Amish do not have a church building; rather, each family takes a turn hosting the service in their barn, garage or home. In this way, every member of the congregation can expect that their fellow worshippers will visit their home at least once a year. Having a central building for worshipping, which is a hallmark of most religions, is considered worldly and a form of idolatry. For the Amish it is the people not the building that matters most. Should the congregation outgrow these modest accommodations, then a new church will be formed. In this way, the Amish expand horizontally rather than vertically. While churches may align themselves with other churches in their area ("districts") and strive to ensure some consistency with them, these alliances are wholly voluntary and by no means prevent differences.

A further defining feature of the Amish is their language. The Amish speak "Pennsylvania Dutch" (PD) which is considered a "West Germanic language with strong Palatinae-dialect roots" (Fisher, et al. 2022: 1). It is predominantly spoken by the Amish and some conservative Mennonite groups. It is considered a remarkable success story since it has not only survived but continues to grow. One can hear it spoken in many American states as well as in the Canadian province of Ontario. Speakers of PD are best classified as diglossic bilinguals, since they speak multiple languages and use each one depending on their particular sociolinguistic contexts." (Grosjean, 2008). The language began forming 250-280 years ago when German-speaking immigrants from Western Europe came to the British Colonies in the 'New World' seeking economic opportunities and, for some, religious freedom. Because these immigrants came from different parts of the German-speaking world, PD represents a melting pot of mostly Southern German dialects the most influential of which is thought to be Palatinate (Christman, 1950). However, the fact that PD was formed in America also means that it has remained in constant contact with English throughout its existence and, remarkably, nearly all speakers are proficient in English and PD.

PD is spoken almost exclusively among the Amish, making it an essential aspect of the Amish culture. Some people who leave the Amish will teach their children PD; others will not. Because language is inherently tied to culture, PD is tied to how the Amish foster an inclusive culture. In a way, the Amish language can also be interpreted as a type of barn building. Language is a social construct that requires a community's collective effort, and while there may be variations in the final product, we nonetheless recognize its outline and relevance. PD creates a foundation for fostering inclusive language within the Amish. It is the language of the home; the language of intimacy. By comparison, when speaking with outsiders the Amish will use English. Because PD is the language that they speak amongst each other, it is the language that gathers all members of the community together, regardless of age, gender, or status. Language can also create a more inclusive community within leadership. By creating a guide to the language used within a workplace, leaders can ensure that all members of their community understand and communicate with each other. This can further heighten a sense of inclusion since they will all speak the same organizational language. By creating a language that all members can speak, leaders can create an inclusive environment where all members of the community express themselves and are heard.

As Wagler (2011: 8) notes, "there is wide variation and a lot of inordinate fussing within Amish circles. Some groups use only hooks and eyes on their clothes; others use buttons and snaps … and so on and on." Among other prohibitions, the Amish do not use public utility electricity or telephones and largely rely on horse-and-buggies for transportation. Yet with their buggies some congregations allow battery-powered lighting (interior and exterior) and disc brakes in place of drum brakes, and some buggies roll on solid rubber tires rather than traditional steel wheels (a good buggy lasts 20-30 years, though 40-50 years is not uncommon). Increasingly, the use of electric bicycles and scooters is gaining acceptance among the Amish, though electric vehicles remain "verboten" (forbidden).

The explosion in the Amish population has brought a unique set of challenges. The Amish were traditionally agrarian and much of their faith and ethos were tied to farming, but this is no longer the case. There is a chronic lack of affordable farmland and farms have been divided so often among children that families struggle to make a living from their small plots. In response, Amish businesses have demonstrated resilience and ingenuity by finding new markets and by reimagining existing industries (Kraybill & Nolt, 2004; Kraybill et al, 2013). Researchers have summarized this transformation by noting that the biggest change within the Amish has been the lunchbox. Rather than working on the family farm, Amish now overwhelmingly "work out"; that is, they work away from home, packing their lunches so that they can eat at the job site before returning home at the end of the day. This change has significantly affected the traditional family dynamic and it has also given rise to the new phenomenon of vacations and travel. No longer are families tied to the farm, nor are they bound to the rhythms of the land. Perhaps more significantly, life away from the farm has also brought a level of economic prosperity unimagined by preceding generations.

Economic growth, however, has also forced the Amish to re-think what it means to be Amish and to renegotiate the line between old practices and new technology. Yet an abiding feature of the Amish is their social cohesion. Members will donate time and money for those who require help. There is no homelessness within the Amish. Economic prosperity has not created haves and have nots. If anything, business success has resulted in greater employment opportunities. The role of leadership in ensuring cohesion while preserving a sense of identity is critical, and the leadership style practiced by the Amish is very different than those found in other contemporary organizations. Bishops are chosen through a type of lottery system ("the lot") and they receive no compensation or formal training; their primary duties are ensuring the harmony of their congregation while interpreting and enforcing the rules governing daily life.

A central argument of this book is that "leadership needs a paradigm shift." Certainly, Amish leadership provides a very different paradigm! Rather than productivity, performance, or shareholder value, Amish leadership is concerned with preserving the harmony and identity of the congregation. In all matters, it is the expression and experience of community as it relates to their faith which guides the Amish. Ferdman, Prime, and Riggio (2021, p. xxvii) find in inclusive leadership a collective advantage, "where ideas, contributions, and direction can come from all types of people; and where equity and social justice are focal goals." As has been argued elsewhere (Keim & Shadnam, 2020), innovation and change come from the periphery but are then decided upon by the group. Thus, leaders present the issues upon which the congregation will decide. In this way, Amish life is a continual negotiation that is conducted in concert. The bishop plays a critical role in this process, since he must decide which issues will be brought to the congregation and must ensure the harmony and identity of the group. Typically, if the introduction of a new technology or practice threatens division or strive, it will be discarded.

## Amish Leadership

Each Amish church is led by a bishop (servant with full powers), two or three ministers (servants of the book) and a deacon (servant to the poor), who oversees the aid given to members in need. Ordained officials (literally called "servants") typically serve for life and receive no formal theological training or lessons in pedagogy. Wagler (2011, p. 26) recalls one preacher, who "had one good sermon in him and we heard it many times." As a formal leader, the bishop occupies a central role and sets the tone for the congregation's behavior. The bishop's duties include conducting marriage ceremonies, funerals, administering the rights of baptism and most importantly, ensuring harmony in the community. The bishop ensures that the rules governing daily life, the *ordnung* (discussed later), are applied fairly and consistently and that business practices conform to it.

The bishop's role is dynamic and not limited to affairs of the church; the bishop guides congregants in all their daily economic and social activities. The bishop's role also varies between churches: some bishops are more involved than others. Although the bishop is not a business leader in the traditional sense of leading a large corporation, his leadership is at the level of directing sets of businesses and other stakeholders in the Amish community to ensure the maintain a close-knit fabric. The bishop also represents the congregation at larger Amish assemblies and is considered a spokesperson and example to the larger English population. The bishop is expected to work closely with the congregation to decide which issues should be addressed and how. Given that bishops are selected from the congregation, they possess intimate knowledge of its norms and how it has responded to issues in the past. Such a model ensures that the bishop knows the congregation and understands its members' sentiments concerning the introduction of new technologies and practices. Since the bishop belongs to the congregation, he also has an appreciation for how his role and the decisions of the congregation will affect his immediate and extended family and the lives of his neighbors. The scale of Amish organization encourages members to build close ties with the bishop, to know the person as a person and not only as a church official.

A defining feature of the Amish is their desire to keep things small. As one Amish carpenter noted, "bigness ruins everything" (Kraybill, 2001, p.80). Most Amish companies are small and employ family members. Thus, a conscious decision will often be made to limit the growth of a business. In other words, businesses will simply say no to opportunities to grow their business so that they can keep their business small. Depending on the situation, however, a business owner may appoint a family member, or other trusted person, to start their own company to meet the demand. This intimacy extends to congregations as well. When a congregation grows too large to gather for church in members' houses or barns, then it is time to form a new congregation. The practice of holding church in this manner ensures that members will visit the home of every family at least once a year. A further feature of Amish leadership is that leaders are known beyond their official station. Thus, bishops will work alongside their members and have numerous social interactions with them.

It is up to each individual congregation to decide which issues should be addressed and how, so while one congregation may worry about members playing golf or vacationing in Florida, another may not. While one congregation may allow electric bicycles for transportation, another may not. Given that the bishop is selected from the congregation, he will possess intimate knowledge of its norms and how it has responded to issues in the past. It is also largely up to the bishop to decide whether an issue should be brought before the congregation or not. The small scale of Amish organization ensures that members have close ties with each other and with their leaders and that they can settle their differences together.

## Selection of the Bishop

Bishops are chosen by a process known as "the lot," which is a combination of careful deliberation and faith. The office of bishop is one that most members wish to avoid. Not only do bishops receive no compensation but they must also interpret and enforce the rules governing daily life while exemplifying the Amish ideals of simplicity in their own lives. These duties must be carried out in addition to the bishop's regular job. Again, no material perks or compensation accompany the role. The pressure of enforcing rules and settling differences between members of the congregation takes a toll, as does the reality that bishops and their families are held to a higher standard. To be a bishop is to live one's life in a type of fishbowl (Keim and Shadnam, 2018) where one's actions are scrutinized and where members may hesitate to disclose their actions or possessions.

The process for selecting a bishop is taken very seriously. After a daylong communion service, church members nominate male church members who have already served as preachers (selecting preachers follows a similar process). Selection is based on how well they are perceived to exemplify Amish values and whether they demonstrate suitable leadership qualities. The most important criterion is how the person has conducted himself in his daily life. Has he been exemplary in his actions and is his family respected? It is believed that the apple does not fall far from the tree, so the attitude and actions of a rebellious child or troublesome family relations are traced to the parent(s). Bishops and other church officials are always male, and yet women are encouraged to voice their opinions and they also vote on issues facing the congregation. Though they may not hold official positions, some women exert significant influence.

Prospective leaders must demonstrate sound judgment and humility. A shoddy and/or disorganized home signals trouble. Financial success or failure may also colour congregants' judgments. Furthermore, members must ask themselves: will every issue, large and small be brought forward, or only those deemed significant? and what is their stance toward technology and other issues? In nominating a member for the position of bishop, members must thus consider the direction they wish their congregation to take since the bishop will exert significant influence. The candidate's wisdom is also considered: is this someone who can successfully help the congregation answer questions that have yet to be asked or navigate solutions to problems posed by technology that have yet to be encountered?

The selection process for leaders is fascinating. Typically, those members who have received at least three votes (the number varies depending on church) are entered in "the lot." Members do not know if they have been selected until their name is called. In keeping with the biblical practice of casting lots, the Amish seek to have the hand of God drawing the name. As such, a slip of paper on which a Bible verse is written is placed inside of a single hymnbook which is then mixed with other hymnbooks, corresponding to the number of candidates. The hymnbooks are mixed multiple times by multiple officials, so that no one knows which book holds the verse. Each candidate must then select a hymnbook. Only when each candidate has a book are the books opened one by one until the slip of paper is found and the candidate's life (and that of his family) is changed forever.

Selection is regarded as a combination of human wisdom and divine providence. Two key concepts undergird the selection: humility and acceptance. First, the Amish place a premium on humility (*gelassenheit*), which is at odds with wider cultural norms of self-interest and self-promotion. Since they are nominated by others, nominees cannot rig the system; furthermore, the value placed on humility ensures that Amish are trained from an early age to embrace its practice. Since nominations depend on the judgment of others, the process ensures that humility is gauged by the group who has known the person their entire life in multiple settings. It is not simply the person's recent performance or how they function in a certain area (specialization) but a lifetime of conduct. Second, acceptance is regarded as a type of submission, not only to the will of God but also to the will of others. In carrying out his duties, the bishop submits himself to the congregation and understands that selection reflects not only the will of his peers but the will of God. Incorporating the lot in the selection process signifies that one's life is guided by a greater force and that one must accept one's lot. In taking the role of bishop, one humbly accepts the responsibility of a lifetime of service.

## Amish Response to Technology

While Amish leadership has always been fraught with challenges, the encroachment of technology has increasingly thrust leaders into uncharted territory. Like their fellow Amish—bishops attend school only for the first eight grades—they do not receive any formal training in theology, management, or pedagogy. Often, they find themselves walking alone the tightrope stretching between accommodating technologies that allow the Amish to provide for their families and prohibiting practices and technologies that compromise long-standing Amish norms and identity. In discussing cell phones and texting with a bishop, his concern was not whether cell phones and texting was worldly or would introduce members to contrary beliefs but rather, the bishop was concerned with the impact such devices would have on the community, especially the family unit. Furthermore, it was soon evident that cell phones and the dizzying array of social media were not well understood by him. But his abiding concerns echoed those often voiced by wider society: how does this technology affect our sense of belonging, does it lead to increasing isolation, and what does it mean for the family unit? Interestingly, the bishop was most worried about how cell phones foster privacy and can lead to a sense of isolation. The bishop held that decisions and communication are best conducted face-to-face with other people.

A core value for the Amish is the integrity of the family unit. They feel it best to have the family together in a room talking or playing games. Conversations around the kitchen table after dinner are very common, a practice which internet and other devices threaten. Yet to simply prohibit internet use would put many Amish businesses out of business. The compromises that have been reached demonstrate ingenuity and a balance between old prohibitions and new realities. One response is to simply hire a non-Amish employee whose job is to operate the computers. The Amish maintain a distinction between the workplace and the home, so Amish construction companies can use power tools at their worksite but not at their home. Though they are allowed to work in a non-Amish workplace and use technology, it is expected that the technology will remain at work. For instance, Noe Yoder (name changed to protect his identity) displayed a technical aptitude that was quickly noticed by his non-Amish managers, so they provided him with training and placed him in charge of their IT system. How strange to watch this computer technician return home at the end of the workday and hitch up his horse and buggy! Most intriguing, however, is that Noe's work is known by everyone in the community, and the congregation agreed that this represented a fair compromise between the demands of his job and the values of their community.

These types of compromises lead to interesting outcomes. Several of the authors' relatives, for instance, have cellphones since they are required and provided by their place of work. The understanding, however, is that they are a necessary evil and are to be used exclusively for work. However, if the authors wish to speak with them, they can simply call them during their hours of work! Another interesting instance concerns Jacob, an elderly bishop, who, after losing his second wife, lived alone. As he grew older, concerns were raised about his safety: what if he suffered a fall or needed assistance? Typically, the elderly either live in a small house next to their children or have family living with them; but this was not the case with Jacob, who relished his independence and looking after his small farm and repairing his favorite tractor. It was impractical to have others checking in on him and the installation of a home phone had been a long-standing prohibition. A compromise was reached by providing him with a cellphone with the internet disabled that he could use in case of an emergency. This was an exceptional circumstance; not everyone would be allowed to own a cellphone. How this was decided demonstrates the inclusive nature of the Amish. The agreement was not reached between the leaders and Jacob, but rather, it involved the entire congregation. The solution was proposed by a member that was concerned with Jacob's safety and then discussed by the congregation until a suitable compromise was unanimously agreed upon.

On the other hand, some technologies are dismissed outright. One member, Roy, decided that it would be beneficial if he would purchase a small riding-lawnmower to take care of his large lawn, which was a popular gathering place for his Amish neighbors to play croquet (a popular Amish pastime). The expertly maintained lawn was a popular place for the custom wooden mallet-wielding players to compete. It was not long, however, before the bishop and a minister paid Roy a visit, and the push mower soon replaced the riding-lawnmower. Roy's willingness to abandon the convenience of the riding-lawnmower exemplifies the spirit of individual sacrifice. It is not clear how word of Roy's purchase had reached the bishop, but in this case, the bishop intervened without taking the issue to the congregation. In other more complicated matters, the bishop would likely take the issue to the congregation.

While secular organizations tend to introduce technology based on productivity or convenience, the Amish consider the effect the technology will have on the congregation and its families. Vehicles, for instance, are rejected not because there is something inherently "evil" with motorized transportation but because it is feared they will compromise the cohesiveness of the community by enabling members to travel farther away from their neighbors. Horse and buggies (and even electric bicycles) help keep neighbors close and things central. As one bishop said, cars make it less likely that you will walk over to your neighbors for a visit or stop by a neighbor to let your horse rest. By extending the range that people can travel, automobiles are believed to erode the fabric of the community. The bishop admitted that vehicles are more efficient for transporting materials and people, but it comes at the expense of the community and redraws boundaries while redefining the concept of neighbor and place. So it is that one finds Amish businesses relying on vehicles for transportation while the owners continue to use the horse and buggy for personal travel. As Nolt (2015, p. 34) observes, for the Amish the goal is "not technological 'purity' but rather a particular expression of community."

Amish leadership stands in stark contrast to existing leadership models, which tend to focus on employees' productivity or organizational performance when examining outcomes. As well, secular leaders often pit employees against each other in the name of "healthy competition"; think of the pink Cadillacs Mary Kay awards to their top salespeople. Revisiting Warren Bennis' (1998) distinction between managers who do things right and leaders who do the right things highlights the radical approach taken by Amish leaders. With any issue brought to church's attention, the underlying issue is how it will affect the life of the community and the integrity of the home. That is, the emphasis is not on whether the technology or practice will lead to greater profits or efficiencies but how it will affect the person and the community. Hence, it is the private and isolating nature of cellphones that are perceived as threatening the cohesiveness of the home and the authority of the church. Besides being viewed as worldly and vain, the pink Cadillacs would be seen as creating strife between members.

## The Shadow of the Past: Tradition in the Amish

Contrary to the narrow focus of business leaders on measures of economic success and impact, even when evaluating projects related to corporate social responsibility (Waldman et al., 2020), industry and business are but one part of life for the Amish. While it is understood that one must make a living, the central concern is living a life consistent with the principles and practices of the Amish faith. All their decisions are made within the long shadow of the past. The *ordnung* is a type of compass guiding them on a path that is consistent with their faith and rooted in the decisions of preceding generations. When most of us encounter new technology, we ask only if it will make our lives better and/or easier or if it will improve our financial standing. Rarely do we ask, "better what?" or do we consider what our parents or grandparents would think. Concerning the promise of technology, Kraybill (2013) noted how the Amish do not buy the hype: "they're more cautious—more suspicious—wondering is this going to be helpful or is it going to be detrimental? Is it going to bolster our life together as a community, or is it going to somehow tear it down?"

What is the *ordnung*? The *ordnung* can be best likened to a kind of mission statement expressing the core beliefs of the congregation. *Ordnung* (German for order) is an oral account of the rules, discipline, organization and system that guides the congregation in their daily life. To be baptized into the church (usually between 18-22 years of age), the individual must agree with the articles of the *ordnung* and solemnly vow to follow them. This is quite different than in most organizations where the mission statement is rarely discussed in interviews, much less in daily interactions. It is the bishop's job to ensure that the *ordnung* is applied fairly and consistently to all members and that business practices are consistent with it. Given the tremendous pace of change, there is continual pressure on the bishop to ensure that current innovations fit within the existing parameters of the *ordnung*.

Nonetheless, there is a lot of leeway for the bishop. For instance, a bishop may decide that while some members are bringing their cell phones home, it is not an issue that the congregation must address. If, however, the bishop believes that a technology or action requires a response, or if members feel strongly, then the issue will be brought before the church. Yet bishops do not make decisions for the church, although they can certainly affect them. So, in the case of cellphones, it would be up to the congregation to reach an agreement on whether cellphones be left at the worksite or be brought home. At such meetings, all members would have the opportunity to bring their concerns forward and all members would cast their vote. All decisions must be unanimous. Formally, each congregation (usually composed of 16–20 households) takes up such questions twice a year during their communion service. At this service, members review the *ordnung* which includes agreed upon parameters for technology use and social practices. Discussion then ensues with members saying why they believe a technology or activity should or should not be allowed as it relates to the *ordnung*. The concluding ritual of communion is not held until all members are "at peace."

There is considerable room for finessing new distinctions for old taboos, and members understand some latitude must be given to ensure that Amish businesses can compete in the marketplace. But again, the marketplace is not the primary consideration; the *ordnung* holds considerable sway. The Amish hold a strong belief in the collective wisdom of the group. Kraybill (2001, p. 99) recounted how a younger bishop sought the counsel of an older bishop. After providing his opinion, the older bishop added, "Don't do it that way just because I told you, go home and work with your Church."

In this way, leadership is not top-down but rather a model of mutual submission in which the leader consults and even submits to the congregation. No special group or "task force" is charged with determining the desirability of adopting change, rather responsibility rests with the congregation. In their discussions, both women and men voice their opinions and cast their votes. Once the votes have been cast, members accept the outcome. The values of humility and submission ensure that members with dissenting opinions will subject themselves to the decision of the group. This includes the bishop. Even though the bishop may not agree with the congregation's decision, he will nonetheless accept it and subject himself to its provisions. Communion, administered at the end of the service, reinforces the bonds of community. Of course, there are some instances where differences cannot be surmounted, and in extreme cases a congregation may split.

While mainstream models of leadership view the domain of culture and identity as one more lever for the change management initiatives of business leaders (Alvesson and Sveningsson, 2016), Amish leaders do not tamper with core values. Although the Amish are remarkably adept at exploiting market openings, they will not compromise their faith as expressed in their congregation—it is more important to be a good Amish person than a successful businessperson. Thus, economic activity takes a backseat to their values. While the Amish work in a variety of fields, they retain their "Amishness" and hold their religious identity paramount. They are guided by an abiding awareness that they belong and are accountable to a community whose roots are intertwined and run deep. It is the integrity and well-being of the community (whose roots are in the home) and the preservation of its guiding principles of faith that are held sacred. The Amish have proven remarkably adept at walking the fine line between being "in the world" but not "of the world" (John 17, v. 14–16), adapting to changing markets while maintaining their identity.

Unlike many organizations that have a mission statement that is on official documents but not employees' minds, the Amish are acutely aware of the *ordnung*. It is a living document written on their heart, not the walls of corporate headquarters. It can change over time but only with assent from all. A defining feature or the Amish is their reverence for tradition. In asking questions about why they engage in certain practices, it is common to hear, "that's what we do." Often this is because the members themselves are unaware why a certain practice has been implemented, but they take it as their responsibility to honor it. The past is the NorthStar by which the Amish compass is calibrated. For the Amish, the biblical injunction to honor one's father and mother is manifested by following in their parent's footsteps or receiving their parent's blessing. Though they may not necessarily belong to the same profession, they seek to imitate their parent's values and mindset. As an example, another bishop, Jonas, pointed to a family that attended a Lutheran church. The parents had attended the church their entire life and now their two boys were attending the church with their own families. "That is how you honor your father and mother," Jonas pointed out; "that is what honor means."

Amish bishops are imbued with a historical sense of their congregation and strive to align current practice with orthodoxy. The negotiation, however, is not a meeting of equals in that the past holds greater authority than the present. If a current practice challenges or contradicts a past precedent, it will likely be abandoned. It is not just technology that is viewed with suspicion, but any new practice or product. Kotter's famous distinction between managers as defenders of the status quo and leaders as agitators of change finds its opposite in the Amish. Here, it is the leaders, the bishops, who are the defenders of the status quo; they are the ones who champion the established way of doing things. Rather than agitate for change, they serve more as shepherds who prevent the congregation from straying off the worn path of tradition.

The centrality of the past can be seen in their introductory question: "who are you?" When meeting a new person, this question will immediately be asked. For us, this question is met with a first name and maybe our surname, soon followed, if you're a Canadian, by a discussion of the weather! For the Amish, however, the question runs much deeper. They will respond by providing at minimum their grandfather's name, followed by their father's and then theirs. Typically, they will include some defining feature of their predecessor (nickname or occupation). Thus, when the lead author is asked who he is, he would reply, "bishop Jonas Keim's Andy's Charles." In this way, he is located within a family and a specific place. In secular society, conversations tend to lead to one asking, "what do you do?" so that the person's occupation and, implicitly, their social status, can be inferred. By contrast, the Amish want to know if they might share someone in common with the person they are speaking with. The occupation is less important. The monikers used by the Amish are often colorful: "Diesel Dan" (a well-known heavy-duty mechanic); "Speck Sammy" (Speck is "chubby" in Pennsylvania Dutch); "Trash Dennis" (known for the collection of "stuff" on his property). These colorful titles serve as touchpoints so that speakers can locate each other within the social fabric of the Amish.

Knowing how to respond to this question signifies that one understands the complex cultural architecture that such a question involves. It also enables people to discover whether they may share people, rather than occupations, in common, while signifying the tight-knit nature of this community. One Amish bishop remarked how important it is to know a person's family because, "the nut doesn't fall far from the tree." One's name, then, brings to the fore the history of preceding generations and situates the individual within the larger fabric of the community. The sense of belonging, then, is reiterated every time a new person is met; the name represents a long-standing link with the community and a point of contact between the speakers.

## Discussion

Ferdman (2021, p. 3) argues how inclusive leadership "involves fostering equity and fairness across multiple identities." Amish leadership underscores the close connection between leaders and members and their equality. All members submit themselves to the *ordnung* and to each other; they submit to the bishop, but the bishop also submits to the members. Such a relationship transcends common workplace practices like information sessions, team-building activities, or feedback surveys. In pursuing new ventures or conducting their existing business, business leaders consult with the bishop to ascertain how their business practices align with the core tenets of the Amish faith. Similarly, Noe's occupation was scrutinized by his neighbors to ensure that it aligned with the values of the congregation. This is more than being accountable to a board of directors or shareholders and the economic justification is secondary. Furthermore, equity is considered within the context of the past so that one's predecessors are also fairly represented and honored.

Our study highlights an instance where leadership is practiced within the context of community and engages the panoply of human experience. Bishops and business leaders are fundamentally members of the community; they are husbands, fathers, brothers, relatives, neighbors and fellow worshippers. Such a role contrasts with the analytical, economic and finance-driven perspectives that are typically ascribed to contemporary leadership (Pirson and Lawrence, 2010). Such dichotomized or even schizophrenic approaches that see work one way and personal life another, too often interpret leadership as a role assumed by a profit maximizer, and leadership itself as the privileged domain of the few. Thus, leaders occupy a different physical space and move in different organizational circles. Amish leadership does not separate the person from the position, and the person lives his/her life and fulfills his/her role within the context of community life. The bishop and other business leaders are seen by and interact with all members of the congregation across the spectrum of human activity; they are not only leaders but also people who work and live alongside community members.

For Ferdman, leadership is the "fulcrum of inclusion" since it magnifies and connects inclusion at the micro and macro level. Effective leadership requires a sophisticated skillset (van Knippenberg et al., 2013; Bennett, 2014; Hannum et al., 2010) and a delicate touch to ensure that people feel included and valued. As demonstrated earlier, including and valuing all members is at the core of the Amish faith. Wasserman (2021, p. 83) argues that the challenge of leading in uncertain times is fundamentally adaptive, involving "situations in which there is no clear answer and issues that require experimentation and improvisation." The Amish response to this uncertainty is instructive. They have successfully navigated government legislation, technological change and increased competition while retaining a strong identity and vital community. Yet the leadership style practiced by Amish leadership cannot be labeled as "transformational leadership"; if anything, it is more reactive than proactive. Yet it is a style that strives to include everyone and has passed the test of time and the encroachment of technology.

Booysen (2014, p. 306) regards inclusive leadership as an ongoing cycle of learning "directed, aligned and committed toward the shared outcomes for the common good of all while retaining a sense of authenticity and uniqueness." The Amish provide practical lessons for how we can define and protect the common good without sacrificing core identity. In formulating these lessons, the Amish expression of community is paramount. There is a place for everyone in the Amish community and everyone knows their place. There is no homelessness in the Amish community, and members know that if they need help of any kind, their community will provide it. Amish community expresses Gergen's (2009) conviction that meaning is the consequence of coordinated action, which is to say that only within the context of relationship is meaning achieved. The practical steps taken by Amish leaders in establishing and maintaining this relationship has been the focus of this chapter.

## CONCLUSION

Amish leadership holds important lessons for creating a culture of belonging. Like the barns they build and the language they speak, each person is critical to the integrity of the community, and only when joined together is such a structure possible. Amish leadership has many methods for ensuring that all members of the community feel that they belong. Even though the bishop is the leader and features prominently within the community, humility and service to the community define this leadership. Decisions are the result of the community's collective wisdom as it is expressed in the long shadow of the past. Amish leadership presents a different paradigm that has much to teach us about building an inclusive community. As the strength of a barn results from the integrity of its construction and the assembly of its parts, so the Amish understand that the strength of a community depends on its people and that the sum is greater than its parts. The Amish know that they belong and are accountable to a community whose strength lies in its cohesion. And yet, every Amish barn-raising requires the supervision and direction of a single person. Without this person conducting and coordinating the activity, the mighty enterprise would be confusion, not construction. Amish leadership provides practical lessons for how leaders can construct their own organizational barns.

## REFERENCES


Alvesson, M., & Sveningsson, S. (2016). *Changing Organizational Culture: Cultural Change Work in Progress*. Routledge.

Bennet, J. (2014). *Intercultural competence: Vital perspectives for diversity and inclusion.*

Bennis, W. (1998). Managers do things right. Leaders do the right thing. In C. Kennedy (Ed.), *Management Gurus* (pp. 47–52). Springer. doi:10.1007/978-3-322-82771-5_7

Christmann, E. (1950). Das Pennsylvanianiadeutsch als pfälzishe Mundart. *Rheinstiches Jahrbuch fur Volkskunde*, *1*, 47–82.

Cunliffe, A. L. (2010). Retelling tales of the field: In search of organizational ethnography 20 years on. *Organizational Research Methods*, *13*(2), 224–239. doi:10.1177/1094428109340041

Donnermeyer, J. (2015). Doubling time and population increase of the Amish. *Journal of Amish and Plain Anabaptist Studies*, *3*(1), 94–109. doi:10.18061/1811/69364

Donnermeyer, J. F., Anderson, C., & Cooksey, E. C. (2013). The Amish Population: County Estimates and Settlement Patterns. *Journal of Amish and Plain Anabaptist Studies*, *1*(1), 72–109. doi:10.18061/1811/54896

Ferdman, B. M. (2021). Inclusive Leadership: the fulcrum of inclusion. In B. M. Ferdman, J. Prime, & R. E. Riggio (Eds.), *Inclusive Leadership: transforming diverse lives, workplaces, and societies* (pp. 3–24). Taylor & Francis.

Ferdman, B. M., Prime, J., & Riggio, R. E. (Eds.). (2021). *Inclusive Leadership: transforming diverse lives, workplaces, and societies*. Taylor & Francis.

Fisher, R., Natvig, D., Pretorius, E., Putnam, Mi., & Schuhmann, K. (2022). Why is inflectional morphology difficult to borrow? Distributing and lexicalizing plural allomorphory in Pennsylvania Dutch. *Languages (Basel, Switzerland)*, *7*(86), 1–25.

Gergen, K. (2009). *Relational beings: Beyond self and community*. Oxford University Press.

Gobo, G. (2008). *Doing Ethnography*. Sage. doi:10.4135/9780857028976

Grosjean, F. (2008). *Studying Bilinguals*. Oxford University Press.

Guest, G., MacQueen, K. M., & Namey, E. E. (2012). *Applied Thematic Analysis*. Sage. doi:10.4135/9781483384436

Hannum, K., McFeeters, B. B., & Booysen, L. (Eds.). (2010). *Leading across differences: Casebook*. Pfeiffer.

Hurst, C., & McConnell. (2010). *An Amish Paradox: Diversity and Change in the World's Largest Amish Community*. Johns Hopkins University Press.

Keim, C., & Shadnam, M. (2018). Through the looking glass: Leadership in the age of surveillance. *Journal of Leadership Studies*, *12*(3), 57–59. doi:10.1002/jls.21596

Keim, C., & Shadnam, M. (2020). Leading in an Amish paradise: Humanistic leadership in the Old Order Amish. *Cross Cultural & Strategic Management*, *27*(3), 473–485. doi:10.1108/CCSM-01-2020-0024

Keim & Shadnam. (2020, July). Leading in an Amish paradise: Humanistic leadership in the Old Order Amish. *Cross Culture & Strategic Management*.

Kraybill, D. (2001). *The Riddle of Amish Culture* (Revised edition). Johns Hopkins University Press.

Kraybill, D., Johnson-Weiner, K., & Nolt, S. (2013). *The Amish*. Johns Hopkins University Press. doi:10.56021/9781421409146

Kraybill, D. B., & Nolt, S. M. (2004). *Amish Enterprise: From Plows to Profits*. Johns Hopkins University Press. doi:10.56021/9780801878046

Nolt, S. (2015). 'You hold the whole world in your hand': Cell phones and discernment in Amish churches. *Vision (Basel)*, *16*(2), 27–37.

Nolt, S., & Meyers, T. (2007). *Plain Diversity: Amish Cultures and Identities*. Johns Hopkins University Press. doi:10.1353/book.3499

Pirson, M. (2017). *Humanistic Management: Protecting dignity and promoting well-Being*. Cambridge University Press. doi:10.1017/9781316675946

Pirson, M., Steinvorth, U., Largacha-Martinez, C., & Dierksmeier, C. (2014). *From Capitalistic To Humanistic Business*. Palgrave Macmillan. doi:10.1057/9781137468208

Studies, A. (2019). Is the Amish population growing? Available at: http://groups.etown.edu/ amishstudies/frequently-askedquestions/?doing_wp_cron51578415405.4935638904571533203125

Studies, A. (2020). *Population growth*. Available at: https://groups.etown.edu/amishstudies/ social-organization/population-growth/

Terry, G., Hayfield, N., Clarke, V., & Braun, V. (2017). Thematic analysis. In C. Willig & W. S. Rogers (Eds.), *The SAGE Handbook of Qualitative Research in Psychology* (pp. 17–37). Sage. doi:10.4135/9781526405555.n2

Van Knippenberg, D., van Ginkel, W. P., & Homan, A. C. (2013). Diversity mindsets and the performance of diverse teams. *Organizational Behavior and Human Decision Processes*, *121*(2), 183–193. doi:10.1016/j.obhdp.2013.03.003

Van Maanen, J. (1988). *Tales of the Field: On Writing Ethnography*. The University of Chicago Press.

Wagler, I. (2011). *Growing up Amish: A Memoir*. Tyndale House Publishing.

Waldman, D. A., Siegel, D. S., & Stahl, G. K. (2020). Defining the socially responsible leader: Revisiting issues in responsible leadership. *Journal of Leadership & Organizational Studies*, *27*(1), 5–20. doi:10.1177/1548051819872201

Wasserman, I. C. (2021). Complex times: Leading with vulnerability and integrity. In B. M. Ferdman, J. Prime, & R. E. Riggio (Eds.), *Inclusive Leadership: transforming diverse lives, workplaces, and societies* (pp. 83–96). Taylor & Francis.

# Chapter 13
# The Path of an Independent Thinker to an Inclusive Leader:
## The Journey of Leadership Transformation

**Ansar Abbas**
https://orcid.org/0000-0003-4521-1920
*Airlangga University, Indonesia*

**Dian Ekowati**
https://orcid.org/0000-0001-9726-4720
*Airlangga University, Indonesia*

**Raziq Husain**
*Muslim Youth University, Pakistan*

**Fendy Suhariadi**
https://orcid.org/0000-0001-9679-2185
*Airlangga University, Indonesia*

**Rakotoarisoa Maminirina Fenitra**
https://orcid.org/0000-0002-1045-3404
*Universitas Indonesia, Indonesia*

## ABSTRACT

*Students may have increased motivation when they engage with a tale told about the transformative journey of a world leader. Specifically, when a personality has five decades of charisma, transformation, and fame amassed in their identity, it might aid in gathering much data to validate the idea. This is because such a personality has a complete picture of their life. The story of Imran Khan is instructive because it follows his journey as a transformative leader. It should be a strategic way to keep an individual's persistence in the face of personal and communal adversity. The author hopes that young readers will take heart from his story of grit and persistence, which chronicles his quest for success. The lives of ordinary people who rose to prominence in their communities through extraordinary commitment can be excellent examples to follow and a source of motivation when read as biographies.*

DOI: 10.4018/978-1-6684-8822-5.ch013

## INTRODUCTION

Employees are more likely to embrace change when their leaders cultivate a culture of honesty, transparency, and independence (Vollero et al., 2020). To foster an atmosphere where democratic values can flourish, a society's transformative leaders must first set an example via their personas (Abbas, Ekowati, Suhariadi, & Fenitra, 2022a; Alon & Higgins, 2005). To a point where people feel safe giving and receiving feedback and where a universal language is actively encouraged to spread. In addition, these leaders recognize that their followers are their greatest asset. People like them cause the world to shift and evolve. We can take a cursory look at current leadership literature to realize that there is a wide variety of theories, each of which has specific preferences (Horner, 1997). Historically democratic and autocratic leaders exercise power to seek solutions (Jooste, 2004). Leaders that empower others to influence their followers to participate in decision-making and are authentic, spiritual, transformational, and transactional have a place in organizations (Avolio & Gardner, 2005; Avolio & Wernsing, 2008; Clapp-Smith et al., 2009; George & Bettenhausen, 1990; Hannah et al., 2009; Saroglou et al., 2008; Zou et al., 2015). It is enough to make one's head spin just thinking about all the different leadership theories proposed throughout the years. The list gives the impression that it will never end. However, transformational leaders are more prominent in specific contexts and are regarded as positive leadership that impacts other theories (Abbas, Saud, et al., 2022; Blanch et al., 2016; Jordan, 2016). It is essential to note that leadership is not a trait that can be applied universally. Instead, it is a collection of intrinsic qualities that set certain people apart from others, allowing them to occupy a more prominent position within this job. Due to the prevalence of modern organizations, it is vital to synchronize leadership philosophies with existing theories in this domain. Researchers must consistently adjust their methodology based on the circumstances' demands and whom they perceive to be in a leadership position in every situation (Jago, 1982). A leadership journey is a loud struggle to reveal the fundamental core components tested when one's persistence is confronted with a challenge. With the elimination of survival bias, decisions based on the self-determination theory become more reliable (Koivisto, 2020).

Among many ambient theories, it is hard to distinguish which kind of leadership is vital and fit for a complete definition of a leader. Perhaps, a genuine personality, a living legend of a great man, can be observed so that a complete leadership theory fits in to make it complete. Discussing what makes great leaders great is essential because humans are indispensable to successful leadership in any setting (Boerma et al., 2017). How can one possibly know what criteria must meet in considering a successful leader? Since many distinct categories of leaders are already operating worldwide, what makes them great? Are there any characteristics that all good leaders should have in common? These are valid questions about what constitutes a leader (Ciulla, 1995). Non-cognitive skills are important predictors of an individual's ultimate success in life, based on general mental ability, abstract reasoning, memory, knowledge, and vocabulary. Research has shown that high intelligence and cognitive skills are not always sufficient to lead individuals to the highest levels of success and achievement (Davidson, 2014). However, there is a growing understanding of these variables, which are as significant, if not more important, in determining an Individual's success eventually. These include characteristics such as grit, motivation, self-control, hope, self-discipline, persistence, and resiliency, which appear to play an enormous influence in determining the final success of an individual (Caza & Posner, 2021).

Popular approaches to the conceptualization of charismatic leadership have arguably become essential to the field of the personal leadership journey (Conger & Kanungo, 1987, 1988). However, academics have highlighted many concerns about these methods enabling leadership qualities (Porter

& McLaughlin, 2006; Yukl, 1999). This chapter aims to draw attention to various issues associated with the difficulty of understanding the leadership journey from a practical life example (Yost & Plunkett, 2009). As little thought has been given to teaching leadership journey lessons, this chapter will concentrate on the individual (Hogan et al., 1994). The argument has centered on the personality of Imran Khan, whose leadership style helped shape him into a towering leadership hero. However, his story has previously been barely touched upon in scholarly discourse. Creating leadership journey lessons is twofold: to motivate and encourage academicians to think creatively about how leadership theories are interconnected and can be linked to individuals (Ahmad et al., 2023). Second, a storytelling idea from the charismatic journey could inspire readers to know different aspects of consistency of leadership, opening academic debate for theoretical arenas. Learners could benefit from a leadership journey of individuals who become inclusive leaders and self-directed established leaders. Learners seeing these leaders' life journeys could be motivated by reading the various episodic developments of these leaders in a narrative style, e.g., (Abbas et al,. 2023)

In this chapter's subsections, the authors will continue to use the literature study as a foundation for our arguments about why Imran Khan's character is well-suited to scholarly discussion. In the following sessions, this chapter will show the relevance of published material by presenting theories, literature support, and argument. This chapter contains the conclusions and suggestions made in the preceding page and the theoretical scopes of development of leadership studies based on an assessment of his life.

## PURPOSE OF THE STUDY

Scholars place a premium on arguments and discussions concerning diverse theories of leadership. Due to this and other factors, a lot is written on effective leadership. Because of this fascination, scholars from sectors as varied as business and education have garnered many benefits from studying leadership. This chapter is essential to the rallying point, e.g., an exciting way of engaging readers. For additional research into influential leadership theories in the face of societal transformation, as evidenced by the longevity of prominent leaders' careers, e.g., any life span of a year or decades.

## JUSTIFICATION OF THE STUDY

A debate is a way of idea comparison and contrast where the importance of grit and persistence of leadership is highlighted to get to a theoretically relevant and trustworthy decision. All disputes are settled on three foundations: claims, evidence, and consequences. The arguer wishes their audience will come to their point of view, and they say that here in the claim. One school of thought maintains that exceptional leaders are innate, while another maintains that they can only be cultivated. The consenting party has supplied evidence or independent verification to support the claim. This chapter compiles research favoring the leadership idea of tenacity, determination, and self-awareness, which is vital for the leadership journey.

## SIGNIFICANCE OF THE STUDY

Leadership and influence theories set the stage for the claim and show why the audience should care about growth. To better understand the leadership issue, we will first explore the theoretical explanation for each side's position before moving on to a point-by-point evaluation of the evidence and counterargument for that position. The same literary patterns are used to depict all major current theories. There has been no clear winner in this scholarly dispute because all sides have made valid points. Leaders may be "bred" or "developed." In a typical theory, both camps have a fair chance to ask pertinent questions about the former notion, which is why studying is more advantageous. Our goal in writing this chapter is to help readers gain some understanding of the bare essentials of what a leadership journey should include.

## RESEARCH QUESTIONS

Whether or if skills and knowledge can be taught also remains a mystery. However, the essential arguments and ideologies of all leadership theories remain unchanged. This argument highlights why a steadfast leader is necessary for resolving the conflict. We picked the biography of a famous individual whose rise to power was well-documented and widely felt. Despite extensive investigation, no conclusive results were found. This study has the potential to show how the leadership journey hypothesis can be mapped, constructed, and founded.

## LITERATURE REVIEW

This discussion regarding the fact that leadership, like art, is fluid and experienced through living makes it difficult to describe, as shown in the United Nations argument regarding efforts to comprehend leadership. It is a diagnosis and possible solution for what some people today call a leadership crisis, leadership extinction, or leadership survival. Leaders learn about themselves, others, and their environments throughout their lifetime, so learning what they have seen is essential. These perceptions have proliferated over the past few years, making it seem everyone is thinking about it. The UN questions leadership development, everything, perhaps more than anywhere else[1]. Given the significance of behavior in preventing negativity from maintaining the quality of life, understanding the elements that inspire human ideology has substantial merits for research (Mumford & Fried, 2014). Literature shows that applying Self-Determination Theory is vital to the motivational challenges of challenging conditions linked to topics discussed in the context of some fundamental questions (Ryan & Deci, 2000). The first question that comes to mind that does the quality of motivation regulating a self-directed behavior "matters?" (Ryan et al., 2008). Is it a personal ideology that stimulates a human behavior to achieve some vision through innate abilities or learned behavior? (Abbas, Ekowati, Suhairidi, & Hamid, 2022). Alternatively, life's experiences shape and inform individuals, fueling their resolve and motivation to realize their goals (Paulhus & John, 1998). The second question is related to the importance of basic psychological and physical needs within the aim and vision of a leader (Watts et al., 2019). It shows how contextual understanding can be drawn from their innate behavior vs. the challenges they undertook. It is also vital to know whether contextual variables can be manipulated to create adaptive environments for the extent of their dreams/visions/missions. e.g., A trip that has been self-directed and sustained throughout time demonstrates a stable course and a kind of unwavering motivation (Rana et al., 2016). It stimulates a person's determination to want more until they reach the summit of their potential. These details matter in a scholarly discussion because they illustrate a person's geographic development (Paradiso-Testa, 2022).

Academics of leadership should seek out and work on new approaches to the subject of leadership education. A determined leader's journey can be an academic input for the learning of younger generations (Ansar Abbas, Dian Ekowati, & Aisha Anwar, 2023; Sinclair, 2004). This chapter aims to provide qualitative results from reflections on learning leadership concepts after watching multiple episodes of a legendary leader's exhibition. Examining the relevant literature would reveal that the researchers can draw parallels between the leadership situations depicted in the manifestations and those they might face.

## SELF-DIRECTED LEADERSHIP

Despite increasing research on self-regulation in the organizational and industrial domain, such research proposals in human resource development are not highly evolved (Nesbit, 2012). The focus management engagement and motivation are focused on operational performance rather than learning. Leaders tend to pay less attention to the learning possibilities inherent in their experiences than they do to the performance consequences of those events. Self-directed learnings from life experience and conscience actions require significant cognitive effort (Rothstein & Burke, 2010). While numerous researchers have stressed the importance of self-reflection for charismatic leadership, few have provided concrete instructions for evaluating one's abilities. The term "self-concept" refers to an individual's mental image of themselves and is often used. The individual's philosophical view of themselves is what is referred to as their identity. It includes his sense of self-worth, the basis for their continued existence, and the societal acceptance they enjoy. Social acceptance can lead to acceptance and understanding and pave the road toward establishing one's sense of direction. A person's sense of self-value, esteem, self-confidence, attitude, and motivation constitutes behavior. Therefore, an individual's views regarding their self-concept are essential components of any leadership development program embedded inside an ideology (Ross, 2014).

Similarly, having a healthy outlook on one's self-concept can help one become more self-assured and, ultimately, a more self-directed but effective leader, e.g. (Ross, 2014). The barriers to leaders' awareness and inspiration to start engaging in self-directed learning are " sameness with the identity belief systems, moral standards, and preferences of leaders, or the natural order of environments and lifestyle in which leaders operate. Specifically, the first challenge is related to attention, while the second is related to motivation (Boyce et al., 2010). The ability and motivation of leaders to engage in self-development and learn from experiences vary from person to person. It expects leaders to be socially accountable for updating and maintaining the relevance of their abilities to use power, e.g. (Fathiaa, 2022).

## AN INDEPENDENT THINKERS' CAREER AND LEADERSHIP JOURNEY

Imran Ahmad Khan Niazi was a great cricketer who turned politician, socialist, and philanthropist. After winning the 1992 cricket world cup for Pakistan, we saw his epiphany initiative of Universities, Cancer hospitals through to fruition, idealizing impossible to turn into possibilities. He became a politician later and was elected as the 22nd Prime Minister of Pakistan. His leadership career is one of self-directed, entrusted, and intriguing storylines that can provide valuable lessons for the academic world, particularly in the journey of a persistent leader that showed grit as an independent thinker, e.g. (Daft & Lengel, 1998).

Imran Khan debuted for the Pakistan National Cricket Team when he was 16. He competed in a One-Day International (ODI) match against England at Edgbaston 1971. In 1976, Khan became associated with Kerry Packer's World Series Cricket. From this point of view, he has been a well-known celebrity for the past 50 years. His authentic person's journey begins with defending a famous ball-tampering case that emerged; Khan maintained his composure and clarity and remained a successful defendant. His initiative to include neutral umpires on the cricketing ground was an idea that inspired cricket to be played all around the world. When he answers questions, he does it with more effective methods. He is known for his unwavering commitment to his vision and ability to hold his nervousness better to overcome all challenges. His resolute in his obstacles made his journey clear. He would stand up for what he believed in whenever he felt necessary, backed by his charm and philosophy. Academically, he has penned books, expressed opinions in news articles, and amassed public gathering history that better illustrates his trek. Imran Khan has published six non-fiction works, including his autobiography, co-written with Patrick Murphy. These include-- West and East (1975), Imran: The Autobiography of Imran Khan (1983), Imran Khan's cricket skills (1989), Indus Journey: A Personal View of Pakistan (1991), All Round View (1992), Warrior Race: A Journey Through the Land of the Tribal Pathans (1993), Pakistan: A Personal History (2011) [2]. He could keep working as a commentator and author after retirement, given his talents. He subsequently served as a cricket analyst on several occasions, earning a reputation for his foresight in the future of the sport. His notoriety helped him get the funding he needed to fulfill his dream of establishing a free cancer hospital in his homeland. Having witnessed his mother's battle with cancer, he decided to devote his life to helping those battling this fatal disease. Perhaps around this time, in his position as a social worker and humanitarian, he started working toward constructing a hospital for people with cancer.

## AUTHENTICITY

When a person aspires to become an ethical leader, business leader, or team captain, they must have specific attributes. Personal tenets and character traits make a leader distinctive, affirming the authentic leadership theory (Avolio et al., 2005; Avolio & Walumbwa, 2014; Begley, 2006; Fathiaa, 2022; Gardner et al., 2005; Gatling et al., 2016). Those who possess these abilities are known for always being "genuine" people grounded in reality and authentic in their interactions with others. Balanced processing, self-awareness, relational transparency, and a solid moral code in one's behavior are all components of authenticity in persons (Ansar Abbas, Dian Ekowati, & Aisha Anwar, 2023). Self-awareness, self-regulation, and ethical behavior are the three pillars that enable leaders to develop authenticity. They help to form trusting relationships with the people they lead (Beddoes-Jones & Swailes, 2015). The authors researched analyzing a leadership character to understand better leadership development and the value of supportive social networks, social fabric, and fabric of mind (Abbas, Ekowati, & Suhariadi, 2022; Abbas, Saud, Ekowati, & Suhariadi, 2021; Chance, 2015). Leaders are expected to be interested in expanding their knowledge based on innate abilities. Leadership formation's importance cannot be completely understated without self-development that takes under social process.

Because their social ties have grown, emerging leaders can draw upon a more excellent range of options. These learning tools promote self-development goals, progress assessments, and motivating approaches. Validating one's status as an authentic leader is a challenging and multi-stage process (Shamir & Eilam, 2005). The most compelling evidence of a leader's abilities and progression in their leadership role is the evidence of their actual actions and the time that has passed since they emerged as a leader (Sosik & Jung, 2011). There are four distinct phases to the authentic journey, the first of which involves the formation of a leader identity. What are the most formative experiences that have allowed them to form their ideology? Second, the maturation of a distinct sense of who one is, what one stands for, and how one got that way. These beliefs and self-awareness allow individuals to make peace with their path. An individual's successes and setbacks can be reconciled through balanced processing. Holding these moral and ethical principles allows one to see the future confidently—third, self-congruent goal-setting growth in understanding one's identity and values. They can chart a leadership course and change their objectives by tying together past, present, and future ideas. Fourth, they were able to solidify their vision thanks to their increasing levels of self-expression, namely the congruence between a leader's actions and their sense of identity as a leader. Even if everyone has the potential to lead, those who hold positions of authority are frequently required to carry out responsibilities that appear to be completely random. However, to truly succeed as a leader, one must be prepared to have his philosophy called into question.

Maintaining authentic serenity under pressure is crucial for leaders. Given that every individual is one of a kind, anyone can become a leader, but not everyone can hold authenticity. Nevertheless, they must be consistent in their moral views and actions to be truly effective. Since Khan's path for social reform appears transparent, achieving logical consistency in the educational landscape should not be difficult. This contentious political career has created an opportunity to gain insight into this individual's moral constancy and his chosen strategies to maintain his viewpoint.

## SERVANTHOOD

The research examines the role of attributions in leadership processes. It shows how it contributes to our understanding of leadership today and in the future (Martinko et al., 2007). We believe this topic should be extensively discussed in the context of leadership because servanthood is another part of leaders' personalities. The literature refers to the approach that a leader is a fabrication in the mind of human beings, e.g., depends upon their life experiences. Leadership is a creation in the minds of individuals; it does not operate independently from people but only from the perspective of others, e.g. (Winkler, 2010). Winkler emphasized that observed or determined conduct could be different from the behavior of other group members if it is regarded through the lens of attribution theory (Winkler, 2010). It was suggested that an analyzer could make a clear differentiation; differences in a person's conduct patterns must be compared with those of others who fall into the same group. Minor differences with other behaviors of group members would not enable us to differentiate. However, suppose we can witness the detection of a particular activity. In that case, the analysis should concentrate on differences in those behaviors. Assuming they have been made out, significant distinctions can be quickly adopted as the foundation for attribution because distinct patterns of conduct are identifiable. Under the guise of celebrity wisdom, many famous people are active in charitable and philanthropic causes. For instance, Al Gore is well-known for his efforts to raise public awareness about the effects of climate change and social awareness about the challenges posed by the world's weather (Abbas, Ekowati, Suhariadi, & Fenitra, 2022b).

A mindset that places the needs of others ahead of one's own is an essential component of servanthood, a leadership quality (Abbas, Saud, Ekowati, Usman, et al., 2021; Brewer, 2010; Greenleaf, 1998; Greenleaf et al., 2002). It is a more altruistic kind of leadership in which a leader devotes his life to fostering compassion, social equality, and unmerited favor (Sendjaya & Sarros, 2002; Serrat, 2017; Spears, 1996; Wong & Page, 2003). A person who demonstrates servant leadership interacts with others in management or a fellow employee position (Greenleaf et al., 2002). a servant leadership theory covers style and philosophy through the inner intention to achieve moral authority rather than power (Waterman, 2011). The indigenous Islamic perspective and global views are compatible with the servanthood theory (Ahmad & Ogunsola, 2011).

The beliefs, practices, convictions, attributes, integrity, intuition, and honesty form the basis of this approach to moral leadership. It promotes the idea that those in positions of authority should serve those in their charge, assisting those individuals in reaching their full potential (Ahmad et al., 2016). Leaders gain the respect of their followers when they prioritize meeting the requirements of their followers, such as providing access to primary healthcare, education, and justice. There is typically a shared vision and a more robust level of trust, enabling individuals to share their thoughts in decision-making (Williams et al., 2017). " This ultimately results in improved outcomes and individual progress in a supportive environment." Khan's journey to being a catalyst which acts as a servant leader, has been established by the opportunities he was awarded in his many political and leadership responsibilities. His unwavering commitment to issues of equality and the alleviation of poverty, as well as to the preservation of the environment and the advancement of social reform, is the driving force behind his job. Because of this, he is in a far better position to demonstrate that the qualities he possesses set him apart from the individuals he is competing against.

## SPIRITUALITY

Even if its roots went back to the 1980s, a model for spiritual leadership did not dominate scholarly discussions since early 2000 (Dent et al., 2005; Freeman, 2011; Fry & Matherly, 2006; Malone & Fry, 2003). This paradigm was developed due to the growing enthusiasm at the time by both researchers and practitioners to apply spiritual themes to work environments (Contreras, 2016). This interest created the paradigm in business settings as a popular notion (Ansar Abbas et al., 2023; Abbas, Suhariadi, et al., 2022). According to this, spiritual leadership theory has a unique conception. Spiritual leadership entails understanding the thoughts, feelings, and actions essential to one's own and the dedication and membership of an organization's followers (Ansar Abbas et al., 2023; Abbas, Suhariadi, et al., 2022; Bayighomog & Arasli, 2022; Bayighomog & Araslı, 2019; Samul, 2020; Sari et al., 2019). Fry advocated a more significant notion of spiritual leadership. He argued that a lack of spiritual leadership hinders an organization's ability to forge a shared vision (Fry & Nisiewicz, 2013). Spiritual leaders establish shared values between employees and management and equip teams. None will likely generate the dedication and output resulting from strong spiritual leadership (Fry, 2003). Ultimately, Fry concluded that spiritual leadership is essential to raise employee engagement and output in the workplace (Fry et al., 2006). The difference between servant leadership, which focuses on the moral character of leaders, and spiritual leadership, which attributes lead to the behavior and performance of the organization as a whole, is highlighted in this first illustration. However, both approaches, spirituality, and spiritual leadership, rely on the intended members' meaningful life, intrinsic motivation, dedication, and membership

(Dent et al., 2005). Spiritual leaders must draw on their human and divine strengths to influence the Faithful for God's purposes. The best use of one's inherent talents and abilities—which are not of one's own making but of God's—is in the service of the Lord and also for His holiness, e.g. (Danz, 2022). The spirituality of a predominantly Muslim country like Pakistan, with a 93% Muslim population, is fraught with global, academic, and practical implications (Jafari & Scott, 2014). To achieve God's goals, philosophical persons must carry out spiritual work using spiritual means, e.g., a leader. Thus, a spiritual leader's primary role is to unite and inspire the native population toward a more purposeful way of life, regardless of their demographic makeup (Hill & Edwards, 2013). According to Crossman, this approach emerged as a different alternative to understanding the human factors in work settings in contrast to the traditional perspective that focuses on productivity, e.g., social and business (Crossman, 2010). This approach contrasts with the fact that the traditional perspective is only concerned with increasing output because the conventional viewpoint solely concentrates on the efficiency with which individuals perform their jobs (Crossman, 2011).

It is not a title or a position that determines spiritual leadership, but rather the leader's soul or religious nature. Individual well-being is central to this leadership philosophy. The term "leader" implies those who follow an academic definition of spirituality. Imran Khan's spiritual development has been an ongoing process spanning decades. After his mother passed away, he was motivated to pursue social work, and he eventually built a free cancer hospital. He is always found carrying on meaningful conversations about life. A goal that was not just human-centric but also nationalistic, patriotic, and, most likely, divine[3] . That is why he is destined for a role of spiritual leadership. Some claim that during his time as prime minister, Khan ignored the country's structural issues in favor of a moral crusade motivated by his desire to be a spiritual leader to the people and atonement for his youthful indiscretions in the West [4]. Leaders take the next logical step in their spiritual life because they recognize they are imperfect. Khan is especially interested in delving into Sufi mysticism once one has begun honing their (Sufi's) wits and methods to reach God.

## THE THEORY

Leaders who are inclusive by their nature are tenacious individuals who are more committed to their vision. They have the confidence to face challenges since they know their identity. Their inquisitive nature lets them make societal change happen and derive cultural and social savvy from collaborating at large scales. This journey, from this point forward for various reasons, includes discrete occurrences and an ongoing methodical battle to achieve the peak of leadership. This type of leader will exercise their authority in leadership positions in a democratic way, e.g., ethically and responsibly accepted ways only (Abbas, 2022; Abbas, Ekowati, et al., 2021). It is a central theme in the classic works of leadership theory. Success, influence, and power beyond most people's imagination are possible because of a leader's conception or evolution. However, when they look to the future, they are united by a common understanding of what it means to be a leader and a desire to dominate the public sphere. It was not for selfish gain, fraud, or manipulation; rather, it was to advance the broad vision or scheme of the leader (Krausz, 1986; Lam & Xu, 2019; Lunenburg, 2012). Any person in a position of authority needs to be able to direct their course of events. Great leaders have the authority to influence society and preserve and improve human dignity. For this reason, their followers need to be coordinated with their vision under power, e.g., social exchange (Blau, 1964; Cook & Rice, 2001).

The traditional leadership development method involves delving into successful leaders' personal histories. Leaders go through strenuous activity to pinpoint the times and places crucial to their development, and they come to terms with these experiences. Many scholars and writers have concentrated on the occurrences and experiences that occurred early in a leader's life or career (Blakeley & Higgs, 2014; Laschinger et al., 2013; Savage-Austin & Honeycutt, 2011; van Droffelaar, 2021; Weiss et al., 2018; Zhang et al., 2019). These include the death of a parent, the successful precision of an early life crisis, and challenging or nurturing life circumstances, e.g. (Ellison et al., 2014; Jeronimus et al., 2014; Morton et al., 2019). High personal ambitions, travel history, cultural assimilations, relationships with mentors or role models, and participation in several leadership roles during the early stages of one's life are also significant (Abbas, Ekowati, & Suhariadi, 2022; Kostikov, 2014; Marques, 2016; Voss, 2000). Literature establishes a link between these events and experiences and the growth of pertinent leadership characteristics and abilities, such as identity, independence, willingness to take risks, drive for achievement, and motivation for power, e.g. (Winkler, 2010). However, leaders at the top echelons need to maintain a consistent character, trajectory, identity, and ideology to maintain their rightful place in society (Maxwell, 2014). Under the description of the postmodern leader method, this argument is valid. The fundamental focus of neo-charismatic leadership is the change that occurs. As a direct result, their personal development also leads to followers' development or transformation. This process's visionary and charismatic features are particularly understood to be located in the qualities and simultaneous behavior patterns exhibited by the person in charge. According to this interpretation, leaders must be persistent and have grit. They must be able to transform people who perceive and follow their vision and give them a powerful sense of purpose and meaning. When a journey becomes planned, leadership would be most beneficial for many things, such as designing training within the determination. It is based on the ideas and values of individuals, such as having a strong will and staying committed. How do people learn to reflect on their beliefs and learn and grow from their experiences? One problem with this way of evolution is that it puts too much weight on human self-ideology. For instance, observing a journey, learning from their biological psychology, and seeing lives change or what they learn are typical patterns that can only be grasped over time. In a quest to answer this question, we may see the role of social psychology in persistence that leads to self-determination, innate psychology, or any learned behavior in early childhood. During the first several decades of a person's existence, many different circumstances contribute to the formation of their mind. These particular aspects of individuals in leadership roles should be considered for studying intensely to understand their journey. Often these keynotes are present in the storyline of any leader. For example, Imran Khan always refers to these memories he had in his mind, reconciling them to explain his thoughts. This could be a beginning point to discovering social psychology education and how ideology, grit, and leadership formation affect a persistent person or leader. This can indicate one's ideologies when posed as a serious comment about the worth of looking back on one's conceptions of autonomy. Social psychology, intrinsic philosophy, and human upbringing play a role in developing a sense of agency and can also be understood this way. So that it can be additionally ascertained whether the properties were acquired through natural means or whether it was a preexisting trait of the individual. Public speeches and interviews, various pieces of literature on Imran Khan's stories that are already available, would make for interesting data for analysis. His personality is dynamic and can function in numerous dimensions, making him an ideal scenario for researchers in leadership studies. Storytelling methods, recordings, interview analysis, and scanning older news stories or magazine pieces could help readers better grasp the subject. It will shed light on numerous hitherto hidden dimensions and provide an in-depth analysis of leaders' challenges. Nobody can expect to lead others effectively if they cannot even lead themselves. Accepting personal accountability and self-discipline are prerequisites to leadership (Neck & Manz, 2010). To some extent, the leadership journeys of people who have a firm grasp on the concept of leadership as a journey can serve as the inspiration for developing novel leadership theories. The most convincing leaders emphasize transformational leadership, which inspires their followers to alter their goals, values, and skills in the face of profound social upheaval. The self-leadership model is a network of superior mediators that affects an individual's behavior selection and determination (Ross, 2014). Bandura identified and explained the role of self-esteem and self-concept as crucial personal influences (Bandura et al., 2003). This argument supports a person's sense of competence, e.g., human capital creation; it increases when they demonstrate that they can succeed despite facing challenges (Abbas, Ekowati, Suhairidi, & Anwar, 2022; Abbas, Ekowati, Suhariadi, Fenitra, et al., 2022). The high-level group of the United Nations supports such a framework. Norm-based, principled, inclusive, responsible, multi-dimensional, transformative, multi-stakeholder, collaborative, self-applied, pragmatic, and action-oriented leadership qualities are essential and could be insightful for upcoming research, e.g. (Thompson & Matkin, 2020; Van Knippenberg & van Ginkel, 2022).

## METHOD

Intelligible synthesis is the process of bringing together disparate parts into a whole. Scholars often use this term when delegating work like a literature review or an extensive citation of multiple sources. The conceptual strength approach can create convincing arguments during its review, e.g., (Machi & McEvoy, 2021; Xiao & Watson, 2019). Given that we have stated that people's personal experiences (in this case, leadership through adversity) can be instructive, we hope you will find this book fascinating. The case study will center on the life story of a single person, such as Imran Khan, to show how they embody the traits of a transformative leadership personality in the context of the global landscapes, as outlined in this chapter. We have compiled evidence from various sources, including academic literature and other materials.

## CONCLUSION, RECOMMENDATION, AND FUTURE DIRECTIONS

The central element of the process is the development of a theory of transformative but self-directed leadership based on grit, persistence, self-concept, direction, and ideology. Research on charismatic leadership has not explained the mechanism by which it has the dramatic effects that it does. Therefore, only specific types of transformation can be recognized. For example, charismatic, persistent personalities with grit or determination frequently motivate their followers to improve their moral character. No inspirational justifications can be provided until charismatic leaders influence their followers to alter their core beliefs, priorities, and objectives. We can conclude that effects on followers' sense of identity are particularly salient. By skillfully linking the followers' sense of identity to the purpose, charismatic leaders can increase the worth of their efforts and the significance of their aims. Charismatic but persistent, and inclusive nature leaders can achieve their missions and goals through three distinct patterns of behavior: (1) behavior that emphasizes collective values and ideologies and that links the mission, goals, and expected behavior to the values and ideologies of the followers; (2) behavior that emphasizes the collective identity of the organization, and that links the mission, goals, and expected behaviors to the identity of the followers; and (3) leader behavior that demonstrates the mission, goals, and expected behaviors. The persistence of a leader, inclusive in all circumstances, is a substitute for oxygen for leadership theory. This circumstance is possible during times of crisis or any other moment when stability and predictability are low. Leaders in these situations must display charismatic traits and behaviors as catalysts. However, adherents have a reputation for being flammable during social change, and most change agents face resistance. It is common knowledge that when social upheaval brings about conflicts, those in charge are the first to be looked to for direction. Crisis and poor judgment have robbed many world leaders of their identities. As a result, their followers are misled, or their opponents are allowed to exploit their false stances. Therefore, some experts feel that charismatic leaders may influence people of any background or belief system. However, charisma alone would not suffice if there was no persistence. The emergence of charismatic leadership would be how to deal with different kinds of usual circumstances. That is what strategic leaders do, yet inclusive leaders are charismatic too and always mend their position with social support. Thus, their survival can last.

The context, philosophies, and exemplary lives of specific individuals who have played the leadership role are the factors that contribute to the limitations of this chapter. The author seems to think that the path of a leader to be inclusive goes through the cyclical advances of a person's self-training and character development. Developing this approach to reasoning through story and identity journey is crucial if individuals are to forge their own identities and succeed in the world. Students should be taught various techniques for cultivating the leadership traits that will serve them professionally. Charisma is one of them, but it is invisible unless combined with the freedom of choice. Many leaders have succeeded and been remembered for their charm.

Nevertheless, others have failed because they relied only on their charisma. From this point of view, persistence, determination, and self-direction in managing their journey could be all important. After the voyage, each thought will explore "inclusiveness" naturally (Abbas, 2023). In the most fundamental sense, self-directed leaders must have 'everyone' in mind, considering unique social factors. Such factors include age, cultural differences, gender identity, religion, handicap, personal attributes, working styles, and building social fabric. Authenticity, spirituality, altruism, and persistence are all characteristics that stand out. The self-directed leadership experience would unfold in organic chunks, making it more welcoming to all social members (Goltz, 2023). This method would help them maintain an endless journey.

Therefore, leaders of the current and next generations must be optimistic if they are to have a positive impact on their followers. Employees rely heavily on their leaders since they are their gateways to the professional world and the sources of critical support and guidance. A growing body of literature on effective leadership focuses on an organization's top executives' impact on their teams' morale and productivity. A leader's optimistic outlook will always have more weight and sway over followers, regardless of the circumstances. A motivational leader is typically inclusive in nature and a trainer. Though setting goals and targets (for self and others) are significant in determining an organization's success, the inspiring qualities of its leader are equally crucial. Leaders can drive their teams by instilling a feeling of purpose, high standards, and challenging but achievable goals. As a result, a leader's ability to inspire his team members improves their output. A good outlook is also related to high levels of motivation. A leader's optimistic demeanor creates a conducive setting for their followers, who are consequently more likely to follow in the leader's footsteps and achieve success. This chapter shows us that a leader's character must be consistent across time to effect change and that the stories of several contemporary figures can serve as instructive examples. In addition, it demonstrates that leadership is not about a single moment in time but about a continuous journey and ongoing transformation. That character is the foundation of effective and lasting leadership; they could only demonstrate that change requires determination and resilience others should learn from.

## REFERENCES


Abbas, A. (2022). *Individual psychological distance: A leadership task to assess and cope with invisible change* [PhD Dissertation]. Airlangga University.

Abbas, A. (2023). The Potential of Ethically Responsible and Persistent Leadership Theory. In Ç. Doğru (Ed.), *Role of Human Resources for Inclusive Leadership, Workplace Diversity, and Equity in Organizations* (pp. 111–123). IGI Publisher. doi:10.4018/978-1-6684-6602-5.ch011

Abbas, A., Ekowati, D., & Anwar, A. (2023). Authentic Leadership Journey: An empirical Discussion from Pakistani higher education employing the Lay theory of Psychology. *International Journal of Public Leadership*. Advance online publication. doi:10.1108/IJPL-04-2022-0020

Abbas, A., Ekowati, D., Suhairidi, F., & Anwar, A. (2022). Human Capital Creation: A Collective Psychological, Social, Organizational and Religious Perspective. *Journal of Religion and Health*. Advance online publication. doi:10.100710943-022-01665-8 PMID:36109469

Abbas, A., Ekowati, D., Suhairidi, F., & Hamid, A. R. (2022). Negative Vs Positive Psychology: A Review of Science of Well-being. *Integrative Psychological & Behavioral Science*. Advance online publication. doi:10.100712124-022-09708-1 PMID:35759165

Abbas, A., Ekowati, D., & Suhariadi, F. (2021). Individual psychological distance: A leadership task to assess and cope with invisible change. *Journal of Management Development*, *40*(3), 168–189. doi:10.1108/JMD-09-2020-0304

Abbas, A., Ekowati, D., & Suhariadi, F. (2022). Social Perspective: Leadership in Changing Society. In M. I. Hassan, S. Sen Roy, U. Chatterjee, S. Chakraborty, & U. Singh (Eds.), *Social Morphology, Human Welfare, and Sustainability* (pp. 89–107). Springer International Publishing. doi:10.1007/978-3-030-96760-4_4

Abbas, A., Ekowati, D., Suhariadi, F., & Anwar, A. (2023). Workplace: Empirical study on spiritual leadership in Pakistani Higher Education. *International Journal of Business and Systems Research*, *17*(4), 367–386. doi:10.1504/IJBSR.2023.131721

Abbas, A., Ekowati, D., Suhariadi, F., Anwar, A., & Fenitra, R. M. (2023). Technology acceptance and COVID-19: A perspective for emerging opportunities from crisis. *Technology Analysis and Strategic Management*, 1–13. doi:10.1080/09537325.2023.2214642

Abbas, A., Ekowati, D., Suhariadi, F., & Fenitra, R. M. (2022a). Health Implications, Leaders Societies, and Climate Change: A Global Review. In U. Chatterjee, A. O. Akanwa, S. Kumar, S. K. Singh, & A. Dutta Roy (Eds.), *Ecological Footprints of Climate Change: Adaptive Approaches and Sustainability* (pp. 653–675). Springer International Publishing. doi:10.1007/978-3-031-15501-7_26

Abbas, A., Ekowati, D., Suhariadi, F., & Fenitra, R. M. (2022b). Health implications, Leaders Societies, and Climate Change: A Global Review. In *Ecological footprints of climate change: Adaptive Approaches and Sustainability*. Springer. doi:10.1007/978-3-031-15501-7_26

Abbas, A., Ekowati, D., Suhariadi, F., Fenitra, R. M., & Fahlevi, M. (2022). Human Capital Development in Youth Inspires Us With a Valuable Lesson: Self-Care and Wellbeing. In K. L. Clarke (Ed.), *Self-Care and Stress Management for Academic Well-Being* (pp. 80–101). IGI Global. doi:10.4018/978-1-6684-2334-9.ch006

Abbas, A., Saud, M., Ekowati, D., & Suhariadi, F. (2021). Social Psychology and Fabrication: A Synthesis of Individuals, Society, and Organization. In B. Christiansen & H. Chandan (Eds.), *Handbook of Research on Applied Social Psychology in Multiculturalism* (Vol. 1, pp. 89–109). IGI Global. doi:10.4018/978-1-7998-6960-3.ch005

Abbas, A., Saud, M., Ekowati, D., Usman, I., & Suhariadi, F. (2021). Servant leadership: A strategic choice for organisational performance. An empirical discussion from Pakistan. *International Journal of Productivity and Quality Management, 34*(4), 468–485. doi:10.1504/IJPQM.2021.120599

Abbas, A., Saud, M., Suhariadi, F., Usman, I., & Ekowati, D. (2022). Positive leadership psychology: Authentic and servant leadership in higher education in Pakistan. *Current Psychology (New Brunswick, N.J.), 41*(10), 5859–5871. doi:10.100712144-020-01051-1

Abbas, A., Suhariadi, F., Ekowati, D., Anwar, A., & Saud, M. (2022). Spirituality at Workplace: Role of Spiritual Leadership, Productivity, and Emotional Exhaustion. *Pre Print Available at* Research Square, 1-18 Doi. doi:10.21203/rs.3.rs-492746/v1

Ahmad, K., & Ogunsola, O. K. (2011). An empirical assessment of Islamic leadership principles. *International Journal of Commerce and Management, 36*(4), 379–387. doi:10.1108/10569211111165325

Ahmad, S., Rofie, M. K. H., & Salim, S. (2016). Rewards and commitment in social development: Equipping modern muslim communities with knowledge on Islamic work ethics towards better living conditions. *Mediterranean Journal of Social Sciences, 7*(S1), 395-400. doi:10.5901/mjss.2016.v7n1s1p395

Ahmad, T., Hamid, A., Abbas, A., Anwar, A., Ekowati, D., Fenitra, R., & Suhariadi, F. (2023). Empowering leadership: Role of Organizational Culture of Self-Esteem, and Emotional Intelligence on Creativity. *Journal of Management Development, 42*(3), 201–214. doi:10.1108/JMD-10-2021-0288

Alon, I., & Higgins, J. M. (2005). Global leadership success through emotional and cultural intelligences. *Business Horizons, 48*(6), 501–512. doi:10.1016/j.bushor.2005.04.003

Avolio, B. J., & Gardner, W. L. (2005). Authentic leadership development: Getting to the root of positive forms of leadership. *The Leadership Quarterly, 16*(3), 315–338. doi:10.1016/j.leaqua.2005.03.001

Avolio, B. J., & Walumbwa, F. O. (2014). Authentic leadership theory, research and practice: Steps taken and steps that remain. In I. D. V. Day (Ed.), *The Oxford handbook of leadership and organizations: Oxford library of psychology*. Oxford University Press.

Avolio, B. J., & Wernsing, T. S. (2008). Practicing authentic leadership. In S. J. Lopez (Ed.), *Positive psychology: Exploring the best in people* (Vol. 4, pp. 147–165). Greenwood.

Bandura, A., Caprara, G. V., Barbaranelli, C., Gerbino, M., & Pastorelli, C. (2003). Role of affective self-regulatory efficacy in diverse spheres of psychosocial functioning. *Child Development*, *74*(3), 769–782. doi:10.1111/1467-8624.00567 PMID:12795389

Bayighomog, S. W., & Araslı, H. (2019). Workplace spirituality–customer engagement Nexus: The mediated role of spiritual leadership on customer–oriented boundary–spanning behaviors. *Service Industries Journal*, *39*(7-8), 637–661. doi:10.1080/02642069.2019.1570153

Bayighomog, S. W., & Arasli, H. (2022). Reviving employees' essence of hospitality through spiritual wellbeing, spiritual leadership, and emotional intelligence. *Tourism Management*, *89*, 104406. doi:10.1016/j.tourman.2021.104406

Beddoes-Jones, F., & Swailes, S. (2015). Authentic leadership: Development of a new three pillar model. *Strategic HR Review*, *13*(4), 94–99. doi:10.1108/SHR-04-2015-0032

Begley, P. T. (2006). Self-knowledge, capacity and sensitivity: Prerequisites to authentic leadership by school principals. *Journal of Educational Administration*, *44*(6), 570–589. doi:10.1108/09578230610704792

Blakeley, K., & Higgs, M. (2014). Responsible leadership development–crucible experiences and power relationships in a global professional services firm. *Human Resource Development International*, *17*(5), 560–576. doi:10.1080/13678868.2014.954192

Blanch, J., Gil, F., Antino, M., & Rodríguez-Muñoz, A. (2016). Positive leadership models: Theoretical framework and research. *Psychologist Papers*, *37*(3), 170–176.

Blau, P. (1964). *Power and exchange in social life*. Wiley & Sons.

Boerma, M., Coyle, E. A., Dietrich, M. A., Dintzner, M. R., Drayton, S. J., Early, J. L., ... Lin, A. Y. F. (2017). Point/counterpoint: Are outstanding leaders born or made? *American Journal of Pharmaceutical Education*, *81*(3), 1–5. doi:10.5688/ajpe81358 PMID:28496278

Boyce, L. A., Zaccaro, S. J., & Wisecarver, M. Z. (2010). Propensity for self-development of leadership attributes: Understanding, predicting, and supporting performance of leader self-development. *The Leadership Quarterly*, *21*(1), 159–178. doi:10.1016/j.leaqua.2009.10.012

Brewer, C. (2010). Servant leadership: A review of literature. *The Online Journal for Workforce Education and Development*, *4*(2), 1–8.

Caza, A., & Posner, B. Z. (2021). Mixed associations between grit and transformational leadership behavior. *Journal of Leadership Studies*, *15*(3), 6–20. doi:10.1002/jls.21781

Chance, M. R. (2015). *Social fabrics of the mind*. Psychology Press. doi:10.4324/9781315728186

Ciulla, J. B. (1995). Leadership ethics: Mapping the territory. *Business Ethics Quarterly*, *5*(1), 5–28. doi:10.2307/3857269

Clapp-Smith, R., Vogelgesang, G. R., & Avey, J. B. (2009). Authentic leadership and positive psychological capital: The mediating role of trust at the group level of analysis. *Journal of Leadership & Organizational Studies*, *15*(3), 227–240. doi:10.1177/1548051808326596

Conger, J. A., & Kanungo, R. N. (1987). Toward a behavioral theory of charismatic leadership in organizational settings. *Academy of Management Review*, *12*(4), 637–647. doi:10.2307/258069

Conger, J. A., & Kanungo, R. N. (1988). The empowerment process: Integrating theory and practice. *Academy of Management Review*, *13*(3), 471–482. doi:10.2307/258093

Contreras, F. (2016). Servant and spiritual leadership theories: Are they two different notions? *Journal of Human Values*, *22*(3), 202–208. doi:10.1177/0971685816650578

Cook, K. S., & Rice, E. R. (2001). Exchange and power: Issues of structure and agency. In J. H. Turner (Ed.), Handbook of sociological theory (pp. 699-719). Springer.

Crossman, J. (2010). Conceptualising spiritual leadership in secular organizational contexts and its relation to transformational, servant and environmental leadership. *Leadership and Organization Development Journal*, *31*(7), 596–608. doi:10.1108/01437731011079646

Crossman, J. (2011). Environmental and spiritual leadership: Tracing the synergies from an organizational perspective. *Journal of Business Ethics*, *103*(4), 553–565. doi:10.100710551-011-0880-3

Daft, R. L., & Lengel, R. H. (1998). *Fusion leadership: Unlocking the subtle forces that change people and organizations*. Berrett-Koehler Publishers.

Danz, C. (2022). God and Evil—Systematic-Theological Reflections on the Doctrine of God. *Religions*, *13*(11), 1075. doi:10.3390/rel13111075

Davidson, B. (2014). Examining the relationship between non-cognitive skills and leadership: The influence of hope and grit on transformational leadership behavior [Doctor of Education]. University of Kansas.

Dent, E. B., Higgins, M. E., & Wharff, D. M. (2005). Spirituality and leadership: An empirical review of definitions, distinctions, and embedded assumptions. *The Leadership Quarterly*, *16*(5), 625–653. doi:10.1016/j.leaqua.2005.07.002

Ellison, N. B., Wohn, D. Y., & Greenhow, C. M. (2014). Adolescents' visions of their future careers, educational plans, and life pathways: The role of bridging and bonding social capital experiences. *Journal of Social and Personal Relationships*, *31*(4), 516–534. doi:10.1177/0265407514523546

Fathiaa, A. (2022). Authentic and relatable UN leadership: Interview with Fathiaa Abdalla. In M. Jacquand, V. Tywuschik-Sohlström, P. Nordlund, H. Hammargren, & S. Gruener (Eds.), *The Art of Leadership in the United Nations: Framing What's Blue*. Dag Hammarskjöld Foundation.

Freeman, G. (2011). Spirituality and servant leadership: A conceptual model and research proposal. *Emerging Leadership Journeys, 4*(1), 120-140.

Fry, L. W. (2003). Toward a theory of spiritual leadership. *The Leadership Quarterly*, *14*(6), 693–727. doi:10.1016/j.leaqua.2003.09.001

Fry, L. W., & Matherly, L. L. (2006). *Spiritual Leadership and Organizational Performance*. Paper presented at the Paper to be presented at the Academy of Management Meeting, Atlanta, GA, United States.

Fry, L. W., & Nisiewicz, M. S. (2013). *Maximizing the triple bottom line through spiritual leadership*. Stanford University Press.

Gardner, W. L., Avolio, B. J., & Walumbwa, F. O. (2005). Authentic leadership development: Emergent trends and future directions. *Authentic leadership theory practice: Origins, effects development*, 387-406. doi:10.1016/j.leaqua.2005.03.001

Gatling, A., Kang, H. J. A., & Kim, J. S. (2016). The effects of authentic leadership and organizational commitment on turnover intention. *Leadership and Organization Development Journal*, *37*(2), 181–199. doi:10.1108/LODJ-05-2014-0090

George, J. M., & Bettenhausen, K. (1990). Understanding prosocial behavior, sales performance, and turnover: A group-level analysis in a service context. *The Journal of Applied Psychology*, *75*(6), 698–709. doi:10.1037/0021-9010.75.6.698

Goltz, S. M. (2023). Team Spiritual Power: A Resource for Managing Toxic Leadership. *Journal of Management, Spirituality & Religion*, *12*(2), 1–11. doi:10.51327/LUQX5612

Greenleaf, R. K. (1998). *The power of servant-leadership: Essays.* Berrett-Koehler Publishers.

Greenleaf, R. K., Spears, L. C., & Covey, S. R. (2002). *Servant Leadership: A Journey Into the Nature of Legitimate Power and Greatness*. Paulist Press.

Hannah, S. T., Woolfolk, R. L., & Lord, R. G. (2009). Leader self-structure: A framework for positive leadership. *Journal of Organizational Behavior*, *30*(2), 269–290. doi:10.1002/job.586

Hill, P. C., & Edwards, E. (2013). Measurement in the psychology of religiousness and spirituality: Existing measures and new frontiers. In K. I. Pargament, J. J. Exline, & J. W. Jones (Eds.), APA handbook of psychology, religion, and spirituality: Vol. 1. *American Psychological Association*. doi:10.1037/14045-003

Hogan, R., Curphy, G. J., & Hogan, J. (1994). What we know about leadership: Effectiveness and personality. *The American Psychologist*, *49*(6), 493–509. doi:10.1037/0003-066X.49.6.493 PMID:8042818

Horner, M. (1997). Leadership theory: Past, present and future. *Team Performance Management*, *3*(4), 270–287. doi:10.1108/13527599710195402

Jafari, J., & Scott, N. (2014). Muslim world and its tourisms. *Annals of Tourism Research*, *44*, 1–19. doi:10.1016/j.annals.2013.08.011

Jago, A. G. (1982). Leadership: Perspectives in theory and research. *Management Science*, *28*(3), 315–336. doi:10.1287/mnsc.28.3.315

Jeronimus, B. F., Riese, H., Sanderman, R., & Ormel, J. (2014). Mutual reinforcement between neuroticism and life experiences: A five-wave, 16-year study to test reciprocal causation. *Journal of Personality and Social Psychology*, *107*(4), 751–764. doi:10.1037/a0037009 PMID:25111305

Jooste, K. (2004). Leadership: A new perspective. *Journal of Nursing Management*, *12*(3), 217–223. doi:10.1111/j.1365-2834.2003.00450.x PMID:15089960

Jordan, S. R. (2016). Positive Leadership Behavior. In A. Farazmand (Ed.), *Global Encyclopedia of Public Administration, Public Policy, and Governance* (pp. 1–6). Springer International Publishing.

Koivisto, M. (2020). Self-Directed Adult Learners and the Paradox of Choice. *Proceedings of the 13th International Conference on E-Learning in the Workplace*.

Kostikov, E. D. (2014). The Great-Power Ambitions and Frontier Policy of the Peking Leadership. *Chinese Law & Government*, *6*(4), 8–21. doi:10.2753/CLG0009-460906048

Krausz, R. R. (1986). Power and leadership in organizations. *Transactional Analysis Journal*, *16*(2), 85–94. doi:10.1177/036215378601600202

Lam, L. W., & Xu, A. J. (2019). Power imbalance and employee silence: The role of abusive leadership, power distance orientation, and perceived organisational politics. *Applied Psychology*, *68*(3), 513–546. doi:10.1111/apps.12170

Laschinger, H. K. S., Wong, C. A., & Grau, A. L. (2013). Authentic leadership, empowerment and burnout: A comparison in new graduates and experienced nurses. *Journal of Nursing Management*, *21*(3), 541–552. doi:10.1111/j.1365-2834.2012.01375.x PMID:23405976

Lunenburg, F. C. (2012). Power and leadership: An influence process. *International Journal of Management, Business, and Administration, 15*(1), 1-9.

Machi, L. A., & McEvoy, B. T. (2021). The literature review: Six steps to success (3rd ed.). SAGE Publications Ltd.

Malone, P., & Fry, L. W. (2003). *Transforming schools through spiritual leadership: A field experiment.* Paper presented at the Annual Meeting of the Academy of Management, Seattle, WA.

Marques, J. (2016). *Leadership: Finding balance between ambition and acceptance.* Routledge. doi:10.4324/9781315695662

Martinko, M. J., Harvey, P., & Douglas, S. C. (2007). The role, function, and contribution of attribution theory to leadership: A review. *The Leadership Quarterly*, *18*(6), 561–585. doi:10.1016/j.leaqua.2007.09.004

Maxwell, J. C. (2014). *The 5 Levels of Leadership: Proven Steps to Maximize Your Potential.* Center Street.

Morton, E., Hole, R., Murray, G., Buzwell, S., & Michalak, E. (2019). Experiences of a web-based quality of life self-monitoring tool for individuals with bipolar disorder: A qualitative exploration. *JMIR Mental Health*, *6*(12), e16121. doi:10.2196/16121 PMID:31799936

Mumford, M. D., & Fried, Y. (2014). Give them what they want or give them what they need? Ideology in the study of leadership. *Journal of Organizational Behavior*, *35*(5), 622–634. doi:10.1002/job.1921

Neck, C. P., & Manz, C. C. (2010). *Mastering self-leadership: Empowering yourself for personal excellence* (5th ed.). Pearson Prentice Hall.

Nesbit, P. L. (2012). The role of self-reflection, emotional management of feedback, and self-regulation processes in self-directed leadership development. *Human Resource Development Review*, *11*(2), 203–226. doi:10.1177/1534484312439196

Paradiso-Testa, M. (2022). A Reflective Essay of a Conceptual Model for Self-Directed Learning for the Adult Learner. In *Self-Directed Learning and the Academic Evolution From Pedagogy to Andragogy* (pp. 163–172). IGI Global. doi:10.4018/978-1-7998-7661-8.ch009

Paulhus, D. L., & John, O. P. (1998). Egoistic and moralistic biases in self-perception: The interplay of self-deceptive styles with basic traits and motives. *Journal of Personality*, *66*(6), 1025–1060. doi:10.1111/1467-6494.00041

Porter, L. W., & McLaughlin, G. B. (2006). Leadership and the organizational context: Like the weather? *The Leadership Quarterly*, *17*(6), 559–576. doi:10.1016/j.leaqua.2006.10.002

Rana, S., Ardichvili, A., & Polesello, D. (2016). Promoting self-directed learning in a learning organization: Tools and practices. *European Journal of Training and Development*, *40*(7), 470–489. doi:10.1108/EJTD-10-2015-0076

Ross, S. (2014). A conceptual model for understanding the process of self-leadership development and action-steps to promote personal leadership development. *Journal of Management Development*, *33*(4), 299–323. doi:10.1108/JMD-11-2012-0147

Rothstein, M. G., & Burke, R. J. (2010). *Self-management and leadership development*. Edward Elgar Publishing. doi:10.4337/9781849805551

Ryan, R. M., & Deci, E. L. (2000). Self-determination theory and the facilitation of intrinsic motivation, social development, and well-being. *The American Psychologist*, *55*(1), 68–78. doi:10.1037/0003-066X.55.1.68 PMID:11392867

Ryan, R. M., Huta, V., & Deci, E. L. (2008). Living well: A self-determination theory perspective on eudaimonia. *Journal of Happiness Studies*, *9*(1), 139–170. doi:10.100710902-006-9023-4

Samul, J. (2020). Spiritual Leadership: Meaning in the Sustainable Workplace. *Sustainability (Basel)*, *12*(1), 1–16. doi:10.3390u12010267

Sari, M., Nasution, M. I., & Wahyuni, S. F. (2019). The strategy of Spiritual Leadership: The Role of Spiritual Survival, Workplace Spirituality and Organizational Commitment at Private Universities. *International Journal of Research in Business Social Science*, *8*(1), 64–72. doi:10.20525/ijrbs.v8i1.194

Saroglou, V., Buxant, C., & Tilquin, J. (2008). Positive emotions as leading to religion and spirituality. *The Journal of Positive Psychology*, *3*(3), 165–173. doi:10.1080/17439760801998737

Savage-Austin, A. R., & Honeycutt, A. (2011). Servant leadership: A phenomenological study of practices, experiences, organizational effectiveness, and barriers. *Journal of Business & Economics Research*, *9*(1), 49–54. doi:10.19030/jber.v9i1.939

Sendjaya, S., & Sarros, J. C. (2002). Servant leadership: Its origin, development, and application in organizations. *Journal of Leadership & Organizational Studies*, *9*(2), 57–64. doi:10.1177/107179190200900205

Serrat, O. (2017). Exercising servant leadership. In *Knowledge solutions: Tools, methods, and approaches to drive organizational performance* (pp. 649–655). Springer. doi:10.1007/978-981-10-0983-9_72

Shamir, B., & Eilam, G. (2005). "What's your story?" A life-stories approach to authentic leadership development. *The Leadership Quarterly*, *16*(3), 395–417. doi:10.1016/j.leaqua.2005.03.005

Sinclair, A. (2004). Journey around leadership. *Discourse (Abingdon)*, *25*(1), 7–19. doi:10.1080/0159630042000178455

Sosik, J. J., & Jung, D. (2011). *Full range leadership development: Pathways for people, profit and planet*. Psychology Press. doi:10.4324/9780203843161

Spears, L. C. (1996). Reflections on Robert K. Greenleaf and servant-leadership. *Leadership and Organization Development Journal, 17*(7), 33–35. doi:10.1108/01437739610148367

Thompson, H., & Matkin, G. (2020). The Evolution of Inclusive Leadership Studies: A literature review. *Journal of Leadership Education, 19*(3), 15–30. doi:10.12806/V19/I3/R2

van Droffelaar, B. (2021). Episodic memories of wilderness experiences foster sustainable leadership style transformation. *Journal of Management Development, 40*(6), 486–502. doi:10.1108/JMD-12-2020-0393

Van Knippenberg, D., & van Ginkel, W. P. (2022). A diversity mindset perspective on inclusive leadership. *Group & Organization Management, 47*(4), 779–797. doi:10.1177/1059601121997229

Vollero, A., Siano, A., Palazzo, M., & Amabile, S. (2020). Hoftsede's cultural dimensions and corporate social responsibility in online communication: Are they independent constructs? *Corporate Social Responsibility and Environmental Management, 27*(1), 53–64. doi:10.1002/csr.1773

Voss, B. L. (2000). The Arc of Ambition: Defining the Leadership Journey. *The Journal of Business Strategy, 21*(2), 47–56.

Waterman, H. (2011). Principles of 'servant leadership'and how they can enhance practice. *Nursing Management, 17*(9), 24–26. doi:10.7748/nm2011.02.17.9.24.c8299 PMID:21473215

Watts, L. L., Steele, L. M., & Mumford, M. D. (2019). Making sense of pragmatic and charismatic leadership stories: Effects on vision formation. *The Leadership Quarterly, 30*(2), 243–259. doi:10.1016/j.leaqua.2018.09.003

Weiss, M., Razinskas, S., Backmann, J., & Hoegl, M. (2018). Authentic leadership and leaders' mental well-being: An experience sampling study. *The Leadership Quarterly, 29*(2), 309–321. doi:10.1016/j.leaqua.2017.05.007

Williams, W. A. Jr, Brandon, R.-S., Hayek, M., Haden, S. P., & Atinc, G. (2017). Servant leadership and followership creativity. *Leadership and Organization Development Journal, 38*(2), 178–193. doi:10.1108/LODJ-02-2015-0019

Winkler, I. (2010). *Contemporary leadership theories: Enhancing the understanding of the complexity, subjectivity and dynamic of leadership*. Springer Science & Business Media.

Wong, P. T., & Page, D. (2003). Servant leadership: An opponent-process model and the revised servant leadership profile. *Proceedings of the Servant Leadership Research Roundtable*.

Xiao, Y., & Watson, M. (2019). Guidance on conducting a systematic literature review. *Journal of Planning Education and Research, 39*(1), 93–112. doi:10.1177/0739456X17723971

Yost, P. R., & Plunkett, M. M. (2009). *Real time leadership development* (Vol. 7). John Wiley & Sons.

Yukl, G. (1999). An evaluation of conceptual weaknesses in transformational and charismatic leadership theories. *The Leadership Quarterly, 10*(2), 285–305. doi:10.1016/S1048-9843(99)00013-2

Zhang, W., Sun, S. L., Jiang, Y., & Zhang, W. (2019). Openness to experience and team creativity: Effects of knowledge sharing and transformational leadership. *Creativity Research Journal*, *31*(1), 62–73. doi:10.1080/10400419.2019.1577649

Zou, W.-C., Tian, Q., & Liu, J. (2015). Servant leadership, social exchange relationships, and follower's helping behavior: Positive reciprocity belief matters. *International Journal of Hospitality Management*, *51*, 147–156. doi:10.1016/j.ijhm.2015.08.012

## ADDITIONAL READING

Alvesson, M., & Spicer, A. (2012). A Stupidity-Based theory of organizations. *Journal of Management Studies*, *49*(7), 1194–1220. doi:10.1111/j.1467-6486.2012.01072.x

Alvesson, M., & Spicer, A. (2012). Critical leadership studies: The case for critical performativity. *Human Relations*, *65*(3), 367–390. doi:10.1177/0018726711430555

Bischak, D. P., & Woiceshyn, J. (2016). Leadership virtues exposed: Ethical leadership lessons from leading in rock climbing. *Journal of Leadership & Organizational Studies*, *23*(3), 248–259. doi:10.1177/1548051815617629

Locke, E. A. (2003). Foundations for a theory of leadership. In *The future of leadership development* (pp. 55–72). England Psychology Press.

Riley, K. (2003). 'Democratic leadership'–A contradiction in terms? *Leadership and Policy in Schools*, *2*(2), 125–139. doi:10.1076/lpos.2.2.125.15543

## KEY TERMS AND DEFINITIONS

**Inclusive:** The term inclusive has a wide-ranging and all-encompassing connotation. To make better decisions and work more successfully with others, inclusive leaders are self-aware and actively seek out and consider multiple points of view.

**Leadership:** A key individual who is capable of leading a group or organization.

**Leadership Journey:** In the process of being a Leader, this term is best understood through a life-trial metaphor.

**Persistence:** Continues or attempts to perform something with determination but often invisibility (inner motivation).

**Self-Directed:** Deciding and organizing own work rather than being taught what to do.

**Social Change:** Interpersonal relationships that change cultural and societal organizations.

## ENDNOTES

1. The Art of Leadership in the United Nations Framing What's Blue.
2. Khan's literary work: https://www.jagranjosh.com/general-knowledge/imran-khan-1587658645-1
3. Spiritual Democracy - Episode 1 - Journey of Self Discovery By Salman Ahmed (https://twitter.com/sufisal) Credits: Junoon.
4. https://www.theguardian.com/commentisfree/2022/apr/12/imran-khan-pakistan-ousted-leader-prime-minister

# Chapter 14
# Effect of Leadership and Motivation on Performance and Engagement of Employees in an Albanian Private Organisation:
## A Case Study of Agna Group

**Alma Duklaska**
*University of Sunderland, UK*

**Alessandro Ferrazza**
*University of Sunderland, UK*

**Giuseppe Umberto Cantafio**
https://orcid.org/0000-0001-5399-8300
*University of Sunderland, UK*

## ABSTRACT

*The aim of the study was to find the influence of leadership on employee motivation and performance in the private sector in Albania. The project used a case study as the research design. A questionnaire and semi-structured interviews were used as the primary means of data collection to gain an understanding of how employees form their opinions about the Agna Group. Agna Group employees were selected to meet the target demographic and a random sample of 112 employees was selected for this study. The study revealed that motivational variables such as management, pay, work environment, perception of organizational support, training, recognition, and rewards influence employees' motivation levels and job satisfaction. The study showed that Agna Group employees had a good relationship between management and employee performance and productivity, but it had no effect on talent prevention. The study results can be useful for employers and employees to increase awareness of the aspects that lead to high levels of motivation and job satisfaction.*

DOI: 10.4018/978-1-6684-8822-5.ch014

## INTRODUCTION

Organizational success is the result of a combination of components that are integrated to achieve the desired results according to the purpose of the company. Human capital is the most important; that is why companies are constantly looking for the best people to lead and implement this path to success. In the last decade, much emphasis has been placed on employees, their motivation level and job satisfaction. In the discipline of human resource management, people in any organization are viewed as an asset that is both valuable and difficult to capture. Many business leaders believe that motivation, not ability, is the most important factor in developing human effectiveness and efficiency in any field.

Employees are considered to possess certain characteristics that ensure that their efforts will benefit the company (Ragothaman, 2020). These remarkable people are visionary leaders who inspire others to achieve. Leaders use different strategies to influence followers; some focus on work, while others are more concerned with bonding in the workplace. The organization "Agna Group", the focus of this case study, uses all available resources, including human, material and financial resources, to achieve the desired results. If a company wants to achieve and maintain success, its employees and employees must have exceptional skills and consistent application. In today's rapidly changing business environment where competition is fiercer, companies must use different survival strategies to succeed. Active employee involvement is one of the best possible results-driven techniques. As Ragothaman (2020) argues, organizational leadership styles can affect employee motivation; Therefore, when employees are excited about their work, they perform better and perform at their best. According to him, this means that modern workplaces are more focused on human resources, which requires a change in management style and the creation of a more collaborative work environment. Leadership and the multiple styles associated with it have a significant impact on the performance and development of individuals, leading to favourable organizational outcomes. The main reason for this research is to further expand the body of knowledge in human resources and the effects of different leadership styles on people's motivational levels and commitment as predictors for organizational success

## CONTEXT BACKGROUND: AGNA GROUP

This study focuses on motivation in general and the impact of corporate leadership style on motivation on employee performance in an organization. With the complexity of doing business today, the need for employees to perform at their best and be loyal to the organization is greater than ever. According to the founder of IBM, Thomas J. Watson, it is possible to get financing and build buildings, but to develop a business, employees are needed (Plessis et al., 2016). Motivated and inspired employees are fully committed to the organization and work to their full potential, which can help the company achieve its goals and produce results quickly, efficiently and effectively. Agna Group was founded in 1991 after the fall of communism in Albania and operates in the following sectors: retail, food and beverages, tobacco, manufacturing, real estate, advertising and energy investments nationally and internationally. This company has accumulated a significant investment portfolio over the years. Agna Grupp, a forward-looking and progressive organization, formulated the conceptual belief that the company's employees are its most important and fundamental asset; Therefore, a company should never stop investing in the professional growth opportunities of its employees. The mission and philosophy of the organization emphasize the importance of the progress of each employee within the organization. After the conceptual foundation of the Academy established at the Agna site in 2019, the structure of the organization's philosophy is as follows: The organization has three options: to continue training and maintain the existing workforce, to terminate the employment relationship of the employees. Who do not meet or fail to meet performance expectations, which would lead to the acceptance of mediocrity as the norm, which would harm both the performance of the employee and the company (Agna Academy Management). It is undeniable that leaders directly influence the actions, efforts, contributions and ultimately the outputs of their subordinates (Iqbal et al., 2015). "Agna Management Academy" opened its doors for the first time in 2012 with the aim of training and nurturing managers and employees motivated by achievement concepts and values. According to Gibson (2011) and Lofsten (2016), building a business unit according to modern efficiency and competitiveness, as well as nurturing long-term personnel and organizational goals, are important factors for organizational success and sustainability. Basically, people strive for progress, whether it is their environment or expectations. Employees are led to believe that their predetermined or chosen actions directly affect the achievement of their ideal outcome, including task performance (Elliot et al., 2017).

Based on a preliminary study of the Albanian market, the study identified the problem of general staffing in the private sector and the large number of young people moving to Europe. As a result of this phenomenon, the country is now facing a huge new dilemma called brain drain.

The Balkan Barometer (2019) states that the general order of problems in the region has not changed for decades, pointing to unemployment, economy, corruption, crime and brain drain. Outflows of human capital usually result from many interrelated reasons beyond the simple push and pull variables of the region.

This can be illustrated by Leitner (2021), who states that skilled workers account for approximately 40% of all human resources leaving Albania in the entire period studied, suggesting a brain drain in the country. Albania's brain drain is high among people in their 20s, suggesting that many leave within a few years of graduating. Highly educated people are most likely to leave in both periods, and the net change is about 40,700 people between 2012 and 2019, or almost 40 per cent of the total number of 105,000 people.

On one hand, this is harmful to the Albanian labour market and to the country's economy; on the other hand, it is difficult for Albanian companies to effectively retain or encourage employees to work. The number of people who want to work in the private sector is also decreasing. That is why Agna Group implements a comprehensive idea of inspiration through education and training, which makes it possible to recruit new employees and maintain existing staff. Despite this, people feel dissatisfied and depressed because of the country's long political and economic transition period. Thus, the research discovers what motivates people to develop their careers within the organization and improve their work results.

## SCOPE AND SIGNIFICANCE

The main purpose and significance of the study was to assess the current understanding of the business world and how managers influence human resources to be more motivated and perform better in business organizations. Agna Group has attracted attention because it is one of the biggest players in the market. The study also focuses on employee retention. Therefore, this study aims to understand the main factor that makes employees stay longer in an organization and increase productivity, also addressing the lack of research in the Albanian private sector and making a modest contribution to the extensive previous literature. The purpose of the research is to present results that help organizations develop strategies to retain people and increase market competitiveness in local and European markets.

## AIMS AND OBJECTIVES

The aim of this study is to investigate and further analyse the relationship between employee motivation and organizational competitiveness in Albania. The purpose of this review is to identify how and when organizational leadership affects the motivation and performance of private sector employees and how this is consistent with national competitiveness.

## OBJECTIVES OF THE RESEARCH

- Understanding how motivation affects the improvement of organizational performance
- Finding out the factors that mainly affect the motivation of the personnel of Agna Group.
- Determining the link between rewards and employee performance.
- Assessing the relationships between leadership, talent retention and employee commitment to the organization.

## RESEARCH QUESTIONS

In order to answer the main question of the project, auxiliary questions were developed based on the objectives. These questions divide the research into four main parts to define and analyse all the factors influencing the motivation of Agna Group.

- What are the key issues to motivate private sector employees in Albania (especially Agna Group)?
- How can HRM improve strategies and training to improve motivation and performance?
- Why can dissatisfaction with work life be harmful to companies and how can it be alleviated?
- To what extent does the incentive affect the productivity and competitiveness of the company?

## CONCEPTUAL FRAMEWORK

The findings of Farrell and Rusbult (1992) show a positive correlation between training and employee loyalty. Employee loyalty affects how long an employee stays with a company (Wu and Norman, 2006; Turkyilmaz et al., 2011). Similarly, Dalziel (2010) argues that an organization's ability to retain employees is greatly improved if it provides a learning environment and career opportunities that encourage employees to grow and appreciate their skills and knowledge. According to Chen (2014), training increases employee engagement by making employees feel accountable to their employers. Therefore, they stay with the company longer after training. Training, on the other hand, helps employees feel supported by the organization and trust the employer.

Motivation is a very complex topic because its effectiveness depends on variables such as the type of company and the culture of the staff. Although there are many studies on motivation, not much has been written about how leadership affects motivation in post-communist countries or how motivation affects employee performance in the private sector in Albania. The aim of this study was therefore to analyse the impact of employee motivation on work performance in Albanian private sector companies, using Agna Group employees as a case study.

## RESEARCH METHODOLOGY

The study utilised questionnaires that were used for quantitative statistical analysis. Positivist research occasionally extends to other data gathering methods and strives to quantify qualitative data, for instance, by applying hypothesis testing to data initially gathered through in-depth interviews. The study employed a deductive approach with an organised methodology to allow for replication, which is critical for ensuring dependability.

## PURPOSE OF RESEARCH

The goal of this research is to fulfil a variety of objectives related to the Albanian labour market, namely staff retention and loyalty within the Agna Group. Furthermore, the research attempts to identify the best HR strategic ways to educate and motivate employees in order to improve the company's performance and competitiveness in the Albanian market.

## TYPES OF RESEARCH

For the aim of this study, the research has utilised a mixed methods approach in order to understand HR practices and employee perceptions Anderson et al., (2020). For example, to get a clear idea of how employees form their opinion for the Agna Group and their leadership style necessitated interviews, but to identify the major predictor of turnover intention and staff engagement in the organisation, this research needs to use a quantitative approach. Utilising quantitative approaches, rather than focusing on statistical measures, relies on the comprehension, explanation, and interpretation of empirical facts, which serves as the foundation for the formation of hypotheses and innovative ideas.

## RESEARCH PROCESS AND DESIGN

This study employed an exploratory research design in which a case study design was used to allow the study to undertake an in-depth inquiry, which included the use of various data collection techniques, sample procedures, data analysis, and presentation (Yin, 2017).

## METHODS OF DATA COLLECTIONS

This study makes use of mixed methods and is employed by the research since the research philosophy is positivism, and the tactic used is a case study. Thus, according to Saunders et al., (2019), mixed approaches utilised both data to generate mutually enlightening conclusions. Also, noticed the case study method as a good tool for expanding the theory that already exists by using new contemporary sources of information.

## DIFFERENT METHODS OF GATHERING DATA

A face-to-face survey was conducted inside Agna Group for the objectives of this study. Contacting a large number of respondents is straightforward and inexpensive because the design is intended to reduce prejudice, and surveys are standardised to ensure reliability and validity. However, according to Brewerton and Millward (2001), developing questionnaire/survey instruments is a difficult task that necessitates the research to consider many factors on the possible quality and amount of data gathered. Likert-type scales are utilised for the purpose of the study, which implies the responder being presented with a statement and being asked to indicate how she/he feels about the statement's correctness or otherwise, ranging from 'Strongly agree' to 'Neither agree nor disagree.' However, Likert answer scales have downsides in that some response sets are visible in some respondents; for example, some people's proclivity to rely on the neutral response a bit too much, while others only employ extreme replies.

## SAMPLING TECHNIQUES

The population of the study refers to all individuals who possess the characteristics that the research aims to explore in the context of a certain research subject (Ram, 2009). A total of 2768 Group's employees were included in the sample selection to match the target demographic, and a random sample of 112 employees was chosen for this study. Brown (2006) outlines the benefits of sampling as making any type and scale of study possible, saving research funds, and resulting in more accurate research findings.

## TYPES OF SAMPLING

Methods of non-probability sampling include purposive, quota, convenience, and snowball sampling. For this research a random probability sampling has been chosen.

## FINDINGS, RESULTS, AND DISCUSSION

Urošević et al. (2016) found interactions between demographic characteristics and employees' perceptions of job satisfaction and motivation.

These are the demographic characteristics utilised for statistical analysis:

- Gender
- Age
- Degree of education
- Years of work experience
- Department of work

## RELIABILITY TEST

The reliability test was conducted and found that Cronbach's Alpha is 0.861, meaning that the Alpha value indicates a high reliability of the questionnaire instrument and internal consistencies of the five point Likert-type scales. Out of 112 responses, 68.75% were male workers, and 31.25% were female employees, bringing the number of male employees to a larger proportion than the number of female employees in the organisation. 26.79% of respondents were in the age group of 40-50 years, followed by 25% in the age group of 30- 40 years and 24.11% for the age groups of 20-30 and 50 and above years, respectively. According to the demographics, 47.32% of respondents have a high school diploma, 30.36% have a bachelor's degree, and 21.43% have a master's degree followed by 0.89% PhDs. In terms of years of experience, the results showed that most participants (36.61%) have been working at Agna Group for more than 12 years; however, 0-2 years, 28.57% is a considerable fraction as well.

## DEPARTMENT OF WORK

Most participants (20.54%) were affiliated with the Sales department, while the majority (54.46%) chose 'Other' departments, which were not mentioned in the list.

13.39% of participants held the position of manager, while 64.29% of participants selected the 'Others' option. This option may encompass positions such as drivers warehouse labours and office positions. In terms of financial incentives, the Salary (Mean 4.71, Std 0.663) is significant, followed by Reward, (Mean, 4.20, Std 0.733) which would influence the motivation of Agna Group's employees. Leadership performed better in non-financial motivators (Mean 4.47, Std 0.759). However, it appears that employees think that job security (Mean, 4.42) and performance appraisal (Mean, 4.42) is crucial. The working practises increase the likelihood that employees will feel motivated. More than half of the respondents, 50.9% ticked, strongly agree with the importance of training. Only a 0.9% and 8.95% disagreed or strongly disagreed with the importance of training. According to the outcomes, employees will likely feel motivated when organisation' management provides support and appreciation. However, employees did not share this perception about salary increases (Mean 3.9) and prospects for advancement (Mean 3.51). The outcomes reveal that the scale's categories scored well, implying that leadership (Mean,4.58) and all of its strategic components would significantly influence performance. Performance Appraisal (Mean 4.09 and Std 0.742) and financial incentives (Mean 4.02 and Std 0.794) scored highly in terms of all intrinsic and extrinsic variables that influence motivation and performance. According to the means comparison analysis, Performance Appraisal and Financial Incentives have a greater impact on performance. Financial motivators are vital and 60.7% of respondents agreed that financial incentives would influence their motivation to work. Only 0.9% strongly disagree that money is not a driver to them. The Chi-Square value is 22.307[a] and the df is 12 indicates that there is a significant correlation between all of the group ages and whether financial incentives would motivate individuals to perform better at work. Therefore, in this comparison of age and motivation in the financial incentives is seen that 21.43% of those aged 50+, 16.96%, 16.07% and 15.18% from the other groups agreed that financial incentives are essential. The examination of the non-financial motivators indicates that 71.43% of respondents believed that non-financial incentives would affect their motivation and performance. Only 1.8% strongly disagreed with such a remark, while 13.39% strongly agreed. Those over the age of 50 were the most likely to think that monetary and non-monetary incentives would have the same effect on motivation as seen in the graph. The chi-square score of 20.845[a] exceeds the df value of 12 for statistical significance. It is noticeable that the value of Chi-square (51.553[a]) was substantially higher than the df (15), indicating a significant correlation between age disparity and tenure in the organisation. Furthermore, this indicates that there is an issue with employee turnover after 0-2 years of employment with the organisation. Besides that, when compared to the statistics supplied by HR, this number has grown in the latter year. Analysing the data of the corporation gathered from the yearly reports submitted to the research by the company's HR, it has been seen that the net profit has climbed, but so has the staff turnover, which has risen to 206 in the last year.

## INTERVIEWS TO EXECUTIVES

The research included discussions with several executives. To address the research aims and questions, semi-structured interview questions were devised. Following that, seven major questions were included in the conversations, along with two additional questions addressed by the HR Partner. The in-person interviews were conducted online due to time constraints and logistics reason. However, most of the interviews took place within the firm after work hours, as agreed upon prior to the meeting. The conversation was pleasant and took place in a peaceful and secure environment. The researchers requested permission to record the talk while also taking notes. The questions were emailed to the Executives ahead of time to help them feel at ease during the interview. The respondents were asked identical questions, and all responses were utilised to inform the study.

1. If you were to define the concept of motivation, what would that be?
   According to their responses to the first question, respondents generally agree that "motivation" is not a simple idea. It invokes a state of mind in which one aspires to inspire and motivate others to provide their best effort. According to Agna Group, an individual's sense of appreciation and belonging to the organisation's culture motivates them to do their best each day.
2. Why do you think the organisation's leadership is responsible for motivating employees?
   The leadership establishes the strategy and mission and guides the personnel in the appropriate direction. A successful leader recognises employees as assets and leads with vision; if the leader does not inspire, employees will not follow. However, they pointed out that motivating staff is not necessarily a one-way process. To maintain morale, leadership must locate the right people to work for the organisation and establish the optimal culture. Agna Leadership Academy is a fantastic example of how the organisation understands and implements employee guidance and support.
3. What is the opinion you hold about the correlation between employee motivation and team productivity?

In response to this question, participants agreed that motivation is a critical component of team productivity. Unmotivated team members will rather keep the team behind and demotivate their coworkers. Also, the respondents argued that the correlation is crucial for the team because of the high standards set for the team by motivated employees.

4. Why do monetary incentives influence motivation and performance?
   People like obtaining praise and a reward for their work, and in this context, we also incorporate thanks. Financial prosperity is a measure of both success and progress, and it is, without a doubt, a component, but it is not the only one that influences performance. Furthermore, the directors anticipated that an immediate benefit-based approach would be highly appreciated by the company's employees. It is vital to highlight that this implies that the organisation is continually seeking new ways to improve motivation.
5. What impact does effective training have on motivation?
   Training will boost self-motivation and ensure that everyday requirements are met to the fullest. People would perform better if they received training to provide them with the necessary information and credentials. According to the respondents, if employees believe they can deliver, they will be encouraged to go above and beyond for the organisation. Moreover, they contended that training fosters self-confidence and is an essential component of having competent personnel.
6. How does motivation affect employee loyalty and engagement?
   It is worth noting that in response to this question, half of the respondents who come from the communist educational system believed loyalty is an integral aspect of one's integrity and is unaffected by motivation. And engagement is an essential component of the education that you receive from your family, meaning that; you contribute to the organisation in this regard. On the other hand, the younger generation of executives do not have the same viewpoint; they feel that motivation should rather focus on establishing relationships characterised by trust and belongingness.
7. How essential is workplace esteem in encouraging employees?
   The accumulation of the replies demonstrates that workers have an expectation that their value as assets of the organisation would be evaluated and acknowledged by its leaders. They referred to Richard Branson when they stated that consumers come second, and staff come first. Considering this, if you want to have the finest brand, you need to have your staff act as ambassadors for your company and provide the ideals that you have promised. The esteem that is held for employees is of critical significance since it ensures that employees will flourish in their work environment and advance their relationships with clients in meaningful ways.

## INTERVIEWING HR

1. How would HR assist in encouraging employees, in your opinion?
   The answer to the first question for the HR Department demonstrates that HR managers must be aware of the dynamics and any external factors that influence the workforce. The company's concept is to approach the best individuals to recruit first and then design a plan to help and encourage them. The emphasis is on employees receiving the necessary training to become a member of the organisation's culture and to generate possibilities for growth. The managers stated that the organisation prioritises employee well-being and job happiness and conducts surveys to gauge job

satisfaction and learn about employee needs in the workplace. This emphasises the need to encourage employees to stay with the organisation for a longer period.

2. Why a great strategic plan and effective training would increase employee satisfaction and commitment to the organisation? Group is devoted to assisting personnel and providing advancement opportunities to all workers seeking personal achievement within the organisation. The corporation develops a strategic plan and invests significant resources year after year, knowing that this investment will result in skilled employees, expertise, and effectiveness. Agna Group's training is thoroughly researched to meet the organisation's and its employees' demands. The HR budget for training is critical and represents a smart investment in the organisation's future. The HR director stated that HR is responsible for developing a strategic plan based on market demands and boosting employee confidence and work satisfaction. The Leadership Academy is delivering training according to plan, as evidenced by 45% of staff achieving outstanding results each year.

## DISCUSSION

To answer the research questions, the research included a questionnaire divided into four sections (the first and second are statement and consent form). The third section was about population demographics, and the fourth was prepared in the form of a Likert scale made up of 5 questions. Male employees constituted 68.75% of the sample, while female employees comprised 31.25% of 112 participants. Respondents in the 40-50 age group had a minor advantage (26.79%), but other age groups were equally represented, indicating that the company is an equal-opportunity employer. Regarding educational attainment, although 47.32% of respondents earned a high school diploma, they were in the minority compared to the rest of the respondents who held a bachelor's degree, 21.43% a master's degree, and 0.89% a PhDs. With regards to the type of the respondents' employment, the majority (64.29%) occupied the 'Other' option of the list, whereas 13.39% held the position of manager, 10.7% were affiliated with sales, 7.1% fulfils executive roles, and only 4.5% had administration posts.

### Do Employees Respond Better to Intrinsic or Extrinsic Motivators?

The analysis revealed that among the financial motivators such as rewards, salary, bonus, company fringe benefits, food, and medical allowances, participants scored more on salary, with Mean of 4.71 and Std deviation of 0.663, as the most crucial fiscal incentive, which motivates them in their job. As per Yousaf et al., (2014), every individual is expected to earn money for meeting their requirements, and thereby they consider "Salary" as an expectation in return for the job they have undertaken. The second important motivator (Mean 4.20, Std deviation of 0.733) is "Reward", as this instance evidently displays. Nevertheless, what can be clearly seen from the analysis of non-financial factors is the fact that leadership had the highest Mean score of 4.47 and Std deviation of 0.759, among the other factors. Although, it is worth noting that all the other factors in the case of non-financial motivators scored high, between 4.22-4.30, suggesting that the employees see these elements as necessary.

## Organisational Support: Perception and Misperception of Progression

Another important finding was that analysis of the impact of motivational factors on employee perception and performance revealed that employees had a positive perception of organisational support, Mean 4.26, and Std 0.791. Contrary to expectations, they were less enthusiastic about the option of periodic salary increases and growth opportunities based on performance, (Mean 3.92, 3.51); this suggests that employees do not perceive that the company provides fair salary increases or growth opportunities, which can lead to dissatisfaction. This study revealed that the impact of leadership approaches on performance for no surprise, rated high, which is consistent with the literature (Mean 4.58 and standard deviation 0.718). This is inferred by the high rating of all supported items of the Likert scale on Question four. It can thus be inferred that excellent leadership strategies influence followers and improve performance. This viewpoint is supported by Al-Hosam et al. (2016) in a study with 160 bank employees, which indicated a substantial positive correlation between psychological empowerment and transformational leadership and job satisfaction. Further analysis of intrinsic and extrinsic motivational factors agreed with the literature regarding the motivational factors, as 60.7% of respondents agreed and 32.1% strongly agreed that financial incentives positively influence their motivation and performance (Mean 4.02, Std 0.794). On the other hand, surprisingly, they expressed the same opinion on the statement, "The performance appraisal motivates me to achieve my goals and perform efficiently" (Mean 4.09 Std 0.742). This tells us that the motive behind the performance appraisal of recognising their contribution by rewarding high performance stimulates employee motivation and leads to an inner commitment to improved performance. Consequently, there is a correlation between these two motivators with the rearwards as a driving force.

## Correlations

According to the variable analysis, there appears to be a correlation between age and incentive components. The influence of financial incentives on motivation and performance was strongly acknowledged or agreed with by all the group ages. The Chi-Square value of 22.307[a] is greater than df 12 and P=0.034 0.05 suggests that the result is not significantly important.

## What Are the Effects on Motivation?

Analysing the data provided from the survey at Agna group is notable that motivation level increases when traits such as leadership implement robust strategies in organising and supporting employees. Additionally, employees are more likely to put out their best effort when they know their leaders value and acknowledge them, as stated by Salasiah et al., (2010). On the other hand, Rita et al., (2018) argued that a leader who fails to motivate the subordinates and succeed in their planned goals is less likely to show productive performance in the organisation. The study found when employees perceive organisational support are ready to "Go the extra mile" for their organisation. Consequently, there are parallels between this study and the literature evaluation in terms of the association between employee motivation, performance, and productivity. As evidenced by the Group's subsequent Net profit, which is the greatest in the past three years (€ 14,000,000), employee motivation leads to improved performance, which boosts business productivity and performance. This is consistent with the findings of Hanaysha and Majid (2018), who discovered comparable results, providing empirical evidence that motivation has a substantial positive effect on organisational commitment and that employee motivation is a crucial predictor of organisational commitment.

## Final Discussion

The research showed a dissimilar pattern in the duration of tenure in the organisation when examining the variables to identify a link between motivation and performance. As a result, a cross tabulation test was performed to compare the difference in group age and duration of the experience. Pearson's ChiSquare value was high (51.553[a]) and the df 15, P< 0.001, showing that there is a strong link between age disparity and tenure in the organisation. This draws attention to the need to dive further into the reasons why the 0-2 years category, group age 20-30 scored (16.96%) and 12+, group age 50+ scored (16.96%) outperformed the other categories in terms of length of tenure in the organisation. That is, the 30-50 age group is departing the firm after a few years. Comparing the figures from the company's data, employee turnover is rising in the latter years: In 2019 was 188, in 2020 was 161 and in 2021 increased to 206. Therefore, the correlation with the findings from the analysis is valid. According to the research, employee retention is influenced by extrinsic and intrinsic motivation. Employee retention varies depending on how employees perceive the organisation's support and exists an important mediating role between motivation and staff retention. This is exemplified by the research conducted by Indermun, and Bayat, (2013), who found that satisfied employees develop a link with their employer, take pride in their organisation membership, and exhibit high levels of performance and productivity. In contrast, unsatisfied employees exhibit low productivity, absenteeism, and staff turnover. Employee motivation and satisfaction require both intrinsic and extrinsic rewards. Motivated personnel have a more favourable attitude toward the business and remain with it for a longer period of time. Individuals who are happy with their jobs are more loyal and committed to the firm. According to Taylor's theory of scientific management, money is a primary concern for most employees, and praising or appreciating them without financial incentives is ineffective (Forson et al., 2021). Nonetheless, the Net profit has increased, suggesting that the performance and productivity of the employee have enhanced. According to Herzberg (1966), extrinsic elements are connected with an employee's general attitude toward their connection with an immediate supervisor. A healthy supervisor-employee connection impacts the quality of two-way communication, trust, and performance while improving work satisfaction, organisational commitment, and decreasing quit intentions (Harris, Harris and Eplion, 2007). The research reported similar findings as those in the literature: that enhanced employee motivation leads to better performance, which boosts the organisation's efficiency and productivity.

# CONCLUSIONS AND RECOMMENDATIONS

The research endeavoured to determine what influences work motivation, performance, and talent prevention among Agna Group workers and what elements are related to and contribute to their job happiness. Employees' demographics were also investigated to learn more about the factors in employees' backgrounds that contribute to work motivation and job satisfaction. The findings shed light on the correlation between motivated personnel, their performance, and corporate output.

## Summary of Findings

The study's questionnaire on job satisfaction and motivation was deemed to have a high-reliability coefficient (Cronbach's Alpha = 0.861). Using the sampled workforce, we may infer that the study has a high degree of dependability, as evidenced by the solid internal consistency of the scale's items. Despite the fact that motivated employees contribute more to the company's productivity, increasing staff retention will necessitate further development of tactics from the organisation's perspective. According to (Karatepe, 2014), good examples to follow include workplace relationship management, training opportunities, monetary and non-monetary rewards, career advancement plans, demonstrating a leadership style that captures the most imagination among workers, and an individualised approach. It has been demonstrated that workers' salary is an essential driver of their motivation and output (Paais & Pattiruhu, 2020). According to Weibel et al., (2010) project that laid forth a theoretical foundation for performance-based remuneration, workers are primarily motivated by financial rewards. A competitive salary is preferred above other monetary rewards because it enables workers to meet their basic needs and those of their families (Hidayati & Zulher, 2022). Similar studies examining the impact of intrinsic and extrinsic motivation on productivity were also found in the literature. The outcomes of this study corroborate the conclusions of numerous other studies that found employee motivation to be a strong predictor of organisational loyalty, work satisfaction and improve performance (Martono and Khoiruddin, 2018., Kuswati,2020). Nevertheless, Alhaji and Yusoff (2012) argue that there is more than one approach to increasing employees' enthusiasm for the workplace and loyalty to the company they work for and that the most successful methods may vary depending on the specifics of the job, the business, and the individual. They also noted that management's skill in dealing with human resource issues is directly related to employees' levels of dedication to their jobs.

## Components of Employee Motivation

The study concluded that motivational factors play a major role in improving employee performance, thus, finances, especially salary, are influential in determining employee performance. Additionally, it was revealed that rewarding employees significantly correlates with employee performance and theories and literature confirmed these findings. Lastly, the study concluded that employees of Agna Group showed a high correlation between leadership and employee performance and productivity but could not show any impact on talent prevention.

## Correlation Between Employee Motivation and Organisation Success

As this study shows, there is a favourable correlation between employee commitment to the firm and their output. Aimed at this reason, it is vital for the business to implement incentive systems for employees who contribute significantly to the company's success, whether monetarily or otherwise. This paper's findings suggest that human resource managers should prioritise boosting employee motivation and happiness on the job (Farouk et al., 2016). Based on the study's outcomes, the training programme has also improved the productivity of Agna Group's staff. According to Agna Group's HRD, 45% of the employees successfully passed the "Agna Leadership Academy" training on the latter year. As indicated in the literature review, some of the training's outcomes include enhanced performance, less turnover, and a narrowing of the skills gap between jobs needs and those needed to do the work. The findings also indicate that initiatives to provide organisational support inside the workplace are crucial for retaining effective individuals.

## Limitation of the Study

For the purpose of this study, participants were chosen at random from each of the Albanian establishments of Agna Group. The fact that the study took place in Albania over the summertime posed both financial and time constraints for the researchers. Only four of the six companies that make up the Group were investigated because of the physical distance between the nation's capital, where the Group's headquarters are situated, and the southern region, where another significant portion of the Group operates. Since English is not the country's primary language, a questionnaire translation was completed in advance, and copies were printed and given out to the workforce. Due to these additional costs, the number of people included in the study's sample was lessened. There were a total of 112 questionnaires filled out, and seven interviews were conducted. This leads to concerns over the extent to which the findings of the study may be generalised to encompass all workers in the private sector in Albania.

## Future Studies

This research brings post-communist developing countries like Albania into the spotlight. Therefore, it may shed light on the unique requirements of these nations in terms of leadership training and staff morale enhancement as they progress toward EU membership. Since this market and its distinctive culture have received little if any academic attention to date, due to the importance of motivation and the scale of Brain Drain, further study of the topic is recommended. There are still several open ends currently. Alternate methodologies that use a bigger sample size and quantitative measures of effect may be feasible in future study.

## Recommendations

Agna Group could consider implementing strategies that support employees' personal and professional growth, as suggested by Maslow's Hierarchy of Needs, due to the diversity of employees. Accordingly, if an employee's fundamental and psychological requirements have already been met, HR should move its focus to the second tier of the pyramid in order to maintain their engagement and loyalty to the organisation. As soon as they reach that point of satisfaction, they must ascend to the pyramid's pinnacle. As a result of being driven to achieve their best, employees automatically enhance efficiency and corporate productivity while also being more innovative and loyal to the organisation. Workplace motivation and satisfaction may be increased by following recommendations that highlight the significance of competitive pay and benefits, job security, and frequent communication between upper- and lower-level management and the workers on the front lines. This may be accomplished with the use of many motivational strategies, such as individual, group, and organisational incentive programmes. An additional suggestion is that organisations arrange workshops to ensure that all employees are aware of their reward system so that they can easily fulfil the criteria. Various tasks are tied to specific rewards to ensure equal and fair rewards. It would influence their behaviour and productivity, which affect overall employee performance and satisfaction Agna Leadership Academy may train a greater number of leaders to be accountable for the inspiration and contentment of their team's employees through accomplishing established goals as a group. New leaders should be given the opportunity to lead teams by setting achievable targets and working together with other individuals to improve coordination and motivation to achieve higher levels of productive performance. As leaders, they would be able to inspire others to continue carrying out their work, and the organisation as a whole need to have a higher level of motivation and performance.

## REFERENCES


Agna Group. (2022). Available at: https://agnagroup.com/new/home

Al-Hosam, A., Ahmed, S., Ahmed, F., & Joarder, M. (2016). Impact of Transformational Leadership on Psychological Empowerment and Job Satisfaction Relationship: A case study of Yemeni Banking. *Binus Business Review.*, *7*(2), 109. Advance online publication. doi:10.21512/bbr.v7i2.1584

Albania Tax Office. (n.d.). Available at: https://www.tatime.gov.al/c/7/154/per-sipermarresit

Alhaji, I. A., & Yusoff, W. F. (2012). Does motivational factor influence organisational commitment and effectiveness? A review of literature. *E3 Journal of Business Management and Economics, 3*(1), 1-9. Available at: https://ideas.repec.org/a/etr/series/v3y2012i1p001-009.html

Bartol, K. M., & Martin, D. C. (1998). Management. McGraw-Hill College.

Bass, B. M. (1998). *Transformational leadership: Industrial, military, and educational impact*. Lawrence Erlbaum Associates.

Bell, E., & Bryman, A. (2007). The Ethics of Management Research: An Exploratory Content Analysis. *British Journal of Management, 18*, 63 - 77. doi:10.1111/j.1467-8551.2006.00487

Boxall, P., & Purcell, J. (2011). *Strategy and human Resource Management* (3rd ed.). Palgrave MacMillan.

Brown, A. T. (2006). *Confirmatory factor analysis for applied research*. Guilford.

Carrell, M.R., & Dittrich, J.E. (1978). Equity theory: The Recent Literature, Methodological Considerations, and New Directions. *The Academy of Management Review, 3*(2), 202.

Chen, M. (2014). *The Effect of Training on Employee Retention*. Atlantis Press. 10.2991/gecss-14.2014.90

Chhabra, T. N. (2010). *Fundamentals of Management* (4th ed.). K.V. SINGH.

Chowdhury, R. G. (2014). *A Study on the Impact of Leadership Styles on Employee Motivation and Commitment: An Empirical Study of Selected Organisations in Corporate Sector*. Available at: https://www.scribd.com/document/410086648/A-study-of-the-Impact-of-Leadership-Styles-onEmployee-Motivation-and-Commitment-An-empirical-study-of-selected-organisations-in-Corporatesector-Rima

Dalziel, P. (2010). *Leveraging "Training Skills Development in SMEs: An Analysis of Canterbury Region, New Zealand"*. Local Economic and Employment Development (LEED). Available at: https://www.academia.edu/23347071/Leveraging_training_and_skills_development_in_SMEs_a_regional_skills_eco-system_case_study

Deci, E., & Ryan, R. (2010). *Intrinsic Motivation*. doi:10.1002/9780470479216.corpsy0467

Elliot, A. J., Dweck, C. S., & Yeager, D. S. (Eds.). (2017). *Handbook of competence and motivation: Theory and application*. Guilford Publications.

Farrell, D., & Rusbult, C. E. (1992). Exploring the exit, voice, loyalty, and neglect typology: The influence of job satisfaction, quality of alternatives, and investment size. *Employee Responsibilities and Rights Journal*, *5*(3), 209–225. doi:10.1007/BF01385048

Forouk, S., Abu Elanain, H. M., Obeidat, S. M., & Al-Nahyan, M. (2016). HRM practices and organisational performance in the UAE banking sector: The mediating role of organisational innovation. *International Journal of Productivity and Performance Management*, *65*(6), 773–791. doi:10.1108/IJPPM-01-2016-0010

Forson, J. A., Ofosu-Dwamena, E., Opoku, R. A., & Adjavon, S. E. (2021). Employee motivation and job performance: A study of basic school teachers in Ghana. *Future Business Journal*, *7*(1), 1–12. doi:10.118643093-021-00077-6

Gibson, R. (2011). *Rethinking the future: rethinking business, principles, competition, control and complexity, leadership, markets and the world*. Hachette.

Harris, K., Harris, R., & Eplion, D. (2007). Personality, leader-member exchanges, and work outcomes. *Journal of Behavioral and Applied Management*, *8*(2), 92–107. doi:10.21818/001c.16715

Hidayati, L., & Zulher, Z. (2022). The Effect of Leadership and Compensation on Employee Performance with Motivation as Moderating Variables at the Pangeran Hotel Pekanbaru. *International Journal of Entrepreneurship and Business Development*, *5*(1), 82-91. Available at: https://repo.stiebangkinang.ac.id/19/1/1601-Article%20Text-4642-1-10-20220208.pdf

Husebø, S. E., O'Regan, S. S. S., & Nestel, D. (2015). Reflective Practice and Its Role in Simulatio. *Clinical Simulation in Nursing*, *11*(8), 368-375. doi:10.1016/j.ecns.2015.04.005

Indermun, V., & Bayat, M. (2013). The Job Satisfaction-Employee performance relationship: a theoretical perspective. *International Journal of Innovative Research in Management*, *11*(2), 1-9. Available at: https://nanopdf.com/download/the-job-satisfaction-employee_pdf

Iqbal, N., Anwar, S., & Haider, N. (2015). Effect of Leadership Style on Employee Performance. *Arabian Journal of Business and Management Review.*, *5*, 146.

Kanfer, R. (1990). Motivation Theory and Industrial and Organisational Psychology. In Handbook of industrial and organisational psychology (Vol. 1, pp. 75-170). Consulting Psychology Press.

Karatepe, O.M., & Vatankhah, S, (2014). The Effect of High-Performance Work practices on Perceived Organisational Support and Turnover Intention: Evidence from the Airline Industry. *Journal of Human Resources in Hospitality & Tourism*, *13*, 103-119. . doi:10.1080/15332845.2014.847292

Kuswati, Y. (2020). The effect of motivation on employee performance. Budapest International Research and Critics Institute. Humanities and Social Sciences, 3(2), 995-1002. https://doi.org/10.33258/birci.v3i2.928

Leitner, S. M. (2021). *Net Migration and its Skill Composition in the Western Balkan Countries between 2010 and 2019.* Results from a Cohort Approach Analysis, The Vienna Institute for International Economic Studies Wiener Institut für Internationale Wirtschaftsvergleiche. Available at: https://wiiw.ac.at/net-migration-and-its-skill-composition-in-the-western-balkancountries-between-2010-and-2019-results-from-a-cohort-approach-analysis-dlp-5695.pdf

Löfsten, H. (2016). New technology-based firms and their survival: The importance of business networks, and entrepreneurial business behaviour and competition. *Local Economy*, *31*(3), 393–409. doi:10.1177/0269094216637334

Martono, S., Khoiruddin, M., & Wulansari, N. A. (2018). Remuneration reward management system as a driven factor of employee performance. *International Journal of Business & Society*, *19*(S4), 535–545.

Nel, P. S., Werner, A., Poisat, P., Du Plessis, A., & Sono, T. (2011). *Human resources management* (8th ed.). Oxford University Press. https://www.jstor.org/stable/40270884?origin=JSTOR-pdf

Nickerson, C. (2022). *What is Positive Reinforcement"?* Simply Psychology. Available at: www.simplypsychology.org/positive-reinforcement.html

Paais, M., & Pattiruhu, J. R. (2020). Effect of Motivation, Leadership, and Organizational Culture on Satisfaction and Employee Performance. The Journal of Asian Finance, Economics and Business, 7(8), 577–588. doi:10.13106/jafeb.2020.vol7.no8.577

Plessis, A., Douangphichit, N., & Dodd, P. (2016). HRM in Relation to Employee Motivation and Job Performance in the Hospitality Industry. *Journal of International Business Research and Marketing, 1*(4). doi:10.18775/jibrm.1849-8558.2015.14.3002

Porter, M. E. (1998). *The competitive advantage of nations: With a new introduction*. doi:10.1007/978-1-349-14865-3

*QKB*. (2022). Albania National Business Centre. Available at: https://qkb.gov.al/kerko/kerkone-regjistrin-tregtar/kerko-per-subjekt/

Ragothaman, C. B. (2020). Leadership Style and its Impact on Employee Motivation in IT / ITES Sector. *International Journal of Mechanical and Production Engineering Research and Development*, *10*(3), 7141–7150. doi:10.24247/ijmperdjun2020675

Ram, R (2009). Government Spending and Happiness of the Population: Additional Evidence from Large Cross-Country Samples. *Public Choice, 138*(3-4), 483-490. Available at: https://www.jstor.org/stable/40270884

Rita, M., Payangan, O. R., Rante, Y., Tuhumena, R., & Erari, A. (2018). Moderating effect of organizational citizenship behavior on the effect of organizational commitment, transformational leadership and work motivation on employee performance. *International Journal of Law and Management*.

Riyanto, S., Endri, E., & Herlisha, N. (2021). Effect of work motivation and job satisfaction on employee performance: Mediating role of employee engagement. *Problems and Perspectives in Management*, 162-174. doi:10.21511/ppm.19(3).2021.14

Salasiah, H.H., Zainab, I., Rosmawati, M., & Ermy, A.R. (2010). Methods of Increasing Learning Motivation among Students. *Procedia Social and Behavior Science, 18*, 138-147. doi:10.1016/j.sbspro.2011.05.021

Sekaran, U., & Bougie, R. (2010). Research Methods for Business: A Skill Building Approach (5th ed.). John Wiley & Sons.

Turkyilmaz, A., Akman, G., Ozkan, C., & Pastuszak, Z. (2011). *Empirical study of public sector employee loyalty and satisfaction: Industrial Management & Data Systems.* Academic Press.

Urošević, S., Karabasevic, D., Maksimovic, M., & Stanujkic, D. (2016). Impact Of Demographic Factors on Motivation and Satisfaction of Employees in The Leather and Footwear Industry. *Tekstilna Industrija,* 45-55. Available at: https://www.researchgate.net/publication/309617116

Uysal, G. (2019). 3rd Definition of SHRM: HR Systems Approach. *Management Studies*, *7*(5). Advance online publication. doi:10.17265/2328-2185/2019.05.011

Waltz, C. W., & Bausell, R. B. (1981). *Nursing Research: Design, Statistics and Computer Analysis.* F.A. Davis.

WordSense Dictionary. (n.d.). Available at https://www.wordsense.eu/

Wright, P. M., & McMahan, G. C. (1992). Theoretical perspectives for strategic human resource management. *Journal of Management*, *18*(2), 295–320. doi:10.1177/014920639201800205

Wu, L., & Norman, I. J. (2006). *An investigation of job satisfaction, organizational commitment and role conflict and ambiguity in a sample of Chinese undergraduate nursing students* (Vol. 26). Nurse Education Today. doi:10.1016/j.nedt.2005.10.011

Yin, R. K. (2017). *Case Study Research: Design and Methods* (6th ed.). Sage Publications.

Yousaf, S., Latif, M., Aslam, S., & Saddiqui, A. (2014). Impact of Financial and non-Financial Rewards on Employee Motivation. *Middle East Journal of Scientific Research*, *21*, 1776–1786.

# Chapter 15
# Motivational Theories of Leadership

**Muhammad Junaid Ahsan**
https://orcid.org/0000-0002-5754-8187
*University of Pisa, Italy*

## ABSTRACT

*This chapter offers an overview of pertinent leadership and motivational theories and how they relate to social work. For social work organizations, effective leadership is essential, and managers who have a solid theoretical foundation in motivation and leadership are more likely to achieve positive outcomes. Before diving into an in-depth analysis of each motivational theory, the chapter looks at the evolution and history of these theories. The most well-known motivational theories of leadership, including the Trait Theory of Leadership, Contingency Theory of Leadership, Need for Achievement Theory, Expectancy Theory, Transformational Leadership Theory, Situational Leadership Model, Emotional Intelligence and Leadership Theory, Positive Psychology and Resilience in Leadership Theory, Path-Goal Theory, Authentic Leadership Theory, and Self-Determination Theory are explored in detail.*

## INTRODUCTION

Leaders are essential for leading staff members and inspiring them to work in the field of social work (Redmond & Dolan, 2016; Schmid, 2006). The success of social work organizations depends on effective leadership, and managers with a strong theoretical grounding in human motivation and leadership are more likely to produce favorable results (Fisher, 2009; Żadkowska, Dowgiałło, Gajewska, Herzberg-Kurasz, & Kostecka, 2022). The leadership approach adopted by any manager will have an impact on the motivational status and response of the people who work for them. This chapter explores various leadership approaches linked to the motivation of workers to inform practitioners of leadership roles on how to influence the motivation of their colleagues better. While practical experience is crucial, a theoretical foundation can offer a framework for comprehending how to inspire and motivate workers, resulting in better outcomes for the organization and the people it serves. In organizational behavior and

DOI: 10.4018/978-1-6684-8822-5.ch015

management, motivation is a complex and multifaceted concept that has been extensively researched (Q. Zhang, Oo, & Lim, 2019). Several theories have attempted to explain motivation, and each theory provides a different viewpoint on the elements that influence behavior (Barba-Sánchez & Atienza-Sahuquillo, 2017; Fisher, 2009). Understanding these ideas and how they apply to leadership may be helpful in the field of social work. Effective social work leaders must inspire their staff to advance the organization's overall mission, in addition to helping them reach their own personal and professional objectives (i.e., a mental model that steers the leader's behavior).

To provide a comprehensive overview, this chapter includes a brief comment on key contributors such as Abraham Maslow's Hierarchy of Needs, Herzberg's Motivation-Hygiene Theory, and the works of Deci and Ryan, among others. These theories provide insightful information on the elements that influence people's motivation and job satisfaction at work.

The purpose of this conceptual chapter is to provide an overview of relevant theories of motivation and leadership, and how they apply to social work. The primary focus of this chapter is to explore how a leader's approach influences staff motivation, emphasizing the importance of understanding leadership approaches and their impact on motivation for the leader's development and future effectiveness.

The most well-known motivational theories of leadership will be specifically discussed in this chapter, including the Trait Theory of Leadership, Contingency Theory of Leadership, Need for Achievement Theory, Expectancy Theory, Transformational Leadership Theory, Situational Leadership Model, Emotional Intelligence and Leadership Theory, Positive Psychology and Resilience in Leadership Theory, Path-Goal Theory, Authentic Leadership Theory, and Self-Determination Theory. The history and development of motivational theories are briefly discussed in this chapter before delving into a thorough analysis of each theory.

The theories discussed in this chapter offer a framework for comprehending the critical elements affecting employee motivation and performance. Leaders may learn more about motivating and inspiring their staff by applying these theories to actual social work environments (Rofuth & Piepenbring, 2019). Ultimately, this may result in better outcomes for the organization and the people it supports. In this chapter, we examine each theory in depth, going through its main ideas and tenets as well as its advantages and disadvantages. We will also examine how these ideas may be used in the field of social work leadership, giving specific instances of how they might be put to use. The chapter will come close with a summary of the main points from each theory and a discussion of their larger leadership implications in social work. We will also provide recommendations for further study and real-world implementation of these theories in the administration of social work.

The goal of this chapter is to provide social work administrators and educators with a strong theoretical basis for leadership and motivation. We aimed to provide insights and solutions for inspiring and motivating staff in the quest for organizational success by examining the most important leadership motivational theories and their application to social work.

## HISTORY AND DEVELOPMENT OF MOTIVATIONAL THEORIES OF LEADERSHIP

Over the years, there have been many studies and debates on the topics of leadership and motivation, two closely intertwined notions (Galbreath & Rogers, 1999; Isaac, Zerbe, & Pitt, 2001). Leaders looking to enhance their leadership abilities and effectiveness should be aware of the evolution of motivational theories of leadership and their history. The characteristic theory of leadership, which first appeared in the early 20th century, was one of the earliest approaches for understanding motivation and leadership (Barker, 2001). Good leaders possess specific innate abilities and traits that are present at birth. Smarts, inventiveness, charm, and aggressiveness are qualities frequently linked to good leaders (Bakker & Leiter, 2017; Barker, 2001). Although the characteristic theory of leadership has recently been criticized for its flaws, it nevertheless represents a significant early advancement in the knowledge of leadership and motivation (Hajiali, Kessi, Budiandriani, Prihatin, & Sufri, 2022; Tierney, Farmer, & Graen, 1999). Psychologists began paying more attention to the contextual and environmental elements that affected leadership and motivation in the 1930s and the 1940s. The contingency theory of leadership, which contends that the most effective leadership style relies on the circumstance and the requirements of the followers, was created as a result of this (Kerr, Schriesheim, Murphy, & Stogdill, 1974; Peters, Hartke, & Pohlmann, 1985). This notion suggests that, rather than depending on a single fixed style, leaders should modify their approach to suit the demands of their followers (Caniëls, Semeijn, & Renders, 2018).

Researchers started concentrating on the role that a person's personality and motivation play in leadership in the 1960s and the 1970s (Herzberg, 1967; Maslow, 1998). McClelland, Atkinson, Clark, and Lowell (1976) Need for Achievement theory, which postulated that people have a basic need to succeed and that this urge is a primary driver of behavior, was one of the most prominent ideas to emerge during this time. McClelland et al. (1976), people who have a strong need for success are more inclined to establish difficult objectives, persevere in the face of challenges, and take calculated risks to succeed. Vroom, Porter, and Lawler (2015) Expectancy theory, which contends that a person's motivation is impacted by their expectations of the results of their activities, is another significant theory that developed around this time. Vroom et al. (2015), people are motivated to act in certain ways when they think doing so will result in positive consequences such as prizes or praise. People are also more driven when they have high expectations for achievement and cherish the benefits or acknowledgments they obtain (Ronnie & Philip, 2021).

Previous studies concentrating on the function of transformational leadership in motivation and output in the 1980s and the 1990s (Bass, 1997; Podsakoff, MacKenzie, Moorman, & Fetter, 1990). Transformational leadership aims to motivate people to realize their maximum potential (Bass, 1998; Bass & Avolio, 1990). This idea contends that transformational leaders inspire followers, offer direction and support, and give them the tools that they need to succeed. Burns (2004) created one of the most well-known ideas of transformational leadership, arguing that these leaders inspire their subordinates with a feeling of direction and motivation.

The situational leadership model, which contends that the most effective leadership style relies on the developmental stage of followers, was another significant idea that emerged during this time (Podsakoff, Niehoff, MacKenzie, & Williams, 1993). This idea suggests that rather than relying on a single, fixed style, leaders should modify their approach depending on the developmental stage of their subordinates. This model places strong emphasis on the significance of offering followers the proper amount of support and challenges to foster their growth and development (Blanchard, Zigarmi, & Nelson, 1993). In recent years, new ideas and models have been developed as a result of scholars' sustained attention to the connection between motivation and leadership. Some of the most recent ideas have concentrated on the function of positive psychology and resilience in leadership as well as the function of emotional intelligence in leadership and motivation. These theories stress the significance of an atmosphere that encourages and supports motivation and output and contend that emotionally intelligent and resilient leaders are more likely to be successful in inspiring and motivating their followers.

## THEORIES

### 1. Trait Theory of Leadership

Trait theory of leadership is one of the earliest and best-known theories of leadership. Good leaders possess specific innate abilities or attributes from birth (Tierney et al., 1999). These characteristics are regarded as major factors in determining leadership aptitude, as they are believed to be quite stable and constant across many settings and scenarios. Trait Theory has its roots in the early 1900s, when psychologists started looking at the personality qualities of leaders for the first time (Kerr et al., 1974; Peters et al., 1985).

Cohen (2012) studied the characteristics of great military commanders in depth in the 1920s and the 1930s and concluded that these leaders often possessed specific personality qualities, including aggressiveness, inventiveness, and intellect. These discoveries served as the basis for the creation of trait theory, a methodological framework for comprehending leaders' personality traits. The features of great leaders have been studied and identified over time, and the trait theory has grown to include a variety of traits that are believed to be connected to good leadership. The most frequently examined characteristics include dominance, extraversion, emotional stability, intellect, and friendliness (Fleeson & Jayawickreme, 2015; Gehring, 2007).

The trait theory of leadership is a popular theory that focuses on leaders' inherent qualities of leaders (Fleeson & Jayawickreme, 2015). This theory argues that leaders possess a distinct set of character qualities that distinguish them from followers (Bakker, Hetland, Olsen, & Espevik, 2022). These traits are considered to be stable and consistent across various situations and settings, and therefore are believed to be a significant factor in determining leadership potential (Bakker et al., 2022). To determine these leadership qualities, researchers use a variety of methods, such as self-report measures including personality inventories or questionnaires, as well as observer evaluations and other assessment techniques. Trait theory also suggests that businesses should use characteristic-based selection techniques to identify and choose successful leaders based on their distinct and recognizable qualities. Overall, the trait theory of leadership emphasizes the importance of innate qualities in determining leadership potential, and has significant implications for leadership selection and development.

Despite its widespread acceptance and influence in the field of leadership studies, Trait Theory has drawn criticism from scholars on several fronts. One major criticism is the lack of empirical support for this theory (Colbert, Judge, Choi, & Wang, 2012; Kotiaho, 2001). Some argue that there is little scientific data to support the notion that leaders possess a distinct set of inherent characteristics that distinguish them from their followers. Additionally, detractors of Trait Theory claim that they fail to account for contextual and situational factors that can impact leadership effectiveness (Zaccaro, 2007). For instance, the theory ignores the needs and motivations of followers, the nature of the work being performed, and the broader organizational and cultural context (Judge, Piccolo, & Kosalka, 2009). Another critique of the Trait Theory is that it pays little attention to developmental processes in leadership (Bolden, Gosling, Marturano, & Dennison, 2003). Gandolfi and Stone (2018); Mendenhall (2017), effective leaders are not just born with certain traits but also acquire new skills and abilities over time. Finally, the theory has been criticized for overemphasizing the importance of leader attributes, while ignoring the methods through which leaders motivate and influence their followers. To lead effectively, some argue that leaders need to engage in effective communication, motivation, and other leadership activities in addition to possessing certain personality traits. A well-researched and important paradigm for analyzing leaders' personality traits is the trait theory of leadership. Despite its popularity, the theory has drawn criticism for its paucity of empirical evidence, little attention to situational and contextual elements, and disregard for leadership and growth processes.

## 2. Contingency Theory of Leadership

Contingency theory of leadership provides a framework for comprehending how situational and contextual elements affect leadership effectiveness. According to this notion, no one's best leadership style applies to all circumstances; instead, the best style of leadership will change based on the particular requirements and limitations of the circumstances. In this chapter, we will give an outline the Contingency Theory of Leadership, including its history, development, essential elements, and main objections.

Researchers first started to question the tenets of trait-based theories of leadership in the 1960s, when Contingency Theory emerged (Luthans, 1973). The demands and motivations of followers, the nature of the work, and the larger organizational and cultural backdrop are just a few examples of the situational and contextual aspects that these early academics recognized as having an impact on leadership effectiveness.

Contingency Theory of Leadership was created as a strategy to account for these situational and contextual elements in leadership, building on these early observations. The ideal leadership style will rely on the particular requirements and limitations of the circumstance, and leaders must modify their style to meet the circumstances in order to be effective (Kerr et al., 1974; Stogdill, 1975).

The Contingency Theory of Leadership is a prominent leadership theory that emphasizes the importance of situational and contextual factors in determining effective leadership (Oc, 2018). This theory, a wide range of situational elements, such as the demands and motivations of followers, the nature of the work, and the larger organizational and cultural environment, all affect the effectiveness of a leader (Avolio, 2007). Furthermore, the theory suggests that the optimal leadership style matches the demands of the situation, and leaders must modify their style to suit the circumstances to be effective. Contingency Theory, effective leaders are adaptable and can change their leadership style to suit the requirements of various scenarios (Yukl, 2011). This means that good leaders may employ a variety of different styles depending on their circumstances. Therefore, the theory acknowledges that there is no single optimal style of leadership and that leaders must be flexible and able to adjust their approach depending on the demands of the situation. Overall, the Contingency Theory of Leadership highlights the importance of considering the situational context of leadership and has significant implications for leadership development and practice.

Contingency Theory of Leadership has been widely accepted as an important concept for understanding how situational and contextual factors affect leadership effectiveness. However, despite its influence, the theory has faced several criticisms. Additionally, critics have highlighted the lack of clear and consistent definitions for key terms, such as situational needs and leadership style, making it difficult to apply the theory in real-world situations. The theory has also been criticized for not providing clear and practical instructions for leaders on how to modify their style to match various situations, despite providing a fundamental framework for understanding the function of the situational and contextual aspects of leadership. Finally, some critics have argued that the theory overemphasizes situational events while downplaying the importance of leadership quality and skills. Nevertheless, the Contingency Theory of Leadership remains a crucial paradigm for understanding leadership effectiveness despite these concerns.

## 3. Situational Leadership Model

The Situational Leadership Model is a commonly used leadership theory that contends that the best leaders are those who can modify their style of leadership to suit the requirements and developmental stage of the people they are leading. Since Paul Hersey and Ken Blanchard initially presented this idea in the late 1960s and early 1970s, it has grown to be one of the most well-known and extensively studied theories of leadership (Hersey & Blanchard, 1997; Hersey, Blanchard, & Natemeyer, 1979). The fundamental tenet of the situational leadership model is that leaders must be able to evaluate the aptitude and dedication of their followers before tailoring their leadership approach to suit these demands. This idea, there are four main leadership philosophies, each of which is suitable for individuals with varying degrees of skills and dedication. The four types of leadership are delegation, coaching, assisting, and directing.

The instruction technique is suitable for followers who are inexperienced in the work at hand or who lack the skills and dedication necessary to do it on their own. High amounts of directive behavior and low levels of supporting conduct define this type. The coaching approach is suitable for followers who possess the necessary skills to finish the assignment, but lack confidence or dedication to do so. A well-balanced combination of directive and supporting conduct defines this approach.

The supportive approach is suitable for followers who are capable and committed to finishing their work but who require assistance and encouragement to do so (W. Zhang, Liu, Das, & De, 2008). High amounts of supporting conduct and minimal levels of directive behavior define this type. The delegation technique is suitable for followers who possess the necessary skills and dedication to perform the assignment independently. Low degrees of directive and supporting conduct define this leadership style, in which the leader delegates work ownership to the followers. The situational leadership model has significant ramifications for both individuals and organizations. This idea offers a framework for leaders to modify their leadership style to suit the requirements and developmental stages of their followers (W. Zhang et al., 2008).

Situational leadership is crucial to modify one's leadership approach depending on the followers' developmental stage and the task at hand (Tett & Guterman, 2000). Leaders can adjust their style to give their followers the appropriate amount of direction, support, and autonomy by considering the followers' developmental stage. It is possible for leaders to successfully adapt their leadership style to their team members' unique needs by considering the varying skill levels, experience, and motivation of their followers. We emphasize the importance of situational leadership in promoting development, skill acquisition, and overall performance within the organizational context by incorporating followers' developmental stage.

Situational leadership may increase employee engagement, job happiness, and firm performance, which can enhance financial results. Business, education, healthcare, and the military are just a few areas where the situational leadership model has been used. This idea has been applied in each of these contexts to better comprehend how leaders might modify their leadership style to suit the requirements and developmental stages of their followers. This idea has also been applied to the creation of leadership training programs, as well as the assessment of their efficacy.

The Situational Leadership Model, a well-known and extensively studied leadership theory, contends that the most successful leaders are those who can modify their leadership styles to match the demands and developmental stages of their followers. The idea offers a useful framework for comprehending how leaders may successfully lead and manage their followers, and it has significant consequences for both leaders and organizations. As a result, the Situational Leadership Model is still relevant and beneficial to the area of leadership study, and in the years to come, it is expected to be extensively researched and used.

## 4. Need for Achievement Theory

The Need for Achievement Theory, commonly referred to as n-Ach theory, is a popular theory of motivation that aims to explain why people are motivated to succeed. It was initially presented by psychologist David McClelland in the early 1960s and has since grown to be one of the most thoroughly studied and used motivation theories. The central claim of achievement theory is that people have a natural desire to succeed and achieve their objectives (McClelland, Koestner, & Weinberger, 1989). This urge or drive is molded by each person's distinctive personality and experiences, and it may affect how they establish goals, behave when making decisions, and how motivated they are. It is believed that the urge for accomplishment is a reasonable and stable personality feature because it does not change greatly over time (McClelland et al., 1976).

Goal-oriented, accomplishment-driven, and self-motivated adjectives are frequently used to characterize people who have a high demand for achievement. They are frequently willing to take on difficult jobs and initiatives because they are determined to succeed in both their personal and professional lives (Covington, 2000). The contrast between the two categories of achievement motives—accomplishment motivation and affiliation motivation—is one of the core ideas of achievement theory. Affiliation motivation is the desire for someone to establish and uphold social ties, whereas achievement motivation is the desire for someone to succeed and achieve their goals (Peterson, 2007). Focusing on accomplishments and wanting to succeed are frequent traits of those with a high demand for achievement. They frequently accept difficult assignments and projects, make ambitious personal objectives, and put up great effort to realize those goals. On the other hand, people who have a strong desire for affiliation tend to be less concerned with self-actualization and are frequently more focused on establishing and sustaining social ties. The Need for Achievement has significant ramifications in comprehending workplace motivation (Ramlall, 2004). Others who have a strong need for accomplishment, for instance, could be more driven by the challenges and praise that come with success, whereas people who have a high need for affiliation might be more driven by the social ties and connections they make at work. Need-for-achievement theory has been used in leadership to comprehend and explain the drive and conduct of effective leaders. This implies that leaders who have a strong need to succeed are frequently more inventive and effective because they are motivated to take on difficult jobs, set lofty objectives, and make great efforts to attain them. The Need for Achievement has also been used to explain why certain people are more driven than others to assume leadership positions. People who have a strong desire for achievement, for instance, could be more prone to pursue leadership positions because they perceive these positions as opportunities to succeed and accomplish their goals.

In summary, achievement theory is a well-known and well-investigated theory of motivation that aims to explain why people are motivated to succeed. It may aid people in better understanding their motivations and drives, and has significant implications for understanding motivation in the workplace, particularly leadership. As a result, the Need for Achievement theory continues to be a significant and useful contribution to the study of motivational psychology, and is expected to be extensively studied and used in the years to come.

## 5. Expectancy Theory

A well-known theory of motivation called expectation aims to explain why people choose to participate in particular actions and how their expectations of the results of such acts affect their motivation. Victor Vroom initially presented this idea in 1964, and since then, it has grown to be one of the most extensively studied and utilized theories of motivation (Vroom et al., 2015). The central claim of anticipation Theory is that expectancy, instrumentality, and valence are the three main drivers of an individual's incentive to engage in a certain action (Correia & Moital, 2009). An individual's expectation is that their efforts will result in an anticipated performance outcome. An individual's assumption that achieving a specific level would lead to a desired outcome, such as a reward or recognition, is referred to as instrumentality (Barba-Sánchez & Atienza-Sahuquillo, 2017). Value describes the importance a person accords with the results of their actions. Expectancy Theory states that the sum of these three elements influences an individual's overall incentive to engage in specific conduct. An individual will be more motivated to engage in the behavior if they perceive a strong relationship between their effort and performance (high expectancy), believe that performing at a certain level will lead to a desired outcome (high instrumentality), and place high value on the outcomes associated with their behavior (high valence) (Pritchard & Sanders, 1973).

Expectancy Theory has significant ramifications for comprehending motivation at work. For instance, it argues that people are more likely to be motivated when they think their efforts will result in desirable performance outcomes, and that those results will be appreciated and rewarded. To create motivating systems that meet employees' needs and expectations, and boost their motivation and performance, businesses might apply Expectancy Theory. Expectancy Theory has been used in the study of leadership because it offers a framework for understanding how leaders might affect the motivation of their followers. For instance, a leader is more likely to inspire their followers than a leader who does not express clear expectations, offer suitable resources and assistance, and connect incentives and recognition with performance results (Isaac et al., 2001). In summary, expectancy theory is a well-known and extensively investigated theory of motivation that aims to understand why people choose to participate in particular actions and how their views on the results of such acts impact their motivation. This theory has significant implications for understanding leadership and motivation in the workplace, and it offers companies and leaders a useful foundation for creating motivating systems that are in line with workers' wants and requirements. Expectancy Theory is still an important and useful addition to the study of motivated psychology, and is thus expected to be extensively studied and used in the years to come.

## 6. Transformational Leadership Theory

The role of leaders in inspiring and motivating followers to do great things is the subject of transformational leadership theory, which is an extensively studied and used leadership theory. James MacGregor Burns initially presented the idea in 1978, and since then it has grown to be one of the most well-known and extensively studied theories of leadership (Burns, 2004, 2012). Fundamentally, the transformational leadership theory holds that by establishing a vision, establishing ambitious goals, and offering assistance and direction to help followers achieve those goals, leaders may inspire and motivate their followers to accomplish great things (Burns, 2012). Idealized influence, inspirational motivation, intellectual stimulation, and individualized consideration are the four key behaviors that define transformational leaders

(Zacher, Pearce, Rooney, & McKenna, 2014). The capacity of a leader to serve as a role model, modeling the attitudes and actions they want their followers to adopt, is referred to as idealized influence. The term "inspirational motivation" describes a leader's capacity to uplift and encourage followers to pursue excellence. A leader's capacity to encourage followers to think critically and creatively is referred to as intellectual stimulation. Additionally, individualized consideration refers to a leader's capacity to support and mentor their followers to advance their careers and realize their full potential (Barling, Slater, & Kelloway, 2000).

Transformational leadership theory has significant ramifications for both leaders and organizations. This theory offers leaders a guide for encouraging and motivating followers to accomplish great things.

Transformational leadership can increase employee engagement, job satisfaction, and organizational performance, all of which can enhance financial results. Additionally, the theory of transformational leadership has been used in a variety of contexts, including business, education, healthcare, and military. In each of these settings, the theory has been used to better understand how leaders can inspire and motivate their followers to achieve great goals. Additionally, this theory has been used to develop leadership development programs and evaluate the effectiveness of leadership training programs.

In conclusion, transformational leadership theory is a well-known and extensively researched school of thought that emphasizes the importance of a leader's ability to inspire and motivate followers to accomplish great things. The theory offers a useful framework for comprehending how leaders can encourage and motivate their followers to accomplish great things, and it has significant implications for both leaders and organizations. As such, the Transformational Leadership Theory remains a relevant and valuable contribution to the field of leadership research and is likely to continue to be widely studied and applied in the years to come.

## 7. Emotional Intelligence and Leadership Theory

The capacity to identify, comprehend, and control one's own emotions as well as those of others is referred to as emotional intelligence (Salovey & Mayer, 1990). In recent years, this concept has drawn considerable attention, especially in light of its implications for leadership. Ahsan and Khalid (2023); George (2000); Koubova and Buchko (2013); Wong and Law (2002), emotional intelligence is a crucial component of good leadership and has a significant impact on a person's ability to succeed as a leader. Daniel Goleman, a psychologist, initially presented the idea of emotional intelligence in his 1995 book "Emotional Intelligence: Why it May Matter More Than IQ." In this book, Daniel Goleman makes the case that emotional intelligence is as significant as standard intelligence tests such as IQ, if not more so. He contended that emotional intelligence enables people to successfully negotiate the challenging emotional terrain of relationships, employment, and personal life. The idea of emotional intelligence has been extensively researched since the release of Goleman's book and has been connected to many advantageous outcomes including improved communication abilities, increased empathy and compassion, improved conflict resolution, and higher levels of job satisfaction. These characteristics are essential for effective leadership as well, which is why the study of emotional intelligence has gained popularity in the field of leadership studies. Self-awareness, an essential element of emotional intelligence, is the capacity to identify and comprehend one's emotions. Having a deeper knowledge of their emotional states and the ability to base their judgments on this understanding is crucial for leaders. Moreover, self-awareness enables leaders to see how their emotions affect others and, as a result, behave more skillfully.

Empathy, or the capacity to comprehend and experience another person's feelings, is another essential element of emotional intelligence (Humphrey, 2013). This is crucial for leaders who must be able to comprehend the emotional states of their subordinates to lead them successfully. As they can comprehend their team members' views and cater to their needs, leaders who exhibit empathy are better able to forge close bonds with their team members.

Self-regulation, another crucial element of emotional intelligence, is the capacity of an individual to regulate and control their emotions. Leaders need to be able to do so because they enable them to remain emotionally stable even under demanding or stressful circumstances. Leadership decisions may be significantly improved using reason rather than emotion when self-regulation is used to assist leaders in making judgments (Goleman, 2017). The capacity to successfully communicate and connect with others is referred to as social skills, which is a crucial component of emotional intelligence. Social abilities are important for leaders because they enable them to establish trusting connections with team members, which is crucial for effective leadership.

To inspire and motivate their teams, leaders must be able to effectively convey their vision and goals. In conclusion, emotional intelligence is a crucial component of good leadership and has a significant impact on leadership performance. Self-awareness, empathy, self-regulation, and social skills, the four pillars of emotional intelligence, are especially crucial for leaders because they enable them to understand their own emotions and those of others, come to rational decisions, forge lasting relationships, and communicate clearly. Leaders may improve their effectiveness in their positions and have a greater impact on their businesses by increasing their emotional intelligence.

## 8. Positive Psychology and Resilience in Leadership Theory

The notion of leadership is complicated and diverse, requiring not only the capability to inspire and encourage followers, but also the ability to deal with difficulties and adversity in a wise and resourceful manner. As they shed light on the psychological and emotional resources necessary for effective leadership, positive psychology and resilience have become significant areas of research in the field of leadership (Riggio & Reichard, 2008). A subfield of psychology known as "positive psychology" is concerned with the study of positive events, feelings, and personality qualities, and how these contribute to well-being and human flourishing. In recent years, it has been used in leadership to emphasize the impact of positive emotions and attitudes on stimulating creativity and innovation, improving organizational performance, and establishing a happy work environment. Positive feelings like pleasure, appreciation, and optimism can increase someone's drive, involvement, and resilience, making them better leaders (Lyubomirsky & Layous, 2013). In contrast, resilience is the capacity to overcome hardship and preserve or reclaim a sense of well-being in the face of stress, trauma, and obstacles. This is a crucial element of leadership because leaders frequently encounter challenging circumstances and must be able to react effectively and adaptively (Jackson, Firtko, & Edenborough, 2007). Resilience is a dynamic and ongoing process that can be fostered and nurtured through deliberate practices. This is not a static quality. Mounting evidence suggests that resilience and positive psychology may be incorporated into leadership theory and practice, and that they can help individuals become more effective leaders. For instance, leaders with strong emotional intelligence and resilience may be better able to control their emotions, manage their stress, and react to difficulties and adversity in an adaptable manner, which eventually leads to better outcomes for their business and followers.

Many theories incorporating resilience and positive psychology into leadership theory have surfaced in recent years. The Positive Leadership Framework contends that using positive feelings, attitudes, and character traits may improve leadership effectiveness. This theory contends that good psychological states may boost a leader's motivation, creativity, and well-being. Leaders can foster positive psychological states by engaging in practices, such as gratitude, mindfulness, and optimism. The Resilient Leadership Framework, which emphasizes the importance of resilience in effective leadership, is another paradigm that incorporates resilience and positive psychology into leadership theory. Resilient leaders are better equipped to handle difficult and demanding circumstances because they can maintain good attitudes and recover from adversity. In addition, resilient leaders can foster followers' resilience and an environment at work that encourages engagement and well-being.

Because of their ability to shed light on the psychological and emotional resources necessary for effective leadership, positive psychology and resilience are significant areas of research in the field of leadership. The development of more capable leaders and supportive and encouraging work environments can benefit from the integration of positive psychology and resilience into leadership theory. We may better understand the psychological and emotional aspects of leadership and provide the groundwork for future studies and applications of this fascinating and dynamic topic by underlining the importance of positive emotions, attitudes, and resilience in leadership.

## 9. Path-Goal Theory

Path-Goal Theory is a leadership theory that outlines how leaders may motivate and influence their followers by laying out a clear path for them to follow and remove barriers in their way. This theory, which Robert House established in 1971, is predicated on the notion that leaders may improve the performance and contentment of their followers by tailoring their leadership style to their followers' requirements and by offering them assistance, direction, and support (House, 1971). Path-goal theory, leaders may sway their followers by exhibiting one of four different leadership styles: directive, supporting, participatory, or achievement-oriented. Giving followers directions and instructions in a clear and precise manner is known as directive conduct. Showing care for the welfare and work happiness of followers is a sign of supportive conduct (House & Mitchell, 1975). Participatory conduct encourages the participation of followers in decision making. Setting high expectations and criteria for followers' performance, as well as praising and rewarding their successes, are all examples of achievement-oriented conduct. The qualities of the followers and the environment in which they operate determine the style of leadership conduct that is most effective (House, 1996). For instance, directive leadership works best when followers require advice and direction (House & Mitchell, 1975). Supportive leadership works best when followers are extremely capable but still requires encouragement and acclaim (House & Mitchell, 1975).

Path-goal theory offers a clear and useful framework for leaders to comprehend and modify their leadership style to fulfill the demands of their followers, which is one of its main advantages. Leaders may improve their efficiency by being aware of the environment in which their subordinates work and changing their approach to leadership appropriately. The fact that the path-goal theory has received extensive investigation and is backed by data is another asset. The theory has proven to be a useful predictor of leader success in a range of organizational settings, including military, educational, and business groups. This idea has also been linked to other significant outcomes including performance, motivation, and work satisfaction. The Path-Goal paradigm has certain drawbacks despite its advantages. The assumption that all followers have comparable wants and traits is a limitation, which may not always be true. In addition, when followers have diverse objectives and reasons, this idea might not be applicable.

The Path-Goal theory is a useful leadership theory that has received extensive investigation and is supported by empirical data. This idea has been proven to be a predictor of leader effectiveness and is connected to significant outcomes, such as job satisfaction, motivation, and performance. It provides leaders with a helpful framework for analyzing and modifying their leadership style to fulfill the demands of their followers. Notwithstanding its flaws, Path-Goal theory is nevertheless a useful tool for managers and leaders who want to be more successful and persuade their subordinates.

## 10. Authentic Leadership Theory

A leader who exhibits self-awareness, transparency, ethics, and confidence is said to practice authentic leadership. William L. Eiler Jr. organizational psychologist, first discussed it in 2003. Effective leaders may cultivate strong relationships with their followers, create an atmosphere that encourages growth and development, and integrate personal and professional principles (Gardner, Avolio, & Walumbwa, 2005). The concept of self-awareness lies at the heart of authentic leadership theory. This refers to a leader's capacity to comprehend their own feelings, ideas, motives, and behaviors. This self-awareness is a tool that authentic leaders utilize to be truthful with their followers, act by following their principles, and lead with integrity. They are also self-assured in their skills and convictions, but are modest and receptive to criticism.

Genuine leaders first establish their followers' connections. They establish a supportive workplace that encourages growth and development by paying attention to the needs and concerns of their teams. This is accomplished by fostering open communication, developing trust, and emphasizing employee well-being. Genuine leaders also work to give their people the freedom and assistance that they require. The focus placed on moral conduct in Authentic Leadership Theory is one of its main features. Genuine leaders make decisions that are fair and just while led by a strong moral compass. They put the needs of the organization and its stakeholders ahead of their own interests out of a commitment to the greater good. An increase in job satisfaction, engagement, and motivation, as well as a decrease in absenteeism and turnover have all been associated with authentic leadership. Authentic leaders have a favorable effect on company culture, fostering a more upbeat, successful, and inclusive workplace. Various techniques can be employed to hone genuine leadership abilities. This entails developing self-awareness through introspective exercises, engaging in open communication, valuing moral behavior, and looking for opportunities to advance oneself. Leaders can also seek coaching and mentoring from more seasoned leaders to assist them in overcoming obstacles and advancing their leadership abilities.

In summary, Authentic Leadership theory offers a useful framework for comprehending the significance of self-awareness, moral conduct, and constructive connections in leadership. Authentic leadership has grown in importance as companies place greater emphasis on the welfare of their workers and moral conduct. Leaders may build a more happy and productive work environment that ultimately benefits the organization and its stakeholders by emphasizing self-awareness, ethical behavior, and positive relationships.

## 11. Self-Determination Theory

Self-Determination Theory (SDT), a popular psychological theory of motivation, emphasizes the interplay between internal and external influences on behavior control. Richard Ryan and Edward Deci first developed it in 1985, and since then, it has been widely used in a variety of fields, such as leadership, education, sports, and the workplace (Deci & Ryan, 2004). SDT's central claim of SDT is that three basic psychological needs—autonomy, competence, and relatedness—underlie human conduct. Yearning for control and freedom in one's life is referred to as autonomy. The need to feel capable and successful in one's endeavors is referred to as competence. The term "relatedness" describes the desire to be accepted and cared for by others. When these requirements are satisfied, people are more likely to engage in fun and satisfying activities, which increases their levels of intrinsic motivation and well-being (Deci & Ryan, 2012). SDT has significant ramifications for how leaders can influence and engage their followers productively. Leaders may encourage followers' intrinsic motivation and engagement by fostering an atmosphere that values autonomy, competence and relatedness. Allowing for control and choice is one method of achieving this. Delegating tasks and responsibilities, offering opportunities for personal growth and development, and enabling open and honest communication are ways to accomplish this.

By offering suitable challenges and assistance, as well as praising and rewarding individual accomplishments, competence can be encouraged. Leaders can also promote relatedness by fostering a sense of belonging and promoting social contact among team members. SDT not only emphasizes the importance of inner motivation, but also the detrimental impacts of extrinsic motivation on behavior. People are less likely to engage in fun and gratifying activities when driven by external rewards, such as money or acclaim, which lowers levels of intrinsic motivation and well-being. Hence, it is more likely that leaders who concentrate on fostering an environment that encourages intrinsic motivation will successfully attract and maintain their followers. By understanding the values of autonomy, competence, and relatedness, leaders can establish a productive workplace that promotes engagement, motivation, and well-being. All things considered, the Self-Determination Theory offers a useful foundation for comprehending how to foster intrinsic drive in leadership scenarios (Deci, Olafsen, & Ryan, 2017). Leaders may build a supportive and interesting work environment that encourages positive outcomes for both themselves and their followers by concentrating on the demands for autonomy, competence, and relatedness.

# DISCUSSION

## Pros and Cons of Leadership Theories

The Trait Theory of Leadership, which contends that leaders are born with particular qualities or traits that enable them to be successful in their position, was one of the first theories on leadership. It is believed that certain qualities such as intelligence, charm, and assertiveness are innate and cannot be acquired through education or experience. Although this idea is no longer commonly held, it nevertheless has some application in the field of leadership today because many firms still search for specific traits when hiring leaders.

On the other hand, Contingency Theory of Leadership adopts a more situational approach. This notion, the best leadership approach depends on the circumstances.

For instance, a leader who is successful in one setting may not be successful in another. This theory emphasizes how crucial it is for leaders to have the flexibility to modify their approach depending on the demands of their circumstances.

According to the Need for Success Theory, people are driven to act in ways that result in success and personal accomplishment. This theory is especially pertinent to leadership since successful leaders frequently want to succeed and leave a lasting impression. A proactive, goal-oriented, and always improving leader has a strong need for success.

According to expectation theory, people are driven because they think their efforts will result in the desired outcomes. This means that, in the context of leadership, leaders who can articulate a compelling vision and give their followers the tools and support they need to succeed are likely to be more successful motivators.

According to the transformational leadership theory, leaders have the power to motivate and change the people they are in charge of. Leaders who can communicate their vision and give their people a feeling of direction are more likely to be powerful motivators. Individual considerations, intellectual stimulation, and inspirational motivation are the traits of transformational leaders.

Situational Leadership Model is the best leadership approach is adapted to the developmental stage of followers. As a result, leaders must modify their approach to fit the needs of their followers and offer the right amount of advice, support, and direction as those needs alter over time.

According to Emotional Intelligence and Leadership Theory, managers who can comprehend and control their own emotions, as well as those of others, perform better in their positions. Managers who can control their emotions, sympathize with others, and amicably resolve problems are more likely to motivate their teams.

The theory of positive psychology and resilience in leadership emphasizes the significance of optimistic feelings, inner resources, and resilience. Leaders who develop psychological virtues, such as optimism and emotional intelligence, as well as positive emotions, such as appreciation and hope, are more likely to be effective motivators. Likewise, leaders who can develop resilience—the capacity to recover from difficulties and failures—are more likely to be successful in their positions.

Path-Goal Theory states that leaders can inspire followers by offering advice, encouragement, and direction that aids in accomplishing their objectives. Leaders are more likely to be powerful motivators if they can assist their followers in clarifying their goals, providing appropriate resources and support, and eliminating impediments. According to Authentic Leadership Theory, motivating leaders are more likely to be authentic, transparent, and true to themselves. Leaders who can gain the trust of their subordinates and act sincerely and authentically are more likely to succeed in their position.

## Discerning Leadership in Different Contexts

It is critical to remember that different theories may apply better to particular circumstances and people when evaluating many leadership motivational ideas.

For instance, the attribute theory of leadership may be especially pertinent in situations where leaders are chosen for their intrinsic traits, such as intelligence, creativity, and charisma. On the other hand, contingency theory of leadership emphasizes the significance of contextual elements and may be particularly applicable in organizations that are dynamic and undergoing rapid change. The significance of motivation in leader behavior and decision-making is emphasized in both need for accomplishment theory and expectancy theory. According to expectation theory, effort will result in performance, and performance will provide particular results. On the other hand, the need for accomplishment theory places strong emphasis on the desire to achieve one's own goals as well as the value of positive reinforcement and acknowledgment in assisting with goal achievement.

The situational leadership model, emotional intelligence and leadership theory, and transformational leadership theory all stress the significance of a leader's character traits and interpersonal abilities in inspiring followers. Transformational leadership theory focuses on the leader's capacity to motivate and enable followers to perform at higher levels. While emotional intelligence and leadership theory highlight the significance of emotional intelligence in effective leadership, the situational leadership model emphasizes the need to adapt leadership styles to match the demands of followers. Insights into the function of motivation in leadership can also be gained from positive psychology, resilience in leadership theory, path goal theory, authentic leadership theory, and self-determination theory. The role of positive emotions, strengths, and resilience in building effective leadership is emphasized by positive psychology and resilience in leadership theory. The leader's responsibility for outlining the strategy for achieving the goal and giving followers encouragement and guidance is highlighted by the path-goal theory. While self-determination theory highlights the value of creating supportive settings that address followers' psychological needs, authentic leadership theory emphasizes leaders who are sincere and open in their relationships with followers.

Finally, numerous leadership motivational theories provide insightful perspectives on the intricate and dynamic processes of motivating followers. All theories stress the significance of a leader's character traits and interpersonal abilities, as well as the significance of situational elements in promoting good leadership, even though different theories may be more applicable to various situations and people. These theories help us to understand the significance of motivation in leadership, including the trait theory of leadership, contingency theory of leadership, need for achievement theory, expectancy theory, transformational leadership theory, situational leadership model, emotional intelligence and leadership theory, positive psychology and resilience in leadership theory, path-goal theory, authentic leadership theory, and self-determination theory.

## Best Approaches for Motivating Social Workers

To help social work managers motivate their staff, we suggest giving them specific recommendations. We offer helpful advice that can be quickly put into practice in the context of motivating social workers by drawing on theories and concepts that are most beneficial and applicable to social work leadership.

Examining the various theories covered in this chapter, it becomes clear how important the motivation is leadership. These theories cover the need for achievement theory, which takes into account people's desire to succeed; the trait theory of leadership, which emphasizes personal traits as factors influencing leadership effectiveness; the contingency theory of leadership, which focuses on situational factors; and expectancy theory, which emphasizes the role of expectations in motivation. The situational leadership model emphasizes tailoring the leadership style to the particular needs and developmental stage of the followers for a particular task, in contrast to transformational leadership theory, which also emphasizes inspiring and motivating followers. Our understanding of how motivation can be successfully used in leadership is furthered by ideas of emotional intelligence and leadership, positive psychology and resilience in leadership, path-goal theory, authentic leadership, and self-determination theory.

Based on these theories, we suggest several of the most effective methods for inspiring social workers. These strategies include establishing a motivating workplace that values sincerity, emotional intelligence, and supportive work culture. They entail giving direction, encouragement, and appreciation to promote the competence and independence of social workers. Additionally, by combining directive, supportive, participative, and goal-oriented leadership, leaders can modify their styles of leadership to suit various contexts. Social work managers can effectively motivate their staff, improve job satisfaction, and ultimately contribute to the success and general well-being of their social work teams by implementing these suggested strategies.

## CONCLUSION

Researchers and practitioners have both shown a strong interest in leadership and motivation, and numerous theories have been developed over time. Each idea offers distinct perceptions and insights into the intricate nature of motivation and leadership. A variety of theories have been developed to understand the motivational aspects of leadership, ranging from the trait theory of leadership, which emphasizes personal traits as the primary factors influencing leadership effectiveness, to contingency theory, which concentrates on the situational factors that influence the leader's behavior, and path-goal theory, which emphasizes the role of the leader in assisting followers in achieving their goals. The advent of transformational leadership, which emphasizes the role of the leader in inspiring and motivating followers to achieve better levels of performance, is one of the more recent innovations in the subject of leadership and motivation. In addition, the expansion of emotional intelligence and positive psychology has facilitated the development of theories emphasizing the significance of leaders' emotional and psychological well-being for effective leadership.

Situational settings in which leaders and followers engage are another crucial component of leadership and motivation. For instance, the situational leadership model emphasizes how important it is for the leader to modify their approach to fit the requirements and capabilities of their followers, while expectancy theory emphasizes how expectations play a part in motivating others. There are still many unsolved questions in the realm of leadership and motivation, despite the abundance of theories and research in this area. For instance, the best ways to assess the essential elements of motivation and leadership are not universally agreed upon, and the connections between these ideas are still poorly understood. Additional studies are required to understand how individual variations such as gender, culture, and other factors affect leadership and motivation. Notwithstanding these drawbacks, research on motivation and leadership has shed light on important aspects of what motivates and sustains effective leadership. As additional studies shed light on the intricate nature of these issues in the future, these theories will probably continue to develop and improve.

In conclusion, research and theories in the fields of motivation and leadership have advanced significantly in recent years, shedding light on fundamental principles of effective leadership. Future studies could improve these findings by examining the interactions among organizational, situational, and individual elements that affect motivation and leadership. By doing this, we can learn more about what leadership is and how it can be developed and enhanced in groups and communities.

This method has a wide range of practical applications. Social work managers and leaders may take action to create a more encouraging and empowering work environment by understanding the fundamental theories of leadership and motivation. By doing so, they will have a better understanding of the factors that influence employee engagement and motivation. Additionally, managers and leaders can improve their effectiveness in their positions and aid staff in realizing their full potential by concentrating on their emotional intelligence, psychological health, and leadership abilities.

Ultimately, motivation and leadership research has the potential to boost not only organizational effectiveness, but also people's and communities' general quality of life. Leaders can create environments that support personal and professional growth, have a significant impact, and promote the well-being of those they serve by implementing the suggested theories and practices. In conclusion, this chapter emphasizes the significance of comprehending and utilizing theories of leadership and motivation in the field of social work. Social work managers can effectively inspire their teams, promote positive outcomes, and significantly improve the lives of people and communities they serve by incorporating these principles into their leadership strategies.

## Conflict of Interest

All the authors in this paper have no conflict of interest.

## Funding

This research was conducted without any external funding.

## REFERENCES

Ahsan, M. J., & Khalid, M. H. (2023). Laissez-Faire Leadership. In *Leadership Approaches in Global Hospitality and Tourism* (pp. 61–72). IGI Global. doi:10.4018/978-1-6684-6713-8.ch004

Avolio, B. J. (2007). Promoting more integrative strategies for leadership theory-building. *The American Psychologist*, *62*(1), 25–33. doi:10.1037/0003-066X.62.1.25 PMID:17209677

Bakker, A. B., Hetland, J., Olsen, O. K., & Espevik, R. (2022). Daily transformational leadership: A source of inspiration for follower performance? *European Management Journal*. Advance online publication. doi:10.1016/j.emj.2022.04.004

Bakker, A. B., & Leiter, M. (2017). Strategic and proactive approaches to work engagement. *Organizational Dynamics*, *46*(2), 67–75. doi:10.1016/j.orgdyn.2017.04.002

Barba-Sánchez, V., & Atienza-Sahuquillo, C. (2017). Entrepreneurial motivation and self-employment: Evidence from expectancy theory. *The International Entrepreneurship and Management Journal*, *13*(4), 1097–1115. doi:10.100711365-017-0441-z

Barker, R. A. (2001). The nature of leadership. *Human Relations*, *54*(4), 469–494. doi:10.1177/0018726701544004

Barling, J., Slater, F., & Kelloway, E. K. (2000). Transformational leadership and emotional intelligence: An exploratory study. *Leadership and Organization Development Journal*, *21*(3), 157–161. doi:10.1108/01437730010325040

Bass, B. M. (1997). Does the transactional–transformational leadership paradigm transcend organizational and national boundaries? *The American Psychologist*, *52*(2), 130–139. doi:10.1037/0003-066X.52.2.130

Bass, B. M. (1998). *Transformational leadership: industrial*. Military, and Educational Impact.

Bass, B. M., & Avolio, B. J. (1990). *Transformational leadership development: Manual for the multifactor leadership questionnaire*. Consulting Psychologists Press.

Blanchard, K. H., Zigarmi, D., & Nelson, R. B. (1993). Situational Leadership® after 25 years: A retrospective. *The Journal of Leadership Studies*, *1*(1), 21–36. doi:10.1177/107179199300100104

Bolden, R., Gosling, J., Marturano, A., & Dennison, P. (2003). *A review of leadership theory and competency frameworks*. Academic Press.

Burns, J. M. (2004). *Transforming leadership: A new pursuit of happiness*. Grove Press.

Burns, J. M. (2012). *Leadership*. Open Road Media.

Caniëls, M. C., Semeijn, J. H., & Renders, I. H. (2018). Mind the mindset! The interaction of proactive personality, transformational leadership and growth mindset for engagement at work. *Career Development International*, *23*(1), 48–66. doi:10.1108/CDI-11-2016-0194

Cohen, E. A. (2012). *Supreme command: Soldiers, statesmen and leadership in wartime*. Simon and Schuster.

Colbert, A. E., Judge, T. A., Choi, D., & Wang, G. (2012). Assessing the trait theory of leadership using self and observer ratings of personality: The mediating role of contributions to group success. *The Leadership Quarterly*, *23*(4), 670–685. doi:10.1016/j.leaqua.2012.03.004

Correia, A., & Moital, M. (2009). Antecedents and consequences of prestige motivation in tourism: An expectancy-value motivation. In *Handbook of tourist behavior* (pp. 34–50). Routledge.

Covington, M. V. (2000). Goal theory, motivation, and school achievement: An integrative review. *Annual Review of Psychology*, *51*(1), 171–200. doi:10.1146/annurev.psych.51.1.171 PMID:10751969

Deci, E. L., Olafsen, A. H., & Ryan, R. M. (2017). Self-determination theory in work organizations: The state of a science. *Annual Review of Organizational Psychology and Organizational Behavior*, *4*(1), 19–43. doi:10.1146/annurev-orgpsych-032516-113108

Deci, E. L., & Ryan, R. M. (2004). *Handbook of self-determination research*. University Rochester Press.

Deci, E. L., & Ryan, R. M. (2012). *Self-determination theory*. Academic Press.

Fisher, E. A. (2009). Motivation and leadership in social work management: A review of theories and related studies. *Administration in Social Work*, *33*(4), 347–367. doi:10.1080/03643100902769160

Fleeson, W., & Jayawickreme, E. (2015). Whole trait theory. *Journal of Research in Personality*, *56*, 82–92. doi:10.1016/j.jrp.2014.10.009 PMID:26097268

Galbreath, J., & Rogers, T. (1999). Customer relationship leadership: A leadership and motivation model for the twenty-first century business. *The TQM Magazine*, *11*(3), 161–171. doi:10.1108/09544789910262734

Gandolfi, F., & Stone, S. (2018). Leadership, leadership styles, and servant leadership. *Journal of Management Research*, *18*(4), 261–269.

Gardner, W., Avolio, B. J., & Walumbwa, F. O. (2005). *Authentic leadership theory and practice: Origins, effects and development*. Academic Press.

Gehring, D. R. (2007). Applying traits theory of leadership to project management. *Project Management Journal*, *38*(1), 44–54. doi:10.1177/875697280703800105

George, J. M. (2000). Emotions and leadership: The role of emotional intelligence. *Human Relations*, *53*(8), 1027–1055. doi:10.1177/0018726700538001

Goleman, D. (2017). *What Makes a Leader?* Harvard Business Press.

Hajiali, I., Kessi, A. M. F., Budiandriani, B., Prihatin, E., & Sufri, M. M. (2022). Determination of Work Motivation, Leadership Style, Employee Competence on Job Satisfaction and Employee Performance. *Golden Ratio of Human Resource Management*, *2*(1), 57–69. doi:10.52970/grhrm.v2i1.160

Hersey, P., & Blanchard, K. H. (1997). *Situational leadership*. Paper presented at the Dean's Forum.

Hersey, P., Blanchard, K. H., & Natemeyer, W. E. (1979). Situational leadership, perception, and the impact of power. *Group & Organization Studies*, *4*(4), 418–428. doi:10.1177/105960117900400404

Herzberg, P. A. (1967). *The parameters of cross-validation*. University of Illinois at Urbana-Champaign.

House, R. J. (1971). A path goal theory of leader effectiveness. *Administrative Science Quarterly*, *16*(3), 321–339. doi:10.2307/2391905

House, R. J. (1996). Path-goal theory of leadership: Lessons, legacy, and a reformulated theory. *The Leadership Quarterly*, *7*(3), 323–352. doi:10.1016/S1048-9843(96)90024-7

House, R. J., & Mitchell, T. R. (1975). *Path-goal theory of leadership*. Academic Press.

Humphrey, R. H. (2013). The benefits of emotional intelligence and empathy to entrepreneurship. *Entrepreneurship Research Journal*, *3*(3), 287–294.

Isaac, R. G., Zerbe, W. J., & Pitt, D. C. (2001). Leadership and motivation: The effective application of expectancy theory. *Journal of Managerial Issues*, 212–226.

Jackson, D., Firtko, A., & Edenborough, M. (2007). Personal resilience as a strategy for surviving and thriving in the face of workplace adversity: A literature review. *Journal of Advanced Nursing*, *60*(1), 1–9. doi:10.1111/j.1365-2648.2007.04412.x PMID:17824934

Judge, T. A., Piccolo, R. F., & Kosalka, T. (2009). The bright and dark sides of leader traits: A review and theoretical extension of the leader trait paradigm. *The Leadership Quarterly*, *20*(6), 855–875. doi:10.1016/j.leaqua.2009.09.004

Kerr, S., Schriesheim, C. A., Murphy, C. J., & Stogdill, R. M. (1974). Toward a contingency theory of leadership based upon the consideration and initiating structure literature. *Organizational Behavior and Human Performance*, *12*(1), 62–82. doi:10.1016/0030-5073(74)90037-3

Kotiaho, J. S. (2001). Costs of sexual traits: A mismatch between theoretical considerations and empirical evidence. *Biological Reviews of the Cambridge Philosophical Society*, *76*(3), 365–376. doi:10.1017/S1464793101005711 PMID:11569789

Koubova, V., & Buchko, A. A. (2013). Life-work balance: Emotional intelligence as a crucial component of achieving both personal life and work performance. *Management Research Review*, *36*(7), 700–719. doi:10.1108/MRR-05-2012-0115

Luthans, F. (1973). The contingency theory of management: A path out of the jungle. *Business Horizons*, *16*(3), 67–72. doi:10.1016/0007-6813(73)90026-8

Lyubomirsky, S., & Layous, K. (2013). How do simple positive activities increase well-being? *Current Directions in Psychological Science*, *22*(1), 57–62. doi:10.1177/0963721412469809

Maslow, A. H. (1998). *Maslow on management*. John Wiley & Sons.

McClelland, D. C., Atkinson, J. W., Clark, R. A., & Lowell, E. L. (1976). *The achievement motive*. Academic Press.

McClelland, D. C., Koestner, R., & Weinberger, J. (1989). How do self-attributed and implicit motives differ? *Psychological Review*, *96*(4), 690–702. doi:10.1037/0033-295X.96.4.690

Mendenhall, M. E. (2017). Leadership and the birth of global leadership. In *Global leadership* (pp. 3–27). Routledge. doi:10.4324/9781315232904-1

Oc, B. (2018). Contextual leadership: A systematic review of how contextual factors shape leadership and its outcomes. *The Leadership Quarterly*, *29*(1), 218–235. doi:10.1016/j.leaqua.2017.12.004

Peters, L. H., Hartke, D. D., & Pohlmann, J. T. (1985). Fiedler's Contingency Theory of Leadership: An application of the meta-analysis procedures of Schmidt and Hunter. *Psychological Bulletin*, *97*(2), 274–285. doi:10.1037/0033-2909.97.2.274

Peterson, T. M. (2007). Motivation: How to increase project team performance. *Project Management Journal*, *38*(4), 60–69. doi:10.1002/pmj.20019

Podsakoff, P. M., MacKenzie, S. B., Moorman, R. H., & Fetter, R. (1990). Transformational leader behaviors and their effects on followers' trust in leader, satisfaction, and organizational citizenship behaviors. *The Leadership Quarterly*, *1*(2), 107–142. doi:10.1016/1048-9843(90)90009-7

Podsakoff, P. M., Niehoff, B. P., MacKenzie, S. B., & Williams, M. L. (1993). Do substitutes for leadership really substitute for leadership? An empirical examination of Kerr and Jermier' s situational leadership model. *Organizational Behavior and Human Decision Processes*, *54*(1), 1–44. doi:10.1006/obhd.1993.1001

Pritchard, R. D., & Sanders, M. S. (1973). The influence of valence, instrumentality, and expectancy on effort and performance. *The Journal of Applied Psychology*, *57*(1), 55–60. doi:10.1037/h0034197

Ramlall, S. (2004). A review of employee motivation theories and their implications for employee retention within organizations. *The Journal of American Academy of Business, Cambridge*, *5*(1/2), 52–63.

Redmond, S., & Dolan, P. (2016). Towards a conceptual model of youth leadership development. *Child & Family Social Work*, *21*(3), 261–271. doi:10.1111/cfs.12146

Riggio, R. E., & Reichard, R. J. (2008). The emotional and social intelligences of effective leadership: An emotional and social skill approach. *Journal of Managerial Psychology*, *23*(2), 169–185. doi:10.1108/02683940810850808

Rofuth, T. W., & Piepenbring, J. (2019). *Management and leadership in social work: A competency-based approach*. Springer Publishing Company. doi:10.1891/9780826130686

Ronnie, J.-B., & Philip, B. (2021). Expectations and what people learn from failure. In *Expectations and actions* (pp. 207–237). Routledge. doi:10.4324/9781003150879-10

Salovey, P., & Mayer, J. D. (1990). Emotional intelligence. *Imagination, Cognition and Personality*, *9*(3), 185–211. doi:10.2190/DUGG-P24E-52WK-6CDG

Schmid, H. (2006). Leadership styles and leadership change in human and community service organizations. *Nonprofit Management & Leadership*, *17*(2), 179–194. doi:10.1002/nml.142

Stogdill, R. M. (1975). The Evolution of Leadership Theory. *Academy of Management Proceedings*.

Tett, R. P., & Guterman, H. A. (2000). Situation trait relevance, trait expression, and cross-situational consistency: Testing a principle of trait activation. *Journal of Research in Personality*, *34*(4), 397–423. doi:10.1006/jrpe.2000.2292

Tierney, P., Farmer, S. M., & Graen, G. B. (1999). An examination of leadership and employee creativity: The relevance of traits and relationships. *Personnel Psychology*, *52*(3), 591–620. doi:10.1111/j.1744-6570.1999.tb00173.x

Vroom, V., Porter, L., & Lawler, E. (2015). Expectancy theories. *Organizational Behavior, 1*, 94-113.

Wong, C.-S., & Law, K. S. (2002). The effects of leader and follower emotional intelligence on performance and attitude: An exploratory study. *The Leadership Quarterly*, *13*(3), 243–274. doi:10.1016/S1048-9843(02)00099-1

Yukl, G. (2011). Contingency theories of effective leadership. The SAGE Handbook of Leadership, 24(1), 286-298.

Zaccaro, S. J. (2007). Trait-based perspectives of leadership. *The American Psychologist*, *62*(1), 6–16. doi:10.1037/0003-066X.62.1.6 PMID:17209675

Zacher, H., Pearce, L. K., Rooney, D., & McKenna, B. (2014). Leaders' personal wisdom and leader–member exchange quality: The role of individualized consideration. *Journal of Business Ethics*, *121*(2), 171–187. doi:10.100710551-013-1692-4

Żadkowska, M., Dowgiałło, B., Gajewska, M., Herzberg-Kurasz, M., & Kostecka, M. (2022). The Sociological Confessional: A Reflexive Process in the Transformation From Face-To-Face to Online Interview. *International Journal of Qualitative Methods*, *21*. doi:10.1177/16094069221084785

Zhang, Q., Oo, B. L., & Lim, B. T. H. (2019). Drivers, motivations, and barriers to the implementation of corporate social responsibility practices by construction enterprises: A review. *Journal of Cleaner Production*, *210*, 563–584. doi:10.1016/j.jclepro.2018.11.050

Zhang, W., Liu, Y., Das, S. K., & De, P. (2008). Secure data aggregation in wireless sensor networks: A watermark based authentication supportive approach. *Pervasive and Mobile Computing*, *4*(5), 658–680. doi:10.1016/j.pmcj.2008.05.005

Section 4

# Leadership, Change Management, Emotional Intelligence, Sustainability, and Teamwork

# Chapter 16
# Complexities of Change Management Strategy During Healthcare Mergers

**William L. Quisenberry**
*Purdue University Global, USA*

**Darrell Norman Burrell**
https://orcid.org/0000-0002-4675-9544
*Marymount University, USA*

**Allison J. Huff**
https://orcid.org/0000-0001-6102-8013
*College of Medicine, University of Arizona, USA*

**Kevin Richardson**
https://orcid.org/0009-0002-3212-8669
*Capitol Technology University, USA*

**Sharon L. Burton**
https://orcid.org/0000-0003-1653-9783
*Capitol Technology University, USA*

**Margaret Crowe**
https://orcid.org/0000-0002-9862-5265
*JM Consulting LLC, USA*

**Quatavia McLester**
https://orcid.org/0000-0003-1596-0517
*The Chicago School of Professional Psychology, USA*

**Kiana Zanganeh**
*Florida Institute of Technology, USA*

## ABSTRACT

*Change management and leadership is a complex set of efforts and processes that frequently lead to failure for many organizations due to a need for more sound organizational development techniques. For healthcare organizations, change management and leadership can be even more difficult than in other industries, with implications that could lead to unhealthy patient care and, for some patients, ultimately, death. The COVID-19 global pandemic helped to shed light on the need and importance of ongoing first-order and second-order change in healthcare organizations to remain relevant and continue providing adequate, quality care. This research utilized the case of Apollo Global Management's acquisition of Wilson Medical Center to shed light on the difficulties associated with various forms of change in healthcare settings and the critical need for leveraging good organizational development, strategy, and leadership practices.*

DOI: 10.4018/978-1-6684-8822-5.ch016

## BACKGROUND

Mergers and acquisitions (M&A) in the healthcare industry have become an increasingly important tool for hospitals to grow and expand their business, increase quality of care, manage risk, and reduce financial pressures in recent years (Hall, 2021). According to a report by the American Hospital Association (AHA), there were 753 mergers and acquisitions completed between 2000 and 2017 in the United States (AHA, 2018). Despite the potential benefits of M&A activity, such as increased market-share and improved bargaining power, the success of these transactions is far from guaranteed (Jiang et al., 2022; Patel, 2017). Mergers and acquisitions in the healthcare industry have grown substantially in recent years, with the number of completed deals increasing from 49 in 2000 to 222 in 2017 (AHA, 2018).

A study by Jiang et al (2022) revealed that multihospital system membership was not consistently a barrier to closure in this cohort analysis of US rural hospitals. In contrast to hospitals that were initially financially sound, system membership was linked to a greater probability of closure for hospitals that were in financial difficulties. However, not all of these deals have been successful, and there are several public examples of M&A deals that have failed. One of the most cited failures is that of the merger between Catholic Health Initiatives (CHI) and Dignity Health in 2018 (Patel, 2017). Although the deal was initially expected to create a $28 billion health system, the merger ultimately failed due to disagreements between the two parties over the governance structure of the combined entity (Patel, 2017).

Wilson Medical Center, formerly Wilson Memorial Hospital, opened its doors to the community in 1968. The hospital initially served as a gateway to healthcare for citizens of this rural town and presumed its reputation as an efficient leader. However, things have taken a drastic and unfathomable turn. Like many rural hospitals nationwide, Wilson Memorial Hospital was bought out by a private equity firm. Apollo Global Management, one of the largest private equity firms in the world, acquired 70 rural hospitals in 2018 for 5.6 billion dollars, one of which was Wilson Memorial Hospital.

Like many for-profit organizations, Apollo Global Management has placed profit over patient care and safety. The private equity business model is unsuited for sound healthcare that services patients. Now known as Wilson Medical Center: Apollo Global Management, the hospital needs change management. Drastic budget cuts have placed the safety and well-being of patients in harm's way by forcing staff to do more with less. What was once a fully functioning 294-bed hospital system now only cares for 50 patients at a time, with an emergency room waiting times ranging from one to three days, thus creating a triage nightmare for the nurses and healthcare staff alike.

While complaints surrounding the hospital's doctors and nurses exist, they are not to blame; management is based on analysis. The avaricious for-profit mission associated with such management companies has led to chronic understaffing that needs to be improved for the needs of community. On June 24, 2022, the hospital received a letter from the Centers for Medicare and Medicaid Services (CMS). CMS reported immediate jeopardy to patients' health, resulting in two patient deaths (Long, 2022). The federal regulators alerted Wilson Medical Center that Medicare payments to the hospital would end if specific corrective measures were not addressed. This is a rare regulatory threat that carries dire implications for both the organization and the community. The once creditable hospital now joins the less than 3 percent of hospitals surveyed by CMS that receive such notices (Tkacik, 2022).

## PROBLEM STATEMENT

Over the past few decades, private equity firms have infiltrated the healthcare sector with mergers and acquisitions (M&A) of hospitals emphasizing revenue over patient care (Baloh et al., 2017; Cerullo, 2023). For example, healthcare professionals working in rural communities face massive budget cuts leading to a lack of resources, forcing healthcare clinicians into exacerbation, and declining patient satisfaction and health outcomes (Hall, 2021). As a result, at least 140 rural hospitals have closed since 2010 due to what private firms deem as "financial strains" (Tkacik, 2022).

According to a study by the American Hospital Association (AHA), the most common cause of failed M&A deals is due to a lack of strategic fit between the two parties (AHA, 2018; Hall, 2021). This is often due to a lack of due diligence on the part of one or both of the parties involved. Other factors that can contribute to failed M&A include poor communication, cultural clashes, and unrealistic expectations (AHA, 2018).

The general problem is that private equity business models are fundamentally incompatible with comprehensive healthcare prioritizing patients' over monetary gain. The specific problem is that when private healthcare firms acquire rural hospitals, there needs to be a plan to integrate employee relations and employ a positive workplace culture from an organization's human resources department.

## LITERATURE REVIEW

### "Human Resources" Department

The term Human Resources (H.R.) needs to be updated due to the need for universality and diversity in the role it represents. Modern organizations are moving towards calling a traditional *Human Resources* department "employee affairs, employee services, personnel informatics, people operations, etc." (Fallon & McConnell, 2007) The new terms are being pushed more in the workforce because H.R. departments are more than just employee benefits, hiring, and firing. They engage, empower, enhance employee experiences, and build an evolving culture (Biro, 2016). All of these are necessary to ensure learning and development within the organization, and personnel is of the topmost priority.

The term Human Resources (HR) began in 1893, coined by economist John R. Commons to paint workers as a kind of capital asset to the company. HR used to be more of an administrative function than a strategic one that was essential to the organization's performance. It included processing payroll, sending birthday presents to workers, planning corporate trips, and ensuring sure paperwork were accurately filled out (Sheffield, 2019; University of Minnesota, n.d.). In recent years, the term H.R. does not capture the current business landscape because people are not resources that organizations must capitalize on. Instead, the role of H.R. should be to use the current financial and operational resources to better the culture and atmosphere of the people employed at the facilities.

In the case of Wilson Medical Center, the Human Resources department has a lot at stake because they are responsible for their employee's well-being and indirectly influencing the patients and their loved one's well-being. The H.R. department of Wilson Medical Center should take a step back in its reevaluation process because the underlying problem extends beyond financial health. Instead of adjusting funding for the newly acquired medical center, the larger organization should stress a better development and process of culture and organization of the underperforming rural medical center.

## Organizational Development

Organizational Development (O.D.) is not the same as the role of the human resources department because it applies behavioral science to understand, develop, and implement organizational changes. O.D. focuses on overall organizational enhancements, high productivity, behavioral changes needed for this shift, planning interventions for better effectiveness, building and managing the health of an organization, striving for overall process improvements for tasks, projects, and services, and reaching the objectives of the organization. (Cheung-Judge & Holbeche, 2021). The objective of O.D. principles is to improve the effectiveness of an organization's performance by supporting people that sustainably work within the system. They consider the values and importance of cultural differences for commitment to growth and the ability to self-renew the values of the organization and the individual. (Cheung-Judge and Holbeche, 2021)

## Bottom-Up Management

The principles of O.D. are very similar to an existing concept of bottom-up management (Cheung-Judge & Holbeche, 2021). Bottom-up management is a concept that states organizational decisions are made mainly through employee feedback and input. In contrast, a traditional, top-down approach is defined as higher-level management determining policies and processes for organizational success. In many cases and applied research instances, there is overwhelming evidence that bottom-up management success leads to increased organizational productivity and efficiency (Klundert et al., 2020). Additionally, employees and consumers of the organization's products reported greater satisfaction. (Klundert et. al., 2020). Bottom-level management's practical and evidence-backed success has brought more attention to the approach and endorsed its relevance.

Although bottom-up management has yielded more tremendous success than the top-down approach in many instances, when the two are used in conjunction, the results can be even more excellent than if the two methods are used individually. The study of the "Hybrid" approach discussed by Klundert et al. (2020) provided similar evidence. The researchers found that using a hybrid management approach can contribute to successful leadership and getting inputs from experts in the field to overcome barriers. They could also use bottom-up practices to innovate solutions that fit the local needs of the communities served.

## Kotter's Model of Change

Kotter's model of change is designed to guide leaders to implement change and increase success rates. Kotter outlines eight steps that change leaders should leverage to foster improvement. These steps include establishing a sense of urgency for change, creating a guiding coalition, developing a vision and strategy, communicating the change vision, empowering broad-based action, generating short-term wins, consolidating gains, producing more change, and anchoring the new approaches into their culture (Kang et al., 2020; Baloh et al., 2017). Kotter highlights the importance that each step builds upon one another, and while skipping a step does not translate to failure, it imposes the risk of failure in the future. The TeamSTEPPS is an evidence-based comprehensive patient safety program established by the U.S. Agency for Healthcare Research and Quality (AHRQ) that somewhat integrates the Kotter model to guide change efforts within small rural hospitals. This tailored program allows hospitals full sovereignty to develop their strategies and objectives (Baloh et al., 2017).

Within these strategies, Wilson Medical Center is suggested to incorporate team huddles. With patient satisfaction nearly nonexistent and patient safety lacking in great magnitude, team huddles may assist the healthcare organization in mitigating risks. It is noted that poor quality of care and patient safety is mainly partly due to the lack of communication among staff, resulting in 60-80 percent of unfavorable events (Baloh et al., 2017).

Team huddles are short briefing sessions typically held during the beginning and the end of shifts. These huddles can be applied to both clinical and administrative staff. During these huddles, pertinent information about patient status, organizational management, and other critical information concerning the hospital's daily functioning is shared. Team huddles are proven to improve patient safety by reinforcing and refining the safety culture and sustaining high dependability (Baloh et al., 2017).

## Employee Engagement and Disengagement

Employee engagement is critical when dealing with change management on an organizational level. Ensuring the workforce is engaged in the change process will help ensure that opinions and understanding are considered at different levels of the organization. Making a genuinely effective change at scale requires everyone that will be touched by the change to be informed and supported. However, there are definite consequences to not ensuring a certain level of engagement is achieved. In the book *Human Resource Management in health care: Principles and Practice*, a concept is discussed to help understand those consequences known as the cost of ignored employees (McConnell, 2021). Employee disengagement has costly implications for the organization, mainly due to lost output and expenses associated with turnover. In this instance, Apollo's purchase of Wilson Medical Center is something the employees have no voice in how the organization is changing. Organizations must make sure that their training activities promote employee performance and contribute to overall organizational success by assessing the training requirements of their workers, creating clear business goals, and offering top-down support (Temples et al., 2019). However, their buy-in for the merger's success is essential for organizational success and patient care.

Ignored and disengaged employees do not bode well for an organization that changes as significant as a large-scale acquisition. New ownership brings new processes, systems, and people, requiring significant transition and output to integrate effectively (May et al., 2021). Disengagement can lead to higher labor costs due to various factors, such as ineffective execution of tasks and responsibilities. Expenses like more monitoring of employees, training, and even bringing on extra employees are methods to help offset the loss in productivity.

Still, more hidden costs are mainly associated with the administrative burden of developing and implementing solutions (Levins, 2023). Systems and records must be updated to document and track the new efforts. There are ways to proactively address the risks presented here, which would be critical to maximizing the success of the merger or acquisition. Those methods include defining the employee's role in fulfilling the organization's purpose, selecting employees with capability and passion, supporting and valuing the employee, creating sustainable reward systems, and developing feedback and reinforcement mechanisms (Halm, 2011).

## Cultural Conflicts

A significant risk when merging two organizations is creating a uniform organizational culture where both sides can feel represented. With Duke LifePoint/Apollo Global Management being an extensive, for-profit health system, there are bound to be cultural differences between it and Wilson Medical Center. Wilson Medical Center is a small, hometown-type medical center familiar to the surrounding community. Apollo's management style has resulted in existential problems for the hospital and the patients that visit. The contrast in culture between a for-profit company's management style and a small community provider could not be more different. Apollo is a private equity firm to increase the profitability of investments for shareholders, while the hospital is meant to be a community resource for Wilsonians of all stripes. The misalignment of missions and cultures between the organizations leaves gaps in provider coverage and a patient experience that affects health outcomes.

Organizational cultures tend to reflect the industries they are a part of, and at the outset, there is a conflict between a healthcare provider and a private equity firm (Boan & Funderburk, 2003). Values and success metrics differ significantly between those two industries, and the effects can be seen in Wilson's hospital. The literature shows that ethical values are associated with high-quality patient care, like compassion, trust, and caring – all values in Wilson have been reported as lacking in recent years (Carney, 2011). Carney (2011) also states that a wealth of ethical and cultural knowledge lies within the healthcare profession, not just the organizations. Therefore, when an organization like Apollo ventures into healthcare, it must learn to navigate that unique aspect of healthcare to be effective. To combat recent drops in patient safety, Apollo and Wilson Medical Center leadership must collaborate on approaches to treat patients with cost-effectiveness in mind safely. The hospital's current state of being in jeopardy of losing its CMS partnership reflects the threat that cultural conflicts can pose to an organization during a corporate takeover. Reversing the impact of a negative organizational culture can be a daunting task, given its deep-rooted nature and resistance to change (Karabati, 2021).

## Diversity Management

### Diversity Strategic Plan

Recently, a significant shift has been made to positively impact diversity, equity, inclusion, and belonging in healthcare. However, since these goals and shifts are so new within society, implementing these processes and protocol changes has become even more challenging. Although we have effective change management techniques that can help facilitate behavior changes, there still needs to be more data and research on fostering greater diversity, equity, inclusion, and belonging in an organization. There is no cookie-cutter approach to these solutions because all organizations have varying types of cultures, people, and services they provide. Thus each needs a unique solution.

A study that explored leadership experiences and knowledge about their own organization found that only 50% of the responses of the 131 executives reported having a plan that addresses diversity targeted to marginalized groups 75% of the time (Standford, 2020). Although the numbers are deficient, a more significant underlying problem is not applying the bottom-up approach. Management should seek employee input to facilitate these changes because the employees are the ones who experience this firsthand and thus would be more effective in obtaining a solution that fits the needs of the organization., the more people that are part of the brainstorming for a project, the greater the chances of success because a lot more experiences and perspectives are presented.

## Diversity Training

In healthcare, only some care team members represent the people they serve. Although recruitment efforts for more diverse employees are necessary, more is needed. Many resources and other factors need to align to increase the retention of a more diverse and qualified healthcare team. On the other hand, providing diversity training ensures all the care team members receive culturally competent resources to help them in patient care and employee communication, especially when the patient is of a different cultural background than the provider (Tulane University School of Public Health and Tropical Medicine, 2021).

In the research and analysis by Fatima Stanford (2020), she claims that there are high language and cultural responsibility barriers and disparities in the current teachings of medical professionals and the care team. She states there is a dire need for better curricula and training that encompasses the various ways medical diagnoses are obtained in people of color and how those are communicated to patients who need to improve in English. (Cardinal et. al., 2016; Standford, 2020).

Several studies referenced by Stanford (2020) suggested that there was not a lack of disinterest in diversity training as much as there was a lack of information from experts about diversity, equity, inclusion, and belonging, especially for gender and sexuality groups. There was a persistent underrepresentation of minority groups in many of the research and data collected, which led to further disengagement and miscommunication of healthcare practices. As seen time and time again, the most significant barriers in healthcare delivery and patient satisfaction are the lack of communication from the care team to the patients and their families, which is challenging to address, as there is an absence of diversity training that properly provides them with tools of effective communication. To ensure Wilson Medical Center can prevail in the next few years post-expansion, more significant efforts will need to be put towards equipping the care team with appropriate cultural competencies, inclusion criteria, and diversity to reduce health disparities, improve communication, and increase patient satisfaction.

## Job Dissatisfaction

Job dissatisfaction contributes to the culture of an organization. A strong organizational culture is of utmost importance as it connects people to purpose and fosters a sense of belonging among employees (Lamo, 2019). It influences various aspects of business, including job performance, retention, strategy, and implementation, resulting in heightened engagement and commitment towards the company's mission, vision, and overall success. A hospital system whose employees appear disgruntled needs to be more motivated to contribute to the mission and vision outlined for the organization. In healthcare, this often trickles down to deficiencies in patient care. Wilson medical center is currently experiencing job dissatisfaction across various departments. However, the medical center can combat this crisis by implementing shared decision-making. Shared decision-making in the planning stages of organizational change grants employees a greater sense of responsibility in the workplace (Turja, 2022).

## Toxic Workplace Cultures

The term "toxic" has grown ubiquitous in various settings and applied to several relationships among people, places, and things. Both parties suffer when toxicity enters any environment dependent upon an efficient partnership. However, in healthcare, a third party is involved, the patients. Toxic workplaces can make or break a company (Sull & Sull, 2022). Those who allow toxicity to fester within their work environment often witness a reduction in employee productivity, disengagement in culture, and, to make matters worse, an increase in resignations (Grace, 2022).

Toxic work environments are frequently noticeable in employees' physical and emotional symptoms. Toxicity can translate to a minor imperfection in an organization, drive the need for change, or cause permanent implications such as closures (Grace, 2022). In *Character and crisis: Toxic Workplaces and culture change,* the authors note that most often, a toxic culture results from a number of people acting in ways that are inconsistent with the organization's goal and vision (Grace, 2022).

Organizational culture includes expectations, experiences, philosophy, and values that drive member behavior. Culture often shifts during change management, mergers, critical deadlines, restructuring, and acquisitions (Grace, 2022). Employees who were once defined as content often experience an adverse change when a new Chief executive officer enters an organization with different views than the preceding management team (Grace, 2022). When an organization's culture has shifted tremendously from its mission and vision, it is safe to say it is experiencing a crisis, just like Wilson Medical Center.

The Washington State Department of Social and Health Services states that three things must be present for an organization to experience a true crisis. One, a stressful situation; two, difficulty coping; and third, the timing of intervention (Grace, 2022). However, where problems exist, so do solutions. The literature outlines ways to fix workplace toxicity. Crisis and toxic workplace environments may be diverted by following five principles and strategies outlined in *Character and crisis: Toxic Workplaces and culture change.* These include implementing cultural change amongst the team, organization, and individual, linking individual beliefs to organizational results, establishing a planned and disciplined application cascade, implementing a "leader-led learning" style, and utilizing technology to document and reinforce cultural change (Grace, 2022).

## Employee Commitment

An organization's commitment to its employees is essential to all healthcare organizations. Without such commitment, organizations are at risk for low-quality service, high turnover rates resulting in increased personnel costs, and decreased patient satisfaction (Indradevi & Veronica, 2019). As stated in, *The Outcome of Employee Commitment in the Healthcare Industry,* employee commitment can be defined as a psychological binding of an individual to the job and the organization, and it encompasses the bond employees share with their organization (Indradevi & Veronica, 2019). The majority of data surrounding this topic can be found in Human Resources Literature, as many employees find their level of commitment tethered to their salary, paid time off, health benefits, retirement contributions, and tuition assistance (Indradevi & Veronica, 2019). Employees who demonstrate commitment report a sense of belonging, and their everyday workings assist the organization in reaching its goal and objectives (Indradevi & Veronica, 2019). With committed employees, organizations can avoid extended periods of decreased productivity from their employees. Also, establishing a positive work environment for employees support employee commitment (Unger et al., 2019).

Three scopes have been established to understand a committed employee's characteristics further. They include "a strong belief in and acceptance of the organization's goals and values, a willingness to exert considerable effort on behalf of the organization, and a strong desire to maintain membership in the organization" (Indradevi & Veronica, 2019). When all three aspects are demonstrated, organizations reap the benefits of low employee turnover, low nonattendance, and improved employee job performance (Indradevi & Veronica, 2019). While employee commitment is essential to all organizations, it is critical in the healthcare industry and within Wilson Medical Center. Healthcare has witnessed remarkable evolution over the past decades, with medical technology at the forefront. However, it is never the technology that a company should hold value to; instead, the individuals behind the technology. Moreover, while technology equates to more significant health outcomes, healthcare remains a people-intensive business (Indradevi & Veronica, 2019).

The correlation between employee engagement and patient care and satisfaction is undeniable. Indradevi and Veronica (2019) stated that, according to a recent Gallup study, positive employee engagement illustrated higher nurse engagement scores, leading to lower patient mortality and complications. When human resource managers can interconnect organizational commitment with employee commitment, they develop the ability to drive a healthcare organization's performance further (Indradevi & Veronica, 2019).

## Inclusive Workplace

### Importance of an Inclusive Workplace

Inclusion in a workplace is very different from diversity; however, they work best when integrated into the organizational practices together. In the Harvard Business Review article by Sherbin and Rashid (2017), they state that "diversity without inclusion is a story of missed opportunities, of employees so used to being overlooked that they no longer share ideas and insights. On the other hand, a powerful combination of talent retention and engagement is provided by diversity and inclusion. This compelling statement accompanies the psychological safety aspect of workplaces, ensuring all employees feel comfortable and empowered to speak up, voice their opinions, and challenge their leaders with constructive insights to advance organizational practices (Hadley, 2023). This can only occur when the employees feel like the company is just as invested in them as they are in the company. It should be a mutually beneficial relationship that enhances the performance of each party involved.

Furthermore, employees that are adequately included in the organization's values and decisions have a unique sense of belonging and uniqueness reflected in the workplace (Boekhorst, 2014). Each theme allows employees to have respect and opportunities in a psychologically safe environment and fosters commonalities between employees. Additionally, having an inclusive, diverse healthcare workforce is crucial because this helps the customers being served feel included, valued, and satisfied. There are many instances where the patients feel out of place or incapable of speaking up due to language or other cultural barriers, which can hinder the quality of patient care. Ultimately this is a colossal dissatisfaction and disservice to their health and well-being.

## Strategies to Create an Inclusive Workplace

The meta-analysis research provided by Sherbin and Rashid (2017) suggests there are four pillars of inclusion in the workplace: inclusive leaders, authenticity, networking and visibility, and outlining a clear career path. Inclusive leaders are a crucial and powerful tool that all team members widely appreciate because they ensure their team members have all the resources they need to succeed (Fagan et al., 2022). These leaders value the bottom-up approach and employee engagement because they realize the importance of feedback and the involvement of employees in critical decisions.

Authenticity is a large part of inclusion, and it builds on diversity. However, a survey conducted by The Center for Talent Innovation suggests that over 40% of leaders with a multicultural background feel compelled to conform their beliefs to the organization and retract their authenticity (Hewlett et al., 2012). As organizations build and hire diverse individuals, their authenticity must be preserved in the workplace because that will inherently enhance and develop the organization further from the varying experiences and outlooks. A plan to preserve and boost the authenticity of leaders so they feel empowered to speak on their beliefs in a respectful and appropriate workplace demeanor (Fagan et al., 2022) is crucial for developing and advancing hospital performance (Sherbin & Rashid, 2017). The establishment of employee resource groups can easily accomplish this. A study by Judith Casey from the University of Maryland - Baltimore states numerous benefits of having resource and affinity groups in an organization because it promotes inclusion practices and a sense of belonging between employees and the overall organization (Casey, 2021).

Following the preservation of authenticity, there is a higher chance of success from the next pillar, networking and visibility because those authentic leaders can attract and coach mentees with similar backgrounds and goals (Fagan et al., 2022). Every good leader knows the importance of succession planning and mentoring the next generation of leaders who will be just as, if not more, competent. It is especially crucial for people who are part of any marginalized group and in a leadership position to advocate and offer mentorship to others who might look up to them as a role models, and this starts by making yourself available to networking opportunities with early careerists and giving them that visibility (Sherbin & Rashid, 2017). It has also been proven in the book by Sylvia Ann Hewlett that *the chance of being happy with the pace of job progress rises with the presence of a sponsor* versus the *probability of leaving within a year* as a result of employee dissatisfaction (Hewlett, 2013).

Having good mentors invested in the mentee and their success helps the mentees have a more distinguished and straightforward career path. Most people with someone to look up to that shares their demographic can anticipate the challenges and are more prepared for what is to come. With greater visibility from mentor and mentee relationships, early careerists will likely advance and climb that ladder sooner. For example, about 45% of women are taken away from their leadership positions due to familial obligations and fail to advance in their careers (Sherbin & Rashid, 2017). However, with early advancement in their career, they do not have to continue to climb the ladder while they are executing family obligations; they remain stagnant during that period but still have a satisfying job that helps them hold their position on the ladder rather than making it seem like an impossible task to climb.

## Ongoing Commitment to Inclusive Workplace

Ongoing commitment to having an inclusive workplace means constant changes are being implemented, and employees are always in a psychologically safe place at work, along with high patient satisfaction (Fagan et al., 2022). However, this commitment is more manageable said than done, but just simple trends and methods to open lines of communication between the frontline team, patients, and administrators can assist greatly. Change management and organization development call for these theories and methods to ensure an organization is flexible enough to handle changes and avoid breaking apart (Cheung-Judge & Holbeche, 2021).

There has to be a great need and desire to establish psychological safety for employees to speak up and communicate with their team (O'Donohoe & Kleinschmit, 2021). This can boost the brainstorming of novel ideas that enhance the workplace, make it more inclusive and integrative for various people, and make people feel more valued. As an organization, they need to be aware of cultural shifts, such as employee turnover. The need to make organizations flexible enough to handle those cultural shifts without affecting patient care is crucial, especially for Wilson Medical Center (Edmondson, 1999).

## PRACTICE AND APPLICATIONS OF LITERATURE REVIEW CONCEPTS

### Current State of Wilson Medical Center

Rural hospitals such as Wilson Medical Center face unprecedented closures compared to urban areas. Currently, 892 rural hospitals across America are at risk of closure (Tkacik, 2022). If Wilson Medical Center continues to extract money without investing in patient care, the hospital will deteriorate and ultimately face closure. Since 2010, at least 140 rural hospitals in America have closed (Tkacik, 2022).

Unfortunately, Wilson Medical Center is the only hospital accessible to the citizens of the small rural town. To receive a more outstanding quality of care, some residents must travel more than 20 miles, with every minute being the difference between life and death (Long, 2022). Upon acquiring Wilson Memorial Hospital, Apollo Global Management agreed to provide its patients with the same or similar clinical hospital services. Recent news reports show they are falling short (Tkacik, 2022).

With many hospitals still recuperating from the pummeling caused by COVID-19, those in rural areas may never witness recovery. While rural hospital closures can be seen nationwide, those in the Midwest and Southern parts are at greater risk. Our nation's Southern region has already witnessed disproportionate hospital closures (Tkacik, 2022). This undesirable phenomenon can be identified in many rural healthcare organizations bought out by for-profit firms. With patient care and safety falling second to revenue, implications could be better. Physicians are forced to relocate, transportation and waiting time for patients increase, and facilities face overcrowding, thus leading to a higher rate of unwarranted and preventable death rates.

### Implications of No Change

Without an immediate change to Wilson Medical Center, the organization, its patients, and the community of the small rural town will ultimately suffer. The culture of Wilson Medical Center has led to an undesirable place to work with the acquisition drastically shifting the culture, thus trickling down to unsatisfied patients and families, disgruntled employees, a toxic work environment, and an overall healthcare organization that is non-dependable (Tkacik, 2022). The hospital will continue to lose valuable nurses, doctors, environmental services, and nutrition staff as the toxic work environment will render high staff turnover. Employee disengagement will continue to seep through the organization's fabric, and staff will continue to face the possibility of workplace anxiety and dissatisfaction, all while lacking a supportive system to address these issues (Robotham & Plaza, 2020). Lawsuits will continue to transpire as patient safety ultimately suffers (Tkacik, 2022).

Wilson's citizens will ultimately seek a more outstanding quality of care elsewhere despite the distance. When patients leave, so does the revenue. Unfortunately, the reality for many Wilsonians does not involve travel for medical care, and many will be forced to encounter a healthcare system that cannot meet the community's needs. The hospital also faces the potential risk of losing Medicaid and Medicare funding provided by The Centers for Medicare and Medicaid if changes are not implemented and successful (Tkacik, 2022). To reiterate the significance of such a consequence, much of the hospital's funding derives from Medicaid and Medicare recipients. Thus, potentially leaving a whole town of vulnerable individuals without a haven. Wilson medical center is the community's only source of emergent medical care; thus, these implications must not be brought to life.

## Recommendations of Change to the Current State

Given the current state of Wilson Medical Center and the rapid changes being acquired from the acquisition by Apollo Global Management, there is a dire need for changes. There are three sections where management consultants want to see changes being brought about, and those are on the organizational level, facilities level, and individual level. The organization is experiencing a lack of H.R. integration and attention, and through developing orientation curriculum and practices that improve understanding of communities served by the hospital, understanding and broadcasting needs of the new and existing teams, and estimated changes that will inevitably come about following the merger and acquisition of Wilson Medical Center by Apollo Global Management will be of the utmost priority.

The combined organization must consider all parts of the social-ecological model of public health that states individuals, relationships, community, and society are of great concern and focus when making significant, impactful decisions. Firstly, there will need to be a massive push for a cultural shift, starting with senior leaders being on board to lead by example. The combined organization will also need policy changes to accommodate positive, inclusive resources such as affinity and resource groups for the employees.

The combined organization must also have a written statement of their employment and benefits status. Post mergers and acquisitions, there is a lot of angst from employees of the liquidating organization about job security, and most cultural shift notices in the Wilson Medical Center are due to this anxiety. Senior leaders will need to introduce any changes to the team and the entire hospital and explain the importance of why H.R. is doing this and what we desire to see happen for this organization.

## Implementation Plan

**Recommendation 1.** This recommendation aims to have the Wilson Medical Center reflect the community it serves through its mission, vision, and values. To implement this, we propose creating a committee of key community stakeholders to represent and communicate what the people want from their medical center. This committee would create and hire a permanent position with real access to medical center leadership, constantly tasked with advocating the community interest. This would take an estimated total of 8 months to complete: four months to create the committee, create a committee charter, and define meeting logistics. Then another four months to recruit and onboard WMC community advocate positions. The human resources leadership from both Wilson Medical Center and Apollo Global Management will be responsible for implementing this recommendation. It would cost an estimated $129,000: $85,000 for a community advocate salary, $36,000 to incentivize committee participation, and about

$8,000 to facilitate the committee meetings. To measure and control these efforts, we plan to monitor metrics like patient satisfaction, employee satisfaction, and patient safety (e.g., readmit rates, quality scores, and medical errors).

**Recommendation 2.** This recommendation aims to create an efficient, safe, and desirable facility to receive care in Wilson. To do this, we recommend identifying the most at-risk service lines needing improvement and departmental leadership collaborating with Apollo and WMC employees to balance each interest against constraints. The management consultants believe this will take roughly five months to achieve; three months to collect/analyze data and conduct interviews to identify problem areas and two months to craft viable, sustainable solutions. Because this recommendation focuses on operational efficiency, the facility's Chief Operating Officer and the business administrators in each department would be responsible for its successful implementation. There are no extra costs for this recommendation since the tasks can be seen as regular duties for those involved, but there will be labor hours and software literacy necessary as inputs. The metrics measuring this recommendation's progress include asset turnover rate, staff-to-patient ratio, patient rooms occupied, E.R. usage rates dropping, and admission rates.

**Recommendation 3.** This recommendation aims to create a standard training curriculum for all employees to merge the two organizations into a more cohesive and consistent culture. Wilson Medical Center and Apollo need to determine and document the ideal culture for the hospital, community, and the necessary stakeholders to implement this recommendation. Once an agreement is reached, they must train the workforce on what is expected of them when representing WMC. This would take an estimated ten months: two months to create content for training materials, one month for review and acceptance by leadership, four months to produce the materials at scale to meet needs at WMC, and three months to schedule and conduct training for the entire workforce. Even though the ideal culture flows from the bottom up, Apollo's leadership would ultimately be responsible for implementing and spreading a positive organizational culture as hospital owners. It would cost roughly $75,000 to implement this solution. It would be measured using employee engagement, employee satisfaction, ROI on training staff, turnover and retention rates, and revenue generated per employee.

## Desired State of Organization

The desired state of Wilson Medical Center is similar to that of any healthcare organization that sets out to be a leader in care for their community. A change in workplace culture fosters psychological safety for all employees in the organization. The standard training curriculum will ensure all staff is utilizing best practice methods when delivering care to its consumers, thus resulting in better patient outcomes. The desired outcome for all service lines is efficiency and quality. After identifying the most at-risk lines, it is desired that patients experience a smooth transition through the healthcare system. We want employees to be confident in their abilities and report medical errors, safety concerns, and suggestions that may result in a more efficient work environment (Indradevi & Veronica, 2019).

Wilson medical center must also avoid the top-down approach it adopted from Apollo management. Ideally, Apollo Management should embrace a bottom-up approach with the staff of Wilson medical center to ensure all employees are included in change throughout the organization to keep them satisfied and committed (Indradevi & Veronica, 2019). A sense of comradery is ultimately the desired outcome for both entities. The hospital's goal is to meet the community's needs. Wilson Medical Center must ensure that all services rendered align with the hospital's mission, vision, and values. The medical center will improve patient safety, health outcomes, and employee satisfaction by aligning its services with its core beliefs. Historically, the reputation of Wilson Medical Center has been dreadful. The desired outcome for the center is to change its reputation, foster faith in its community, and ultimately maintain patient revenue (Tkacik, 2022).

## CONCLUSION

The patient safety and quality measures of Wilson Medical Center were declining after being acquired by a more extensive hospital system. Significant cultural shifts also occurred due to the merger and acquisition with Apollo Global Management. As healthcare leaders and providers, our primary and uniting measures in a facility are patient care and their well-being. However, an H.R. department must ensure that our leaders and employees are well cared for and have a healthy workplace culture. The WMC acquisition jeopardized this dynamic. The implications are that it has caused cultural conflicts and variable power dynamics between staff already present at the facility and the new employees arriving. Integrating the new employees, securing the old staff, and accommodating both parties, while ensuring sound, cutting-edge quality care is provided for patients and their families is of utmost priority in our three OD-focused recommendations.

These recommendations were tiered to consider all parts of the social-ecological model of public health that states individuals, relationships, community, and society are of great concern and focus when making significant, impactful decisions (Stokhold, 1996). A hospital is a primary location in the community that significantly impacts public health and well-being. It has footprints extending beyond the immediate community and reaches the entire United States via healthcare policies and community health. Making these changes now might feel small, but there is research and other indicators that show the profitable returns of human resources' impact on the health and well-being of not just the employees we serve but also the patients and their communities.

## REFERENCES

AHA. (2018). *Mergers & Acquisitions: Trends & Insights.* Author. https://www.aha.org/publications/market-trends-insights/mergers-acquisitions-trends-insights

Baloh, J., Zhu, X., & Ward, M. M. (2017). Implementing team huddles in small rural hospitals: How does the Kotter model of change apply? *Journal of Nursing Management*, *26*(5), 571–578. doi:10.1111/jonm.12584 PMID:29250892

Biro, M. M. (2016, August 12). *'Human Resources' Just Doesn't Tell You What H.R. Really Does.* Entrepreneur. https://www.entrepreneur.com/growing-a-business/human-resources-just-doesnt-tell-you-what-hr-really-does/279916

Boan, D., & Funderburk, F. (2003). Healthcare quality improvement and organizational culture. *Delmarva Foundation*, *5*, 1–18.

Boekhorst, J. A. (2015). The Role of Authentic Leadership in Fostering Workplace Inclusion: A Social Information Processing Perspective. *Human Resource Management*, *54*(2), 241–264. doi:10.1002/hrm.21669

Cardinal, L. J., Maldonado, M., & Fried, E. D. (2016). A National Survey to Evaluate Graduate Medical Education in Disparities and Limited English Proficiency: A Report from the AAIM Diversity and Inclusion Committee. *The American Journal of Medicine*, *129*(1), 117–125. doi:10.1016/j.amjmed.2015.09.007 PMID:26453990

Carney, M. (2011). Influence of organizational culture on quality healthcare delivery. *International Journal of Health Care Quality Assurance*, *24*(7), 523–539. doi:10.1108/09526861111160562 PMID:22204086

Casey, J. C. (2021, November 1). *Employee Resource Groups: A Strategic Business Resource for Today's Workplace*. The UMB Digital Archive. https://archive.hshsl.umaryland.edu/handle/10713/17334

Cerullo, M., Yang, K. K., McDevitt, R. C., Maddox, K. J., Roberts, J. W., & Offodile, A. C., II. (2023). When private equity firms buy hospitals? *Harvard Business Review*. https://hbr.org/2023/03/research-what happens-when-private-equity-firms-buy-hospitals

Cheung-Judge, M.-Y., & Holbeche, L. (2021). *Organizational Development: A practitioner's guide for O.D. and H.R. Essay*. Kogan Page Limited.

Edmondson, A. (1999). Psychological Safety and Learning Behavior in Work Teams. *Administrative Science Quarterly*, *44*(2), 350–383. doi:10.2307/2666999

Fagan, H. A. S., Guenther, S., Wells, B., & Matkin, G. S. (2022). The path to inclusion: A literature review of attributes and impacts of inclusive leaders. *Journal of Leadership Education*. https://journalofleadershiped.org/wp-content/uploads/2022/01/21_1_fagan.pdf

Grace, M. A. (n.d.). *Character and crisis: Toxic workplaces and culture change*. https://digitalud.dbq.edu/ojs/index.php/character/article/view/107

Hadley, C. N., Mortensen, M., & Edmondson, A. C. (2023). Make it safe for employees to speak up: Especially in risky times. *Harvard Business Review*. https://hbr.org/2023/04/make-it-safe-for-employees-to-speak-up-especially-in-risky-times

Hall, K. (2021). *Partnerships, mergers, and acquisitions can provide benefits to certain hospitals and Communities*. American Hospital Association. https://www.aha.org/system/files/media/file/2021/10/KH-AHA-Benefits-of-Hospital-Mergers-Acquisitions-2021-10-08.pdf

Halm, B. (2011). Employee engagement: A prescription for organizational transformation. *Advances in Health Care Management*, *10*, 77–96. doi:10.1108/S1474-8231(2011)0000010011 PMID:21887939

Hewlett, S. A. (2013). *Forget a mentor; find a sponsor, the new way to fast-track your career*. Harvard Business Review Press.

Hewlett, S. A., Allwood, N., Sumberg, K., Scharf, S., & Fargnoli, C. (2012). *Cracking the Code: Executive Presence and Multicultural Professionals*. Center for Talent Innovation. https://coqual.org/wp-content/uploads/2020/09/29_crackingthecode_keyfindings-1.pdf

Jennifer Molinsky, J. (2022). *Housing for America's older adults: Four problems we must address*. Joint Center for Housing Studies of Harvard University. https://www.jchs.harvard.edu/blog/housing-americas-older-adults-four-problems-we-must-address

Jiang, H. J., Fingar, K. R., Liang, L., & Henke, R. M. (2022). Risk of Closure Among Independent and Multihospital-Affiliated Rural Hospitals. *JAMA Health Forum*, *3*(7), e221835. doi:10.1001/jamahealthforum.2022.1835 PMID:35977220

Kang, S. P., Chen, Y., Svihla, V., Gallup, A., Ferris, K., & Datye, A. K. (2020). Guiding change in higher education: An emergent, iterative application of Kotter's change model. *Studies in Higher Education*. Advance online publication. doi:10.1080/03075079.2020.1741540

Karabati, S. (2021). Organizational outcomes of destructive leadership: Summary and evaluation. In S. M. Camgöz & Ö. T. Ekmekci (Eds.), *Destructive Leadership and Management Hypocrisy* (pp. 117–127). Emerald Publishing Limited. doi:10.1108/978-1-80043-180-520211008

Klundert, J. V., de Korne, D., Yuan, S., Wang, F., & van Wijngaarden, J. (2020). Hybrid top down bottom up health system innovation in rural China: A qualitative analysis. *PLoS One*, *15*(10), e0239307. doi:10.1371/journal.pone.0239307 PMID:33027287

Lamo, E. (2019). *The center of success: a case study on Hilton's company culture.* California Polytechnic State University. https://digitalcommons.calpoly.edu/cgi/viewcontent.cgi?article=1002&context=expindsp

Levins, H. (2023). *Hospital consolidation continues to boost costs, narrow access, and impact care quality.* Penn Leonard Davis Institute of Health Economics. https://ldi.upenn.edu/our-work/research-updates/hospital-consolidation-continues-to-boost-costs-narrow-access-and-impact-care-quality/#:~:text=As%20hospital%20consolidations%20swept%20the,consistently%20produced%20higher%20care%20prices

Long, C. (2022, July 5). *Wilson Medical Center Needs Radical Change*. The East Carolinian. http://www.piratemedia1.com/theeastcarolinian/article_94f4dcc0-fcd4-11ec-bc47-c320bb2001d0.html

May, S., Noether, M., & Stearns, B. (2021). *Hospital merger benefits: an econometric analysis revisited executive summary.* American Hospital Association. https://www.aha.org/guidesreports/2021-08-18-hospital-merger-benefits-econometric-analysis-revisited-executive-summary

McConnell, C. R. (2021). Chapter 5: The Manager-Employee Relationship. In Human Resource Management in health care: Principles and practice (pp. 83–98). Academic Press.

McConnell, C. R., & Fallon, F. (2007). Chapter 1: An Overview of Human Resources. In Human Resource Management in health care: Principles and practice (pp. 7–8). Academic Press.

O'Donohoe, J., & Kleinschmit, K. (2021). *Psychological safety for teams.* University of Utah. https://accelerate.uofuhealth.utah.edu/improvement/psychological-safety-for-teams

Patel, S. (2017, December 12). Why the Catholic Health Initiatives, Dignity Health Merger Failed. *Becker's Hospital Review*. https://www.beckershospitalreview.com/hospital-transactions-and-valuation/why-the-catholic-health-initiatives-dignity-health-merger-failed.html

Robotham, D., & Plaza, C. H. (2020). *Employee disengagement and the impact of leadership.* Penn State Extension. https://extension.psu.edu/employee-disengagement-and-the-impact-of-leadership#:~:text=Disengagement%20is%20often%20defined%20by,toward%20their%20work%20and%20organization

Sheffield, L. (2019, April 3). *Renaming human resources: People operations or team culture?* Human Interest. https://humaninterest.com/learn/articles/whats-name-hr-people-operations-team-culture/

Sherbin, L., & Rashid, R. (2021, August 27). *Diversity doesn't stick without inclusion*. Diversity and Inclusion. https://hbr.org/2017/02/diversity-doesnt-stick-without-inclusion

Stanford, F. C. (2020). The Importance of Diversity and Inclusion in the Healthcare Workforce. *Journal of the National Medical Association*, *112*(3), 247–249. doi:10.1016/j.jnma.2020.03.014 PMID:32336480

Stokols, D. (1996). Translating Social Ecological Theory into Guidelines for Community Health Promotion. *American Journal of Health Promotion*, *10*(4), 282–298. doi:10.4278/0890-1171-10.4.282 PMID:10159709

Sull, D., & Sull, C. (2022). How to fix a toxic culture. *MIT Sloan School of Management Review*. https://sloanreview.mit.edu/article/how-to-fix-a-toxic-culture/

Temples, A., Simons, D., & Atkinson, M. (2019). Strategic employee training and development in a changing world. *International Journal of Training and Development*, *23*(1), 1–10.

Tkacik, M. (2022, August 16). *'A place to die': For-profit health care crisis exposed* [Video] YouTube. https://www.youtube.com/watch?v=xzaCZs_qtI4

Tulane University School of Public Health and Tropical Medicine. (2021). *How to improve cultural competence in health care*. Author. https://publichealth.tulane.edu/blog/cultural-competence-in-health-care/

Turja, T. (2022, March). Rather sooner than later: Participatory change management associated with greater job satisfaction in Healthcare. *Journal of Advanced Nursing*. https://www.ncbi.nlm.nih.gov/pmc/articles/PMC9306817/

Unger, D., Goh, S. K., Whelan, J., & Burns, P. (2019). Toxic leadership: A meta-analytic review of negative outcomes for individuals and teams. *Journal of Occupational and Organizational Psychology*, *92*(3), 577–599.

University of Minnesota. (n.d.). *1.1 What is human resources?* Author. https://open.lib.umn.edu/humanresourcemanagement/chapter/1-1-what-is-human-resources/

# Chapter 17
# The Relationship Between Emotional Intelligence and Leadership Styles of Managers in Small and Medium Enterprises

**Ashly Nyathi**
*International University of Management, Namibia*

**Sadrag Panduleni Shihomeka**
https://orcid.org/0000-0001-9874-3133
*University of Namibia, Namibia*

## ABSTRACT

*This study investigated the relationship between emotional intelligence and leadership styles of managers in small and medium enterprises at Dog Forces Security Services (DFSS), Namibia. The study used a quantitative correlation research design and a case study strategy. The results show a positive correlation between emotional intelligence and transformational (SD=2.06), transactional (SD=1.59), and laissez-faire leadership styles (SD=0.49). Further confirmation was done using Structural Equation Modelling (SEM) by creating a path analysis, and to confirm the hypotheses where a comparative fix index of .748 between emotional intelligence and transformational, .770 between emotional intelligence and transactional, .183 between emotional intelligence and laissez-faire was found resulting in the acceptance of all hypotheses. The study recommended that DFSS management should strengthen leadership initiatives that promote emotional intelligence and leadership styles in order to achieve their goals and intentions.*

DOI: 10.4018/978-1-6684-8822-5.ch017

## INTRODUCTION

Over the years, several studies on emotional intelligence and leadership styles were conducted (McCleskey, 2014). This can be traced back to Galton's Hereditary Genius, which was published in 1869 (Zaccaro, 2007). Galton placed an emphasis on two fundamental notions that have contributed to contemporary conceptions of leadership. The first notion is that leadership is an exceptional skill that can only be possessed by very exceptional people, whose choices, as a result, have the potential to significantly impact the way our past unfolds. The second idea establishes a connection between the unique characteristics of these people and their genetic makeup. This notion of leadership, which is often referred to as the Great Man theory, held that the characteristics that determine successful leadership were naturally bestowed and handed down from generation to generation (Zaccaro, 2007).

Researchers from a wide range of disciplines have investigated and documented the correlational effects that exist between emotional intelligence and leadership styles in a variety of organisational contexts and situations (Badri-Harun et al., 2016; Batool, 2013; Chepng'eno & Ngui, 2017). Also, several studies so far have been conducted on emotional intelligence in relation to organisational leadership (Singh, 2007); emotional leadership theory (Bataeva & Vavilina, 2018); transformational leadership; Pillay et al. (2019), leader-member exchange (LMX) (Erdogan & Bauer, 2015); and leadership emergence in small groups (Goleman et al., 2013).

Thus, findings from the above studies were that Singh (2007) indicated a positive and significant correlation of emotional intelligence with organisational leadership for both genders. Bataeva and Vavilina (2018) revealed the essence of emotional intelligence and emotional competence which indicated a correlation between the level of managers' emotional intelligence and their business performance. It further considered specific features of emotional leadership of various styles, namely resonant, dissonant, demagogue, and ignorant. Spano-Szekely et al. (2016) focused on emotional intelligence and transformational leadership of managers in the medical field. Their findings revealed a positive correlation between EI and transformational leadership.

Pillay et al. (2019), conducted a study on the relationship between EI and leadership styles in the South African petrochemical sector. It was revealed that a correlation exists between emotional intelligence, transactional and transformational leadership styles. In contrast to the foregoing, Weinberger (2009) discovered that there is no association between emotional intelligence and perceived leadership effectiveness amongst a sample of managers of a manufacturing business in the United States. However, the above studies did not focus more on the constructs of emotional intelligence and leadership styles which lives a gap that this study intends to cover and non-was from the security industry.

Researchers in this study did not find any trace of a study done on Emotional Intelligence and leadership styles within the setting of private security SMEs in Namibia or within the SME fraternity as a whole. As a result, a study is required to ascertain whether there is a relationship between emotional intelligence and leadership styles within the context of SMEs in Namibia, particularly within the private security industry.

As a result of the effects of globalisation, SMEs in Namibia's private security industry provide an attractive context in which to investigate the relationship between emotional intelligence and leadership styles (Mukata & Swanepoel, 2017). In the same way as other industries in Namibia, the private security industry has been compelled to implement new business strategies, new management systems, changes in technology, and shifts in the policy to align with government policies. It is inevitable that change will not only result in the introduction of new procedures and methods inside an organisation, but it will also have an impact on the individuals that make up that organization's environment (Arindam & Atik, 2015). It should come as no surprise that the behaviour of leaders is emphasised as a crucial factor of the overall performance of an organisation (Chatterjee & Kulakli, 2015; Chepng'eno & Ngui, 2017). Therefore, the ability of leaders to control their own emotions as well as those of their subordinates will have an impact on the success of their company (Crowne et al., 2017). In this sense, the assessment and development of emotional intelligence as it relates to effective leadership may play a vital role in assisting the private security industry to drive high performance (Crowne et al., 2017).

By establishing a relationship between emotional intelligence and leadership style, one might argue that there is a positive link between the two concepts. In other words, the primary goal of this study is to determine whether or not emotional intelligence can accurately predict an effective leadership style within a Namibian SME private security organisation. These leadership styles are represented by transformational leadership, transactional leadership, and laissez-faire leadership (Dey & Carvalho, 2014).

Established in 2013, Dog Force Security Services (DFSS) is one of the widely growing Small Medium Enterprises (SMEs) in the private security industry in Namibia whose operations are in Windhoek, Gobabis, Okahanja, Walvis Bay, Arandis, and Swakopmund. The organisation employs a total of 330 people both technical and managerial staff. The organization operates in an extremely competitive security industry with competitors such as G4S, Namibia Protection Services, Omega Security, Shilimela Security and Windhoek Security. Customers have become more informed about what could be affecting the performance of personnel and the organisation. The way of living has become faster-more paced, and customers are now accustomed to a wide range of choices and on the go, customers constantly want more flexibility (Banda, 2018).

Over the past 8 years, it has been observed from the annual reports of DFSS that the inability to manage change and manage the emotional aspects of changes whether with employees or with a client is a large problem that deserves attention (Kampandu, 2019). The security industry is in flux, and the demand of security services in such a turbulent environment, coupled with the need for employees to deliver excellent service, is stronger than ever (Banda, 2018).

Without adequately applying leadership styles to adapt to the changes managers in private security enterprises often experience frustration and are not able to manage either their emotions or the emotions of others within the organization (Alkahtani, 2016), that is intrapersonal, interpersonal, adaptability, stress management and general mood. Such reactions are witnessed whenever employees behave negatively towards clients, when they have not performed their duties as expected, or when involved in theft on the client's premises (Banda, 2018). Recommendations from DFSS annual reports were that the organisation needs leaders who can manage the daily stress, create a learning organization and lead their associates to excel in delivering great service (Kampandu, 2019). Additionally, in such a complex and changing environment, managers lack the ability to articulate a vision for success, inspire others to embrace the vision, and show empathy in the workplace. The organization operates in an industry characterised with more of managing industrial relations and cordial relationships with clients. Employers tend to punish employees for bad behaviour without managing their emotions which later results in labour conflicts or losses (Musa et al., 2017).

Several studies (Allameh et al., 2015; Musa et al., 2017; Muthembwa, 2019) based on organisations that do not fall under SME sector settings and have found that EI is a useful predictor of leadership style, but few studies have been done to test this in SMEs and mostly in Namibia. The study, therefore, examines the relationship between Emotional Intelligence and the leadership styles of managers in SMEs at DFSS.

## Namibia Context

The central problem for this study was the issue of emotional intelligence and leadership styles. As a basis for this study, the researcher found three key problems that demanded an investigation. The first major issue identified as a basis for this study was the issue regarding emotional intelligence which is the non-cognitive capabilities, competencies, and skills that influence one's abilities to succeed in coping with organisational demands in SMEs. The emotional intelligence of leaders has been recognised as a significant factor in the positive attitudes, actions, and results of employees in the workplace (Ajia, 2021). More critically, SMEs need capable leaders who possess the essential trait of emotional intelligence as their defining characteristic in managing employees (Baaha & Mekpor, 2017).

The second major issue as a basis for this study was the leadership styles and how they are influenced by emotional intelligence within SMEs specifically in the private security sector. With its headquarters in Windhoek, Namibia, DFSS operates as a private entity. The company has a staff complement of 330 employees from the director, management, and technical employees. Out of this figure, 300 make up the technical staff (Security guards), 3 Executives, 5 Top managers, and 22 lower-level managers. As a manager, one is expected to apply leadership styles to achieve organisational objectives. Although, the organisation does not have a specific training budget for its management staff. Since the company was formed, managers have been attending several workshops related to leadership. However, little is known of the relationship between emotional intelligence and leadership styles; and the extent to which it affects the operations of the organisation. This in turn causes distress within the operations and running of the business. As stated by Muthembwa (2019) the emotional intelligence and leadership style of organizational leaders impacts the employees which serve under them and their outputs. Organizational leaders guide the organization and its members in many areas that include fulfilling the mission of the organization, marketing, work environment, staff morale, clients, and job satisfaction (Muthembwa, 2019).

Moreover, the private security industry is characterised by more of managing industrial relations and cordial relationships with clients as witnessed by conflicts arising in the industry (Banda, 2018). Banda (2018) further indicated that 64% of employee turnover is voluntary and nearly one-third of this employee turnover is attributable to the leader's management style. Leadership behaviors that include support and consideration of staff, high visibility, and a willingness to share leadership responsibilities might positively influence staff retention.

Thirdly, the major issue found as a basis for this study was the currently limited literature on the relationship between emotional intelligence and leadership styles in SMEs. Although the areas of emotional intelligence and leadership style have been well documented and are sometimes conflicting (Lee, 2019), a gap in the literature exists regarding the relationship that links emotional intelligence and leadership styles to organizational effectiveness from an SMEs perspective, especially in the private security industry in Namibia. This also prompted the researcher to carry out this research. Thus, the purpose of this study was to explore whether or not there is a relationship between Emotional Intelligence and leadership styles and to evaluate whether or not Emotional Intelligence can predict a successful leadership style among SMEs operating in the private security industry in Namibia.

## Hence the Objectives for This Study Were

(i) To investigate the relationship between emotional intelligence and transactional leadership as perceived by managers at DFSS.
(ii) To investigate the relationship between emotional intelligence and transformational leadership as perceived by managers at DFSS.
(iii) To investigate the relationship between emotional intelligence and laissez-faire leadership style as perceived by managers at DFSS.
(iv) To proffer recommendations to DFSS on the improvement of leaders' emotional intelligence so that it assists them to become better, more transformational leaders.

## MATERIALS AND METHODS

The study adopted a positivist philosophy as it facilitated researchers' ability to compile numerical data to provide numerical representations of the correlation between emotional intelligence and leadership styles.

The study used a correlation research design. The quantitative correlational design methodologies examined current theories of leadership and emotional intelligence. Building on a transformational leadership paradigm, the correlation analysis sought to quantify the link between the dependent variable of leadership practices on the subscales of leadership and Emotional Intelligence. The correlational research design allowed for multiple variable analyses that contain predictive design, that is, the analyses identified predictors of leadership behaviours from the variables investigated in the study through the Multifactor Leadership instrument. The inclusion criteria for success in this research was the leadership practices of a sample of managers from the security industry. When investigating a vast topic of study such as leadership, the choice of the research strategy is critical. The suitability of a research technique is determined by the design that provides the "best fit" for answering the research objectives (Prezerakos, 2018).

This was due to the fact that a case study provides support for the kinds of questions that were utilised in the research, the level of control that the researcher had over real behavioural occurrences, and the degree to which attention was paid to current concerns. A researcher can make use of a variety of research approaches while using a case study, which is another benefit of using this research method.

The targeted population for this study was 80 managerial employees and supervisors of DFSS. It was fit to include both management and supervisors in this study as they all played leadership roles in various areas of their duties. In this study, a straightforward random sample approach was employed since this strategy was found to be consistent with both the research method and the philosophy that was utilised. A simple random method was adopted so that each individual who was going to be considered for the research may have an equal probability of being picked from a pool of people. Names of the population were requested from the organisation in order to carry out a simple random sampling. These names were written on small pieces of paper which were then folded and put in a small box. The box was placed in a higher place of about 1.5m where the research firstly steered all the small papers before picking one. This process was repeated until 66 participants were selected from a pool of 80 people.

In determining the sample size, De-Morgan's sample determination table was used in this study. Table 1 below shows various sample sizes depending on a researcher's population.

*Figure 1. De-Morgan's sample determination table*
*Source: Krejcie and Morgan (1970, p. 608)*

| N | S | N | S | N | S |
|---|---|---|---|---|---|
| 10 | 10 | 220 | 140 | 1200 | 291 |
| 15 | 14 | 230 | 144 | 1300 | 297 |
| 20 | 19 | 240 | 148 | 1400 | 302 |
| 25 | 24 | 250 | 152 | 1500 | 306 |
| 30 | 28 | 260 | 155 | 1600 | 310 |
| 35 | 32 | 270 | 159 | 1700 | 313 |
| 40 | 36 | 280 | 162 | 1800 | 317 |
| 45 | 40 | 290 | 165 | 1900 | 320 |
| 50 | 44 | 300 | 169 | 2000 | 322 |
| 55 | 48 | 320 | 175 | 2200 | 327 |
| 60 | 52 | 340 | 181 | 2400 | 331 |
| 65 | 56 | 360 | 186 | 2600 | 335 |
| 70 | 59 | 380 | 191 | 2800 | 338 |
| 75 | 63 | 400 | 196 | 3000 | 341 |
| 80 | 66 | 420 | 201 | 3500 | 346 |
| 85 | 70 | 440 | 205 | 4000 | 351 |
| 90 | 73 | 460 | 210 | 4500 | 354 |
| 95 | 76 | 480 | 214 | 5000 | 357 |
| 100 | 80 | 500 | 217 | 6000 | 361 |
| 110 | 86 | 550 | 226 | 7000 | 364 |
| 120 | 92 | 600 | 234 | 8000 | 367 |
| 130 | 97 | 650 | 242 | 9000 | 368 |
| 140 | 103 | 700 | 248 | 10000 | 370 |
| 150 | 108 | 750 | 254 | 15000 | 375 |
| 160 | 113 | 800 | 260 | 20000 | 377 |
| 170 | 118 | 850 | 265 | 30000 | 379 |
| 180 | 123 | 900 | 269 | 40000 | 380 |
| 190 | 127 | 950 | 274 | 50000 | 381 |
| 200 | 132 | 1000 | 278 | 75000 | 382 |
| 210 | 136 | 1100 | 285 | 1000000 | 384 |

The figure above shows De-Morgan's sample determination table, the total population for this study was 80 managers and supervisors employed by Dog Force Security Services. Hence, the sample size was 66 employees. The sample used in this study was selected from the middle and senior managers of the organisation.

## Research Instruments

The study adopted a structured questionnaire to gather primary data.

*The Emotional intelligence questionnaire (MSCEIT) by* Mayer et al. (2002): This questionnaire was used in the study to assess the emotional intelligence of managers. The questionnaire consisted of five micro scales that measure self-awareness, self-management, self-motivation, empathy, and social skills on a five-value Likert scale (0=Not at all, 1=Once in a while, 2=Sometimes, 3=Fairly often, 4=Frequently if not always). The justifiability of this questionnaire has been validated by scholars with relevant expertise, and after measuring its perpetuity, its validity was determined to be 0.83. Additionally, Mavroveli et al. (2009) used splitting and Cronbach's alpha as ways to report the justifiability and perpetuity of this questionnaire. They found that the correlation between the two was between 0.76 and 0.84.

*The Multifactor Leadership Questionnaire (MLQ), by* (Bass & Avolio, 1996): The microscale measurement of transformative leadership is provided by this questionnaire. The questionnaire takes the form of a Likert 5-point scale with one item having the following options: 0 for "not at all," 1 for "sometimes," 2 for "sometimes," 3 for "fairly often," and 4 for "often if not usually." In the current study, five different micro scales of transformational leadership were utilised. These micro scales were as follows: individualised consideration, inspirational motivation, intellectual stimulation, idealised influence (spiritual influences), and idealised influence (behavioural influences). The justifiability of this questionnaire has been validated by scholars, and the perpetuity of the survey was validated by an evaluation using Cronbach alpha (0.86). According to Bass and Avolio's (1996) findings, this questionnaire has a validity of between 0.74 and 0.94 reliability.

The pilot study was carried out at DFSS with top supervisors who were not part of the study. In order to carry out this test, a simple method of random sampling was used, and 5 supervisors were given questionnaires to complete. All the participants who participated in the pilot study responded to the questionnaire which was found to be reliable and valid after producing a Cronbach Alpha value of 0.869. The structure, layout, and simplicity of the language were found to be good as well.

The SPSS Amos version 22 was used in sorting, coding, and analyzing statistical calculations. An Excel spreadsheet was used in capturing primary data and later on imported into SPSS for analysis.

In order to determine the nature of the link between the two questionnaires, the product-moment correlation coefficient was used. Following that, hierarchical linear regression, also known as hierarchical regression, was used as a method to examine whether or not the independent variables (Emotional Intelligence) had any predictive qualities on the dependent variables (Leadership styles).

In this research, the constructs that make up the leadership styles are classed as dependent variables. The four emotional intelligence components are the independent variables. The benefit of this technique is that the true link between variables is disclosed, which previously may have been masked.

## FINDINGS AND DISCUSSIONS

### Demographic Characteristics

The managers that chose to participate in this study were requested to complete the questionnaires, which included several demographic questions including Emotional Intelligence (EI) and Transformational Leadership (TL) questions. Participants were approached by the research assistant to participate and an explanation of the study, its procedure, process, and reasons to participate were highlighted. After completing the survey, data was collected coded, inputted, and analysed using the SPSS Amos version 22 a statistical software. Demographic characteristics of participants are presented as well as correlation scores of the relationship between Emotional Intelligence (EI) and Transformational Leadership (TL).

### Gender Distribution

From the questionnaire, respondents were requested to signify their gender by putting a tick in the relevant box that was provided. The questionnaires further provided the results below:

*Table 1. Gender (n=66)*

| Gender | | | | | |
|---|---|---|---|---|---|
| | | Frequency | Percent | Valid Percent | Cumulative Percent |
| Valid | Male | 46 | 69.6 | 69.6 | 70.2 |
| | Female | 20 | 30.3 | 30.3 | 100.0 |
| | Total | 66 | 100.0 | 100.0 | |

Table 1 above table shows the gender distribution of participants who took part in this study. From the above results, the majority were male (69.6%) whilst females were the minority participants (30.3%). This shows that male employees dominate managerial positions in the organisation.

## Participants' Age

The questionnaire went further to ask for the participant's ages and participants were requested to signify their answers by ticking the relevant box provided. From the given answers, below is the summary from the respondents:

*Table 2. Age (n=66)*

| Age | | | | | |
|---|---|---|---|---|---|
| | | Frequency | Percent | Valid Percent | Cumulative Percent |
| Valid | <30 | 3 | 4.5 | 4.5 | 3.7 |
| | 30-45 | 51 | 77.1 | 77.1 | 81.5 |
| | 46-50 | 12 | 18.2 | 18.2 | 100.0 |
| | Total | 66 | 100.0 | 100.0 | |

The study examined the age of participants, it can be shown above that 77.1% being the majority are between 30-45 years, 18.2% are between 46-50 years, and 4.5% being the minority are less than 30 years.

## Participant's Experience

The participants were requested to signify their working experience on the same questionnaire by ticking their answers in the provided boxes. From the answers given, below is a summary of their responses:

*Table 3. Experience (n=66)*

| | | Experience | | | |
|---|---|---|---|---|---|
| | | Frequency | Percent | Valid Percent | Cumulative Percent |
| Valid | 1-5 | 29 | 43.8 | 44.4 | 44.4 |
| | 5-10 | 27 | 40.9 | 40.7 | 85.2 |
| | 15-20 | 7 | 10.6 | 10.6 | 96.3 |
| | 20+ | 3 | 3.7 | 4.5 | 100.0 |

The above table shows the work experience of participants in the organisation. The results show that the majority of the participants 44.4% have 1-5 years experience working in the organisation, 40.7% have 5-10 years, 11,1% have 15-20 years and the minority 3.7% have more than 20 years of working experience. From the results, it can be seen that people stay longer with the organization, signifying a possibility of a good retention policy for employees.

## Participants' Qualifications

The researcher also sought to assess the qualifications of the participants. Participants were requested to show their educational level by ticking the appropriate box provided on the questionnaire.

*Table 4. Qualification (n=66)*

| | | Qualification | | | |
|---|---|---|---|---|---|
| | | Frequency | Percent | Valid Percent | Cumulative Percent |
| Valid | Matric | 32 | 48.4 | 48.4 | 48.1 |
| | Bachelor's degree | 29 | 43.9 | 43.9 | 92.6 |
| | Master's degree | 5 | 7.5 | 7.5 | 100.0 |
| | Total | 66 | 100.0 | 100.0 | |

From the above table, the results revealed that a large number of employees (48.4%) still have matric qualifications, 43.9% have bachelor's degrees, and the minority 7.5% have master's degrees. The results show that most employees could be failing to further their level of education and this could bring up challenges when it comes to leadership management and management of emotions.

As highlighted earlier, the objectives of the study involved testing the relationship between EI and transformational, transactional and leadership styles. Thus, various regressions and correlations were performed.

Research question 1: *What if any correlation exists between EI and transactional leadership among DFSS managers?*

The first study question showed a favourable association between Emotional Intelligence (EI) scores and Transactional leadership style (TNSL). While the correlation findings between the overall EI scores and TNSL demonstrated a positive significant association between the variables as displayed in table 5 below, the correlations among each of the four constructs of EI and TNSL.

*Table 5. Correlation between EI scores and TNSL*

| Correlations | | | | | | | |
|---|---|---|---|---|---|---|---|
| | | | TNSL | ME | MO | SS | EM |
| Spearman's rho | TNSL | Correlation Coefficient | 1.000 | .993** | .992** | .997** | .991** |
| | | Sig. (2-tailed) | . | .000 | .000 | .000 | .000 |
| | | N | 66 | 66 | 66 | 66 | 66 |
| | ME | Correlation Coefficient | .993** | 1.000 | .991** | .993** | .993** |
| | | Sig. (2-tailed) | .000 | . | .000 | .000 | .000 |
| | | N | 66 | 66 | 66 | 66 | 66 |
| | MO | Correlation Coefficient | .992** | .991** | 1.000 | .995** | .991** |
| | | Sig. (2-tailed) | .000 | .000 | . | .000 | .000 |
| | | N | 66 | 66 | 27 | 66 | 66 |
| | SS | Correlation Coefficient | .997** | .993** | .995** | 1.000 | .993** |
| | | Sig. (2-tailed) | .000 | .000 | .000 | .000 | .000 |
| | | N | 66 | 66 | 66 | 66 | 66 |
| | EM | Correlation Coefficient | .989** | .993** | .992** | .997** | 1.000 |
| | | Sig. (2-tailed) | .000 | .000 | .000 | .000 | . |
| | | N | 66 | 66 | 66 | 66 | 66 |

**. Correlation is significant at the 0.01 level (2-tailed).

The research question was investigated by examining the Spearman's rho correlation between pairs of total scores of biological (Managing Emotions-ME; Motivating Oneself-MO; Social Skill-SS; Empathy-EM) factors of the Emotional Intelligence questionnaire and the MLQ5x-TL. It is believed that if the results obtained a significant correlation of ($p < .05$), a positive correlation would be accepted. As observed in table 5 there was a statistically significant and moderate correlation between two pairs from the range ($r=.989$, $N=27$, $p < .001$) to ($r=.997$, $N=27$, $p < .001$) meaning that the correlation was strong.

In support of these findings, from the literature, a substantial relationship was discovered between EI and TNSL style and some of its components, such as idealised influence, inspiring motivation, and individual concern (Dogru, 2022). Another study from the literature links the positive association between EI and contingent reward to the assumption that this dimension has certain shared qualities with transactional leadership (Chepng'eno & Ngui, 2017). However, the findings do not agree with a study by Shahhosseini and Daud (2013) which revealed no association between EI and TNSL.

As a result, as the magnitude of emotional intelligence scores increased, there was a propensity for scores in transactional leadership to rise as well. According to Clarke (2010) criteria, the association between these two variables in the sample would be judged strongly based on the size of the link. Total EI scores are plotted along the horizontal axis, and total MLQ5x-TL scores are plotted along the vertical axis, in order to visually represent the relationship between pairs of EI and MLQ-TL scores. Total EI scores and total MLQ-TL scores are plotted along the horizontal and vertical axes, respectively, in Figure 2 below.

*Figure 2. EI scores and TNSL scatter plots*

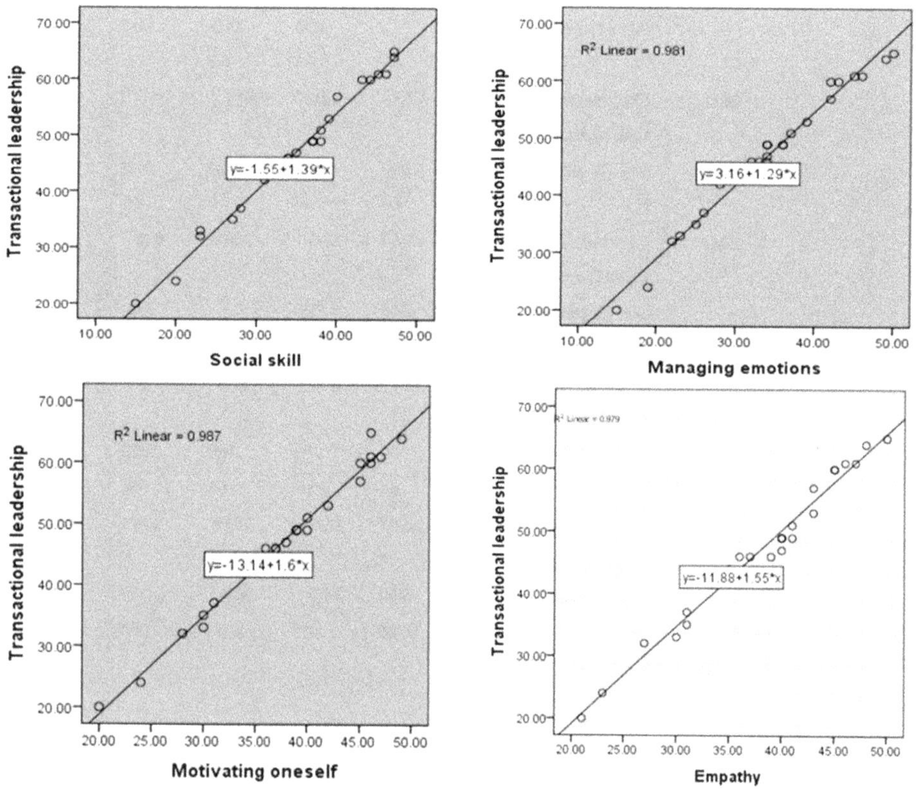


Further to table 5, which observed a statistically significant relationship between TNSL, ME, MO, EM, and SS. TNSL and ME [(r=.993, N=27, p < .001), TNSL and MO (r=.992, N=27, p < .001), TNSL and EM (r=.989, N=27, p < .001)]; and TNSL and SS (r=.997, N=27, p < .001)]. The 4 emotional intelligence scales were able to predict a linear relation with TL scores, resulting to $R^2 = 0.988$

and $R^2 = 0.981$. The variability in the distribution of empathy scores was able to account for about 98% of the variability in the distribution of total TL scores. The unstandardized regression equation for this particular analysis was TL=18.54+1.68 ME; 2.17 + 2.07 MO and 12.62 + 1.81 SS.

*Table 6. Correlation between EI Score and TNSL*

**Correlations**

| | | TNSL | SA |
|---|---|---|---|
| TNSL | Pearson Correlation | 1 | .990** |
| | Sig. (2-tailed) | | .000 |
| | N | 66 | 66 |
| SA | Pearson Correlation | .990** | 1 |
| | Sig. (2-tailed) | .000 | |
| | N | 66 | 66 |

**. Correlation is significant at the 0.01 level (2-tailed).

Another aim was to measure how social awareness as a construct of EI would affect the overall relationship between EI and TNSL. From the table above, a Pearson Correlation between the scales was conducted. The correlation statistics were in the same range as other factors that were analyzed above. The findings of the study conclude that there is a statistically significant and moderate correlation between TNSL and behavioral factors variable. TNSL and SA (r=.990, N=27, $p < .001$).

Further to Table 6 which observed a statistically significant relationship between TNSL and SA (r=.990, N=27, $p < .001$). The self-awareness scale was able to predict a linear relation with TNSL scores, resulting to $R^2 = 0.988$. The variability in the distribution of empathy scores was able to account for about 98% of the variability in the distribution of total TNSL scores. The unstandardized regression equation for this particular analysis was TNSL= 6.24 + 2.04 SS.

As interpreted above, from a literature point of view, Batool (2013) confirmed that transactional leadership style had a positive correlation with all the components of emotional intelligence. The results are also further in line with Campbell-Evans (2014) who found the emotional intelligence construct to be positively correlated with transformational leadership style.

Research question 2: *What if any correlation exists between EI and transformational leadership among DFSS managers?*

The emotional intelligence scale consisted of individual factors ME, MO, EM, and SS. The research question was investigated by testing Spearman's rho correlation coefficient between pairs of total scores of individual factors (ME, MO & SS) factors of the Emotional Intelligence questionnaire and the MLQ5x-TL. The correlations revealed positive significant relationships among the four constructs. The table below shows the correlation statistics.

*Table 7. Correlation between EI scores and TL*

**Correlations**

| | | | TL | ME | MO | SS | EM |
|---|---|---|---|---|---|---|---|
| earman's | TL | Correlation Coefficient | 1.000 | .998** | .995** | .998** | .993** |
| ) | | Sig. (2-tailed) | . | .001 | .001 | .001 | .001 |
| | | N | 66 | 66 | 66 | 66 | 66 |
| | ME | Correlation Coefficient | .998** | 1.000 | .991** | .993** | .991** |
| | | Sig. (2-tailed) | .001 | . | .001 | .001 | .001 |
| | | N | 66 | 66 | 66 | 66 | 66 |
| | MO | Correlation Coefficient | .995** | .991** | 1.000 | .995** | .995** |
| | | Sig. (2-tailed) | .001 | .001 | . | .001 | .001 |
| | | N | 66 | 66 | 66 | 66 | 66 |
| | SS | Correlation Coefficient | .998** | .993** | .995** | 1.000 | .998** |
| | | Sig. (2-tailed) | .001 | .001 | .001 | . | .001 |
| | | N | 66 | 66 | 66 | 66 | 66 |
| | EM | Correlation Coefficient | .993** | .991** | .995** | .998** | .991** |
| | | Sig. (2-tailed) | .001 | .001 | .001 | .001 | .001 |
| | | N | 66 | 66 | 66 | 66 | 66 |

Correlation is significant at the 0.01 level (2-tailed).

After conducting Spearman's rho correlation coefficient, the above findings reviewed that a statistically and moderate correlation exists between TL and Individual factors variables. TL and ME (r=.998, N=27, $p < .001$), TL and MO (r=.995, N=27, $p < .001$), TL and EM (r=.993, N=27, $p < .001$) and TL and SS (r=.998, N=27, $p < .001$).

An increase in individual factors of emotional intelligence is associated with an increase in transformational leadership scores, according to positive correlations found in the data. Further analysis is presented in scatter plots below.

Further to Table 7 which observed a statistically significant relationship between TL, ME, MO, EM and SS. TL and ME [(r=.998, N=27, $p < .001$), TL and MO (r=.995, N=27, $p < .001$) and TL and SS (r=.998, N=27, $p < .001$)]. The 4 emotional intelligence scales were able to predict a linear relation with TL scores, resulting to $R^2 = 0.988$ and $R^2 = 0.981$. The variability in the distribution of empathy scores was able to account for about 98% of the variability in the distribution of total TL scores. The unstandardized regression equation for this particular analysis was TL=18.54+1.68 ME; 2.17 + 2.07 MO and 12.62 + 1.81 SS. Also, a statistically significant relationship between TL and EM (r=.993, N=27, $p < .001$) was observed. The EM scales were able to predict a linear relation with TL scores, resulting to $R^2 = 0.987$. The variability in the distribution of empathy scores was able to account for about 98% of the variability in the distribution of total TL scores. The unstandardized regression equation for this particular analysis was TL=1.1+2.02EM

Another measurement was done using Social Awareness as a construct of EI to measure the relationship between EI and TL. From the table above, a Pearson Correlation between the scales was conducted. The correlation statistics were in the same range as other factors that were analyzed above. The findings above found a statistically and moderate correlation between TL and behavioral factors variables. TL and SA (r=.994, N=27, $p < .001$).

*Figure 3. EI scores and TL scatter plots*

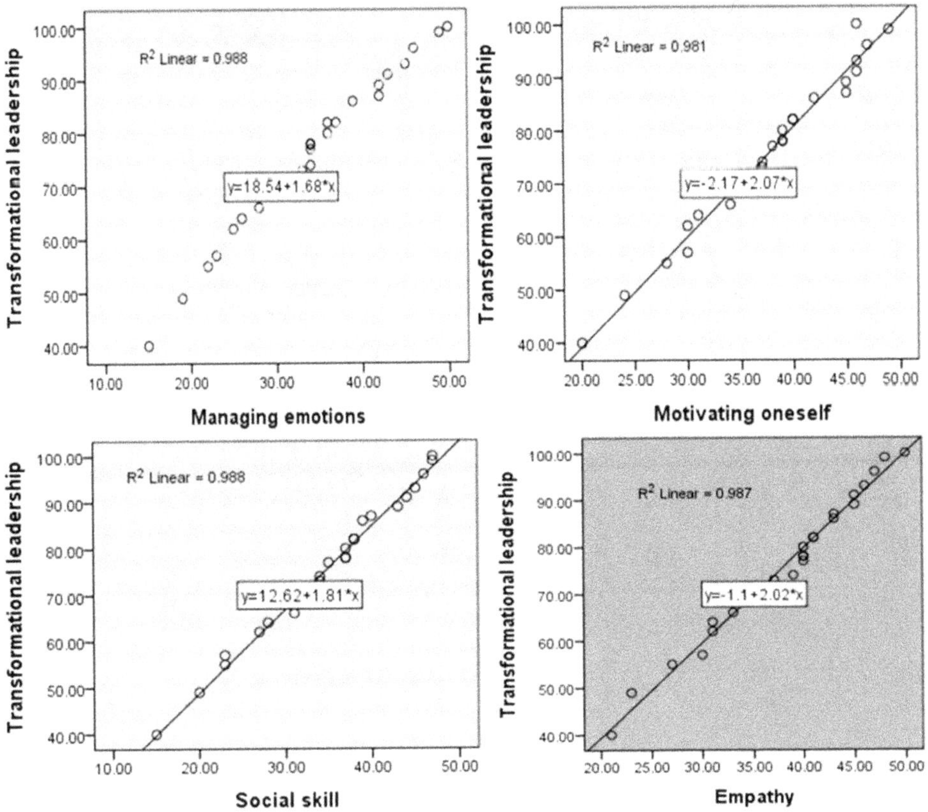


*Table 8. Correlation between EI score and TL*

| Correlations | | | |
|---|---|---|---|
| | | SA | TL |
| SA | Pearson Correlation | 1 | .994** |
| | Sig. (2-tailed) | | .001 |
| | Sum of Squares and Cross-products | 1398.038 | 2851.346 |
| | Covariance | 55.922 | 114.054 |
| | N | 66 | 66 |
| TL | Pearson Correlation | .994** | 1 |
| | Sig. (2-tailed) | .001 | |
| | Sum of Squares and Cross-products | 2851.346 | 5883.115 |
| | Covariance | 114.054 | 235.325 |
| | N | 66 | 66 |

**. Correlation is significant at the 0.01 level (2-tailed).

*Figure 4. EI score and TL scatter plot*

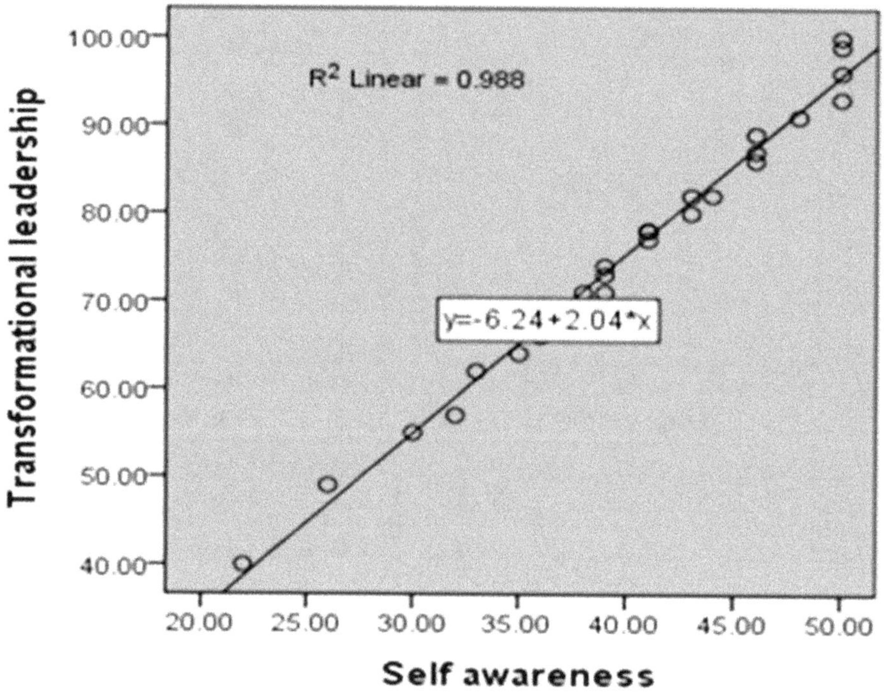


Further to Table 8 which observed a statistically significant relationship between TL and SA (r=.994, N=27, p < .001). The self-awareness scale was able to predict a linear relation with TL scores, resulting to $R^2 = 0.988$. The variability in the distribution of empathy scores was able to account for about 98% of the variability in the distribution of total TL scores. The unstandardized regression equation for this particular analysis was TL= 6.24 + 2.04 SA.

The positive relationships between EI constructs and TL further confirm the findings of previous studies (Fannon, 2018; Garg & Jain, 2013; Harms & Credé, 2010) that reported positive correlations between TL and managing emotions, motivating oneself, empathy and social skills. EI equips leaders with the ability to acquire the trust and confidence of their followers, to portray an appealing vision, and to build confidence in others that such a goal is attainable. Leaders that are emotionally intelligent are also able to recognise the one-of-a-kind qualities that others possess and, as a result, will interact with their followers on a one-on-one basis, rather than seeing them just in the context of groups (Hebert, 2011). The qualities of leaders who are grateful, empathetic, and attentive to the specific needs of others form the connection between emotional intelligence and empathy.

Important ramifications stem from the highest positive correlations between EI constructs and TNSL. Leadership is rooted in emotional intelligence's relationship management, which is captured in influence, the ability to coach and mentor, conflict management, inspirational leadership, and teamwork skills (Jain & Duggal, 2016). Leaders who have a good impact on others and who are able to convince people to acquire their support are successful leaders who are capable of motivating and directing others toward the attainment of objectives. Given that leadership is influence, a leader's capacity to influence others is contingent upon the leader's ability to establish and manage relationships with those others (Kaur, 2020).

This strongest connection consequently suggests that leaders who are capable of controlling emotions in their relationships with followers earn the trust and confidence of followers and create an atmosphere that is favourable to the accomplishment of objectives.

Research question 3: *There is a significant positive correlation between emotional intelligence abilities and the laissez-faire leadership style of DFSS managers?*

The third research question sought to determine whether a correlation existed between emotional intelligence and laissez-faire leadership style. The emotional intelligence scale consisted of individual factors ME, MO, EM, and SS. The research question was investigated by testing Spearman's rho correlation coefficient between pairs of total scores of individual factors (ME, MO & SS) factors of the Emotional Intelligence questionnaire and the MLQ5x-TL. The correlations revealed positive significant relationships among the four constructs. The table below shows the correlation statistics.

*Table 9. Correlation between EI scores LFL*

**Correlations**

| | | | LFL | ME | MO | SS | EM |
|---|---|---|---|---|---|---|---|
| Spearman's rho | LFL | Correlation Coefficient | 1.000 | .976** | .982** | .971** | .961** |
| | | Sig. (2-tailed) | . | .000 | .000 | .000 | .000 |
| | | N | 66 | 66 | 66 | 66 | 66 |
| | ME | Correlation Coefficient | .976** | 1.000 | .991** | .993** | .982** |
| | | Sig. (2-tailed) | .000 | . | .000 | .000 | .000 |
| | | N | 66 | 66 | 66 | 66 | 66 |
| | MO | Correlation Coefficient | .982** | .991** | 1.000 | .995** | .983** |
| | | Sig. (2-tailed) | .000 | .000 | . | .000 | .000 |
| | | N | 66 | 66 | 66 | 66 | 66 |
| | SS | Correlation Coefficient | .971** | .993** | .995** | 1.000 | .986** |
| | | Sig. (2-tailed) | .000 | .000 | .000 | . | .000 |
| | | N | 66 | 66 | 66 | 66 | 66 |
| | EM | Correlation Coefficient | .961** | .982** | .983** | .986** | 1 |
| | | Sig. (2-tailed) | .000 | .000 | .000 | .000 | |
| | | N | 66 | 66 | 66 | 66 | 66 |

**. Correlation is significant at the 0.01 level (2-tailed).

According to the data shown in Table 9, the association between the components of emotional intelligence and the laissez faire leadership style is only fairly strong. The results mean that when EI is high, LFL will be low or when LFL is high EI becomes low. Because EI answers and scores were right-skewed (the majority were at the upper end). LFL and ME ($r=.976$, $N=27$, $p < .001$), LFL and MO ($r=.982$, $N=27$, $p < .001$), LFL and EM ($r=.961$, $N=27$, $p < .001$) and LFL and SS ($r=.971$, $N=27$, $p < .001$).

An increase or decrease in individual factors of emotional intelligence is associated with an increase or decrease in laissez-faire leadership scores, according to positive correlations found in the data. Further analysis is presented in scatter plots below.

*Figure 5. EI scores and LFL scatter plots*

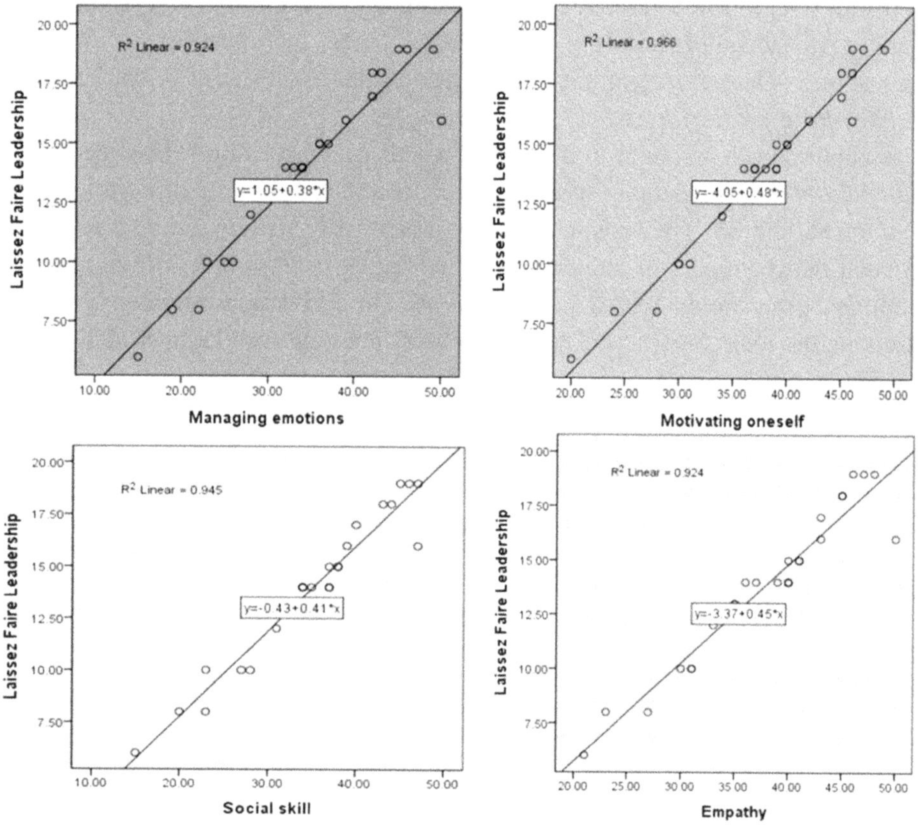


In addition to Table 9 which observed a statistically significant relationship between LFL, ME, MO, EM and SS. LFL and ME [(r=.924, N=27, $p < .001$), LFL and MO (r=.966, N=27, $p < .001$), LFL and EM (r=.924, N=27, $p < .001$)]; and LFL and SS (r=.945, N=27, $p < .001$)]. The 4 emotional intelligence scales were able to predict a linear relation with TL scores, resulting to $R^2 = 0.978$ and $R^2 = 0.971$. It was shown that the variation in the distribution of empathy scores could explain around 95% of the variation in the distribution of overall LFL scores. The unstandardized regression equation for this particular analysis was TL=18.54+1.68 ME; 2.17 + 2.07 MO and 12.62 + 1.81 SS.

A third research question found another positive relationship between EI and Laissez-faire Leadership style. The correlation between the total EI scores of leaders and laissez-faire leadership (LFL) revealed a positive relationship as shown in table 4.11 and figure 4.4. This contradicts the findings of previous studies (Alexander, 2016; Arindam & Atik, 2015; Badri-Harun et al., 2016) This conflicts with the results of earlier research (Alexander,2016; Arindam & Atik,2015; Badri-Harun et al.,2016) that suggests that emotionally competent leaders would neither shirk responsibilities nor be absent when necessary and will not play a passive position in leadership. These leaders have strong relationship management attributes, such as coaching and mentoring, teamwork, and influencing people by working with them towards shared objectives; on the other hand, leaders who dodge accountability are unable to comprehend their own thoughts and emotions as well as the feelings and emotions of others, and they are unable to successfully regulate them (Chepng'eno & Ngui, 2017).

*Table 10. Correlation between EI score and LFL*

**Correlations**

| | | LFL | SA |
|---|---|---|---|
| **LFL** | Pearson Correlation | 1 | .973** |
| | Sig. (2 tailed) | | .000 |
| | N | 66 | 66 |
| **SA** | Pearson Correlation | .973** | 1 |
| | Sig. (2-tailed) | .000 | |
| | N | 66 | 66 |

**. Correlation is significant at the 0.01 level (2-tailed).

Another measurement was done using Social Awareness as a construct of EI to measure the relationship between EI and LFL. From the table above, a Pearson Correlation between the scales was conducted. The correlation statistics were in the same range as other factors that were analyzed above. The above findings found a statistically and moderate correlation between LFL and behavioral factors variable. LFL and SA (r=.973, N=27, p < .001).

*Figure 6. EI score and LFL scatter plot*

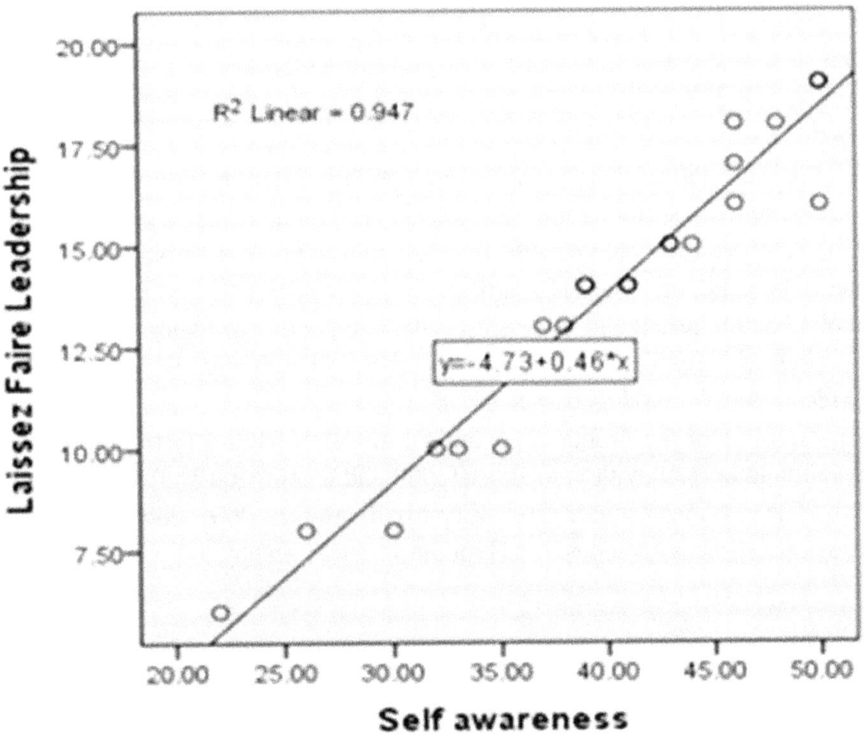

Further to Table 10 which observed a statistically significant relationship between LFL and SA (r=.973, N=27, $p < .001$). The self-awareness scale was able to predict a linear relation with LFL scores, resulting to $R^2 = 0.947$. It was shown that the variability in the distribution of empathy scores was able to explain around 98% of the variability in the distribution of overall LFL scores. Employees with high self-awareness are said to have strong emotionality and can be expected to show little of a laissez-faire leadership style.

## Hypothesis Testing

Hypothesis testing was done to further confirm the relationship between EI and transformational leadership with the use of the Structural Equation Model (SEM). According to Kumar and Kumar (2015) SEM refers to a mixture of two analyses, multiple regressions, and exploratory factors. SEM allows researchers to test theoretical propositions regarding how constructs are theoretically linked and the directionality of significant relationships. Schreiber et al. (2006) indicated that SEM could be viewed as a CFA and multiple regressions since it uses a confirmatory method and can be used in exploratory research.

They extended their argument by articulating that "SEM, in comparison with CFA, extends the possibility of relationships among the latent variables and encompasses two components: a measurement model that is essentially the CFA and a structural model." (Schreiber et al., 2006, p. 326). Before one can test SEM, factor loadings, modification indexes, and unique variances are estimated to enable researchers to come up with latent variables. The measurement model of SEM can thus be regarded as the CFA and it represents the pattern of observed variables for the latent variables in the hypothesised model (Schreiber et al., 2006). In addition, Schreiber et al. (2006) expounded the notion that in a SEM, testing the reliability of variables is the main issue of Confirmatory Factor Analysis. Hence the measurement model is used to examine the extent of covariation and interrelationships among the latent variables (Schreiber et al., 2006).

## Testing Hypothesis 1

From the results of the correlation, there is a substantial positive relationship between each of the four EI scores and the TRNL style, as seen in Tables 5 and 6 above. The link was further evaluated using SPSS Amos software. In the structural equation model of EI and transactional leadership style, the measurement model was found to be valid, and there is a perfect match between data and the model. The structural equation model of EI and transactional leadership is depicted below in Figure 7.

Hypothesis $_1$: *There is a significant positive correlation between emotional intelligence abilities and transactional leadership style of DFSS managers?*

The model fit summary of the structural equational model of EI and TRNL leadership style shows the standard deviation to be 1.59 with a *p*-value of .000 and a comparative fit index of. 770 which are acceptable ranges. The root mean square error of approximation is .000, which was also an acceptable range. The analysis, therefore, concludes that Hypothesis 1 was accepted.

*Table 11. Baseline comparisons (EM and TRNL)*

| Model | NFI Delta1 | RFI rho1 | IFI Delta2 | TLI rho2 | CFI |
|---|---|---|---|---|---|
| Default model | .195 | -.251 | .205 | -.270 | .183 |
| Saturated model | 1.000 | | 1.000 | | 1.000 |
| Independence model | .000 | .000 | .000 | .000 | .000 |

*Table 12. RMSEA (EM and TRNL)*

| Model | NFI Delta1 | RFI rho1 | IFI Delta2 | TLI rho2 | CFI |
|---|---|---|---|---|---|
| Default model | .757 | .490 | .776 | .517 | .770 |
| Saturated model | 1.000 | | 1.000 | | 1.000 |
| Independence model | .000 | .000 | .000 | .000 | .000 |

*Figure 7. Structural equation model of EI and TRNL style*

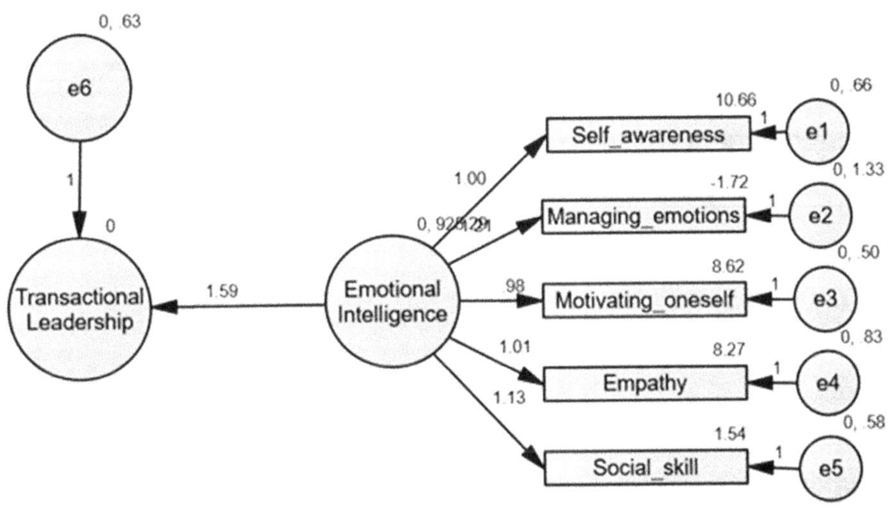


## Testing Hypothesis 2

According to the findings of the correlation, there is a substantial positive association between each of the four EI scores and the TL leadership style, as seen in Tables 7 and 8 above. The link was further evaluated using SPSS Amos software. In the structural equation model of emotional intelligence and transformational leadership style, the measurement model was found to be valid, and there is a good match between the data and the model. The structural equation model of EI and TL leadership is depicted in Figure 8.

Hypothesis $_2$: *There is a significant positive correlation between EI abilities and TL leadership style of DFSS managers?*

The model fit summary of the structural equational model of emotional intelligence and transformational leadership style shows the standard deviation to be 2.06 with a *p*-value of .000 and a comparative fit index of. 748 which are acceptable ranges. The root mean square error of approximation is .000, which was also an acceptable range. The analysis, therefore, concludes that Hypothesis 2 was accepted.

*Table 13. CMIN (EM and TL)*

| Model | NPAR | CMIN | DF | P | CMIN/DF |
|---|---|---|---|---|---|
| Default model | 17 | 106.722 | 10 | .000 | 10.672 |
| Saturated model | 27 | .000 | 0 | | |
| Independence model | 6 | 404.961 | 21 | .000 | 19.284 |

*Table 14. Baseline Comparisons (EM and TL)*

| Model | NFI Delta1 | RFI rho1 | IFI Delta2 | TLI rho2 | CFI |
|---|---|---|---|---|---|
| Default model | .736 | .447 | .755 | .471 | .748 |
| Saturated model | 1.000 | | 1.000 | | 1.000 |
| Independence model | .000 | .000 | .000 | .000 | .000 |

*Table 15. RMSEA (EI and TL)*

| Model | RMSEA | LO 90 | HI 90 | PCLOSE |
|---|---|---|---|---|
| Default model | .610 | .508 | .717 | .000 |
| Independence model | .839 | .768 | .911 | .000 |

*Figure 8. Structural equation model of EI and TL style*

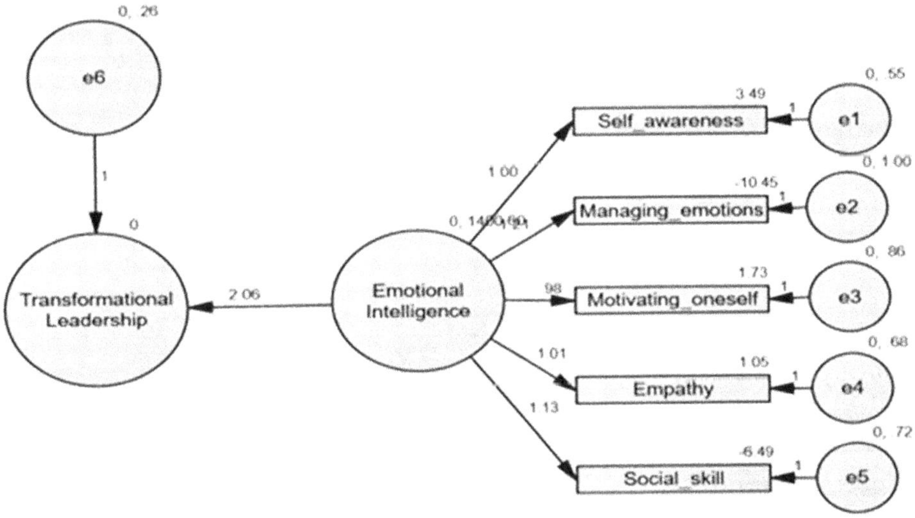


## Testing Hypothesis 3

As shown in Tables 9 and 10, the findings of correlation analysis showed that there was a substantial positive link between all four clusters of emotional intelligence and the laissez-faire leadership style. The link was further evaluated using SPSS Amos software. In the structural model of EI and the laissez-faire leadership style, the measurement model was found to be valid, and there is a good match between the data and the model. Therefore, the correlation value of.49, which is closer to 0 than it is to 1, indicates that there is a weak but significant association between the respondents' levels of emotional intelligence and their Laissez Fair Leadership styles. The structural model of EI and the laissez-faire leadership style is depicted in Figure 4.8.

Hypothesis $_3$: *There is a significant positive correlation between EI abilities and the LFL style of DFSS managers?*

The model fit summary of the structural equational model of emotional intelligence and laissez-faire leadership style shows the standard deviation to be 0.49 with a $p$-value of .000 and a comparative fit index of. 183 which is slightly above acceptable ranges. The root mean square error of approximation is .000, which was also an acceptable range. The analysis, therefore, concludes that Hypothesis 3 was accepted.

*Table 16. CMIN (EM and LFL)*

| Model | NPAR | CMIN | DF | P | CMIN/DF |
|---|---|---|---|---|---|
| **Default model** | 17 | 325.796 | 18 | .000 | 18.100 |
| **Saturated model** | 35 | .000 | 0 | | |
| **Independence model** | 7 | 404.961 | 28 | .000 | 14.463 |

*Table 17. RMSEA (EM an LFL)*

| Model | RMSEA | LO 90 | HI 90 | PCLOSE |
|---|---|---|---|---|
| Default model | .811 | .735 | .889 | .000 |
| Independence model | .720 | .658 | .783 | .000 |

*Table 18. Baseline comparisons (EM and LFL)*

| Model | NFI Delta1 | RFI rho1 | IFI Delta2 | TLI rho2 | CFI |
|---|---|---|---|---|---|
| Default model | .195 | -.251 | .205 | -.270 | .183 |
| Saturated model | 1.000 | | 1.000 | | 1.000 |
| Independence model | .000 | .000 | .000 | .000 | .000 |

*Figure 9. Structural equation model of EI and LFL style*

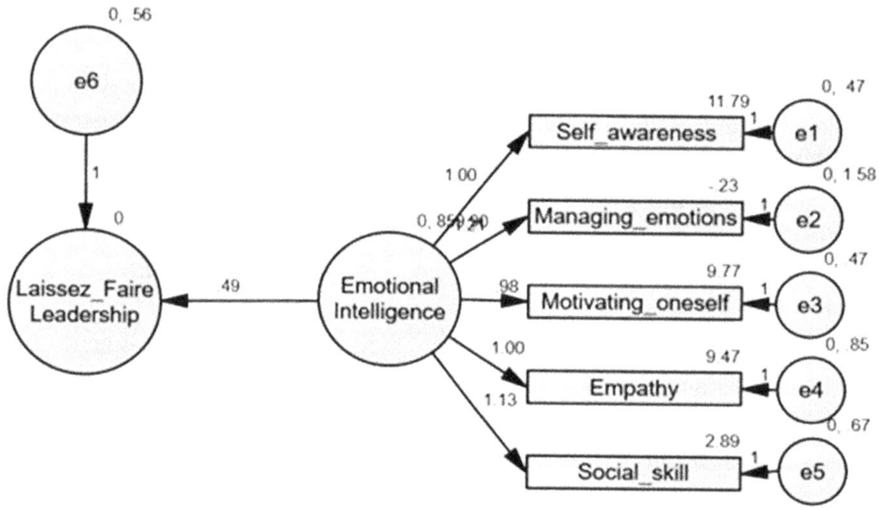


## CONCLUSION

As mentioned earlier, the study investigated and analysed the relationship between the overall EI scores or components and leadership styles (TNSL, TL and LFL) of managers in Small and Medium Enterprises at Dog Forces Security Services, Namibia. First and foremost, the study in Chapter 1 provided the background of the study, problem statement, research objectives/questions, research hypothesis, and significance of the study.

Chapter 2 which is the literature review, focused on the development of emotional intelligence, leadership, leadership styles as well as how emotionally intelligent leadership may have a beneficial influence on organisational performance and assist organisations in bringing about good change that is sustainable. There have been a lot of studies done on the relationship between EI and leadership, but since EI is still a relatively new area, not as much attention has been paid to the ways in which an individual's degree of emotional intelligence might influence their leadership style and, more significantly, the reasons why it should influence the leadership style they choose. This deficiency is especially noticeable in the private security sector organisations. When reviewing the findings of the study, it is important to realise that the majority of individuals don't leave their occupations; they leave their leaders. Increased awareness and sensitivity in the workplace as a result of increased emotional intelligence have the potential to enhance the general atmosphere, as well as the effectiveness of leaders and the level of satisfaction experienced by employees (Matjie, 2018).

In chapter 3, the researcher discussed the research technique that was employed for the investigation, along with the research philosophy, design, and strategy. The survey instruments that were used to collect data, as well as the reliability and validity of those survey instruments were presented. The chapter also covered the strategy for data collection, which included the target demographic as well as the technique for analysing the data. In Chapter 4, the results of the study were discussed in further depth. According to the findings of the research, emotional intelligence has a significant positive link with all three types of leadership styles: transformational, transactional, and laissez-faire.

## The Relationship Between Emotional Intelligence and Transactional Leadership Style

The first objective of this study was to investigate the relationship between emotional intelligence and transactional leadership style as perceived by DFSS managers. The research came to the conclusion that there was a positive connection between EI and the TNSL style of management at DFSS. The study had a standard deviation of 1.59, Pearson r =997, and p>.001 to determine the significance of the correlation. In support of that, the literature also concludes that various research but limited to the security industry have found a link between EI and TNSL style. A further positive hypothesis cemented the results.

## The Relationship Between Emotional Intelligence and Transformational Leadership Style

The second objective of the study was to investigate the relationship between EI and TL style as perceived by DFSS managers. The study concluded regarding this objective in that the link between EI and transformational leaders is still an issue that requires more research from the Namibia context. The results presented a standard deviation of 2.06, Pearson $r = 0.987$, and $p > .001$. As presented in the literature review, a number of studies have found that there is a relationship between emotional intelligence and leadership style. The most linked emotional intelligence constructs were managing emotions and social skills. It shows that managers at DFSS highly apply these constructs in determining the type of leadership style to apply.

## The Relationship Between Emotional Intelligence and Laissez-Faire Leadership Style

The third objective was to investigate the relationship between EI and LFL as perceived by managers at DFSS. The study concluded that a positive correlation existed between emotional intelligence and laissez-faire leadership style, with a standard deviation of 0.49, Pearson $r = 0.971$, and $p > .001$. Although literature had concluded that a negative correlation existed, this study further concluded with positive and accepted hypotheses as depicted by SEM results (CFI=183). Managers and leaders who see themselves as passive are more frequently than not incapable of identifying their feelings and emotions, comprehending the feelings and emotions of others; managing their emotions; and exercising effective control over them.

The research hypotheses that were investigated in this study were concerned with the relationship that exists between the emotional intelligence of managers and the perceptions that their subordinates hold regarding the leadership style of those managers as well as the various outcomes of leadership. The populations that were looked at consisted of employees working for DFSS. The findings of the study pertain to the personnel members who took part in the research study. Because of this, it is not suitable to draw broad conclusions for practice based on the findings of a single research; rather, it is more appropriate to draw specific implications for practice based on the findings of many studies that build upon each other. Further replication of this kind of research and empirical verification would assess the importance of the suggestions outside the confines of the firm.

## Conclusion

The first objective of this study was to investigate at the relationship between emotional intelligence and transactional leadership style as perceived by DFSS managers. The research came to the conclusion that there was a positive connection between EI and the TNSL style of management at DFSS. The study had a standard deviation of 1.59, Pearson r =997, and p>.001 to determine the significance of the correlation. In support of that, literature also concludes that various researches but limited to the security industry have found a link between EI and TNSL style. A further positive hypothesis cemented the results.

While the second objective of the study was to investigate on the relationship between EI and TL style as perceived by DFSS managers. The study concluded regarding this objective in that the link between EI and transformational leaders is still an issue that require more research from the Namibia context. The results presented standard deviation of 2.06, Pearson $r = 0.987$ and $p > .001$. As presented in the literature review, a number of studies have found that there is a relationship between emotional intelligence and leadership style. The most linked emotional intelligence constructs were managing emotions and social skills. It shows that managers at DFSS highly apply these constructs in determining the type of leadership style to apply.

Additionally, the third objective was to investigate the relationship between EI and LFL as perceived by managers at DFSS. The study concluded that a positive correlation existed between emotional intelligence and laissez faire leadership style, standard deviation 0.49, Pearson $r = 0.971$ and $p > .001$. Although literature had concluded that a negative correlation existed, this study further concluded with a positive and accepted hypotheses as depicted by SEM results (CFI=183). Managers and leaders who see themselves as passive are more frequently than not incapable of identifying their own feelings and emotions, comprehending the feelings and emotions of others; managing their emotions; and exercising effective control over them.

The research hypotheses that were investigated in this study were concerned with the relationship that exists between the emotional intelligence of managers and the perceptions that their subordinates hold regarding the leadership style of those managers as well as the various outcomes of leadership. The populations that were looked at consisted of employees working for DFSS. The findings of the study pertain to the personnel members who took part in the research study. Because of this, it is not suitable to draw broad conclusions for practice based on the findings of a single research; rather, it is more appropriate to draw specific implications for practice based on the findings of many studies that build upon each other. Further replication of this kind of research and empirical verification would assess the importance of the suggestions outside the confines of the firm.

## Recommendations

After having carried out the study, the following recommendations were drawn:

- The concept of emotional intelligence and leadership is an issue that most SMEs do not put into consideration when operating their organisation and how it can positively or negatively affect their employee performance, and morale. DFSS and other organisations in the industry should separate themselves from the leadership styles being applied in the defence forces as such becomes difficult when dealing with personnel from civilian society.
- The private security industry is one of the biggest employing industries in Namibia and is of a sensitive nature. Failing to apply proper leadership styles may ruin DFSS or the entire industry by disgruntled employees through industrial actions, sabotage, and loss of clients.
- Transformational leadership style should be well considered by the organisation during leadership training programs and this can also apply to other organisations or Namibia at large. During leadership conferences and other relevant training, emotional intelligence and the components that have been recognised in this study should be represented as part of a successful leadership curriculum. This should be done to ensure that these topics are adequately covered.
- Experts in leadership development should have a deeper understanding of the laissez-faire style of leadership as a sort of leadership that has the potential to be successful if the circumstances allow for it. As most research from the literature have found no relationship between emotional intelligence and laissez faire leadership style, these were not from the private security point of view since there has been less research from the field. Thus researchers need to conduct more research on this leadership style in the security industry.
- Leaders have a responsibility to assess the circumstances surrounding their situations and make every effort to modify their leadership approach appropriately. The degree of emotional intelligence offers a new way for leaders to improve their effectiveness and recognise the responses of their subordinates. Every leader has to be aware of their own leadership style and direct his or her focus toward the accomplishment of a shared objective using a fruitful leadership style.
- More studies should be done and published in Namibia other than the private security industry with a bigger sample to determine how others see and value emotional intelligence and leadership styles.

## ACKNOWLEDGMENT

Part of this chapter was submitted as a Dissertation for a Master of Business Administration at the International University of Management, Namibia under the direct supervision of Dr Sadrag Panduleni Shihomeka at The School of Education, Facutly of Education and Human Sciences, University of Namibia.

## REFERENCES

Ajia, A. Y. (2021). The Impact of Transformational Leadership and Perceived Leadership Effectiveness on Organizational Commitment of Public Sector Workers in Kwara State, Nigeria. *Management Analysis Journal*, *10*(1), 115–130. doi:10.15294/maj.v10i1.43641

Alexander, E. D. (2016). *Examination of Emotional Intelligence and Transformational Leadership Profiles of Directors and Managers of Human Resources at Starwood Hotels and Resorts*. Virginia Polytechnic Institute and State University.

Alkahtani, A. H. (2016). The influence of leadership styles on organizational commitment: The moderating effect of emotional intelligence. *Business and Management Studies*, *2*(1), 23–34. doi:10.11114/bms.v2i1.1091

Allameh, S. M., Pool, J. K., Kazemi, R. V., & Mostafavi, M. (2015). The impact of emotional intelligence on transformational leadership and leader effectiveness. *Latin American Journal of Management for Sustainable Development*, *2*(1), 83–93. doi:10.1504/LAJMSD.2015.067473

Arindam, C., & Atik, K. (2015). An Empirical investigation of the relationship between Emotional Intelligence, Transactional and Transformational Leadership Styles in banking sector. *Procedia: Social and Behavioral Sciences*, *210*, 291–300. doi:10.1016/j.sbspro.2015.11.369

Baaha, K. D., & Mekpor, B. (2017). Emotional Intelligence: Does Leadership Style Matter? Employees Perception in Ghana's Banking Sector. *International Journal of Business Insights & Transformation*, *22*(1), 42–54.

Badri-Harun, A., Zainol, M. R., Amar, A., & Shaari, Z. H. (2016). Emotional intelligence as mediator between leadership styles and leadership effectiveness: A theoretical framework. *International Review of Management and Marketing*, *6*(1), 116–121.

Banda, T. E. (2018). The Challenges Facing Private Security Companies. In *Retaining Clients: A Case Study In Gauteng Shopping Malls*. University Of South Africa.

Bass, B. M., & Avolio, B. J. (1996). Multifactor leadership questionnaire. *Western Journal of Nursing Research*.

Bataeva, B., & Vavilina, A. (2018). Emotional Leadership in Organizations: Theoretical and Applied Aspects. Leadership for the Future Sustainable Development of Business and Education.

Batool, B. F. (2013). Emotional Intelligence and Effective Leadership. *Journal of Business Studies Quarterly*, *4*(3), 84–94.

Chatterjee, A., & Kulakli, A. (2015). An Empirical Investigation of the Relationship Between emotional Intelligence, Transactional and Transformational Leadership Styles in Banking Sector. *Procedia: Social and Behavioral Sciences*, *210*, 291–300. doi:10.1016/j.sbspro.2015.11.369

Chepng'eno, M., & Ngui, T. (2017). Relationship between Emotional Intelligence and Leadership Styles: A Case Study of Leaders in Selected Banking Institutions in Kenya. *International Journal of Research in Humanities and Social Studies*, *4*(2), 1 12.

Clarke, N. (2010). Emotional intelligence and its relationship to transformational leadership and key project manager competencies. *Project Management Journal*, *41*(2), 5–20. doi:10.1002/pmj.20162

Crowne, K. A., Young, T. M., Goldman, B., Patterson, B., Krouse, A. M., & Proenca, J. (2017). Leading nurses: Emotional intelligence and leadership development effectiveness. *Leadership in Health Services*, *30*(3), 217 232. doi:10.1108/LHS-12-2015-0055 PMID:28693391

Dartey-Baah, K., & Mekpor, B. (2017). Emotional Intelligence: Does Leadership Style Matter? Employees Perception in Ghana's Banking Sector. *International Journal of Business Insights & Transformation*, *22*(1), 41–54.

Dey, R., & Carvalho, S. (2014). Are transactional leaders also emotionally intelligent? An analysis of sales executives in India. *International Journal of Business Insights & Transformation*, *7*(2), 42–49.

Erdogan, B., & Bauer, T. (2015). *Leader–Member Exchange Theory*. International Encyclopedia of the Social & Behavioral Sciences. doi:10.1093/oxfordhb/9780199326174.013.23

Fannon, D. (2018). The relationship between emotional intelligence and leadership style in educational leaders. *Theses and Dissertations*, *930*, 1–114.

Garg, S., & Jain, S. (2013). Mapping Leadership Styles of Public and Private Sector Leaders Using Blake and Mouton Leadership Model. *A Management Journal, 4*.

Goleman, D., Boyatzis, R., & McKee, A. (2013). *Primal leadership: Unleashing the power of emotional intelligence*. Harvard Business Review Press.

Harms, P. D., & Credé, M. (2010). Emotional Intelligence and Transformational and Transactional Leadership: A Meta-Analysis. *Journal of Leadership & Organizational Studies*, *17*(1), 5–17. doi:10.1177/1548051809350894

Hebert, E. B. (2011). *The Relationship between Emotional Intelligence, Transformational Leadership, and Effectiveness in School Principals*. Georgia State University.

Jain, P., & Duggal, T. (2016). The influence of transformational leadership and emotional intelligence on organizational commitment. *Journal of Commerce and Management Thought*, *7*(3), 586–598. doi:10.5958/0976-478X.2016.00033.1

Kampandu, R. (2019). *Dog Force Security Services cc Anualy Report - Financial and Operations.* Academic Press.

Kaur, N. (2020). *Role of Leader's Emotional Intelligence in Organizational Learning: A Quantitative Analysis*. Rochester Institute of Technology. doi:10.1177/001316447003000308

Krejcie, R. V., & Morgan, D. W. (1970). Determining Sample Size for Research Activities. *Educational and Psychological Measurement*, *30*(3), 607–610. doi:10.1177/001316447003000308

Kumar, S., & Kumar, S. (2015). Structure equation modeling basic assumptions and concepts: A novices guide. *Asian Journal of Management Sciences*, *3*(7), 25–28.

Lee, Y. H. (2019). Emotional intelligence, servant leadership, and development goal orientation in athletic directors. *Sport Management Review*, *22*(3), 395–406. doi:10.1016/j.smr.2018.05.003

Maamari, B., & Majdalani, J. (2017). Emotional intelligence, leadership style & organizational climate. *The International Journal of Organizational Analysis*, *25*(2), 1–25. doi:10.1108/IJOA-04-2016-1010

Matjie, T. (2018). The relationship between the leadership effectiveness and emotional competence of managers in the public sector. *International Journal of Public Administration*, *41*(15), 1271–1278. doi:10.1080/01900692.2017.1387140

Mavroveli, S., Petrides, K. V., Sangareau, Y., & Furnham, A. (2009). Exploring the relationships between trait emotional intelligence and objective socio-emotional outcomes in childhood. *The British Journal of Educational Psychology*, *79*(2), 259–272. doi:10.1348/000709908X368848 PMID:18950549

Mayer, J. D., Salovey, P., & Caruso, D. R. (2002). *Mayer-Salovey-Caruso Emotional Intelligence Test (MSCEIT)*. Users Manual.

McCleskey, J. (2014). Emotional intelligence and leadership. *The International Journal of Organizational Analysis*, *22*(1), 76–93. doi:10.1108/IJOA-03-2012-0568

Mukata, C. M., & Swanepoel, E. (2017). Development support for small and medium enterprises in the fi nancially constrained north-eastern regions of Namibia. *Southern African Business Review*, *21*, 198–221.

Musa, H., Azmi, F., Abdullah, A., Sedek, M., & Saad, N. (2017). Emotional intelligence and stress among SME entrepreneurs in Melaka: A case of entrepreneurial education. *Proceedings of Mechanical Engineering Research Day*, *2017*, 248–249.

Muthembwa, M. (2019). *Effect of managers' emotional intelligence on performance of small and micro-enterprises in Nakuru East Sub-County*. Kabarak University. doi:10.31871/WJIR.7.5.11

Nanjundeswaraswamy, T. S., & Swamy, D. R. (2014). Leadership styles. *Advances In Management*, *7*(2), 57–62.

Pillay, M., Viviers, R., & Mayer, C.-H. (2019). The relationship between emotional intelligence and leadership styles in the South African petrochemical industry. *SA Journal of Industrial Psychology*, *39*(1), 1–12.

Prezerakos, P. E. (2018). Nurse managers' emotional intelligence and effective leadership: A review of the current evidence. *The Open Nursing Journal*, *12*(86), 86–92. doi:10.2174/1874434601812010086 PMID:29997711

Schreiber, J. B., Nora, A., Stage, F. K., Barlow, E. A., & King, J. (2006). Reporting structural equation modeling and confirmatory factor analysis results: A review. *The Journal of Educational Research*, *99*(6), 323–338. doi:10.3200/JOER.99.6.323-338

Singh, S. (2007). Emotional intelligence and organisational leadership: A gender study in Indian context. *Int. J. Indian Culture and Business Management*, *1*(1/2), 48. Advance online publication. doi:10.1504/IJICBM.2007.014470

Spano-Szekely, L., Griffin, M. T. Q., Clavelle, J., & Fitzpatrick, J. J. (2016). Emotional intelligence and transformational leadership in nurse managers. *The Journal of Nursing Administration*, *46*(2), 101–108. doi:10.1097/NNA.0000000000000303 PMID:26796823

Weinberger, L. A. (2009). Emotional intelligence, leadership style, and perceived leadership effectiveness. *Advances in Developing Human Resources*, *11*(6), 747–772. doi:10.1177/1523422309360811

Zaccaro, S. J. (2007). Trait-based perspectives of leadership. *The American Psychologist*, *62*(1), 6–16. doi:10.1037/0003-066X.62.1.6 PMID:17209675

# Chapter 18
# Leadership for Longevity and Sustainability in Antigua and Barbuda, West Indies:
## The Offshore Islands Conservation Program

**Christell M. Chesney**
https://orcid.org/0000-0001-8593-7772
*University of Guyana, Guyana*

**Shanna C. Challenger**
*Environmental Awareness Group, Antigua and Barbuda*

**Simon A. Black**
https://orcid.org/0000-0003-4931-7992
*Wildwood Trust, UK*

**Arica Hill**
*Environmental Awareness Group, Antigua and Barbuda*

## ABSTRACT

*Effective leadership is a critical component of adaptive management. Within the conservation realm, novel insights into leadership can be gleaned in the areas of longevity, sustainability, and legacy that offer lessons for sectors in the business, scientific, and technological worlds. This chapter examines the historical leadership and management of the Offshore Islands Conservation Program (OICP) found in the Small Island Developing State (SIDS) of Antigua and Barbuda. Utilizing a mixed method approach involving the Conservation Excellence Model (CEM), desk-based review, and stakeholder feedback, observations on governance and management were generated and used to improve the program's operational approach and sustainability of conservation efforts. The benefits arising from the use of the CEM assessment, in this case, illustrate that evaluations of this type should be encouraged for use by practitioners within their organization. Thus, the passing on of leadership skills and the careful recruitment of diverse talents is essential to the maintenance of high-performing organizations.*

DOI: 10.4018/978-1-6684-8822-5.ch018

Transformational Leadership describes the approach of leaders to enable change and improvement in organisations and outcomes by engaging followers to commit to change, and make it happen through effort, initiative and improvement, with wider engagement of stakeholders partners, accounting for the complexities of political, legal, commercial and social environment (Bass, 2000; Kouzes & Posner, 2007). Within the current globally recognised environmental crisis, the challenge of preserving and restoring biological diversity and ecosystem functions to support sustainability of human systems is a key area requiring transformation in human effort and engagement, and leadership will play a critical part in this process (Black, 2021).

Whilst some elements of biodiversity recovery demand, at least at face value, highly variable climatic, ecosystem and landscape-level recovery and change (so are outside direct human control), all aspects of leadership are under the control of managers whose role is to coordinate effort to reverse global extinction rates. Although wildlife conservation seems a niche area of activity, leadership and management insights within the conservation realm can provide novel insights into addressing key dilemmas across various fields (including strategy, communication, engagement, resource utilisation, and professional development). This is because elements of leadership, finances, resource management, people management, stakeholder relations, processes, and results influence the effectiveness of work, as is true in any sector of the business, scientific and technological world (Black, Groombridge & Jones, 2011a).

In recent times, transformational leadership has proven especially advantageous to the conservation field. Transformational leadership adopts the treatment of employees beyond tangible compensation, but rather it inculcates employee interest, aspiration and drive for the organisation and develops and or/ enhances those qualities for greater collaborative commitment to the organisation's cause (Barnett et al., 2001; Bass, 2000; Hay, 2006; Kouzes & Posner, 2007). According to Hay (2006) "transformational leadership fosters capacity development and brings higher levels of personal commitment amongst 'followers' to organizational objectives" (p. 4). As such, a number of specialist conservation leadership training programmes have arisen including: 1) short-courses (e.g. the African Wildlife Foundation Conservation Management Training Programme), 2) training for new conservation professionals (e.g. the WWF Russell E. Train Fellowships, and the ZSL EDGE Fellow Programme) and 3) postgraduate development programmes (notably, the MSc in Conservation Project Management at the University of Kent, UK; the Masters in Conservation Leadership Through Learning at Colorado State, USA; the MBA for Conservation Leaders at the African Leadership University, Rwanda, and the Masters in Conservation Leadership at the University of Cambridge in the UK (Sandrook et al., 2021).

Conservation work itself usually takes the form of focused programmes or projects either as fixed-term actions by a specialist team focused on particular outcomes, or longer-term often landscape-based interventions which are usually part of national or regional commitments to biodiversity (Copsey et al., 2018). Activities can often be collaborative involving local people, NGOs, government departments and academic research institutions (Black, 2021).

In the Caribbean, conservation programs are on the forefront to protect this biodiversity hotspot containing approximately 7000 endemic plants and 800 endemic vertebrates (all found nowhere else on earth) (WWF, 2018). One of the challenges faced in the regional effort, is maintaining the longevity of programs due to constraints in funding, manpower and remote locations (Bell et al., 2019; Daltry, 2001; Daltry, 2010; Myers et al., 2000; Black; 2019). Programs that indirectly conserve species through the eradications of threats such as Invasive Alien Species (IAS) are especially under strain. These IAS are directly implicated in predation, spread of disease, and competition for food and habitat of endemic species. Invasive species eradication programs require continuous effort and are often undertaken to counteract these impacts, resulting in the recovery of ecosystems and native species abundance (Atkinson, 1985; Bell et al., 2019; Daltry et al., 2001; Daltry, 2010; Witmer et al., 2011). Due to the continuity of effort, strong transformational leadership is crucial to the outworking those programs.

Such leadership is evidenced by an award-winning program that has been the pioneer for rewilding in the region, operating for twenty-eight-years to eradicate invasive species. One critical success factor has been straightforward, effective leadership that sustains the longevity of this program, has halted the extinction of endemics, encouraged work which has generated evidence of successful rewilding and landscape recovery in our time, and has fostered local people's love for less charismatic creatures.

This chapter provides novel insights into the transformational leadership, performance and management of Caribbean conservation program. Using Antigua and Barbuda as the case study, this chapter introduces the Environmental Awareness Group's Offshore Islands Conservation Program (OICP) and provides historical background of the program, discussing management structure in the OICP, its conservation victories in recovery of the Antiguan Racer Snake (*Alsophis antiguae*) and a summary of a performance evaluation of OICP using the Conservation Excellence Model (CEM) and its improvements due to transformational leadership.

## TRANSFORMATIONAL LEADERSHIP IN CONSERVATION

In conservation as with other sectors, leadership has the ability to affect the outcomes of a project or program (Black, 2019). The last two decades have seen research into leadership in conservation which has led to novel insights on psychological aspects of leaderships in areas such as governance, and performance measurement as well as, interpersonal skills such as behaviours, personal qualities, skills that draws upon and resonates with learning on transformational leadership (Black, 2019; 2021). However, with currently only one empirically-derived model of conservation leadership, linking crucial conservation practices to theories of psychology, conservation science and, leadership (Black, 2021), more research is needed to understand and improve leadership and management in the conservation realm (Englefield et al., 2019). Black (2021) recommends a transformational leadership approach to conservation leaders adding that "new skills influencing team development, stakeholder engagement, and managing improvement" are needed to influence staff, advisors, volunteers, external communities and donors (see also Bruyere, 2015). Such competencies should be prioritized alongside technical skills through training schemes for higher efficiency and effectiveness in conservation (Englefield et al., 2019). Transformational leadership skills have recently been shown in conservation scenarios to be advantageous to both male and female leaders, providing a balance in respective management and decision-making styles (Nery Silva et al., 2022).

Although, there is no clear consensus to the all the attributes of transformational leadership, Leithwood & Jantzi (2000) identified six attributes of transformational leadership as:

1. Building vision and goals.
2. Providing intellectual stimulation.
3. Offering individualized support.
4. Symbolizing professional practices and values.
5. Demonstrating high performance expectations.
6. Developing structures to foster participation in decisions.

Hay (2006) later collated and summarised the four factors of Transformational Leadership, namely:

1. Idealized influence-Charismatic vision and behavior that inspires others to follow.
2. Inspirational motivation -Capacity to motivate others to commit to the vision.
3. Intellectual stimulation- Encouraging innovation and creativity.
4. Individualized consideration-Coaching to the specific needs of followers.

However, the factors outlined by Hay (2006) and Leithwood & Jantzi (2000) described general attributes to transformational leadership, but not within the context of conservation. In response, Black et al. (2011a) specifically devised a four-category model of characteristics, qualities, and action for contemporary leadership in conservation, encompassing:

1. Ability to share a clear, long-term vision.
2. Orientation toward "hands-on" management
3. Ability to switch attention between wider context and details.
4. Willingness to encourage learning, improvement, and receptiveness to alternative solutions.

Since, transformational leadership can have significant impact on the motivation, innovation and positive drive within conservation organisations, examinations of case studies can provide insights in the benefits of this leadership style when embedded in conservation programs.

One such case study is the Jaguars of Iguaçu Program in Brazil focused on the mitigation of human conflict with Jaguar (*Panthera onca*) utilizing transformational leadership to enable significant community ownership and engagement. Strategic planning from leadership enabled the program to have a clear vision, wider perspective of the issues with community input, innovated and collaborative solutions to have a practical, hands-on approach to the Jaguar conservation (Nery Silva et al., 2022).

In contrast, the Po'ouli *(Melamprosops phaeosoma)* case study in Hawaii demonstrates the dire consequences of failing to inculcate transformational leadership. A static, hierarchical leadership approach resulted in a lack of clear, long-term vision for the species conservation, an unresponsive management approach due to bureaucracy and the absence of innovative solutions, ultimately leading to the presumed extinction of the species. (Black et al., 2011a; Powell, 2008).

In this chapter we use a detailed examination of the Offshore islands Conservation program (OICP) to provide more insights into the benefits of transformational leadership to conservation. Thus, the chapter aims to: 1) evaluate the performance of the OICP to its conservation of the Racer Snake, 2) benchmark the OICP with similar islands base programs in for the identification of crucial conservation practices for excellence, and 3) to highlight the importance of evaluations to enhancement of transformational leadership in conservation programs.

## BACKGROUND OF CONSERVATION IN ANTIGUA AND BARBUDA

Antigua and Barbuda is a Small Island Developing State (SIDS) found in the Leeward Islands in the Caribbean. Antigua occupies an area of 280 $km^2$, while Barbuda occupies 160 $km^2$, and together the twin islands cover a total area of only 440 $km^2$. A total of 85,567 residents live on the islands giving rise to heterogeneous communities of resource users including fisherfolk, tour operators and vendors (DOE, 2012; PAHO/ WHO, 2008).

The country boasts a wide range of biodiversity including 1150 species of plants belonging to 149 families, as well as, 180 species of birds (DOE, 2012). There are 13 Key Biodiversity Areas (KBAs) with 8 KBAs having no protected coverage (SCBD & UNDP, 2021). Most of the marine and terrestrial wildlife are protected by the largest Marine Reserve in the country, the North East Marine Management Area (Birdlife International, 2009; DOE, 2012; Walker & Lawrence, 2022).

The North-East Marine Management Area (NEMMA) was designated in 2005 and declared a Marine Reserve under Section 22 of the Fisheries Act Cap. 173 and published on December 29, 2005 in the Official Gazette XXV No. 82 (DOE, 2012; Ecoengineering, 2007; Jackson, 2008). Before this, there was no formal legislation or mandate for protecting the critical wildlife and ecosystems in the North East of Antigua.

The NEMMA Marine Reserve is an area of over 78 km$^2$ covering parts of the Atlantic and Caribbean Oceans on the windward north-eastern coast of Antigua. The objectives of the reserve are focused upon: biodiversity and ecosystem protection, research and monitoring, management of tourism, education and awareness, traditional livelihoods, and the promotion of economic and social benefits (DOE, 2012; Ecoengineering, 2007; Jackson, 2008; Walker& Lawrence, 2022). Marine Reserve contains several marine and coastal habitats such as mangroves, coral reefs and seagrass beds that sustain many marine creatures such as Hawksbill Turtle, Queen Conch and Caribbean Spiny Lobster that breed and forage in those habitats. In addition to these major habitat types, the NEMMA also contains 30 small islands, islets and rocky outcrops ranging from an elevation of 3m to 75m (DOE, 2012; Jackson, 2008; Walker & Lawrence, 2022).

However, even with the establishment of the NEMMA, Jackson (2008) states "no staff [is] dedicated to management of the NEMMA or central management office" (p. 25). While this statement was made in 2008, it is important to note that there is still no governmental management and oversight of NEMMA to date, such that other organisations have needed to step in to maintain the NEMMA (in light of external threats) and to protect and conserve Antigua and Barbuda's ecosystems and biodiversity, particularly the important endemics. The efforts of the Environmental Awareness Group (EAG), along with regional and international partners enabled development of the Antiguan Racer Conservation Project (ARCP) and subsequently, the Offshore Islands Conservation Program (OICP) to specifically conserve and protect specific offshore islands and surrounding marine ecosystems of Antigua (ARCP, 1999; CANARI, 2019; Jackson, 2008).

The EAG, Antigua and Barbuda's longest functioning environmental Non-Governmental Organisation (NGO), has sought to support the protection and management of priority areas within this critical Marine Reserve through the implementation of various programs. The EAG, established in 1989, is an independent, volunteer-based organisation, which aims to collaborate with agencies, communities and individuals for the sustainable management of natural resources and the overall benefit of people and wildlife. Specifically, the EAG's mission is "We work collaboratively towards shaping a mindful and responsible society that sustainably uses biodiversity, fosters sustainable livelihoods, and promotes nature-based solutions supported by science." The EAG has been advocating for the NEMMA's protection for over twenty-five years without a mandate (CANARI, 2019) and continues to have the leading role in the resource management in the NEMMA.

## HISTORY AND MANAGEMENT OF THE OFFSHORE ISLANDS CONSERVATION PROGRAM (OICP)

The presence of endemics reptiles such as the Critically Endangered snake, the Antiguan Racer (*Alsophis antiguae*) and the Antiguan Ground Lizard (*Pholidocelis griswoldi*) found on the offshore islands and islets have long interested local and international conservationists (Daltry, 2007; Smith et al., 2002; Varnham et al., 1998). This interest arose in 1995, when the Antiguan Forestry Unit of the Ministry of Agriculture and Fisheries embarked on a faunal survey of the offshore islands to collect baseline data on the population status of the Antiguan Racer after the Racers were erroneously declared extinct in 1936 from the mainland of Antigua and Barbuda. The survey led to a startling discovering of only fifty (50) individual racers isolated to the offshore islet, Great Bird Island – a mere 8.4 hectares in size (ARCP, 1999; Daltry et al., 2001; Jackson, 2008; Soorae, 2010; Varnham et al., 1998). With such low population numbers, this finding led to the Racer being declared the World's rarest snake in 1995 (Durrell, n.d.).

Recognizing the likelihood of the Racer's demise, a plan was devised to remove harmful invasive rats from the island in an effort to save the species from extinction. This discovery led to the formation of *Antiguan Racer Conservation Project (ARCP)*. This project formed the foundation for key leadership of the national conservation efforts to date. The partnership consisted six national and international organisations, namely: The Forestry Unit, Environmental Awareness Group, Fauna & Flora International, Durrell Wildlife Conservation Trust, Black Hills State University and the Island Resources Foundation. Key representatives from each organisation have provided technical expertise in efforts to conserve the Antiguan racer on the offshore islands through research, education and awareness, ecological restoration, conservation breeding and habitat management (ARCP, 1999; Daltry et al., 2001, 2003; Jackson, 2008; Soorae, 2010; Varnham et al., 1998).

However, realising that the work of rewilding the offshore islands and rescuing the 'World's Rarest Snake' would entail greater management, time and resources, the ARCP was expanded from a having solely a species-focus to taking a fuller ecosystem-focus through the development of the *Offshore Islands Conservation Program (OICP)* as a basis for formal leadership in 2003 (Lawrence et al., 2013). The award winning OICP was then co-managed by the six aforementioned organisations with divisions of technical, financial and administrative support (Dando et al., 2022; DOE, 2012).

In the year 2010, a Memorandum of Understanding (MoU) was drafted by the EAG to formalize the relationships between itself and the OICP program partners, and to define the roles and responsibilities of each partner in achieving the goals of the OICP. Amongst all the partners, the EAG was the only locally-based NGO, so the most fitting to accommodate the program.

This new management structure facilitated the development of key personnel positions such as the OICP Coordinator who is tasked with day-to-day operations of the program. The Coordinator reports to the EAG Executive Director, who in turn reports to the voluntary EAG Board of Directors and OICP program partners. Subordinate positions of Wildlife Officer and Invasive Species Officer were also created on a seasonal basis to assist the Coordinator when needed, along with ten scientifically trained volunteers and dozens of other volunteers from the general public. The programme also attracts international scientific volunteers each year.

In 2020, the OICP partnerships were revived to re-engage local and international environmental organizations, and long serving EAG members. The OICP Coordinator and program partners meet annually to discuss the future conservation management activities of the species and ecosystems under the program. Continual conservation and preservation of the endemic species and offshore island ecosystems from 1995 to date was enabled through adaptive management and strong leadership roles in the OICP. Throughout the evolution of the program, the critically endangered endemic Antiguan Racer and other wildlife have increased in population on the offshore islands.

*Figure 1. The critically endangered Antiguan racer (Alsophis antiguae)*
*Source: © Jenny Daltry*

## CONSERVATION VICTORIES: THE ANTIGUAN RACER

It is believed that the Antiguan Racer evolved on Antigua and Barbuda's mainland but due to extensive threats, the species' numbers dwindled so significantly that only a small population existed offshore. In the initial stages of the ARCP, it was found that the declining populations of Racers was due to human disturbance (foot traffic, habitat destruction and intentional killing), hurricanes, fluctuating prey populations and most notably invasive alien species. Further field observations indicated that out of all the threats, the invasive mammalian species (mongooses and black rats) were quite detrimental to the snake species as they mangled adults and destroyed eggs. Since Racers are non-venomous and lack natural defence mechanisms to effectively ward off invasives, the snake population dwindled significantly to only fifty (50) individuals isolated on Great Bird Island (ARCP, 1999; Daltry et al., 2001, 2003, 2007; Varnham et al., 1998). Thus, decisive conservation actions were taken by leadership of then ARCP to save the species from extinction.

## Captive Breeding

The first of the conservation actions recorded was the attempt at captive breeding in 1996. Five of the Racers were transported from Great Bird Island to Jersey Zoo on the island of Jersey in the English Channel to understand the feasibility and success rate of captive breeding (Daltry et al., 2001). Under the supervision of OICP Partner Durrell Wildlife Conservation Trust, this process allowed for closer observation of the species and to understand its biology, as well as, provided a satellite ex-situ population in case the in-situ populations became extinct. However, snakes succumbed to an allergic response to the common snake mite (*Ophionyssus natrici)*, so captive breeding was abandoned as it could not provide reintroduction stock; effort was then focussed on eradication of invasives in the existing wild habitats (Daltry et al., 2001).

## Eradication of mammalian invasive Species

In the early stages of scientific ground surveys, mangled and mutilated Racers were discovered due to the negative impact of the mammalian IAS, so eradication was primarily focused on rats to alleviate predation pressure (Daltry et al., 2001; Lawrence et al., 2013; Varnham et al., 1998). Eradication efforts were centred on the main habitat of Great Bird Island and other offshore islands and Islets that could potentially sustain Racer populations in future re-location efforts and prevent rats from using the islands as stepping stones (Jackson, 2008). Teams of volunteers, the OICP Coordinator, EAG members and an Invasive Species Consultant would spend weeks at a time camping on the offshore islands, and each day replenishing bait stations on the offshore islands with brodifacoum poison bait. Maintaining pest-free islands has been quite difficult due to their distances from the mainland, and the constant visits by tourist boats made reinvasion inevitable. Regular monitoring needs to be conducted every five weeks by staff, volunteers and invasive species monitors on the islands (Daltry et al., 2001). These biosecurity efforts have successfully led to the revegetation of offshore islands and the recovery of endemic and migratory faunal species.

## Re-introduction of Antiguan Racer Snakes

Subsequent to the eradications, the Antiguan Racer was reintroduced to other small offshore islands from 1999 to 2012 to diversify gene pool and expand the home range. To date, Racers can be found on four of the offshore islands namely: Great Bird, Green, York and Rabbit Island (Daltry et al., 2017). The last reliable census conducted in 2017 using population estimate software and modelling reported an increase of Antiguan Racers from 50 to more than 1,000 individuals (Daltry et al., 2017). Higher densities and density of vegetation, birds, invertebrates and reptiles were also observed on the islands in response to their pest-free status. Overall, this represents a significant conservation victory for the Caribbean.

# PERFORMANCE MANAGEMENT AND LEADERSHIP OF THE OICP

Caribbean eradication programs tend focus on the extermination of *Rattus sp.* (*R. norvegicus, R. rattus, and R. exulans*) on offshore Islands, as they are one of the most destructive IAS. Black Rats suppress the abundance of avian and reptilian endemics that are restricted to those offshore habitats (Atkinson,

1985; Bell et al., 2019; Daltry et al., 2001; Daltry, 2010; Witmer et al., 2011). The removal of rodent IAS is therefore critical to conservation and the protection of marine and terrestrial ecosystems found in the NEMMA, but these eradication programs come at a significant cost. On average, eradication in the Caribbean has cost upwards of US $1,615,200 annually (accounting for inflation) from factors such as land area, target species, and geographical remoteness of locations (Martin et al., 2006; Daltry et al., 2017).

Therefore, to ensure prudent use of resources for eradication campaigns and continued biosecurity monitoring, conservation programs must be evaluated (Ferraro & Pattanayak, 2006; Veitch et al., 2011; Zavaleta et al., 2001). Performance evaluations of management, leadership, and approaches and their link to the results of the program allow current and future leaders to adapt and modify effort for better efficiency and effectiveness (Black & Groombridge, 2010). Given the OICP's years of operations, it is imperative for such evaluations to be conducted.

One well-established assessment tool that can be used to assess the OICP is the Conservation Excellence Model (CEM). A CEM assessment seeks to understand links between approaches undertaken by a conservation program and the results it achieves to assess overall performance (Black & Groombridge, 2010; Black & Copsey, 2014).

*Figure 2. The conservation excellence model*
*Source: Black and Groombridge (2010)*

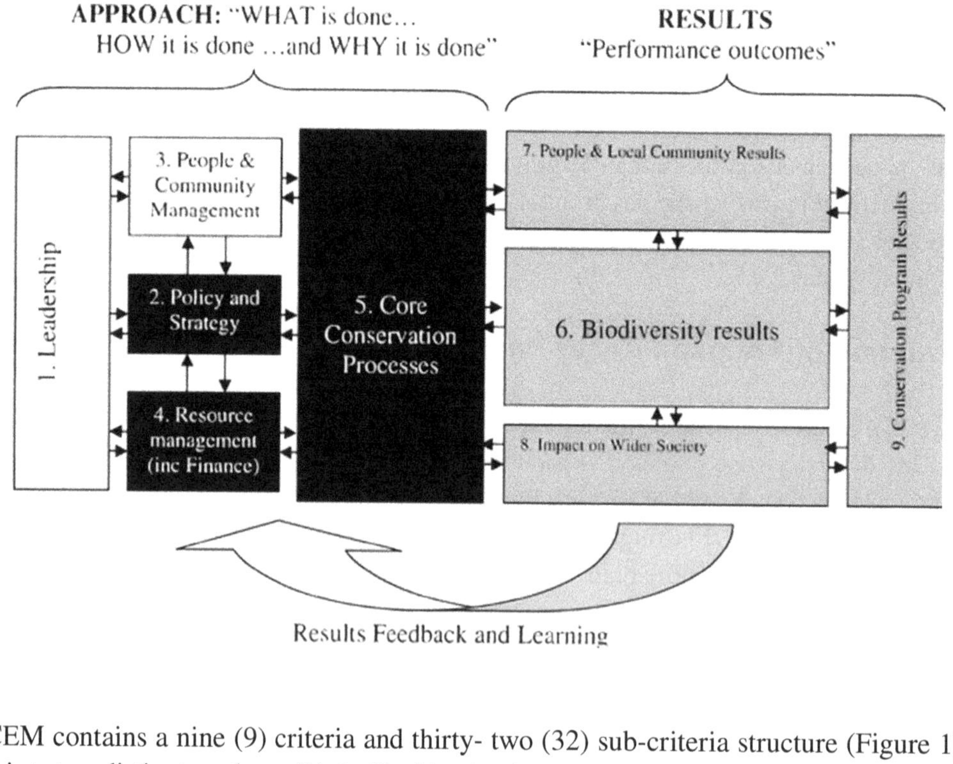


The CEM contains a nine (9) criteria and thirty- two (32) sub-criteria structure (Figure 1) that are separated into two distinct sections: (1) the Enabler (or Approach) criteria that discusses policy, strategy, management and technical interventions, operational activities and (2) the Results criteria which include operational, financial and biodiversity results (Black & Groombridge, 2010; Black et al., 2011b). The CEM follows sound organizational theory but is non-prescriptive and can form the basis for self-assessment by the organisation's own management team, an independent review by external experts, or comparative benchmarking with other conservation organizations (Black & Groombridge, 2010; Moore et al., 2018).

The CEM is used to assess many varied conservation projects globally. Published accounts include an amphibian project in East Africa (Black et al., 2011b), a bird recovery project in the Pacific (Black & Groombridge, 2010), reforestation in North Africa (Opfer & Black 2019) and across Indian Ocean islands (Amavassee et al., 2022), big cat recovery in Brazil (Nery Silva et al., 2022), plus a range of other programs spanning forestry, island protected areas, reptile conservation and mammal conservation (Moore et al., 2018).

## INTEGRATING STAKEHOLDER FEEDBACK INTO CEM PERFORMANCE ASSESSMENT

Feedback from key stakeholders is a useful performance indicator to many action-oriented organizations to improve the overall management, prevent inappropriate trade-off (for example the loss of goodwill, support, and participation of locals) when pursuing successful outcomes (Black, 2015; Bou-Llusar et al., 2009; Williams et al., 2006; Veitch et al., 2011; Moore et al., 2018). The integration of a plurality of methods in an evaluation provides a complete picture for improvement of governance, conservation efforts and management (Bennett, 2016); evidence can be triangulated to provide a more complete picture. Although the CEM places biodiversity results as the focus for the performance of conservation organizations (Black et al., 2011b), stakeholder feedback and processes involving people are also required in the evaluation since it is the people that produce those results of the project (Oakland et al., 2002). The CEM is useful in covering these social aspects within the evaluation (Black & Groombridge, 2010).

Moore et al. (2018) indicated that the CEM is a rapid, robust, and efficient tool for conservation organizations, particularly those that are donor dependent. Thus, the CEM was used to conduct a performance assessment of the OICP in 2020 and collation of current stakeholder perceptions supplemented the process. The research also examined how easily stakeholder feedback could be integrated into the CEM assessment. The research was conducted during the COVID- 19 pandemic, with travel restrictions and covid-19 regulations, so usual forms of assessment involving site visits and face-to-face interviews were prevented.

This research provided opportunity for novel insights into understanding usefulness of the CEM to the OICP's performance and management. Whether an effective third-party evaluation can still be delivered in restricted conditions (Covid-19 and/or remote assessment) is important in terms of constraints, feasibility, burden on the organization, and overall cost-effectiveness. The following research questions were examined: (1) Can the CEM provide valuable insights into the performance of OICP, amidst constraints of COVID-19 pandemic? (2) Does the use of stakeholder feedback enhance the CEM assessment, thereby enabling the identification of direct problems and critical areas of improvement in the program? (3) Can the management of EAG and the OICP benefit from the performance evaluations?

## METHOD

For three months (June-August 2020) an independent Primary assessor, alongside an assessor team, conducted a desktop review of the Offshore Islands Conservation Program in Antigua.

## Data Collection

Due to the onset of COVID-19, the Primary assessor was prevented from making an on-site visit, but a mixed-methods assessment was conducted using the organization's key documents, social media platforms, newspaper, and journal articles. The documents collected comprised eradication and biosecurity activities, environmental education, and awareness projects as well as biodiversity monitoring by the organization.

Semi-structured interviews were also conducted to supplement the evaluation process with a primary focus on stakeholder perceptions of the program (Barriball & While, 1994; Black & Groombridge, 2010). The interviews involved key informants who gave written and spoken consent. Each interview was conducted by telephone or Zoom and lasted for an average of 45 minutes. Notes were taken alongside digital recordings. The respondents were asked questions on how the program addressed certain aspects relating to the 32 sub-criteria of the CEM and about their perceptions of the program as seen in Table 1. Some questions were modified or omitted based on the relevance to respondents.

*Table 1. Interview template used to guide discussions with the EAG staff, partners, and associates*

| *Criteria* | *Questions* |
|---|---|
| ***1. Leadership*** | • *What is your perception of the past Program Coordinator?*<br>• *Do you think she was effective at biodiversity conservation and awareness?* |
| | • *How did she show support for the OICP?*<br>• *Do financial resources, people and priorities reflect this commitment?* |
| | • *Do you feel appreciated; were your efforts recognized by the past program officer?* |
| | • *What are your thoughts on the interim program coordinator?* |
| ***2. Policy and Strategy*** | • *Are you aware of policies for each conservation activity of the OICP? Can you list a few? (biosecurity, biodiversity, awareness, Establishing MPAs)*<br>• *Are there any processes that do not have policies or strategy document?*<br>• *Who creates or sets these policies? What is the process? Any scientific basis?*<br>• *How are these policies communicated to field staff? Partners? Government?* |
| | • *Are policies and strategies regularly updated? How is that done? Based on new data?*<br>• *Is there a policy or strategy that differentiates what the OICP is for MARINE RESERVE against the MARINE RESERVE management body?* |
| ***3. People & Community Management*** | • *Is there a set system for hiring, firing, and discipling staff?*<br>• *How are volunteers and consultants recruited?*<br>• *Is there a community awareness and school outreach strategy?*<br>• *How do you select a community or school to educate?*<br>• *What provisions are made for project teams, experts, community team/volunteers?* |
| | • *Are provisions made for staff training and development?*<br>• *Are appraisals conduced? How do you evaluate staff performance?*<br>• *How are staff roles assigned? Is there a job description?*<br>• *Who managed field staff? The program coordinator?*<br>• *Is staff wellbeing included in daily management?*<br>• *Can staff complain or raise concerns? Who handles that? Is it dealt with?*<br>*Results*<br>• *Does the program have a high staff turnover?*<br>• *Is the community fully involved/support with the OICP activities?*<br>• *Have you ever had past conflicts with the community/ Govt, landowner?*<br>• *Past conflict in the organization?*<br>• *Is there Government Support? How so?*<br>• *Do you think the OICP has good partnerships? Could it be improved? How?*<br>• *Is there national recognition? Any awards won?*<br>• *Can all staff contribute to the way the program is run?* |

*continues on following page*

*Table 1. Continued*

| Criteria | Questions |
|---|---|
| **4. Resource management (including Finance)** | • Who handles the finances? (budgets, bank accounts, records, authorization, reports)? |
| | • How keeps the financial documents? Has access?<br>• Does the OICP own any assets?<br>• What are the financial streams? Enough? Need more?<br>• Financially sustainable?<br>• Are audits conducted? Who conducts it? How often?<br>• How materials/equipment purchases/decisions are made? (supplier, contract, order)<br>• How is this equipment maintained? Is it accounted for in the budget?<br>• How are they stored? Who has access them? Who maintains them?<br>Non-financial<br>• Tell me about Information management: access, structures, validity, security<br>• How is data (scientific, management, financial) validated, stored, shared, updated? |
| | • Is relevant information utilized and protected? |
| **5. Core Conservation Processes** | • How do staff know what the focus is every year?<br>• How are core activities and processes identified? Scientific/expert/local knowledge?<br>• Is there a document for each of the processes?<br>• Do you have access to it? Is it easily readable for all staff/partners in the OICP? |
| | • Is there a system for managing processes? Who knows what they are going to do?<br>• Who allocates task, and how the resources are used? Can you give any input?<br>• How monitors the work and who checks and validates?<br>• Are reports submitted? Who does the reports? Who reviews the reports? |
| | • Is there a monthly or annual review of how the processes are undertaken?<br>• Does it change the future processes? |
| | • Are improvements undertaken including using new scientific knowledge/findings? |
| | • Are the new changes monitored and evaluated for improvement?<br>• Do you think the OICP fulfils all its goals and objectives in set out annually?<br>• Is the budget sufficient?<br>• Are activities conducted within a fixed timeline?<br>• Are current processes still relevant? Should they be maintained?<br>• What is the OICP roles in MARINE RESERVE? |
| **6. Biodiversity Results** | • What species does the OICP monitor? What are the indicators used?<br>• Does the program monitor entire islands?<br>• Would you say these species are improving?<br>• Do you think any other forms of Wildlife should be monitored? |

*Note.* The questions were adopted from Amavassee et al. (2022) and modified for the OICP.

## Data Analysis

### Interviews

The interviews were conducted using a purposive sample of key stakeholders of the program to receive feedback from all the groups of stakeholders that were integral to the formation and continuity of the OICP. Names of participants have been changed to protect confidentiality. Recordings were audio transcribed for thematic analysis against the CEM's People and Local Community Results and Impact on Wider Society Results criteria. Novel themes, when found, were compared across other the CEM criteria where applicable.

### CEM Assessment-Position Document

The assessment of the organization's documents was conducted using the Five-Step Approach, as outlined in Black and Groombridge (2010). Subsequently, the information was organized under headings of the CEM's 9 criteria to produce a Position Document describing the Great Bird Eradication Program (EFQM, 2003; Black & Groombridge, 2010; Moore et al., 2018). The Position document was then sent to EAG to ensure accuracy of the description of its Approaches and Results.

### Consensus Workshop and Benchmarking

The Position document was reviewed in a virtual Consensus Workshop (on Zoom) by a six-member panel of independent assessors, inclusive of the primary assessor, who were all trained in CEM assessment and scoring (Black & Groombridge, 2010; Moore et al., 2018). Each assessor reviewed the document ten (10) days before the Consensus workshop and assigned scores to the program using the Assessment Scoring Process as outlined in Moore et al. (2018). This process takes account of the principles of Results, Approach, Deployment and Review (EFQM 2003), but more particularly emphasizes the purpose of the program, the results achieved, subsequent learning and improvement (Black et al., 2011b). The assessors' scores were later reviewed after discussions at a Consensus meeting (two 3-hour zoom sessions in consecutive days) to produce a final agreed panel score. Highly effective programs receive scores of ~800 and programs with less effective management produce scores of ~250 (Black & Groombridge, 2010). Assessors noted the strengths and areas for improvement against each criterion for inclusion in the Assessment report. Finally, the OICP's scoring profile was benchmarked with three other island conservation programs to compare performance across the nine criteria.

## RESULTS

### CEM Scoring: Offshore Islands Conservation Program

The overall CEM weighted score for the OICP was 293 (See Table 2 and Table 3). A score of 350 represents a program of average development, so in scoring less than 300 despite being established for 25 years, suggests that there is opportunity for improvement of the program. Across the nine criteria, the average score was 28 $\pm$5.5. Leadership achieved the highest, if modest, Approach criterion score of 30, since at least the appropriate personnel are involved in overall Governance. The Biodiversity results achieved the highest Results criteria score of 37, since the program recovered one of the world's rarest snake from extinction. But reinvasion by IAS still occurs due to anthropogenic activities on the offshore islands, placing the racer in a constant vulnerable state.

Unfortunately, several areas underpinned the program's generally low level of performance. For the Approaches, the Resource Management Criterion received the lowest score of 19 due to the inadequate systems for scientific data and financial management, which hampered the program's management response and weakened its ability to be transparent and credible. The Policy and Strategy and the Core Conservation Process criteria were awarded scores of 24 and 25, respectively. Policy shortfalls had crippling effects on the results, since a lack of an education and awareness strategy, financial strategy, volunteer recruitment strategy, partnership strategy and biodiversity monitoring strategy resulted in little to no systemic guidance of core conservation work. Without clear management of processes, the program's results were less than satisfactory, particularly those involving key stakeholders as seen in the People and Community Results criterion which received the lowest score among the other results criteria. Results and recommendations from the CEM assessment (See Table 4) were used in the recent OICP Strategic Meeting held in 2021.

*Table 2. Raw and weighted scores for the nine criteria of OICP after the consensus meeting*

| Results | | Results/ Approach | Scope/ Deployment | Overall Criteria Score | Weighting per criterion | Weighted Score |
|---|---|---|---|---|---|---|
| Results | Biodiversity results | 42 | 33 | 37 | 2 | 74 |
| | Conservation Program results | 38 | 28 | 33 | 1.5 | 49.5 |
| | Impact on Society | 41 | 37 | 33 | 0.6 | 19.8 |
| | People and Community results | 27 | 25 | 26 | 0.9 | 23.4 |
| Approaches | Core Conservation Process | 28 | 22 | 25 | 1.4 | 35 |
| | People and Community Management | 29 | 27 | 28 | 0.9 | 25.2 |
| | Resource Management | 19 | 19 | 19 | 0.9 | 17.1 |
| | Policy and strategy | 23 | 24 | 24 | 0.8 | 19.2 |
| | Leadership | 39 | 21 | 30 | 1 | 30 |
| **Total CEM Score (Weighted)** | | | | | | **293** |

*Note.* This summarizes final scores agreed by assessors through consensus after consideration of the program's strengths and areas for improvement for each criterion during the CEM assessment workshop.

*Table 3. Raw and weighted scores for the 9 criteria of OICP before the consensus meeting*

| Results | | Results/ Approach | Scope/ Deployment | Overall Criteria Score | Weighting per Criterion | Weighted Score |
|---|---|---|---|---|---|---|
| Results | Biodiversity results | 48 | 40 | 44 | 2 | 88 |
| | Conservation Program results | 38 | 27 | 32 | 1.5 | 48 |
| | Impact on Society | 49 | 36 | 43 | 0.6 | 25.8 |
| | People and Community results | 33 | 29 | 30 | 0.9 | 27 |
| Approaches | Core Conservation Process | 30 | 32 | 31 | 1.4 | 43.4 |
| | People and Community Management | 33 | 30 | 32 | 0.9 | 28.8 |
| | Resource Management | 21 | 26 | 22 | 0.9 | 19.8 |
| | Policy and strategy | 26 | 25 | 26 | 0.8 | 20.8 |
| | Leadership | 34 | 22 | 28 | 1 | 28 |
| **Total CEM Score (Weighted)** | | | | | | **330** |

*Note.* The table shows average scores from the individual scores generated by assessors independently before the workshop.

*Table 4. Identification of fourteen key areas of improvement of the OICP from the CEM assessment*

| CEM Criteria | Recommendations Identified for OICP |
|---|---|
| Results Criteria | 1. Identify the target audience (i.e. focal groups of people and organizations) and devise a protocol to engage, educate and monitor perceptions. |
| | 2. Identify critical indicators to monitor species and ecosystem recovery after IAS eradication. |
| Policies and strategies | 3. Conduct strategic meeting to reassess the direction of Program (vision, objectives). |
| | 4. Produce guiding documents for financial management, data management, human resource management, research, biodiversity monitoring and education and awareness. |
| | 5. Negotiate the terms for co-management of the Marine Reserve with Government. |
| Resource management | 6. Build internal capacities for data management and financial management. |
| People and Community management | 7. Build permanent capacities within the program (paid roles for locally employed competent people, plus on-going training, skill development, and where possible, progression). |
| | 8. Identify, train, and certify local experts for eradication and biodiversity monitoring integrate volunteers as members of a wider team- give them updates and recognition. |
| | 9. More robust engagement of key stakeholders (landowner, Government agencies, international partners) in planning, implementation, and evaluation. |
| Leadership | 10. Formation of an Executive Managing Board with relevant supporting competence (political, financial, partnership/tourism, possible academic). |
| | 11. Conduct Leadership training across the organization. |
| | 12. Strategic collaborations with partners to align priorities, work plans and cost. |
| Core Conservation Process | 13. Identify core processes from guiding policy and strategies and establish relevant indicators. |
| | 14. Establish systemic monitoring process that feedbacks back. |

## Benchmarking

The OICP was benchmarked with score profiles from three island conservation programs which involved similar strong multi sectoral partnerships. These programs, however, differed in conservation focus, age, and location. When benchmarked, the mean score across all the programs was 416±146 with OICP attaining the lowest total weighted score of 294 (Table 5). The OICP and the Community-based Landscape Program (Program 3) both scored below 300 and reported similar discrepancies in 'Policy and Strategy', 'Resource Management', 'People and Community Management' and 'Core Conservation Processes'.

In contrast, Program 1 (Bird Conservation) and Program 2 (Island Protected Area) were scored as the 'good performing organization' due to their strengths in Leadership, Resource management, People and Community Management. High performance is not necessarily program age-related, but instead excellence is achieved when approach and results are actively managed and improved by the organization.

*Table 5. Benchmarking between OICP and three other island conservation programs*

| | Criteria | Program 1 | Program 2 | Program 3 | Program 4 (OICP) |
|---|---|---|---|---|---|
| | **Years of Operation** | **3 years** | **37** | **7 years** | **25 years** |
| | **Programme Description** | Bird Conservation | Remote Island Protected Area | Community-based landscape conservation | IAS eradication Programme |
| | **Region** | Madagascar | Indian Ocean Island | Pacific Island | Caribbean Island |
| Results | Biodiversity results | 51 | 52 | 28 | 37 |
| | Conservation Programme results | 64 | 38 | 25 | 33 |
| | Impact on Society | 42 | 48 | 28 | 33 |
| | People and Community results | 66 | 48 | 37 | 26 |
| Approaches | Core Conservation Process | 60 | 50 | 29 | 25 |
| | People and Community Management | 59 | 42 | 31 | 28 |
| | Resource Management | 59 | 66 | 20 | 19 |
| | Policy and strategy | 54 | 44 | 25 | 24 |
| | Leadership | 68 | 58 | 41 | 30 |
| | **Aggregated criterion scores** | **523** | **446** | **264** | **255** |
| | **Total CEM Scores (weighted)** | **584** | **494** | **294** | **293** |
| | ------------------------------→ | | | | |
| | **Decreasing Performance** | | | | |

*Note.* Benchmarking of Raw Criterion scores (out of 100 points) between OICP and three other island conservation programs. Total weighted scores (out of 1000 points) are given for overall comparison. Programs are listed from higher performing (on CEM criteria) on the left to lower performing on the right.

## Stakeholder Feedback

### Perceptions of the Program

Thirty-one (31) key informants participated in individual interviews. The interviews contained the local respondents (n=24) consisting of OICP staff, EAG Board members, regular volunteers, Community Ambassadors and Government officials who work closely with the program. The regional and international respondents (n=7) comprised of international and regional organizations and program partners as seen in Table 6.

### Perceptions to the Conservation of the Antiguan Racer

When discussing the success of the OICP, all the respondents (quoted under pseudonyms below) praised the rewilding successes of the offshore island's ecosystem and the recovery of the endemic snake species, which was on the brink of extinction. Nathaniel (Government official and volunteer) stated, "Scientifically that is a wonder story."

*Table 6. List of the number of respondents and their roles*

| Respondent's Role | Number of Persons |
|---|---|
| EAG's Full Time Staff | 4 |
| EAG Board Members | 3 |
| Regular Volunteers | 3 |
| Community Ambassadors | 3 |
| Government Officials | 5 |
| Local Partners | 3 |
| International Partners | 3 |
| Regional Partners | 2 |
| Consultants | 2 |
| Offshore Island Owners | 3 |
| **Total** | **31** |

*The snakes starting from where they were in 1995 with less than 50 individual and the projection is there is more than 1000, that is the biggest positives of the project. (Shirley, Regular Volunteer)*

Overall, the respondents (n= 28) emphasized the increased population of the critically endangered endemic snake and the natural regeneration of the offshore islands.

## Development and Management of the Marine Reserve: NEMMA

Respondents (n=28) indicated that the private ownership and constant development of the offshore islands threaten the future of the program.

*Majority of the islands are privately owned by Chinese Developers who will do whatever they want to do with it when they want to do with it. The main island with the snakes is up for sale. So, the decades of work we have done is just wasted, so a lot of their effort although I think is very well intentioned, very passionate, well managed... is wasted. (John, Tour Operator)*

The interviews also revealed that the lack of management from the relevant Ministries was a major factor impeding the sustainability of OICP efforts. Through the actions and contributions of the OICP the NEMMA was created, however, since its legal instalment, the mandate and management rights have not been relinquished to the EAG. Therefore, with a lack of management from the mandated Government agencies coupled with lack of mandate and unsustainable funding systems of the OICP, the continued protection of the offshore islands and dependent biodiversity is always threatened. Donald (EAG Board member) states, "we have never been given the mandate to manage our program and conduct our work. The opportunity has not been realized. We can do the exercises we need to do but to benefit or have control, we do not have it."

The eradication processes became even more complex during peak tourism season where international tourist and locals freely traverse the offshore islands, while unknowingly transferring invasive alien mammalian species with them. The lack of political will to levy payments from tourists to subsidize the OICP as the sole active management body, has led to further financial burdens of the program.

*The Marine Reserve has not had the opportunity to function as a protected area. One of the reasons over the years is that [Fisheries Division] cannot collect fees from the users and be able to claim it when deposited in consolidated funds. (Carolyn, Government Official)*

Respondents (n= 12) stated that dependency on Government agencies has also complicated management efforts, since the agencies legislated to manage the marine reserve suffered from a lack of resources and workforce. Eve (Government official) states, "unfortunately we are now in the position where Government has a hiring freeze, so we cannot have any staff at the moment although we desperately need staff."

The respondents also stated that it is not clear which Government agency is responsible for the management and protection of the offshore island given the inactivity of the NEMMA management. This ambiguous assignment of roles and duties hinders direct and purposive efforts which quite often results in little to no protection from the Government who are more often persuaded by the tangible economic benefits associated with developments within the area. Hence, it is the OICP that graciously picks up the mantle and advocates for biodiversity conservation for the ultimate benefit of people and wildlife.

## Perceptions of Leadership of the OICP

The OICP now embedded within the EAG is spearheaded by the Coordinator, who relies on the Executive Director of the EAG for administrative support. The Executive Director is tasked with the daily management of the EAG and its subsidiary programs. However, it has not always been the case that the position of an Executive Director was filled. Due to several constraints of the voluntary EAG Board to accumulate funds to hire an Executive Director, that post was left vacant for over a decade leaving the burden of funding, administrative support and technical support solely on the Coordinator.

Although difficult, it was sheer dedication of the OICP Coordinator of past, that pushed for the continual protection of the Antiguan Racers. Another EAG Board member stated: "I think that the program coordinator was extremely loyal because she stuck around despite having no leadership." Another EAG Board member described the past Coordinator as "a tower of commitment."

It must also be stated that the OICP partners and long standing EAG members have also greatly contributed the OICP's success. Although the OICP consisted of several organisational partners, it is individuals from those organisations that stayed and volunteered their time and talents for over twenty-eight years to see the program evolve. One EAG Board member laments: "It has been a labour of love for OICP." Similar sentiments were expressed by James, a long serving international partner: "it has been individual who are really pushing things and making sure that it doesn't just die with us."

*I think we have every reason to be very proud of what we have accomplished. It's commitment, that's what has kept it going really. Through thick, and there's been a lot of thin periods too, but we managed to keep going... there aren't many organizations that have a project running for 25 years as you know the ARCP started in 1995. We've been very fortunate. I also must say we've been very fortunate in the partners that we have had. (Job, Regional Partner)*

The interviews indicated that with the recent presence of an Executive Director (from 2018 to current) spearheading the philanthropic activities as resulted in further evolution of the OICP, along with the recruitment of new staff members. The OICP now has a new vibrant Coordinator, an Invasive Species Officer, a Wildlife Officer and two long serving biosecurity monitors and a cadre of trained volunteer wildlife and invasive species monitors.

The recruitment of staff has been a huge encouragement to everyone in the program as the legacy of the OICP can be passed on. Jessica, an international partner indicated: "having different people coming in, can create fresh ideas- different people have different strengths."

## DISCUSSION

### Insights Into OICP Performance Through CEM Assessment

The CEM assessment was a useful tool to unearth areas of improvement for the OICP. Although the program was able to boast high biodiversity results through species and ecosystem recovery, the low overall score suggests that the underlying principles of the program were problematic, leading to the ranking of unsatisfactory performance for a program of this longevity.

Though leadership was evidenced in the documentation of the program and echoed in sentiments of past and current program partners, the shift in program management with missing organisational roles (Executive Director) created a cascade of adverse effects to the OICP, as is typical in many cases (Black et al., 2011b).

As such, the program needed to review its direction, guiding documents and adjust its processes to improve. A systems-thinking approach would be beneficial to the organization to allow for a greater understanding of the relationship between the approaches and results of the program (Black, Meredith & Groombridge, 2011; Black & Copsey, 2014). Higher achievements, however, are now expected from the program in the coming few years as the results of CEM assessment was used in the recent OICP Strategic Planning Meeting (October 2020) to guide adaptive management of the program.

Following the 2021- 2023 OICP Strategic Planning workshop, the OICP Partnership been renewed and consists of the Environmental Awareness Group, Fisheries Division, Department of the Environment, Forestry Unit, the Ministry of Tourism and Investment, the National Parks Authority and Fauna & Flora International. Having signed a Memorandum of Understanding (MoU) in 2021, renewed its this cooperative partnership is working towards achieving OICP's has renewed its vision to 'Adaptively managed, flourishing offshore island ecosystems where wildlife thrives and sustainable use is practiced by all.' It is important to note that the development of the OICP Strategic Plan identifies clear conservation and community goals that the organisation wishes to achieve. These goals allow the OICP to clearly define its scope of work and identify the critical pathways (and means of verification) for improving habitats for critically endangered species.

Further, in follow-up interviews with the EAG, it has been noted that the organisation has incorporated CEM considerations. Some of the key factors have been strengthening organisational resilience through the election of a new EAG Board of Directors who are equipped with clear guidance on how to manage the organisation based on existing gaps. Through the 'Board Buddy' system, each board member is assigned to a member of staff and provides mentorship to staff to foster collaborative actions and renew commitment to the cause of the OICP.

The EAG has long identified the need for the development of a sustainable financing mechanism, that gives rise to the generation of unrestricted funding for the organisation. It is anticipated that in 2023 the EAG will establish a Sustainable Financing Unit that will help to generate unrestricted funding streams and ultimately relieve the pressure for consistent grant writing.

The OICP has also built the capacity of volunteers to better assist in monitoring wildlife and involving them in the decision-making process for the conservation management of the offshore islands as frequently as possible. Hence, between 2020 and 2023 the EAG has built the conservation capacity of approximately 10 volunteers in wildlife and invasive species monitoring techniques, through a combination of classroom training workshops and field exercises. These volunteers, notably trained and capable, collect ecological data and make contributions as citizen scientists as team leads in various projects and educators in the Floating Classroom. Programmes are being developed to encourage further recruitment and retention which will be finalised in 2024.

Transformational leadership has provided the impetus for change and it is clearly identifiable that the EAG has improved in its operations as a result of consistent leadership from the Executive Director. Staff have reported there is now accommodations for new innovative ideas using technology, staff exchange and training, thereby improving conservation initiatives and the sustainability of conservation efforts. This sets the foundation for the organisation and will lead to even more ambitious projects over time.

## Understanding Excellence in Conservation Management

In evaluations to date, conservation programs have always exhibited intermediate performance, which means that a program could generally identify good practise by benchmarking (Sutherland & Peel, 2011; Moore et al., 2018). Benchmarking the OICP with the three island conservation programs underlined the need, as a general principle, for programs to have strong leadership and governance; better-performing programmes had those things in place (Black et al., 2011a).

Program 1 and Program 2 exhibited prime leadership and, people and community management, which essentially enable the production of sound policies, core processes and adept resource management. Therefore, once the OICP improved such processes, it should be able to increase its CEM scores resulting in the sustained improvement of its overall performance and positive impact on biodiversity outputs.

This study also demonstrates that a substantial CEM assessment can be conducted during periods of constraints of a global pandemic or financial deficiencies preventing face to face meetings and site visits. Interviews gave unique insights into the program that would have otherwise been obtained during site visits such as descriptions of offices, terrain, and weather conditions of field sites. The use of a desk-based mixed methods approach was successful in assessing the case study, and such a method is encouraged for researchers and practitioners with financial, geographical, and logistical constraints.

## Integration of Stakeholder Interviews to Supplement the CEM

The goal of conservation is not only to improve the science but to enhance conservation actions and outcomes (Bennett, 2016). Perception research is crucial to that process as it provides novel information on governance and management shortcomings, of which contemporary quantitative methods (such as hard results on species population size, habitat quality and budgets) provide limited insight (Bennett, 2016). Stakeholder feedback, as seen in this case study, helpfully supplemented the organizational assessment by providing in-depth explanations to support the assessor's identification of areas for improvement. Nevertheless, incorporating information from interviews into the CEM assessment requires some consideration.

In this assessment, some information could be included in the Position Document (including key themes and specific perceptions), but other information was better shared verbally by the Lead Assessor during the confidential CEM assessment meeting. The information from interview themes (organisational breakdown, data management, volunteer recruitment, partnership, management of Marine Reserve) informed assessment of various CEM criteria.

A case in point is the information needed to assess against the CEM Leadership criterion. An initial, superficial review of the OICP documentation would suggest that leadership appears strong in terms of external profile, leader's apparent commitment to conservation, and recognition for conservation activity. However, when stakeholder feedback is examined against other aspects prompted by the CEM criteria, discrepancies in leadership approach were identified. The lack of an Executive Director to support the OICP Coordinator reduced the program's ability to manage its processes and update its policies adaptively (Amah et al., 2013). Loss of these critical roles also hindered the program's ability to secure funds and recruit additional staff which led to an over-reliance on the Government and delegation of these duties to funding NGOs (e.g. recruitment of key roles, reporting, training). The stakeholder feedback also indicated a lack of legitimate governance (i.e., oversight and decision-making authority at the correct level) in the program, pinpointing breakdowns of internal people processes (e.g., role definition, recruitment, training, pay & reward) that fragmented the program's direction, execution, and evaluation (Black & Groombridge, 2010; Oakland et al., 2002). Understanding the importance of maintaining key positions and roles in the program was a vital output of this assessment.

Stakeholder feedback provided insights to understand how the inadequacies of external governance and management had altered the program outcomes (Bennett & Dearden, 2014). Mandates governing the Marine Reserve are significantly weakened by funding, rendering those protected areas, paper parks (Garrod & Wilson, 2003; van Wilgen & Wannenburgh, 2016). For the OICP, Government departments were unable to set up a fee-charging system for users of the marine reserve, thereby reducing its ability to produce the funding mechanism needed for resources to support conservation efforts and core management activities. In this case, the Government agendas primarily concentrated efforts on national politics and modernization rendering conservation (and by extension management of the Marine Reserve) a low priority concern (van Wilgen & Wannenburgh, 2016). Consequently, the EAG became the forerunners for conservation locally and are widely known amongst the public for their work within the NEMMA. Nonetheless, the EAG was significantly inhibited by the lack of an actively functioning Government body with necessary legislative power to oversee the Marine Reserves and enforce regulations. Thus, for decades the EAG merely addressed the symptoms of the conservation dilemma through on-going and repeated IAS eradication and stakeholder outreach, while the major underlying problem was the lack of policing and effective management of the Marine Reserve by the Government to prevent re-invasion by undesirable species (van Wilgen & Wannenburgh, 2016).

## CONCLUSION

Balancing organizational performance with limited resources and human capacity is difficult for many practitioners. Whilst leadership has a key role in this, so do broader disciplines of organisation design and programme improvement. In the core case examined in this study, the CEM has proven to be effective in assessing the OICP and identifying relevant areas of improvement. This research has demonstrated that the integration of stakeholder perceptions and feedback within the CEM assessment is invaluable to understanding underlying governance and management issues.

People-related processes which are often overlooked can be the difference between an effective organization and one that is underperforming. Hence, strong leadership goes beyond 'tick-box' checks of tasks, but rather, the act of clear management and the legacy of passing on lessons learned to the new generations. Cultivating an atmosphere of support and openness to new ideas and technologies is imperative to finding novel ways of adapting to global climatic changes and their effects especially as SIDS.

It is therefore essential for conservation organizations to facilitate regular evaluations (e.g., within a 3-year or 5-year repeating cycle) of their programs to identify underperforming processes obscuring efficiency and effectiveness. Program evaluations must include stakeholder perceptions and feedback (e.g. from staff, volunteers, partners, government, public), as these are the keys to recognizing crucial areas of governance, management, and leadership. The CEM process ensures effective triangulation of information and incisive questioning of the approaches taken and results achieved, allowing helpful insight to improve conservation effectiveness. This study indicates that, where needed, remote data collection and assessment is an effective option when conducted within the CEM methodology.

Additionally, transformational leadership has proven to beneficial to the continued longevity of a number of conservation programs. Leaders need to install systems for communication to understand the needs of staff and the level of motivations and commitment that exist in order to fortify trust, respect and loyalty for collaborative conservation efforts. When leadership is strong and proactive, conservation initiates are strengthened, policy development is conducted in a more inclusive manner thereby engaging local people, businesses and civic institutions and fortifying the sustainability of programs.

It is the effort, time and goodwill of people that make conservation work. Consequently, gathering, integrating, and learning from stakeholder feedback should no longer be optional, but instead be a pertinent part of conservation processes. What people say matters; conservation professionals need to stop, listen, and adapt so that the programs that are put in place are relevant, set up correctly, and capable of evolving over time.

**Conflict of interest:** The authors declare that there is no conflict of interest.

## REFERENCES

Amah, E., Daminabo-weje, M., & Dosunmu, R. (2013). Size and Organizational Effectiveness: Maintaining a Balance. *Advances in Management & Applied Economics*, *3*(5), 115–123.

Amavassee, E.J., Lee, M.A.G., Ingram, G., & Black, S.A. (2022). Using the conservation excellence model to improve ecosystem restoration undertaken by organisations working in biodiversity hotspots. *International Journal of Avian & Wildlife Biology*, *6*(1), 11–19. DOI: doi:10.15406/ijawb.2022.06.00178/

Racer Conservation Project. (1999). *Re-introduction of the Antiguan Racer, Alsophis antiguae (Serpentes: Colubridae) to Offshore Islands Around Antigua, West Indies*. Proposal to the IUCN/SSC Re-introduction Specialist Group, Fauna & Flora International, Cambridge, UK. doi:Antiguan

Atkinson, I. A. E. (1985). The spread of commensal species of Rattus to oceanic islands and their effects on island avifaunas. In Conservation of island birds (pp. 35–81). International Council for Bird Preservation (ICBP).

Barnett, K., McCormick, J., & Conners, R. (2001). Transformational leadership in schools – panacea, placebo or problem? *Journal of Educational Administration*, *39*(1), 24–46. doi:10.1108/09578230110366892

Barriball, K., & While, A. (1994). Collecting data using semi structured interviews: A discussion Paper. *Journal of Advanced Nursing*, *19*(2), 328–335. doi:10.1111/j.1365-2648.1994.tb01088.x PMID:8188965

Bass, B. M. (2000). The Future of Leadership in Learning Organizations. *The Journal of Leadership Studies*, *7*(3), 18–40. doi:10.1177/107179190000700302

Bell, E., Daltry, J., Mukhida, F., Connor, R., & Varnham, K. (2019). The eradication of black rats (Rattus rattus) from Dog Island, Anguilla, using ground-based techniques. In *Island Invasives: Scaling up to meet the challenge* (pp. 162-166). IUCN.

Bennett, N. J. (2016). Using perceptions as evidence to improve conservation and environmental management. *Conservation Biology*, *30*(3), 582–592. doi:10.1111/cobi.12681 PMID:26801337

Bennett, N. J., & Dearden, P. (2014). From measuring outcomes to providing inputs: Governance, management, and local development for more effective marine protected areas. *Marine Policy*, *50*, 96–110. doi:10.1016/j.marpol.2014.05.005

BirdLife International. (2009). *The Caribbean Islands Biodiversity Hotspot*. Final Draft for Submission to the CEPF Donor Council.

Black, S., & Groombridge, J. (2010). Use of a business excellence model to improve conservation programs. *Conservation Biology*, *24*(6), 1448–1458. doi:10.1111/j.1523-1739.2010.01562.x PMID:20825449

Black, S. A. (2015). A Clear Purpose is the Start Point for Conservation Leadership. *Conservation Letters*, *8*(5), 383–384. doi:10.1111/conl.12203

Black, S. A. (2019). Psychological Knowledge Relevant to Leadership in Wildlife Conservation. *Open Journal of Leadership*, *8*(3), 114–141. doi:10.4236/ojl.2019.83007

Black, S. A. (2021). A Leadership Competence Framework to Support the Development of Conservation Professionals. *Open Journal of Leadership*, *10*(4), 300–337. doi:10.4236/ojl.2021.104019

Black, S. A., & Copsey, J. A. (2014). Does Deming's "System of Profound Knowledge" Apply to Leaders of Biodiversity Conservation? *Open Journal of Leadership*, *03*(2), 53–65. doi:10.4236/ojl.2014.32006

Black, S. A., Groombridge, J. J., & Jones, C. G. (2011a). Leadership and conservation effectiveness: Finding a better way to lead. *Conservation Letters*, *4*(5), 329–339. doi:10.1111/j.1755-263X.2011.00184.x

Black, S. A., Meredith, H. M. R., & Groombridge, J. J. (2011b). Biodiversity conservation: Applying new criteria to assess excellence. *Total Quality Management & Business Excellence*, *22*(11), 1165–1178. doi:10.1080/14783363.2011.624766

Bou-Llusar, J. C., Escrig-Tena, A. B., Roca-Puig, V., & Beltrán-Martín, I. (2009). An empirical assessment of the EFQM Excellence Model: Evaluation as a TQM framework relative to the MBNQA Model. *Journal of Operations Management*, *27*(1), 1–22. doi:10.1016/j.jom.2008.04.001

Bruyere, B. L. (2015). Giving Direction and Clarity to Conservation Leadership. *Conservation Letters*, *8*(5), 378–382. doi:10.1111/conl.12174

Caribbean Natural Resources Institute (CANARI). (2019). *Case study on Environmental Awareness Group: Supporting collaboration for the restoration of Redonda Island, Antigua and Barbuda*. CANARI.

Copsey, J. A., Black, S.A., Groombridge, J.J., & Jones, C.G. (2018). Species conservation: Lessons from islands. Cambridge University Press.

Daltry, J. (2010). Observations on the Ecology of Dog Island, Anguilla. Anguilla Development Company. Anguilla National Trust, Department of Environment (Government of Anguilla) and DEFRA-Fera (UK Government).

Daltry, J. C. (2007). An introduction to the herpetofauna of Antigua, Barbuda and Redonda, with some conservation recommendations. *Journal of Applied Herpetology*, *4*(2), 97–130. doi:10.1163/157075407780681338

Daltry, J. C., Bloxam, Q., Cooper, G., Day, M. L., Hartley, J., Henry, M., Lindsay, K., & Smith, B. E. (2001). Five years of conserving the 'world's rarest snake', the Antiguan racer Alsophis antiguae. *Oryx*, *35*(2), 119–127. doi:10.1046/j.1365-3008.2001.00169.x

Daltry, J. C., Lindsay, K., Lawrence, S. N., Morton, M. N., Otto, A., & Thibou, A. (2017). Successful reintroduction of the Critically Endangered Antiguan racer *Alsophis antiguae* to offshore islands in Antigua, West Indies. *International Zoo Yearbook*, *51*(1), 97–106. doi:10.1111/izy.12153

Daltry, J. C., Morton, M., Smith, B. E., & Sylvester, I. (2003). *Antiguan Racer Census and Re-introduction*. Antiguan Racer Conservation Project.

Dando, T. R., Crowley, S. L., Young, R. P., Carter, S. P., & McDonald, R. A. (2022). Social feasibility assessments in conservation translocations. *Trends in Ecology & Evolution*. Advance online publication. doi:10.1016/j.tree.2022.11.013 PMID:36567154

Department of Environment (DOE). (2012). *Action Plan for Implementing the Program of Work on Protected Areas of the Convention on Biological Diversity*.

Durrell. (n.d.). *Saving the world's rarest snake*. https://www.durrell.org/news/saving-the-world-s-rarest-snake/

Ecoengineering Caribbean Limited. (2007). *Environmental and Socio-Economic Studies for North East Marine Management Area (NEMMA), Antigua Site Report*. Organization of Eastern Caribbean States – ESDU.

Englefield, E., Black, S. A., Copsey, J. A., & Knight, A. T. (2019). Interpersonal Competencies Define Effective Conservation Leadership. *Biological Conservation*, *235*, 18–26. doi:10.1016/j.biocon.2019.03.043

European Foundation for Quality Management (EFQM). (2003). *EFQM Model for Business Excellence*. https://www.efqm.org/index.php/efqm-model/

Ferraro, P. J., & Pattanayak, S. K. (2006). Money for nothing? A call for empirical evaluation of biodiversity conservation investments. *PLoS Biology*, *4*(4), 482–488. doi:10.1371/journal.pbio.0040105 PMID:16602825

Garrod, B., & Wilson, J. (Eds.). (2003). Marine Ecotourism: Issues and Experiences. Channel View Publications. *Journal of Sustainable Tourism*, *12*(2), 107–111.

Hay, I. (2006). Transformational leadership: characteristics and criticisms. *EJournal of Organizational Learning and Leadership*, *5*(2). http://www.weleadinlearning.org/ejournal.htm

Jackson, I. (2008). *Northeast Marine Management Area (NEMMA) 2007-2010 Management Plan.* Updated to include OPAAL Baseline Studies and related documentation (EDITED). Eastern Caribbean States (OECS) Environment and Sustainable Development Unit (ESDU).

Kouzes, J. M., & Posner, B. Z. (2007). *The Leadership Challenge* (4th ed.). Jossey-Bass Publishers.

Lawrence, N., James, K., Otto, A., Ross, T. N., & Daltry, C. J. (2013). Is Eradicating Rats Worth It? Impacts Observed on Antigua's Offshore Islands. *19th Regional Meeting*, Society for the Conservation and Study of Caribbean Birds, Grenada.

Leithwood, K., & Jantzi, D. (2000). The effects of transformational leadership on organizational conditions and student engagement with school. *Journal of Educational Administration*, *38*(2), 112–129. doi:10.1108/09578230010320064

Martins, T. L. F., Brooke, M. D. L., Hilton, G. M., Farnsworth, S., Gould, J., & Pain, D. J. (2006). Costing eradication of alien mammals from islands. *Animal Conservation*, *9*(4), 439–444. doi:10.1111/j.1469-1795.2006.00058.x

Moore, A. A., Weckauf, R., Accouche, W. F., & Black, S. A. (2018). The value of consensus in rapid organization assessment: Wildlife programs and the Conservation Excellence Model. *Total Quality Management & Business Excellence*, *0*, 1–15.

Myers, N., Mittermeier, R. A., Mittermeier, C. G., da Fonseca, G., & Kent, J. (2000). Biodiversity hotspots for conservation priorities. *Nature*, *403*(6772), 853–858. doi:10.1038/35002501 PMID:10706275

Nery Silva, L., Diederichsen, A., Talbert, L., Leslie, S. C., & Black, S. A. (2022). Insights into leadership, Gender and Organisational Effectiveness Revealed by Benchmarking Conservation Programs against the Conservation Excellence Model. *Open J. Leadership*, *11*(4), 370–397. doi:10.4236/ojl.2022.114020

Oakland, J., Tanner, S., & Gadd, K. (2002). Best practice in business excellence. *Total Quality Management*, *13*(8), 1125–1139. doi:10.1080/0954412020000008

Opfer, K., & Black, S.A. (2019). Assessing community reforestation projects for biodiversity improvement and poverty alleviation. *Forestry Engineering and Research International, 3*(1), 32-37.

Pan American Health Organization/ World Health Organization (PAHO/WHO). (2008). *Antigua and Barbuda Health Systems Profile. Monitoring and Analizing Health- Systems Change/Reform.* U.S. Government Printing Office.

Powell, A. (2008). *The race to save the world's rarest bird: the discovery and death of the Po'ouli.* Stackpole Books.

Sandbrook, C., Nelson, H. P., Bolderson, S., & Leader-Williams, N. (2022). Evaluating the impact of the first 10 years of the Cambridge Masters in Conservation Leadership. *Oryx, 56*(5), 710–719. doi:10.1017/S0030605321000818

Secretariat of the Convention on Biological Diversity (SCBD) and United Nations Development Programme (UNDP). (2021). *Aichi Biodiversity Target 11 Country Dossier: ANTIGUA & BARBUDA*. https://www.cbd.int/pa/doc/dossiers/antigua-and-barbuda-abt11-country-dossier2021.pdf

Smith, B. E., & Colbert, P. L. (2002). *Surveys of the Lizard Anolis wattsi on Antiguan Offshore Islands III: Summer 2001*. Antiguan Racer Conservation Project Report No. 7. Black Hills State University.

Soorae, P. S. (Ed.). (2010). Global Re-Introduction Perspectives: Additional case-studies from around the globe. Journal of the IUCN/SSC Re-Introduction Specialist Group, 8, 352.

van Wilgen, B. W., & Wannenburgh, A. (2016). Co-facilitating invasive species control, water conservation and poverty relief: Achievements and challenges in South Africa's Working for Water program. *Current Opinion in Environmental Sustainability, 19*, 7–17. doi:10.1016/j.cosust.2015.08.012

Varnham, K., Ross, T., Daltry, J., Day, M., Cooper, G., & Lindsay, K. (1998). Recovery of the Antiguan racer. *Journal of the IUCN/SSC Invasive Species Specialist Group, 8*, 21.

Veitch, C. R., Clout, M. N., & Towns, D. R. (Eds.). (2011). *Island Invasives: Scaling up to meet the challenge*. Occasional Paper SSC No. 62. IUCN.

Walker, T. B., & Lawrence, N. (2022). *Advocacy for Protected Areas in the Caribbean: A Collaborated Approach to Ecotourism in Antigua and Barbuda. CABI Books.* CABI International. doi:10.1079/9781789249033.0005

Williams, R., Bertsch, B., Van Der Wiele, A., Van Iwaarden, J., & Dale, B. (2006). Self-assessment against business excellence models: A critique and perspective. *Total Quality Management & Business Excellence, 17*(10), 1287–1300. doi:10.1080/14783360600753737

Witmer, G.W., & Hall, P. (2011). Attempting to eradicate invasive Gambian giant pouched rats (Cricetomys gambianus) in the United States: Lessons learned. *Island invasives: Eradication and management,* 131–134.

World Wildlife Fund (WWF). (2018). *Living planet report 2018: Aiming Higher*. WWF International.

Zavaleta, E. S., Hobbs, R. J., & Mooney, H. A. (2001). Viewing invasive species removal in a whole-ecosystem context. *Trends in Ecology & Evolution, 16*(8), 454–459. doi:10.1016/S0169-5347(01)02194-2

# Chapter 19
# Happiness at Work in Colombian Companies:
## A Perspective Under the Rise Model

**Rafael Ignacio Pérez-Uribe**
https://orcid.org/0000-0001-9924-6657
*La Salle University, Colombia & UNAD, Colombia*

**David Ocampo-Guzman**
https://orcid.org/0000-0002-6497-5646
*Universidad EAN, Colombia*

**Fabio Fernando Moscoso-Duran**
*UNAD, Spain*

**Carlos Salcedo-Perez**
https://orcid.org/0000-0002-4433-5537
*Politécnico Grancolombiano, Colombia*

**Carlos M. Munoz Maya**
https://orcid.org/0000-0003-1451-1648
*University of La Salle, Colombia*

## ABSTRACT

*Between 2017 and 2021, the RISE model (route of innovation and business sustainability) structured by the authors of this chapter and Ean University colleagues, has been applied in 126 organizations of different sizes and economic sectors in Colombia. This model is composed of nine factors (innovation, sustainable production, leadership and strategic management, collaborative processes, organizational culture, recognition, new markets, technology, and financial indicators). Four dimensions are analyzed for each factor and in turn, these dimensions are described in 48 variables, among which is happiness at work. The objective of this chapter is to present the analysis of the variables that best explain happiness at work in Colombian companies. The data of the 106 organizations were processed with the statistical package Statgraphic centurión XVI, using factorial analysis using multiple regression, and three variables explain between 46.95% and 48.45% of the managerial decision to strengthen happiness at work to generate a harmonious organizational culture.*

DOI: 10.4018/978-1-6684-8822-5.ch019

## INTRODUCTION

The current business environment is changing at a rapid pace. Markets and workers' priorities change over time. Companies usually study their needs and external trends but eventually, forget or put in second place the way their workers feel at their workplace.

In Colombia, only 32% of workers are pleased with their jobs, 62% state that they feel a certain level of physical exhaustion, and 56% feel some level of emotional or mental exhaustion, according to research performed by HubSpot, a CRM platform (Portafolio, 2022). In Latin America, according to Microsoft (2022) in its Work Trend Index, 48% of workers and 53% of managers inform that they have a certain level of exhaustion at work, and 43% of employees say that their companies ask for their opinions at least once a year, meaning that over 57% of companies rarely knows about the experiences of their workers at the workplace; the same Index states that 55% of workers consider that working in a different company, different to the one they currently work at, is the best way to develop their skills. These numbers provide an overview of how workers feel about their jobs in Colombia and Latin America, showing that there is room for improvement.

Thus, in this chapter, the authors will present the results obtained through organizational diagnoses that took place in several Colombian organizations, both public and private, using utilizing the RISE Model (Route for Innovative and Sustainable Enterprises), a model designed to help organisations in their endeavours and efforts to enhance their managerial practices, thus allowing them to become World-Class Organizations (Pérez-Uribe et al., 2021; Ramírez-Salazar et al., 2019). This chapter will concentrate specifically on the study results focusing on finding the aspects that strongly influence happiness in the workplace. Until the first half of 2022, the RISE Model has been applied in 126 organisations and companies of all types and sizes. However, for this chapter's purposes, the database of 106 of those 126 organisations was used.

Hence, the author's purpose with this chapter is to analyze the results obtained using assessing those 106 institutions by dint of the RISE Model and thereby get a more crystal-clear idea of what organisational factors, descriptors and/or variables can contribute or hamper a company's corporate climate, factors that can affect happiness at work. This element has a tremendous influence on competitiveness and organizational sustainability.

Therefore, the authors will provide several theoretical pillars sustaining the concept of "happiness at work", the methodology that entails the RISE Model and present the results of the statistical method used for the validation of the data concerns, using multivariate multiple regression analysis. This will undoubtedly help the authors provide recommendations to the academic and entrepreneurial communities based on this study's conclusions, aiming to improve a company's organisational climate and happiness at work.

The authors expect that the conclusions and recommendations provided in this chapter will prove helpful in improving the organisational climate and culture in organizations.

# CONCEPTUAL FRAMEWORK: RISE MODEL

## Origins

The RISE Model originates from the Model of Modernization for Organizational Management (MMOM)" (all copyrights EAN University), which was designed in 2003 by the joint work of researchers of the G3Pymes Research Group (research group devoted to the study of management practices and strategies in Small, Medium, and Large Enterprises), which is a research group of the Universidad EAN. The MMOM includes sixteen organizational components to diagnose Small and Medium-sized Enterprises (MSMEs) properly; the Model also highlights the best management practices to be followed by SMEs' management to be more competitive and sustainable over time. (Pérez-Uribe et al., 2021, Pérez-Uribe et al., 2009, 2013 and 2015).

The MMOM is a thorough situational analysis approach that situates a business on a management level while, at the same time, identifying the critical points for developing a clear pathway that leads to change, improvement, innovation, and management modernization:

*It systematically establishes the priorities for the modernization and innovation projects and offers descriptions of the actions and elements that the company should consider whilst defining the pathways that allow the optimization of said key elements. Given its broad spectrum, this Model applies to both service and manufacturing companies. (Pérez-Uribe et al., 2021; Pérez-Uribe & Ocampo-Guzmán, 2015, mentioned by Pérez-Uribe & Ramirez, 2015)*

Between 2017 and 2020, the RISE Model - Route for Innovative and Sustainable Enterprises (Pérez-Uribe et al., 2021; Ramírez-Salazar et al., 2019) was applied in organizations from all walks of life within the Colombian economy. These organizations are of different sizes and belong to other economic sectors, which has created many possibilities for the hypotheses' construction.

Just like its forebear, the Model of Modernization for Organizational Management (MMOM), the RISE model was "born and bred" at EAN University, and it is a product of years of devoted efforts and resources to study the genesis of Colombian and Bogotá´s MSMEs. Such efforts have come to fruition in designing several business and organizational assessment models, the MMOM and the RISE.

## Factors Analyzed

The RISE Model allows any organization's upper management to thoroughly assess the company by analyzing nine (9) organizational factors (1. innovation, 2. sustainable production, 3. leadership and strategic direction, 4. corporate culture, 5. acknowledgement and recognition, 6. collaborative processes, 7. new markets, 8. technology and 9. financial indicators) concerning four (4) specific dimensions (social, environmental, managerial, and economic) (Pérez-Uribe et al., 2021, Pérez-Uribe, et al., 2018). (Table 1).

*Table 1. Factors, dimensions, and descriptors of the RISE model*

| No | Factors | Dimension | Descriptors |
|---|---|---|---|
| 1 | **Innovation** is the creation or transformation of a product, process, market strategy and business model. It is a process of change and invention into something useful and valuable for the market; the final consumer validates the usefulness when satisfying a need. In this factor, the level of innovation of the organisations is measured. | Social | Way to innovate |
| | | Environmental | Ecodesign-Circular economy |
| | | Managerial | Type of innovation |
| | | Economic | Value creation |
| 2 | **Sustainable Production:** to promote the efficient use of resources to improve the quality of life of present and future generations. It aims to improve human quality of life without overflowing the capacity of ecosystems. | Social | Suppliers- Raw materials and/or components necessary for the operation |
| | | Environmental | Efficient use of water-wastewater-Energy-polluting emissions, solid waste |
| | | Managerial | Plans, Environmental certifications |
| | | Economic | Budget for environmental management- Circular economy model |
| 3 | **Leadership and Strategic Direction:** Managerial focus from which top management sets a path and promotes the necessary actions so all the organization moves in the same direction. | Social | Social trends, Mobilization capabilities-Ethics, Values, Anti-Corruption Policies |
| | | Environmental | Accountability-Value of sustainability |
| | | Managerial | Corporate government-Knowledge Management-Corporate Strategies. |
| | | Economic | Environment Analysis-Decision-making |
| 4 | **Organisational Culture:** Basic assumptions and beliefs shared by members of an organisation. Top management can plan and influence them to create organisational change. | Social | Work environment |
| | | Environmental | Paradigm change |
| | | Managerial | Communication |
| | | Economic | Shared-value |
| 5 | **Recognition:** Practice valuing and recognizing people's contributions through symbols, actions, and material compensations. | Social | Happiness-at-work |
| | | Environmental | Environmentally conscious worker |
| | | Managerial | Motivation practices |
| | | Economic | Value of work |
| 6 | **Collaborative Processes:** Actions in which people, organizations or industries get involved to develop projects with the same objective of getting mutual benefits. | Social | Associativeness |
| | | Environmental | Work safety |
| | | Managerial | Agreements -Consensus |
| | | Economic | Corporate volunteering |
| 7 | **New Markets:** Set of new consumers able to buy the products of the enterprise. | Social | Degree of influence on other markets |
| | | Environmental | Green markets |
| | | Managerial | Strategic plan to enter new markets |
| | | Economic | Commercial strategy |
| 8 | **Technology:** System of knowledge and information that arise from research, experimentation, or experience that, along with production, commercialization and management processes, allow the creation of new, improved products or procedures. | Social | Wider Access to technology |
| | | Environmental | Clean technologies |
| | | Managerial | Prospective |
| | | Economic | Technological transfer |
| 9 | **Financial Indicators:** Metrics that show the financial situation of the enterprise regarding its liquidity, efficiency, performance, productivity, debt, and economic assessment. | Social | Impact on stakeholders |
| | | Environmental | Environmental protection and/or recovery |
| | | Managerial | ROA |
| | | Economic | EBITDA |

Source. Perez-Uribe and Ramírez-Salazar (2020, p.7)

## Evaluation of Results

The RISE model employs a 0 to 100 per cent scale to classify the results obtained by its application (Pérez-Uribe, et al., 2019), thus organizing the organization in 5 possible stages, described as follows:

1. **Stage One – Incipient/Nascent, 0 to 20%**: An organization in its early stages; therefore, all its processes are incipient and/or in the location of creation. It is a stage of great uncertainty for the organization because the founders/managers are comfortable and seldom need to be advised into better managerial practices.
2. **Stage Two – Survival/Livelihood, 21 to 40%:** An organization with more than 4 years of existence, a gargantuan accomplishment. Colombian MSMEs endure the harshest conditions; little governmental support and little to null financial assistance from the banking system. Amid these adversities lies the entrepreneur, fighting tooth and nail to survive, to keep their endeavor afloat. This is a level of bridges, of recognizing the enormous value of relations. It is a time for getting acquainted with the company's surroundings in the most aggressive fashion possible. Becoming part of business innovation systems and/or regional clusters is essential during this stage.
3. **Stage Three – Development, 41 to 60%:** An organization experiencing growth in sales and market share. Purchasing technology, trying new and innovative manners to manufacture goods and provide services, hiring new personnel, searching for external sources to finance its growth and highly likely immersing in foreign trade using importing, but most importantly, by exporting. It is a stage where entrepreneurs experiment through trial and error, and it is a stage where funding is the key: growing is always expensive, so it is paramount to know how much the company can grow organically and how much it will cost to obtain external funding.
4. **Stage Four – Outstanding, 61 to 80%:** An organization that separates itself from other companies from the same sector. It is a consolidation phase, where the market niche is highly differentiated, and the company enjoys financial stability, both attained by reaching high-quality standards in products and/or services. These are crucial times, however. Success leads to complacency, and Colombian idiosyncrasy is especially vulnerable to this fact. Now it is the time to begin the succession planning, a succession that will keep the organization on the route to success, satisfying all stakeholders' needs and expectations.
5. **Stage Five – World Class, 81 to 100%:** Organizations that are universally recognized and valued within the society, not only for the outstanding quality of their products and services but because of their business management and corporate policies, considered as references, not only in Colombia but internationally as well. Mass media praises these organizations' achievements and performance while their executives/founders are exalted in different societal levels, such as the academic community and public and private management associations. Their social work is also a trademark. Customers and non-customers recognize the company's brand; it has transcended boundaries. It is a stage where the entrepreneur must stay ahead of trends, and competition, of large companies looking to imitate and absorb the organization. It is a time for profound introspection, for the temptation of selling to a more prominent company will be hard to ignore!

## Dimensions Studied

For each of the nine factors analyzed, the RISE Model studies four types of dimensions, social, environmental, managerial, and economic. The dimensions composing the RISE Model are thoroughly described below (Ramírez-Salazar et al., 2019):

A. **Social Dimension:** 1) Innovation factor; considers all the organizations' stakeholders and asks these questions: Whom do we innovate with? Are all company members considered, or only management? 2) Sustainable production; Commercial inventories, raw materials, other supplies, and purveyors are analyzed. 3) Leadership and strategic direction; analyses the moral fabric of the organization. What social tendencies are considered? 4) Organizational Culture; assesses the working environment. Is it toxic? Is it healthy? Does it promote camaraderie and trust? Is the workforce imbued with a sense of belonging and pride? 5) Acknowledgement and recognition; How do company members feel at work; are they happy? Are they miserable? Are they successful in maintaining a balance between work and family? How can that be evidenced and measured? 6) Collaborative processes; Is management favouring subscribing to guilds and associations? Is the company a member of any guild and/or association? Are experts from other areas and companies consulted to develop new projects? 7) New markets; Has the company defined one or several market niches? If so, does the company have an impact and clout in those? Does the company possess a clear and deep understanding of the culture and idiosyncrasy of the communities where it makes its presence? 8) Technology; Do all company members have easy access to technology, or is this a privilege reserved for a few? 9) Financial indicators; Has the company impacted the communities where it is present?

B. **Environmental Dimension:** 1) Innovation factor; Does management enforces eco-design strategies? Is the company promoting and enforcing a circular economy policy? 2) Sustainable production; What policies and practices does the company enforce regarding efficient water use, wastewater management, storage of hazardous materials, disposal of solid residues (organic and inorganic), energy use and atmospheric emissions? 3) Leadership and strategic direction; Regarding sustainability, has the company improved transparency and accountability in this domain? 4) Organizational Culture; Has the company been able to produce a paradigm shift in all its stakeholders? Has it been able to update how it approaches current and potential customers and markets utilizing the available new technologies and social media or does it still generate most sales with a fixed retail sale outlet? 5) Acknowledgement and recognition; Has the company made the necessary efforts to prepare and train staff in Environmental Awareness? 6) Collaborative processes; Is personnel safety and wellness a priority for the company? Is information regarding industrial safety and technical specifications routinely updated and made public domain, leading to fewer hazards, risks, and accidents? 7) New markets; Is the company buying in green markets? Where? How much of its material demands are met by green markets purveyors? 8) Technology; Is the company an advocate and utilizer of clean technologies? Which ones does it utilize? Has this led to an improvement in the production process and its impact on the environment? 9) Financial indicators; Does the company pursue and enforce a policy of investing in the recovery of its surroundings, therefore mitigating the impact of its presence there? Has the company invested in recuperating/building sidewalks, parks, squares, boulevards, riversides, handicap access, signaling, and/or streets? In reforestation?

C. **Managerial Dimension:** 1) Innovation factor; What innovation processes are undertaken? Are they circumscribed solely on products and services, or do they include marketing as well? Is the company at the forefront of innovative marketing strategies? Of organization structure, production processes, and business model? Does it promote social innovation, where the most vulnerable members are favored and benefited? 2) Sustainable production; Are the company's sustainable production processes and policies certified by a proper environmental authority? 3) Leadership and strategic direction; Are function and procedure manuals for corporate management, knowledge management and corporate strategies available? If so, how often are they updated? 4) Organizational Culture; Does the company use cross-company communication or is it a hierarchical process? Is communication assertive, confusing, transparent, and open? 5) Acknowledgement and recognition; How is personnel motivated? Is it an incentive-based policy? Merit and public recognition are used. A combination? 6) Collaborative processes; How are agreements reached? Does the company allow and promote coexistence and community committees? Are various protocols and agreements available so that the parties have proper monitoring during negotiations? 7) New markets; Is the entry into a new market a consequence of a thorough research and strategic process, or is it done to meet customer demand or by a management hunch? 8) Technology; Is perspective used to plan the company's future? 9) Financial indicators; Does the company deliver on its promise to generate added value for its stakeholders?

D. **Economic Dimension**: 1) Innovation factor; Is the company striving to generate value for its customers and other stakeholders? Is the value added derived from innovation processes? 2) Sustainable production; Does the company have a defined environmental governance, and if that is the case, does this governance have a specific budget available and a circular economy model attached to it? 3) Leadership and strategic direction; Is the company's upper management invested in executing periodically thorough environmental analyses to sustain decision-making? 4) Organizational Culture; What is the company's shared value with its stakeholders? 5) Acknowledgement and recognition; Is personnel getting just and righteous gratification and recognition for their performance? Is the recognition above or below market average? 6) Collaborative processes; Are company members and stakeholders invested in corporate volunteerism? 7) New markets; Has management developed a sound, coherent, clear commercial strategy? 8) Technology; Is the company a regular participant in scientific and business symposiums, congresses, discussions, and other events where technology transfer occurs? Does the company embark on a two-way technology transfer process with stakeholders, such as purveyors and same-sector companies? 9) Financial indicators; From the financial standpoint, is the company enjoying good health? Do the short-term and long-term liquidity, profitability and indebtedness indicators reassure this state of good health?

## THEORETICAL FRAMEWORK

### Happiness at Work

Happiness at work is a variable assessed in the RISE Model as a descriptor from the Social Dimension analyzed within the Recognition factor. According to Misra and Srivastava (2023) and Salas (2017), most researchers and investigators have approached the notion from two (2) concepts amply developed and discussed by Greek philosophers, both appearing in the works of Aristotle and Epicurus.

On the one hand, there is the approach from the hedonistic experience of pleasure, leisure, delight, and enjoyment and/or positive experiences derived from variables such as satisfaction at work, positive emotions, and emotional commitment. And then there is the other Greek concept, similar to hedonism in its pursuit of happiness, but diverging from it in the means to achieve it successfully. Eudaimonia attempts to attain happiness via personal development and individual growth.

As stated by the mentioned authors, happiness is a sentiment that has an immensity importance in individuals and organizations alike, and most theoretical constructs used to measure happiness at work converge around three (3) levels:

i. A transitional level includes concepts like satisfaction ad work, momentaneous affection, flowing state, emotional state, commitment, task enjoyment, enthrallment, and intrinsic motivation.
ii. A personal level entails personal satisfaction, acknowledgement and affection, emotional bond with the organization, involvement beyond mere obligations, vigor, blooming and an overall welfare status at work.
iii. A unity level pertains to collective morale and eudemonia.

Eckhaus (2021) and Moccia (2016) affirm that several dimensions should be approached when happiness and satisfaction at work are to be assessed: 1) The tasks themselves (the actual job). 2) The job with its specifications (salary, work environment, colleagues, supervisor/immediate boss) and 3) The organization, including, but not circumscribing exclusively to, feelings of belonging and attachment.

Kun & Gadanecz (2022) and Turban (2016) have served as revisionists of The Welfare Theory and its relationship with a performance at work, both from the Hedonistic perspective and from Eudaimonia. By these authors, early research was based on hedonism, leading to the adoption of policies aiming at motivating the workforce from that perspective, such as bonuses, benefits, gaming rooms, and buffets with gourmet foods.

It is vox populi that a happy employee is a more productive one and under this thesis) and Peiró et al., (2021) and Turban (2016) propose to merge hedonism and eudemonia to create the hypothesis that combining those two is the best way to procure better work satisfaction, performance, commitment, disposition and hence, happiness at work. These authors' work has been instrumental in determining that hedonism is most related to satisfaction at work while eudemonia is most related to purpose, personal growth, and social significance. Consequently, both perspectives must be considered when procuring an environment where employees will find work satisfaction and benefits and opportunities to grow both as humans and as professionals.

Lozano-Correa (2020) and Pérez–Uribe (2021) both have concluded in their respective doctoral theses that modern organisations attain sustainable and holistic success when they can create a healthy work atmosphere that aims at providing happiness, commitment, and productiveness while it is guaranteeing equal opportunities and diversity.

Fitriana (2022) and Palomar (2005) maturated a multidimensional scale aimed at measuring happiness at work, while Busser & Shulga (2018), in turn, conducted a study that addresses a research gap by developing a conceptually grounded and psychometrically sound scale of value, research matured by following a multi-step, multi-stage methodology, verifying the scale in different tourism and hotel contexts. Both research projects yielded exciting findings. Firstly, the concept of "happiness at work" involves several dimensions associated with the personal interactions between employees and their individual experiences and the organisations' experiences, where a high amount of happiness at work is related to the work environment and the support they feel within organisations.

Contrariwise, if individuals do not feel comfortable with their work and feel an absence of meaningful tasks, they will present lower levels of happiness at work. The dimensions found and proposed by the authors above include the following: 1) The intrinsic flow and motivation that meaningful activities provide, giving the employee constant creative stimuli as well as promoting collaborative practices with colleagues, 2) Feelings of repulse and spurn at work, especially when the relations with immediate superior are a source of angst and stress, where there are confusing and conflicting messages in regards to daily tasks when the immediate superior often steals subordinate ideas and initiatives and presents them as if they were their own. Such toxic behaviours provoke ailments such as insomnia, depression, stress and overall diminished quality of life 3) Creating a support group where different adjuvant organisational experiences are shared, stimulating the conditions for employees to be happy at work.

Hernández & Serravalle (2014) came to the following conclusions in their investigation conducted in Argentine and Spanish companies:

- Most workers are happy at work, if they feel respected and supported by their colleagues, especially their superiors.
- Employees consider securing a job essential but by no means decisive. They believe it is necessary, but it does not condition their happiness.
- For the employed and the unemployed, happiness will always be a factor that influences greatly performance and productivity.
- Interviewees consider personal fulfilment a fourth place need and prioritise stability over happiness at work.
- A healthy working environment with camaraderie and companionship is essential for work happiness.
- A motivated employee who does not receive the proper company support will develop frustration and unhappiness.
- In turn, when the organization is supportive, but employees do not like their jobs, they will do the strictly necessary in compliance with their job description, but nothing more. A parasitical relationship will result, and the organisations will lose the most.
- Disgruntled employees dislike their jobs and do not receive and/or perceive organisational support; a latent environment arises, making both parties losers.

## METHODOLOGY

As mentioned in the Introduction, one of the foundations for this research was the RISE analysis in 106 companies located throughout Colombian soil. A second foundation comes in the form of descriptive analysis (Hernández-Sampieri, 2018; Hernández-Sampieri, Fernández - Collado and Baptista-Lucio, 2014, p. 92) utilised to specify better the general characteristics of the convenience samples employed. (Otzen, & Manterola, 2017, p. 230). 'Thirdly, a factorial analysis was deployed to learn the grade of association between our dependent variable (Happiness at Work) and the remaining 35 descriptors the RISE Model entails. (Hernández-Sampieri, et al., 2018)

Various analyses utilising multiple regression models were made. Such a method is ideal for this type of research, for it allows a higher percentage of correlation and assumes the existence of many causes (independent variables, in this case, RISE Model's factors and dimensions) to pair against the analysed dependent variable mentioned above.

Statgraphics Centurion XVI (Perez-Uribe and Ramírez-Garzón, 2020) was the statistical package chosen to undergo this research, providing a total of 31 analyses, the 31st being the one that provided the most accurate and adjusted equation that showcases the variables that best explain the behavior of our dependent variable, thus enabling the authors to prescribe recommendations to managers, directors, executives and administrators alike about attaining a harmonic organizational culture containing the best managerial practices, like this providing all the elements necessary to achieve the main objective and this chapter's leitmotiv: Happiness at work.

## FINDINGS

As mentioned priorly, the statistical package Statgraphics Centurion XVI was the "weapon of choice" to conduct the analyses using multiple regression, carrying out a total of 31 investigations before "striking gold" in analysis No. 31, when the output finally yielded the results of adjusting a multiple regression analysis model to verify the relation between happiness at work and three independent variables that best explain such correlation. Hence, the resulting equation was the following:

Happiness at work = 5,1772 + 0,277204*Work Environment + 0,26417*Motivation Practices + 0,181335*Occupational Safety

Since the value P depicted in Table 4 is less than 0,05, a statistically significant relationship between the variables with a confidence level of 95,0% is existent. The R-squared ($R^2$) indicates that the adjusted model expresses at a level of 48,4536%% the variability of Happiness at Work.

It is well known that the $R^2$ is an appropriate statistic when comparing models with a different number of independent variables. In this case, the value was 46,9522%, with a standard deviation ($\sigma$) of 13,0544. This $\sigma$ value will be helpful in future research. The Mean Absolute Error (MAE%) was 16,4862, the average residual (e).

Utilizing the Durbin–Watson (DW) statistic the (e) value was examined to further confirm the results' validity, as shown in table 2.

*Table 2. Multiple regression analyses results*

| | |
|---|---|
| R2 | 48,4536% |
| $R^2$ (modified.) = | 46,9522% |
| Standard Deviation (•) = | 13,0544 |
| Mean absolute deviation (MAD) = | 16,4862 |
| Durbin–Watson (DW) statistic = | 1,63837 (P=0,0306) |
| Average residual (e).1 = | 0,178841 |

Source. Authors from Statgraphics Centurion XVI

To determine if the model was prone to simplification, it is imperative to acknowledge that the highest P value from the independent variables is 0,0031, corresponding to the "Occupational Safety" variable. Since this value is less than 0,05, that term is statistically significant with a 95,0% level of trust. This determined that none of the variables employed needs to be eliminated (Tables 3 and 4)

*Table 3. Analysis 31 results*

| Parameter | Estimate | Standard Error | T Statistics | P-Value |
|---|---|---|---|---|
| CONSTANT | 5,1772 | 4,45181 | 1,16294 | 0,2475 |
| Work Environment | 0,277204 | 0,0718367 | 3,85881 | 0,0002 |
| Motivation Practices | 0,26417 | 0,0754661 | 3,50051 | 0,0007 |
| Occupational Safety | 0,181335 | 0,0597854 | 3,03309 | 0,0031 |

Source. Authors from Statgraphics Centurion XVI.

*Table 4. Variance analysis*

| Source | Sum of Squares | FD | Middle Square | F-Index | P-Value |
|---|---|---|---|---|---|
| Model | 26315,1 | 3 | 8771,69 | 32,27 | 0,0000 |
| Residual | 27994,8 | 103 | 271,794 | | |
| Total (Corr.) | 54309,9 | 106 | | | |

Source. Authors from Statgraphics Centurion XVI

The research concludes that work happiness is explained in 47% - 48% by the independent variables mentioned previously: Work Environment, Motivation Practices, and Occupational Safety. Therefore, the authors believe that strengthening these three variables as a priority through implementing activities explained in the recommendations will benefit organizations immensely in their pursuit of providing an ambience conducive to happiness at work. According to this study, they are the variables that have the most impact, but they are far from being the only variables that affect happiness at work (Figure 1).

## CONCLUSION

Almost half of the happiness workers experience at their jobs is related to the environment, motivation, and safety their enterprises provide. These three descriptors represent 8,33% of all descriptors analyzed to explain the forces behind the happiness that workers experience at their jobs; their importance cannot be underrated. So, companies should emphasize and prioritize policies aimed at improving these three factors but must remember all others since all of them combined also represent the remaining half of the happiness experienced by workers. These three primary descriptors belong to social, environmental, and managerial dimensions, showing that improving happiness at work is a comprehensive process involving more than just a specific dimension in enterprises.

Factors and variables such as the type of technology in which the core-business is set on, the variables that a PESTEL analysis assesses (political, economic, social, technological, ecological, legal, which will inevitable vary from one country to another), stakeholders' idiosyncrasies, ambitions, morals and principles, the manner in which the organization establishes relations with shareholders and stakeholders, local, municipal and national government policies and regulations, if the organization is private or public, profit or non-profit, a public-private partnership (PPP), a consortium of various organizations, a non-government organization (NGO), a Small and Medium Enterprise (SME), a holding or a multinational company, the tasks entailed in the jobs' descriptions, the leadership approach utilised by the upper-echelons, the preferences in information and communications technologies (ICT), in software and hardware and finally the MYU- μ: those aspects that cannot be controlled, nor foreseen, such as pandemics, natural disasters, sudden deaths of critical members, among others.

*Figure 1. Aspects affecting organisations' complexity*
*Source. Authors*

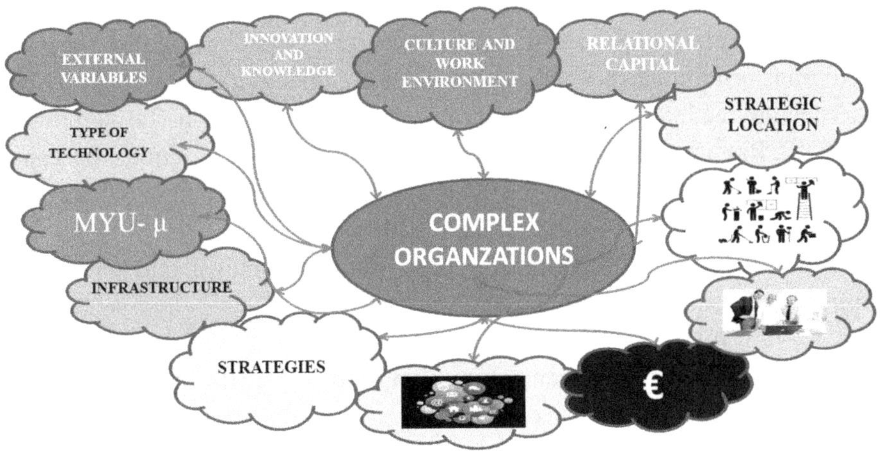


## RECOMMENDATIONS

As explained erstwhile, the authors determined three independent variables with the most significant influence on the dependent variable (happiness at work). The Conceptual Framework details how the RISE Model comprises a series of activities to allow organisations to evolve from stage to stage, and those activities, as well as the four analysed variables, will be explained as follows:

1. Happiness at work (the independent variable)
2. Organization culture factor, social dimension, variable Work Environment
3. Acknowledgement factor, managerial dimension, variable Motivation Practices
4. Collaborative processes factor, environmental dimension, variable Occupational Safety

## 1) Happiness at Work

Under similar conditions, any two given companies that are direct competitors have the same access to the necessary resources to manufacture their products and provide their services. Given that they are similar in size, tradition, sales volume, cash flow and assets, they are bound to obtain pretty much the same prices from purveyors, the same interest rates from banks; they're using the same type of machinery, there is virtually no possibility of outdoing the other using tangible assets. Take that comparison to intangible assets, and a whole different story is unveiled. That is why concepts such as intangible assets, intellectual capital, and of course, human talent has experienced an enormous appreciation within the business world. Through these concepts, a competitive advantage can be obtained, and what's more, it can resist the test of time. As we move deeper and deeper into the Knowledge Era, companies must construct strong, hefty organizational capacities and be founded on human talent.

Organizations must constantly validate with their stakeholders how effective their processes designed to attain happiness at work are and keep those results properly analyzed, documented, and reported to interested parties (Fernandez, 2015).

Leadership has become one of the most challenging skills senior managements needs to develop nowadays because all company areas require leaders. Leaders are in high demand if the new world requires an organization to transform into a knowledge-networked organization comprising highly effective and high-performance teams. Leaders must lead by example, and their actions must be methodically measured by KPIs (Sierra, 2022; Ramírez-Salazar, 2021). One of the most decisive actions the upper echelons of organisations must take is to utilise state-of-the-art ICTs to continuously communicate current company affairs with its stakeholders (Álvarez-Nobell & Lesta, 2011).

Perez-Uribe (2021) enumerates other activities organisations' senior-management must embrace to generate the proper conditions to secure happiness at work:

- Structure and release human management mission, policies, goals, and strategies and uniformly develop them throughout the company.
- Align, execute, and evaluate the human management strategic plan by the company's strategic direction and periodically check that it works perfectly.
- Implement and assess from time to time the documents, procedures and assessment and improvement mechanisms related to human management.
- Permanently use and evaluate the selection process (interviews, tests, background check, references, etc.), including outsourcing, the company's priorities regarding the skills, capabilities and values of the candidates, and the physical and health criteria to determine if the candidate fits the position. Develop tests for their entrance.
- Develop and periodically evaluate the hiring policies and inside and outside consultation sources to prepare employment and draft contracts.
- Permanently use: 1) mechanisms to inform the new employee of essential aspects such as History, evolution and objectives, organization chart, Work Regulations, duties and coordination relations with other company areas and 2) mechanisms to promote and measure adaptation of a new worker.

- Develop and frequently assess 1) training programs that are useful for the company's workers, 2) training with clear criteria, known and used by all the areas of the organization, 3) improvement and innovation of the training programs in all the company´s areas and processes, 4) proof of achievement by the workers trained and implementation of the concepts learned in their daily, operational or technical work throughout the areas or processes.
- Implement criteria that evaluate the employees´ development in their daily work and their achievements in applying the training process with the collaborators, both at the administrative and operational or technical levels and provide them with indicators in all areas or functions.
- Implement criteria to promote workers (by merit, years of service, etc.) and verify them with statistical data throughout all areas or methods showing the promotion criteria; the positions promoted, and their effectiveness in the company's productivity.
- Implement an Assessment and Merit process that reveals worker improvement needs and a performance evaluation with objectives and factors relevant to each position, rotation, or work area.
- Implement: 1) Fair criteria to determine the salary for a work position, readjustment regularity and salary policies; 2) management indicators to determine the salary scale concerning the industry and 3) payroll system with the latest technology in the sector.
- Develop and follow-up on programs demonstrated by indicators in all areas or processes: 1) of Social Welfare, 2) creating an environment favoring the worker´s collaboration and willingness, and 3) communicating to disclose to the workers the existing welfare programs.
- Throughout the company, statistics show an increase in productivity y a decrease in absenteeism and workplace accidents because of the implementation and execution of welfare programs.
- Implement and evaluate safeguard measures against labor-related risks that may affect the individual or collective health in the workplace.

## 2) Work Environment

It has been mentioned that every descriptor contained by the RISE Model has several actions detailed to promote the best managerial practices. The steps the authors recommend to constantly promote respect and dignity and to counter the sentiments of alienation, uprooting, anguish, and stress, are a combination of those described within the RISE Model, activities that lead organizations to transform themselves into great places to work (Mckinsey, 2021; Furstenberg, 2015; Carro et al., 2017).

Fair criteria to determine the salary for a work position, readjustment regularity and compensation policies, management indicators to determine the salary scale concerning the industry and implementing a payroll system with the latest technology in the sector are paramount (López, et al., 2019).

When designing the organisations' strategic planning, programmes to uphold the code of ethics and anti-corruption policy should be included. That code must be systematically ingrained in the organisational culture, and stakeholders must be held to its due fulfilment. Results must be measured and benchmarked with international standards, in such a way that they serve as input for future strategic projects (Montenegro, 2021). Organisations must strive to best respond to the demands and expectations of society, constantly exceeding expectations, and international standards in Corporate Governance through dynamic and adequate processes where organisational culture and quality of life are achieved (Yanka et al., 2021).

Perez-Uribe (2021) itemizes other actions organizations could execute to create good scenarios to improve their work environment further:

- Adjust the structure to guarantee the success of the Strategies mentioned and make them known to everyone involved in the company.
- Utilize, evaluate and make periodically known each worker's role or position descriptions to further improve processes.
- Evaluate, update and get feedback on the process maps, manual and organisation chart to enhance the process and strategies of the company.
- Adopt a space for dialogue with all the parties involved in your decision-making process. Decisions should always be in line with Strategic Management. This should be shown with the indicators and the results over time.
- Standardization and normalization should be part of the collaborators' usual rhythm and, whenever possible, it should count with international certification.
- Strategic management should be the guideline for any structural, manual or system upgrades.
- Developing activities that allow collaborators to create and work in teams is a common characteristic of their job. This should be shown through indicators and results.
- The way the company is run should enable project work permanently and all records are to be complete, updated and used to improve the learning curve and facilitate decision-making processes.
- Carry out transformation in the company structure that follows the guidelines established by Strategic Management.
- Create systematic and integrated databases that contribute to the value-added in measuring efficiency indicators of the system about strategic management. This should facilitate decision-making for the construction of change.

## 3) Motivation Practices

Management should be attentive to employee initiatives providing creative solutions to improve their environment, and strive to implement these (Osborne et al., 2017). A healthy, objective, and permanent feedback process is critical to the program's success (Andrade & Bravo, 2014).

Leadership has become one of the most challenging skills senior managements needs to develop nowadays because all company areas require leaders. Leaders are in high demand if the new world requires an organisation to transform into a knowledge-networked organisation comprising highly effective and high-performance teams. Leaders must incorporate the best management practices into their managerial approach to best satisfy the expectations of those stakeholders who have put their trust in them; the satisfaction that will be attained using developing a proper strategic direction, solid and healthy, that leads organizations to the "promised land" and out of the wilderness (Parapat et al., 2020).

Organizations' strategic direction must be disseminated and interiorized by all stakeholders, especially those wielding power and influence within the governing bodies. It should serve as a working guide in which different scenarios are studied and evaluated, allowing upper management to feed this process with adequate indicators to assess organisations' direction and change their course if needed (Perez-Uribe, 2018).

Here are some other activities that could prove helpful to promote happiness at work via motivation practices, as stated by Perez-Uribe (2021):

- Define, document, and make explicit the responsibilities of the company's directives (Board of Directors, Family counsel) to all interested.
- With indicators show the role and involvement of the business management as a leader in creating, promoting and maintaining a harmonious work culture.
- Make explicit throughout the company the activities that promote leadership development at all levels.
- With indicators make explicit the results of the diagnosis and improvements of a management culture.
- With indicators reveal the results of the activities that promote the improvement of each person's handling of authority and autonomy in their job.
- Develop strategies to consolidate work teams that help achieve the company's objectives easier.
- Put into practice a process to develop formal and manifest commitments of the management to quickly respond and satisfy the employee's initiatives.
- Create and carry out development plans for the workers that show their results in their everyday work in the business.
- Set up programs to prepare employees that are soon to be retired.
- Employ referencing and comparison methods to recognize and contrast your company's management policies and practices with the best national and international development practices. Use this information when engaging in decision-making processes.
- Create, implement, and give feedback to a process of acknowledgement for the tasks that each individual and group perform and that contribute to achieving the company's objectives.
- Come up with methods to analyse and adequately tackle the feelings of rootlessness, angst, and stress that some workers might have because of their work environment.
- Use activities to promote respect and human dignity among employees and collaborators of the company.
- Conceive future situations and evaluate their occurrence probability, alongside a long-term vision, supported by a validation system, a simulation, or a mathematical model as a planning tool.
- Achieve a total alignment of the enterprise's planning requirements and those of its labor force.
- Deploy a system for the company's objectives. This should be a working tool for all employees.
- Develop a programme so that the fulfilment of the business values becomes not only a motivation factor but a source of stability and commitment from and for its members.
- Permanently evaluate and implement the strategies, adjusting them according to the market's and the business' stakeholders' requirements.
- Devise an indicator system that evaluates the effectiveness and reach of the strategies (a Balanced Scorecard is highly recommended).

## 4) Occupational Safety/Safety at Work

It is evident that we are in a new working environment, which is constantly mutating into new labor forms; all is way different from what it used to be, and so much more complex. Employees do not need to be present at their workplace to be connected to their jobs; the Information Age proudly welcomes flexible organization of working schedules, for example, part-time work, work from home and teleworking; Social networks accelerate the dissemination of information. Organizational culture is no longer developed exclusively at the company's premises, it is also produced within the Cloud, and as such, the cloud must be included as a place of work. These elements must be taken into consideration when upper management is defining the working environment. Leadership is now exercised via social networks, and the higher-ups must find new and creative ways to imbue their employees with powerful, motivating messages (Tilbaut et al., 2020). Therefore, organizations must go the extra mile and implement additional and complementary industrial health and safety services to those required by law (Ramírez, 2012).

All activities, actions and initiatives designed to promote innovation and sustainable production practices must be encouraged and made explicit at all organisational levels alongside a healthy and safe workplace environment (Muñoz-La Rivera, et al., 2021).

Perez-Uribe (2021) strongly recommends the design and implementation of communicable disease surveillance, prevention and control, and overall employee welfare programmes which entail the following activities:

- Promote welfare at work using stimulating physical activities, substituting junk food for healthy options, and supporting football, basketball, baseball, hockey, and team sports in general.
- Always be attentive and ready to intervene when mental illnesses are detected, such as depression, anxiety, mourning and overall sadness.
- Always be attentive and ready to intervene when addictions are detected, such as alcohol, nicotine and recreational drugs, Performance Enhancing Drugs (PEDs), and/or painkillers.
- Have adequations made within office grounds to permit employees to take renowned and proven healthy practices such as Yoga, Pilates, HIIT, martial arts and other physical activities.
- Implement a "health passport" where employees can keep track of key health indicators such as HDL, LDL, glucose, triglycerides, blood pressure, and body mass index, among others.
- Make it accessible and expected to talk about sensitive issues, such as VD ailments, AIDS, breast cancer and testicular.
- Enable employee access to the domains of financial security, physical health and wellness, mental health, social environment, and intellectual pursuits via experts.
- Enable direct employee access to experts in physiotherapy, Yoga, Pilates, fitness, chiropractors, nutrition, and others.
- Enable support lines for accidents, crises, and diseases, both mental and physical.
- Enable support lines for those employees who have experienced a traumatic event, such as the passing on of loved ones.
- Already mentioned, but worth mentioning again, enable employee access to a sound financial education, where they can learn how the best utilize credit cards, mortgages, loans, wages, bonuses, redundancy payments, family grant payments, funeral services and pension and healthcare contributions.

## REFERENCES

Álvarez-Nobell, A., & Lesta, L. (2011). Medición de los aportes de la gestión estratégica de comunicación interna a los objetivos de la organización. *Palabra Clave (La Plata), 14*(1), 11–30. http://www.scielo.org.co/scielo.php?script=sci_arttext&pid=S0122-82852011000100002&lng=en&tlng=es

Andrade, O. A., & Bravo, H. R. (2014). *Estudio exploratorio acerca de la calidad de vida laboral de trabajadores de una empresa proveedora de productos y servicios en la industria cuprífera.* Tesis para optar al título de Sociólogo y al grado de Licenciado en Sociología. Universidad Academia de Humanismo Cristiano. Chile. http://bibliotecadigital.academia.cl/xmlui/handle/123456789/3221

Busser, J., & Shulga, L. (2018). Co-created value: Multidimensional scale and nomological network. *Tourism Management, 65*, 69-86. doi:10.1016/j.tourman.2017.09.014

Carro, J., Sarmiento, S., & Rosano, G. (2017). La cultura organizacional y su influencia en la sustentabilidad empresarial: La importancia de la cultura en la sustentabilidad empresarial, *EST. GER, 33*(145), 352–365. doi:10.1016/j.estger.2017.11.006

De Smet, A., Dowling, B., Mugayar, M., & Schaninger, B. (2021). *Great Attrition' or 'Great Attraction'? The choice is yours.* https://www.mckinsey.com/capabilities/people-and-organizational-performance/our-insights/great-attrition-or-great-attraction-the-choice-is-yours#/

Eckhaus, E. (2021). *The Fourth Dimension of Happiness and Work Satisfaction.* doi:10.2478/mmcks-2021-0008

Fernandez, I. (2015). *Felicidad organizacional. Como construir felicidad en el trabajo.* Ediciones B. Chile S.A. https://books.google.es/books?hl=es&lr=&id=zlQsDwAAQBAJ&oi=fnd&pg=PT5&dq=felicidad+en+el+trabajo&ots=CfkE_X1KXd&sig=L3Eq_Hg6ZWqp8f01BpoMVPEqCCY#v=onepage&q=felicidad%20en%20el%20trabajo&f=false

Fisher, C. (2003). Why do lay people believe that satisfaction and performance are correlated? Possible sources of a commonsense theory. *Journal of Organizational Behavior, 24*(6), 753–777. doi:10.1002/job.219

Fitriana, N., Hutagalung, F. D., Awang, Z., & Zaid, S. M. (2022). Happiness at work: A cross-cultural Validation of happiness at the work scale. *PLoS One, 17*(1), e0261617. doi:10.1371/journal.pone.0261617 PMID:34986180

Flores Konja, J. V., & Rozas Flores, A. E. (2008). El gobierno corporativo: Un enfoque moderno. *Quipukamayoc, 15*(29), 7–22. doi:10.15381/quipu.v15i29.2065

Frías Castro, P. (2014). Compromiso y satisfacción laboral como factores de permanencia de la generación Y. Tesis de grado para optar al grado de Magíster en Gestión de Personas y Dinámica Organizacional. Universidad de Chile. Santiago de Chile.

Furstenberg, C. (2015). La dignidad inherente al hombre a respetar, proteger y promover en todo ser humano: Una lucha que merece la pena para la protección de la humanidad. *Horizonte de Enfermería, 26*(2), 47–56. doi:10.7764/Horiz_Enferm.26.2.47

GRI. (2016). *Global Reporting Initiative.* GRI 103: Management Approach 2016. https://www.globalreporting.org/standards/gri-standards-download-center/?g=30f6860d-7c3e-4d29-b3ae-98549f76774f

Hernández, R., & Serravalle, C. D. (2014). *Felicidad en el trabajo.* Trabajo de investigación final. Universidad Argentina de la Empresa – UADE. https://repositorio.uade.edu.ar/xmlui/bitstream/handle/123456789/2483/Hernandez.pdf?s

Hernández-Sampieri, R., & Mendoza, C. (2018). Metodología de la investigación. Las rutas cuantitativa, cualitativa y mixta. Ciudad de México, México: Editorial Mc Graw Hill Education.

Hernández-Sampieri, R., Fernández-Collado, C., & Baptista-Licio, MdeP. (2014). *Metodología de la investigación.* McGraw-Hill. https://docs.google.com/viewer?a=v&pid=sites&srcid=ZGVmYXVsdGRvbWFpbnxjb250YWR1cmlhcHVibGljYTk5MDUxMHxneDo0NmMxMTY0NzkxNzliZmYw

Kun, A., & Gadanecz, P. (2022). Workplace happiness, well-being, and their relationship with psychological capital: A study of Hungarian Teachers. *Current Psychology (New Brunswick, N.J.), 41*(1), 185–199. doi:10.100712144-019-00550-0

López Chanes, F., Casique Guerrero, A., & Ferrer Guevara, J. (2019). La Satisfacción hacia el Trabajo. Un Análisis Basado en las Teorías de las Expectativas y de Equidad. *Administración y Organizaciones, 9*(17), 117-134. https://rayo.xoc.uam.mx/index.php/Rayo/article/view/249

Lozano-Correa, L. J., Pérez-Uribe, R. I., & Ocampo-Guzmán, D. (2020). Truthfulness as a critical factor in competitiveness in medium-sized companies in Colombia. doi:10.4018/978-1-7998-2019-2.ch015

Microsoft. (2022). *Resumen del Reporte del Índice de Tendencias Laborales 2022.* https://news.microsoft.com/es-xl/resumen-del-reporte-del-indice-de-tendencias-laborales-2022/

Misra, N., & Srivastava, S. (2023). Happiness at Work: A Psychological Perspective. *Inertechopen.* doi:10.5772/intechopen.108241

Moccia, S. (2016). Felicidad en el Trabajo. *Papeles del Psicólogo, 37*(2), 143-151. https://www.redalyc.org/pdf/778/77846055007.pdf

Montenegro, S. L. F. (2021). *El código de ética y su influencia en la política anticorrupción de una entidad pública del oriente peruano.* Escuela de Posgrado Programa académico de Maestría en Gestión Pública. Universidad Cesar Vallejo. https://hdl.handle.net/20.500.12692/73000

Muñoz-La Rivera, F., Hermosilla, P., Delgadillo, J., & Echeverría, D. (2021). Proposal for constructing innovation skills in engineering education in the context of Industry 4.0 and sustainable development goals (SDG). *Formación Universitaria, 14*(2), 75–84. doi:10.4067/S0718-50062021000200075

Osborne & Hammoud. (2017). Effective Employee Engagement in the Workplace. *International Journal of Applied Management and Technology, 16*(1), 50–67.

Otzen, T., & Manterola, C. (2017). Técnicas de Muestreo sobre una Población a Estudio. *International Journal of Morphology, 35*(1), 227–232. doi:10.4067/S0717-95022017000100037

Palomar, L. J. (2005). *Estructura del bienestar subjetivo: construcción de una escala multidimensional.* https://books.google.com.mx/books?hl=es&lr=&id=j16GIakxXpgC&oi=fnd&pg=PA113&dq=ESCALA+MULTIDIMENSIONAL+PARA+MEDIR+LA+FELICIDAD+EN+EL+TRABAJO+&ots=0XZbgHBupo&sig=dfSQZnqwf0Ap8msAfA23ZXexhZ0#v=onepage&q&f=false

Parapat, Y., Sabdono, E., Agus, M., Djati, P., & Hidayat, A. (2020) Moses Leadership Transition - A Moses Leadership Transition Model - A Successful Succession Management Model. *International Journal of Innovative Science and Research Technology.*

Peiró, J. M., Montesa, D., Soriano, A., Kozusznik, M. W., Villajos, E., Magdaleno, J., Djourova, N. P., & Ayala, Y. (2021). Revisiting the Happy-Productive Worker Thesis from a Eudaimonic Perspective: A Systematic Review. *Sustainability, 13*, 3174. doi:10.3390/su13063174

Pérez-Uribe, R., Nieto, M., Velásquez, A., Castellanos, G., Garzón, M., Vargas, H., Alfonso, N. (+), Calixto, N., Rodríguez, A., Palacio, M., López, L.G., Vidal, M., & López De Mesa, J. (2013). Modelo De Modernización Para La Gestión De Organizaciones (MMGO). Universidad Ean. Libro: 624 P. Primera Impresión, agosto de 2009. Segunda Impresión, diciembre de 2011. Tercera Impresión, febrero de 2013.

Perez-Uribe, R. (2018). *Gerencia Estratégica Corporativa*. Primera edición. ECOE ediciones.

Perez-Uribe, R. (2020). Innovación y sostenibilidad en la Empresa L. *Revista Citas, Universidad Santo Tomas.* . doi:10.15332/24224529.6365

Perez-Uribe, R., Ocampo-Guzman, D., Moscoso-Duran, F., & Ramirez-Salazar, M. P. (2021). Innovation and Sustainability Management as a Key Factor in Global Purpose-Driven Micro, Small, and Medium-Sized Bogotanas Companies: Its Impact on Financial Results in MSMEs. *Advances in Business Strategy and Competitive Advantage*, *26*, 354–379. doi:10.4018/978-1-7998-4909-4.ch019

Perez-Uribe, R., & Salcedo-Perez, C., & Correa- Lozano, L.J. (2022). *Ebitda is a key indicator of sustainability in colombian companies.* IGI Global Publishing. doi:10.4018/978-1-7998-9301-1.ch009

Perez-Uribe, R., Salcedo-Perez, C., & Lozano-Correa, L.J. (2022). *Ebitda as a key indicator of sustainability in colombian companies.* doi:10.4018/978-1-7998-9301-1.ch009

Pérez-Uribe, R. I., & Ramírez-Garzón, M. T. (2020). Human Resources Management and its contribution to Colombian SMEs Sustainability. doi:10.4018/978-1-7998-2019-2.ch012

Pérez-Uribe R. (2012). *El ambiente laboral y su incidencia en el desempeño de las organizaciones: estudio de las mejores empresas para trabajar en Colombia.* Tesis doctoral. Universidad Nebrija. http://edicionesean.ean.edu.co/index.php/es/productos-de-investigacion1/tesis-doctorales/23-publicaciones/192-el-ambiente-laboral-y-su-incidencia-en-el-desempeno-de-las-organizaciones-estudio-en-las-mejores-empresas-para-trabajar-en-colombia

Perez-Uribe, R., & Ramírez-Salazar, M. D. P. (2020). *Guía para el manejo del modelo de innovación y sostenibilidad empresarial (RISE = Ruta de Innovación y Sostenibilidad Empresarial).* doi:10.13140/RG.2.2.13026.45762

PNUMA. (2016). *Manual del Convenio de Viena para la protección de la capa de Ozono.* Décima edición de 2016. https://observatoriop10.cepal.org/sites/default/files/documents/treaties/vc-handbook-2016-spanish.pdf

Portafolio. (2022). *¿Qué tan felices son los colombianos en su trabajo?* https://www.portafolio.co/economia/empleo/colombianos-que-tan-felices-son-en-sus-trabajos-estudio-de-hubspot-575238

Ramírez, A. (2012). Servicios de salud ocupacional. *Anales de la Facultad de Medicina, 73*(1), 63-69. http://www.scielo.org.pe/scielo.php?script=sci_arttext&pid=S1025-55832012000100012&lng=es&tlng=es

Ramírez-Salazar, M. P. (2016). *Modelo De Innovación Abierta Colaborativa Para La Banca De Fomento: Caso Bancóldex.* Tesis Doctoral. Doctorado en Gestión. Universidad Ean.

Ramírez-Salazar, C. F. (2021). Happiness at Work Through Recognition and Reward Programs: Cases in Colombian and American Companies. *Advances in Business Strategy and Competitive Advantage, 21*, 310–330. doi:10.4018/978-1-7998-4909-4.ch017

Ramírez-Salazar, M. D. P., Salcedo-Perez, C., & Castañeda, S. E. (2021). Open Collaborative Innovation at Colombia's National Spectrum Agency. *Advances in Business Strategy and Competitive Advantage, 24*, 169–192. Advance online publication. doi:10.4018/978-1-7998-3568-4.ch009

Ramirez-Salazar, M. P., Perez-Uribe, R. I., Salcedo-Perez, C., & Huffington-Smith, J. (2019). RISE Model: Its application on diving enterprises located in the San Andres Archipelago. In *Entrepreneurship and Family Business Vitality–Surviving and Flourishing in the Long Term*. Ediciones Springer. https://www.springer.com/gp/book/9783030155254

Razzouk, R., & Shute, V. (2012, September). What Is Design Thinking and Why Is It Important? *Review of Educational Research, 82*(3), 330–348. doi:10.3102/0034654312457429

Salas, A. (2017). La felicidad en el trabajo: un reto alcanzable para las empresas. *Capital Humano*, 325.

Salas, V. A., Alegre, V. J., & Fernández, G. R. (2013). *La medición de la felicidad en el trabajo y sus antecedentes: un estudio empírico en el área de alergología de los hospitales públicos españoles.* Universidad de Huelva. https://rabida.uhu.es/dspace/handle/10272/9306

Serrano, O. B. J., & Portalanza, A. (2014). Influencia del liderazgo sobre el clima organizacional. *Suma Neg., 5*(11), 117-125. http://www.scielo.org.co/pdf/sdn/v5nspe11/2027-5692-sdn-5-spe11-117.pdf

Sierra, M. J. E. (2022). *Liderazgo con valores. Visión Cristiana de la RSE.* Digital Reasons. https://books.google.es/books?hl=es&lr=&id=qtd-EAAAQBAJ&oi=fnd&pg=PT5&dq=liderazgo+con+valores&ots=w5_HexieRE&sig=kMy22YALTLfzAU46QE7D-kg6Wbk#v=onepage&q=liderazgo%20con%20valores&f=false

Tilbault, L., Schweyer, A., & Whillans, A. (2018). *Winning the War for Talent: Modern Motivational Methods for Attracting and Retaining Employees.* doi:10.1177/0886368718808152

Turban Wan Yan, D. (2016). Relationship of eudaimonia and hedonia with work outcomes. *Journal of Managerial Psychology, 31*(6), 1006–1020. doi:10.1108/JMP-07-2015-0271

Yanka Perkasa & Fardinal. (2021). *The Influence of Organizational Culture.* Internal Control.

## KEY TERMS AND DEFINITIONS

**G3PYMES:** Research group managing small and medium-sized companies of the EAN University in Bogota, Colombia.

**RISE:** Route for Innovative and Sustainable Enterprises is a business diagnosis model allowing organizations' upper echelons to make a thorough assessment of their organization using analysing four (4) specific dimensions (social, environmental, managerial, and economic) concerning nine (9) organisational factors: 1. innovation, 2. sustainable production, 3. leadership and strategic direction, 4. organisational culture, 5. acknowledgement and recognition, 6. collaborative processes, 7. new markets, 8. technology, and 9. financial indicators.

# Chapter 20
# The Art of Team Science:
## Exploring Team Dynamics and Implications for Leadership Practice

**Ralph A. Gigliotti**
*Rutgers University, USA*

**Alexis M. Rotondo**
*Rutgers University, USA*

**Daniel B. Horton**
https://orcid.org/0000-0002-1831-1339
*Rutgers University, USA*

**Nancy E. Reichman**
*Rutgers University, USA*

## ABSTRACT

*Clinical and translational science research collaborations rely on the effectiveness of high-performing teams and on the ability of leaders to stimulate, support, and encourage team effectiveness. The objective of this study was to explore insights related to teamwork, team dynamics, and team collaboration from professionals outside biomedical science that might otherwise be overlooked within the context of traditional disciplinary biomedical training. Five dominant themes emerged from this exploratory qualitative study—communication, trust, culture, learning orientation, and consistency. These themes are relevant for the study and practice of team science and underscore the need for leaders to attend to relationships, processes, and structures in support of team effectiveness. The chapter concludes with recommendations for applied leadership practice that can inform the literature on this topic and could be implemented by biomedical researchers and others engaged in leading translational science and translational research.*

DOI: 10.4018/978-1-6684-8822-5.ch020

## INTRODUCTION

It has become increasingly apparent that high-impact biomedical research requires collaborative cross-disciplinary teamwork and the ability of leaders to stimulate, support, and encourage team effectiveness (Disis & Slattery, 2010; Pitzen et al., 2020; Surratt et al., 2023). The composition of teams and the dynamics that help and hinder team effectiveness are the focus of the emerging field of team science, defined as the empirical examination of "processes by which large and small scientific teams, research centers, and institutes organize, communicate, and conduct research" (Cooke & Hilton, 2015, p. 3) in biomedical sciences. The Clinical and Translational Science Awards (CTSA) program of the National Center for Advancing Translational Sciences (NCATS) seeks to foster team science by engaging "all relevant expertise across disciplines, fields, and professions to produce research that advances translation" and integrating "concepts, theories, methods, technologies, and approaches from the range of disciplines, fields, and professions that can advance research goals" (National Center for Advancing Translational Sciences, n.d.). Recognizing the need to work across the boundaries of disciplinary silos, biomedical researchers have increasingly engaged in such collaborations in order to secure grant funding and conduct high impact research. However, successful transdisciplinary research requires a set of competencies that extend beyond most biomedical researchers' traditional disciplinary training.

Research on the science of team science (SciTS) has typically focused on identifying factors that aid or hinder the formation and functioning of research teams. For example, Gilliland et al. (2019) provided a high-level view of the basic traits or characteristics of a translational scientist independent of the individual's unique area(s) of expertise. These include boundary crosser, domain expert, process innovator, skilled communicator, systems thinker, rigorous researcher, and, most germane to the subject of this article, team player (Gilliland et al., 2019). The authors describe the team player as one who "practices a team science approach by leveraging the strengths and expertise and valuing the contributions of all players on the translational science team" (p. 215). Lotrecchiano et al. (2020) found that much of the literature on team science competencies has focused on the knowledge, skills, and abilities of the individual and not the team and identified sets of both individual and group-related competencies organized around five domains: team communication, collaborative problem-solving, managing team research, facilitating team affect (bonding), and team leadership. The authors emphasized the following individual competencies associated with effective translational science: facilitating awareness and exchange, cognitive openness and intersubjectivity, self-awareness, interdisciplinary research management, passion, and perseverance. They also noted the following team competencies: team roles, team-based communication, shared visioning, understanding complexity, team learning and adaptive behaviors, meeting management, interdisciplinary collaboration, and building trust.

Effective leadership, whether one individual is tasked with formal leadership or leadership responsibilities are distributed across individuals, is well-documented as a key ingredient for research team performance. Consistent with the foundational writing on transformational leadership (Bass, 1985; Burns, 1978; Rafferty & Griffin, 2004), transformational leaders have a profound impact on follower motivation and performance. With a focus on individualized consideration, intellectual stimulation, inspirational motivation, and idealized influence (Bass & Avolio, 1994), transformational leaders have the ability to connect with follower interests and goals, solicit input in ways that leverage the expertise of the team, inspire others towards a desired future state, and establish trust in pursuit of shared goals. As widely documented in the literature, transformational leaders motivate followers to achieve performance that exceeds expectations—in both traditional in-person environments and when working in virtual teams

(Goldthwaite et al., 2023; Greimeil et al, 2023; Grošelj et al., 2021). Although studies have highlighted the importance of transformational leadership for effective team science (Hustead, 2018; Wang et al, 2011), there is no one-size-fits-all leadership approach for enhancing team effectiveness (Cooke & Hilton, 2015). Acknowledging the shifting needs of multidisciplinary teams, Cooke and Hilton suggest that "team science leaders would benefit from developing skills and behaviors that would allow them to practice directive as well as more participative, collaborative, or shared styles of leadership depending on team needs" (p. 137). Research on transformative leadership and the SciTS points to various competencies required to lead highly effective multidisciplinary teams (Lotrecchiano et al., 2020). This exploratory study adds to this literature by investigating what makes teams work across varying disciplines and industries and extracting lessons for effective leadership of high-impact multidisciplinary biomedical research projects.

Although lessons about teamwork from other disciplines and sectors may not translate seamlessly to biomedical research collaborations, the ability to learn about teamwork, team dynamics, and team collaboration from the vantage point of other fields can reveal insights that might otherwise be overlooked within the context of traditional disciplinary training and may be useful for biomedical researchers and others engaged in leading translational science and translational research. With a goal of soliciting input across diverse units, centers, or schools to broaden how biomedical researchers understand and enact the principles of team science, some CTSA hubs have sought expertise from partners outside of biomedical sciences to learn about successful team competencies and to encourage conversations regarding team dynamics. For example, the Wake Forest School of Medicine Clinical and Translational Science Institute partnered with faculty from their School of Business to develop and implement a team science training program for biomedical faculty and research staff (Brower, et al., 2020). Our own New Jersey Alliance for Clinical and Translational Sciences (NJ ACTS) CTSA hub, which includes Rutgers University, Princeton University, New Jersey Institute of Technology, and other institutional, industry, and community organizations, has partnered with the Rutgers Center for Organizational Leadership and the Alan Alda Center for Communicating Science at the School of Communication and Journalism at Stony Brook University to offer a communication-centered perspective that may not be considered in traditional biomedical and health-related disciplines. As noted by Keyton, Ford, and Smith (2008), communication is not merely a component of collaboration; rather, communication is "the essence of collaboration" (p. 376). Communication lies at the heart of transdisciplinary research, and it is through communication that collaborations and the leadership of such efforts can succeed (Ruben & Gigliotti, 2016, 2017).

In the spirit of deepening understanding of the study and practice of team science across disciplines, this paper focuses on a unique initiative sponsored by the team science core of NJ ACTS—a seminar series entitled "Secrets of Successful Team Building: What Can Academia Learn from Non-Academia?" This series featured input from invited guests outside of biomedical research and, in many cases, beyond academia to learn from team leaders and members representing diverse fields and industries about their strategies for building, leading, and working on successful teams. The premise was that learning about experiences in teamwork from a variety of settings and perspectives could reveal new insights and ideas about successful teamwork and leadership that might directly or indirectly translate to biomedical research settings. In this paper, we describe this initiative, highlight the themes and practical lessons about teams and teamwork that emerged and how they correspond to team science competencies identified in the literature to date, and explore the implications for applied leadership practice.

## MATERIALS AND METHODS

The seminar series, launched in April 2021, consisted of six bi-monthly events, each of which featured a team or speaker from a different industry, organization, or field where collaborative teamwork is essential. The virtual seminars featured team leaders and members from athletics, biotechnology, aerospace, architecture, performing arts, and cybersecurity to learn about the formation of teams and the ways in which these teams operate in pursuit of shared goals. Each session was organized around five specific questions that presenters were asked to address (Table 1). The sessions were recorded, professionally edited, and published on the NJ ACTS website for general viewership.

*Table 1. Teamwork seminar questions*

| | |
|---|---|
| 1 | Academia has long rewarded individual accomplishment over team success (e.g., principal authorship and Principal Investigator status on grants are highly rewarded for promotion and raises). In your industry or sector, how do you incentivize team members to work for the good of the team and not just their individual success? How do you attempt to strike the right balance? |
| 2 | How do you balance talent and toxicity when you have a team member who is very valuable because he/she brings needed expertise to the endeavor but creates a difficult work environment for other team members? |
| 3 | How do you maintain team integrity as individuals enter and leave the team? How do you maintain team productivity during such transitions? |
| 4 | Do you have specific processes for communication and conflict resolution when problems arise that can affect everyone on a team? What works and what doesn't work? |
| 5 | What do you see as the greatest challenges in leading a team? |

To identify the emergent themes from the seminar series, our research team engaged in a systematic approach to qualitatively analyze the data. Initially, we reviewed and transcribed the content of the videos, compiled the key messages and statements into an Excel spreadsheet, and synthesized the material using several rounds of open coding to identify central themes and supporting evidence. Using a constant comparative method (Glaser & Strauss, 1967), we sorted through the raw data and organized responses into groupings with similar themes. We then examined the items within and across groups and identified five dominant themes and multiple sub-themes related to effective team dynamics. We also extracted various practical lessons from the panel conversations that complement the prominent themes. Finally, we compared the five dominant themes and supporting sub-themes with the other dominant SciTS competency frameworks to explore areas of overlap and uniqueness. This study was approved by the Rutgers University Institutional Review Board.

## RESULTS

The participants of this seminar series drew upon a wide range of experiences in their responses to questions and offered substantive reflections regarding the ways in which they understand and engage in the practice of teamwork. Despite their unique disciplines, professions, and roles, five central themes emerged from the conversations—communication, trust, culture, learning orientation, and consistency—along with multiple sub-themes (see Figure 1 for a summary of the dominant themes and sub-themes and Table

2 for selected illustrative quotes for each of the supporting sub-themes). Given that these themes center on effective team dynamics and emerged from the narratives and examples offered in response to a set of shared questions, there is some expected overlap and interdependence across themes.

*Table 2. Selected quotations*

| Theme | Subtheme With Selected Quotation |
|---|---|
| Communication | **Open Lines of Communication**<br>"Ask, don't assume." - *Aerospace*<br>**Open-Mindedness**<br>"There (are) a lot of preconceived notions that we come into conversation with, and we can sometimes miss what the other is trying to communicate." – *Architecture*<br>**Active Listening**<br>"Active listening is important. We tend to put our own filters and judgement on what others are saying to us." – *Architecture*<br>"Communication occurs at the ear of the listener." – *Architecture*<br>**Feedback**<br>"Use conflicts as teaching opportunities. Most often everyone wants to learn how to do things right, so exploring where things went wrong brings a lot of value." – *Architecture*<br>**Follow-Up**<br>"Follow-up is very important, sometimes people will seem fine to make their managers happy but will be silently brewing." – *Biotechnology*<br>**Transparency**<br>"Having a culture of transparency builds trust in leadership." – *Cybersecurity* |
| Trust | **Delegation**<br>"The secret of casting is that once you've cast, your job is to get out of their way and support their process. A bad director is a puppeteer." – *Performing Arts*<br>**Sacrifice**<br>"Having team players who are willing to give up their preferences for the good of the team are vital." – *Performing Arts*<br>**Flexibility**<br>"People must have enough flexibility to maneuver because you trust them, and you must earn their trust for them to rely on you as a leader." – *Architecture*<br>**Engagement**<br>"Believing in your purpose and project can keep a team unified, even through changes and losses." – *Performing Arts* |
| Culture | **Collaboration**<br>"Team success is always sweeter than the individual." – *Athletics*<br>**Unification**<br>"Team success and individual success are not mutually exclusive." – *Cybersecurity*<br>**Sense of Belonging**<br>"Without teamwork, there is a near 0% chance of success. The patients need us, so we must have extreme dependency and trust in each other." – *Biotechnology*<br>**Equality**<br>"It is very important to have the same set of standards for all, and to never choose favorites." – *Biotechnology*<br>**Motivation**<br>"Stop to smell the accomplishments, both teamwide and on an individual level." – *Aerospace*<br>**Agency**<br>"Communicating and collaborating with so many people should allow some freedom of other opinions, thoughts, and feelings." – *Performing Arts* |

*continues on following page*

*Table 2. Continued*

| Theme | Subtheme With Selected Quotation |
|---|---|
| Learning Orientation | **Mentorship**<br>"Involve everyone in leadership, as a collective property." – *Performing Arts*<br>"We make sure to have enough mentorship happening that there will always be backfill for when someone leaves." – *Cybersecurity*<br>"Everyone is incentivized to mentor any new hires because you want to always be working with the best." – *Cybersecurity*<br>**Willingness to Learn**<br>"What comes along with being a good mentor is being mentored"<br>– *Aerospace*<br>**Curiosity**<br>"Someone may suggest something, and another will vehemently disagree – a third will say "let's try it". That is important that we test these things to see if they do work. Someone may hate their own idea, or others may find their own spin on it." – *Performing Arts*<br>**Self-Awareness**<br>"All team members can lead in some way, and as a leader you should aim to find everyone's leadership strengths." – *Performing Arts*<br>"Leaders must come with the same attitude they want their players to have." – *Athletics*<br>**Seeking Understanding**<br>"Seek to understand before seeking to be understood." – *Biotechnology* |
| Consistency | **Routines and Schedules**<br>"Call sheets are distributed to give everyone a schedule, but also short-term goals. This keeps everyone on the same page and reinforces this notion of a joint endeavor." – *Performing Arts*<br>**Goal Setting**<br>"Tracking goals and sticking with them is important, as well as keeping accurate perspectives based on reality over desired outcome." – *Athletics*<br>"There is a goal cycle that balances team and individual accomplishments, as well as end of the year bonuses to incentivize." – *Cybersecurity*<br>**Role Clarity**<br>"If you are repeatedly defining roles and keeping an open dialogue, it allows for easier onboarding and loss of team members." – *Architecture*<br>"Clearly defined roles on the team and personal ownership of these components builds camaraderie, which is critical to project success." – *Architecture*<br>"We build in some degree of redundancy and awareness of everyone's role and implement something similar to a succession plan." – *Biotechnology*<br>"Having a solid bench that can replace individuals that leave helps to maintain team integrity." – *Cybersecurity*<br>**Expectation Setting**<br>"Communication, validation, and understanding of expectations are the main foundations for teamwork." – *Aerospace*<br>"It is important to set the culture and expectations and put it in writing."<br>– *Aerospace*<br>"Teamwork isn't that hard, it just needs to constantly be addressed."<br>– *Aerospace*<br>**Accountability**<br>"Conflicts should always be addressed early and often, bringing the individuals back to the team vision and expectations to hold them accountable." – *Athletics* |

*Figure 1. Emergent themes and sub-themes*

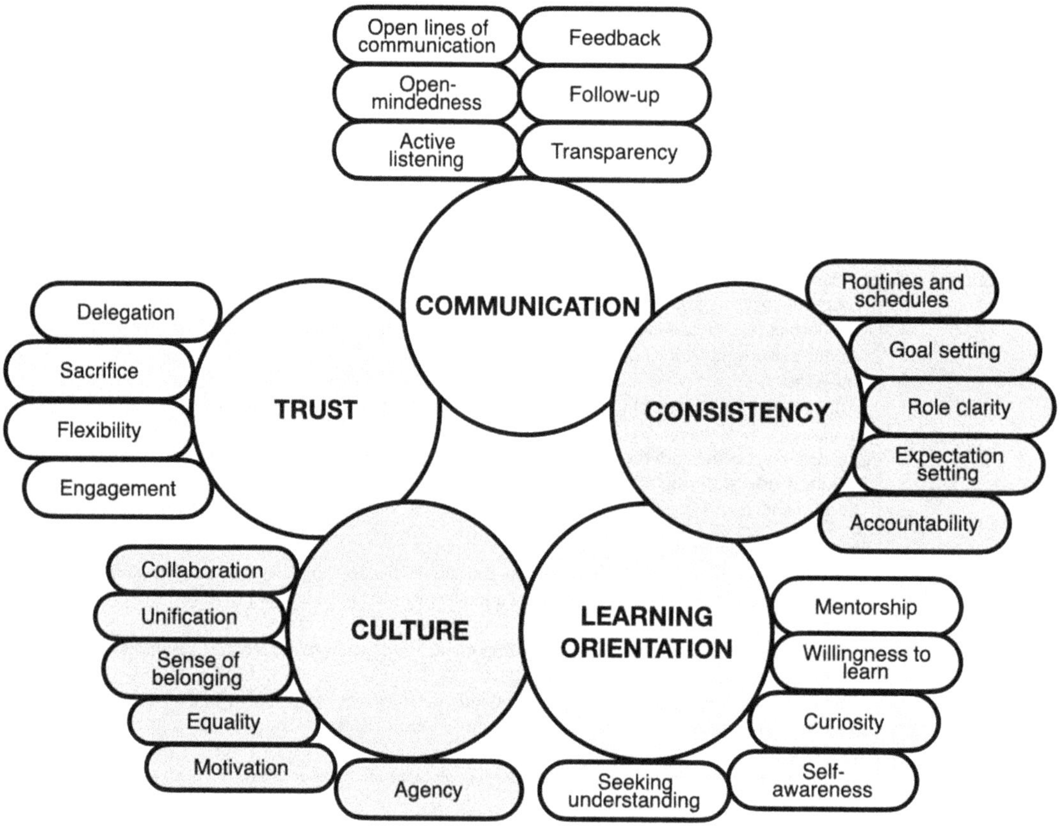


## Communication

The theme of communication centered on interactions among team members and with team leaders. All panels stressed the importance of communication for the cultivation, development, and performance of teams. Relevant sub-themes included open lines of communication, open-mindedness, active listening, feedback, follow-up, and transparency. Stressing the importance of open-mindedness, one professional in the architecture industry noted, "we tend to put our own filters and judgement on what others are saying to us; there (are) a lot of preconceived notions that we come into conversation with, and we can sometimes miss what the other is trying to communicate." The ability to understand the perspective of others and come to a shared understanding is critical for effective team performance. The value of communication was a recurring point of emphasis of panelists across disciplines when leaders need to respond to questions regarding team conflict. As an aerospace professional noted, "where there are people, there will be conflict," and as noted by this individual and the team from biotechnology, there is value in "separating the person from the issue." When addressing conflict or engaging in difficult conversations, a leader in cybersecurity argued that the ability to personalize the communication based on the unique style and preferences of others can contribute to a more effective dialogue, make the task run far more smoothly, and ultimately contribute to a culture of transparency and psychological safety for members of the team. Discussing the value of feedback and follow-up, this individual noted that "If there are people causing issues, we must have those courageous conversations with them. Sometimes they're unaware of their behavior, and that is enough to cause a change. Sometimes it doesn't work, so then a performance improvement plan must be implemented; if that doesn't work, they're gone."

## Trust

Unlike groups of loosely connected individuals, teams consist of interconnected and interdependent individuals and require trust among members and in team leaders to optimize performance. Some of the sub-themes associated with trust included delegation, sacrifice, flexibility, and engagement. Referring to experiences in working with others in a chamber orchestra, one of the panelists highlighted the importance of "having team players who are willing to give up their preferences for the good of the team." Another panelist from the architecture sector noted that: "People must have enough flexibility to maneuver because you trust them, and you must earn their trust for them to rely on you as a leader." The ability to earn and maintain trust appears to be a core competency for both ensuring team synergy and effectively leading teams. Interdisciplinary teams bring together individuals from diverse backgrounds who possess unique perspectives, goals, expectations, skills, and disciplinary expertise. This theme of trust reinforces an important point noted by many of the respondents—that the work of a team can almost never be performed solely by one person, and that by leaning on one another and working together to produce a result, the whole remains greater than the sum of its parts.

## Culture

The theme of culture permeated the discussions, with supporting sub-themes of collaboration, unification, sense of belonging, equality, motivation, and agency. As an athletics coach noted, "team success is always sweeter than the individual," and as the cybersecurity expert described, "team success and individual success are not mutually exclusive." The ability to contribute to a greater goal can help to sustain, motivate, and inspire the members of a team. As multiple panelists noted, the experience of working on a team can be more fulfilling and rewarding if leaders attend to issues of team culture. Some of the strategies for building a cohesive culture were discussed, included recognizing individuals for their contributions, celebrating individual and team accomplishments, ensuring consistent and equitable standards, and creating an environment to support open and honest communication.

## Learning Orientation

The fourth dominant theme to emerge from the panel conversations was the importance of team leaders and members adopting a learning orientation. Unlike the theme of communication, which involves interactions with others, this learning orientation focuses more specifically on one's individual mindset and the ways in which one approaches interpersonal and team dynamics from a position of curiosity. As described by Senge (2006), successful groups consist of "people [who] continually expand their capacity to create the results they truly desire, where new and expansive patterns of thinking are nurtured, where collective aspiration is set free, and where people are continually learning to see the whole together" (p. 3). The panelists focused on several sub-themes that speak to the importance of cultivating a learning perspective, including self-awareness, seeking understanding, mentorship, willingness to learn, and curiosity. Panelists working in settings as diverse as athletics and biotechnology highlighted the importance of building awareness of both the self and organization. As one of the performing arts panelists noted, "the idea of keeping an open mind...goes a long way to solve many conflicts, before they even arise." Recalling one of Covey's (2004) seven habits of effective leadership, effective teams rely on the ability of members to "seek first to understand before seeking to be understood" (p. 196).

### Consistency

Another dominant theme was the importance of consistency in relation to team policies, procedures, roles, and practices. Supporting sub-themes included routines and schedules, role clarity, goal setting, expectation setting, and accountability. The broad theme of consistency captures the managerial and organizational behaviors that allow for an efficient, organized, and coordinated approach to team activities. For example, as a filmmaker described: "Call sheets are distributed to give everyone a schedule but also short-term goals. This keeps everyone on the same page and reinforces this notion of a joint endeavor." As described from the architecture perspective: "Clearly defined roles on the team and personal ownership of these components builds camaraderie, which is critical to project success." Teams and their members may thrive with an awareness of roles and expectations, along with a mechanism for pursuing individual and collective goals in a coordinated manner. Finally, as several respondents recognized, a consistent and purposeful approach to setting and incentivizing goals and expectations is critical for effective team leadership and performance.

## DISCUSSION

The five dominant themes that emerged from this exploratory study—communication, trust, culture, learning orientation, and consistency—may be viewed as imperatives for the study, practice, and leadership of team science. These attributes have been associated with high-performing teams and, when not heeded, may be the cause of blame for team dysfunction. Leadership plays an important role in helping to build and cultivate teams that support these five imperatives. Described as the process of social influence, those engaged in the practice of formal or informal leadership help to model what is both accepted and expected in these settings (Gigliotti et al., 2017; Gigliotti & Goldthwaite, 2021). Despite the enthusiasm for crossing disciplinary boundaries in pursuit of team science, barriers to the success of such efforts can be formidable. For example, tensions and challenges that are difficult to overcome often stem from "ontological and epistemological differences and power inequalities between the disciplines" (Thorpe, et al., 2020, p. 362). Limited by existing institutional and organizational structures, interdisciplinary and translational collaborations require a reimagined organization that can motivate and support such initiatives (Rhoten, 2004; Sa´, 2007; Whitmer, et al, 2010). A review of the literature on interdisciplinarity by Siedlok et al. (2015) notes, "a gap exists in our knowledge of how such collaborations are accomplished and the kinds of emergent organizational forms in which it occurs" (p. 96). In addition to organizational limitations, other factors contribute to the failure of interdisciplinary efforts; including leadership deficits, mismatched skill sets, and dysfunction in project organization or team dynamics (Brown et al., 2019; Gehlert, 2010; Klein & Porter, 1990; Siedlok & Hibbert, 2014).

Given the challenges and potential barriers associated with team science, leaders in biomedical research can turn to successful team efforts across disciplines for additional insights into the subject. Representing a range of disciplines outside of the biomedical sciences, the findings from this study reinforce at least two major ideas. In much the same way as there is no one best way to lead such teams, there is no one size fits all approach to effective team science, although certain principles appear to be universal. As such, an approach that is grounded in established principles, but at the same time remains flexible, is warranted. Secondly, effective team science requires an understanding of self, other, and context. Straddling theory and practice, the emergent themes from our seminar series and the recommendations put forward by the panelists capture the challenges and opportunities associated with team dynamics. As illustrated in the Figure 1, communication, trust, culture, learning orientation, and consistency are crucial branches that allow strongly rooted teams to flourish and withstand the pressures that might otherwise jeopardize effective team performance.

Key competencies for translational science have previously been described in the clinical and translational science literature (Gilliland et al., 2019; Lotrecchiano et al., 2020). These existing frameworks place an emphasis on the skills of the individual researcher and the ways in which the researcher engages with others to advance the goals of the team. The results from this study align nicely with these existing frameworks, and the major themes to emerge from these panel discussions appear broad enough to capture the various practices documented in these alternative frameworks. Lotrecchiano et al. (2020) noted the importance of trustworthiness as a critical feature of all individual and team-based domains, echoing the theme of trust and related subthemes (delegation, sacrifice, flexibility, engagement) captured in our study. The emphasis on communication, trust, culture, learning orientation, and consistency resonate across the fields, disciplines, and industries represented in this exploratory study and may provide a useful foundation for future research exploring team science and team dynamics from both within *and beyond* biomedical science. This ability to extend our perspective beyond traditional disciplines can enrich the study, practice, and leadership of team science, introduce new ways of approaching shared challenges, and facilitate the integration of lessons learned from other sectors into the core activities of clinical and translational science.

The featured seminar series was but one component of the general inductive approach our NJ ACTS team science core has engaged in to identify central competencies for effective team science. Additional initiatives include a mini-conference with a diverse group of experts from across the country (including professors of English and sociology) featuring approaches to reward team science in promotion and tenure processes; virtual modules from the Alan Alda Center for Communicating Science on the topics of communication essentials, creating connections, and writing for your audience; and a seminar series that spotlights scientific teams and leaders across the consortium that have secured funding through one of the federal grant mechanisms designed to foster interdisciplinary, high-impact research—e.g., R01 (research grants) with multiple principal investigators (MPIs), U01 (Research Grants - Cooperative Agreements), and P-series (Program Project Grants and Center Grants). We also developed a semester-long team science course that includes readings; guest lectures from scholars and practitioners across NJ ACTS, other universities, and other sectors (industry and government); guided discussions; and opportunities for experiential learning. In addition, we launched a Team Science microcredential badge to encourage learners to explore team science and a consulting service to support current and prospective interdisciplinary research teams. Moving forward, we intend to explore additional strategies for integrating current SciTS research into our programs and service offerings, with a careful and coordinated emphasis on communication, trust, culture, learning orientation, and consistency.

## Recommendations for Applied Practice

The dominant themes from this project have the potential to inform how leaders think about, engage in, and contribute to the practice of team science. As concepts, these themes reflect some of the dominant thinking on the dynamics and practices associated with effective teams. The themes discussed in this chapter tend to underscore the importance of relationships, processes, and structures to support team efforts. Furthermore, the focus on communication, trust, culture, learning orientation, and consistency sit at the nexus of self, other, and context—units of analysis that come together and inform one another as teams engage in their core activities and practices. The themes introduced in this chapter also reflect the spirit of transformational leadership and the need for leaders to co-construct with team members a shared vision and to tie this vision to actionable steps that might be fully implemented (Yukl, 1999).

In addition to reflecting dominant thinking on the theoretical concepts and principles that contribute to their understanding of team dynamics, the panelists shed light on a wide range of recommendations for applied practice that can inform the literature on this topic and can be implemented by teams across the biomedical sciences and those engaged in leading these teams. Using the five dominant themes as a guiding framework, we mapped these recommendations to those themes (Table 3). Although some of the anecdotes and proposed strategies include unique terms, concepts, and modes of engagement that are sector-specific, the recommended practices can be broadened into actionable strategies that transcend fields. For example, as one of the coaches noted, "Top players can help their teammates competing in lower brackets carry equipment." As one of the architects described, "The inspiration of architects is the final, tangible result, which takes a team." Finally, as one of the performing artists proposed, "The team appreciating their beautiful joint product is great for the team culture." Although these recommendations might reflect one's unique frame of reference and may directly align with the vocabulary and context unique to one's discipline or professional occupation, leaders in biomedical research could translate these insights and recommendations into actionable strategies that bear relevance for the enactment of team science.

## Limitations

In the spirit of describing the "art of team science," we acknowledge the inherent subjectivity of the responses to the question prompts. We also acknowledge that our coding and organization of the themes may not directly align with the ways in which the panelists may have categorized these focal themes, and that some of the panel participants may not consistently demonstrate these practices across all team settings and contexts. Rather, by curating and consolidating varied perspectives on team effectiveness, as opposed to observing team dynamics through an experiential research design, the synthesis of emergent themes to surface from this seminar series reflects the socially constructed, improvisational, and variable dynamics of team functioning.

*Table 3. Practical lessons*

| Theme | Practical Lessons |
|---|---|
| Communication | • Self-awareness sometimes is the problem, so frank discussions and reminders about the value of combined effort can help. (Biotechnology)<br>• It is important to listen to issues when they arise, pick up on cues, and address problems as soon as possible. (Architecture)<br>• If you are not active in remedying toxic situations, you are part of the problem. (Architecture)<br>• If there are people causing issues, we must have those "courageous conversations" with them. Sometimes they're unaware of their behavior, and that is enough to cause a change. Sometimes that doesn't work, so a performance improvement plan must be implemented. If that doesn't work, they're gone. (Cybersecurity)<br>• Toxicity must be addressed, and not balanced. We cannot gloss over it. We must talk about it until we figure it out. (Performing Arts)<br>• When transitions occur, maintain solid communication, give time, and ensure everyone's needs are met and satisfied. (Biotech)<br>• Approach the conflict without a pre-determined view, with no assumptions, and talk to everyone involved; separate the person from the event - once the person becomes the issue, then you are stuck. (Biotech)<br>• What doesn't work: Ignoring the problem, but also not jumping into it too early and making the issue bigger than it is. (Biotech)<br>• Follow-up is very important, sometimes people will seem fine to make their managers happy but will be silently brewing. (Biotechnology)<br>• Leaders must be capable of having hard conversations and addressing the issues. There must be an action plan and follow-up, and it is important to focus on problematic behavior rather than the whole person. (Aerospace)<br>• Ask, don't assume. (Aerospace)<br>• Technology allows for communication that is consistent. (Architecture)<br>• Active listening is important. We tend to put our own filters and judgement on what others are saying to us. There are a lot of preconceived notions that we come into conversation with, and we can sometimes miss what the other is trying to communicate. (Architecture)<br>• Never scold; rather, use conflicts as teaching opportunities. Most often people want to learn how to do things right, so exploring where things went wrong brings a lot of value—if done with sensitivity. (Architecture)<br>• Communication occurs at the ear of the listener. There is much work that goes into really ensuring someone gets your message and understands it, and the listener must be careful to not judge. (Architecture)<br>• Keeping an open mind and listening to each other goes a long way to solve many conflicts before they even arise. (Performing Arts)<br>• Approach negative feedback or changes from the perspective of those we're communicating it to. Anticipate the questions they'll ask and their reactions and be prepared for those. Deciding on group meetings vs. one-on-ones is also important because some people will have different reactions to news and be impacted differently. (Cybersecurity)<br>• Putting yourself in the person's shoes helps them receive bad news. (Cybersecurity)<br>• It is important to keep up with everyone individually, which is a constant work in progress. (Athletics) |
| Trust | • Talk about sacrifice to achieve team goals from day one. (Athletics)<br>• Encourage relationships and trust among team members. (Biotechnology)<br>• Years are spent together on teams, so there must be relationships and trust between members. (Architecture)<br>• Encourage flexibility. (Athletics)<br>• It is important to match your leadership approach to your team, some people require micromanaging, and some benefit more from being assigned tasks and trusted to perform them independently. (Aerospace)<br>• It can help to communicate the issues upward to higher management too, to spread the issue out to multiple people so you don't need to tackle it alone. (Aerospace)<br>• Keeping everyone engaged, which requires you to know them well and have a connection with all of your team members. (Architecture)<br>• Building and earning trust work in both directions. (Architecture)<br>• Being able to give your trust to someone requires mutual respect. (Architecture) |

*continues on following page*

*Table 3. Continued*

| Theme | Practical Lessons |
|---|---|
| Culture | • Stress that we need individual "stars" but that everyone must work together, and nobody can do it alone. (Athletics)<br>• Build a culture of equality—e.g., top players can help their teammates competing in lower brackets carry equipment. Encourage, spotlight, and praise small but important things like that. (Athletics)<br>• Use standards based on team performance - individual performance is incentivized, but just as important is the idea that improvement makes the whole team better, by raising our average—even if you are last. (Athletics)<br>• Make the message clear that every part of our work is so important and diverse, which necessitates teamwork; without teamwork, there is a near 0% chance of success. (Biotechnology)<br>• Give time and visibility to individuals in less glamorous roles. (Biotechnology)<br>• Stress that when we have succeeded, everyone can be proud of their individual contributions. (Biotechnology)<br>• Foster a strong institutional culture. Motivation is key, everyone wants to know why we do what we do and where we are going with it. Having that purpose and end goal, and reminding the team of that, makes teamwork come more easily. (Biotechnology)<br>• Leveraging and celebrating strengths helps to motivate the team be the best it can be. (Biotechnology)<br>• Stop to smell the accomplishments, both teamwide and on an individual level. (Aerospace)<br>• Encourage team members to recognize the accomplishments of their peers, which is important for building a united team front. (Aerospace)<br>• The inspiration of architects is the final, tangible result, which takes a team—stress that message. (Architecture)<br>• Motivating people is achieved through recognition of individual contributions within the team. (Architecture)<br>• The team appreciating their beautiful joint product is great for the team culture. (Performing Arts)<br>• Have the same set of standards for all and never choose favorites. (Biotechnology)<br>• Make clear that talent will never outweigh teamwork. (Cybersecurity)<br>• It helps to have collaborators that embody healing and care about mental health. (Performing Arts)<br>• Remind everyone of the common aim. (Performing Arts)<br>• Keep the team motivated and minimize the burden on others when someone leaves or is out. (Biotechnology)<br>• Shared beliefs in your purpose and project (group culture) can keep a team unified, even through changes and losses. (Performing Arts)<br>• Stress that the collaboration is the most important aspect of what you're doing, and everyone in the room is a part of that process. Performing Arts)<br>• Building success through failure is very difficult but important. (Athletics)<br>• Motivation is always the biggest challenge, keeping the team on task, focused, and working toward a goal. Communication, validation, and understanding of expectations are the main foundations for teamwork. With relationship building and these foundations, teamwork isn't that hard, it just needs to constantly be addressed. (Aerospace)<br>• The hardest part is the interaction of the varying personality types and backgrounds that can sometimes clash. Through coaching and communication, we can either acclimate people into our culture, or remove them if they do not fit with the team. Having a cohesive team that can put their best foot forward for our clients is so crucial. (Cybersecurity) |
| Learning Orientation | • It is important to remember that everyone wants to do well and be successful, even if their actions or words don't seem to reflect that. (Athletics)<br>• Pairing teammates up to have one mentor the other, so that the mentee's success can be at least partially attributed to the mentor. (Athletics)<br>• Leaders must come with the same attitude they want their players to have. (Athletics)<br>• Identifying strengths and playing them up can help players naturally work in a way that benefits the team by making them feel better about themselves. (Athletics)<br>• Mentoring and cross-training helps to build team depth and synergy even as new members join. (Aerospace)<br>• Make sure to have enough mentorship happening that there will always be backfill for when someone leaves. (Cybersecurity)<br>• Be willing to learn from people beneath you in the hierarchy. (Aerospace)<br>• Wide demographics in terms of age has posed a challenge because every generation has a different value and way of viewing performance and job satisfaction. There is massive merit in understanding diverse views. (Biotechnology) |

*continues on following page*

*Table 3. Continued*

| Theme | Practical Lessons |
|---|---|
| Consistency | • Clearly defined roles on the team and personal ownership of those components build comradery, which is critical to success. (Architecture)<br>• Short-term goals are key. Call sheets are distributed to give everyone a schedule, but these provide short term goals. This keeps everyone on the same page and reinforces the notion of a joint endeavor. (Performing Arts)<br>• Set goals that balance team and individual accomplishments and reward effective teamwork. (Cybersecurity)<br>• Build in some degree of redundancy and awareness of others' roles and implement something similar to a succession plan. (Cybersecurity)<br>• Establish a culture and put it in writing. This includes expectations, philosophy, and team culture. As individuals join, reinforce this culture both with the new person and existing team members to manage expectations and encourage mutual responsibility. (Aerospace)<br>• Consistently make roles clear and keep an open dialogue; this allows for easier onboarding and loss of team members and provides a clear understanding of where slack must be picked up or how roles can be delegated. (Architecture)<br>• Build in some redundancy, e.g., always have multiple people with various skillsets. (Biotechnology)<br>• Make sure that everything is communicated as things happen and making sure that standards are met. Track goals and stick with them. (Athletics)<br>• Put the right people in the right place at the right time (Architecture) |

## CONCLUSION

The findings from this study add to the evolving knowledge of the science of team science through insights and lessons from leaders and other professionals outside biomedical science that might otherwise be overlooked in traditional biomedical training and research settings. The recognition, teaching, and fostering of communication, trust, culture, learning orientation, and consistency among team leaders, team members, and trainees may enhance the dynamics and performance of research collaborations. These approaches may also enhance the practice of transformational leadership. As an exploratory study, the findings from this work can inform future research on team science across biomedical and non-biomedical teams and may be applied as a framework for studying the experiential dynamics of team science. We invite researchers to further consider the ways in which the five themes from this study interact with one another and play out in interdisciplinary team science and to continue to solicit input from leaders and professionals outside of biomedical sciences to inform this work. Furthermore, future studies may also take a closer look at the ways in which transformational leaders support and foster high-performing teams across a diversity of team settings. By expanding upon the findings of this study and by investigating the art of team science across a broader range of non-biomedical disciplines, we may be able to see which of these five practices are common as leaders and their teams continue to adapt to a post-pandemic work and learning environment, and to determine which of these practices are most critical for the development, cultivation, and effectiveness of diverse transdisciplinary teams.

## ACKNOWLEDGMENT

The authors would like to thank the seminar participants as well as Judith Argon, Rachana Bhatt, Pamela Dahlen, Cassandra Burrows, William Jester, Biju Parekkadan, and Reynold Panettieri for their support of the seminar series. This research was supported by the National Center for Advancing Translational Sciences, a component of the National Institutes of Health under award number UL1TR003017 (Gigliotti, Rotondo, Horton, Reichman) and the Robert Wood Johnson Foundation through its support of the Child Health Institute of New Jersey under Grant 74260 (Reichman).

## REFERENCES

Applegate, J. (Eds.), *Leadership in healthcare and public health*. Press Books.

Bass, B. M. (1985). *Leadership and performance beyond expectations*. Free Press.

Bass, B. M., & Avolio, B. J. (1994). Improving organizational effectiveness through transformational leadership. *Sage (Atlanta, Ga.)*.

Brower, H. H., Nicklas, B. J., Nader, M. A., Trost, L. M., & Miller, D. P. (2020). Creating effective academic research teams: Two tools borrowed from business practice. *Journal of Clinical and Translational Science*, *5*(1), e74. doi:10.1017/cts.2020.553 PMID:33948292

Brown, R., Werbeloff, L., & Raven, R. (2019). Interdisciplinary research and impact. *Global Challenges (Hoboken, NJ)*, *3*(4), 1900020. Advance online publication. doi:10.1002/gch2.201900020 PMID:31565373

Burns, J. M. (1978). *Leadership*. Harper & Row.

Cooke, N. J., & Hilton, M. L. (Eds.). (2015). *National Research Council. Enhancing the effectiveness of team science*. The National Academies Press.

Covey, S. R. (2004). *The seven habits of highly effective people: Powerful lessons in personal change (15th Anniversary)*. Free Press.

Disis, M. L., & Slattery, J. T. (2010). the road we must take: Multidisciplinary team science. *Science Translational Medicine*, *2*(22), 22cm9. Advance online publication. doi:10.1126citranslmed.3000421 PMID:20374998

Feller, I. (2002). New organizations, old cultures: Strategy and implementation of interdisciplinary programs. *Research Evaluation*, *11*(2), 109–116. doi:10.3152/147154402781776862

Gehlert, S., Murray, A., Sohmer, D., McClintock, M., Conzen, S., & Olopade, O. (2010). The importance of transdisciplinary collaborations for understanding and resolving health disparities. *Social Work in Public Health*, *25*(3), 408–422. doi:10.1080/19371910903241124 PMID:20446184

Gigliotti, R. A., & Goldthwaite, C. (2021). *Leadership in academic health centers: Core concepts and critical cases*. Kendall Hunt.

Gigliotti, R. A., Ruben, B. D., & Goldthwaite, C. (2017). *Leadership: Communication and social influence in personal and professional settings*. Kendall Hunt.

Gilliland, C. T., White, J., Gee, B., Kreeftmeijer-Vegter, R., Bietrix, F., Ussi, A. E., Hajduch, M., Kocis, P., Chiba, N., Hirasawa, R., Suematsu, M., Bryans, J., Newman, S., Hall, M. D., & Austin, C. P. (2019). The Fundamental Characteristics of a Translational Scientist. *ACS Pharmacology & Translational Science, 2*(3), 213–216. doi:10.1021/acsptsci.9b00022 PMID:32259057

Glaser, B., & Strauss, A. (1967). *The discovery of grounded theory: Strategies for qualitative research*. AldineTransaction.

Goldthwaite, C., Gigliotti, R. A., & Spear, S. E. (2023). Leadership in digital contexts. Kendall Hunt.

Greimel, N. S., Kanbach, D. K., & Chelaru, M. (2023). Virtual teams and transformational leadership: An integrative literature review and avenues for further research. *Journal of Innovation & Knowledge, 8*(2), 100351. Advance online publication. doi:10.1016/j.jik.2023.100351

Grošelj, M., Černe, M., Penger, S., & Grah, B. (2021). Authentic and transformational leadership and innovative work behaviour: The moderating role of psychological empowerment. *European Journal of Innovation Management, 24*(3), 677–706. doi:10.1108/EJIM-10-2019-0294

Hustead, E. (2018). Team science and transformational leadership in the healthcare field. Academic Press.

Keyton, J., Ford, D. J., & Smith, F. L. (2008). A mesolevel communicative model of collaboration. *Communication Theory, 18*(3), 376–406. doi:10.1111/j.1468-2885.2008.00327.x

Klein, J. T., & Porter, A. L. (1990). Preconditions for interdisciplinary research. In P. H. Birnbaum, F. A. Rossini, & D. R. Baldwin (Eds.), *International Research Management*. Academic. doi:10.1093/acprof:oso/9780195062526.003.0002

Lotrecchiano, G. R., DiazGranados, D., Sprecher, J., McCormack, W. T., Ranwala, D., Wooten, K., Lackland, D., Billings, H., & Brasier, A. R. (2020). Individual and team competencies in translational teams. *Journal of Clinical and Translational Science, 5*(1), e72. doi:10.1017/cts.2020.551 PMID:33948290

National Center for Advancing Translational Sciences. (n.d.). *Translational science principles*. https://ncats.nih.gov/training-education/translational-science-principles

Pitzen, J. H., Dieter, H. L., Gronseth, D. L., Dahl, A. K., Boyle, V. L., Maran, T., Harper, C. M. Jr, & Gores, G. J. (2020). Transforming the practice of medicine through team science. *Health Research Policy and Systems, 18*(104), 104. Advance online publication. doi:10.118612961-020-00619-4 PMID:32943070

Rafferty, A. H., & Griffin, M. A. (2004). Dimensions of transformational leadership: Conceptual and empirical dimensions. *The Leadership Quarterly, 15*(3), 329–354. doi:10.1016/j.leaqua.2004.02.009

Rhoten, D. R. (2004). *Interdisciplinary research: Trend or transition*. Social Science Research Council. https://items.ssrc.org/from-our-archives/interdisciplinary-research-trend-or-transition/

Ruben, B. D., & Gigliotti, R. A. (2016). Leadership as social influence: An expanded view of leadership communication theory and practice. *Journal of Leadership & Organizational Studies, 23*(4), 467–479. doi:10.1177/1548051816641876

Ruben, B. D., & Gigliotti, R. A. (2017). Communication: Sine qua non of organizational leadership theory and practice. *International Journal of Business Communication*, *54*(1), 12–30. doi:10.1177/2329488416675447

Sa´, C. M. (2007). Interdisciplinary strategies in U.S. research universities. *Higher Education*, *55*(5), 537–552. doi:10.100710734-007-9073-5

Senge, P. (2006). *The fifth discipline: The art and practice of the learning organization* (2nd ed.). Cornerstone.

Siedlok, F., & Hibbert, P. (2014). The organization of interdisciplinary research: Modes, drivers, and barriers. *International Journal of Management Reviews*, *16*(2), 194–210. doi:10.1111/ijmr.12016

Siedlok, F., Hibbert, P., & Sillince, J. (2015). From practice to collaborative community in interdisciplinary research contexts. *Research Policy*, *44*(1), 96–107. doi:10.1016/j.respol.2014.07.018

Surratt, H., Otachi, J., Slade, E., Kern, P., King, V., Kelly, T., & DiPaola, R. (2023). Optimizing team science in an academic medical center: A qualitative examination of investigator perspectives. *Journal of Clinical and Translational Science*, *7*(1), E57. doi:10.1017/cts.2023.3 PMID:37008610

Thorpe, H., Brice, J., Clark, M., & Sims, S. (2020). The transdisciplinary health research apparatus: A Baradian account of knowledge boundaries and beyond. *Health*, *26*(3), 361–384. doi:10.1177/1363459320961429 PMID:33012195

Wang, G., Oh, I.-S., Courtright, S. H., & Colbert, A. E. (2011). Transformational leadership and performance across criteria and levels: A meta-analytic review of 25 years of research. *Group & Organization Management*, *36*(2), 223–270. doi:10.1177/1059601111401017

Whitmer, A., Ogden, L., Lawton, J., Sturner, P., Groffman, P. M., Schneider, L., Hart, D., Halpern, B., Schlesinger, W., Raciti, S., Bettez, N., Ortega, S., Rustad, L., Pickett, S. T. A., & Killilea, M. (2010). The engaged university: Providing a platform for research that transforms society. *Frontiers in Ecology and the Environment*, *8*(6), 314–321. doi:10.1890/090241

Yukl, G. (1999). An evaluation of conceptual weaknesses in transformational and charismatic leadership theories. *The Leadership Quarterly*, *10*(2), 285–305. doi:10.1016/S1048-9843(99)00013-2

# Chapter 21
# The Intersection of Social Entrepreneurship, Sustainability, and Environmental Public Health

**Kevin Richardson**
https://orcid.org/0009-0002-3212-8669
*Capitol Technology University, USA*

**Darrell Norman Burrell**
https://orcid.org/0000-0002-4675-9544
*Capitol Technology University, USA*

## ABSTRACT

*Social entrepreneurship and sustainability are two important concepts that have gained increasing attention in recent years. Social entrepreneurship refers to the process of creating new ventures that address social problems and generate social value. Sustainability, on the other hand, refers to the ability of a system or process to maintain ecological, economic, and social well-being over time. The intersection of social entrepreneurship and sustainability has the potential to drive positive change in society by promoting environmentally sustainable practices, addressing social problems, and creating sustainable business models. In this chapter, the authors explore the intersection of social entrepreneurship and sustainability, with a focus on the contributions of social entrepreneurship to sustainability and environmental public health.*

## INTRODUCTION

Social entrepreneurship and sustainability leadership are two essential concepts that have gained increasing attention in recent years. Social entrepreneurship creates new ventures that address social problems and generate social value (Dees, 1998). Sustainability, on the other hand, refers to the ability

DOI: 10.4018/978-1-6684-8822-5.ch021

of a system or process to maintain ecological, economic, and social well-being over time (Hart, 2005). The intersection of social entrepreneurship and Sustainability has the potential to drive positive change in society by promoting environmentally sustainable practices, addressing social problems, and creating sustainable business models.

The rise of social entrepreneurship and sustainability leadership has become an increasingly important part of social change efforts in today's society. Social entrepreneurs and sustainability leaders are individuals and organizations that create innovative solutions to social, economic, and environmental challenges. These individuals and groups often take risks, experiment with new ideas, and use creative and innovative approaches to address pressing social issues (Hanson, 2020). By providing innovative solutions to social problems, they can create systemic change, which leads to a more equitable and sustainable global society. However, the work of social entrepreneurs and sustainability leaders is often undervalued, and it is often difficult for them to gain access to the resources they need to succeed.

Social entrepreneurship and sustainability leadership are essential for positive social change in society, organizations, and communities. Social entrepreneurs are individuals and organizations that develop new approaches to solving social problems (Hanson, 2020). They often use business principles to create sustainable solutions to social and environmental challenges. They use their knowledge and skills to identify and address gaps in the existing systems and to create new products, services, and organizations that have the potential to make a lasting impact (Hanson, 2020).

Sustainability leaders are individuals and organizations committed to creating a more sustainable world (Hanson, 2020). They use their knowledge, skills, and resources to develop innovative solutions to environmental and social challenges. They often seek to change their communities and organizations and influence local, national, and international policy decisions (Hanson, 2020). They focus on creating long-term solutions that address the underlying causes of environmental and social issues (Hanson, 2020).

Social entrepreneurs and sustainability leaders often play an essential role in developing a more equitable and sustainable global society (Hanson, 2020). They are often the first to recognize and address existing system gaps and provide innovative solutions to social and environmental challenges (Hanson, 2020). Taking risks and experimenting with new ideas can create systemic change, leading to lasting social and environmental improvements (Hanson, 2020).

Social impact is defined as the "creation of a positive, lasting change in the well-being of a community's constituents" (Williamson, 2011). Social entrepreneurs use this concept to change the business sector (Mair & Marti, 2006). OD traditionalists also encourage practitioners to promote positive social change and corporate citizenship (Cummings & Worley, 2008). Measuring this social impact is a challenge recently addressed by the concept of "scaling social impact" (Bradach, 2003). This concept refers to increasing the impact of social-purpose organizations to meet better the magnitude of the social need or problem (Dees, 2008). Managers of social entrepreneurial organizations and the donors and agencies that fund them are interested in learning how to scale social impact to reach a wider population (Bloom & Smith, 2010).

The concept of social entrepreneurship refers to the process of creating innovative solutions to social and environmental problems. It is a form of entrepreneurship that combines the purpose of a traditional for-profit business to create positive social change (Farny & Binder, 2021). Social entrepreneurs identify a need in society, develop a solution to address that need, and then use business principles to create a sustainable and profitable organization that can scale up and reach more people in need. Social entrepreneurs are driven by a desire to bring about positive change and are often passionate about the causes they are working to address (Farny & Binder, 2021).

The intersection of social entrepreneurship and Sustainability has been the subject of increasing attention in recent years (Farny & Binder, 2021). Scholars have highlighted the potential of social entrepreneurship to drive positive change in society by promoting Sustainability (Austin et al., 2006). Social entrepreneurship can contribute to Sustainability in several ways. First, social entrepreneurship can promote environmental Sustainability by creating businesses that use renewable resources, minimize waste and pollution, and promote sustainable production and consumption practices. By promoting sustainable practices, social entrepreneurs can help reduce the environmental impact of business activities and create a more sustainable future for all.

Second, social entrepreneurship can promote social Sustainability by addressing social problems such as poverty, inequality, and exclusion (Mair & Marti, 2006). Social entrepreneurs can create businesses that provide goods and services to underserved communities, such as affordable healthcare, education, and housing (Bansal et al., 2019). Social entrepreneurs can help create a more inclusive and equitable society that benefits all community members by addressing social problems. Third, social entrepreneurship can promote economic Sustainability by creating sustainable business models that generate social and economic value (Mair & Marti, 2006). Social entrepreneurs can create businesses that provide employment opportunities, generate income for local communities, and contribute to local economic development. According to Bansal et al. (2019), by creating sustainable businesses, social entrepreneurs can help build resilient and prosperous communities that can meet the needs of both current and future generations.

While social entrepreneurship has the potential to promote Sustainability, several challenges need to be addressed. One of the main challenges is the need for more clarity around the concept of Sustainability, making it difficult for social entrepreneurs to incorporate Sustainability into their business models. In order to address this challenge, more research is needed to develop a clear and comprehensive framework for Sustainability that social entrepreneurs can easily apply. Another challenge is more funding and support for social entrepreneurship and sustainability initiatives (Mair & Marti, 2006). Social entrepreneurs often face significant financial and institutional barriers when trying to create sustainable businesses, which can limit their impact and Sustainability (Gupta et al., 2020). In order to address this challenge, more funding and support are needed for social entrepreneurship and sustainability initiatives, including government support, philanthropic funding, and private investment.

## Problem Statement

According to Stobierski (2021), 95 percent of workers believe that a company's primary responsibility is maximizing returns for all its stakeholders, not just its shareholders. These stakeholders include the company's employees, customers, and suppliers. According to Stobierski (2021), seventy percent of Americans believe that it is either "somewhat important" or "imperative" for businesses to work toward making the world a better place. According to Stobierski (2021), seventy-seven percent of consumers are motivated to purchase from businesses devoted to improving the world, and seventy-three percent of investors indicate that efforts to enhance the environment and society contribute to their investment decisions. According to Stobierski (2021), only 16 percent of baby boomers and 27 percent of Gen X investors make considerable efforts to understand a company's corporate social responsibility (CSR) procedures. This compares to 41 percent of investors who are millennials. According to Stobierski (2021), more than half of consumers in the United States think businesses must take a stance on significant social, political, and environmental issues.

Sustainability is an essential element of CSR, and organizations increasingly focus on initiatives promoting long-term environmental and social benefits. A survey by the World Business Council for Sustainable Development (2010) found that 83% of companies had adopted sustainability policies, while 86% had adopted specific sustainability goals. Environmental public health is another critical element of CSR initiatives. Organizations are increasingly focusing on initiatives that promote public health and environmental protection. A study by the World Health Organization (2015) found that environmental factors cause 80% of global diseases and that organizations have a role in reducing these negative impacts.

## METHODOLOGY

In order to explore the intersection of social entrepreneurship and Sustainability, we conducted a systematic literature review of academic articles, reports, and case studies on the topic. We searched several databases, including Google Scholar, Scopus, and Web of Science, using keywords such as "Corporate Social Responsibility," "social entrepreneurship," "sustainability," "green entrepreneurship," "environmental public health," and "social innovation." We also searched the websites of relevant organizations, such as the Schwab Foundation for Social Entrepreneurship and Ashoka, for relevant case studies and reports. We selected articles and reports based on their relevance to the topic and the quality of their research methods. We analyzed the selected articles and reports using thematic analysis, which involved identifying key themes and patterns in the data (Byrne, 2022). We coded the data based on these themes and patterns and then organized the data into categories to facilitate our analysis. The themes that emerged from the literature review were:

- Social Entrepreneurship and Environmental Sustainability
- Social Entrepreneurship and Social Sustainability
- Social Entrepreneurship and Economic Sustainability
- Challenges and Barriers to social entrepreneurship and Sustainability
- Corporate social responsibility
- Community change and organizational change

### Contexts From the Literature

Although social entrepreneurship and sustainability leadership can significantly impact society and community social change, these leaders face many challenges and opportunities (Kamaludin et al., 2021). One of the most significant challenges is the need for access to resources. Social entrepreneurs often need help accessing the capital and resources they need to succeed, limiting their ability to develop innovative solutions and create lasting change (Kamaludin et al., 2021). In addition, cultural and institutional barriers often prevent social entrepreneurs and sustainability leaders from making an impact.

Many existing systems and institutions are designed to maintain the status quo, making it difficult for social entrepreneurs to introduce new ideas and create meaningful change (Kamaludin et al., 2021). Finally, political and economic challenges often limit the impact of social entrepreneurship and sustainability leadership. Political and economic systems often favor the status quo, making it difficult for social entrepreneurs and sustainability leaders to create the necessary systemic changes (Kamaludin et al., 2021).

For social entrepreneurship and sustainability leadership to have a lasting impact on society and community social change, governments, businesses, and communities need to support these leaders. Governments can provide financial and other support to social entrepreneurs and sustainability leaders. They can also create policies and regulations that encourage innovation and support the development of new solutions to social and environmental challenges (Kamaludin et al., 2021).

Businesses can also be essential in supporting social entrepreneurs and sustainability leaders. Businesses can provide financial support, mentorship, and access to resources. They can also use their platform to raise awareness about social and environmental issues and to encourage their customers and employees to support social entrepreneurs and sustainability leaders (Kamaludin et al., 2021). Communities can provide platforms for collaboration, mentorship, and networking. They can also create opportunities for social entrepreneurs and sustainability leaders to share their stories and connect with potential customers and supporters (Kamaludin et al., 2021).

The trend of intense competition and a rapidly changing environment calls for Change Management (CM) leadership approaches (Cameron & Green, 2019). There are different perspectives on how change is viewed and managed, which can be seen as an opportunity or a problem (Cameron & Green, 2019).

On the other hand, the traditional view perceives the purpose of change as a way of stopping, slowing down, or disrupting a planned change. With this knowledge, change agents can anticipate resistance and make the necessary interventions (Cameron & Green, 2019). It is also vital for organizations to execute their strategies effectively for a competitive advantage; this includes creating change programs that deliver the strategy and allocating and managing resources to execute the change programs.

## Environmental Public Health

Environmental public health is the study of how environmental factors, such as air pollution, chemicals, and other contaminants, impact the health of individuals and communities (Abad-Segura et al., 2019). It is a field of research that focuses on preventing and controlling health risks from environmental hazards. Environmental public health aims to reduce the disease burden and improve public health by identifying and controlling environmental hazards (Abad-Segura et al., 2019).

Organizational leadership is essential for the success of environmental public health initiatives within organizations. Leaders must create a culture of safety and accountability, set clear expectations and goals, and ensure that all employees know the organization's environmental public health policies and practices. Leaders must also be able to identify and develop opportunities for environmental public health initiatives, assess the impact of these initiatives, and ensure that they are sustainable in the long run.

When considering CSR initiatives, companies, leaders, and organizations should focus on areas with tremendous potential to improve public health outcomes. These areas include improving air and water quality, reducing the use of hazardous materials, and promoting energy efficiency (Abad-Segura et al., 2019). Improving air and water quality is essential for public health, as air and water pollution can have serious health consequences (Abad-Segura et al., 2019). Companies, leaders, and organizations should focus on reducing emissions from production and transportation processes and improving waste management (Abad-Segura et al., 2019). Additionally, they should seek to reduce the use of hazardous materials in production processes, as these materials can harm public health. Finally, companies, leaders, and organizations should focus on promoting energy efficiency, as this can reduce emissions, reduce costs, and improve public health outcomes (Abad-Segura et al., 2019).

It is essential to recognize that CSR initiatives have the potential to have a lasting impact on environmental public health (Abad-Segura et al., 2019). When companies, leaders, and organizations focus on improving public health outcomes, the benefits can extend beyond the immediate outcomes. For example, improved air and water quality can improve public health outcomes for generations, while reduced hazardous materials can lead to improved health outcomes for humans and animals. Additionally, improved energy efficiency can reduce emissions and lower costs for companies, leaders, and organizations, which can help ensure long-term Sustainability (Abad-Segura et al., 2019).

## CSR

The role of Corporate Social Responsibility (CSR) in business is continually expanding as stakeholders across the globe require firms to take a more proactive stance in tackling socio-economic issues (Ismail, 2009). This has placed a weight on corporate leaders to transform how businesses are structured and operated (Mahmood & Humphrey, 2013). To ensure CSR is successfully integrated and accepted in the organization, efficient management of the integration process is necessary for many leaders (Boubakary, 2016). Boubakary (2016) posits that a Change Management (CM) process is essential to ensure the successful integration of CSR within the organization.

Rodriguez (2015) proposed that in order to ensure successful CSR integration within a firm, leaders should utilize Kotter's 8-step change model. This model includes steps such as creating a sense of urgency, forming a powerful coalition, developing a vision, communicating the vision, empowering others to act on the vision, generating quick wins, consolidating gains, and anchoring the change in the culture (Kotter & Cohen, 2002). According to Rodriguez (2015), these steps will result in successful CSR integration within a firm.

# FINDINGS

## Social Entrepreneurship and Environmental Sustainability

One of the critical contributions of social entrepreneurship to Sustainability is the promotion of environmental Sustainability (Galindo-Martín et al., 2020; Sadiq et al., 2022). Social entrepreneurs can create businesses that use renewable resources, minimize waste and pollution, and promote sustainable production and consumption practices. For example, B-Corporations such as Patagonia and Ben & Jerry's have incorporated environmental Sustainability into their business models by using recycled materials, reducing waste, and promoting sustainable farming practices (Venkatesan, 2022; Blasi & Sedita, 2022). In addition to creating sustainable businesses, social entrepreneurs can promote environmental Sustainability through advocacy and education. For example, the social enterprise Plastic Bank works to reduce plastic pollution by establishing recycling centers in developing countries and incentivizing people to collect plastic waste (Katz, 2019). Plastic Bank also educates communities about reducing plastic waste and promoting sustainable practices.

## Social Entrepreneurship and Social Sustainability

Social entrepreneurship can also contribute to social Sustainability by addressing social problems such as poverty, inequality, and exclusion (Ahmad & Bajwa, 2023). Social entrepreneurs can create businesses that provide goods and services to underserved communities, such as affordable healthcare, education, and housing. For example, the social enterprise Embrace Innovations has developed a low-cost infant warmer to help reduce infant mortality in developing countries (Iwelunmor et al., 2022; Mitra et al., 2019). The warmer is designed to be portable, low-cost, and easy to use, making it accessible to communities with limited access to healthcare (Iwelunmor et al., 2022). Social entrepreneurship can also address social Sustainability by promoting social innovation and entrepreneurship (Ahmad & Bajwa, 2023). Social entrepreneurs can provide mentorship and support to aspiring entrepreneurs from underrepresented communities, helping to promote diversity and inclusion in the business world (Ahmad & Bajwa, 2023). For example, Deberry-Spence and Torres (2019) note how the organization Endeavor Global provides mentorship and support to entrepreneurs from emerging markets, helping to create a more inclusive and diverse global economy.

## Social Entrepreneurship and Economic Sustainability

Social entrepreneurship can also contribute to economic Sustainability by creating sustainable business models that generate social and economic value (Bansal et al., 2019). Social entrepreneurs can create businesses that provide employment opportunities, generate income for local communities, and contribute to local economic development. For example, the social enterprise Natura &Co, which includes the brands Natura, Aesop, and The Body Shop, has a business model prioritizing Sustainability, social responsibility, and fair trade (Simões-Coelho et al., 2023). The company has created sustainable supply chains that support local communities and promote economic development. Moreover, social entrepreneurship can promote economic Sustainability by promoting innovation and entrepreneurship. Social entrepreneurs can create networks and partnerships that support entrepreneurship and innovation, helping to create new opportunities for economic growth and development (Phillips et al., 2019). For example, the Skoll Foundation supports social entrepreneurs worldwide by providing funding, mentorship, and networking opportunities (Shekhawat, 2022).

## Challenges and Barriers to Social Entrepreneurship and Sustainability

Despite the potential of social entrepreneurship to promote Sustainability, several challenges and barriers need to be addressed. One of the main challenges is the need for more clarity around the concept of Sustainability (Meuer et al., 2020; ElAlfy et al., 2020). Lack of clarity can make it difficult for social entrepreneurs to incorporate Sustainability into their business models. In order to address this challenge, more research is needed to develop a clear and comprehensive framework for Sustainability that social entrepreneurs can easily apply. Another challenge is more funding and support for social entrepreneurship and sustainability initiatives (Gupta et al., 2020; Fatima & Elbanna, 2023). Social entrepreneurs often need help with significant financial and institutional barriers when creating sustainable businesses, which can limit their impact and Sustainability. In order to address this challenge, more funding and support are needed for social entrepreneurship and sustainability initiatives, including government support, philanthropic funding, and private investment.

## DISCUSSION

The intersection of social entrepreneurship and Sustainability can potentially drive positive societal change (Bansal et al., 2019; Karwowski & Raulinajtys-Grzybek, 2021). This can happen through promoting environmentally sustainable practices, addressing social problems, and creating sustainable business models. Social entrepreneurs play a crucial role in driving this change. They create businesses prioritizing social and environmental impact and economic Sustainability (Sun et al., 2020). However, some challenges and barriers must be addressed to fully realize the potential of social entrepreneurship and Sustainability. More research is needed to develop a comprehensive framework for Sustainability that social entrepreneurs can easily apply. Additionally, more funding and support are needed to help social entrepreneurs overcome financial and institutional barriers and create sustainable businesses.

In order to promote social entrepreneurship and Sustainability, governments, philanthropists, investors, and other stakeholders must recognize the value of these initiatives and provide the necessary support and resources. Working together can create a more sustainable and equitable future for all. One potential area for future research in social entrepreneurship and Sustainability is the role of social entrepreneurship in promoting sustainable consumption patterns (Wang et al., 2019; Karwowski & Raulinajtys-Grzybek, 2021). Social entrepreneurs can create businesses that promote sustainable consumption by providing alternatives to traditional products and services that are more environmentally friendly and socially responsible. For example, social enterprises such as The Renewal Workshop and ThreadUp use innovative business models to promote sustainable fashion by repurposing and upcycling clothing (Bassett, 2021).

Another potential area for future research is the impact of social entrepreneurship on environmental and social justice (Tien et al., 2019). Social entrepreneurs can promote environmental and social justice by addressing systemic issues such as climate change, pollution, and inequality. For example, the social enterprise GRID Alternatives provides access to clean energy for low-income communities, promoting both environmental and social justice. The intersection of social entrepreneurship and Sustainability is a complex and multifaceted field that can potentially drive positive societal change (Bansal et al., 2019; Karwowski & Raulinajtys-Grzybek, 2021). By promoting sustainable business practices, addressing social and environmental issues, and creating sustainable economic models, social entrepreneurs can play a crucial role in creating a more equitable and sustainable future for all (Farny & Binder, 2021; Karwowski & Raulinajtys-Grzybek, 2021). However, more research and support are needed to fully realize social entrepreneurship's and sustainability's potential and overcome existing challenges and barriers.

In addition to research, practical steps can be taken to promote social entrepreneurship and sustainability (Alter, 2013; Karwowski & Raulinajtys-Grzybek, 2021). One such step is to increase awareness and education around these topics. This can include training and resources for aspiring social entrepreneurs and educating consumers about supporting sustainable businesses. Another practical step is to provide funding and support for social entrepreneurs (Farinha et al., 2020; Fatima & Elbanna, 2023). This can include grants, loans, and other forms of financial support, as well as mentorship and networking opportunities (Farinha et al., 2020). Governments, philanthropists, and investors can all play a role in providing this support and helping social entrepreneurs overcome financial and institutional barriers (Bansal et al., 2019; Fatima & Elbanna, 2023). Creating a supportive policy environment for social entrepreneurship and Sustainability is also vital. This can include policies encouraging sustainable business practices, such as tax incentives for environmentally-friendly businesses and policies promoting social justice and equity. By creating a supportive policy environment, we can encourage more social entrepreneurs to start and grow sustainable businesses and create a more equitable and sustainable society (Gupta et al., 2020; Fatima & Elbanna, 2023). The intersection of social entrepreneurship and Sustainability can drive positive change in society by promoting sustainable business practices, addressing social and environmental issues, and creating sustainable economic models (Gupta et al., 2020; Fatima & Elbanna, 2023). However, more research and support are needed to fully realize this potential and overcome the existing challenges and barriers. We can create a more equitable and sustainable future for all by working together to promote social entrepreneurship and Sustainability.

According to Ren & Jackson (2020), it is critical to recognize that the intersection of social entrepreneurship and Sustainability is not a one-size-fits-all solution. Different regions and communities face unique challenges and opportunities, and solutions must be tailored to these contexts. For example, a sustainable business model that works in one region may not be feasible or effective in another (Bozhikin et al., 2019). Therefore, it is essential to take a context-specific approach to social entrepreneurship and Sustainability and work closely with local communities to develop relevant and practical solutions. Social entrepreneurship and Sustainability are constantly evolving (Haidar, 2019; Fatima & Elbanna, 2023). New challenges and opportunities will continue to arise, and it is crucial to remain adaptive and responsive in the face of these changes. This requires ongoing research, education, stakeholder collaboration, and a willingness to experiment and innovate. According to Hermann & Bossle (2020), social entrepreneurship and Sustainability are closely intertwined and have the potential to drive positive change in society. By promoting sustainable business practices, addressing social and environmental issues, and creating sustainable economic models, social entrepreneurs can play a crucial role in creating a more equitable and sustainable future for all (Bozhikin et al., 2019). However, more research and support are needed to fully realize this potential and overcome the existing challenges and barriers. We can create a better future for ourselves and generations by working together to promote social entrepreneurship and Sustainability.

The intersection of social entrepreneurship and Sustainability represents an exciting and dynamic field that has the potential to create a better future for all (Bockel et al., 2021). According to Lang & Fink (2019), social entrepreneurs are at the forefront of creating sustainable businesses that prioritize social and environmental impact alongside economic Sustainability. Social entrepreneurs can drive positive societal change by promoting sustainable business practices, addressing social and environmental issues, and creating sustainable economic models (Tykklainen & Ritala, 2021). However, some challenges and barriers must be addressed to fully realize the potential of social entrepreneurship and Sustainability. Research is needed to understand the complexities of this intersection better and to identify practical solutions for overcoming these challenges (Tykklainen & Ritala, 2021). Furthermore, funding and support must be provided to social entrepreneurs to enable them to create sustainable businesses and overcome financial and institutional barriers. A supportive policy environment is also crucial for promoting social entrepreneurship and Sustainability, including tax incentives, funding schemes, and policies promoting social justice and equity.

According to Agarwal (2020), social entrepreneurship and Sustainability must be approached context-specific and remain adaptive and responsive to ongoing changes and challenges. We must work together to promote social entrepreneurship and Sustainability and to create a more equitable and sustainable future for all. Through collaboration, innovation, and a commitment to positive change, we can unlock social entrepreneurship's and sustainability's full potential and build a better world for ourselves and future generations (Bockel et al., 2021; Fatima & Elbanna, 2023). Governments, businesses, and individuals need to recognize the importance of social entrepreneurship and Sustainability (Bassett, 2021; Fatima & Elbanna, 2023). This means investing in research, education, and funding for social entrepreneurs and sustainable businesses and creating a supportive policy environment that promotes sustainable practices and social justice (Simões-Coelho et al., 2023; Fatima & Elbanna, 2023). It also means supporting sustainable consumption patterns and creating awareness of sustainable businesses' importance.

It addressed the challenges and barriers that prevent social entrepreneurs' and sustainable businesses' growth and success (Venkatesan, 2022; Blasi & Sedita, 2022). This can include financial and institutional barriers, lack of access to funding, lack of education and training, and lack of awareness around sustainable practices. Addressing these challenges will require collaboration and partnership between various stakeholders, including governments, philanthropists, investors, and communities (Meuer et al., 2020; Fatima & Elbanna, 2023

## Challenges and Opportunities in Promoting Social Entrepreneurship and Sustainability

### Opportunities

As social entrepreneurship and Sustainability continue gaining prominence, it is crucial to recognize that these concepts are relevant to businesses, organizations, and individuals (Galindo-Martín et al., 2020; Sadiq et al., 2022). Consumers and citizens can play a crucial role in promoting social entrepreneurship and Sustainability by making conscious decisions that support sustainable businesses and practices (Mair & Marti, 2006; Fatima & Elbanna, 2023). Consumers can support businesses prioritizing social and environmental impact and opt for sustainable products and services with a reduced environmental impact. Similarly, citizens can advocate for sustainable policies and practices and hold businesses and governments accountable for their social and environmental impact.

According to Deberry-Spence and Torres (2019), by recognizing the power of individuals to drive change, we can promote a more inclusive and equitable approach to social entrepreneurship and Sustainability. It is essential to recognize that Sustainability is about protecting the environment and promoting social justice and equity (Ahmad & Bajwa, 2023). According to Lang & Fink (2019), promoting social entrepreneurship and Sustainability requires a holistic approach prioritizing social and environmental impact alongside economic Sustainability. The intersection of social entrepreneurship and Sustainability presents a unique opportunity to drive positive societal change. Social entrepreneurs are creating innovative businesses prioritizing social and environmental impact alongside economic Sustainability and promoting sustainable business practices and models that can help create a more equitable and sustainable world.

### Challenges

However, some challenges and barriers must be addressed to fully realize the potential of social entrepreneurship and Sustainability. By investing in research, education, and funding for social entrepreneurs and sustainable businesses, creating a supportive policy environment, and experimenting with new models of social entrepreneurship and Sustainability, we can overcome these challenges and unlock the full potential of social entrepreneurship and Sustainability (Sadiq et al., 2022; Fatima & Elbanna, 2023). Moreover, promoting social entrepreneurship and Sustainability is not just about creating sustainable businesses but also about a more just and equitable society. Therefore, it is crucial to recognize the power of individuals to drive change and promote a holistic approach to social entrepreneurship and Sustainability that prioritizes social and environmental impact alongside economic Sustainability. By working together to promote social entrepreneurship and Sustainability, we can create a better future for ourselves and future generations (Haidar, 2019; Fatima & Elbanna, 2023). It is up to governments, businesses, and individuals to recognize the importance of social entrepreneurship and Sustainability and to address the challenges and barriers that prevent its full potential from being realized (Haidar, 2019; Fatima & Elbanna, 2023).

## Emerging Trends

In addition to the challenges and opportunities discussed above, several emerging trends are shaping the future of social entrepreneurship and Sustainability. According to Ren & Jackson (2020), these trends reflect changing social, environmental, and economic conditions and offer new opportunities for social entrepreneurs and sustainable businesses to create an impact. One such trend is the rise of impact investing, which refers to investments made to generate both financial returns and social or environmental impact. Impact investing is overgrowing and is expected to reach $1 trillion by 2020 (Global Impact Investing Network, 2019). This trend is creating new opportunities for social entrepreneurs and sustainable businesses to access capital and is helping to mainstream the idea that business can be a force for social and environmental good.

Another emerging trend is the growth of the circular economy, which refers to an economic system regenerative by design and seeking to minimize waste and pollution. According to Hermann & Bossle (2020), the circular economy offers new opportunities for social entrepreneurs and sustainable businesses to create value from waste and promote sustainable production and consumption. For example, social enterprises such as TerraCycle and Rubicon Global are creating innovative solutions to reduce waste and promote recycling. A third emerging trend is an increasing focus on social innovation, which refers to developing and implementing new ideas and approaches to addressing social and environmental challenges (Bockel et al., 2021; Fatima & Elbanna, 2023). Social innovation is becoming increasingly important as traditional approaches to social and environmental problems are inadequate (Bockel et al., 2021; Fatima & Elbanna, 2023). Social entrepreneurs are pivotal in driving social innovation and creating new social and environmental impact models that challenge the status quo (Bockel et al., 2021; Fatima & Elbanna, 2023).

These emerging trends offer new opportunities for social entrepreneurs and sustainable businesses to create impact and reflect a growing recognition that business can be a force for social and environmental good. However, they also present new challenges and barriers that must be addressed to realize their potential fully. For example, impact investing requires a supportive policy environment that encourages and incentivizes investment in social and environmental impact. The circular economy requires new business models and supply chain solutions that promote Sustainability and minimize waste (Haidar, 2019). Social innovation requires a supportive ecosystem that fosters collaboration, experimentation, and learning (Tykklainen & Ritala, 2021; Fatima & Elbanna, 2023). In order to address these challenges and unlock the full potential of emerging trends in social entrepreneurship and Sustainability, it is crucial to continue to invest in research, education, and funding for social entrepreneurs and sustainable businesses (Bozhikin et al., 2019; Fatima & Elbanna, 2023). It is also vital to create a supportive policy environment that promotes sustainable practices and social justice and experiment with new social entrepreneurship and sustainability models prioritizing social and environmental impact (Bozhikin et al., 2019; Fatima & Elbanna, 2023).

## CONCLUSION

The intersection of social entrepreneurship, Sustainability, and public health presents a unique opportunity to drive positive societal change (Bansal et al., 2019). Social entrepreneurship and sustainability leadership are essential for positive social change in society and communities. These individuals and organizations often take risks, experiment with new ideas, and use creative and innovative approaches to address pressing social issues. However, social entrepreneurs and sustainability leaders often need help accessing the resources they need to succeed, and cultural and institutional barriers often prevent them from making an impact. For social entrepreneurship and sustainability leadership to have a lasting impact on society and community social change, governments, businesses, and communities must support these leaders. Social entrepreneurs are creating businesses prioritizing social and environmental impact alongside economic Sustainability and promoting sustainable business practices and models that can help create a more equitable and sustainable world. However, some challenges and barriers must be addressed to fully realize the potential of social entrepreneurship and Sustainability. The challenges and barriers include the need for a comprehensive framework for Sustainability, more funding and support for social entrepreneurs, and a supportive policy environment.

Furthermore, social entrepreneurship and Sustainability must be approached context-specific and remain adaptive and responsive to ongoing changes and challenges. To address these challenges, it is essential to invest in research, education, and funding for social entrepreneurs and sustainable businesses and to create a supportive policy environment that promotes sustainable practices and social justice (Bozhikin et al., 2019; Fatima & Elbanna, 2023). It is also essential to address the financial and institutional barriers that prevent the growth and success of social entrepreneurs and sustainable businesses and experiment with new social entrepreneurship and Sustainability models that prioritize social and environmental impact.

Organizational leadership is essential for the success of social entrepreneurship, Sustainability, and environmental public health initiatives within organizations. Leaders must create a culture of innovation, Sustainability, and safety, set clear goals and objectives, and ensure all employees know the organization's policies and practices. Leaders must also be able to identify and develop opportunities for initiatives, assess the impact of these initiatives, and ensure that they are sustainable in the long run. By doing so, organizations can promote social change and protect the health and well-being of their employees and the environment.

Ultimately, promoting social entrepreneurship and Sustainability is not just about creating sustainable businesses but also about a more just and equitable society. This means addressing poverty, inequality, and discrimination and creating a more inclusive and equitable world. We can create a better future for ourselves and generations by working together to promote social entrepreneurship and Sustainability. It is up to governments, businesses, and individuals to recognize the importance of social entrepreneurship and Sustainability and to address the challenges and barriers that prevent its full potential from being realized. Doing so can create a more equitable and sustainable future for all.

Corporate social responsibility (CSR) and social impact are two essential concepts that have become increasingly important in today's business world. Many organizations are now integrating social responsibility and social impact into their corporate strategies to improve their corporate image and achieve their broader business objectives. In order to successfully implement these strategies, leaders must understand the roles they can play in promoting corporate social responsibility and social impact within their organizations and communities.

In order to understand the steps that leaders can take to promote CSR and social impact, it is vital to understand the theoretical framework behind these concepts. According to Crane and Matten (2016), corporate social responsibility involves a company's commitment to its stakeholders to ensure that its operations are conducted in a socially responsible manner. This commitment can come from ethical business practices, environmental protection, and community engagement. Similarly, social impact refers to the positive effect that an organization's activities can have on society (Crane & Matten, 2016; Fatima & Elbanna, 2023).

## Steps Leaders Can Take to Promote CSR and Social Impact

Leaders are crucial in promoting corporate social responsibility and social impact in their organizations and communities. There are several steps that leaders can take to ensure that their organizations are promoting CSR and social impact (Crane & Matten, 2016; Fatima & Elbanna, 2023). First, leaders can ensure that their organizations adhere to ethical business practices (Crane & Matten, 2016). This includes ensuring that their organizations are following applicable laws and regulations and that their operations are conducted in a socially responsible manner. Second, leaders can ensure their organizations engage in environmental protection efforts (Crane & Matten, 2016; Fatima & Elbanna, 2023). This can include reducing waste, using energy-efficient practices, and promoting sustainability initiatives. Third, leaders can create opportunities for organizations to engage in local communities. This can include sponsoring community events, engaging in volunteer activities, and donating resources to local organizations (Crane & Matten, 2016; Fatima & Elbanna, 2023).

## REFERENCES


Abad-Segura, E., Cortés-García, F. J., & Belmonte-Ureña, L. J. (2019). The Sustainable Approach to Corporate Social Responsibility: A Global Analysis and Future Trends. *Sustainability (Basel)*, *11*(19), 5382. doi:10.3390u11195382

Agarwal, S., Lenka, U., Singh, K., Agrawal, V., & Agrawal, A. M. (2020). A qualitative approach towards crucial factors for sustainable development of women social entrepreneurship: Indian cases. *Journal of Cleaner Production*, 274. doi:10.1016/j.jclepro.2020.123135

Ahmad, S., & Bajwa, I. A. (2023). The role of social entrepreneurship in socio-economic development: A meta-analysis of the nascent field. *Journal of Entrepreneurship in Emerging Economies*, *15*(1), 133–157. doi:10.1108/JEEE-04-2021-0165

Alter, K. (2013). Social Entrepreneurship and Sustainability: Why the social element is Important for Environmental and Economic Sustainability. *Journal of Business Ethics*, *115*(3), 481–494. doi:10.100710551-013-1808-6

Andersson, L. (2015). Resistance to change: A literature review. *International Journal of Management Reviews*, *17*(1), 1–13.

Austin, J. E., Stevenson, H., & Wei-Skillern, J. (2006). Social and commercial entrepreneurship: Same, different, or both? *Entrepreneurship Theory and Practice*, *30*(1), 1–22. doi:10.1111/j.1540-6520.2006.00107.x

Bansal, S., Garg, I., & Sharma, G. D. (2019). Social entrepreneurship as a path for social change and driver of sustainable development: A systematic review and research agenda. *Sustainability (Basel), 11*(4), 1091. doi:10.3390u11041091

Bareil, C. (2013). Understanding resistance to change. *Human Resource Management International Digest, 21*(2), 40–43.

Bassett, N. (2021). *Sustainable Fashion Through Circular Business Innovations: New Business Models Reduce Waste. Sustainable Textile and Fashion Value Chains: Drivers*, Concepts, Theories and Solutions.

Blasi, S., & Sedita, S. R. (2022). Mapping the emergence of a new organisational form: An exploration of the intellectual structure of the B Corp research. *Corporate Social Responsibility and Environmental Management, 29*(1), 107–123. doi:10.1002/csr.2187

Bloom, I., & Smith, J. (2010). Scaling Social Impact. *Stanford Social Innovation Review, 8*(3), 46–51.

Böckel, A., Hörisch, J., & Tenner, I. (2021). A systematic literature review of crowdfunding and Sustainability: highlighting what really matters. *Management Review Quarterly, 71*, 433-453. https://link.springer.com/article/10.1007/s11301-020-00189-3

Boubakary, A. (2016). Change management: The need for successfully integrating corporate social responsibility in organizations. *The International Journal of Organizational Analysis, 24*(2), 231–250.

Bozhikin, I., Macke, J., & da Costa, L. F. (2019). The role of government and key non-state actors in social entrepreneurship: A systematic literature review. Journal of Cleaner Production, 226, 730–747. doi:10.1016/j.jclepro.2019.04.076

Bradach, J. (2003). *Scale and Scope: The Dynamics of Industrial Capitalism*. Harvard University Press.

Byrne, D. (2022). A worked example of Braun and Clarke's approach to reflexive thematic analysis. *Quality & Quantity, 56*(3), 1391–1412. doi:10.100711135-021-01182-y

Cameron, E., & Green, M. (2019). *Making sense of change management: A complete guide to the models, tools, and techniques of organizational change*. Kogan Page Publishers.

Crane, A., & Matten, D. (2016). *Business ethics: Managing corporate citizenship and Sustainability in the age of globalization* (4th ed.). Oxford University Press.

Cummings, T. G., & Worley, C. G. (2008). *Organization Development & Change*. South-Western/Cengage Learning.

Deberry-Spence, B. E. N. E. T., & Torres, L. T. (2019). Multinational Corporation Approaches to Corporate Social Responsibility and Entrepreneurship in Africa. The Oxford Handbook of Corporate Social Responsibility: Psychological and Organizational Perspectives, 391.

Dees, J. G. (2001). The meaning of social entrepreneurship. *Stanford Social Innovation Review, 1*(1), 1–8. https://ssir.org/articles/entry/the_meaning_of_social_entrepreneurship

Dees, J. G. (2008). Scaling Social Impact: What Every Social Entrepreneur Should Know. *Stanford Social Innovation Review, 6*(3), 35–41.

ElAlfy, A., Palaschuk, N., El-Bassiouny, D., Wilson, J., & Weber, O. (2020). Scoping the evolution of corporate social responsibility (CSR) research in the sustainable development goals (SDGs) era. *Sustainability (Basel), 12*(14), 5544. doi:10.3390u12145544

Farinha, L., Sebastião, J. R., Sampaio, C., & Lopes, J. (2020). Social innovation and social entrepreneurship: Discovering origins, exploring current and future trends. *International Review on Public and Nonprofit Marketing, 17*(1), 77–96. doi:10.100712208-020-00243-6

Farny, S., & Binder, J. (2021). Sustainable entrepreneurship. In *World Encyclopedia of Entrepreneurship* (pp. 605–611). Edward Elgar Publishing. doi:10.4337/9781839104145.00076

Fatima, T., & Elbanna, S. (2023). Corporate social responsibility (CSR) implementation: A review and a research agenda towards an integrative framework. *Journal of Business Ethics, 183*(1), 105–121. doi:10.100710551-022-05047-8 PMID:35125567

Franken, E., Edwards, D., & Lambert, S. (2009). Strategy execution: Making it happen. *Strategy and Leadership, 37*(4), 12–17.

Galindo-Martín, M. A., Castaño-Martínez, M. S., & Méndez-Picazo, M. T. (2020). The relationship between green innovation, social entrepreneurship, and sustainable development. *Sustainability (Basel), 12*(11), 4467. doi:10.3390u12114467

Global Impact Investing Network. (2019). *What is impact investing?* Retrieved from https://thegiin.org/impact-investing/need-to-know/#what-is-impact-investing

Griebel, T. (2018). Corporate social responsibility: An overview and introduction. *Journal of Corporate Citizenship*, (72), 5–24.

Gupta, P., Chauhan, S., Paul, J., & Jaiswal, M. P. (2020). Social entrepreneurship research: A review and future research agenda. Journal of Business Research, 113, 209–229.

Haldar, S. (2019). Towards a conceptual understanding of sustainability-driven entrepreneurship. *Corporate Social Responsibility and Environmental Management, 26*(6), 1157–1170. doi:10.1002/csr.1763

Hanson, S. (2020). *What Is Social Entrepreneurship?* Retrieved April 13, 2021, from https://www.entrepreneur.com/article/352759

Hao, J., & Yazdanifard, R. (2015). Change management: Strategies and practices in different contexts. *International Journal of Business Research and Management, 3*(2), 157–167.

Harvard Business School. (2013). *Understanding the Impact of Corporate Social Responsibility on Companies*. Retrieved from https://www.hbs.edu/socialenterprise/research/Pages/understanding-the-impact-of-corporate-social-responsibility-on-companies.aspx

Hermann, R. R., & Bossle, M. B. (2020). Bringing an entrepreneurial focus to sustainability education: A teaching framework based on content analysis. *Journal of Cleaner Production*, 246. doi:10.1016/j.jclepro.2019.119038

International Institute for Management Development (IMD). (2010). *Corporate Social Responsibility: A role for senior management*. Retrieved from https://www.imd.org/publications/corporate-social-responsibility-role-senior-management/

Ismail, K. (2009). Corporate social responsibility: An Islamic perspective. *International Journal of Social Economics*, *36*(8), 704–717.

Iwelunmor, J., Blackstone, S., Nwaozuru, U., Obiezu-Umeh, C., Uzoaru, F., Mason, S., ... Airhihenbuwa, C. (2022). Social Enterprises for Child and Adolescent Health in Sub-Saharan Africa: A Realist Evaluation. *Child Behavioral Health in Sub-Saharan Africa: Towards Evidence Generation and Policy Development*, 317-332.

Kamaludin, M. F., Xavier, J. A., & Amin, M. (2021). Social entrepreneurship and Sustainability: A conceptual framework. *Journal of Social Entrepreneurship*, 1–24. doi:10.1080/19420676.2021.1900339

Karwowski, M., & Raulinajtys-Grzybek, M. (2021). The application of corporate social responsibility (CSR) actions for mitigation of environmental, social, corporate governance (ESG), and reputational risk in integrated reports. *Corporate Social Responsibility and Environmental Management*, *28*(4), 1270–1284. doi:10.1002/csr.2137

Katz, D. (2019). Plastic bank: launching social plastic® revolution. *Field Actions Science Reports. The Journal of Field Actions*, (19), 96–99.

Kotter, J. P., & Cohen, D. S. (2002). *The heart of change: Real-life stories of how people change their organizations*. Harvard Business Press.

Lang, R., & Fink, M. (2019). Rural social entrepreneurship: The role of social capital within and across institutional levels. *Journal of Rural Studies*, *70*, 155–168. doi:10.1016/j.jrurstud.2018.03.012

Mahmood, Z., & Humphrey, D. (2013). The impact of corporate social responsibility on organizational performance in Malaysian manufacturing firms. *International Journal of Business and Social Science*, *4*(2), 145–154.

Mair, J., & Marti, I. (2006). Social entrepreneurship research: A source of explanation, prediction, and delight. *Journal of World Business*, *41*(1), 36–44. doi:10.1016/j.jwb.2005.09.002

Meuer, J., Koelbel, J., & Hoffmann, V. H. (2020). On the nature of corporate Sustainability. *Organization & Environment*, *33*(3), 319–341. doi:10.1177/1086026619850180

Mitra, P., Kickul, J., Gundry, L., & Orr, J. (2019). The Rise of Hybrids: A Note for Social Entrepreneurship Educators. *International Review of Entrepreneurship*, *17*(2).

Nicholls, A. (2007). *Social Entrepreneurship: New Models of Sustainable Social Change*. Oxford University Press.

Phillips, W., Alexander, E. A., & Lee, H. (2019). Going it alone won't work! The relational imperative for social innovation in social enterprises. *Journal of Business Ethics*, *156*(2), 315–331. doi:10.100710551-017-3608-1

Prabhu, J. U. (2015). *Social entrepreneurship: A global perspective*. Palgrave Macmillan.

Ren, S., & Jackson, S. E. (2020). HRM institutional entrepreneurship for sustainable business organizations. *Human Resource Management Review*, *30*(3), 100691. doi:10.1016/j.hrmr.2019.100691

Rodriguez, R. (2015). Corporate social responsibility: An analysis of corporate social responsibility practices in the Indian Companies Act, 2013. *International Journal of Management and Applied Science, 1*(7), 15–21.

Sadiq, M., Nonthapot, S., Mohamad, S., Chee Keong, O., Ehsanullah, S., & Iqbal, N. (2022). Does green finance matter for sustainable entrepreneurship and environmental corporate social responsibility during COVID-19? *China Finance Review International, 12*(2), 317–333. doi:10.1108/CFRI-02-2021-0038

Shekhawat, D. (2022). A Comparative Analysis Of Organizations Supporting Social Entrepreneurship. *Social Innovations Journal, 15*.

Simões-Coelho, M., Figueira, A. R., & Russo, E. (2023). Motivations for a sustainable ethos: Evidence from the globally present Brazilian multinational Natura &Co. *Environment Systems & Decisions, 43*(3), 1–16. doi:10.100710669-022-09890-y PMID.36628130

Stobierski, T. (2021, June 21). 15 eye-opening corporate social responsibility statistics. *Harvard Business Review*. Retrieved from: https://online.hbs.edu/blog/post/corporate-social-responsibility-statistics

Sun, H., Pofoura, A. K., Mensah, I. A., Li, L., & Mohsin, M. (2020). The role of environmental entrepreneurship for sustainable development: Evidence from 35 countries in Sub-Saharan Africa. *The Science of the Total Environment, 741*, 140132. doi:10.1016/j.scitotenv.2020.140132 PMID:32886991

Tien, N. H., Anh, D. B. H., Ngoc, N. M., & Do Thi, Y. N. (2019). Sustainable social entrepreneurship in Vietnam. *International Journal of Entrepreneurship, 23*(3), 1–12.

Todnem, R. (2005). Change management: A review of current thinking. Leadership &amp. *Organization Development Journal, 26*(3), 195–204.

Tykkyläinen, S., & Ritala, P. (2021). Business model innovation in social enterprises: An activity system perspective. *Journal of Business Research, 125*, 684–697. doi:10.1016/j.jbusres.2020.01.045

Vedenik, J., & Leber, P. (2015). Change management: The view through the prism of three different models. Management &amp. *Marketing Challenges for the Knowledge Society, 10*(1), 5–17.

Venkatesan, M. (2022). Marketing Sustainability: A Critical Consideration of Environmental Marketing Strategies. In Products for Conscious Consumers (pp. 151-166). Emerald Publishing Limited. doi:10.1108/978-1-80262-837-120221009

Wang, C., Ghadimi, P., Lim, M. K., & Tseng, M. L. (2019). A literature review of sustainable consumption and production: A comparative analysis in developed and developing economies. *Journal of Cleaner Production, 206*, 741–754. doi:10.1016/j.jclepro.2018.09.172

Williamson, P. C. (2011). *Social Impact: A Definition*. Retrieved from http://www.socialimpactcenter.com/social-impact/

World Business Council for Sustainable Development. (2010). *Sustainability: A Global Survey of Corporate Practices*. Retrieved from https://www.wbcsd.org/web/publications/WBCSD_Survey_2010.pdf

World Health Organization. (2015). Retrieved from https://www.who.int/

# Chapter 22
# The Case for the Chief Strategic Transformational Officer

**Simon Cleveland**
https://orcid.org/0000-0001-9293-3905
*Purdue University Global, USA*

**Marisa Cleveland**
*Northeastern University, USA*

## ABSTRACT

*Transformation leaders are the relationship builders and change champions in their organizations. To succeed in these roles, such leaders require reskilling and upskilling on specific key performance indicators and techniques to determine issues and corrective actions, the use of data gathering, analysis, as well as data-based decision making. Moreover, as strategists, transformation leaders improve organizational learning; however, to accomplish this, they need to create a shared vision, team leading and systems thinking approach, as well as promoting action learning through problem solving and build a learning culture in the organization. The goal of this chapter is to examine these roles and propose an approach to solve the overarching theme of the study – the need for the establishment of a Chief Transformation Officer at the C-Suit level who would be involved in facilitating change initiatives, which emerge from the factors explored in the literature review.*

## INTRODUCTION

The need to remain competitive in the marketplace drives organizations to constant evolution, which is driven by changes introduced through projects that support the strategic organizational objectives (Cleveland, 2022). During this process, organizations are faced with change, often due to the introduction of innovation (Holbeche, 2005). This change creates conflict and impacts the organizational atmosphere in a variety of ways.

DOI: 10.4018/978-1-6684-8822-5.ch022

Garg and Garg (2008) referred to organizational atmosphere as the factors focused on improving the work culture, the organizational operating results and overall performance. An atmosphere where everyone is informed and aware about the organizational goals, the methods to address change are communicated and the productivity for all stakeholders, leads to increased employee satisfaction and highly performing organization. Garg and Talwar (2017) proposed that the organizational atmosphere typically improves as the decision-making process of senior leadership influences employees' overall perceptions of the company's performance and direction. Moreover, the authors argued that senior leadership quality and recognition of employees' contributions increases the corporate atmosphere. Finally, Msc (2013) noted that the organizational atmosphere improves where employees feel more responsible for their roles and contribution to the overall company performance, which ultimately increases their positive attitude toward the company's direction.

## PROBLEM STATEMENT

While factors, such as learning, leadership training, change management, and shared vision, are critical to the leader's role and have been investigated in the literature, there is a gap in understanding how transformational leadership plays a role in converting organizations into highly performing integrated units. As a result, the research question for this study is: In what ways do transformational leaders strengthen organizations?

## PURPOSE STATEMENT

This chapter examines factors that need consideration in building highly performing organizations and proposes one approach to address challenges with these factors - the need for the creation of a Chief Transformation Officer at the C-Suit level who would be involved in facilitating change initiatives, which emerge from the factors explored in the literature review.

The remainder of the chapter is structured as follows: a review of the transformational leader role is performed, followed by exploration of several critical factors that challenge high performing organizations. The chapter concludes with the examination of the and recommendations for the new role of the chief strategic transformational officer (CSTO).

## LITERATURE REVIEW

Transformational leaders recognize when the organizational atmosphere is in peril and in these situations become relationship builders and change champions in their organizations (Pasovska & Miceski, 2017). In these roles, transformational leaders communicate the urgency of change required to build momentum, hold focus groups or use external consultants to identify causes and make critical decisions on recommended improvements (Wadhawan et al., 2022).

Additionally, as change champions, transformational leaders provide direction for the change, which incorporates knowledge on how to build commitment, shared vision with everyone and to build coalitions (McKnight, 2013). They create ownership and support for the change, which includes strong communication, knowledge about rewarding deserving employees and encouragement of active involvement from everyone (Agbaeze & Eyisi, 2010). They implement and manage the change, integrate the change and measure, and monitor the impact of the change (Yaslioglu & Erden, 2018). To do so, reskilling and upskilling for transformational leaders should focus on acquiring knowledge of specific key performance indicators and techniques to determine issues and corrective actions, the knowledge on data gathering, analysis, as well as data-based decision making (Yadav & Agrawal, 2017).

As strategists, transformational leaders improve organizational learning, which leads to growth and improvement in employees' perceived attitude toward commitment to the organization. To accomplish this, transformational leaders create a shared vision, team leading and systems thinking approach, as well as promoting action learning through problem solving and building a learning culture in the organization (Akkaya & Tabak, 2020).

## Employee Privacy and the Transformational Leader

No improvement to an organization's performance and capabilities can happen without addressing employee privacy in the workplace (Ferrell et al., 2019) as individual behaviors in organizations are influenced by employee privacy, including ethical issues intensify. Anton and Ward (1998) argued that employee privacy is considered an urgent issue, which should be addressed. They defined employee privacy as the right of employees to decide where, what and how knowledge about them is shared with other stakeholders.

Transformational leaders need to understand why businesses monitor employees' internet use and social media posts, before engaging in decision-making on how to improve employee performance. Ambalavanan and Lister (2020) provided four critical reasons for consideration with regards to employee privacy. The authors argued that companies track employees in order to: 1) determine employee productivity, 2) prevent data theft, 3) guard company assets, and 4) protect employees and the company from potential cyberbullying, or sexual harassment claims. By engaging in monitoring of employee internet and system use, a company is aiming to enhance specific desirable and eliminate undesirable behaviors from its employees.

Therefore, the question transformational leaders should answer is: Is it ethical for employers to monitor/track employees and if so, why? Joseph (2020) argued that while such monitoring practices may seem to violate employees' rights under the Fourth Amendment of the U.S. Constitution, the equipment used for such activities are usually owned by the companies and as such employers have the right to track activities that may damage such equipment or minimize their own productivity for which they are paid. In the instances where employees are using personal equipment and personal social media accounts to share information, employers should be able to track and monitor any information sharing that pertain to the intellectual property of the company. Based on this argument, transformational leaders need to ensure that, while focusing on improving productivity through technology and tracking, such surveillance is made with employees' consent and with their knowledge that the company will engage in such monitoring and tracking as a condition of the employee's work agreement (Spiggle, 2020).

## Whistleblowers and the Transformational Leader

Jeon (2017) defined whistleblowing as the act of engaging in reporting of any wrongdoing to one's manager or to the media. The Sarbanes–Oxley Act provides employees whistle-blower protection (Ferrell et al, 2019). This ensures that employers can't engage in retaliation against whistle-blowers who expose fraud. The act also provides whistle-blowers coverage for damages, including attorney's fees. Furthermore, the Dodd–Frank Wall Street Reform and Consumer Protection Act provides additional protection for whistle-blowers in the financial industry.

Using these acts as foundation, transformational leaders can create programs following the framework proposed by OSHA.Org (n.d.) which contains five key elements: 1) Management Commitment – where management is responsible for providing employees with a system to report concerns and these are examined, evaluated and enforced; 2) Compliance Concern Response System – where there are multiple channels for employees to report their concerns; 3) Anti-Retaliation Response System – where confidentiality is maintained, transparency with employees is demonstrated, investigation is objective and actions are taken; 4) Anti-Retaliation Training – specific training is provided to address issues; and 5) Program Oversight – where monitoring and auditing is conducted on a regular basis.

The use of such programs will allow transformational leaders to ensure their organizations have anti-retaliation programs, which allow employees to feel safe in expressing their concerns about behaviors that do not conform to the organization's code of conduct.

## Tolerance, anti-Harassment, and the Transformational Leader

Sotelo (2000) defined tolerance as the readiness to extend basic rights and liberties to all social groups. Work harassment is defined as the act of bullying against someone who is engaged in completing a task at work (Brunetto et al., 2016).

Transformational leaders should examine and work to remove potentially dangerous corporate policies. For example, in the landmark case between Equal Employment Opportunity Commission vs. Abercrombie & Fitch Stores, Inc., the company had instated a policy known as 'Look Policy' which forbade employees from wearing black clothing or caps. As a result, a prospective employee, who was a practicing Muslim and wore a hijab during the interview, was prevented from being hired due to her wearing a headscarf. A lawsuit was filed by the Equal Employment Opportunity Commission (EEOC) on behalf of the perspective employee against Abercrombie on the basis of the company violating Title VII of the Civil Rights Act of 1964. The case made its way to the United States Supreme Court, which ruled in favor of the EEOC (Abercrombie & Fitch Stores, Inc., 2015). Among other protections, Title VII guards employees against employer's refusal to hire someone on the basis of their religion (Noe et al., 2021).

The outcome for the company was not only public embarrassment, but also loss of customer loyalty. If a transformational leader engaged during the policy envisioning, the situation could have been averted. The implication for transformational leaders from the Abercrombie's case is to ensure they work to establish clear policies in their organizations on how management should work, in conjunction with their company's legal team, to establish equitable practices for tolerance and dress code accommodations for all current and perspective employees. These policies should ensure that the organizations do not engage in discrimination based on any religious practices and observances of their employees and prospective employees. Additionally, transformational leaders should create training programs that educate employees and their managers about the importance of tolerance and acceptance of everyone's religious beliefs.

In the case of Christiansen versus Omnicom Group, which examined a scenario where a gay man was harassed by his employer for his sexual orientation and health status (AIDS victim), transformational leaders could learn another lesson, to take part in the creation of anti- harassment policies in the organization. In that case, the plaintiff (Christiansen) claimed he was subjected to bullying and harassment based on him exhibiting feminine traits (Christiansen v. Omnicom Group, Inc., 2017). The plaintiff received no help from the HR department for his complaint and consequently filed a lawsuit claiming sexual harassment on the basis of Title VII violations by the employer. The trial court dismissed the case as it was unable to reconcile the plaintiff's claim of gender stereotype and sexual orientation. The appellate court reinstated the case and ruled in favor of the plaintiff since they found that the employer sexually discriminated against the employee under Title VII.

Transformational leaders should be familiar with Title VII, which protects employees against sexual discrimination (Noe et al., 2021). As a result, the implications for transformational leaders from this case include the need for instituting clear anti-harassment policies which protect employees from sexual harassment and bullying practices. Transformational leaders should safeguard employees and give them the ability to file complaints without fear of retaliation by others. Furthermore, transformational leaders should create and disseminate training programs that target sexual harassment and bullying behaviors, prohibit such behaviors, and educate employees on penalties for practicing such behaviors. Finally, since employees tend to mirror the behaviors of their supervisors and leaders (Dietz et al., 2020), transformational leaders should work with senior management to create a culture of acceptance of employee's differences, inclusivity, and safety in the workplace. To accomplish this, transformational leaders should be regarded as a strategic partner and included in the strategy planning meetings by senior management to help set the course for all-inclusive workforce in the organization.

## Corporate Social Responsibility and the Transformational Leader

In addition to knowledge about privacy, tolerance and anti-harassment policies, transformational leaders s should be aware whether their organizations act in a socially responsible manner. This is accomplished through the practice of corporate social responsibility, or as Farrell et al. (2019) defined it: the obligation of the company to increase its impact on stakeholders in a positive way, while minimizing the negative impact, by any economic, legal, ethical, and philanthropic means. Specifically, Farrell et al. focused on the need for corporate citizenship expressed through four dimensions: strong economic performance, compliance, ethical actions and contributions that advance stakeholder commitment. To ensure this, transformational leaders should focus on the organizational stakeholders – the employees who have stakes in the success of the corporations and who brings their own values and standards with regards to consumer rights, environmental protection, privacy protection and acceptable work conditions.

For example, Edmans (2019) demonstrated that between 1984 and 2009, companies which focused on the well-being of their stakeholders and ensured employee satisfaction, increased their financial value up to 3% year over year. In other words - companies which treat their workers better realize increased firm value and as a result, acting in a socially responsible way translates into a great business sense.

Friedman (1970) argued that the mission of any business is to maximize the contribution to each shareholder and therefore businesses should focused on making as much money as possible rather on corporate social responsibility. The economist's main focus is the owner of the company, rather than the employee. This argument is in a sharp contrast to Edmans and Farrell et al.'s perspectives because it proposes that companies should be solely responsible to their 'owners' and should ignore social responsibility toward their stakeholders. While this approach was adopted throughout the 1970s, it led to ethical misconduct and poor decisions which result in damaged employee relationships, damaged corporate reputation and diminished consumer confidence during the following three decades (ECI, n.d.). As a result, transformational leaders should work with senior leaders to ensure their organizations adopt approaches to acting social responsibility.

## Forecasting and the Transformational Leader

Fitz-Enz and Mattox (2014) argued that one way transformational leaders ensure the same problems do not occur over and over in the organization is to use predictive analytics to analyze employee issues in the first place. The analysis should include what is occurring and what would happen if the problem is not resolved. The process of predictive analytics includes the use of statistical modeling and data mining based on historical data in order to make certain predictions about the future. For example, many organizations struggle with locating the right talent. Often, companies find that key personnel had left and by the time this had occurred proper turnover forecast had not been done in a timely manner leading to productivity declines, lower sales quotas or incomplete job duties.

As a result, transformational leaders should engage in educating management on proper forecasting practices of the supply and demand for the positions in their company and how to predict where the labor shortages may occur over a period of several years (Noe et al., 2021). The second lesson for transformational leaders is to teach management how to set clear goals and engage in sound strategic planning. In these scenarios, the need for talent should be tied to the company's strategic plan.

One type of data to be used in the forecasting process is for transformational leaders to study university recruitment yield ratios of their organizations and determine whether there are any declines from prior quarter. If there are, this will suggest that the company is not utilizing their recruitment resource effectively in order to fulfill their strategic plans. To improve on this strategy, it is recommended that the transformational leaders work with senior leaders to offer hiring bonuses for university graduates, provide creative job perks such as relaxed work environment, free lunches, and work-life balance, and create internship programs that give course credits.

Another approach to predicting poor university recruitment is for transformational leaders to examine the company's image branding. Ineffective image branding campaigns typically impact recruitment processes and thus transformational leaders should be involved with marketing during the decision-making on the type of marketing campaigns necessary to promote flexible work environment, work-life balance and showcase engaging teamwork. transformational leader, in conjunction with the marketing team, should consult on the type of innovative social media channels required to promote corporate image to university graduates.

Additionally, transformational leaders may engage in predictive analysis on the number of internal referrals. Management out to be educated and be on the lookout for annual yield ratios across several years. Any declines in such ratios would suggest that the company is not using one of the best sources for candidates, their own employees. To capitalize on this source, transformational leaders should work in finance departments to provide bonuses for referrals.

All these analyses, coupled with the use of sound statistical tools, would ensure that transformational leaders are actively engaged in supporting senior management in making the appropriate decisions to predict the issues causing recruitment problems and implement strategies to prevent such problems from occurring in the future.

## IMPLICATIONS AND RECOMMENDATIONS: THE ROLE OF THE CHIEF STRATEGIC TRANSFORMATIONAL OFFICER (CSTO)

The implications from this analysis suggest that transformational leaders should become integral stakeholders during the strategic decision-making steps in organizations. As a result, the main recommendation is the need for organizations to establish a role called Chief Strategic Transformational Officer (CSTO). This role would serve as the strategic advisor in the C-Suit. One of the critical roles of the CSTO would be to take part in the decision-making process at the C-level on how the strategy of the firm will be executed at large in the organization and the specific roles employees will play in the execution of the strategy.

In line with the factors presented in this chapter, the CSTO's input would be critical for the strategy formulation of the organization in the areas of: 1) employee privacy; 2) prevention of harassment as well as whistleblowers protection; 3) ensuring socially responsible corporate actions; and 4) ensuring proper forecasting of the workforce development.

First, in ensuring employee privacy, the CSTO would be focused on identifying long-term strategies that can be used to ensure privacy protection of employee data. Decisions around how employee monitoring of systems access and their use of social media impact employees performance should be made. The CSTO should participate in the strategic discussions and provide recommendations on appropriate strategies that motivate employees to improve negative behaviors, rather than penalize them.

Next, the CSTO should take part in the conversations and the development of anti-harassment and anti-bullying policies. This will ensure that the organization engages in diversity, equity and inclusion considerations and practices to protect the organization's most precious asset – the employee.

Third, the CSTO should work with senior executives to ensure that the organization is acting in a socially and ethically responsible way in the marketplace. This approach would ensure that the corporate social image is enhanced and brand loyalty is sustained with the customers, which would also translate into increase employee commitment to the company culture and improved productivity.

Finally, the CSTO should ensure senior executives rely on data when making decisions through proper forecasting techniques. For example, the CSTO should drive the discussions toward areas of external and internal analysis of the organization and would assist in identifying strengths, weaknesses, opportunities, and threats in order develop strategic alternatives on how to best establish the positioning of the company. The CSTO with critical evaluation skills, who demonstrates strong information interpretation for better decision-making and recommendations, would be especially valuable to the organization. The CSTO with strong business acumen, who is focused on developing skills that analyze information useful for the development of the company's strategic plan (SHRM, n.d), would also be of great value to the organization.

## REFERENCES

Abercrombie & Fitch Stores, Inc. 575 U.S. (2015). *14-86 EEOC v. Abercrombie & Fitch Stores, Inc. (06/01/2015) (supremecourt.gov)

Agbaeze, E. K., & Eyisi, A. S. (2010). The role of leaders in organizational transformation. *The Nigerian Journal of Research and Production, 16*(2).

Akkaya, B., & Tabak, A. (2020). The link between organizational agility and leadership: A research in science parks. *Academy of Strategic Management Journal*, *19*(1), 1–17.

Ambalavanan, B., & Lister, K. (2020, August 24). *Should Employers Use Software to Monitor Remote Workers?* SHRM. Retrieved from https://www.shrm.org/hr-today/news/hr-magazine/fall2020/pages/should-employers-use-software-to-monitor-remote-workers.aspx

Anton, G., & Ward, J. J. (1998). Every Breath You Take: Employee Privacy Rights in the Workplace-An Orwellian Prophecy Come True? *Labor Law Journal*, *49*(3), 897.

Brunetto, Y., Xerri, M., Trinchero, E., Farr-Wharton, R., Shacklock, K., & Borgonovi, E. (2016). Public–private sector comparisons of nurses' work harassment using SET: Italy and Australia. *Public Management Review*, *18*(10), 1479–1503. doi:10.1080/14719037.2015.1114136

Christiansen v. Omnicom Group, Inc. 16-748 F.3d (2017). Christiansen v. Omnicom Group, Inc., No. 16-748 (2d Cir. 2017): Justia

Cleveland, S. (2022). *Critical Impact Factors and Leadership Competencies for Project Success* [Doctoral dissertation]. Northeastern University.

Dietz, C., Zacher, H., Scheel, T., Otto, K., & Rigotti, T. (2020). Leaders as role models: Effects of leader presenteeism on employee presenteeism and sick leave. *Work and Stress*, *34*(3), 300–322. doi:10.1080/02678373.2020.1728420

ECI. (n.d.). *Timeline of business ethics and compliance*. Retrieved from https://www.ethics.org/resources/free-toolkit/ethics-timeline/

Edmans, A. (2019). *Does corporate social responsibility improve firm value?* Retrieved from https://alexedmans.com/blog/investment-strategies/does-corporate-social-responsibility-improve-firm-value/

Ferrell, O. C., Fraedrich, J., & Ferrell, L. (2019). *Business ethics: Ethical decision making and cases* (12th ed.). Cengage Learning.

Fitz-Enz, J., & John Mattox, I. I. (2014). *Predictive analytics for human resources*. John Wiley & Sons. doi:10.1002/9781118915042

Friedman, M. (1970). The Social Responsibility Of Business Is to Increase Its Profits A Friedman business doctrine. *The NY Times*. Retrieved from https://www.proquest.com/historical-newspapers/friedman-doctrine/docview/117933451/se-2?accountid=11091

Garg, N. K., & Garg, A. (2008). Inculcating A Corporate Revolution in the New Millennium. *Journal of Commerce and Trade*, *3*(2), 23–25.

Holbeche, L. (2005). *The high performance organization creating dynamic stability and sustainable success*. Elsevier Butterworth-Heinemann.

Jeon, S. H. (2017). Where to report wrongdoings? Exploring the determinants of internal versus external whistleblowing. *International Review of Public Administration*, *22*(2), 153–171. doi:10.1080/12294659.2017.1315235

Joseph, C. (2020). *Why Should Employers Track Employees' Online Habits?* Chron. Retrieved from https://smallbusiness.chron.com/ethical-issues-employer-monitoring-internet-usage-12617.html

McKnight, L. L. (2013). Transformational leadership in the context of punctuated change. *Journal of Leadership, Accountability and Ethics*, *10*(2), 103–112.

Msc, F. B. (2013). The relationship between Antecedents (Job Stressors) and Burnout in Iranian Nurses. *International Journal of Academic Research in Business & Social Sciences*, *3*(12), 550.

Noe, R., Hollenbeck, J., Gerhart, B., & Wright, P. (2021). *Human Resource Management: Gaining a Competitive Advantage* (12th ed.). McGraw Hill.

OSHA.gov. (n.d.). *Recommended Practices for Anti-Retaliation Programs*. Retrieved from https://www.osha.gov/sites/default/files/publications/OSHA3905.pdf

Pasovska, S., & Miceski, T. (2017). Application of transformational leadership as an incentive for innovation ie developing subordinates with durable values. *Journal of Economics*, *2*(2), 28–35.

Sotelo, M. J. (2000). Individual differences in political tolerance among adolescents. *Social Behavior and Personality*, *28*(2), 185–192. doi:10.2224bp.2000.28.2.185

Spiggle, T. (2020, May 21). Can Employers Monitor Employees Who Work From Home Due To The Coronavirus? *Forbes*. Retrieved from https://www.forbes.com/sites/tomspiggle/2020/05/21/can-employers-monitor-employees-who-work-from-home-due-to-the-coronavirus/?sh=bae29122fb78

Wadhawan, S., Gupta, N., Kaur, A., & Bhardwaj, A. (2022). Transformational leadership and employee performance amid COVID-19 crisis. *Journal of Information and Optimization Sciences*, *43*(6), 1431–1441. doi:10.1080/02522667.2022.2117345

Yadav, S., & Agrawal, V. (2017). Challenges Face by Transformational leader and suggestions to solve the challenges. *International Journal of Research in IT and Management*, *7*(5), 34–43.

Yaslioglu, M. M., & Erden, N. S. (2018). Transformational leaders in action: Theory has been there, but what about practice? *IUP Journal of Business Strategy*, *15*(1), 42–53.

# Compilation of References


Aasebo, T. S., Midtsundstad, J. H., & Willbergh, I. (2017). Teaching in the age of accountability: Restrained by school culture? *Journal of Curriculum Studies*, *49*(3), 273–290. doi:10.1080/00220272.2015.1072249

Abad-Segura, E., Cortés-García, F. J., & Belmonte-Ureña, L. J. (2019). The Sustainable Approach to Corporate Social Responsibility: A Global Analysis and Future Trends. *Sustainability (Basel)*, *11*(19), 5382. doi:10.3390u11195382

Abbas, A. (2022). *Individual psychological distance: A leadership task to assess and cope with invisible change* [PhD Dissertation]. Airlangga University.

Abbas, A., Suhariadi, F., Ekowati, D., Anwar, A., & Saud, M. (2022). Spirituality at Workplace: Role of Spiritual Leadership, Productivity, and Emotional Exhaustion. *Pre Print Available at* Research Square, 1-18 Doi. doi:10.21203/rs.3.rs-492746/v1

Abbas, A. (2023). The Potential of Ethically Responsible and Persistent Leadership Theory. In Ç. Doğru (Ed.), *Role of Human Resources for Inclusive Leadership, Workplace Diversity, and Equity in Organizations* (pp. 111–123). IGI Publisher. doi:10.4018/978-1-6684-6602-5.ch011

Abbas, A., Ekowati, D., & Anwar, A. (2023). Authentic Leadership Journey: An empirical Discussion from Pakistani higher education employing the Lay theory of Psychology. *International Journal of Public Leadership*. Advance online publication. doi:10.1108/IJPL-04-2022-0020

Abbas, A., Ekowati, D., Suhairidi, F., & Anwar, A. (2022). Human Capital Creation: A Collective Psychological, Social, Organizational and Religious Perspective. *Journal of Religion and Health*. Advance online publication. doi:10.100710943-022-01665-8 PMID:36109469

Abbas, A., Ekowati, D., Suhairidi, F., & Hamid, A. R. (2022). Negative Vs Positive Psychology: A Review of Science of Well-being. *Integrative Psychological & Behavioral Science*. Advance online publication. doi:10.100712124-022-09708-1 PMID:35759165

Abbas, A., Ekowati, D., & Suhariadi, F. (2021). Individual psychological distance: A leadership task to assess and cope with invisible change. *Journal of Management Development*, *40*(3), 168–189. doi:10.1108/JMD-09-2020-0304

Abbas, A., Ekowati, D., & Suhariadi, F. (2022). Social Perspective: Leadership in Changing Society. In M. I. Hassan, S. Sen Roy, U. Chatterjee, S. Chakraborty, & U. Singh (Eds.), *Social Morphology, Human Welfare, and Sustainability* (pp. 89–107). Springer International Publishing. doi:10.1007/978-3-030-96760-4_4

Abbas, A., Ekowati, D., Suhariadi, F., & Anwar, A. (2023). Workplace: Empirical study on spiritual leadership in Pakistani Higher Education. *International Journal of Business and Systems Research*, *17*(4), 367–386. doi:10.1504/IJBSR.2023.131721

Abbas, A., Ekowati, D., Suhariadi, F., Anwar, A., & Fenitra, R. M. (2023). Technology acceptance and COVID-19: A perspective for emerging opportunities from crisis. *Technology Analysis and Strategic Management*, 1–13. doi:10.1080/09537325.2023.2214642

Abbas, A., Ekowati, D., Suhariadi, F., & Fenitra, R. M. (2022a). Health Implications, Leaders Societies, and Climate Change: A Global Review. In U. Chatterjee, A. O. Akanwa, S. Kumar, S. K. Singh, & A. Dutta Roy (Eds.), *Ecological Footprints of Climate Change: Adaptive Approaches and Sustainability* (pp. 653–675). Springer International Publishing. doi:10.1007/978-3-031-15501-7_26

Abbas, A., Ekowati, D., Suhariadi, F., Fenitra, R. M., & Fahlevi, M. (2022). Human Capital Development in Youth Inspires Us With a Valuable Lesson: Self-Care and Wellbeing. In K. L. Clarke (Ed.), *Self-Care and Stress Management for Academic Well-Being* (pp. 80–101). IGI Global. doi:10.4018/978-1-6684-2334-9.ch006

Abbas, A., Saud, M., Ekowati, D., & Suhariadi, F. (2021). Social Psychology and Fabrication: A Synthesis of Individuals, Society, and Organization. In B. Christiansen & H. Chandan (Eds.), *Handbook of Research on Applied Social Psychology in Multiculturalism* (Vol. 1, pp. 89–109). IGI Global. doi:10.4018/978-1-7998-6960-3.ch005

Abbas, A., Saud, M., Ekowati, D., Usman, I., & Suhariadi, F. (2021). Servant leadership: A strategic choice for organisational performance. An empirical discussion from Pakistan. *International Journal of Productivity and Quality Management*, *34*(4), 468–485. doi:10.1504/IJPQM.2021.120599

Abbas, A., Saud, M., Suhariadi, F., Usman, I., & Ekowati, D. (2022). Positive leadership psychology: Authentic and servant leadership in higher education in Pakistan. *Current Psychology (New Brunswick, N.J.)*, *41*(10), 5859–5871. doi:10.100712144-020-01051-1

Abdolvand, N., Albadvi, A., & Ferdowsi, Z. (2008). Assessing readiness for business process reengineering. *Business Process Management Journal*, *14*(4), 497–511. doi:10.1108/14637150810888046

Abercrombie & Fitch Stores, Inc. 575 U.S. (2015). *14-86 EEOC v. Abercrombie & Fitch Stores, Inc. (06/01/2015) (supremecourt.gov)

Aceves, T. C., & Orosco, M. J. (2014). *Culturally responsive teaching*. University of Florida: Collaboration for Effective Educators. Retrieved May 25, 2020 from https://ceedar.education.ufl.edu/tools/innovationconfigurations/

Adams, J., King, C., & Hook, D. (2010). *Global research report Africa*. https://hedbib.iau-aiu.net/pdf/Thompson-Reuters_globalresearchreport-africa.pdf

Addow, A. A. (2022). The influence of leadership styles on employee performance in higher education-case study from the University of Somalia (UNISO). *EPRA International Journal of Environmental Economics, Commerce and Educational Management*, *9*(7), 743.

African Development Bank Group. (2020). *Impact of COVID-19 on Africa's education: Reflection on promising interventions and challenges, towards a new normal*. https://www.afdb.org/en/news-and-events/events/impact-covid-19-africas-education-reflecting-promising-interventions-and-challenges-towards-new-normal-36810

African Union. (2021). *Policy brief on school reopening in Africa during the COVID-19 pandemic*. https://cieffa.au.int/en/documents/2021-10-18/policy-brief-school-reopening-africa

Agarwal, S., Lenka, U., Singh, K., Agrawal, V., & Agrawal, A. M. (2020). A qualitative approach towards crucial factors for sustainable development of women social entrepreneurship: Indian cases. *Journal of Cleaner Production*, 274. doi:10.1016/j.jclepro.2020.123135

Agbaeze, E. K., & Eyisi, A. S. (2010). The role of leaders in organizational transformation. *The Nigerian Journal of Research and Production, 16*(2).

Agna Group. (2022). Available at: https://agnagroup.com/new/home

AHA. (2018). *Mergers & Acquisitions: Trends & Insights.* Author. https://www.aha.org/publications/market-trends-insights/mergers-acquisitions-trends-insights

Ahmad, S., Rofie, M. K. H., & Salim, S. (2016). Rewards and commitment in social development: Equiping modern muslim communities with knowledge on Islamic work ethics towards better living conditions. *Mediterranean Journal of Social Sciences, 7*(S1), 395-400. doi:10.5901/mjss.2016.v7n1s1p395

Ahmad, K., & Ogunsola, O. K. (2011). An empirical assessment of Islamic leadership principles. *International Journal of Commerce and Management, 36*(4), 379–387. doi:10.1108/10569211111165325

Ahmad, S., & Bajwa, I. A. (2023). The role of social entrepreneurship in socio-economic development: A meta-analysis of the nascent field. *Journal of Entrepreneurship in Emerging Economies, 15*(1), 133–157. doi:10.1108/JEEE-04-2021-0165

Ahmad, T., Hamid, A., Abbas, A., Anwar, A., Ekowati, D., Fenitra, R., & Suhariadi, F. (2023). Empowering leadership: Role of Organizational Culture of Self-Esteem, and Emotional Intelligence on Creativity. *Journal of Management Development, 42*(3), 201–214. doi:10.1108/JMD-10-2021-0288

Ahmed, S., Khalil, M. I., Chowdhury, B., & Haque, R., bin S Senathirajah, A. R., & bin Omar Din, F. M. (2022). Motivators and barriers of artificial intelligent (AI) based teaching. *Eurasian Journal of Educational Research, 100*(100), 74–89.

Ahsan, M. J., & Khalid, M. H. (2023). Laissez-Faire Leadership. In *Leadership Approaches in Global Hospitality and Tourism* (pp. 61–72). IGI Global. doi:10.4018/978-1-6684-6713-8.ch004

Ajia, A. Y. (2021). The Impact of Transformational Leadership and Perceived Leadership Effectiveness on Organizational Commitment of Public Sector Workers in Kwara State, Nigeria. *Management Analysis Journal, 10*(1), 115–130. doi:10.15294/maj.v10i1.43641

Akkaya, B., & Tabak, A. (2020). The link between organizational agility and leadership: A research in science parks. *Academy of Strategic Management Journal, 19*(1), 1–17.

Akman, Y., & Imamoglu Akman, G. (2017). Ogretmenlerin cok kulturlu egitim tutumunun sosyal zeka algisina gore incelenmesi [Examination of multicultural education attitude of teachers according to social intelligence perception]. *Sakarya University Journal of Education, 7*(1), 34–48. doi:10.19126uje.306954

Albania Tax Office. (n.d.). Available at: https://www.tatime.gov.al/c/7/154/per-sipermarresit

Alblooshi, M., Shamsuzzaman, M., & Haridy, S. (2021). The relationship between leadership styles and organisational innovation: A systematic literature review and narrative synthesis. *European Journal of Innovation Management, 24*(2), 338–370. doi:10.1108/EJIM-11-2019-0339

Alemu, S. K. (2018). The meaning, idea and history of University/Higher education in Africa: A brief literature review. *FIRE: Forum for International Research in Education, 4*(3), 210–227.

Alessa, G. S. (2012). The dimensions of transformational leadership and its organizational effects in public universities in Saudi Arabia: A systematic review. *Frontiers in Psychology, 12*, 1–16. doi:10.3389/fpsyg.2021.682092 PMID:34867578

Alexander, E. D. (2016). *Examination of Emotional Intelligence and Transformational Leadership Profiles of Directors and Managers of Human Resources at Starwood Hotels and Resorts.* Virginia Polytechnic Institute and State University.

Alhaji, I. A., & Yusoff, W. F. (2012). Does motivational factor influence organisational commitment and effectiveness? A review of literature. *E3 Journal of Business Management and Economics, 3*(1), 1-9. Available at: https://ideas.repec.org/a/etr/series/v3y2012i1p001-009.html

Al-Hosam, A., Ahmed, S., Ahmed, F., & Joarder, M. (2016). Impact of Transformational Leadership on Psychological Empowerment and Job Satisfaction Relationship: A case study of Yemeni Banking. *Binus Business Review.*, *7*(2), 109. Advance online publication. doi:10.21512/bbr.v7i2.1584

Al-Husseini, S., El Beltagi, I., & Moizer, J. (2021). Transformational leadership and innovation: The mediating role of knowledge sharing amongst higher education faculty. *International Journal of Leadership in Education*, *24*(5), 670–693. doi:10.1080/13603124.2019.1588381

Alkahtani, A. H. (2016). The influence of leadership styles on organizational commitment: The moderating effect of emotional intelligence. *Business and Management Studies*, *2*(1), 23–34. doi:10.11114/bms.v2i1.1091

Allameh, S. M., Pool, J. K., Kazemi, R. V., & Mostafavi, M. (2015). The impact of emotional intelligence on transformational leadership and leader effectiveness. *Latin American Journal of Management for Sustainable Development*, *2*(1), 83–93. doi:10.1504/LAJMSD.2015.067473

Alon, I., & Higgins, J. M. (2005). Global leadership success through emotional and cultural intelligences. *Business Horizons*, *48*(6), 501–512. doi:10.1016/j.bushor.2005.04.003

Alonso-Yanez, G., Preciado-Babb, A., Brown, B., & Friesen, S. (2021). Emergence in school systems: Lessons from complexity and pedagogical leadership. *Canadian Journal of Educational Administration and Policy / Revue Canadienne en administration et politique de l'éducation*, (196), 65–82. https://doi.org/ doi:10.7202/1078518ar

Alter, K. (2013). Social Entrepreneurship and Sustainability: Why the social element is Important for Environmental and Economic Sustainability. *Journal of Business Ethics*, *115*(3), 481–494. doi:10.100710551-013-1808-6

Al-Thawabiya, A., Singh, K., Al-Lenjawi, B. A., & Alomari, A. (2023). Leadership styles and transformational leadership skills among nurse leaders in Qatar, a cross-sectional study. *Nursing Open*, *10*(6), 3440–3446. doi:10.1002/nop2.1636 PMID:36760040

Álvarez-Guerrero, G., de Aguileta, A. L., Racionero-Plaza, S., & Flores-Moncada, L. G. (2021). Beyond the school walls: Keeping interactive learning environments alive in confinement for students in Special Education. *Frontiers in Psychology*, *12*, 662646. Advance online publication. doi:10.3389/fpsyg.2021.662646 PMID:33897572

Álvarez-Nobell, A., & Lesta, L. (2011). Medición de los aportes de la gestión estratégica de comunicación interna a los objetivos de la organización. *Palabra Clave (La Plata)*, *14*(1), 11–30. http://www.scielo.org.co/scielo.php?script=sci_arttext&pid=S0122-82852011000100002&lng=en&tlng=es

Alvesson, M., & Sveningsson, S. (2016). *Changing Organizational Culture: Cultural Change Work in Progress.* Routledge.

Amador, J. M., Rogers, M. A. P., Hudson, R., Phillips, A., Carter, I., Galindo, E., & Akerson, V. L. (2022). Novice teachers' pedagogical content knowledge for planning and implementing mathematics and science. *Teaching and Teacher Education*, *115*, 103736. doi:10.1016/j.tate.2022.103736

Amah, E., Daminabo-weje, M., & Dosunmu, R. (2013). Size and Organizational Effectiveness: Maintaining a Balance. *Advances in Management & Applied Economics*, *3*(5), 115–123.

Amanchukwu, R. N., Stanley, G. J., & Ololube, N. P. (2015). A review of leadership theories, principles and styles and their relevance to educational management. *Management*, *5*(1), 6–14.

Amavassee, E.J., Lee, M.A.G., Ingram, G., & Black, S.A. (2022). Using the conservation excellence model to improve ecosystem restoration undertaken by organisations working in biodiversity hotspots. *International Journal of Avian & Wildlife Biology*, *6*(1), 11–19. Doi:10.15406/ijawb.2022.06.00178/

Ambalavanan, B., & Lister, K. (2020, August 24). *Should Employers Use Software to Monitor Remote Workers?* SHRM. Retrieved from https://www.shrm.org/hr-today/news/hr-magazine/fall2020/pages/should-employers-use-software-to-monitor-remote-workers.aspx

Anand, R., & UdayaSuriyan, G. (2010). Emotional intelligence and its relationship with leadership practices. *International Journal of Business and Management*, *5*(2), 65.

Andersson, L. (2015). Resistance to change: A literature review. *International Journal of Management Reviews*, *17*(1), 1–13.

Andrade, O. A., & Bravo, H. R. (2014). *Estudio exploratorio acerca de la calidad de vida laboral de trabajadores de una empresa proveedora de productos y servicios en la industria cuprífera.* Tesis para optar al título de Sociólogo y al grado de Licenciado en Sociología. Universidad Academia de Humanismo Cristiano. Chile. http://bibliotecadigital.academia.cl/xmlui/handle/123456789/3221

Andrews, T. C., Speer, N. M., & Shultz, G. V. (2022). Building bridges: A review and synthesis of research on teaching knowledge for undergraduate instruction in science, engineering, and mathematics. *International Journal of STEM Education*, *9*(66), 66. Advance online publication. doi:10.118640594-022-00380-w

Andriani, S., Kesumawati, N., & Kristiawan, M. (2018). The influence of the transformational leadership and work motivation on teachers' performance. *International Journal of Scientific & Technology Research*, *7*(7), 19–29.

Annala, J. (2022). What knowledge counts-boundaries of knowledge in cross-institutional curricula in higher education. *Higher Education*. Advance online publication. doi:10.100710734-022-00891-z

Antonakis, J., Avolio, B. J., & Sivasubramaniam, N. (2003). Context and leadership: An examination of the nine-factor full-range leadership theory using the multifactor leadership questionnaire. *The Leadership Quarterly*, *14*(3), 261–295. doi:10.1016/S1048-9843(03)00030-4

Antonakis, J., Cianciolo, A. T., & Sternberg, R. J. (2004). *The nature of leadership*. Sage.

Anton, G., & Ward, J. J. (1998). Every Breath You Take: Employee Privacy Rights in the Workplace-An Orwellian Prophecy Come True? *Labor Law Journal*, *49*(3), 897.

Applegate, J. (Eds.), *Leadership in healthcare and public health*. Press Books.

Apriwandi, A., Asrin, A., & Sudirman, S. (2019). Implementation of character education management in junior high school 1 Praya. *International Journal of Multicultural and Multireligious Understanding*, *6*(6), 381–389.

Arbaoui, L. (2012, October 2). *World News*. http://www.moroccoworldnews.com

Ardianto, H., Sunaryo, W., & Sumardi. (2020). increasing learning organization through transformational leadership and self-efficacy of Buddhist private junior high school teachers throughout Banten Province. *Journal of Education Management*, *8*(1), 1–6.

Arindam, C., & Atik, K. (2015). An Empirical investigation of the relationship between Emotional Intelligence, Transactional and Transformational Leadership Styles in banking sector. *Procedia: Social and Behavioral Sciences*, *210*, 291–300. doi:10.1016/j.sbspro.2015.11.369

Arnold, R. (2005). *Empathic intelligence: Teaching, learning, relating*. UNSW Press.

Arokiasamy, A. R. A., Abdullah, A. G. K., Ahmad, M. Z., & Ismail, A. (2016). Transformational leadership of school principals and organizational health of primary school teachers in Malaysia. *Procedia: Social and Behavioral Sciences*, *229*, 151–157. doi:10.1016/j.sbspro.2016.07.124

Asadi, S. P., & Samimi, A. J. (2023). Local development challenge in lagging-behind areas: Insights from new and evolutionary economic geography. *GeoJournal*, *88*(1), 397–407. doi:10.100710708-022-10612-9 PMID:35261430

Aspers, P., & Corte, U. (2019, February 27). What is qualitative in qualitative research? *Qualitative Sociology*, *42*(2), 139–160. doi:10.100711133-019-9413-7 PMID:31105362

Asrar-ul-Haq, M., & Anwar, S. (2018). The many faces of leadership: Proposing research agenda through a review of literature. *Future Business Journal*, *4*(2), 179–188. doi:10.1016/j.fbj.2018.06.002

Asri, D. N., Cahyono, B. E. H., & Trisnani, R. P. (2021). Early reading learning for special needs students: Challenges on inclusive primary school during COVID-19 pandemic. *Linguistics and Culture Review*, *5*(S1), 1062–1074. doi:10.21744/lingcure.v5nS1.1489

Assie-Lumumba, N. (2005). Higher education in Africa: Crises, reforms and transformation. Senegal: Council for the Development of Social Science Research in Africa (CODSERIA).

Atkinson, I. A. E. (1985). The spread of commensal species of Rattus to oceanic islands and their effects on island avifaunas. In Conservation of island birds (pp. 35–81). International Council for Bird Preservation (ICBP).

Atuzarirwe, C., Mkwizu, K. H., & Matama, R. (2020). Standardization and internationalization of tourism small businesses: A study of Hotels in Kampala, Uganda. *ATLAS Tourism and Leisure Review*, *2020*(1), 11–22.

Austin, J. E., Stevenson, H., & Wei-Skillern, J. (2006). Social and commercial entrepreneurship: Same, different, or both? *Entrepreneurship Theory and Practice*, *30*(1), 1–22. doi:10.1111/j.1540-6520.2006.00107.x

Avolio, B. J., & Walumbwa, F. O. (2014). *Authentic leadership theory, research and practice: Steps taken and steps that remain*. Academic Press.

Avolio, B. J. (2007). Promoting more integrative strategies for leadership theory-building. *The American Psychologist*, *62*(1), 25–33. doi:10.1037/0003-066X.62.1.25 PMID:17209677

Avolio, B. J. (2011). Full range leadership development. *Sage (Atlanta, Ga.)*.

Avolio, B. J., & Bass, B. M. (1997). *Full range leadership development: Manual for the MLQ multifactor leadership questionnaire*. Mindgarden.

Avolio, B. J., & Bass, B. M. (2004). *Multifactor leadership questionnaire* (TM). Mind Garden, Inc. Menlo Park, CA.

Avolio, B. J., & Bass, B. M. (2004). *Multifactor leadership questionnaire: Manual and sample set* (3rd ed.). Mind Garden.

Avolio, B. J., Bass, B. M., & Jung, D. I. (1995). *MLQ multifactor leadership questionnaire: Technical report*. Mindgarden.

Avolio, B. J., Bass, B. M., & Jung, D. I. (1999). Re-examining the components of transformational and transactional leadership using the multifactor leadership questionnaire. *Journal of Occupational and Organizational Psychology*, *72*(4), 441–462. doi:10.1348/096317999166789

Avolio, B. J., & Gardner, W. L. (2005). Authentic leadership development: Getting to the root of positive forms of leadership. *The Leadership Quarterly*, *16*(3), 315–338. doi:10.1016/j.leaqua.2005.03.001

Avolio, B. J., & Locke, E. E. (2002). Contrasting different philosophies of leader motivation: Altruism versus egoism. *The Leadership Quarterly*, *13*(2), 169–191. doi:10.1016/S1048-9843(02)00094-2

Avolio, B. J., & Walumbwa, F. O. (2014). Authentic leadership theory, research and practice: Steps taken and steps that remain. In I. D. V. Day (Ed.), *The Oxford handbook of leadership and organizations: Oxford library of psychology*. Oxford University Press.

Avolio, B. J., Walumbwa, F. O., & Weber, T. J. (2009). Leadership: Current theories, research, and future directions. *Annual Review of Psychology*, *60*(1), 421–449. doi:10.1146/annurev.psych.60.110707.163621 PMID:18651820

Avolio, B. J., & Wernsing, T. S. (2008). Practicing authentic leadership. In S. J. Lopez (Ed.), *Positive psychology: Exploring the best in people* (Vol. 4, pp. 147–165). Greenwood.

Avolio, B. J., Zhu, W., Koh, W., & Bhatia, P. (2004). Transformational leadership and organizational commitment: Mediating the role of psychological empowerment role and moderating role of structural distance. *Journal of Organizational Behavior*, *25*(8), 951–968. doi:10.1002/job.283

Baaha, K. D., & Mekpor, B. (2017). Emotional Intelligence: Does Leadership Style Matter? Employees Perception in Ghana's Banking Sector. *International Journal of Business Insights & Transformation*, *22*(1), 42–54.

Babbie, E. R. (2020). *The practice of social research* (15th ed.). Cengage.

Bäcklander, G. (2019). Doing complexity leadership theory: How agile coaches at Spotify practise enabling leadership. *Creativity and Innovation Management*, *28*(1), 42–60. doi:10.1111/caim.12303

Badibanga, J. (2019). *Promoting Flow and Generating Profifit: A Study of Millennial Managers Through Gamification* [Doctoral Dissertation]. College of Education and Human Services.

Badri-Harun, A., Zainol, M. R., Amar, A., & Shaari, Z. H. (2016). Emotional intelligence as mediator between leadership styles and leadership effectiveness: A theoretical framework. *International Review of Management and Marketing*, *6*(1), 116–121.

Bajcar, B., & Babiak, J. (2022). Transformational and transactional leadership in the Polish organizational context: Validation of the full and short forms of the multifactor leadership questionnaire. *Frontiers in Psychology*, *13*, 1–18. doi:10.3389/fpsyg.2022.908594 PMID:35645888

Bakker, A. B., Hetland, J., Olsen, O. K., & Espevik, R. (2022). Daily transformational leadership: A source of inspiration for follower performance? *European Management Journal*. Advance online publication. doi:10.1016/j.emj.2022.04.004

Bakker, A. B., & Leiter, M. (2017). Strategic and proactive approaches to work engagement. *Organizational Dynamics*, *46*(2), 67–75. doi:10.1016/j.orgdyn.2017.04.002

Baloh, J., Zhu, X., & Ward, M. M. (2017). Implementing team huddles in small rural hospitals: How does the Kotter model of change apply? *Journal of Nursing Management*, *26*(5), 571–578. doi:10.1111/jonm.12584 PMID:29250892

Banda, T. E. (2018). The Challenges Facing Private Security Companies. In *Retaining Clients: A Case Study In Gauteng Shopping Malls*. University Of South Africa.

Bandura, A., Caprara, G. V., Barbaranelli, C., Gerbino, M., & Pastorelli, C. (2003). Role of affective self-regulatory efficacy in diverse spheres of psychosocial functioning. *Child Development*, *74*(3), 769–782. doi:10.1111/1467-8624.00567 PMID:12795389

Banks, G., McCauley, K., Gardner, W., & Williams, C. (2016). A meta-analytic review of authentic and transformational leadership: A test for redundancy. *The Leadership Quarterly*, *27*(4), 634–652. doi:10.1016/j.leaqua.2016.02.006

Bansal, S., Garg, I., & Sharma, G. D. (2019). Social entrepreneurship as a path for social change and driver of sustainable development: A systematic review and research agenda. *Sustainability (Basel)*, *11*(4), 1091. doi:10.3390u11041091

Barba-Sánchez, V., & Atienza-Sahuquillo, C. (2017). Entrepreneurial motivation and self-employment: Evidence from expectancy theory. *The International Entrepreneurship and Management Journal*, *13*(4), 1097–1115. doi:10.100711365-017-0441-z

Bareil, C. (2013). Understanding resistance to change. *Human Resource Management International Digest*, *21*(2), 40–43.

Barker, R. A. (2001). The nature of leadership. *Human Relations*, *54*(4), 469–494. doi:10.1177/0018726701544004

Barling, J., Slater, F., & Kelloway, E. K. (2000). Transformational leadership and emotional intelligence: An exploratory study. *Leadership and Organization Development Journal*, *21*(3), 157–161. doi:10.1108/01437730010325040

Barnett, K., McCormick, J., & Conners, R. (2001). Transformational leadership in schools – panacea, placebo or problem? *Journal of Educational Administration*, *39*(1), 24–46. doi:10.1108/09578230110366892

Barratt, M., Choi, T. Y., & Li, M. (2021). Qualitative case studies in operations management: Trends, research outcomes, and future research implications. *Journal of Operations Management*, *66*(1-2), 15–36.

Barrett, P., Treves, A., Shmis, T., Amasz, D., & Ustinova, M. (2019). *The impact of school infrastructure on learning: A synthesis of the evidence*. Word Bank Group. doi:10.1596/978-1-4648-1378-8

Barriball, K., & While, A. (1994). Collecting data using semi structured interviews: A discussion Paper. *Journal of Advanced Nursing*, *19*(2), 328–335. doi:10.1111/j.1365-2648.1994.tb01088.x PMID:8188965

Barr, J., & Saltmarsh, S. (2014). "It all comes down to the leadership" the role of the school principal in fostering parent-school engagement. *Educational Management Administration & Leadership*, *42*(4), 491–505. doi:10.1177/1741143213502189

Barth, R. S. (2002). The culture builder. *Educational Leadership*, *59*(8), 6–11.

Bartol, K. M., & Martin, D. C. (1998). Management. McGraw-Hill College.

Barton, G. (2021). *Developing literacy and the arts in schools*. Routledge.

Basham, L. M. (2012). Transformational leadership characteristics necessary for todays leaders in higher education. *Journal of International Education Research*, *8*(4), 343–348. doi:10.19030/jier.v8i4.7280

Bass, B. M., & Riggio, R. E. (2006). *Transformational leadership*. Academic Press.

Bass, B. M. (1981). *Stogdill's Handbook of Leadership*. The Free Press.

Bass, B. M. (1985). *Leadership and performance beyond expectations*. Free Press.

Bass, B. M. (1990). From transactional to transformational leadership: Learning to share the vision. *Organizational Dynamics*, *18*(3), 19–31. doi:10.1016/0090-2616(90)90061-S

Bass, B. M. (1997). Does the transactional–transformational leadership paradigm transcend organizational and national boundaries? *The American Psychologist*, *52*(2), 130–139. doi:10.1037/0003-066X.52.2.130

Bass, B. M. (1998). *Transformational leadership: Industrial, military, and educational impact*. Lawrence Erlbaum Associates.

Bass, B. M. (1998). *Transformational leadership: industrial*. Military, and Educational Impact.

Bass, B. M. (1998). *Transformational Leadership: Industrial*. Military, and Educational Impact.

Bass, B. M. (2000). The Future of Leadership in Learning Organizations. *The Journal of Leadership Studies*, *7*(3), 18–40. doi:10.1177/107179190000700302

Bass, B. M. (2008). *The Bass Handbook of Leadership: Theory, Research, and Managerial Applications*. Free Press.

Bass, B. M., & Avolio, B. J. (1990). Developing transformational leadership: 1992 and beyond. *Journal of European Industrial Training*, *14*(5), 21–27. doi:10.1108/03090599010135122

Bass, B. M., & Avolio, B. J. (1993). Transformational leadership and organizational culture. *Public Administration Quarterly*, 112–121.

Bass, B. M., & Avolio, B. J. (1993). Transformational leadership: A response to critiques. In M. M. Chemers & R. Ayman (Eds.), *Leadership theory and research: Perspectives and directions*. Free Press.

Bass, B. M., & Avolio, B. J. (1994). Improving organizational effectiveness through transformational leadership. *Sage (Atlanta, Ga.)*.

Bass, B. M., & Avolio, B. J. (1994). *Improving organizational effectiveness through transformational leadership*. SAGE.

Bass, B. M., & Avolio, B. J. (1995). *MLQ multifactor leadership questionnaire, leader form, rater form, and scoring*. Mind Garden.

Bass, B. M., & Avolio, B. J. (1996). Multifactor leadership questionnaire. *Western Journal of Nursing Research*.

Bass, B. M., & Avolio, B. J. (1998). *Platoon readiness as a function of transformational/transactional leadership, squad mores and platoon cultures. Second Interim Report*. U.S. Army Research Institute in the Behavioral Sciences.

Bass, B. M., & Avolio, B. J. (2004). *Transformational leadership development: Manual for the multifactor leadership questionnaire*. Consulting.

Bass, B. M., Avolio, B. J., & Atwater, L. E. (1996). The transformational and transactional leadership of men and women. *Applied Psychology*, *45*(1), 5–34. doi:10.1111/j.1464-0597.1996.tb00847.x

Bass, B. M., & Bass, R. (2008). *Handbook of leadership: Theory, research, and application*. Free Press.

Bass, B. M., & Bass, R. (2008). *The Bass Handbook of Leadership* (4th ed.). Free Press.

Bass, B. M., Jung, D., Avolio, B., & Berson, Y. (2003). Predicting unit performance by assessing transformational and transactional leadership. *The Journal of Applied Psychology*, *88*(2), 207–218. doi:10.1037/0021-9010.88.2.207 PMID:12731705

Bass, B. M., & Riggio, R. E. (2006). *Transformational leadership* (2nd ed.). Psychology Press. doi:10.4324/9781410617095

Bass, B. M., & Steidlmeier, P. (1999). Ethics, character, and authentic transformational leadership behavior. *The Leadership Quarterly*, *10*(2), 181–217. doi:10.1016/S1048-9843(99)00016-8

Bass, B. M., & Stogdill, R. M. (1990). *Bass & Stogdill's handbook of leadership: Theory, research, and managerial applications* (3rd ed.). Free Pr.

Bassett, N. (2021). *Sustainable Fashion Through Circular Business Innovations: New Business Models Reduce Waste. Sustainable Textile and Fashion Value Chains: Drivers*, Concepts, Theories and Solutions.

Bataeva, B., & Vavilina, A. (2018). Emotional Leadership in Organizations: Theoretical and Applied Aspects. Leadership for the Future Sustainable Development of Business and Education.

Bates, R., & Khasawneh, S. (2022). Organizational performance and leadership style in the digital age: An exploratory study of the IT sector. *Journal of Business Research*, *134*, 129–141.

Batinoluho, L. (2022b). Tourism business clusters: A tool for transforming MSEMs in the tourism industry in Tanzania. *Journal of Tourism, Culinary and Entrepreneurship, 2*(20). doi:10.37715/jtce.v2i2.2660

Batinoluho, L. (2022a). Training needs assessment for tourism businesses in Tanzania. *Journal of Tourism, Culinary and Entrepreneurship*, *2*(2), 200–225. Advance online publication. doi:10.37715/jtce.v2i2.2671

Batool, B. F. (2013). Emotional Intelligence and Effective Leadership. *Journal of Business Studies Quarterly*, *4*(3), 84–94.

Battiste, M. (2017). *Decolonizing education: Nourishing the learning spirit*. University of British Columbia Press.

Bayighomog, S. W., & Araslı, H. (2019). Workplace spirituality–customer engagement Nexus: The mediated role of spiritual leadership on customer–oriented boundary–spanning behaviors. *Service Industries Journal*, *39*(7-8), 637–661. doi:10.1080/02642069.2019.1570153

Bayighomog, S. W., & Arasli, H. (2022). Reviving employees' essence of hospitality through spiritual wellbeing, spiritual leadership, and emotional intelligence. *Tourism Management*, *89*, 104406. doi:10.1016/j.tourman.2021.104406

Bayrami, L. (2022). *The implications of virtual teaching and learning in Ontario's publicly funded schools, K-12*. Ontario Teachers' Federation.

Bayrami, L. (2022). *The implications of virtual teaching and learning in Ontario's publicly funded schools, K-12*. Ontario Teachers' Federation. https://www.otffeo.on.ca/en/wp-content/uploads/sites/2/2022/05/The-Implications-of-Virtual-Teaching-and-Learning-Lisa-Bayrami-FULL-VERSION.pdf

Beddoes-Jones, F., & Swailes, S. (2015). Authentic leadership: Development of a new three pillar model. *Strategic HR Review*, *13*(4), 94–99. doi:10.1108/SHR-04-2015-0032

Begley, P. T. (2006). Self-knowledge, capacity and sensitivity: Prerequisites to authentic leadership by school principals. *Journal of Educational Administration*, *44*(6), 570–589. doi:10.1108/09578230610704792

Bell, E., & Bryman, A. (2007). The Ethics of Management Research: An Exploratory Content Analysis. *British Journal of Management, 18*, 63 - 77. doi:10.1111/j.1467-8551.2006.00487

Bell, E., Daltry, J., Mukhida, F., Connor, R., & Varnham, K. (2019). The eradication of black rats (Rattus rattus) from Dog Island, Anguilla, using ground-based techniques. In *Island Invasives: Scaling up to meet the challenge* (pp. 162-166). IUCN.

Belrhiti, Z., Giralt, A. N., & Marchal, B. (2018). Complex leadership in healthcare: A scoping review. *International Journal of Health Policy and Management*, *7*(12), 1073–1084. doi:10.15171/ijhpm.2018.75 PMID:30709082

Benmira, S., & Agboola, M. (2021). Evolution of leadership theory. *BMJ Leader*, *5*, 3–5. doi:10.1136/leader-2020-000296

Bennet, J. (2014). *Intercultural competence: Vital perspectives for diversity and inclusion.*

Bennett, N. J. (2016). Using perceptions as evidence to improve conservation and environmental management. *Conservation Biology*, *30*(3), 582–592. doi:10.1111/cobi.12681 PMID:26801337

Bennett, N. J., & Dearden, P. (2014). From measuring outcomes to providing inputs: Governance, management, and local development for more effective marine protected areas. *Marine Policy*, *50*, 96–110. doi:10.1016/j.marpol.2014.05.005

Bennis, W. (1998). Managers do things right. Leaders do the right thing. In C. Kennedy (Ed.), *Management Gurus* (pp. 47–52). Springer. doi:10.1007/978-3-322-82771-5_7

Bennis, W. G. (1989). Managing the Dream: Leadership in the 21st Century. *Journal of Organizational Change Management*, *2*(1), 6–10. doi:10.1108/09534818910134040

Bennis, W., & Nanus, B. (1985). *Leaders: Strategies for taking charge*. Harper and Row.

Benson, L. E. (1991). *A youth leadership case study* [Doctoral dissertation]. The University of Alberta.

Berasategi Santxo, N., Idoiaga Mondragon, N., Ozamiz-Etxebarria, N., & Dosil-Santamaria, M. (2021). Well-being of adolescents in de-escalation situation: Physical, emotional, social, and academic impact. *Frontiers in Psychology*, *12*, 646027. doi:10.3389/fpsyg.2021.646027 PMID:34512431

Berkovich, I. (2016). School leaders and transformational leadership theory: Time to part ways? *Journal of Educational Administration*, *54*(5), 609–622. doi:10.1108/JEA-11-2015-0100

Berkowitz, B. (2010). Orienting Ideas in Leadership. *The Community Tool Box*. Retrieved from: www.ctb.ku.edu/en/

Beyak, T. S. (2021). *Entangled agencies: A rhizomatic exploration of assemblages from a global studies classroom* [Master's Thesis]. University of Manitoba. https://mspace.lib.umanitoba.ca/xmlui/handle/1993/35192?show=full

Beyak, T. S. (2022). "Thing-power": Art, assemblage, and entanglement as practitioner action research. *Canadian Journal of Action Research*, *22*(3), 45–68. https://journals.nipissingu.ca/index.php/cjar/article/view/579

Bird, C. (1940). *Social psychology*. Appleton-century.

BirdLife International. (2009). *The Caribbean Islands Biodiversity Hotspot*. Final Draft for Submission to the CEPF Donor Council.

Biro, M. M. (2016, August 12). *'Human Resources' Just Doesn't Tell You What H.R. Really Does*. Entrepreneur. https://www.entrepreneur.com/growing-a-business/human-resources-just-doesnt-tell-you-what-hr-really-does/279916

Bjornberg, N. H. (2017). *Creativity and Innovation Through the Job Demands-Resources Model*. [PhD Dissertation]. Old Dominion University. https://digitalcommons.odu.edu/psychology_etds/63

Black, S. A. (2015). A Clear Purpose is the Start Point for Conservation Leadership. *Conservation Letters*, *8*(5), 383–384. doi:10.1111/conl.12203

Black, S. A. (2019). Psychological Knowledge Relevant to Leadership in Wildlife Conservation. *Open Journal of Leadership*, *8*(3), 114–141. doi:10.4236/ojl.2019.83007

Black, S. A. (2021). A Leadership Competence Framework to Support the Development of Conservation Professionals. *Open Journal of Leadership*, *10*(4), 300–337. doi:10.4236/ojl.2021.104019

Black, S. A., & Copsey, J. A. (2014). Does Deming's "System of Profound Knowledge" Apply to Leaders of Biodiversity Conservation? *Open Journal of Leadership*, *03*(2), 53–65. doi:10.4236/ojl.2014.32006

Black, S. A., Groombridge, J. J., & Jones, C. G. (2011a). Leadership and conservation effectiveness: Finding a better way to lead. *Conservation Letters*, *4*(5), 329–339. doi:10.1111/j.1755-263X.2011.00184.x

Black, S. A., Meredith, H. M. R., & Groombridge, J. J. (2011b). Biodiversity conservation: Applying new criteria to assess excellence. *Total Quality Management & Business Excellence*, *22*(11), 1165–1178. doi:10.1080/14783363.2011.624766

Black, S., & Groombridge, J. (2010). Use of a business excellence model to improve conservation programs. *Conservation Biology*, *24*(6), 1448–1458. doi:10.1111/j.1523-1739.2010.01562.x PMID:20825449

Blakeley, K., & Higgs, M. (2014). Responsible leadership development–crucible experiences and power relationships in a global professional services firm. *Human Resource Development International*, *17*(5), 560–576. doi:10.1080/13678868.2014.954192

Blanchard, K. H., Zigarmi, D., & Nelson, R. B. (1993). Situational Leadership® after 25 years: A retrospective. *The Journal of Leadership Studies*, *1*(1), 21–36. doi:10.1177/107179199300100104

Blanch, J., Gil, F., Antino, M., & Rodríguez-Muñoz, A. (2016). Positive leadership models: Theoretical framework and research. *Psychologist Papers*, *37*(3), 170–176.

Blasi, S., & Sedita, S. R. (2022). Mapping the emergence of a new organisational form: An exploration of the intellectual structure of the B Corp research. *Corporate Social Responsibility and Environmental Management*, *29*(1), 107–123. doi:10.1002/csr.2187

Blattner, J. F., Karmia, W. P., & Walter, T. J. (2021). How culture, leadership, and engagement helped a small business survive during the pandemic. *Strategic HR Review*, *20*(3), 88–93. doi:10.1108/SHR-11-2020-0096

Blau, P. (1964). *Power and exchange in social life*. Wiley & Sons.

Bligh, M. C. (2016). Introduction: Exploring compelling contexts through paradox, tension, and new approaches to leadership. In C. Peus, S. Braun, & B. Schyns (Eds.), *Leadership lessons from compelling contexts* (pp. 1–27). Emerald Group. doi:10.1108/S1479-357120160000008001

Bloom, I., & Smith, J. (2010). Scaling Social Impact. *Stanford Social Innovation Review*, *8*(3), 46–51.

Boan, D., & Funderburk, F. (2003). Healthcare quality improvement and organizational culture. *Delmarva Foundation*, *5*, 1–18.

Böckel, A., Hörisch, J., & Tenner, I. (2021). A systematic literature review of crowdfunding and Sustainability: highlighting what really matters. *Management Review Quarterly, 71*, 433-453. https://link.springer.com/article/10.1007/s11301-020-00189-3

Boehnke, K., Bontis, N., DiStefano, J. J., & DiStefano, A. C. (2003). Transformational leadership: An examination of cross-national differences and similarities. *Leadership and Organization Development Journal*, *24*(1), 5–15. doi:10.1108/01437730310457285

Boekhorst, J. A. (2015). The Role of Authentic Leadership in Fostering Workplace Inclusion: A Social Information Processing Perspective. *Human Resource Management*, *54*(2), 241–264. doi:10.1002/hrm.21669

Boerma, M., Coyle, E. A., Dietrich, M. A., Dintzner, M. R., Drayton, S. J., Early, J. L., ... Lin, A. Y. F. (2017). Point/counterpoint: Are outstanding leaders born or made? *American Journal of Pharmaceutical Education*, *81*(3), 1–5. doi:10.5688/ajpe81358 PMID:28496278

Bogardus, E. S. (1928). World leadership types. *Social Sociology Resources*, *12*, 573–599.

Bogardus, E. S. (1929). Leadership and attitudes. *Social Sociology Resources*, *13*, 377–387.

Bogardus, E. S. (1931). Leadership and social situations. *Social Sociology Resources*, *16*, 164–170.

Bogotch, I. (2014). Educational theory: The specific case of social justice as an educational leadership construct. International Handbook of Educational Leadership and Social (In) Justice, 51-65.

Bolden, R., Gosling, J., Marturano, A., & Dennison, P. (2003). *A review of leadership theory and competency frameworks*. Academic Press.

Bolden, R., Gosling, J., & Hawkins, B. (2023). *Exploring leadership: Individual, organizational, and societal perspectives* (2nd ed.). Oxford University Press.

Bolman, L. G., & Deal, T. E. (2008). *Reframing organizations: Artistry, choice, and leadership* (4th ed.). Jossey-Bass.

Boschma, R. (2022a). *Evolutionary Economic Geography and Policy. Papers in Evolutionary Economic Geography (PEEG) 2220*. Utrecht University, Department of Human Geography and Spatial Planning, Group Economic Geography. https://ideas.repec.org/p/egu/wpaper/2220.html

Boschma, R. (2022b). Global value chains from an evolutionary economic geography perspective: A research agenda. *Area Development and Policy*, *7*(2), 123–146. doi:10.1080/23792949.2022.2040371

Boschma, R. A., & Frenken, K. (2006). Why is economic geography not an evolutionary science? Towards an evolutionary economic geography. *Journal of Economic Geography*, *6*(3), 273–302. doi:10.1093/jeg/lbi022

Boubakary, A. (2016). Change management: The need for successfully integrating corporate social responsibility in organizations. *The International Journal of Organizational Analysis*, *24*(2), 231–250.

Bou-Llusar, J. C., Escrig-Tena, A. B., Roca-Puig, V., & Beltrán-Martín, I. (2009). An empirical assessment of the EFQM Excellence Model: Evaluation as a TQM framework relative to the MBNQA Model. *Journal of Operations Management*, *27*(1), 1–22. doi:10.1016/j.jom.2008.04.001

Bowditch, J. L., & Buono, A. F. (2005). *A primer on organizational behaviour* (6th ed.). John Wiley & Sons.

Boxall, P., & Purcell, J. (2011). *Strategy and human Resource Management* (3rd ed.). Palgrave MacMillan.

Boyce, L. A., Zaccaro, S. J., & Wisecarver, M. Z. (2010). Propensity for self-development of leadership attributes: Understanding, predicting, and supporting performance of leader self-development. *The Leadership Quarterly*, *21*(1), 159–178. doi:10.1016/j.leaqua.2009.10.012

Bozhikin, I., Macke, J., & da Costa, L. F. (2019). The role of government and key non-state actors in social entrepreneurship: A systematic literature review. Journal of Cleaner Production, 226, 730–747. doi:10.1016/j.jclepro.2019.04.076

Bozkurt, A., & Sharma, R. C. (2020). Education in normal, new normal, and next normal: Observations from the past, insights from the present and projections for the future. *Asian Journal of Distance Education*, *15*(2), i–x.

Bradach, J. (2003). *Scale and Scope: The Dynamics of Industrial Capitalism*. Harvard University Press.

Branch, R. M., & Kritsonis, W. A. (2006). National Agenda: Minority Teacher Recruitment, Development, and Retention. *Online Submission, 3*(1).

Branson, C. M. (2007). Improving leadership by nurturing moral consciousness through structured self-reflection. *Journal of Educational Administration*, *45*(4), 471–495. doi:10.1108/09578230710762463

Braun, V., & Clarke, V. (2006). Using thematic analysis in psychology. *Qualitative Research in Psychology*, *3*(2), 77–101. doi:10.1191/1478088706qp063oa

Brelsford, S. N., Camarillo, E. E., Garcia, A. S., Garcia, G., Lopez, V. R., Montoya, C. P., ... Merchant, B. (2020). Keeping the bus moving while maintaining social distance in a COVID-19 world. *International Studies in Educational Administration*, *48*(2), 12–20. doi:10.3390oc5010136

Bresman, H., & Rao, V. D. (2017). *What Generations X, Y and Z Want From Leadership*. Retrieved from https://knowledge.insead.edu/: knowledge.insead.edu/leadershiporganisations/what-generations-x-y-and-z-want-from-leadership-5716

Breul, M., & Prub, F. (2021). Applying evolutionary economic geography beyond case studies in the global north: Regional diversification in Vietnam. *Singapore Journal of Tropical Geography*, *43*(1), 26–42. doi:10.1111jtg.12412

Brewer, C. (2010). Servant leadership: A review of literature. *The Online Journal for Workforce Education and Development*, *4*(2), 1–8.

Broh, B. A. (2002). Linking extracurricular programming to academic achievement: Who benefits and why? *Sociology of Education*, *75*(1), 69–95. doi:10.2307/3090254

Bromley, J., & Yazdanpanah, L. K. (2021). Teachers' views of parental involvement in the schooling of low literacy refugee and migrant children: An Australian study. *Teaching English as a Second Language for Foreign Language, Electronic Journal, 25*(2), 1–15. https://eric.ed.gov/?id=EJ1314733

Broomhead, K. E. (2018). Perceived responsibility for developing and maintaining home-school partnerships: The experiences of parents and practitioners. *British Journal of Special Education*, *45*(4), 435–453. doi:10.1111/1467-8578.12242

Brouder, P., Clave, S. A., Gill, A., & Ioannides, D. (2020). *Tourism Destination Evolution.* Routledge. https://www.routledge.com/Tourism-DestinationEvolution/Brouder-Clave-Gill-Ioannides/p/book/9780367668259

Brouder, P. (2014). Evolutionary economic geography: A new path for tourism studies? *Tourism Geographies*, *16*(1), 2–7. doi:10.1080/14616688.2013.864323

Brouder, P., & Eriksson, R. H. (2013). Tourism evolution: On the synergies of tourism studies and evolutionary economic geography. *Annals of Tourism Research*, *43*, 370–389. doi:10.1016/j.annals.2013.07.001

Brower, H. H., Nicklas, B. J., Nader, M. A., Trost, L. M., & Miller, D. P. (2020). Creating effective academic research teams: Two tools borrowed from business practice. *Journal of Clinical and Translational Science*, *5*(1), e74. doi:10.1017/cts.2020.553 PMID:33948292

Brown, A. T. (2006). *Confirmatory factor analysis for applied research.* Guilford.

Brown, J., & Green, T. (2023). Leadership in Government Institutions: A Case Study. *Public Administration Review*, *83*(2), 234–248.

Brown, R., Werbeloff, L., & Raven, R. (2019). Interdisciplinary research and impact. *Global Challenges (Hoboken, NJ)*, *3*(4), 1900020. Advance online publication. doi:10.1002/gch2.201900020 PMID:31565373

Brunetto, Y., Xerri, M., Trinchero, E., Farr-Wharton, R., Shacklock, K., & Borgonovi, E. (2016). Public–private sector comparisons of nurses' work harassment using SET: Italy and Australia. *Public Management Review*, *18*(10), 1479–1503. doi:10.1080/14719037.2015.1114136

Bruni, E., Cortellazzo, L., Bonesso, S., & Gerli, F. (2018). *Leadership style scale: conceptualization and initial validation.* Università Ca'Foscari Venezia, Department of Management: Working Paper Series.

Bruyere, B. L. (2015). Giving Direction and Clarity to Conservation Leadership. *Conservation Letters*, *8*(5), 378–382. doi:10.1111/conl.12174

Bryant, K., & Murillo (Graham), C. L. (2023). Leadership skills and attributes needed to run a simulation center. In P. R. Jeffries (Ed.), *Clinical simulations in nursing education: Advanced concepts, trends, and opportunities* (2nd ed., pp. 1-15). Lippincott Williams & Wilkins.

Bryman, A. (1992). *Charisma and Leadership in Organizations.* SAGE.

Buchholz, W. (2001). Open communication climate. Bentley College.

Buil, I., Martinez, E., & Matute, J. (2019). Transformational leadership and employee performance: The role of identification, engagement and proactive personality. *International Journal of Hospitality Management*, *77*, 64–75. doi:10.1016/j.ijhm.2018.06.014

Bulach, C. R. (2001). A 4-step process for identifying and reshaping school culture. *Principal Leadership*, *1*(8), 48–51.

Burke, W. (1986). Leadership as empowering others. In S. Srivastva (Ed.), *Executive Power* (pp. 51–77). Jossey-Bass.

Burns, J. (1978). *Leadership. Harper and Row: New York.* Lexington Books.

Burns, J. M. (1978). *Leadership.* Harper & Row.

Burns, J. M. (1978). Leadership. New York: Harper and Row. *The Leadership Quarterly, 2*(1).

Burns, J. M. (2004). *Transforming leadership: A new pursuit of happiness.* Grove Press.

Busser, J., & Shulga, L. (2018). Co-created value: Multidimensional scale and nomological network. *Tourism Management, 65*, 69-86. doi:10.1016/j.tourman.2017.09.014

Byrne, D. (1998). *Complexity theory and the social sciences.* Routledge.

Byrne, D. (2022). A worked example of Braun and Clarke's approach to reflexive thematic analysis. *Quality & Quantity, 56*(3), 1391–1412. doi:10.100711135-021-01182-y

Byrne, D., & Callaghan, G. (2023). *Complexity theory and the social sciences: The state of the art* (2nd ed.). Routledge. doi:10.4324/9781003213574

Cabrera, J. (2017). *Millennials, Generation Z and the US Army recruiting efforts: Innovative approaches to reach the newest generations yet.* Savannah College of Art and Design. http://ecollections.scad.edu/iii/cpro/DigitalItemViewPage.external?sp=1003864

Cameron, E., & Green, M. (2019). *Making sense of change management: A complete guide to the models, tools, and techniques of organizational change.* Kogan Page Publishers.

Caniëls, M. C., Semeijn, J. H., & Renders, I. H. (2018). Mind the mindset! The interaction of proactive personality, transformational leadership and growth mindset for engagement at work. *Career Development International, 23*(1), 48–66. doi:10.1108/CDI-11-2016-0194

Capp, G., Astor, R. A., & Gilreath, T. D. (2020). Advancing a conceptual and empirical model of school climate for school staff in California. *Journal of School Violence, 19*(2), 107–121. doi:10.1080/15388220.2018.1532298

Cardinal, L. J., Maldonado, M., & Fried, E. D. (2016). A National Survey to Evaluate Graduate Medical Education in Disparities and Limited English Proficiency: A Report from the AAIM Diversity and Inclusion Committee. *The American Journal of Medicine, 129*(1), 117–125. doi:10.1016/j.amjmed.2015.09.007 PMID:26453990

Caribbean Natural Resources Institute (CANARI). (2019). *Case study on Environmental Awareness Group: Supporting collaboration for the restoration of Redonda Island, Antigua and Barbuda.* CANARI.

Carlyle, T. (1907). Heroes and hero worship. Boston: Adams. (Original publication 1841)

Carney, M. (2011). Influence of organizational culture on quality healthcare delivery. *International Journal of Health Care Quality Assurance, 24*(7), 523–539. doi:10.1108/09526861111160562 PMID:22204086

Carney, S. (2022). Reimagining our futures together: A new social contract for education. *Comparative Education, 58*(4), 568–569. doi:10.1080/03050068.2022.2102326

Carrell, M.R., & Dittrich, J.E. (1978). Equity theory: The Recent Literature, Methodological Considerations, and New Directions. *The Academy of Management Review, 3*(2), 202.

Carro, J., Sarmiento, S., & Rosano, G. (2017). La cultura organizacional y su influencia en la sustentabilidad empresarial: La importancia de la cultura en la sustentabilidad empresarial, *EST. GER, 33*(145), 352–365. doi:10.1016/j.estger.2017.11.006

Carson, J. B., & Farh, J. L. (2023). Leading during crises: Can transformational leadership help? *Leadership and Organization Development Journal*, *44*(5), 630–645.

Casey, J. C. (2021, November 1). *Employee Resource Groups: A Strategic Business Resource for Today's Workplace*. The UMB Digital Archive. https://archive.hshsl.umaryland.edu/handle/10713/17334

Cashin, J., Crewe, P., Desai, J., Desrosiers, L., Prince, J., Shallow, G., & Slaney, S. (2000). Transformational leadership.

Casimer, G., Waldman, D. A., Bartram, T., & Yang, S. (2006). Trust and the relationship between leadership and follower performance: Opening the black box in Australia and China. *Journal of Leadership & Organizational Studies*, *12*(3), 68–84. doi:10.1177/107179190601200305

Caza, A., & Posner, B. Z. (2021). Mixed associations between grit and transformational leadership behavior. *Journal of Leadership Studies*, *15*(3), 6–20. doi:10.1002/jls.21781

Cerullo, M., Yang, K. K., McDevitt, R. C., Maddox, K. J., Roberts, J. W., & Offodile, A. C., II. (2023). When private equity firms buy hospitals? *Harvard Business Review*. https://hbr.org/2023/03/research-what-happens-when-private-equity-firms-buy-hospitals

Cervo, C. S., Mónico, L., Santos, N. R., Hutz, C. S., & Pais, L. (2016). Authentic Leadership Questionnaire: Invariance between samples of Brazilian and Portuguese employees. *Psicologia: Reflexão e Crítica*, *29*(1), 40. Advance online publication. doi:10.118641155-016-0046-4

Chanana, N., & Sangeeta. (2020, October 1). Employee engagement practices during COVID-19 lockdown. *Journal of Public Affairs*, *21*(4). Advance online publication. doi:10.1002/pa.2508 PMID:33041656

Chance, M. R. (2015). *Social fabrics of the mind*. Psychology Press. doi:10.4324/9781315728186

Charmaz, K. (2006). *Constructing grounded theory: A practical guide through qualitative analysis*. SAGE.

Chaudhry, N. I., & Roomi, M. A. (2010). Accounting for the development of human capital in manufacturing organizations: A study of the Pakistani textile sector. *Journal of Human Resource Costing & Accounting*, *14*(3), 178–195. doi:10.1108/14013381011095463

Chazan, B. (2022). What is education? *Principles and Pedagogies in Jewish Education*, 5-12. https://link.springer.com/chapter/10.1007/978-3-030-83925-3_2#DOI

Chen, M. (2014). *The Effect of Training on Employee Retention*. Atlantis Press. 10.2991/gecss-14.2014.90

Chenail, R. (2011). Learning to appraise the quality of qualitative research articles: A contextualized learning object for constructing knowledge. *Qualitative Report*, *1*(16), 236–248. doi:10.46743/2160-3715/2011.1049

Chen, H., Wang, X., Liu, X., & Li, X. (2020). Transformational leadership, teacher job satisfaction, and student academic achievement: A moderated mediation model. *Frontiers in Psychology*, *11*, 1181.

Chen, J. (2022). Understanding teacher leaders' behaviours: Development and validation of the Teacher Leadership Inventory. *Educational Management Administration & Leadership*, *50*(4), 630–648. doi:10.1177/1741143220945704

Chepng'eno, M., & Ngui, T. (2017). Relationship between Emotional Intelligence and Leadership Styles: A Case Study of Leaders in Selected Banking Institutions in Kenya. *International Journal of Research in Humanities and Social Studies*, *4*(2), 1–12.

Cherniss, C., & Goleman, D. (Eds.). (2001). *The emotionally intelligent workplace: How to select for, measure and improve emotional intelligence in individuals, groups, and organizations*. Jossey-Bass.

Cheung-Judge, M.-Y., & Holbeche, L. (2021). *Organizational Development: A practitioner's guide for O.D. and H.R. Essay*. Kogan Page Limited.

Chhabra, T. N. (2010). *Fundamentals of Management* (4th ed.). K.V. SINGH.

Choi, S. B., Kim, K., & Kang, S. W. (2017). Effects of transformational and shared leadership styles on employees' perception of team effectiveness. *Social Behavior and Personality*, *45*(3), 377–386. doi:10.2224bp.5805

Chowdhury, R. G. (2014). *A Study on the Impact of Leadership Styles on Employee Motivation and Commitment: An Empirical Study of Selected Organisations in Corporate Sector*. Available at: https://www.scribd.com/document/410086648/A-study-of-the-Impact-of-Leadership-Styles-onEmployee-Motivation-and-Commitment-An-empirical-study-of-selected-organisations-in-Corporatesector-Rima

Christiansen v. Omnicom Group, Inc. 16-748 F.3d (2017). Christiansen v. Omnicom Group, Inc., No. 16-748 (2d Cir. 2017): Justia

Christmann, E. (1950). Das Pennsylvaniadeutsch als pfälzishe Mundart. *Rheinstiches Jahrbuch fur Volkskunde*, *1*, 47–82.

Chukwusa, J. (2018). Autocratic leadership style: Obstacle to success in academic libraries. *Library Philosophy and Practice*, *1*, 1–11.

Ciftgul, R., & Cetinkanat, A. C. (2021). The impact of school principals on teachers' organisational culture perceptions and organisational citizenship behaviors. *Revista de Cercetare si Interventie Sociala*, *72*, 93–108. doi:10.33788/rcis.72.6

Cilliers, P. (1998). *Complexity and postmodernism: Understanding complex systems*. Routledge.

Ciulla, J. B. (1995). Leadership ethics: Mapping the territory. *Business Ethics Quarterly*, *5*(1), 5–28. doi:10.2307/3857269

Ciulla, J. B. (2012). *Ethics Effectiveness: The Nature of Good Leadership." The Nature of Leadership* (2nd ed.). SAGE.

Clapp-Smith, R., Vogelgesang, G. R., & Avey, J. B. (2009). Authentic leadership and positive psychological capital: The mediating role of trust at the group level of analysis. *Journal of Leadership & Organizational Studies*, *15*(3), 227–240. doi:10.1177/1548051808326596

Clarke, N. (2010). Emotional intelligence and its relationship to transformational leadership and key project manager competencies. *Project Management Journal*, *41*(2), 5–20. doi:10.1002/pmj.20162

Clem, O. M., & Dodge, S. B. (1933). The relation of high school leadership and scholarship to post-school success. *Peabody Journal of Education*, *10*(6), 321–329. doi:10.1080/01619563309535159

Cleveland, S. (2022). *Critical Impact Factors and Leadership Competencies for Project Success* [Doctoral dissertation]. Northeastern University.

Cohen, E. A. (2012). *Supreme command: Soldiers, statesmen and leadership in wartime*. Simon and Schuster.

Cohen, W. (1990). *The Art of the Leader*. Prentice Hall.

Colbert, A. E., Judge, T. A., Choi, D., & Wang, G. (2012). Assessing the trait theory of leadership using self and observer ratings of personality: The mediating role of contributions to group success. *The Leadership Quarterly*, *23*(4), 670–685. doi:10.1016/j.leaqua.2012.03.004

Coman, C., Tiru, L. G., Mesesan-Schmitz, L., Stanciu, C., & Bularca, M. C. (2020). Online teaching and learning in higher education during the Coronavirus pandemic: Students' perspective. *Sustainability (Basel)*, *12*(24), 10367. doi:10.3390u122410367

Conger, J. A., & Kanungo, R. N. (1987). Toward a behavioral theory of charismatic leadership in organizational settings. *Academy of Management Review*, *12*(4), 637–647. doi:10.2307/258069

Conger, J. A., & Kanungo, R. N. (1988). The empowerment process: Integrating theory and practice. *Academy of Management Review*, *13*(3), 471–482. doi:10.2307/258093

Contreras, F. (2016). Servant and spiritual leadership theories: Are they two different notions? *Journal of Human Values*, *22*(3), 202–208. doi:10.1177/0971685816650578

Cook, K. S., & Rice, E. R. (2001). Exchange and power: Issues of structure and agency. In J. H. Turner (Ed.), Handbook of sociological theory (pp. 699-719). Springer.

Cooke, N. J., & Hilton, M. L. (Eds.). (2015). *National Research Council. Enhancing the effectiveness of team science*. The National Academies Press.

Cooper, C. D., Scandura, T. A., & Schriesheim, C. A. (2005). Looking forward but learning from our past: Potential challenges to developing authentic leadership theory and authentic leaders. *The Leadership Quarterly*, *16*(3), 475–493. doi:10.1016/j.leaqua.2005.03.008

Copsey, J. A., Black, S.A., Groombridge, J.J., & Jones, C.G. (2018). Species conservation: Lessons from islands. Cambridge University Press.

Corbett, J., & Slee, R. (2000). An international conversation on inclusive education. In Inclusive Education. Policy, context, and comparative perspectives (pp. 133-146). Academic Press.

Cornelißen, T., & Pfeifer, C. (2007). The impact of participation in sports on educational Attainment: New evidence from Germany. *Economics of Education Review*, *29*(1), 94–103. doi:10.1016/j.econedurev.2009.04.002

Correia, A., & Moital, M. (2009). Antecedents and consequences of prestige motivation in tourism: An expectancy-value motivation. In *Handbook of tourist behavior* (pp. 34–50). Routledge.

Courtney, M. E. (1938). Persistence of leadership. *The School Review*, *46*(2), 97–107. doi:10.1086/440187

Covey, S. R. (2004). *The seven habits of highly effective people: Powerful lessons in personal change (15th Anniversary)*. Free Press.

Covington, M. V. (2000). Goal theory, motivation, and school achievement: An integrative review. *Annual Review of Psychology*, *51*(1), 171–200. doi:10.1146/annurev.psych.51.1.171 PMID:10751969

Cowley, W. H. (1928). Three distinctions in the study of leaders. *Journal of Abnormal and Social Psychology*, *23*(2), 144–157. doi:10.1037/h0073661

Cowley, W. H. (1931). Traits of face-to-face leader. *Journal of Abnormal and Social Psychology*, *26*(3), 304–313. doi:10.1037/h0074766

Crampton, S. M., Hodge, J. W., & Mishra, J. M. (1998). The informal communication network: Factors influencing grapevine activity. *Public Personnel Management*, *27*(4), 569–584. doi:10.1177/009102609802700410

Crane, A., & Matten, D. (2016). *Business ethics: Managing corporate citizenship and Sustainability in the age of globalization* (4th ed.). Oxford University Press.

Creswell, J. W. (1998). *Qualitative inquiry and research design: Choosing among five traditions*. Sage.

Creswell, J. W. (2013). *Qualitative inquiry and research design: Choosing among five approaches* (3rd ed.). Sage Publications.

Cribbion, J. I. (1981). *Leadership: Strategies for organizational effectiveness*. AMACOM.

Crossman, J. (2010). Conceptualising spiritual leadership in secular organizational contexts and its relation to transformational, servant and environmental leadership. *Leadership and Organization Development Journal*, *31*(7), 596–608. doi:10.1108/01437731011079646

Crossman, J. (2011). Environmental and spiritual leadership: Tracing the synergies from an organizational perspective. *Journal of Business Ethics*, *103*(4), 553–565. doi:10.100710551-011-0880-3

Crowell, D. M., & Boynton, B. (2020). *Complexity leadership: Nursing's role in health care delivery* (3rd ed.). FA Davis.

Crowne, K. A. (2009). The relationships among social intelligence, emotional intelligence and cultural intelligence. *Organizational Management Journal*, *6*(3), 148–163. doi:10.1057/omj.2009.20

Crowne, K. A., Young, T. M., Goldman, B., Patterson, B., Krouse, A. M., & Proenca, J. (2017). Leading nurses: Emotional intelligence and leadership development effectiveness. *Leadership in Health Services*, *30*(3), 217–232. doi:10.1108/LHS-12-2015-0055 PMID:28693391

Csikszentmihalyi, M. (2004). *Good business: Leadership, flow, and the making of meaning*. Penguin Group.

Cummings, T. G., & Worley, C. G. (2008). *Organization Development & Change*. South-Western/Cengage Learning.

Cunliffe, A. L. (2010). Retelling tales of the field: In search of organizational ethnography 20 years on. *Organizational Research Methods*, *13*(2), 224–239. doi:10.1177/1094428109340041

D'Souza, A. A. (2003). *Leadership: A trilogy on leadership and effective management*. Paulines Publications.

Daft, R. L. (2010). *Management* (9th ed.). South-Western Cengage Learning.

Daft, R. L., & Lengel, R. H. (1998). *Fusion leadership: Unlocking the subtle forces that change people and organizations*. Berrett-Koehler Publishers.

Daltry, J. (2010). Observations on the Ecology of Dog Island, Anguilla. Anguilla Development Company. Anguilla National Trust, Department of Environment (Government of Anguilla) and DEFRA-Fera (UK Government).

Daltry, J. C. (2007). An introduction to the herpetofauna of Antigua, Barbuda and Redonda, with some conservation recommendations. *Journal of Applied Herpetology*, *4*(2), 97–130. doi:10.1163/157075407780681338

Daltry, J. C., Bloxam, Q., Cooper, G., Day, M. L., Hartley, J., Henry, M., Lindsay, K., & Smith, B. E. (2001). Five years of conserving the 'world's rarest snake', the Antiguan racer Alsophis antiguae. *Oryx*, *35*(2), 119–127. doi:10.1046/j.1365-3008.2001.00169.x

Daltry, J. C., Lindsay, K., Lawrence, S. N., Morton, M. N., Otto, A., & Thibou, A. (2017). Successful reintroduction of the Critically Endangered Antiguan racer *Alsophis antiguae* to offshore islands in Antigua, West Indies. *International Zoo Yearbook*, *51*(1), 97–106. doi:10.1111/izy.12153

Daltry, J. C., Morton, M., Smith, B. E., & Sylvester, I. (2003). *Antiguan Racer Census and Re-introduction*. Antiguan Racer Conservation Project.

Dalziel, P. (2010). *Leveraging "Training Skills Development in SMEs: An Analysis of Canterbury Region, New Zealand"*. Local Economic and Employment Development (LEED). Available at: https://www.academia.edu/23347071/Leveraging_training_and_skills_development_in_SMEs_a_regional_skills_ecosystem_case_study

Dando, T. R., Crowley, S. L., Young, R. P., Carter, S. P., & McDonald, R. A. (2022). Social feasibility assessments in conservation translocations. *Trends in Ecology & Evolution*. Advance online publication. doi:10.1016/j.tree.2022.11.013 PMID:36567154

Daniel, J. (2022). Open Schooling: New era, new relevance, new methods. *International Journal of Open Schooling, 1*(1), 1–8. https://www.nios.ac.in/media/documents/IJOS/articles/IJOS_Ch-17.pdf

Danz, C. (2022). God and Evil—Systematic-Theological Reflections on the Doctrine of God. *Religions, 13*(11), 1075. doi:10.3390/rel13111075

Darling, J., & Leffel, A. (2010). Developing the leadership team in an entrepreneurial venture: A case focusing on the importance of styles. *Journal of Small Business and Entrepreneurship, 23*(3), 355–371. doi:10.1080/08276331.2010.10593490

Daudelin, M. W. (1996). Learning from experience through reflection. *Organizational Dynamics, 24*(3), 36–48. doi:10.1016/S0090-2616(96)90004-2

Davidson, B. (2014). Examining the relationship between non-cognitive skills and leadership: The influence of hope and grit on transformational leadership behavior [Doctor of Education]. University of Kansas.

Davis, B. (2008). Complexity and education: Vital simultaneities. In M. Mason (Ed.), *Complexity theory and the philosophy of education* (pp. 46–61). Wiley-Blackwell. doi:10.1002/9781444307351.ch4

Davis, B., & Sumara, D. (2006). *Complexity and education: Inquiries into learning, teaching, and research.* Lawrence Erlbaum.

Davis, B., & Sumara, D. (2012). Fitting teacher education in/to/for an increasingly complex world. *Complicity: An International Journal of Complexity and Education, 9*(1), 30–40. doi:10.29173/cmplct16531

Day, C., Gu, Q., & Sammons, P. (2016) The impact of leadership on student outcomes: how successful school leaders use transformational and instructional strategies to make a difference. *Educational Administration Quarterly, 52*(2), 221-258.

Day, C., Sammons, P., & Gorgen, K. (2020). *Successful School Leadership.* Education Development Trust.

Day, C., Gu, Q., & Sammons, P. (2016). The impact of leadership on student outcomes: How successful school leaders use transformational and instructional strategies to make a difference. *Educational Administration Quarterly, 52*(2), 221–258. doi:10.1177/0013161X15616863

De Leon, J. (2022). 7 things we learned about COVID's impact on education from a survey of 800 schools. *The 74.* Retrieved May 25, 2020, from https://www.the74million.org/article/7-things-we-learned-about-covids-impact-on-education-from-survey-of-800-schools/

De Smet, A., Dowling, B., Mugayar, M., & Schaninger, B. (2021). *Great Attrition' or 'Great Attraction'? The choice is yours.* https://www.mckinsey.com/capabilities/people-and-organizational-performance/our-insights/great-attrition-or-great-attraction-the-choice-is-yours#/

de Vries, R. E., Bakker-Pieper, A., & Oostenveld, W. (2010). Leadership=communication? Relations of leaders' communication styles, knowledge sharing and leadership outcomes. *Journal of Business and Psychology, 25*, 367–380. doi:10.100710869-009-9140-2 PMID:20700375

Deal, T., & Peterson, K. (2016). *The shaping school culture field book.* John Wiley & Sons. doi:10.1002/9781119210214

Debbarma, I., & Durai, T. (2021). Education disruption: Impact of COVID-19 on students from the Northeast states of India. *Elsevier Public Health Emergency Collection, 120*, 105769. https://www.ncbi.nlm.nih.gov/pmc/articles/PMC7708175/

Deberry-Spence, B. E. N. E. T., & Torres, L. T. (2019). Multinational Corporation Approaches to Corporate Social Responsibility and Entrepreneurship in Africa. The Oxford Handbook of Corporate Social Responsibility: Psychological and Organizational Perspectives, 391.

Deci, E. L., & Ryan, R. M. (2012). *Self-determination theory*. Academic Press.

Deci, E., & Ryan, R. (2010). *Intrinsic Motivation*. doi:10.1002/9780470479216.corpsy0467

Deci, E. L., Koestner, R., & Ryan, R. M. (1999). A meta-analytic review of experiments examining the effects of extrinsic rewards on intrinsic motivation. *Psychological Bulletin, 125*(6), 627–700. doi:10.1037/0033-2909.125.6.627 PMID:10589297

Deci, E. L., Olafsen, A. H., & Ryan, R. M. (2017). Self-determination theory in work organizations: The state of a science. *Annual Review of Organizational Psychology and Organizational Behavior, 4*(1), 19–43. doi:10.1146/annurev-orgpsych-032516-113108

Deci, E. L., & Ryan, R. M. (2004). *Handbook of self-determination research*. University Rochester Press.

Dees, J. G. (2001). The meaning of social entrepreneurship. *Stanford Social Innovation Review, 1*(1), 1–8. https://ssir.org/articles/entry/the_meaning_of_social_entrepreneurship

Dees, J. G. (2008). Scaling Social Impact: What Every Social Entrepreneur Should Know. *Stanford Social Innovation Review, 6*(3), 35–41.

Dehghanan, H., Gheltarani, F., Rahimi, S., & Nawaser, K. (2021). A systematic review of leadership organization: Introducing the concept of a task-relationship-change leadership network. *International Journal on Management of Innovation & Technology, 18*(7), 2130007. doi:10.1142/S021987702130007X

Dent, E. B., Higgins, M. E., & Wharff, D. M. (2005). Spirituality and leadership: An empirical review of definitions, distinctions, and embedded assumptions. *The Leadership Quarterly, 16*(5), 625–653. doi:10.1016/j.leaqua.2005.07.002

Department of Environment (DOE). (2012). *Action Plan for Implementing the Program of Work on Protected Areas of the Convention on Biological Diversity*.

Dessler, G. (2011). *Human resource management* (12th ed.). Prentice-Hall.

Dewhurst, S., & Fitzpatrick, L. (2007). Bringing out the excellent communicator in managers. How to help your leaders fulfill their communication responsibilities. *Strategic Communication Management, 11*(5), 20–23.

DeWitt, P. M. (2018). *School climate: Leading with collective efficacy*. Corwin Press. doi:10.4135/9781071873229

DeWitt, P., & Slade, S. (2014). *School climate change: How do I build a positive environment for learning?* ASCD.

Dey, R., & Carvalho, S. (2014). Are transactional leaders also emotionally intelligent? An analysis of sales executives in India. *International Journal of Business Insights & Transformation, 7*(2), 42–49.

Dhiman, S., Sahu, P. K., Reed, W. R., Ganesh, G. S., Goyal, R. K., & Jain, S. (2020). Impact of COVID-19 outbreak on mental health and perceived strain among caregivers tending children with special needs. *Research in Developmental Disabilities, 107*, 103790. doi:10.1016/j.ridd.2020.103790 PMID:33091712

Dias, M. J., Almodóvar, M., Atiles, J. T., Vargas, A. C., & Zúñiga León, I. M. (2020). Rising to the Challenge: Innovative early childhood teachers adapt to the COVID-19 era. *Childhood Education, 96*(6), 38–45. doi:10.1080/00094056.2020.1846385

Dietz, C., Zacher, H., Scheel, T., Otto, K., & Rigotti, T. (2020). Leaders as role models: Effects of leader presenteeism on employee presenteeism and sick leave. *Work and Stress*, *34*(3), 300–322. doi:10.1080/02678373.2020.1728420

Dinh, J. E., Lord, R. G., Gardner, W. L., Meuser, J. D., Liden, R. C., & Hu, J. (2014). Leadership theory and research in the new millennium: Current theoretical trends and changing perspectives. *The Leadership Quarterly*, *25*(1), 36–62. doi:10.1016/j.leaqua.2013.11.005

Disis, M. L., & Slattery, J. T. (2010). the road we must take: Multidisciplinary team science. *Science Translational Medicine*, *2*(22), 22cm9. Advance online publication. doi:10.1126citranslmed.3000421 PMID:20374998

Donkor, F., & Zhou, D. (2019). Complexity leadership theory: A perspective for state-owned enterprises in Ghana. *International Journal of Educational Leadership and Management*, *7*(2), 139–170. doi:10.17583/ijelm.2019.3647

Donnelly, R., & Patrinos, H. A. (2022). Learning loss during COVID-19: An early systematic review. *Prospects*, *51*(4), 601–609. doi:10.100711125-021-09582-6 PMID:34785823

Donnermeyer, J. (2015). Doubling time and population increase of the Amish. *Journal of Amish and Plain Anabaptist Studies*, *3*(1), 94–109. doi:10.18061/1811/69364

Donnermeyer, J. F., Anderson, C., & Cooksey, E. C. (2013). The Amish Population: County Estimates and Settlement Patterns. *Journal of Amish and Plain Anabaptist Studies*, *1*(1), 72–109. doi:10.18061/1811/54896

Dorasanny, N., & Rampersad, R. (2014). Perceptions on a student leadership development initiative. *Corporate Ownership and Control*, *12*(1), 9.

Dou, D., Devos, G., & Valcke, M. (2016). The effects of autonomy gap in personnel policy, principal leadership and teachers' self-efficacy on their organizational commitment. *Asia Pacific Education Review*, *17*(2), 339–353. doi:10.100712564-016-9428-7

Downton, J. V. (1973). *Rebel leadership: Commitment and charisma in the revolutionary process*. Free Press.

Drath, W., & Palus, C. (1994). *Making Common Sense: Leadership as Meaning-Making in a Community of Practice*. Center for Creative Leadership. doi:10.35613/ccl.1994.2004

Duff, A. R., Podesta, M. T., & Horton, S. (2022). Crisis management and transformational leadership: The winning combination. *Journal of Organizational Behavior*, *43*(2), 180–196.

Dunphy, D., & Stace, D. (1993). The Strategic Management of Corporate Change. *Human Relations*, *46*(8), 905–920. doi:10.1177/001872679304600801

Durrell. (n.d.). *Saving the world's rarest snake*. https://www.durrell.org/news/saving-the-world-s-rarest-snake/

Eadson, W., & Veelen, B. (2023). Green and just regional path development. *Regional Studies, Regional Science*, *10*(1), 218–233. doi:10.1080/21681376.2023.2174043

Eastwood, G. (2013). Moral Choices and Leadership. *The International Journal of Ethical*, 2. Available at: https://scholarlycommons.law.case.edu/ijel/vol2/iss1/14

Eaton, L. (2022). *Transformational leadership: A political science theory transformed by management studies. How did this happen, and why does it matter?* [Doctoral dissertation]. Victoria University of Wellington.

Ebert, R. J., & Griffin, R. W. (2011). *Business essentials* (8th ed.). Prentice Hall.

ECI. (n.d.). *Timeline of business ethics and compliance*. Retrieved from https://www.ethics.org/resources/free-toolkit/ethics-timeline/

Eckhaus, E. (2021). *The Fourth Dimension of Happiness and Work Satisfaction*. doi:10.2478/mmcks-2021-0008

Ecoengineering Caribbean Limited. (2007). *Environmental and Socio-Economic Studies for North East Marine Management Area (NEMMA), Antigua Site Report*. Organization of Eastern Caribbean States – ESDU.

Edmans, A. (2019). *Does corporate social responsibility improve firm value?* Retrieved from https://alexedmans.com/blog/investment-strategies/does-corporate-social-responsibility-improve-firm-value/

Edmondson, A. (1999). Psychological Safety and Learning Behavior in Work Teams. *Administrative Science Quarterly*, *44*(2), 350–383. doi:10.2307/2666999

Egbo, B. (2009). *Teaching for diversity in Canadian schools*. Pearson.

ElAlfy, A., Palaschuk, N., El-Bassiouny, D., Wilson, J., & Weber, O. (2020). Scoping the evolution of corporate social responsibility (CSR) research in the sustainable development goals (SDGs) era. *Sustainability (Basel)*, *12*(14), 5544. doi:10.3390u12145544

Eliana, G. E. (2015). An integrative review of literature on learners in the digital era. *Studia Paedagogica*, 161-184.

Elliot, A. J., Dweck, C. S., & Yeager, D. S. (Eds.). (2017). *Handbook of competence and motivation: Theory and application*. Guilford Publications.

Ellison, N. B., Wohn, D. Y., & Greenhow, C. M. (2014). Adolescents' visions of their future careers, educational plans, and life pathways: The role of bridging and bonding social capital experiences. *Journal of Social and Personal Relationships*, *31*(4), 516–534. doi:10.1177/0265407514523546

Engelbrecht, W. H. (2022). *Consistency in leadership during a pandemic: Managing academics at a private higher education institution in South Africa*. https://www.intechopen.com/online-first/80578

Engels, N., Hotton, G., Devos, G., Bouckenooghe, D., & Aelterman, A. (2008). Principals in schools with a positive school culture. *Educational Studies*, *34*(3), 159–174. doi:10.1080/03055690701811263

Englefield, E., Black, S. A., Copsey, J. A., & Knight, A. T. (2019). Interpersonal Competencies Define Effective Conservation Leadership. *Biological Conservation*, *235*, 18–26. doi:10.1016/j.biocon.2019.03.043

Epitropaki, O., Kark, R., Mainemelis, C., & Lord, R. (2016). Leadership and followership identity processes: A multilevel review. *The Leadership Quarterly Yearly Review*, *28*, 104–129.

Epstein, J. L. (2018). School, family, and community partnerships in teachers' professional work. *Journal of Education for Teaching*, *44*(3), 397–406. doi:10.1080/02607476.2018.1465669

Erchick, D. J., George, A. S., Umeh, C., & Wonodi, C. (2017). Understanding internal accountability in Nigeria's routine immunization system: Perspectives from government officials at the national, state, and local levels. *International Journal of Health Policy and Management*, *6*(7), 403–412. doi:10.15171/ijhpm.2016.150 PMID:28812836

Erdogan, B., & Bauer, T. (2015). *Leader–Member Exchange Theory*. International Encyclopedia of the Social & Behavioral Sciences. doi:10.1093/oxfordhb/9780199326174.013.23

Eren, E. (1984). *Yonetim psikolojisi*. Istanbul Universites.

erudera. (2021). *The oldest university in the world*. https://erudera.com/resources/oldest-universities/

European Foundation for Quality Management (EFQM). (2003). *EFQM Model for Business Excellence*. https://www.efqm.org/index.php/efqm-model/

Evans, L. (2022). Is leadership a myth? A 'new wave' critical leadership-focused research agenda for recontouring the landscape of educational leadership. *Educational Management Administration & Leadership*, *50*(3), 413–435. doi:10.1177/17411432211066274

Fagan, H. A. S., Guenther, S., Wells, B., & Matkin, G. S. (2022). The path to inclusion: A literature review of attributes and impacts of inclusive leaders. *Journal of Leadership Education.* https://journalofleadershiped.org/wp-content/uploads/2022/01/21_1_fagan.pdf

Fairman, J. C., & Mackenzie, S. V. (2015). How teacher leaders influence others and understand their leadership. *International Journal of Leadership in Education*, *18*(1), 61–87. doi:10.1080/13603124.2014.904002

Fannon, D. (2018). The relationship between emotional intelligence and leadership style in educational leaders. *Theses and Dissertations*, *930*, 1–114.

Farinha, L., Sebastião, J. R., Sampaio, C., & Lopes, J. (2020). Social innovation and social entrepreneurship: Discovering origins, exploring current and future trends. *International Review on Public and Nonprofit Marketing*, *17*(1), 77–96. doi:10.100712208-020-00243-6

Farny, S., & Binder, J. (2021). Sustainable entrepreneurship. In *World Encyclopedia of Entrepreneurship* (pp. 605–611). Edward Elgar Publishing. doi:10.4337/9781839104145.00076

Farrell, D., & Rusbult, C. E. (1992). Exploring the exit, voice, loyalty, and neglect typology: The influence of job satisfaction, quality of alternatives, and investment size. *Employee Responsibilities and Rights Journal*, *5*(3), 209–225. doi:10.1007/BF01385048

Fathiaa, A. (2022). Authentic and relatable UN leadership: Interview with Fathiaa Abdalla. In M. Jacquand, V. Tywuschik-Sohlström, P. Nordlund, H. Hammargren, & S. Gruener (Eds.), *The Art of Leadership in the United Nations: Framing What's Blue*. Dag Hammarskjöld Foundation.

Fatima, T., & Elbanna, S. (2023). Corporate social responsibility (CSR) implementation: A review and a research agenda towards an integrative framework. *Journal of Business Ethics*, *183*(1), 105–121. doi:10.100710551-022-05047-8 PMID:35125567

Fayol, H. (1949). *General and industrial management.* Pitman.

Feller, I. (2002). New organizations, old cultures: Strategy and implementation of interdisciplinary programs. *Research Evaluation*, *11*(2), 109–116. doi:10.3152/147154402781776862

Fennell, K. (2021). Conceptualisations of leadership and relevance to health and human service workforce development: A scoping review. *Journal of Multidisciplinary Healthcare*, *14*, 3035–3051. doi:10.2147/JMDH.S329628 PMID:34737575

Ferdman, B. M. (2021). Inclusive Leadership: the fulcrum of inclusion. In B. M. Ferdman, J. Prime, & R. E. Riggio (Eds.), *Inclusive Leadership: transforming diverse lives, workplaces, and societies* (pp. 3–24). Taylor & Francis.

Ferdman, B. M., Prime, J., & Riggio, R. E. (Eds.). (2021). *Inclusive Leadership: transforming diverse lives, workplaces, and societies*. Taylor & Francis.

Fernandez, I. (2015). *Felicidad organizacional. Como construir felicidad en el trabajo.* Ediciones B. Chile S.A. https://books.google.es/books?hl=es&lr=&id=zlQsDwAAQBAJ&oi=fnd&pg=PT5&dq=felicidad+en+el+trabajo&ots=CfkE_X1KXd&sig=L3Eq_Hg6ZWqp8f01BpoMVPEqCCY#v=onepage&q=felicidad%20en%20el%20trabajo&f=false

Fernandez, A. A., & Shaw, G. P. (2020). Academic leadership in a time of crisis: The coronavirus and COVID-19. *Journal of Leadership Studies*, *14*(1), 39–45. doi:10.1002/jls.21684

Fernandez, S. (2009). Peter Drucker's leap to faith: Examining the origin of his purpose driven life and its impact on his views of management. *Journal of Management History*, *15*(4), 404–419. doi:10.1108/17511340910987329

Ferraro, P. J., & Pattanayak, S. K. (2006). Money for nothing? A call for empirical evaluation of biodiversity conservation investments. *PLoS Biology*, *4*(4), 482–488. doi:10.1371/journal.pbio.0040105 PMID:16602825

Ferrell, O. C., Fraedrich, J., & Ferrell, L. (2019). *Business ethics: Ethical decision making and cases* (12th ed.). Cengage Learning.

Ferrin, D. L., & Dirks, K. T. (2002). Trust in Leadership: Meta-Analytic Findings and Implications for Research and Practice. *The Journal of Applied Psychology*, *87*(4), 611–628. doi:10.1037/0021-9010.87.4.611 PMID:12184567

Fidanboy, M. (2022). *Organizations and complex adaptive systems*. Routledge. doi:10.4324/9781003182764

Fisher, B. M., & Edwards, J. E. (1988). Consideration and initiating structure and their relationships with leader effectiveness: a meta-analysis. *Proceedings of the Academy of Management*, 201-205. 10.5465/ambpp.1988.4980535

Fisher, C. (2003). Why do lay people believe that satisfaction and performance are correlated? Possible sources of a commonsense theory. *Journal of Organizational Behavior*, *24*(6), 753–777. doi:10.1002/job.219

Fisher, E. A. (2009). Motivation and leadership in social work management: A review of theories and related studies. *Administration in Social Work*, *33*(4), 347–367. doi:10.1080/03643100902769160

Fisher, R., Natvig, D., Pretorius, E., Putnam, Mi., & Schuhmann, K. (2022). Why is inflectional morphology difficult to borrow? Distributing and lexicalizing plural allomorphory in Pennsylvania Dutch. *Languages (Basel, Switzerland)*, *7*(86), 1–25.

Fiske, S. T., & Lee, T. L. (2008). Stereotypes and prejudice create workplace discrimination. *Diversity at Work,* 13-52.

Fitriana, N., Hutagalung, F. D., Awang, Z., & Zaid, S. M. (2022). Happiness at work: A cross-cultural Validation of happiness at the work scale. *PLoS One*, *17*(1), e0261617. doi:10.1371/journal.pone.0261617 PMID:34986180

Fitz-Enz, J., & John Mattox, I. I. (2014). *Predictive analytics for human resources*. John Wiley & Sons. doi:10.1002/9781118915042

Fleeson, W., & Jayawickreme, E. (2015). Whole trait theory. *Journal of Research in Personality*, *56*, 82–92. doi:10.1016/j.jrp.2014.10.009 PMID:26097268

Fleras, A., & Elliott, J. L. (1992). The" nations within": aboriginal-state relations in Canada, the United States, and New Zealand. Oxford University Press.

Flores Konja, J. V., & Rozas Flores, A. E. (2008). El gobierno corporativo: Un enfoque moderno. *Quipukamayoc*, *15*(29), 7–22. doi:10.15381/quipu.v15i29.2065

Fogel, A., Lyra, M., & Valsiner, J. (Eds.) (1997). *Dynamics and indeterminism in developmental and social processes.* Lawrence Erlbaum.

Foon, M. (2016) The theoretical framework of transformational and transactional leadership styles in enhancing job satisfaction of Nurse educators in Malaysia. *International Journal of Social Science and Humanities Research, 4*(1), 590-595.

Ford, C. M. (1996). A Theory of Individual Creative Action in Multiple Social Domains. *Academy of Management Review*, *21*(4), 1112–1142. doi:10.2307/259166

Ford, R. (2009). Complex leadership competency in health care: Towards framing a theory of practice. *Health Services Management Research*, *22*(3), 101–114. doi:10.1258/hsmr.2008.008016 PMID:19633178

Forkosh-Baruch, A., & Hershkovitz, A. (2019). Knowing me, knowing you: Teachers' perceptions of communication with their students on Facebook. *Interdisciplinary Journal of E-Learning & Learning Objects*, *15*, 59–80. doi:10.28945/4256

Forouk, S., Abu Elanain, H. M., Obeidat, S. M., & Al-Nahyan, M. (2016). HRM practices and organisational performance in the UAE banking sector: The mediating role of organisational innovation. *International Journal of Productivity and Performance Management*, *65*(6), 773–791. doi:10.1108/IJPPM-01-2016-0010

Forson, J. A., Ofosu-Dwamena, E., Opoku, R. A., & Adjavon, S. E. (2021). Employee motivation and job performance: A study of basic school teachers in Ghana. *Future Business Journal*, *7*(1), 1–12. doi:10.118643093-021-00077-6

Franken, E., Edwards, D., & Lambert, S. (2009). Strategy execution: Making it happen. *Strategy and Leadership*, *37*(4), 12–17.

Frantz, J., Lawack, V., & Rhoda, A. (2020). Reflection of academic and professional leaders on leadership in a higher education institution. *SA Journal of Human Resource Management*, *18*. doi:10.4102ajhrm.v18i0.1373

Freeman, G. (2011). Spirituality and servant leadership: A conceptual model and research proposal. *Emerging Leadership Journeys, 4*(1), 120-140.

Frei, F. X., & Morriss, A. (2020). Begin with trust. *Harvard Business Review*, *98*(3), 112–121.

Frías Castro, P. (2014). Compromiso y satisfacción laboral como factores de permanencia de la generación Y. Tesis de grado para optar al grado de Magíster en Gestión de Personas y Dinámica Organizacional. Universidad de Chile. Santiago de Chile.

Friedman, M. (1970). The Social Responsibility Of Business Is to Increase Its Profits A Friedman business doctrine. *The NY Times*. Retrieved from https://www.proquest.com/historical-newspapers/friedman-doctrine/docview/117933451/se-2?accountid=11091

Fry, L. W., & Matherly, L. L. (2006). *Spiritual Leadership and Organizational Performance.* Paper presented at the Paper to be presented at the Academy of Management Meeting, Atlanta, GA, United States.

Fry, L. W. (2003). Toward a theory of spiritual leadership. *The Leadership Quarterly*, *14*(6), 693–727. doi:10.1016/j.leaqua.2003.09.001

Fry, L. W., & Nisiewicz, M. S. (2013). *Maximizing the triple bottom line through spiritual leadership*. Stanford University Press.

Fullan, M. (2001). *Leading in a Culture of Change*. Jossey Bass.

Fullan, M. (2004). *Leadership and sustainability: System thinkers in action*. Corwin Press.

Fu, P. P., & Yukl, G. (2000). Perceived effectiveness of influence tactics in the United States and China. *The Leadership Quarterly*, *11*(2), 251–266. doi:10.1016/S1048-9843(00)00039-4

Furstenberg, C. (2015). La dignidad inherente al hombre a respetar, proteger y promover en todo ser humano: Una lucha que merece la pena para la protección de la humanidad. *Horizonte de Enfermería*, *26*(2), 47–56. doi:10.7764/Horiz_Enferm.26.2.47

Gage, N. A., Larson, A., & Chafouleas, S. M. (2016). The meriden school climate survey–student version: Preliminary evidence of reliability and validity. *Assessment for Effective Intervention*, *41*(2), 67–78. doi:10.1177/1534508415596960

Gainey, B. S. (2009). Crisis management's new role in educational settings. *The Clearing House: A Journal of Educational Strategies, Issues and Ideas, 82*(6), 267–274. doi:10.3200/TCHS.82.6.267-274

Galbraith, P. (2004). Organisational leadership and chaos theory: Let's be careful. *Journal of Educational Administration, 42*(1), 9–28. doi:10.1108/09578230410517440

Galbreath, J., & Rogers, T. (1999). Customer relationship leadership: A leadership and motivation model for the twenty-first century business. *The TQM Magazine, 11*(3), 161–171. doi:10.1108/09544789910262734

Galindo-Martín, M. A., Castaño-Martínez, M. S., & Méndez-Picazo, M. T. (2020). The relationship between green innovation, social entrepreneurship, and sustainable development. *Sustainability (Basel), 12*(11), 4467. doi:10.3390u12114467

Gallo, C. (2022). How Great Leaders Communicate. *Business Communication: Harvard Business Review.* https://hbr.org/2022/11/how-great-leaders-communicate

Galton, F. (1869). Hereditary genius. New York: Appleton. doi:10.1037/13474-000

Gandolfi, F., & Stone, S. (2018). Leadership, leadership styles, and servant leadership. *Journal of Management Research, 18*(4), 261 269.

Garbacz, S. A., Herman, K. C., Thompson, A. M., & Reinke, W. M. (2017). Family engagement in education and intervention: Implementation and evaluation to maximize family, school, and student outcomes. *Journal of School Psychology, 62*, 1–10. doi:10.1016/j.jsp.2017.04.002 PMID:28646971

Garcia-Morales, V. J., Garrido-Moreno, A., & Martin-Rojas, R. (2021). The transformation of higher education after the COVID disruption: Emerging challenges in an online learning scenario. *Frontiers in Psychology, 12*, 616059. doi:10.3389/fpsyg.2021.616059 PMID:33643144

García-Moya, I., Bunn, F., Jiménez-Iglesias, A., Paniagua, C., & Brooks, F. M. (2019). The conceptualisation of school and teacher connectedness in adolescent research: A scoping review of literature. *Educational Review, 71*(4), 423–444. doi:10.1080/00131911.2018.1424117

Gardner, W., Avolio, B. J., & Walumbwa, F. O. (2005). *Authentic leadership theory and practice: Origins, effects and development.* Academic Press.

Garg, S., & Jain, S. (2013). Mapping Leadership Styles of Public and Private Sector Leaders Using Blake and Mouton Leadership Model. *A Management Journal, 4.*

Garg, N. K., & Garg, A. (2008). Inculcating A Corporate Revolution in the New Millennium. *Journal of Commerce and Trade, 3*(2), 23–25.

Garrod, B., & Wilson, J. (Eds.). (2003). Marine Ecotourism: Issues and Experiences. Channel View Publications. *Journal of Sustainable Tourism, 12*(2), 107–111.

Gatling, A., Kang, H. J. A., & Kim, J. S. (2016). The effects of authentic leadership and organizational commitment on turnover intention. *Leadership and Organization Development Journal, 37*(2), 181–199. doi:10.1108/LODJ-05-2014-0090

Gawande, A. (2010). *The Checklist Manifesto: How to Get Things Right.* Metropolitan Books.

Gebretsadik, D. M. (2022). An exploration of change leadership at public higher education institutions in Ethiopia. *SAGE Open, 12*(2), 1–11. doi:10.1177/21582440221091256

Gehlert, S., Murray, A., Sohmer, D., McClintock, M., Conzen, S., & Olopade, O. (2010). The importance of transdisciplinary collaborations for understanding and resolving health disparities. *Social Work in Public Health, 25*(3), 408–422. doi:10.1080/19371910903241124 PMID:20446184

Gehring, D. R. (2007). Applying traits theory of leadership to project management. *Project Management Journal, 38*(1), 44–54. doi:10.1177/875697280703800105

Geijsel, F., Sleegers, P., Leithwood, K., & Jantzi, D. (2003). Transformational leadership effects on teachers' commitment and effort toward school reform. *Journal of Educational Administration, 41*(3), 228–256. doi:10.1108/09578230310474403

Geijsel, F., Sleegers, P., Stoel, R., & Kruger, M. (2009). The effect of teacher psychological and school organizational and leadership factors on teachers' professional learning in Dutch schools. *The Elementary School Journal, 109*(4), 406–427. doi:10.1086/593940

George, D., & Mallery, P. (2016). *IBM SPSS statistics 23 step by step: A simple guide and reference* (14th ed.). Routledge. doi:10.4324/9781315545899

George, J. M. (2000). Emotions and leadership: The role of emotional intelligence. *Human Relations, 53*(8), 1027–1055. doi:10.1177/0018726700538001

George, J. M., & Bettenhausen, K. (1990). Understanding prosocial behavior, sales performance, and turnover: A group-level analysis in a service context. *The Journal of Applied Psychology, 75*(6), 698–709. doi:10.1037/0021-9010.75.6.698

Gergen, K. (2009). *Relational beings: Beyond self and community*. Oxford University Press.

Gerwing, C. (2016). Meaning of change agents within organizational change. *Journal of Applied Leadership and Management, 4*, 21–40.

Ghasabeh, M. S., & Provitera, M. J. (2017). Transformational leadership: Building an effective culture to manage organisational knowledge. *The Journal of Values Based Leadership, 10*(2), 1–19. doi:10.22543/0733.102.1187

Gibbs, L. (2021). Leading through complexity in early childhood education and care. *Australasian Journal of Early Childhood, 46*(4), 335–341. doi:10.1177/18369391211050139

Gibbs, L. (2022). Leadership emergence and development: Organizations shaping leading in early childhood education. *Educational Management Administration & Leadership, 50*(4), 672–693. doi:10.1177/1741143220940324

Gibbs, L., Press, F., & Wong, S. (2019). Complexity leadership theory: A framework for leading in Australian early childhood education settings. In P. Strehmel, J. Heikka, E. Hujala, J. Rodd, & M. Waniganayake (Eds.), *Leadership in early education in times of change: Research from five continents* (pp. 173–186). Verlag Barbara Budrich. doi:10.2307/j.ctvmd84fc.16

Gibson, J., Ivancevich, J., Donnelly, J. Jr, & Konopaske, R. (2003). *Organizations: Behavior, structure, processes* (11th ed.). McGraw-Hill/Irwin.

Gibson, R. (2011). *Rethinking the future: rethinking business, principles, competition, control and complexity, leadership, markets and the world*. Hachette.

Gigliotti, R. A., & Goldthwaite, C. (2021). *Leadership in academic health centers: Core concepts and critical cases*. Kendall Hunt.

Gigliotti, R. A., Ruben, B. D., & Goldthwaite, C. (2017). *Leadership: Communication and social influence in personal and professional settings*. Kendall Hunt.

Gillet, N., & Vandenberghe, C. (2014). Transformational Leadership and Organizational Commitment: The Mediating Role of Job Characteristics. *Human Resource Development Quarterly, 25*(3), 321–347. doi:10.1002/hrdq.21192

Gilliland, C. T., White, J., Gee, B., Kreeftmeijer-Vegter, R., Bietrix, F., Ussi, A. E., Hajduch, M., Kocis, P., Chiba, N., Hirasawa, R., Suematsu, M., Bryans, J., Newman, S., Hall, M. D., & Austin, C. P. (2019). The Fundamental Characteristics of a Translational Scientist. *ACS Pharmacology & Translational Science, 2*(3), 213–216. doi:10.1021/acsptsci.9b00022 PMID:32259057

Gill, R. (2002). Change management—Or change leadership? *Journal of Change Management*, *3*(4), 307–318. doi:10.1080/714023845

Glaser, B. G., & Strauss, A. (1967). *The discovery of grounded theory: Strategies for qualitative research.* Aldine.

Global Impact Investing Network. (2019). *What is impact investing?* Retrieved from https://thegiin.org/impact-investing/need-to-know/#what-is-impact-investing

Gobo, G. (2008). *Doing Ethnography.* Sage. doi:10.4135/9780857028976

Goktas, Y., Hasancebi, F., Varisoglu, B., Akcay, A., Bayrak, N., Baran, M., & Sozbilir, M. (2012). Trends in educational research in Turkey: A content analysis. *Educational Sciences: Theory & Practice*, *12*(1), 455–459.

Goldstein, J. (2000). Emergence: A construct amid a thicket of conceptual snares. *Emergence*, *2*(1), 5–22. doi:10.1207/S15327000EM0201_02

Goldthwaite, C., Gigliotti, R. A., & Spear, S. E. (2023). Leadership in digital contexts. Kendall Hunt.

Goleman, D. (1998). *Working with emotional intelligence.* Bantam Books.

Goleman, D. (2017). *What Makes a Leader?* Harvard Business Press.

Goleman, D. (2018). *Emotional Intelligence: Why it can matter more than IQ.* Bantam Books.

Goleman, D., Boyatzis, R., & McKee, A. (2013). *Primal leadership: Unleashing the power of emotional intelligence.* Harvard Business Review Press.

Goltz, S. M. (2023). Team Spiritual Power: A Resource for Managing Toxic Leadership. *Journal of Management, Spirituality & Religion*, *12*(2), 1–11. doi:10.51327/LUQX5612

Gomez, K., Mawhinney, T., & Betts, K. (2019). *Welcome to generation Z.* Available at: https://www2.deloitte.com/content/dam/Deloitte/us/Documents/consumer-business/welcome-to-gen-z.pdf

Gonzales, L. (2023). Global crises and the evolution of leadership: A critical analysis. *Leadership and Organization Development Journal*, *34*(1), 1–14.

Google. (2023). *Google Learning and Development.* Retrieved from https://www.google.com/about/careers/learning-and-development/

Gorton, R. A., & Alston, J. A. (2012). *School leadership and administration: Important concepts, case studies, & simulations* (9th ed.). McGraw-Hill.

Grace, M. A. (n.d.). *Character and crisis: Toxic workplaces and culture change.* https://digitalud.dbq.edu/ojs/index.php/character/article/view/107

Graen, G., & Uhl-Bien, M. (1995). Relationship-based approach to leadership: Development of leader-member exchange (LMX) theory over 25 years: Applying a multi-level multi-domain perspective. *The Leadership Quarterly*, *6*(2), 219–247. doi:10.1016/1048-9843(95)90036-5

Greenleaf, R. K. (1998). *The power of servant-leadership: Essays.* Berrett-Koehler Publishers.

Greenleaf, R. K., Spears, L. C., & Covey, S. R. (2002). *Servant Leadership: A Journey Into the Nature of Legitimate Power and Greatness.* Paulist Press.

Greeshma, G. (2020). *Multinational corporation: Meaning, definitions, concept, characteristics, types, strategic approach, rationale and regulations.* Retrieved from https://www. businessmanagementideas. Com

Greimel, N. S., Kanbach, D. K., & Chelaru, M. (2023). Virtual teams and transformational leadership: An integrative literature review and avenues for further research. *Journal of Innovation & Knowledge*, *8*(2), 100351. Advance online publication. doi:10.1016/j.jik.2023.100351

GRI. (2016). *Global Reporting Initiative.* GRI 103: Management Approach 2016. https://www.globalreporting.org/standards/gri-standards-download-center/?g=30f6860d-7c3e-4d29-b3ae-98549f76774f

Griebel, T. (2018). Corporate social responsibility: An overview and introduction. *Journal of Corporate Citizenship*, (72), 5–24.

Griffith, J. (2004). Relation of principal transformational leadership to school staff job satisfaction, staff turnover, and school performance. *Journal of Educational Administration*, *42*(3), 333–356. doi:10.1108/09578230410534667

Grissom, J. A., & Condon, L. (2021). Leading schools and districts in times of crisis. *Educational Researcher*, *50*(5), 315–324. doi:10.3102/0013189X211023112

Gronn, P. (2002). Distributed leadership as a unit of analysis. *The Leadership Quarterly*, *13*(4), 423–451. doi:10.1016/S1048-9843(02)00120-0

Grošelj, M., Černe, M., Penger, S., & Grah, B. (2021). Authentic and transformational leadership and innovative work behaviour: The moderating role of psychological empowerment. *European Journal of Innovation Management*, *24*(3), 677–706. doi:10.1108/EJIM-10-2019-0294

Grosjean, F. (2008). *Studying Bilinguals.* Oxford University Press.

Gruenert, S., & Whitaker, T. (2015). *School culture rewired: How to define, assess, an transform it.* ASCD.

Guerriero, S. (2017). *Teachers' pedagogical knowledge and the teaching profession.* https://www.oecd.org/education/ceri/Background_document_to_Symposium_ITEL-FINAL.pdf

Guest, G., MacQueen, K. M., & Namey, E. E. (2012). *Applied Thematic Analysis.* Sage. doi:10.4135/9781483384436

Guest, G., Namey, E., & Mitchell, M. (2013). *Qualitative research: Defining and designing.* SAGE Publications, Ltd. doi:10.4135/9781506374680

Guile, D., & Wilde, R. J. (2022). Complexity theory and learning: Less radical than it seems? *Educational Philosophy and Theory*, 1–9. doi:10.1080/00131857.2022.2132934

Gumus, S., Bellibas, M. S., Esen, M., & Gumus, E. (2018). A systematic review of studies on leadership models in educational research from 1980 to 2014. *Educational Management Administration & Leadership*, *46*(1), 25–48. doi:10.1177/1741143216659296

Guo, K. L., & Sanchez, Y. (2009). *Workplace communication.* Retrieved from http:// healthadmin.jbpub.com/Borkowski/chapter4.pdf

Guo, K. L. (2009). Effective communication in health care: Strategies to improve communication skills for managers. *Business Review (Federal Reserve Bank of Philadelphia)*, *12*(2), 8–19.

Gupta, P., Chauhan, S., Paul, J., & Jaiswal, M. P. (2020). Social entrepreneurship research: A review and future research agenda. Journal of Business Research, 113, 209–229.

Gustafson, L. P., Short, A. K., & Hamilton, N. W. (2022). Teaching and Assessing Active Listening as a Foundational Skill for Lawyers as Leaders, Counselors, Negotiators, and Advocates. *Santa Clara Law Review*, *62*, 1.

Habib, U. E. H., Nasir, A. R., Ullah, F., Qayyum, S., & Thaheem, M. J. (2022). BIM roles and responsibilities in developing countries: A dedicated matrix for design-bid-build projects. *Buildings*, *12*(10), 1752. doi:10.3390/buildings12101752

Hadley, C. N., Mortensen, M., & Edmondson, A. C. (2023). Make it safe for employees to speak up: Especially in risky times. *Harvard Business Review*. https://hbr.org/2023/04/make-it-safe-for-employees-to-speak-up-especially-in-risky-times

Hager, P., & Beckett, D. (2019). *The emergence of complexity: Rethinking education as a social science*. Springer. doi:10.1007/978-3-030-31839-0

Hagman, G. (2021). Empathy: Expanding the Capacity for Humanness and Freedom. *Psychoanalytic Review*, *108*(2), 155–168. doi:10.1521/prev.2021.108.2.155 PMID:33999701

Hai, T. N., Van, T. T., & Thi, H. N. (2021). Relationship between transformational leadership style and leadership thinking of provincial administration leaders. *Emerging Science Journal*, *5*(5). https://ijournalse.org/index.php/ESJ/article/view/610

Hajiali, I., Kessi, A. M. F., Budiandriani, B., Prihatin, E., & Sufri, M. M. (2022). Determination of Work Motivation, Leadership Style, Employee Competence on Job Satisfaction and Employee Performance. *Golden Ratio of Human Resource Management*, *2*(1), 57–69. doi:10.52970/grhrm.v2i1.160

Haldar, S. (2019). Towards a conceptual understanding of sustainability-driven entrepreneurship. *Corporate Social Responsibility and Environmental Management*, *26*(6), 1157–1170. doi:10.1002/csr.1763

Hale, L. V. A., Lutter, J. C., & Shultz, G. V. (2016). The development of a tool for measuring graduate students' topic specific pedagogical content knowledge of thin layer chromatography. *Chemistry Education Research and Practice*, *17*(4), 700–710. doi:10.1039/C5RP00190K

Hall, K. (2021). *Partnerships, mergers, and acquisitions can provide benefits to certain hospitals and Communities.* American Hospital Association. https://www.aha.org/system/files/media/file/2021/10/KH-AHA-Benefits-of-Hospital-Mergers-Acquisitions-2021-10-08.pdf

Hallinger, P., & Heck, R. (1999). Can leadership enhance school effectiveness. *Educational management: Redefining theory, policy and practice*, *178*, 190.

Hallinger, P. (2003). Leading educational change: Reflections on the practice of instructional and transformational leadership. *Cambridge Journal of Education*, *33*(3), 329–352. doi:10.1080/0305764032000122005

Hallinger, P. (2018). Bringing context out of the shadows of leadership. *Educational Management Administration & Leadership*, *46*(1), 5–24. doi:10.1177/1741143216670652

Hall, S. (2020). *The work of representation*. Routledge. doi:10.4324/9780429355363-15

Halm, B. (2011). Employee engagement: A prescription for organizational transformation. *Advances in Health Care Management*, *10*, 77–96. doi:10.1108/S1474-8231(2011)0000010011 PMID:21887939

Halpin, A., & Croft, D. (1962). The Organizational Climate of Schools (Vol. 11, No. 7). Midwest Administration Center, University of Chicago.

Hamilton, M. K. (2021). Introspective faculty assessment of self leadership. *SAGE Open*, *11*(3). doi:10.1177/21582440211031902

Hammond, M., Clapp-Smith, R., & Palanski, M. (2017). Beyond (just) the workplace: A theory of leader development across multiple domains. *Academy of Management Review*, *42*(3), 481–498. doi:10.5465/amr.2014.0431

Hannah, S. T., Woolfolk, R. L., & Lord, R. G. (2009). Leader self-structure: A framework for positive leadership. *Journal of Organizational Behavior*, *30*(2), 269–290. doi:10.1002/job.586

Hannum, K., McFeeters, B. B., & Booysen, L. (Eds.). (2010). *Leading across differences: Casebook*. Pfeiffer.

Hanson, S. (2020). *What Is Social Entrepreneurship?* Retrieved April 13, 2021, from https://www.entrepreneur.com/article/352759

Hao, J., & Yazdanifard, R. (2015). Change management: Strategies and practices in different contexts. *International Journal of Business Research and Management*, *3*(2), 157–167.

Harms, P. D., & Credé, M. (2010). Emotional Intelligence and Transformational and Transactional Leadership: A Meta-Analysis. *Journal of Leadership & Organizational Studies*, *17*(1), 5–17. doi:10.1177/1548051809350894

Harris, A. (2013). *Distributed leadership matters: Perspectives, practicalities, and potential*. Corwin Press. doi:10.4324/9780203607909

Harris, A. (2020). COVID-19–school leadership in crisis? *Journal of Professional Capital and Community*, *5*(3/4), 321–326. doi:10.1108/JPCC-06-2020-0045

Harris, A., & Jones, M. (2020). COVID 19–school leadership in disruptive times. *School Leadership & Management*, *40*(4), 243–247. doi:10.1080/13632434.2020.1811479

Harris, K., Harris, R., & Eplion, D. (2007). Personality, leader-member exchanges, and work outcomes. *Journal of Behavioral and Applied Management*, *8*(2), 92–107. doi:10.21818/001c.16715

Harshitha, G., Raj, S., Jake, S., & Nihal, J. (2018). Impact of Leadership on Team's Performance. *Engineering and Technology Management Student Projects*, 1912.

Harvard Business School. (2013). *Understanding the Impact of Corporate Social Responsibility on Companies*. Retrieved from https://www.hbs.edu/socialenterprise/research/Pages/understanding-the-impact-of-corporate-social-responsibility-on-companies.aspx

Hasim, R. A., & Mahmood, R. (2012). How do Malaysian academic staff perceive their leaders' leadership styles in relation to their commitment to service quality? *The International Journal of the Arts in Society*, *5*(3), 231–242.

Hassink, R., & Ma, M. (2017). Tourism area research and economic geography theories: Investigating the notions of co-evolution and regional innovation systems. In P. Brouder, S, Anton Clave, A. Gill., & D. Ioannides (Eds.), Tourism destination evolution. Routledge.

Hay, I. (2006). Transformational leadership: characteristics and criticisms. *EJournal of Organizational Learning and Leadership*, *5*(2). http://www.weleadinlearning.org/ejournal.htm

Hazy, J. K., & Uhl-Bien, M. (2014). Changing the rules: The implications of complexity science for leadership research and practice. In D. V. Day (Ed.), *The Oxford handbook of leadership and organizations* (pp. 709–732). Oxford University Press.

Hebert, E. B. (2011). *The Relationship between Emotional Intelligence, Transformational Leadership, and Effectiveness in School Principals*. Georgia State University.

He, C., He, S., Mu, E., & Peng, J. (2022). Environmental economic geography: Recent advances and innovative development. *Geography and Sustainability*, *3*(2), 152–163. doi:10.1016/j.geosus.2022.05.002

Heifetz, R. A., & Linsky, M. (2017). *Leadership on the Line, With a New Preface: Staying Alive Through the Dangers of Change*. Harvard Business Review Press.

Heinrichs, J. (2018). School leadership based in a philosophy and pedagogy of parent engagement. *School Leadership & Management*, *38*(2), 187–201. doi:10.1080/13632434.2017.1406905

Heiss, K. (2023). *Introduction to leadership*. Kenneth Heiss.

Hemphill, J. K. & Coons, A.E. (1981). Development of the Leader Behavior Description Questionnaire. In *Stogdill's Handbook of Leadership*. New York: The Free Press.

Henning, M. (2019). Time should tell (more): Evolutionary economic geography and the challenge of history. *Regional Studies*, *53*(4), 602–613. doi:10.1080/00343404.2018.1515481

Herman, R., Gates, S. M., Arifkhanova, A., Bega, A., Chavez-Herrerias, E. R., Han, E., ... Wrabel, S. L. (2017). *School leadership interventions under the every student succeeds act: Evidence review*. Academic Press.

Hermann, R. R., & Bossle, M. B. (2020). Bringing an entrepreneurial focus to sustainability education: A teaching framework based on content analysis. *Journal of Cleaner Production*, 246. doi:10.1016/j.jclepro.2019.119038

Hernández, R., & Serravalle, C. D. (2014). *Felicidad en el trabajo*. Trabajo de investigación final. Universidad Argentina de la Empresa – UADE. https://repositorio.uade.edu.ar/xmlui/bitstream/handle/123456789/2483/Hernandez.pdf?s

Hernández-Sampieri, R., & Mendoza, C. (2018). Metodología de la investigación. Las rutas cuantitativa, cualitativa y mixta. Ciudad de México, México: Editorial Mc Graw Hill Education.

Hernández-Sampieri, R., Fernández-Collado, C., & Baptista-Licio, MdeP. (2014). *Metodología de la investigación*. McGraw-Hill. https://docs.google.com/viewer?a=v&pid=sites&srcid=ZGVmYXVsdGRvbWFpbnxjb250YWR1cmlhcHVibGljYTk5MDUxMHxneDo0NmMxMTY0NzkxNzliZmYw

Hersey, P., & Blanchard, K. H. (1997). *Situational leadership*. Paper presented at the Dean's Forum.

Hersey, P., & Blanchard, K. (1969). Life Cycle Theory of Leadership. *Training and Development Journal*, *23*(5), 26–34.

Hersey, P., & Blanchard, K. H. (1977). *The management of organizational behavior* (3rd ed.). Prentice Hall.

Hersey, P., Blanchard, K. H., & Natemeyer, W. E. (1979). Situational leadership, perception, and the impact of power. *Group & Organization Studies*, *4*(4), 418–428. doi:10.1177/105960117900400404

Herzberg, F. (1959). *The motivation to work*. John Wiley & Sons.

Herzberg, P. A. (1967). *The parameters of cross-validation*. University of Illinois at Urbana-Champaign.

Hesselbein, F., Goldsmith, M., & Beckhard, R. (1996). *The leader of the future: The Drucker foundation*. Jossey-Bass.

Hess, F. M., & Kelly, A. P. (2007). Learning to lead: What gets taught in principal-preparation programs 1. *Teachers College Record*, *109*(1), 244–274. doi:10.1177/016146810710900105

Hewlett, S. A., Allwood, N., Sumberg, K., Scharf, S., & Fargnoli, C. (2012). *Cracking the Code: Executive Presence and Multicultural Professionals*. Center for Talent Innovation. https://coqual.org/wp-content/uploads/2020/09/29_crackingthecode_keyfindings-1.pdf

Hewlett, S. A. (2013). *Forget a mentor; find a sponsor, the new way to fast-track your career*. Harvard Business Review Press.

Hidayati, L., & Zulher, Z. (2022). The Effect of Leadership and Compensation on Employee Performance with Motivation as Moderating Variables at the Pangeran Hotel Pekanbaru. *International Journal of Entrepreneurship and Business Development, 5*(1), 82-91. Available at: https://repo.stiebangkinang.ac.id/19/1/1601-Article%20Text-4642-1-10-20220208.pdf

Hiller, N. J., Sin, H. P., Ponnapalli, A. R., & Ozgen, S. (2019). Benevolence and authority as weirdly unfamiliar: A multi-language meta-analysis of paternalistic leadership behaviors from 152 studies. *The Leadership Quarterly*, *30*(1), 165–184. doi:10.1016/j.leaqua.2018.11.003

Hill, P. C., & Edwards, E. (2013). Measurement in the psychology of religiousness and spirituality: Existing measures and new frontiers. In K. I. Pargament, J. J. Exline, & J. W. Jones (Eds.), APA handbook of psychology, religion, and spirituality: Vol. 1. *American Psychological Association*. doi:10.1037/14045-003

Hitt, D. H., Woodruff, D., Meyers, C. V., & Zhu, G. (2018). Principal competencies that make a difference: Identifying a model for leaders of school turnaround. *Journal of School Leadership*, *28*(1), 56–81. doi:10.1177/105268461802800103

Hoffman, D. L., & Shipilov, A. (2022). Successful Leadership Transitions: A Comparative Study. *The Leadership Quarterly*, *33*(1), 101–117.

Hogan, R., Curphy, G. J., & Hogan, J. (1994). What we know about leadership: Effectiveness and personality. *The American Psychologist*, *49*(6), 493–509. doi:10.1037/0003-066X.49.6.493 PMID:8042818

Ho, J., Foo Seong Ng, D., Chua, P. H., & Binte Munir, N. (2021). Leadership across schools to diffuse an education innovation: Applying complexity leadership theory with ecological leadership. *International Journal of Leadership in Education*, 1–23. doi:10.1080/13603124.2021.2010283

Holbeche, L. (2005). *The high performance organization creating dynamic stability and sustainable success*. Elsevier Butterworth-Heinemann.

Hollander, E. P. (1980). Leadership and Social Exchange Processes. In K. J. Gergen, M. S. Greenberg, & R. H. Willis (Eds.), *Social Exchange*. Springer. doi:10.1007/978-1-4613-3087-5_5

Holmes, J. (2012). *Transformational Leadership: Do Great Leaders Share the Same Traits?* Retrieved from Integrating Woman Leaders Foundation: http://integratingwomanleaders.com/transformational-leadership-do-greatleaders-share-the-same-traits/?goback=%2Egde_1022597_member_131169946

Hooper, M. A., & Bernhardt, V. L. (2016). *Creating capacity for leading and equity in schools*. Routledge. doi:10.4324/9781315668697

Hopen, D. (2010). Leadership and change. *Journal for Quality and Participation*, *32*(4), 3–4.

Horner, M. (1997). Leadership theory: Past, present and future. *Team Performance Management*, *3*(4), 270–287. doi:10.1108/13527599710195402

Horvat, A., & Filipovic, J. (2018). Service quality and maturity of health care organizations through the lens of Complexity Leadership Theory. *Journal of Evaluation in Clinical Practice*, *24*(1), 301–307. doi:10.1111/jep.12789 PMID:28714561

House, R. J. (1971). A path goal theory of leader effectiveness. *Administrative Science Quarterly*, *16*(3), 321–339. doi:10.2307/2391905

House, R. J. (1996). Path-goal theory of leadership: Lessons, legacy, and a reformulated theory. *The Leadership Quarterly*, *7*(3), 323–352. doi:10.1016/S1048-9843(96)90024-7

House, R. J., & Mitchell, T. R. (1975). *Path-goal theory of leadership*. Academic Press.

Hoxha, A. (2015). Empowerment and trust as mediators of the relationship between transformational leadership and organizational effectiveness. *European Journal of Economic and Political Studies*, *8*, 43–60.

Hoy, W. K., Miskel, C. G., & Turan, S. (2010). *Educational administration: eğitim yönetimi; teori, araştırma ve uygulama; theory, research, and practice*. Nobel.

Hoyle, J. R. (1985). *Skills for successful school leaders*. Academic Press.

Hoyle, J. R., English, F., & Steffy, B. (2005). *Skills for successful 21st century school leaders*. R&L Education.

Hoy, W. K., & Miskel, C. G. (2013). *Educational administration: Theory, research, and practice* (9th ed.). McGraw-Hill.

Huang, R., Tlili, A., Chang, T. W., Zhang, X., Nascimbeni, F., & Burgos, D. (2020). Disrupted classes, undisrupted learning during COVID-19 outbreak in China: Application of open educational practices and resources. *Smart Learning Environments*, *7*(19), 1–15. doi:10.118640561-020-00125-8

Huckaby, W. O., & Sperling, H. B. (1981). Leadership giftedness: An idea whose time has not yet come. *Roeper Review*, *3*(3), 19–22. doi:10.1080/02783198109552528

Huguet, B. C. S. (2017). Effective leadership can positively impact school performance. *On the Horizon*, *25*(2), 96–102. doi:10.1108/OTH-07-2016-0044

Hui, L., Phouvong, S., & Phong, L. B. (2018). Transformational leadership facilitates innovation capability: The mediating roles of interpersonal trust. *International Journal of Business Administration*, *9*(3), 1–9. doi:10.5430/ijba.v9n3p1

Human Resources and Skills Development Canada (HRSDC). (2011). *Disability in Canada: A 2006 profile.* Cat. No.: HS64-11/2010.

Humphrey, R. H. (2013). The benefits of emotional intelligence and empathy to entrepreneurship. *Entrepreneurship Research Journal*, *3*(3), 287–294.

Hurst, C., & McConnell. (2010). *An Amish Paradox: Diversity and Change in the World's Largest Amish Community.* Johns Hopkins University Press.

Husebø, S. E., O'Regan, S. S. S., & Nestel, D. (2015). Reflective Practice and Its Role in Simulatio. *Clinical Simulation in Nursing, 11*(8), 368-375. doi:10.1016/j.ecns.2015.04.005

Hustead, E. (2018). Team science and transformational leadership in the healthcare field. Academic Press.

Hutton, D. (2011). Revealing the essential characteristics, qualities and behaviours of the high performing principal: Experiences of the Jamaican school system. *The International Journal of Educational Leadership Preparation*, *5*(3), 1–15.

Hutton, D. M. (2016). The rating of high-performing principals' performance on their leadership dimensions by senior administrators, middle managers and classroom teachers. *Research in Comparative and International Education*, *11*(2), 194–207. doi:10.1177/1745499916632423

IBM. (2022). *IBM Tech Re-Entry Program.* Retrieved from https://www.ibm.com/

Ibrahim, M. S., Ghavifekr, S., Ling, S., Siraj, S., & Azeez, M. I. K. (2014). Can transformational leadership influence on teachers' commitment towards organization, teaching profession, and students learning? A quantitative analysis. *Asia Pacific Education Review*, *15*(2), 177–190. doi:10.100712564-013-9308-3

Indermun, V., & Bayat, M. (2013). The Job Satisfaction-Employee performance relationship: a theoretical perspective. *International Journal of Innovative Research in Management, 11*(2), 1-9. Available at: https://nanopdf.com/download/the-job-satisfaction-employee_pdf

International Institute for Management Development (IMD). (2010). *Corporate Social Responsibility: A role for senior management.* Retrieved from https://www.imd.org/publications/corporate-social-responsibility-role-senior-management/

Ioannides, D., Halkier, H., & Lew, A. A. (2014). Evolutionary economic geography and the economies of tourism destinations. *Tourism Geographies*, *16*(4), 535–539. doi:10.1080/14616688.2014.947315

Iqbal, N., Anwar, S., & Haider, N. (2015). Effect of Leadership Style on Employee Performance. *Arabian Journal of Business and Management Review.*, *5*, 146.

Isaac, R. G., Zerbe, W. J., & Pitt, D. C. (2001). Leadership and motivation: The effective application of expectancy theory. *Journal of Managerial Issues*, 212–226.

Isaacson, W. (2011). *Steve Jobs*. Simon & Schuster.

Ismail, K. (2009). Corporate social responsibility: An Islamic perspective. *International Journal of Social Economics*, *36*(8), 704–717.

Ivanec, T. P. (2022). The lack of academic social interactions and student's learning difficulties during COVID-19 Faculty lockdowns in Croatia: The mediating role of the perceived sense of life disruption caused by the pandemic and the adjustment to online studying. *Social Sciences (Basel, Switzerland)*, *11*(2), 42. doi:10.3390ocsci11020042

Iwelunmor, J., Blackstone, S., Nwaozuru, U., Obiezu-Umeh, C., Uzoaru, F., Mason, S., ... Airhihenbuwa, C. (2022). Social Enterprises for Child and Adolescent Health in Sub-Saharan Africa: A Realist Evaluation. *Child Behavioral Health in Sub-Saharan Africa: Towards Evidence Generation and Policy Development*, 317-332.

Jackson, I. (2008). *Northeast Marine Management Area (NEMMA) 2007-2010 Management Plan*. Updated to include OPAAL Baseline Studies and related documentation (EDITED). Eastern Caribbean States (OECS) Environment and Sustainable Development Unit (ESDU).

Jackson, D., Firtko, A., & Edenborough, M. (2007). Personal resilience as a strategy for surviving and thriving in the face of workplace adversity: A literature review. *Journal of Advanced Nursing*, *60*(1), 1–9. doi:10.1111/j.1365-2648.2007.04412.x PMID:17824934

Jacobsen, C. B., Anderson, L. B., Bollingtoft, A., & Eriksen, T. L. M. (2021, January 28). Can leadership training improve organizational effectiveness? Evidence from a randomized field experiment on transformational and transactional leadership. *Public Administration Review*, *82*(1), 117–131. doi:10.1111/puar.13356

Jacobs, H. L. (1976). A critical evaluation of Fiedler's contingency model of leadership effectiveness in its application to interdisciplinary task groups in public school settings. *Dissertation Abstracts International*, 4912.

Jacobs, T. O. (1970). *Human ResourcesResearch Organization*. Leadership and Exchange in Formal Organizations.

Jafari, J., & Scott, N. (2014). Muslim world and its tourisms. *Annals of Tourism Research*, *44*, 1–19. doi:10.1016/j.annals.2013.08.011

Jago, A. G. (1982). Leadership: Perspectives in Theory and Research. *Management Science*, *28*(3), 315–336. doi:10.1287/mnsc.28.3.315

Jain, P., & Duggal, T. (2016). The influence of transformational leadership and emotional intelligence on organizational commitment. *Journal of Commerce and Management Thought*, *7*(3), 586–598. doi:10.5958/0976-478X.2016.00033.1

James, C., Connolly, M., & Hawkins, M. (2020). Reconceptualising and redefining educational leadership practice. *International Journal of Leadership in Education*, *23*(5), 618–635. doi:10.1080/13603124.2019.1591520

Jameson, J. M., Stegenga, S. M., Ryan, J., & Green, A. (2020). Free appropriate public education in the time of COVID-19. *Rural Special Education Quarterly*, *39*(4), 181–192. doi:10.1177/8756870520959659

Jaroliya, D., & Gyanchandani, R. (2022). Transformational leadership style: A boost or hindrance to team performance in IT sector. *Vilakshan - XIMB Journal of Management*, *19*(1), 87–105. doi:10.1108/XJM-10-2020-0167

Jennifer Molinsky, J. (2022). *Housing for America's older adults: Four problems we must address*. Joint Center for Housing Studies of Harvard University. https://www.jchs.harvard.edu/blog/housing-americas-older-adults-four-problems-we-must-address

Jeon, S. H. (2017). Where to report wrongdoings? Exploring the determinants of internal versus external whistleblowing. *International Review of Public Administration*, *22*(2), 153–171. doi:10.1080/12294659.2017.1315235

Jeronimus, B. F., Riese, H., Sanderman, R., & Ormel, J. (2014). Mutual reinforcement between neuroticism and life experiences: A five-wave, 16-year study to test reciprocal causation. *Journal of Personality and Social Psychology*, *107*(4), 751–764. doi:10.1037/a0037009 PMID:25111305

Jeynes, W. H. (2018). A practical model for school leaders to encourage parental involvement and parental engagement. *School Leadership & Management*, *38*(2), 147–163. doi:10.1080/13632434.2018.1434767

Jiang, H. J., Fingar, K. R., Liang, L., & Henke, R. M. (2022). Risk of Closure Among Independent and Multihospital-Affiliated Rural Hospitals. *JAMA Health Forum*, *3*(7), e221835. doi:10.1001/jamahealthforum.2022.1835 PMID:35977220

Jogulu, U. D., & Wood, G. J. (2008). A cross-cultural study into peer evaluations of women's leadership effectiveness. *Leadership and Organization Development Journal*, *29*(7), 600–616. doi:10.1108/01437730810906344

Johns, C. (2009). *Becoming a reflective practitioner*. John Wiley & Sons.

Johnson, N. N. (2016). *10 Skills for Successful School Leaders* [Conference session]. 2016 American Association of School Personnel Administrators Annual Conference, Orlando, FL. 10.13140/RG.2.2.15691.80169

Johnson, N. N. (2017). *Bolman & Deal's Four-Frame Model of Successful Organizational Leadership* [Conference session]. 2017 American Association of School Personnel Administrators Annual Conference, Chandler, AZ. 10.13140/RG.2.2.31126.45121

Johnson, B. (2023). Remote work and leadership: Insights from the pandemic. *Journal of Business and Management*, *35*(3), 280–296.

Johnson, M., & Lee, A. (2020). Transformational leadership, innovation, and performance: A meta-analytic review. *Journal of Leadership & Organizational Studies*, *27*(2), 217–234.

Johnson, M., & Lee, A. (2022). Transformational Leadership and Diversity: Effects on Team Creativity and Innovation. *The Leadership Quarterly*, *33*(2), 253–270.

Johnson, M., & Lee, A. (2023). Managing Conflict in the New Normal: A Transformational Leadership Approach. *Journal of Leadership Studies*, *29*(1), 15–30.

Johnson, M., & Lee, A. (2023). Transformational Leadership in the New Normal: Fostering Learning and Development. *Journal of Leadership Studies*, *29*(1), 35–50.

Johnson, S. K., & Lambert, B. K. (2020). Why diversity needs inclusion and how leaders make it happen. In *Inclusive Leadership* (pp. 60–69). Routledge. doi:10.4324/9780429449673-4

Jones, M. D., & Kober, J. J. (2019). Employee engagement in difficult times. *World Class Benchmarking*. http://worldclassbenchmarking.com/ employee-engagement-in-difficult-times/

Jones, G. R., George, J. M., & Hill, C. W. L. (2000). *Contemporary management* (2nd ed.). Irwin McGraw-Hill.

Jooste, K. (2004). Leadership: A new perspective. *Journal of Nursing Management*, *12*(3), 217–223. doi:10.1111/j.1365-2834.2003.00450.x PMID:15089960

Jordan, S. R. (2016). Positive Leadership Behavior. In A. Farazmand (Ed.), *Global Encyclopedia of Public Administration, Public Policy, and Governance* (pp. 1–6). Springer International Publishing.

Joseph, C. (2020). *Why Should Employers Track Employees' Online Habits?* Chron. Retrieved from https://smallbusiness.chron.com/ethical-issues-employer-monitoring-internet-usage-12617.html

Jovanovic, D., & Ciric, M. (2018). Benefits of transformational leadership in the context of education. *The European Proceedings of Social & Behavioural Sciences*, 496 – 503. doi:10.15405/epsbs.2016.09.64

Judge, T. A., Piccolo, R. F., & Kosalka, T. (2009). The bright and dark sides of leader traits: A review and theoretical extension of the leader trait paradigm. *The Leadership Quarterly*, *20*(6), 855–875. doi:10.1016/j.leaqua.2009.09.004

Jung, S. B., & Sheldon, S. (2020). Connecting Dimensions of School Leadership for Partnerships with School and Teacher Practices of Family Engagement. *School Community Journal*, *30*(1), 9–32.

Junita, I. (2019). Transformational Leadership in Digital Era: Analysis of Nadiem Makarim (Founder of GO-JEK Indonesia) Leadership Figure. *MPRA Paper*, *91575*(1), 80–92. doi:10.33019/ijbe.v3i1.106

Kadiyono, A. L., Sulistiobudi, R. A., Haris, I., Wahab, M. K. A., Ramdani, I., Purwanto, A., ... Sumartiningsih, S. (2020). Develop leadership style model for indonesian teachers performance in Education 4.0 era. *Systematic Reviews in Pharmacy*, *11*(9), 363–373.

Kaehler, B., & Grundei, J. (2019). *HR governance: A theoretical introduction*. Springer. doi:10.1007/978-3-319-94526-2

Kagoya, M. S., & Mkwizu, K. H. (2019). Factors influencing African Youths at Higher Education Institutions to Shop Online: A Study of Uganda. *International Journal of Research Methodology in Social Science*, *5*(2), 70–77. https://zenodo.org/record/3354104#.XZtpk9IzbZs

Kagoya, S. M., & Mkwizu, K. H. (2020). ICT in Panelist Sessions to Enhance Completion of PhD Studies in Public Universities: Study of Uganda and Tanzania. *ATLAS Tourism and Leisure Review*, *2020*(1), 63–73.

Kagoya, S., & Mkwizu, K. H. (2023). Digital Transformation and Mental Health in Higher Learning Institutions. In *Proceedings of the 2nd International Conference on Finance, Information Technology and Management – ICFITM*. SciTePress. 10.5220/0011601400003581

Kai, H., & Zimmer, R. (2016). Does investing in school capital infrastructure improve student achievement? *Economics of Education Review*, *53*, 143–158. doi:10.1016/j.econedurev.2016.05.007

Kaleem, S., Din, M. U., & Rehman, A. (2021). Impact of principals' leadership style on schools climate, teachers' performance and academic achievement of the students in South Districts of Khyber Pakhtunkhwa. *Elementary Education Online*, *20*(6), 518–527. doi:10.17051/ilkonline.2021.06.055

Kalkan, Ü., Altinay, F., Gazi, Z., Atasoy, R., & Dagli, G. (2020). The relationship between school administrators' leadership styles, school culture, and organisational image. *SAGE Open*, *10*(1). Advance online publication. doi:10.1177/2158244020902081

Kamaludin, M. F., Xavier, J. A., & Amin, M. (2021). Social entrepreneurship and Sustainability: A conceptual framework. *Journal of Social Entrepreneurship*, 1–24. doi:10.1080/19420676.2021.1900339

Kampandu, R. (2019). *Dog Force Security Services cc Anualy Report - Financial and Operations*. Academic Press.

Kandlousi, N. S., Ali, A. J., & Abdollahi, A. (2010). Organizational citizenship behavior in concern of communication satisfaction: The role of the formal and informal communication. *International Journal of Business and Management*, *5*(10), 51–61. doi:10.5539/ijbm.v5n10p51

Kanfer, R. (1990). Motivation Theory and Industrial and Organisational Psychology. In Handbook of industrial and organisational psychology (Vol. 1, pp. 75-170). Consulting Psychology Press.

Kang, S. P., Chen, Y., Svihla, V., Gallup, A., Ferris, K., & Datye, A. K. (2020). Guiding change in higher education: An emergent, iterative application of Kotter's change model. *Studies in Higher Education*. Advance online publication. doi:10.1080/03075079.2020.1741540

Kanwar, A., & Sanjeeva, M. (2022). Student satisfaction survey: A key for quality improvement in the higher education institution. *Journal of Innovation and Entrepreneurship*, *11*(1), 27. doi:10.118613731-022-00196-6

Kaplan, A., & Garner, J. K. (2020). Steps for applying the complex dynamical systems approach in educational research: A guide for the perplexed scholar. *Journal of Experimental Education*, *88*(3), 486–502. doi:10.1080/00220973.2020.1745738

Karabati, S. (2021). Organizational outcomes of destructive leadership: Summary and evaluation. In S. M. Camgöz & Ö. T. Ekmekci (Eds.), *Destructive Leadership and Management Hypocrisy* (pp. 117–127). Emerald Publishing Limited. doi:10.1108/978-1-80043-180-520211008

Karadağ, E. (2015). *Leadership and Organizational Outcomes: Meta-Analysis of Empirical Studies*. Springer. doi:10.1007/978-3-319-14908-0

Karadag, E., Bektas, F., Cogaltay, N., & Yalcin, M. (2015). The effect of educational leadership on students' achievement: A meta-analysis study. *Asia Pacific Education Review*, *16*(1), 79–93. doi:10.100712564-015-9357-x

Karakitapoğlu-Aygün, Z., Gumusluoglu, L., Erturk, A., & Scandura, T. A. (2021). Two to Tango? A cross-cultural investigation of the leader-follower agreement on authoritarian leadership. *Journal of Business Research*, *128*, 473–485. doi:10.1016/j.jbusres.2021.02.034

Kara, S. N., & Mkwizu, K. H. (2020). Demographic factors and travel motivation among leisure tourists in Tanzania. *International Hospitality Review*, *34*(1), 81–103. doi:10.1108/IHR-01-2020-0002

Karasel Ayda, N., Bastas, M., Altinay, F., Altinay, Z., & Dagli, G. (2020). Distance education for students with special needs in primary schools in the period of COVID-19 epidemic. *Propósitos y Representaciones*, *8*(3), 587. doi:10.20511/pyr2020.v8n3.587

Karatepe, O.M., & Vatankhah, S, (2014). The Effect of High-Performance Work practices on Perceived Organisational Support and Turnover Intention: Evidence from the Airline Industry. *Journal of Human Resources in Hospitality & Tourism, 13*, 103-119. . doi:10.1080/15332845.2014.847292

Kark, R., & Van Dijk, D. (2007). Motivation to lead, motivation to follow: The role of the self regulatory focus in leadership processes. *Academy of Management Review*, *32*(2), 500–528. doi:10.5465/amr.2007.24351846

Karwowski, M., & Raulinajtys-Grzybek, M. (2021). The application of corporate social responsibility (CSR) actions for mitigation of environmental, social, corporate governance (ESG), and reputational risk in integrated reports. *Corporate Social Responsibility and Environmental Management*, *28*(4), 1270–1284. doi:10.1002/csr.2137

Katz, D. (2019). Plastic bank: launching social plastic® revolution. *Field Actions Science Reports. The Journal of Field Actions*, (19), 96–99.

Katz, D., & Khan, R. L. (1978). *The social psychology of organization* (2nd ed.). John Wiley.

Katz, E., Lazarsfeld, P. F., & Roper, E. (2006). *Personal Influence - The Part Played by People in the Flow of Mass Communications*. Routledge.

Katzell, R. A., & Thompson, D. E. (1990). Work motivation: Theory and practice. *The American Psychologist*, *45*(2), 144–153. doi:10.1037/0003-066X.45.2.144

Katz, R. L. (1955, Jan.). Skills of an effective supervisor. *Harvard Business Review*, 33–42.

Kaur, N. (2020). *Role of Leader's Emotional Intelligence in Organizational Learning: A Quantitative Analysis*. Rochester Institute of Technology. doi:10.1177/001316447003000308

Kedsuda, L., & Ogunlana, S. O. (2008). Performance and leadership outcome correlates of leadership styles and subordinate commitment. *Engineering, Construction, and Architectural Management*, *15*(2), 164–184. doi:10.1108/09699980810852682

Kegan, R., & Lahey, L. L. (2016). *An everyone culture: Becoming a deliberately developmental organization*. Harvard Business Review Press.

Keim & Shadnam. (2020, July). Leading in an Amish paradise: Humanistic leadership in the Old Order Amish. *Cross Culture & Strategic Management*.

Keim, C., & Shadnam, M. (2018). Through the looking glass: Leadership in the age of surveillance. *Journal of Leadership Studies*, *12*(3), 57–59. doi:10.1002/jls.21596

Keim, C., & Shadnam, M. (2020). Leading in an Amish paradise: Humanistic leadership in the Old Order Amish. *Cross Cultural & Strategic Management*, *27*(3), 473–485. doi:10.1108/CCSM-01-2020-0024

Kellar, F., & Slayton, J. (2016). Fostering and achieving organizational change: A framework for studying the complexities of school leadership. *Journal of School Leadership*, *26*(4), 690–715. doi:10.1177/105268461602600406

Kelly, R. (2016). *Creative development: Transforming education through design thinking, innovation, and invention*. Brush Education.

Kerr, S., Schriesheim, C. A., Murphy, C. J., & Stogdill, R. M. (1974). Toward a contingency theory of leadership based upon the consideration and initiating structure literature. *Organizational Behavior and Human Performance*, *12*(1), 62–82. doi:10.1016/0030-5073(74)90037-3

Kets de Vries, M. F. R., & Florent-Treacy, E. (1999). *The new global leaders*. Jossey-Bass.

Keyton, J., Ford, D. J., & Smith, F. L. (2008). A mesolevel communicative model of collaboration. *Communication Theory*, *18*(3), 376–406. doi:10.1111/j.1468-2885.2008.00327.x

Khalil, M. I., Haque, R., Senathirajah, A. B. S., Connie, G., & Chowdhury, B. (2022). Entrepreneurial leadership effect on SME'S performance in Malaysia. *International Journal of Health Sciences*, *6*, 10758–10775. doi:10.53730/ijhs.v6nS5.10879

Khan, H., Rehmat, M., Butt, T. H., Farooqi, S., & Asim, J. (2020). Impact of transformational leadership on work performance, burnout and social loafing: A mediation model. *Future Business Journal, 6*(40). https://fbj.springeropen.com/articles/10.1186/s43093-020-00043-8

Khan, Z. A., Nawaz, A., Khan, I., & Khan, D. I. (2016). Leadership theories and styles: A literature review. *Journal of Resources Development and Management, 16*. https://core.ac.uk/download/pdf/234696192.pdf

Khan, Z. A., Nawaz, A., & Khan, I. (2016). Leadership theories and styles: A literature review. *Journal of Resources Development and Management*, *16*, 1–7.

Kidere, F., & Mkwizu, K. H. (2022). Sustainability Tourism Education in Developing Countries: A Case of Selected Universities in the East African Communities. *Proceedings of the International Conference on Innovation and Education for Sustainable Human Resources Development*. https://drive.google.com/file/d/126m9AFUwCQ9BuhGW7lv7P-AlRUZO8-jV/view

Kikoski, J. (1993). Effective communication in the International workplace: Models for public sector managers and theorists. *Public Administration Quarterly*, *17*(1), 84.

Kilic-Cakmak, E., Cebi, A., Mihci, P., Gunbatar, M. S., & Akcayir, M. (2013). A content analysis of educational technology research in 2011. *Procedia: Social and Behavioral Sciences*, *106*, 74–83. doi:10.1016/j.sbspro.2013.12.010

Kiliç, M. Y., & Yavuz, M. (2021). The evaluation of authentic leadership in terms of trust in managers and schools' levels of openness to change. *Cukurova University Faculty of Education Journal*, *50*(2), 1033–1068. doi:10.14812/cuefd.863251

Kirkpatrick, S. H., & Locke, E. A. (1991). Leadership: Do traits matter? *Academy of Management Education*, *5*(2), 48–60.

Klasmeier, K. N., Schleu, J. E., Millhoff, C., Poethke, U., & Bormann, K. C. (2022). On the destructiveness of laissez-faire versus abusive supervision: A comparative, multilevel investigation of destructive forms of leadership. *European Journal of Work and Organizational Psychology*, *31*(3), 406–420. doi:10.1080/1359432X.2021.1968375

Klein, J. T., & Porter, A. L. (1990). Preconditions for interdisciplinary research. In P. H. Birnbaum, F. A. Rossini, & D. R. Baldwin (Eds.), *International Research Management*. Academic. doi:10.1093/acprof:oso/9780195062526.003.0002

Kline, R. J. (2022). Emotional Intelligence and Its Role in Leadership. *Journal of Leadership Studies*, *16*(1), 46–53.

Kline, T. J. (2022). Emotional intelligence and leadership efficacy: A meta-analysis. *The Leadership Quarterly*, *33*(2), 120–134.

Klundert, J. V., de Korne, D., Yuan, S., Wang, F., & van Wijngaarden, J. (2020). Hybrid top down bottom up health system innovation in rural China: A qualitative analysis. *PLoS One*, *15*(10), e0239307. doi:10.1371/journal.pone.0239307 PMID:33027287

Knight, B. (2022). The classroom as a complex adaptive system (CAS): Credible framing, useful metaphor or misdesignation? *International Journal of Complexity in Education*, *3*(1), 33–59.

Kochan, T. A., Schmidt, S. M., & deCotis, T. A. (1975). Supervisor-subordinate relations: Leadership and headship. *Human Relations*, *28*(3), 279–294. doi:10.1177/001872677502800306

Koivisto, M. (2020). Self-Directed Adult Learners and the Paradox of Choice. *Proceedings of the 13th International Conference on E-Learning in the Workplace*.

Kolzow, D. R. (2014). *Leading from Within: Building Organizational Leadership Capacity*. Available at: https://www.iedconline.org/clientuploads/Downloads/edrp/Leading_from_Within.pdf

Kong, M., & Thompson, L. A. (2020). Considerations for young children and those with special needs as COVID-19 continues. *JAMA Pediatrics*, *174*(10), 1012–1012. doi:10.1001/jamapediatrics.2020.2478 PMID:32870247

Koopmans, M. (2020). Education is a complex dynamical system: Challenges for research. *Journal of Experimental Education*, *88*(3), 358–374. doi:10.1080/00220973.2019.1566199

Korejan, M., & Shahbazi, H. (2016). An analysis of the transformational leadership theory. *Revue des Sciences Fondamentales et Appliquées*, *8*(3), 452. doi:10.4314/jfas.v8i3s.192

Kostikov, E. D. (2014). The Great-Power Ambitions and Frontier Policy of the Peking Leadership. *Chinese Law & Government*, *6*(4), 8–21. doi:10.2753/CLG0009-460906048

Kotiaho, J. S. (2001). Costs of sexual traits: A mismatch between theoretical considerations and empirical evidence. *Biological Reviews of the Cambridge Philosophical Society*, *76*(3), 365–376. doi:10.1017/S1464793101005711 PMID:11569789

Kotler, P., & Armstrong, G. (2006). *Principles of marketing* (11th ed.). Prentice Hall.

Kotter, J. P. (1988). *The Leadership Factor*. Free Press.

Kotter, J. P., & Cohen, D. S. (2002). *The heart of change: Real-life stories of how people change their organizations*. Harvard Business Press.

Kotterman, J. (2006). Leadership vs Management: What's the difference? *Journal for Quality and Participation*, *29*(2), 13–17.

Koubova, V., & Buchko, A. A. (2013). Life-work balance: Emotional intelligence as a crucial component of achieving both personal life and work performance. *Management Research Review*, *36*(7), 700–719. doi:10.1108/MRR-05-2012-0115

Kouzes, J. M., & Posner, B. Z. (1995). *The Leadership Challenge*. JoeyBass.

Kouzes, J. M., & Posner, B. Z. (2017). *The leadership challenge: How to keep getting extraordinary things done in organizations*. Jossey-Bass.

Kouzes, J. M., & Posner, B. Z. (2023). *The leadership challenge: How to make extraordinary things happen in organizations*. John Wiley & Sons.

Kozikoglu, I., & Tosun, Y. (2020). Examining the relationship between teachers' views on culturally sensitive pedagogy and their cultural intelligence. *Journal of Higher Education and Science*, *10*(3), 539–548. doi:10.5961/jhes.2020.414

Krausz, R. R. (1986). Power and leadership in organizations. *Transactional Analysis Journal*, *16*(2), 85–94. doi:10.1177/036215378601600202

Kraybill, D. (2001). *The Riddle of Amish Culture* (Revised edition). Johns Hopkins University Press.

Kraybill, D. B., & Nolt, S. M. (2004). *Amish Enterprise: From Plows to Profits*. Johns Hopkins University Press. doi:10.56021/9780801878046

Kraybill, D., Johnson-Weiner, K., & Nolt, S. (2013). *The Amish*. Johns Hopkins University Press. doi:10.56021/9781421409146

Kruger, M., Witziers, B., & Sleegers, P. (2007). The impact of school leader variables on school level factors: Validation of a causal model. *School Effectiveness and School Improvement*, *18*(1), 1–20. doi:10.1080/09243450600797638

Kruse, K. (2013). *What is Leadership?* Retrieved from Forbes: https://www.forbes.com/sites/kevinkruse/2013/04/09/what-isleadership/#305ccc45b90c

Kruse, S. D. (2021). Hiding in plain sight: Systems thinking and school organization. *Journal of Educational Administration*, *59*(1), 43–58. doi:10.1108/JEA-01-2020-0011

Kumar, S., & Kumar, S. (2015). Structure equation modeling basic assumptions and concepts: A novices guide. *Asian Journal of Management Sciences*, *3*(7), 25–28.

Kun, A., & Gadanecz, P. (2022). Workplace happiness, well-being, and their relationship with psychological capital: A study of Hungarian Teachers. *Current Psychology (New Brunswick, N.J.)*, *41*(1), 185–199. doi:10.100712144-019-00550-0

Kuswati, Y. (2020). The effect of motivation on employee performance. Budapest International Research and Critics Institute. Humanities and Social Sciences, 3(2), 995-1002. https://doi.org/10.33258/birci.v3i2.928

Kytle, A. W., & Bogotch, I. E. (2000). Measuring reculturing in national reform models. *Journal of School Leadership*, *10*(2), 131–157. doi:10.1177/105268460001000202

Labate, H. (2020). *Knowledge access and distribution: The future(s) of what we used to call 'curriculum'*. https://unesdoc.unesco.org/ark:/48223/pf0000374153

LaBonte, R., Barbour, M. K., & Nagle, J. (2021). *Pandemic pedagogy in Canada: Lessons from the first 18 months*. Canadian eLearning Network.

Lam, L. W., & Xu, A. J. (2019). Power imbalance and employee silence: The role of abusive leadership, power distance orientation, and perceived organisational politics. *Applied Psychology*, *68*(3), 513–546. doi:10.1111/apps.12170

Lamo, E. (2019). *The center of success: a case study on Hilton's company culture.* California Polytechnic State University. https://digitalcommons.calpoly.edu/cgi/viewcontent.cgi?article=1002&context=expindsp

Langely, N., & Jacobs, M. M. (2014). *5 Essential Skills for Successful School Leaders: Moving from Good to Great.* Rowman & Littlefield.

Lang, R., & Fink, M. (2019). Rural social entrepreneurship: The role of social capital within and across institutional levels. *Journal of Rural Studies*, *70*, 155–168. doi:10.1016/j.jrurstud.2018.03.012

Larsen–Freeman, D. (2019). On language learner agency: A complex dynamic systems theory perspective. *Modern Language Journal*, *103*, 61–79. doi:10.1111/modl.12536

Laschinger, H. K. S., Wong, C. A., & Grau, A. L. (2013). Authentic leadership, empowerment and burnout: A comparison in new graduates and experienced nurses. *Journal of Nursing Management*, *21*(3), 541–552. doi:10.1111/j.1365-2834.2012.01375.x PMID:23405976

Lashley, C. (1998). Towards an understanding of employee empowerment in hostitality services. *International Journal of Contemporary Hospitality Management*, *7*(1), 27–32. doi:10.1108/09596119510078207

Lawrence, N., James, K., Otto, A., Ross, T. N., & Daltry, C. J. (2013). Is Eradicating Rats Worth It? Impacts Observed on Antigua's Offshore Islands. *19th Regional Meeting*, Society for the Conservation and Study of Caribbean Birds, Grenada.

Lee, Y. H. (2019). Emotional intelligence, servant leadership, and development goal orientation in athletic directors. *Sport Management Review*, *22*(3), 395–406. doi:10.1016/j.smr.2018.05.003

Leithwood, K., Hallinger, P., Furman, G. C., Riley, K., MacBeath, J., & Mulford, B. (2008). Second international handbook of educational leadership: Part one. Academic Press.

Leithwood, K., Harris, A., & Hopkins, D. (2020). Seven strong claims about successful school leadership revisited. *School Leadership & Management*, *40*(1), 5–22. doi:10.1080/13632434.2019.1596077

Leithwood, K., & Jantzi, D. (1990). Transformational leadership: How principals can help reform school cultures. *School Effectiveness and School Improvement*, *1*(4), 249–280. doi:10.1080/0924345900010402

Leithwood, K., & Jantzi, D. (2000). The effects of transformational leadership on organizational conditions and student engagement with school. *Journal of Educational Administration*, *38*(2), 112–129. doi:10.1108/09578230010320064

Leithwood, K., & Jantzi, D. (2005). A review of transformational school leadership research 1996–2005. *Leadership and Policy in Schools*, *4*(3), 177–199. doi:10.1080/15700760500244769

Leithwood, K., & Jantzi, D. (2006). Transformational school leadership for large-scale reform: Effects on students, teachers, and their classroom practices. *School Effectiveness and School Improvement*, *17*(2), 201–227. doi:10.1080/09243450600565829

Leithwood, K., Louis, K., Anderson, S., & Wahlstrom, K. (2004). *How leadership influences student learning. Review of Research.* The Wallace Foundation.

Leithwood, K., & Sun, J. (2012). The nature and effects of transformational school leadership: A meta-analytic review of unpublished research. *Educational Administration Quarterly*, *48*(3), 387–423. doi:10.1177/0013161X11436268

Leithwood, K., Sun, J., & Schumacker, R. (2020). How school leadership influences student learning: A test of "The four paths model". *Educational Administration Quarterly*, *56*(4), 570–599. doi:10.1177/0013161X19878772

Leitner, S. M. (2021). *Net Migration and its Skill Composition in the Western Balkan Countries between 2010 and 2019.* Results from a Cohort Approach Analysis, The Vienna Institute for International Economic Studies Wiener Institut für Internationale Wirtschaftsvergleiche. Available at: https://wiiw.ac.at/net-migration-and-its-skill-composition-in-the-western-balkancountries-between-2010-and-2019-results-from-a-cohort-approach-analysis-dlp-5695.pdf

Levin, B. (2011). Mobilizing research knowledge in education. *London Review of Education*, *9*(1), 15–26. doi:10.1080/14748460.2011.550431

Levins, H. (2023). *Hospital consolidation continues to boost costs, narrow access, and impact care quality.* Penn Leonard Davis Institute of Health Economics. https://ldi.upenn.edu/our-work/research-updates/hospital-consolidation-continues-to-boost-costs-narrow-access-and-impact-care-quality/#:~:text=As%20hospital%20consolidations%20swept%20the,consistently%20produced%20higher%20care%20prices

Lewin, K., Lippet, R., & White, R. K. (1939). Patterns of aggressive behavior in experimentally created social climates. *The Journal of Social Psychology*, *10*(2), 271–301. doi:10.1080/00224545.1939.9713366

Lichtenstein, B. B., Uhl-Bien, M., Marion, R., Seers, A., Orton, J. D., & Schreiber, C. (2006). Complexity leadership theory: An interactive perspective on leading in complex adaptive systems. *Emergence*, *8*(4), 2–12.

Lin Tengi, M., Mansor, M., & Hashim, Z. (2017). A review theory of transformational leadership for school. *International Journal of Academic Research in Business & Social Sciences*, *7*(3), 792–799.

Li, R., Chen, Z., Zhang, H., & Luo, J. (2019). How do authoritarian leadership and abusive supervision jointly thwart follower proactivity? a social control perspective. *Journal of Management*, *47*(4), 930–956. doi:10.1177/0149206319878261

Liu, J., Siu, O. L., & Shi, K. (2010). Transformational leadership and employee well-being: The mediating role of trust in the leader and self-efficacy. *Applied Psychology*, *59*(3), 454–479. doi:10.1111/j.1464-0597.2009.00407.x

Liu, Z., Riggio, R. E., Reichard, R. J., & Walker, D. O. (2022). Everyday leadership: The construct, its validation, and developmental antecedents. *International Leadership Journal*, *14*(1), 3–35.

Lochmiller, C. R. (2021). Rural superintendents' responses to COVID-19: Navigating local control during a public health crisis. *Frontiers in Education*, *6*(617058), 1–14. doi:10.3389/feduc.2021.617058

Locker, K. O., & Findlay, M. (2009). *Business communication now* (Canadian Edition). McGraw-Hill, Ryerson.

Löfsten, H. (2016). New technology-based firms and their survival: The importance of business networks, and entrepreneurial business behaviour and competition. *Local Economy*, *31*(3), 393–409. doi:10.1177/0269094216637334

Long, C. (2022, July 5). *Wilson Medical Center Needs Radical Change.* The East Carolinian. http://www.piratemedia1.com/theeastcarolinian/article_94f4dcc0-fcd4-11ec-bc47-c320bb2001d0.html

López Chanes, F., Casique Guerrero, A., & Ferrer Guevara, J. (2019). La Satisfacción hacia el Trabajo. Un Análisis Basado en las Teorías de las Expectativas y de Equidad. *Administración y Organizaciones, 9*(17), 117-134. https://rayo.xoc.uam.mx/index.php/Rayo/article/view/249

Lopez, A. E. (2014). Re-conceptualising teacher leadership through curriculum inquiry in pursuit of social justice: Case study from the Canadian context. In *International Handbook of Educational Leadership and Social (In) Justice* (pp. 465–484). Springer. doi:10.1007/978-94-007-6555-9_26

Lotrecchiano, G. R., DiazGranados, D., Sprecher, J., McCormack, W. T., Ranwala, D., Wooten, K., Lackland, D., Billings, H., & Brasier, A. R. (2020). Individual and team competencies in translational teams. *Journal of Clinical and Translational Science*, *5*(1), e72. doi:10.1017/cts.2020.551 PMID:33948290

Love, T. S., & Hughes, A. I. (2022). Engineering pedagogical content knowledge: Examining correlations with formal and informal preparation experiences. *International Journal of STEM Education, 9*(1), 29. doi:10.118640594-022-00345-z

Lozano-Correa, L. J., Pérez-Uribe, R. I., & Ocampo-Guzmán, D. (2020). Truthfulness as a critical factor in competitiveness in medium-sized companies in Colombia. doi:10.4018/978-1-7998-2019-2.ch015

Lucas, S. E., & Valentine, J. W. (2002). *Transformational leadership: Principals, leadership teams, and school culture.* Academic Press.

Lundqvist, D., Wallo, A., Coetzer, A., & Kock, H. (2023). Leadership and learning at work: A systematic literature review of learning-oriented leadership. *Journal of Leadership & Organizational Studies, 30*(2), 205–238. doi:10.1177/15480518221133970

Lunenburg, F. C. (2012). Power and leadership: An influence process. *International Journal of Management, Business, and Administration, 15*(1), 1-9.

Lunenburg, F. C. (2011). Leadership versus Management: A Key Distinction - At Least in Theory. *International Journal of Management, Business Administration (London), 14*(1), 15–18. doi:10.24234/miopap.v3i3.15

Lusiani, M., Abidin, Z., Fitrianingsih, D., Yusnita, E., Adiwinata, D., Rachmaniah, D., ... Purwanto, A. (2020). Effect of servant, digital and green leadership toward business performance: Evidence from Indonesian manufacturing. *Systematic Reviews in Pharmacy*, 11.

Lustick, H. (2021). Going restorative, staying tough: Urban principals' perceptions of restorative practices in collocated small schools. *Education and Urban Society, 53*(7), 739–760. doi:10.1177/0013124520974335

Luthans, F. (1973). The contingency theory of management: A path out of the jungle. *Business Horizons, 16*(3), 67–72. doi:10.1016/0007-6813(73)90026-8

Luthans, F. (2011). *Organizational behavior* (11th ed.). McGraw-Hill Irwin.

Lyubomirsky, S., & Layous, K. (2013). How do simple positive activities increase well-being? *Current Directions in Psychological Science, 22*(1), 57–62. doi:10.1177/0963721412469809

Maamari, B., & Majdalani, J. (2017). Emotional intelligence, leadership style & organizational climate. *The International Journal of Organizational Analysis, 25*(2), 1–25. doi:10.1108/IJOA-04-2016-1010

MacDonald, M., & Sánchez, A. (2010). Provoking dialogue: Promote a deeper understanding of teaching and learning through images and documents. *Canadian Children, 35*(2).

Machi, L. A., & McEvoy, B. T. (2021). The literature review: Six steps to success (3rd ed.). SAGE Publications Ltd.

Mackinnon, D., Dawley, S., Pike, A., & Cumbers, A. (2018). *Rethinking Path Creation: A Geographical Political Economy Approach.* Papers in Evolutionary Economic Geography (PEEG) 1825, Utrecht University, Department of Human Geography and Spatial Planning, Group Economic Geography,

Maguire, M., & Delahunt, B. (2017). Doing a thematic analysis: A practical step-by-step learning and teaching scholars. *All Ireland Journal of Higher Education, 9*(2), 3351. https://ojs.aishe.org/index.php/aishe-j/article/view/335

Mahmood, Z., & Humphrey, D. (2013). The impact of corporate social responsibility on organizational performance in Malaysian manufacturing firms. *International Journal of Business and Social Science, 4*(2), 145–154.

Mair, J., & Marti, I. (2006). Social entrepreneurship research: A source of explanation, prediction, and delight. *Journal of World Business, 41*(1), 36–44. doi:10.1016/j.jwb.2005.09.002

Maldonado, T., Vera, D., & Ramos, N. (2018). How humble is your company culture? And, why does it matter? *Business Horizons*, *61*(5), 745–753. doi:10.1016/j.bushor.2018.05.005

Maldonado, T., Vera, D., & Spangler, W. D. (2022). Unpacking humility: Leader humility, leader personality, and why they matter. *Business Horizons*, *65*(2), 125–137. doi:10.1016/j.bushor.2021.02.032

Malone, P., & Fry, L. W. (2003). *Transforming schools through spiritual leadership: A field experiment.* Paper presented at the Annual Meeting of the Academy of Management, Seattle, WA.

Malterud, K., Siersma, V. D., & Guassora, A. D. (2015). Sample size in qualitative interview studies: Guided by information power. *Qualitative Health Research*, *26*(13), 1753–1760. doi:10.1177/1049732315617444 PMID:26613970

Manitoba Education and Advanced Learning. (2015). *Grades 9 to 12 visual arts: Manitoba curriculum framework.* The Government of Manitoba. https://www.edu.gov.mb.ca/k12/cur/arts/visual/framework_9-12.html

Manitoba Education and Early Childhood Learning. (2023, April 10). *Mandate.* Manitoba Education and Early Childhood Learning. https://www.edu.gov.mb.ca/aboutus.html

Manitoba Education and Training. (2017). *Global issues: Citizenship and sustainability.* https://www.edu.gov.mb.ca/k12/cur/socstud/global_issues/full_doc.pdf

Manolopoulos, D. (2007). An evaluation of employee motivation in the extended public sector in Greece. *Employee Relations*, *30*(1), 63–85. doi:10.1108/01425450810835428

Maria, O., & Ilias, K. (2020). The effect of administrative actions on satisfaction of primary and secondary public school principals. *Journal of Contemporary Education Theory & Research*, *4*(1), 21–27. doi:10.5281/zenodo.3769323

Marion, R., & Uhl-Bien, M. (2002, December). *Complexity v. transformation: The new leadership revisited* [Paper presentation]. Managing the Complex IV-Conference on Complex Systems and the Management of Organizations, Ft. Meyers, FL.

Mark, M. A., & Greer, J. E. (1995). The VCR Tutor: Effective instruction for device operation. *Journal of the Learning Sciences*, *4*(2), 209–246. doi:10.120715327809jls0402_3

Marks, M. A., Mathieu, J. E., & Zaccaro, S. J. (2001). A temporally based framework and taxonomy of team processes. *Academy of Management Review*, *26*(3), 356–376. doi:10.2307/259182

Marques, J. (2016). *Leadership: Finding balance between ambition and acceptance*. Routledge. doi:10.4324/9781315695662

Martinko, M. J., Harvey, P., Brees, J. R., & Mackey, J. (2013). A review of abusive supervision research. *Journal of Organizational Behavior*, *34*(S1), S120–S137. doi:10.1002/job.1888

Martinko, M. J., Harvey, P., & Douglas, S. C. (2007). The role, function, and contribution of attribution theory to leadership: A review. *The Leadership Quarterly*, *18*(6), 561–585. doi:10.1016/j.leaqua.2007.09.004

Martin, R., & McCormack, L. (2023). Nurturing emotional intelligence through transformational leadership: New insights for the post-pandemic era. *Journal of Business Ethics*, *170*(1), 101–118.

Martin, R., & Sunley, P. (2022). Making history matter more in evolutionary economic geography. *Advances in Economic Geography*, *66*(2), 65–80. doi:10.1515/zfw-2022-0014

Martins, T. L. F., Brooke, M. D. L., Hilton, G. M., Farnsworth, S., Gould, J., & Pain, D. J. (2006). Costing eradication of alien mammals from islands. *Animal Conservation*, *9*(4), 439–444. doi:10.1111/j.1469-1795.2006.00058.x

Martono, S., Khoiruddin, M., & Wulansari, N. A. (2018). Remuneration reward management system as a driven factor of employee performance. *International Journal of Business & Society*, *19*(S4), 535–545.

Marzano, R. J., Waters, T., & McNulty, B. A. (2001). *School leadership that works: From research to results*. ASCD.

Masi, R. J., & Cooke, R. A. (2000). Effects of transformational leadership on subordinate motivation, empowering norms, and organizational productivity. *The International Journal of Organizational Analysis*, *8*(1), 16–47. doi:10.1108/eb028909

Maslow, A. H. (1998). *Maslow on management*. John Wiley & Sons.

Mason, C., Griffin, M., & Parker, S. (2014). Transformational leadership development: Connecting psychological and behavioral change. *Leadership and Organization Development Journal*, *35*(3), 174–194. doi:10.1108/LODJ-05-2012-0063

Mason, M. (2008a). Complexity theory and the philosophy of education. In M. Mason (Ed.), *Complexity theory and the philosophy of education* (pp. 1–15). Wiley Blackwell. doi:10.1002/9781444307351.ch1

Mason, M. (2008b). What is complexity theory and what are its implications for educational change? In M. Mason (Ed.), *Complexity theory and the philosophy of education* (pp. 32–45). Wiley Blackwell.

Matama, R., & Mkwizu, K. H. (2021). Sense-of- Urgency and Timeliness in Higher Education efficiency: Study of Uganda. *International Journal of Arts. Management and Humanities*, *10*(1&2), 6–17.

Mathende, T., & Yousefi, M. (2021). Transformational leadership role and means efficacy on work performance under volatile uncertain complex and ambiguous environment. *Open Journal of Leadership*, *10*(4), 277–299. doi:10.4236/ojl.2021.104018

Matjie, T. (2018). The relationship between the leadership effectiveness and emotional competence of managers in the public sector. *International Journal of Public Administration*, *41*(15), 1271–1278. doi:10.1080/01900692.2017.1387140

Mavroveli, S., Petrides, K. V., Sangareau, Y., & Furnham, A. (2009). Exploring the relationships between trait emotional intelligence and objective socio-emotional outcomes in childhood. *The British Journal of Educational Psychology*, *79*(2), 259–272. doi:10.1348/000709908X368848 PMID:18950549

Maxwell, J. C. (2014). *The 5 Levels of Leadership: Proven Steps to Maximize Your Potential*. Center Street.

May, S., Noether, M., & Stearns, B. (2021). *Hospital merger benefits: an econometric analysis revisited executive summary*. American Hospital Association. https://www.aha.org/guidesreports/2021-08-18-hospital-merger-benefits-econometric-analysis-revisited-executive-summary

Mayer, J. D., Salovey, P., & Caruso, D. R. (2002). *Mayer-Salovey-Caruso Emotional Intelligence Test (MSCEIT)*. Users Manual.

Mayer, R. E. (1987). *Educational Psychology: A Cognitive Approach*. Little, Brown.

McCarley, T. A., Peters, M. L., & Decman, J. M. (2016). Transformational leadership related to school climate. *Educational Management Administration & Leadership*, *44*(2), 322–342. doi:10.1177/1741143214549966

McCauley, C. D. (2001). Leader training and development. *The nature of organizational leadership: Understanding the performance imperatives confronting today's leaders*, 347-383.

McClelland, D. C., Atkinson, J. W., Clark, R. A., & Lowell, E. L. (1976). *The achievement motive*. Academic Press.

McClelland, D. C., Koestner, R., & Weinberger, J. (1989). How do self-attributed and implicit motives differ? *Psychological Review*, *96*(4), 690–702. doi:10.1037/0033-295X.96.4.690

McCleskey, J. (2014). Emotional intelligence and leadership. *The International Journal of Organizational Analysis*, *22*(1), 76–93. doi:10.1108/IJOA-03-2012-0568

McConnell, C. R. (2021). Chapter 5: The Manager-Employee Relationship. In Human Resource Management in health care: Principles and practice (pp. 83–98). Academic Press.

McConnell, C. R., & Fallon, F. (2007). Chapter 1: An Overview of Human Resources. In Human Resource Management in health care: Principles and practice (pp. 7–8). Academic Press.

McEnrue, M. P., & Groves, K. (2006). Choosing among tests of emotional intelligence: What is the evidence? *Human Resource Development Quarterly*, *17*(1), 9–42. doi:10.1002/hrdq.1159

McFarland, J., Hussar, B., Wang, X., Zhang, J., Wang, K., Rathbun, A., Barmer, A., Forrest Cataldi, E., & Bullock Mann, F. (2018). *The condition of education 2018*. U.S. Department of Education. Washington, DC: National Center for Education Statistics. Retrieved May 25, 2018 from https://nces.ed.gov/pubsearch/pubsinfo. asp?pubid=2018144

McGaha, K. (2018). *An Interpretive Phenomenological Study Of America's Emerging Workforce: Exploring Generation Z's Leadership Preferences* [Dissertation]. University of Phoenix.

McGraw, K. L., & Harbison-Briggs, K. (1989). *Knowledge Acquisition: Principles and Guidelines*. Prentice-Hall.

McKnight, L. L. (2013). Transformational leadership in the context of punctuated change. *Journal of Leadership, Accountability and Ethics*, *10*(2), 103–112.

McLaurin, J. R., & Al Amri, M. B. (2008). Developing an understanding of charismatic and transformational leadership. *Proceeding of the Allies Academies, 15*(2), 333-337.

McShane, S. L., Tasa, K., & Steen, S. L. (2021). *Canadian organizational behaviour* (11th ed.). SAGE.

Mehrad, A., Fernández-Castro, J., & de Olmedo, M. P. G. G. (2020). A systematic review of leadership styles, work engagement and organizational support. *International Journal of Research in Business and Social Science, 9*(4), 66-77.

Mendenhall, M. E. (2017). Leadership and the birth of global leadership. In *Global leadership* (pp. 3–27). Routledge. doi:10.4324/9781315232904-1

Mendes, M., Gomes, C., Marques-Quinteiro, P., Lind, P., & Curral, L. (2016). Promoting learning and innovation in organizations through complexity leadership theory. *Team Performance Management*, *22*(5/6), 301–309. doi:10.1108/TPM-02-2016-0004

Merello, Á. (2021). *Barriers and facilitators for children with special educational needs education during the COVID-19 pandemic: A systematic literature review in 2020* [Unpublished Master's thesis]. Jönköping University. http://www.diva-portal.org/smash/get/diva2:1552898/FULLTEXT01.pdf

Merriam, S. B. (2009). *Qualitative research: A guide to design and implementation*. Jossey-Bass.

Metcalfe, L. S., & Perez, I. (2020). Blinded by the unknown: A school's leader's actions to support teachers and students during COVID-19 school closures. *Journal of School Administration Research and Development*, *5*(S1), 49–54. doi:10.32674/jsard.v5iS1.2746

Meuer, J., Koelbel, J., & Hoffmann, V. H. (2020). On the nature of corporate Sustainability. *Organization & Environment*, *33*(3), 319–341. doi:10.1177/1086026619850180

Meyer, C. B. (2020). Unpacking case selection: A conceptual and empirical analysis. *European Management Journal*, *38*(1), 127–137.

Microsoft. (2022). *Resumen del Reporte del Índice de Tendencias Laborales 2022.* https://news.microsoft.com/es-xl/resumen-del-reporte-del-indice-de-tendencias-laborales-2022/

Mifsud, D. (2023). A systematic review of school distributed leadership: Exploring research purposes, concepts and approaches in the field between 2010 and 2022. *Journal of Educational Administration and History*, 1–26. Advance online publication. doi:10.1080/00220620.2022.2158181

Misra, N., & Srivastava, S. (2023). Happiness at Work: A Psychological Perspective. *Inertechopen.* doi:10.5772/intechopen.108241

Mitchell, K. (2019). Reflection on Leadership. *AASA Journal of Scholarship & Practice*, *16*(2), 4–6.

Mitchell, R., & Turner, J. (2023). Emotionally Intelligent Leadership in Tech Startups: A Case Study. *Journal of Business Venturing*, *38*(1), 80–96.

Mitra, P., Kickul, J., Gundry, L., & Orr, J. (2019). The Rise of Hybrids: A Note for Social Entrepreneurship Educators. *International Review of Entrepreneurship*, *17*(2).

Mizrahitokatli, N., & Guney, S. (2016). Ideal Leadership Perception of Undergraduate and Graduate Students: An Application. *Business Management Dynamics*, *6*(6), 17–34.

Mkwizu, K. H. (2019). *Community and Research in Higher Education: Any Repository opportunities for Thesis?* In 1st Doctoral Research Conference, Dar es Salaam, Tanzania.

Mkwizu, K. H., & Kimeto, J. C. (2022a). Challenges and Strategies for managing Customer Services Education and Tourism in the Post-COVID-19 pandemic: A Comparative Study of Tanzania and Kenya. *Education@ETMA*, *1*(3), 13–26.

Mkwizu, K. H., & Kimeto, J. C. (2022b). *Perspectives: How are citation metrics marginalizing knowledge in developing countries?* Emerald Publishing. https://www.emeraldgrouppublishing.com/opinion-and-blog/how-are-citation-metrics-marginalising-knowledge-developing-countries?fbclid=IwAR3Iby6tVKwCj2XXU7y1PySCxstZuO8yDc9UWq9dvQp1Sh1ti-HDgk3haZg

Mkwizu, K. H. (2020). Digital marketing and tourism opportunities for Africa. *International Hospitality Review*, *34*(1), 5–12. doi:10.1108/IHR-09-2019-0015

Mkwizu, K. H. (2022a). Advertising Dynamics and Destination Evolution in Tourism Promotion for Africa. *African Journal of Hospitality, Tourism and Leisure*, *11*(SE2), 1698–1706.

Mkwizu, K. H. (2022b). Virtual Reality and Open Schooling: Challenges and Opportunities. *International Journal of Open Schooling*, *1*(1), 97–108. https://www.nios.ac.in/media/documents/IJOS/articles/IJOS_Ch-19.pdf

Mkwizu, K. H., & Kagoya, M. S. (2019). Panelist Sessions and PhD Studies: UTAUT Approach. *International Journal of Research Methodology in Social Science*, *5*(2), 49–57. https://zenodo.org/record/3334935#.XS5DJD9KjZs

Mkwizu, K. H., Mtae, G. H., Schultz, J. L., Gardner, B., Otieno, B., Charles, R. P., Belete, B., Koroma, W., & Udoh, A. (2020). Technology Usage in Tourism: Comparative Study of Tanzania and USA. *ATLAS Tourism and Leisure Review*, *2020*(1), 74–88.

Mkwizu, K. H., & Ngaruko, D. D. (2020). Implied benefits of Open and Distance Learning in Tanzania. A qualitative approach on its benefits in Tanzania. *Global and Lokal Distance Education-GLOKALde*, *6*(2), 80–89.

Mkwizu, K. H., & Ngaruko, D. P. (2019). Authorship and collaborative research among scholars in Open and Distance Learning Institutions in Africa. *Asian Journal of Distance Education*, *14*(2), 47–57.

Moccia, S. (2016). Felicidad en el Trabajo. *Papeles del Psicólogo*, *37*(2), 143-151. https://www.redalyc.org/pdf/778/77846055007.pdf

Mohamed, A. A. (2023). A review of curriculum change and innovation for higher education in Somalia. *European Journal of Education Studies*, *10*(5), 135–144. doi:10.46827/ejes.v10i5.4785

Mohan, S. (2022). The hidden powers of vulnerability and humility. *Leader to Leader*, *2022*(105), 40–45. doi:10.1002/ltl.20649

Moldenhauer, E. (2019). Leadership Development: Introspective Foundations. *Leadership As We Know It*, 119.

Molloy, J. C. (2011). The Open Knowledge Foundation: Open data means better science. *PLoS Biology*, *9*(12), e1001195. doi:10.1371/journal.pbio.1001195 PMID:22162946

Mona High School. (2019). *Fortieth Anniversary: 1979 – 2019*. Publishing House Ltd.

Mona High School. (n.d.). *Student Handbook*. monahighschool.org

Montenegro, S. L. F. (2021). *El código de ética y su influencia en la política anticorrupción de una entidad pública del oriente peruano*. Escuela de Posgrado Programa académico de Maestría en Gestión Pública. Universidad Cesar Vallejo. https://hdl.handle.net/20.500.12692/73000

Montgomery, L., Hartley, J., Neylon, C., Gillies, M., Gray, E., Herrmann-Pillath, C., Huang, C. K., Leach, J., Potts, J., Ren, X., Skinner, K., Sugimoto, C. R., & Wilson, K. (2021). *Open knowledge institutions: Reinventing Universities*. https://mobile.eduq.info/xmlui/bitstream/handle/11515/38307/montgomery-et-al-open-knowledge-institutions-mit-press-2021.pdf?sequence=2&isAllowed=y

Moolenaar, N. M., Daly, A. J., & Sleegers, P. J. (2010). Occupying the principal position: Examining relationships between transformational leadership, social network position, and schools' innovative climate. *Educational Administration Quarterly*, *46*(5), 623–670. doi:10.1177/0013161X10378689

Moore, A. A., Weckauf, R., Accouche, W. F., & Black, S. A. (2018). The value of consensus in rapid organization assessment: Wildlife programs and the Conservation Excellence Model. *Total Quality Management & Business Excellence*, *0*, 1–15.

Morales, M. P. (2019). Participatory action research (PAR) in education. In C. A. Mertler (Ed.), *The Wiley handbook of action research in education* (pp. 317–341). Wiley Blackwell. doi:10.1002/9781119399490.ch15

Morgan, P. (2022). Conflict Management in Healthcare: A Case Study. *Health Services Management Research*, *35*(2), 111–123.

Morris, A. (2018). *Increase in CSEC passes*. Jamaica Information Service. https://jis.gov.jm/increase-in-csec-passes/

Morrison, K. (2008). Educational philosophy and the challenge of complexity theory. In M. Mason (Ed.), *Complexity theory and the philosophy of education* (pp. 16–31). Wiley-Blackwell. doi:10.1002/9781444307351.ch2

Morrison, K. (2010). Complexity theory, school leadership and management: Questions for theory and practice. *Educational Management Administration & Leadership*, *38*(3), 374–393. doi:10.1177/1741143209359711

Morton, E., Hole, R., Murray, G., Buzwell, S., & Michalak, E. (2019). Experiences of a web-based quality of life self-monitoring tool for individuals with bipolar disorder: A qualitative exploration. *JMIR Mental Health*, *6*(12), e16121. doi:10.2196/16121 PMID:31799936

Mosadegh Rad, A. M., & Yarmohammadian, M. H. (2016). *A Study of Relationship Between Managers' Leadership Style and Employees' Job Satisfaction*. Retrieved from https://www.researchgate.net/publication/263656844_A_survey_of_relationship_between_managers%27_leadership_style_and_employees%27_job_satisfaction

Mosadeghrad, A. M. (2003). *Principles of Health Care Administration*. Dibagran Tehran.

Msc, F. B. (2013). The relationship between Antecedents (Job Stressors) and Burnout in Iranian Nurses. *International Journal of Academic Research in Business & Social Sciences*, *3*(12), 550.

Msila, V. (2022). Higher education leadership in a time of digital technologies: A South African case study. *International Journal of Information and Education Technology (IJIET)*, *12*(10), 1110–1117. doi:10.18178/ijiet.2022.12.10.1728

Mugimu, C. B. (2021). *Higher Education Institutions (HEIs) in Africa embracing the "New Normal" for knowledge production and innovation: Barriers, realities and possibilities*. https://www.intechopen.com/chapters/79255

Mukata, C. M., & Swanepoel, E. (2017). Development support for small and medium enterprises in the fi nancially constrained north-eastern regions of Namibia. *Southern African Business Review*, *21*, 198–221.

Mukhtar, U., Anwar, S., Ahmed, U., & Baloch, M. A. (2015). Factors effecting the service quality of public and private sector universities comparatively: An empirical investigation. *Research World*, *6*(3), 132.

Mumford, M. D., & Fried, Y. (2014). Give them what they want or give them what they need? Ideology in the study of leadership. *Journal of Organizational Behavior*, *35*(5), 622–634. doi:10.1002/job.1921

Muñoz-La Rivera, F., Hermosilla, P., Delgadillo, J., & Echeverría, D. (2021). Proposal for constructing innovation skills in engineering education in the context of Industry 4.0 and sustainable development goals (SDG). *Formación Universitaria*, *14*(2), 75–84. doi:10.4067/S0718-50062021000200075

Musa, H., Azmi, F., Abdullah, A., Sedek, M., & Saad, N. (2017). Emotional intelligence and stress among SME entrepreneurs in Melaka: A case of entrepreneurial education. *Proceedings of Mechanical Engineering Research Day*, *2017*, 248–249.

Mustofa, M. U. A., Gulton, R. Z., Bayuny, A. F. R., & Mustofa, M. A. H A. (2022). Transactional and transformational leadership in Islamic perspectives. *Indonesian Journal of Development Studies*, 13 – 19.

Musu-Gillette, L., Robinson, J., McFarland, J., KewalRamani, A., Zhang, A., & Wilkinson-Flicker, S. (2016). *Status and trends in the education of racial and ethnic groups 2016*. National Center for Education Statistics. Retrieved May 25, 2021 from https://nces.ed.gov/pubs2016/2016007.pdf

Muthembwa, M. (2019). *Effect of managers' emotional intelligence on performance of small and micro-enterprises in Nakuru East Sub-County*. Kabarak University. doi:10.31871/WJIR.7.5.11

Muzondiwa, Y. T., Swarts, I., & Schultz, C. M. (2022). The relationship between transformational leadership, perceived organisational effectiveness and organisational culture in a selected multinational corporation in Africa. *SA Journal of Human Resource Management*, *20*(1), 1–11. doi:10.4102ajhrm.v20i0.1888

Mwambari, D., Ali, F. A., & Barak, C. (2022). The impact of open access on knowledge production, consumption and dissemination in Kenya's higher education system. *Third World Quarterly*, *43*(2), 1408–1424. doi:10.1080/01436597.2022.2056010

Mwesigwa, R., Tusiime, I., & Ssekiziyivu, B. (2020). Leadership styles, job satisfaction and organizational commitment among academic staff in public universities. *Journal of Management Development*, *39*(2), 253–268. doi:10.1108/JMD-02-2018-0055

Myers, N., Mittermeier, R. A., Mittermeier, C. G., da Fonseca, G., & Kent, J. (2000). Biodiversity hotspots for conservation priorities. *Nature*, *403*(6772), 853–858. doi:10.1038/35002501 PMID:10706275

Myers, P. J. (2019). *Leadership, Empowerment, and Motivation: An Analysis of Modern Management*. CMC Senior Theses.

Nanjundeswaraswamy, T. S., & Swamy, D. R. (2014). Leadership styles. *Advances In Management*, *7*(2), 57–62.

National Center for Advancing Translational Sciences. (n.d.). *Translational science principles*. https://ncats.nih.gov/training-education/translational-science-principles

National Center for Education Statistics. (n.d.). *Fast facts: Back-to-school statistics*. https://nces.ed.gov/fastfacts/display.asp?id=372

Nazim, F., & Mahmood, A. (2016). Transformational and transactional leadership style and job satisfaction of college teachers. *Journal of Education and Practice*, *7*(34), 18–22.

Ndaipa, C. J., Edstrom, K., Langa, P., & Geschwind, L. (2023). Internationalization of the curriculum in higher education: A case from Mozambican university. *Cogent Education*, *10*(1), 2188773. doi:10.1080/2331186X.2023.2188773

Neck, C. P., & Manz, C. C. (2010). *Mastering self-leadership: Empowering yourself for personal excellence* (5th ed.). Pearson Prentice Hall.

Nel, P. S., Werner, A., Poisat, P., Du Plessis, A., & Sono, T. (2011). *Human resources management* (8th ed.). Oxford University Press. https://www.jstor.org/stable/40270884?origin=JSTOR-pdf

Nembhard, I. M., & Edmondson, A. C. (2006). Making it safe: The effects of leader inclusiveness and professional status on psychological safety and improvement efforts in health care teams. *Journal of Organizational Behavior*, *27*(7), 941–966. doi:10.1002/job.413

Nery Silva, L., Diederichsen, A., Talbert, L., Leslie, S. C., & Black, S. A. (2022). Insights into leadership, Gender and Organisational Effectiveness Revealed by Benchmarking Conservation Programs against the Conservation Excellence Model. *Open J. Leadership*, *11*(4), 370–397. doi:10.4236/ojl.2022.114020

Nesbit, P. L. (2012). The role of self-reflection, emotional management of feedback, and self-regulation processes in self-directed leadership development. *Human Resource Development Review*, *11*(2), 203–226. doi:10.1177/1534484312439196

Neuman, W. L. (2003). *Social research methods: Qualitative and quantitative approaches* (5th ed.). Allyn & Bacon.

Newell, C. (2008). The class as a learning entity (complex adaptive system): An idea from complexity science and educational research. *SFU Educational Review*, *2*(1), 5–17. doi:10.21810fuer.v2i.335

Newstrom, J. W., & Davis, K. (2002). *Organizational behavior: Human behavior at work* (11th ed.). McGraw-Hill, Irwin.

Ngang, T. K. (2011). The effect of transformational leadership on school culture in male's primary schools Maldives. *Procedia: Social and Behavioral Sciences*, *30*, 2575–2580. doi:10.1016/j.sbspro.2011.10.503

Nicholls, A. (2007). *Social Entrepreneurship: New Models of Sustainable Social Change*. Oxford University Press.

Nickerson, C. (2022). *What is Positive Reinforcement"?* Simply Psychology. Available at: www.simplypsychology.org/positive-reinforcement.html

Ning-xue, F. (2019). Persistence and change: Evolution of the definitions of education in the past 40 years after the China's reform and opening-up. *US-China Education Review B*, *9*(2), 53–68. doi:10.17265/2161-6248/2019.02.003

Nita, V., & Guțu, I. (2023). The role of leadership and digital transformation in higher education students' work engagement. *International Journal of Environmental Research and Public Health*, *20*(6), 5124. doi:10.3390/ijerph20065124 PMID:36982029

Njos, R., Sjotun, S. G., Jakobsen, S., & Floysand, A. (2020). Expanding analyses of path creation: Interconnections between territory and technology. *Economic Geography*, *96*(3), 266–288. doi:10.1080/00130095.2020.1756768

Noe, R., Hollenbeck, J., Gerhart, B., & Wright, P. (2021). *Human Resource Management: Gaining a Competitive Advantage* (12th ed.). McGraw Hill.

Nolt, S. (2015). 'You hold the whole world in your hand': Cell phones and discernment in Amish churches. *Vision (Basel)*, *16*(2), 27–37.

Nolt, S., & Meyers, T. (2007). *Plain Diversity: Amish Cultures and Identities*. Johns Hopkins University Press. doi:10.1353/book.3499

Nooteboom, S. G., & Termeer, C. J. A. M. (2013). Strategies of complexity leadership in governance systems. *International Review of Public Administration*, *18*(1), 25–40. doi:10.1080/12294659.2013.10805238

Northouse, P. G. (2013). Leadership: Theory and practice (6th ed.). Sage.

Northouse, P. (2022). *Leadership: Theory and practice* (9th ed.). Sage.

Novitasari, D., & Asbari, M. (2021). Leaders Coaching di Sekolah: Apa Perannya terhadap Kinerja Guru? *Edumaspul: Jurnal Pendidikan*, *5*(1), 580–597. doi:10.33487/edumaspul.v5i1.1299

Novita, W., & Sulaiman, M. R. (2022). Work Motivation as an Intermediary Variable in the Relationship between Principal Transformational Leadership, School Climate, and Teacher Professionalism. *International Journal of Social Science and Human Research*, *5*(06), 2285–2291.

O'Donohoe, J., & Kleinschmit, K. (2021). *Psychological safety for teams*. University of Utah. https://accelerate.uofuhealth.utah.edu/improvement/psychological-safety-for-teams

O'Kane, P., Palmer, M., & Hargie, O. (2007). Workplace interactions and the polymorphic role of e-mail. *Leadership and Organization Development Journal*, *28*(4), 308–324. doi:10.1108/01437730710752193

Oakland, J., Tanner, S., & Gadd, K. (2002). Best practice in business excellence. *Total Quality Management*, *13*(8), 1125–1139. doi:10.1080/0954412022000000008

Oc, B. (2018). Contextual leadership: A systematic review of how contextual factors shape leadership and its outcomes. *The Leadership Quarterly*, *29*(1), 218–235. doi:10.1016/j.leaqua.2017.12.004

Odumeru, J. A., & Ogbonna, I. G. (2013). Transformational vs. Transactional Leadership Theories: Evidence in Literature. *International Review of Management and Business Research*, *2*(2), 335–361.

Olson, M. S. (2006). *A model for transformational nurse leadership and intrapreneurism: The nursing leadership cycle of integrity* [Master's Thesis]. Washington State University, Vancouver Campus. https://rex.libraries.wsu.edu/esploro/outputs/graduate/A-Model-for-Transformational-Nurse-Leadership/99900590537001842

Onyekuru, B. U., & Ibegbunam, J. O. (2013). Teaching effectiveness of secondary school Teachers in Emohua local government area of Rivers state, Nigeria. *European Scientific Journal*, 9.

Opfer, K., & Black, S.A. (2019). Assessing community reforestation projects for biodiversity improvement and poverty alleviation. *Forestry Engineering and Research International, 3*(1), 32-37.

Osberg, D., & Biesta, G. J. (2007). Beyond presence: Epistemological and pedagogical implications of 'strong' emergence. *Interchange*, *38*(1), 31–51. doi:10.100710780-007-9014-3

Osborne & Hammoud. (2017). Effective Employee Engagement in the Workplace. *International Journal of Applied Management and Technology*, *16*(1), 50–67.

OSHA.gov. (n.d.). *Recommended Practices for Anti-Retaliation Programs*. Retrieved from https://www.osha.gov/sites/default/files/publications/OSHA3905.pdf

Oshagbemi, T., & Gill, R. (2004). Differences in leadership styles and behaviour across hierarchical levels in UK organisations. *Leadership and Organization Development Journal*, *25*(1), 93–106. doi:10.1108/01437730410512796

Othman, J., Lawrence, J., & Mohammed, K. A. (2012). Review of factors that influence leadership styles among top management in small and medium-size enterprises. *International Business Management*, *6*(3), 384–389. doi:10.3923/ibm.2012.384.389

Otzen, T., & Manterola, C. (2017). Técnicas de Muestreo sobre una Población a Estudio. *International Journal of Morphology*, *35*(1), 227–232. doi:10.4067/S0717-95022017000100037

Owings, W. A., & Kaplan, L. S. (2010). *Leadership and organizational behaviour in education: Theory into Practice*. Pearson.

Paais, M., & Pattiruhu, J. R. (2020). Effect of Motivation, Leadership, and Organizational Culture on Satisfaction and Employee Performance. The Journal of Asian Finance, Economics and Business, 7(8), 577–588. doi:10.13106/jafeb.2020.vol7.no8.577

Page, D. P. (1935). Measurement and prediction of leadership. *American Journal of Sociology*, *41*(1), 31–43. doi:10.1086/217003

Pahi, M. H., Umrani, W. H., Hamid, K. A., & Ahmed, U. (2015). Examining multifactor leadership questionnaire construct: A validation study in the public hospitals of Sindh, Pakistan context. *IPBJ*, *7*(2), 27–39.

Palmer, D., Hermond, D., & Gardiner, C. (2014). Principals' leadership practices and mathematics pass rate in Jamaican high schools. *Administrative Issues Journal: Connecting Education, Practice, and Research*, *4*(2), 35–47. doi:10.5929/2014.4.2.1

Palomar, L. J. (2005). *Estructura del bienestar subjetivo: construcción de una escala multidimensional*. https://books.google.com.mx/books?hl=es&lr=&id=j16GIakxXpgC&oi=fnd&pg=PA113&dq=ESCALA+MULTIDIMENSIONAL+PARA+MEDIR+LA+FELICIDAD+EN+EL+TRABAJO+&ots=0XZbgHBupo&sig=dfSQZnqwf0Ap8msAfA23ZXexhZ0#v=onepage&q&f=false

Pan American Health Organization/ World Health Organization (PAHO/WHO). (2008). *Antigua and Barbuda Health Systems Profile. Monitoring and Analizing Health- Systems Change/Reform*. U.S. Government Printing Office.

Panait, C. (2017). Emotional intelligence in leadership. *Sci. Res. Educ. Air Force*, *19*(2), 133–138.

Paradiso-Testa, M. (2022). A Reflective Essay of a Conceptual Model for Self-Directed Learning for the Adult Learner. In *Self-Directed Learning and the Academic Evolution From Pedagogy to Andragogy* (pp. 163–172). IGI Global. doi:10.4018/978-1-7998-7661-8.ch009

Parapat, Y., Sabdono, E., Agus, M., Djati, P., & Hidayat, A. (2020) Moses Leadership Transition - A Moses Leadership Transition Model - A Successful Succession Management Model. *International Journal of Innovative Science and Research Technology.*

Parmigiani, D., Benigno, V., Giusto, M., Silvaggio, C., & Sperandio, S. (2020). E-inclusion: Online special education in Italy during the Covid-19 pandemic. *Technology, Pedagogy and Education*, *30*(1), 111–124. doi:10.1080/1475939X.2020.1856714

Pasovska, S., & Miceski, T. (2017). Application of transformational leadership as an incentive for innovation ie developing subordinates with durable values. *Journal of Economics*, *2*(2), 28–35.

Patel, S. (2017, December 12). Why the Catholic Health Initiatives, Dignity Health Merger Failed. *Becker's Hospital Review*. https://www.beckershospitalreview.com/hospital-transactions-and-valuation/why-the-catholic-health-initiatives-dignity-health-merger-failed.html

Patterson, E. (2015). 'What are leaders' experiences of reflection?' What leaders and leadership developers need to know from the findings of an exploratory research study. *Reflective Practice*, *16*(5), 636–651. doi:10.1080/14623943.2015.1064386

Paulhus, D. L., & John, O. P. (1998). Egoistic and moralistic biases in self-perception: The interplay of self-deceptive styles with basic traits and motives. *Journal of Personality*, *66*(6), 1025–1060. doi:10.1111/1467-6494.00041

Paulsen, N., Maldonado, D., Callan, V. J., & Ayoko, O. (2009). Charismatic leadership, change, and innovation in an R&D organization. *Journal of Organizational Change Management*, *22*(5), 511–523. doi:10.1108/09534810910983479

Peiró, J. M., Montesa, D., Soriano, A., Kozusznik, M. W., Villajos, E., Magdaleno, J., Djourova, N. P., & Ayala, Y. (2021). Revisiting the Happy-Productive Worker Thesis from a Eudaimonic Perspective: A Systematic Review. *Sustainability*, *13*, 3174. doi:10.3390/su13063174

Pérez-Uribe R. (2012). *El ambiente laboral y su incidencia en el desempeño de las organizaciones: estudio de las mejores empresas para trabajar en Colombia.* Tesis doctoral. Universidad Nebrija. http://edicionesean.ean.edu.co/index.php/es/productos-de-investigacion1/tesis-doctorales/23-publicaciones/192-el-ambiente-laboral-y-su-incidencia-en-el-desempeno-de-las-organizaciones-estudio-en-las-mejores-empresas-para-trabajar-en-colombia

Perez-Uribe, R. (2018). *Gerencia Estratégica Corporativa*. Primera edición. ECOE ediciones.

Perez-Uribe, R. (2020). Innovación y sostenibilidad en la Empresa L. *Revista Citas, Universidad Santo Tomas*. . doi:10.15332/24224529.6365

Pérez-Uribe, R. I., & Ramírez-Garzón, M. T. (2020). Human Resources Management and its contribution to Colombian SMEs Sustainability. doi:10.4018/978-1-7998-2019-2.ch012

Perez-Uribe, R., & Ramírez-Salazar, M. D. P. (2020). *Guía para el manejo del modelo de innovación y sostenibilidad empresarial (RISE = Ruta de Innovación y Sostenibilidad Empresarial).* doi:10.13140/RG.2.2.13026.45762

Pérez-Uribe, R., Nieto, M., Velásquez, A., Castellanos, G., Garzón, M., Vargas, H., Alfonso, N. (+), Calixto, N., Rodríguez, A., Palacio, M., López, L.G., Vidal, M., & López De Mesa, J. (2013). Modelo De Modernización Para La Gestión De Organizaciones (MMGO). Universidad Ean. Libro: 624 P. Primera Impresión, agosto de 2009. Segunda Impresión, diciembre de 2011. Tercera Impresión, febrero de 2013.

Perez-Uribe, R., Ocampo-Guzman, D., Moscoso-Duran, F., & Ramirez-Salazar, M. P. (2021). Innovation and Sustainability Management as a Key Factor in Global Purpose-Driven Micro, Small, and Medium-Sized Bogotanas Companies: Its Impact on Financial Results in MSMEs. *Advances in Business Strategy and Competitive Advantage*, *26*, 354–379. doi:10.4018/978-1-7998-4909-4.ch019

Perez-Uribe, R., & Salcedo-Perez, C., & Correa- Lozano, L.J. (2022). *Ebitda is a key indicator of sustainability in colombian companies.* IGI Global Publishing. doi:10.4018/978-1-7998-9301-1.ch009

Peters, B. (2011). *A formative study of rhythm and pattern: Semiotic potential of multimodal experiences for early years readers* [Doctoral dissertation]. University of Manitoba. https://mspace.lib.umanitoba.ca/handle/1993/4855

Peters, L. H., Hartke, D. D., & Pohlmann, J. T. (1985). Fiedler's Contingency Theory of Leadership: An application of the meta-analysis procedures of Schmidt and Hunter. *Psychological Bulletin*, *97*(2), 274–285. doi:10.1037/0033-2909.97.2.274

Peterson, T. M. (2007). Motivation: How to increase project team performance. *Project Management Journal*, *38*(4), 60–69. doi:10.1002/pmj.20019

Phillips, W., Alexander, E. A., & Lee, H. (2019). Going it alone won't work! The relational imperative for social innovation in social enterprises. *Journal of Business Ethics*, *156*(2), 315–331. doi:10.100710551-017-3608-1

Pillay, M., Viviers, R., & Mayer, C.-H. (2019). The relationship between emotional intelligence and leadership styles in the South African petrochemical industry. *SA Journal of Industrial Psychology*, *39*(1), 1–12.

Pinkas, G., & Bulic, A. (2017). Principal's leadership styles as perceived by teachers, in relation to teachers' experience factor of school climate in elementary schools. *Human Research in Rehabilitation*, *7*(2), 34–50. doi:10.21554/hrr.091705

Pirson, M. (2017). *Humanistic Management: Protecting dignity and promoting well-Being*. Cambridge University Press. doi:10.1017/9781316675946

Pirson, M., Steinvorth, U., Largacha-Martinez, C., & Dierksmeier, C. (2014). *From Capitalistic To Humanistic Business*. Palgrave Macmillan. doi:10.1057/9781137468208

Pittman, A. (2020). Leadership rebooted: Cultivating trust with the brain in mind. *Human Service Organizations, Management, Leadership & Governance*, *44*(2), 127–143. doi:10.1080/23303131.2019.1696910

Pitzen, J. H., Dieter, H. L., Gronseth, D. L., Dahl, A. K., Boyle, V. L., Maran, T., Harper, C. M. Jr, & Gores, G. J. (2020). Transforming the practice of medicine through team science. *Health Research Policy and Systems*, *18*(104), 104. Advance online publication. doi:10.118612961-020-00619-4 PMID:32943070

Pizzolitto, E., Verna, I., & Venditti, M. (2022). Authoritarian leadership styles and performance: A systematic literature review and research agenda. *Management Review Quarterly*. https://link.springer.com/article/10.1007/s11301-022-00263-y

Plessis, A., Douangphichit, N., & Dodd, P. (2016). HRM in Relation to Employee Motivation and Job Performance in the Hospitality Industry. *Journal of International Business Research and Marketing*, *1*(4). doi:10.18775/jibrm.1849-8558.2015.14.3002

PNUMA. (2016). *Manual del Convenio de Viena para la protección de la capa de Ozono*. Décima edición de 2016. https://observatoriop10.cepal.org/sites/default/files/documents/treaties/vc-handbook-2016-spanish.pdf

Podsakoff, P. M., Niehoff, B. P., MacKenzie, S. B., & Williams, M. L. (1993). Do substitutes for leadership really substitute for leadership? An empirical examination of Kerr and Jermier′ s situational leadership model. *Organizational Behavior and Human Decision Processes*, *54*(1), 1–44. doi:10.1006/obhd.1993.1001

Podsakoff, P., MacKenzie, S., Moorma, R., & Fetter, R. (1990). In Transformational leader behaviors and their effects on followers' trust in leader, satisfaction, and organizational citizenship behaviors. *The Leadership Quarterly*, *1*(2), 107–142. doi:10.1016/1048-9843(90)90009-7

Pokhrel, S., & Chhetri, R. (2021). A Literature review on impact of COVID-19 Pandemic on teaching and learning. *Higher Education for the Future*, *8*(1), 133–141. doi:10.1177/2347631120983481

Pollock, K., & Hauseman, D. C. (2015). Principal Leadership in Canada. In H. Arlestig, C. Day, & O. Johansson (Eds.), *A decade of research on school principals: Cases from 24 countries* (pp. 211–244). Springer International Publishing. doi:10.1007/978-3-319-23027-6

Portafolio. (2022). *¿Qué tan felices son los colombianos en su trabajo?* https://www.portafolio.co/economia/empleo/colombianos-que-tan-felices-son-en-sus-trabajos-estudio-de-hubspot-575238

Porter, L. W., & McLaughlin, G. B. (2006). Leadership and the organizational context: Like the weather? *The Leadership Quarterly*, *17*(6), 559–576. doi:10.1016/j.leaqua.2006.10.002

Porter, M. E. (1998). *The competitive advantage of nations: With a new introduction.* doi:10.1007/978-1-349-14865-3

Porter-O'Grady, T. (2020). Complexity leadership: Constructing 21st-century health care. *Nursing Administration Quarterly*, *44*(2), 92–100. doi:10.1097/NAQ.0000000000000405 PMID:32134867

Pounder, J. S. (2001). New leadership and university organizational effectiveness: Exploring the relationship. *Leadership and Organization Development Journal*, *22*(5/6), 281–291. doi:10.1108/EUM0000000005827

Powell, A. (2008). *The race to save the world's rarest bird: the discovery and death of the Po'ouli.* Stackpole Books.

Prabhu, J. U. (2015). *Social entrepreneurship: A global perspective.* Palgrave Macmillan.

Prentice, W. (1961). Understanding Leadership. *Harvard Business Review.* PMID:14723181

Prezerakos, P. E. (2018). Nurse managers' emotional intelligence and effective leadership: A review of the current evidence. *The Open Nursing Journal*, *12*(86), 86–92. doi:10.2174/1874434601812010086 PMID:29997711

Pritchard, R. D., & Sanders, M. S. (1973). The influence of valence, instrumentality, and expectancy on effort and performance. *The Journal of Applied Psychology*, *57*(1), 55–60. doi:10.1037/h0034197

*QKB.* (2022). Albania National Business Centre. Available at: https://qkb.gov.al/kerko/kerkone-regjistrin-tregtar/kerko-per-subjekt/

Raber Hedberg, P. (2009). Learning through reflective classroom practice: Applications to educate the reflective manager. *Journal of Management Education*, *33*(1), 10–36. doi:10.1177/1052562908316714

Racer Conservation Project. (1999). *Re-introduction of the Antiguan Racer, Alsophis antiguae (Serpentes: Colubridae) to Offshore Islands Around Antigua, West Indies.* Proposal to the IUCN/SSC Re-introduction Specialist Group, Fauna & Flora International, Cambridge, UK. doi:Antiguan

Rafferty, A. E., & Griffin, M. A. (2004). Dimensions of Transformational Leadership: Conceptual and Empirical Extensions. *The Leadership Quarterly*, *15*(3), 329–354. doi:10.1016/j.leaqua.2004.02.009

Ragothaman, C. B. (2020). Leadership Style and its Impact on Employee Motivation in IT / ITES Sector. *International Journal of Mechanical and Production Engineering Research and Development*, *10*(3), 7141–7150. doi:10.24247/ijmperdjun2020675

Rahim, M. A. (2002). Toward a theory of managing organizational conflict. *International Journal of Conflict Management*, *13*(3), 206–235. doi:10.1108/eb022874

Rahmani, M., Roels, G., & Karmarkar, U. S. (2018). Team leadership and performance: Combining the roles of direction and contribution. *Management Science*, *64*(11), 5234–5249. doi:10.1287/mnsc.2017.2911

Ram, R (2009). Government Spending and Happiness of the Population: Additional Evidence from Large Cross-Country Samples. *Public Choice, 138*(3-4), 483-490. Available at: https://www.jstor.org/stable/40270884

Ramírez, A. (2012). Servicios de salud ocupacional. *Anales de la Facultad de Medicina, 73*(1), 63-69. http://www.scielo.org.pe/scielo.php?script=sci_arttext&pid=S1025-55832012000100012&lng=es&tlng=es

Ramirez-Salazar, M. P., Perez-Uribe, R. I., Salcedo-Perez, C., & Huffington-Smith, J. (2019). RISE Model: Its application on diving enterprises located in the San Andres Archipelago. In *Entrepreneurship and Family Business Vitality–Surviving and Flourishing in the Long Term*. Ediciones Springer. https://www.springer.com/gp/book/9783030155254

Ramírez-Salazar, C. F. (2021). Happiness at Work Through Recognition and Reward Programs: Cases in Colombian and American Companies. *Advances in Business Strategy and Competitive Advantage*, *21*, 310–330. doi:10.4018/978-1-7998-4909-4.ch017

Ramírez-Salazar, M. D. P., Salcedo-Perez, C., & Castañeda, S. E. (2021). Open Collaborative Innovation at Colombia's National Spectrum Agency. *Advances in Business Strategy and Competitive Advantage*, *24*, 169–192. Advance online publication. doi:10.4018/978-1-7998-3568-4.ch009

Ramírez-Salazar, M. P. (2016). *Modelo De Innovación Abierta Colaborativa Para La Banca De Fomento: Caso Bancóldex*. Tesis Doctoral. Doctorado en Gestión. Universidad Ean.

Ramlall, S. (2004). A review of employee motivation theories and their implications for employee retention within organizations. *The Journal of American Academy of Business, Cambridge*, *5*(1/2), 52–63.

Rana, S., Ardichvili, A., & Polesello, D. (2016). Promoting self-directed learning in a learning organization: Tools and practices. *European Journal of Training and Development*, *40*(7), 470–489. doi:10.1108/EJTD-10-2015-0076

Razzouk, R., & Shute, V. (2012, September). What Is Design Thinking and Why Is It Important? *Review of Educational Research*, *82*(3), 330–348. doi:10.3102/0034654312457429

Real, L. (2004). *Development of youth leadership life skills of Texas youth as San Antonio Livestock Exposition school tour guides* [Master's thesis]. Texas A&M University. Available electronically from https: / /hdl .handle .net / 1969 .1 / 1332

Redmond, S., & Dolan, P. (2016). Towards a conceptual model of youth leadership development. *Child & Family Social Work*, *21*(3), 261–271. doi:10.1111/cfs.12146

Reed, L. C., & Swaminathan, R. (2014). An urban school leader's approach to school improvement: Toward contextually responsive leadership. *Urban Education*, *51*(9), 1096–1125. doi:10.1177/0042085914553675

Reh, F. J. (2018). *The role and responsibilities of today's manager*. Available at: https://www.thebalancecareers.com/what-is-a-manager-2276096

Rennie, D. L. (2012). Qualitative research as methodical hermeneutics. *Psychological Methods*, *17*(3), 385–398. doi:10.1037/a0029250 PMID:22823104

Ren, S., & Jackson, S. E. (2020). HRM institutional entrepreneurship for sustainable business organizations. *Human Resource Management Review*, *30*(3), 100691. doi:10.1016/j.hrmr.2019.100691

Revilla, M. A., Saris, W. E., & Krosnick, J. A. (2013). Choosing the Number of Categories in Agree-Disagree Scales. *Sociological Methods & Research*, *43*(1), 73–97. doi:10.1177/0049124113509605

Rhoten, D. R. (2004). *Interdisciplinary research: Trend or transition*. Social Science Research Council. https://items.ssrc.org/from-our-archives/interdisciplinary-research-trend-or-transition/

Richard, A. (2013). *Theory Building in Applied Disciplines*. Berrett-Koehler Publishers.

Richardson, K., & Cilliers, P. (2001). What is Complexity Science? A view from different directions. *Emergence*, *3*(1), 5–23. doi:10.1207/S15327000EM0301_02

Riggio, R. E., & Reichard, R. J. (2008). The emotional and social intelligences of effective leadership: An emotional and social skill approach. *Journal of Managerial Psychology*, *23*(2), 169–185. doi:10.1108/02683940810850808

Rillo, R. M., & Alieto, E. O. (2018). Indirect markers in Korean and Persian English essays: Implications for teaching writing to EFL learners. *The Journal of English as an International Language, 13*(2.2), 165 – 184. doi:10.2139/ssrn.3588006

Rita, M., Payangan, O. R., Rante, Y., Tuhumena, R., & Erari, A. (2018). Moderating effect of organizational citizenship behavior on the effect of organizational commitment, transformational leadership and work motivation on employee performance. *International Journal of Law and Management.*

Riyanto, S., Endri, E., & Herlisha, N. (2021). Effect of work motivation and job satisfaction on employee performance: Mediating role of employee engagement. *Problems and Perspectives in Management*, 162-174. doi:10.21511/ppm.19(3).2021.14

Rizvi, H. (2022, September 21). *Authentic leadership vs transformational leadership, difference, pros and cons.* Hidayat Rizvi. https://hidayatrizvi.com/authentic-leadership-vs-transformational-leadership/

Robbins, S. P., & Judge, T. A. (2011). *Organizational behavior* (14th ed.). Academic Press. doi:10.1108/13639511011085060

Robbins, S. P., & Judge, T. A. (2010). *Essentials of organizational behavior* (10th ed.). Prentice Hall.

Robotham, D., & Plaza, C. H. (2020). *Employee disengagement and the impact of leadership.* Penn State Extension. https://extension.psu.edu/employee-disengagement-and-the-impact-of-leadership#:~:text=Disengagement%20is%20often%20defined%20by,toward%20their%20work%20and%20organization

Rodriguez, R. (2015). Corporate social responsibility: An analysis of corporate social responsibility practices in the Indian Companies Act, 2013. *International Journal of Management and Applied Science*, *1*(7), 15–21.

Rofuth, T. W., & Piepenbring, J. (2019). *Management and leadership in social work: A competency-based approach.* Springer Publishing Company. doi:10.1891/9780826130686

Ronnie, J.-B., & Philip, B. (2021). Expectations and what people learn from failure. In *Expectations and actions* (pp. 207–237). Routledge. doi:10.4324/9781003150879-10

Rosenstein, A. H., & Naylor, B. (2012). Incidence and impact of physician and nurse disruptive behaviors in the emergency department. *The Journal of Emergency Medicine*, *43*(1), 139–148. doi:10.1016/j.jemermed.2011.01.019 PMID:21421291

Ross, S. (2014). A conceptual model for understanding the process of self-leadership development and action-steps to promote personal leadership development. *Journal of Management Development*, *33*(4), 299–323. doi:10.1108/JMD-11-2012-0147

Rothstein, M. G., & Burke, R. J. (2010). *Self-management and leadership development.* Edward Elgar Publishing. doi:10.4337/9781849805551

Ruben, B. D., & Gigliotti, R. A. (2016). Leadership as social influence: An expanded view of leadership communication theory and practice. *Journal of Leadership & Organizational Studies*, *23*(4), 467–479. doi:10.1177/1548051816641876

Ruben, B. D., & Gigliotti, R. A. (2017). Communication: Sine qua non of organizational leadership theory and practice. *International Journal of Business Communication*, *54*(1), 12–30. doi:10.1177/2329488416675447

Rudasill, K. M., Snyder, K. E., Levinson, H., & Adelson, L, J. (. (2018). Systems view of school climate: A theoretical framework for research. *Educational Psychology Review*, *30*, 35–60. doi:10.100710648-017-9401-y

Russell, R. C., & Aquino-Russell, C. E. (2011). Living and working between two worlds: Using qualitative phenomenological findings to enhance understanding of lived experiences. In *The role of expatriates in MNCs knowledge mobilization* (pp. 177–192). Emerald Group Publishing Limited. doi:10.1108/S1876-066X(2011)0000027012

Ruyter, D., Oades, L., & Waghid, Y. (2019). *Meaning(s) of human flourishing and education: A research brief by the International Science and Evidence Based Education Assessment: An initiative by UNESCO MGIEP*. https://en.unesco.org/futuresofeducation/sites/default/files/2021-03/Flourishing%20and%20Education_ISEEA%20Research%20Brief.pdf

Rwanamiza, E. (2009). Knowledge, education, learning and teaching: Meanings and relationships. *Journal of the American Association for the Advancement of Curriculum Studies, 5.*

Ryan, R. M., & Deci, E. L. (2000). Self-determination theory and the facilitation of intrinsic motivation, social development, and well-being. *The American Psychologist*, *55*(1), 68–78. doi:10.1037/0003-066X.55.1.68 PMID:11392867

Ryan, R. M., Huta, V., & Deci, E. L. (2008). Living well: A self-determination theory perspective on eudaimonia. *Journal of Happiness Studies*, *9*(1), 139–170. doi:10.100710902-006-9023-4

Rycroft-Smith, L. (2022). Knowledge brokering to bridge the research-practice gap in education: Where are we now? *Review of Education*, *10*(1), e3341. doi:10.1002/rev3.3341

Sa´, C. M. (2007). Interdisciplinary strategies in U.S. research universities. *Higher Education*, *55*(5), 537–552. doi:10.100710734-007-9073-5

Sabie, O. M., Brişcariu, R. M., Pîrvu, C., Burcea, Ş. G., & Gâtan, M. L. (2020). The relationship between emotional intelligence and human resources employee performance: A case study for Romanian companies. *Management Research and Practice*, *12*(3), 45–59.

Sabie, S., Malek, J., Kline, T., & Lu, J. (2020). Emotional intelligence and team performance: A meta-analysis. *Psychological Bulletin*, *146*(8), 655–671.

Sadiq, M., Nonthapot, S., Mohamad, S., Chee Keong, O., Ehsanullah, S., & Iqbal, N. (2022). Does green finance matter for sustainable entrepreneurship and environmental corporate social responsibility during COVID-19? *China Finance Review International*, *12*(2), 317–333. doi:10.1108/CFRI-02-2021-0038

Sadri, G., Weber, T. J., & Gentry, W. A. (2011). Empathy in the workplace: A tool for effective leadership. *The Business Review, Cambridge*, *17*(1), 61–66.

Salas, A. (2017). La felicidad en el trabajo: un reto alcanzable para las empresas. *Capital Humano*, 325.

Salas, V. A., Alegre, V. J., & Fernández, G. R. (2013). *La medición de la felicidad en el trabajo y sus antecedentes: un estudio empírico en el área de alergología de los hospitales públicos españoles*. Universidad de Huelva. https://rabida.uhu.es/dspace/handle/10272/9306

Salasiah, H.H., Zainab, I., Rosmawati, M., & Ermy, A.R. (2010). Methods of Increasing Learning Motivation among Students. *Procedia Social and Behavior Science, 18*, 138-147. doi:10.1016/j.sbspro.2011.05.021

Salovey, P., & Mayer, J. D. (1990). Emotional intelligence. *Imagination, Cognition and Personality*, *9*(3), 185–211. doi:10.2190/DUGG-P24E-52WK-6CDG

Samul, J. (2020). Spiritual Leadership: Meaning in the Sustainable Workplace. *Sustainability (Basel)*, *12*(1), 1–16. doi:10.3390u12010267

Sandbrook, C., Nelson, H. P., Bolderson, S., & Leader-Williams, N. (2022). Evaluating the impact of the first 10 years of the Cambridge Masters in Conservation Leadership. *Oryx*, *56*(5), 710–719. doi:10.1017/S0030605321000818

Sanders, P. (1982). Phenomenology: A new way of viewing organizational research. *Academy of Management Review*, *7*(3), 353–360. doi:10.2307/257327

Santos-Hermosa, G., & Atenas, J. (2022). Building capacities in open knowledge: Recommendations for library and information science professionals and schools. *Frontiers in Education*, *7*, 866049. doi:10.3389/feduc.2022.866049

Sari, M., Nasution, M. I., & Wahyuni, S. F. (2019). The strategy of Spiritual Leadership: The Role of Spiritual Survival, Workplace Spirituality and Organizational Commitment at Private Universities. *International Journal of Research in Business Social Science*, *8*(1), 64–72. doi:10.20525/ijrbs.v8i1.194

Saroglou, V., Buxant, C., & Tilquin, J. (2008). Positive emotions as leading to religion and spirituality. *The Journal of Positive Psychology*, *3*(3), 165–173. doi:10.1080/17439760801998737

Sashkin, M. (2004). Transformational leadership approaches. *Revue de Synthese*.

Saskatchewan Ministry of Education. (2015). *Actualizing a needs-based model*. https://publications.saskatchewan.ca/#/products/33546

Saskatchewan Ministry of Education. (2017). *The adaptive dimension for K-12 students*. https://publications.saskatchewan.ca/#/products/86567

Savage-Austin, A. R., & Honeycutt, A. (2011). Servant leadership: A phenomenological study of practices, experiences, organizational effectiveness, and barriers. *Journal of Business & Economics Research*, *9*(1), 49–54. doi:10.19030/jber.v9i1.939

Savovic, S. (2017). The impact of the dimensions of transformational leadership on the post-acquistion performance of the acquired company. *Economic Horizons*, *19*(2), 97–109. doi:10.5937/ekonhor1702095S

Scheffer, A., Braun, N., & Scheffer, M. (2012). *Hanging the mirror: The discipline of reflective leadership*. Wasteland Press.

Schein, E. H. (2004). *Organizational culture and leadership* (3rd ed.). Harper and Row.

Schmid, H. (2006). Leadership styles and leadership change in human and community service organizations. *Nonprofit Management & Leadership*, *17*(2), 179–194. doi:10.1002/nml.142

Schön, D. A. (1983). *The reflective practitioner: How professionals think in action*. Basic Books, Inc.

Schreiber, J. B., Nora, A., Stage, F. K., Barlow, E. A., & King, J. (2006). Reporting structural equation modeling and confirmatory factor analysis results: A review. *The Journal of Educational Research*, *99*(6), 323–338. doi:10.3200/JOER.99.6.323-338

Sebola, M. (2021). South Africa's public education institutions, university research outputs, and contribution to national human capital. *Human Resource Development International*. https://www.tandfonline.com/doi/full/10.1080/13678868.2022.2047147

Secretariat of the Convention on Biological Diversity (SCBD) and United Nations Development Programme (UNDP). (2021). *Aichi Biodiversity Target 11 Country Dossier: ANTIGUA & BARBUDA*. https://www.cbd.int/pa/doc/dossiers/antigua-and-barbuda-abt11-country-dossier2021.pdf

Seetal, I., Gunness, S., & Teeroovengadum, V. (2021). Educational disruption during the COVID-19 crisis in Small Island Developing States: Preparedness and efficacy of academics for online teaching. *International Review of Education*, *67*(1-2), 185–217. doi:10.100711159-021-09902-0 PMID:34024933

Seevers, B., Dormody, T., & Clason, D. (1995). Developing A Scaled To Research And Evaluate Youth Leadership Like Skills Development. *Journal of Agricultural Education*, *28*(36), 28–34. doi:10.5032/jae.1995.02028

Sekaran, U., & Bougie, R. (2010). Research Methods for Business: A Skill Building Approach (5th ed.). John Wiley & Sons.

Seligman, M. E. P. (2000). Positive psychology, positive prevention, and positive therapy. In Handbook of positive psychology. Oxford University Press.

Seligman, M. E., & Csikszentmihalyi, M. (2000). Positive psychology: An introduction. *The American Psychologist, 55*(1), 5–14. doi:10.1037/0003-066X.55.1.5 PMID:11392865

Semetsky, I. (2008). Re-reading Dewey through the lens of complexity science, or: On the creative logic of education. In M. Mason (Ed.), *Complexity theory and the philosophy of education* (pp. 79–90). Wiley-Blackwell. doi:10.1002/9781444307351.ch6

Sendjaya, S., & Sarros, J. C. (2002). Servant leadership: Its origin, development, and application in organizations. *Journal of Leadership & Organizational Studies, 9*(2), 57–64. doi:10.1177/107179190200900205

Senge, P. (2006). *The fifth discipline: The art and practice of the learning organization* (2nd ed.). Cornerstone.

Serrano, O. B. J., & Portalanza, A. (2014). Influencia del liderazgo sobre el clima organizacional. *Suma Neg., 5*(11), 117-125. http://www.scielo.org.co/pdf/sdn/v5nspe11/2027-5692-sdn-5-spe11-117.pdf

Serrat, O. (2017). Exercising servant leadership. In *Knowledge solutions: Tools, methods, and approaches to drive organizational performance* (pp. 649–655). Springer. doi:10.1007/978-981-10-0983-9_72

Sessoms, D. H., & Stevenson, J. L. (1981). *Leadership and group dynamics in recreation services.* Allyn Bacon.

Shaffer, J. (2008). Creating a leadership engine to power performance. *Strategic Communication Management, 12*(6), 28–32.

Shamir, B., & Eilam, G. (2005). "What's your story?" A life-stories approach to authentic leadership development. *The Leadership Quarterly, 16*(3), 395–417. doi:10.1016/j.leaqua.2005.03.005

Shannon, J. R. (1929). The post-school careers of high school leaders and high school scholars. *The School Review, 37*(9), 656–665. doi:10.1086/438921

Sharp, C., Nelson, J., Lucas, M., Julius, J., McCrone, T., & Sims, D. (2020). *Schools' responses to COVID-19: The challenges facing schools and pupils in September 2020.* National Foundation for Educational Research.

Sheffield, L. (2019, April 3). *Renaming human resources: People operations or team culture?* Human Interest. https://humaninterest.com/learn/articles/whats-name-hr-people-operations-team-culture/

Shekhawat, D. (2022). A Comparative Analysis Of Organizations Supporting Social Entrepreneurship. *Social Innovations Journal, 15.*

Sheldon, S. B., & Jung, S. B. (2018). *Student outcomes and parent teacher home visits.* Center on School, Family, and Community Partnerships, Johns Hopkins University. Recuperado de http://www. pthvp. org/wp-content/uploads/2018/12/181130-StudentOutcomesandPTHVReportFINAL. pdf

Sherbin, L., & Rashid, R. (2021, August 27). *Diversity doesn't stick without inclusion.* Diversity and Inclusion. https://hbr.org/2017/02/diversity-doesnt-stick-without-inclusion

Shields, C. M. (2010). Transformative leadership: Working for equity in diverse contexts. *Educational Administration Quarterly, 46*(4), 558–589. doi:10.1177/0013161X10375609

Sholikhati, N. I., Prayogo, M. M., & Santoso, J. (2021). The Effect of Distance Learning on Learning Outcomes of Children with Special Needs in Inclusive Schools in the New Normal. *Indonesian Journal of Disability Studies, 8*(1), 145–154. doi:10.21776/ub.ijds.2021.008.01.11

Showry, M., & Manasa, K. V. L. (2014). Self-Awareness-Key to Effective Leadership. *The IUP Journal of Soft Skills*, *8*(1).

Siedlok, F., & Hibbert, P. (2014). The organization of interdisciplinary research: Modes, drivers, and barriers. *International Journal of Management Reviews*, *16*(2), 194–210. doi:10.1111/ijmr.12016

Siedlok, F., Hibbert, P., & Sillince, J. (2015). From practice to collaborative community in interdisciplinary research contexts. *Research Policy*, *44*(1), 96–107. doi:10.1016/j.respol.2014.07.018

Sierra, M. J. E. (2022). *Liderazgo con valores. Visión Cristiana de la RSE.* Digital Reasons. https://books.google.es/books?hl=es&lr=&id=qtd-EAAAQBAJ&oi=fnd&pg=PT5&dq=liderazgo+con+valores&ots=w5_HexieRE&sig=kMy22YALTLfzAU46QE7D-kg6Wbk#v=onepage&q=liderazgo%20con%20valores&f=false

Simiyu, A. (2015). *Role of Leadership In Organizational Development.* Available at: https://www.researchgate.net/publication/273766248_ROLE_OF_LEADERSHIP_IN_ORGANIZATIONAL_DEVELOPMENT

Simões-Coelho, M., Figueira, A. R., & Russo, E. (2023). Motivations for a sustainable ethos: Evidence from the globally present Brazilian multinational Natura &Co. *Environment Systems & Decisions*, *43*(3), 1–16. doi:10.100710669-022-09890-y PMID:36628130

Sinclair, A. (2004). Journey around leadership. *Discourse (Abingdon)*, *25*(1), 7–19. doi:10.1080/0159630042000178455

Singh, S. (2007). Emotional intelligence and organisational leadership: A gender study in Indian context. *Int. J. Indian Culture and Business Management*, *1*(1/2), 48. Advance online publication. doi:10.1504/IJICBM.2007.014470

Skiba, R. J., Honer, R. H., Chung, C.-G., Rausch, M. K., May, S. L., & Tobin, T. (2011). Race is not neutral: A national investigation of African American and Latino disproportionality in school discipline. *School Psychology Review*, *40*(1), 85–107. doi:10.1080/02796015.2011.12087730

Skogstad, A., Einarsen, S., Torsheim, T., Aasland, M. S., & Hetland, H. (2007). The destructiveness of laissez-faire leadership behavior. *Journal of Occupational Health Psychology*, *12*(1), 80–92. doi:10.1037/1076-8998.12.1.80 PMID:17257068

Smith, B. E., & Colbert, P. L. (2002). *Surveys of the Lizard Anolis wattsi on Antiguan Offshore Islands III: Summer 2001*. Antiguan Racer Conservation Project Report No. 7. Black Hills State University.

Smith, C. (2020). Challenges and opportunities for teaching students with disabilities during the COVID-19 pandemic. *International Journal of Multidisciplinary Perspectives in Higher Education*, *5*(1), 167–173. doi:10.32674/jimphe.v5i1.2619

Smith, H. L., & Krueger, L. M. (1933). *A brief summary of the literature on leadership.* Indiana University, School of Education Bulletin.

Smith, L. T., Tuck, E., & Yang, K. W. (Eds.) (2019). *Indigenous and decolonising studies in education: Mapping the long view*. Routledge.

Smith, P., Francis, D., & Harper, A. (2015). Reframing transformational leadership for education and nation building in the Caribbean. *Caribbean Educational Research Journal*, *3*(2), 76–89.

Smith, T., & Shouppe, G. (2018). *Is there a relationship between schools' climate ratings and student performance data? National Teacher Education Journal, 11(1).*

Smoak-Mancheno, L., Endres, G. M., Potak, R., & Athanasaw, Y. (2009). The individual cultural values and job satisfaction of the transformational leader. *Organization Development Journal*, *27*(3), 9–22.

Snyder, H. (2019). Literature review as a research methodology: An overview and guidelines. *Journal of Business Research*, *104*, 333–339. doi:10.1016/j.jbusres.2019.07.039

Sohmen, V. S. (2013). Leadership and teamwork: Two sides of the same coin. *Journal of IT and Economic Development*, *4*(2), 1–18.

Solan, A. M. (2008). The relationships between emotional intelligence, visionary leadership, and organizational citizenship behavior in continuing higher education. *Dissertation Abstracts International, 69*(8), B. (UMI No. 3325538)

Soorae, P. S. (Ed.). (2010). Global Re-Introduction Perspectives: Additional case-studies from around the globe. Journal of the IUCN/SSC Re-Introduction Specialist Group, 8, 352.

Sosik, J. J., & Jung, D. (2011). *Full range leadership development: Pathways for people, profit and planet*. Psychology Press. doi:10.4324/9780203843161

Sotelo, M. J. (2000). Individual differences in political tolerance among adolescents. *Social Behavior and Personality*, *28*(2), 185–192. doi:10.2224bp.2000.28.2.185

Spano-Szekely, L., Griffin, M. T. Q., Clavelle, J., & Fitzpatrick, J. J. (2016). Emotional intelligence and transformational leadership in nurse managers. *The Journal of Nursing Administration*, *46*(2), 101–108. doi:10.1097/NNA.0000000000000303 PMID:26796823

Sparks, J. (2021). Understanding Transformational Leadership during a Time of Uncertainty. *Alabama Journal of Educational Leadership.*, *8*, 10–15.

Spears, L. C. (1996). Reflections on Robert K. Greenleaf and servant-leadership. *Leadership and Organization Development Journal*, *17*(7), 33–35. doi:10.1108/01437739610148367

Spector, P. E., & Fox, S. (2005). A model of counterproductive work behavior. In S. Fox & P. E. Spector (Eds.), *Counterproductive workplace behavior: Investigations of actors and targets* (pp. 151–174). American Psychological Association. doi:10.1037/10893-007

Spiggle, T. (2020, May 21). Can Employers Monitor Employees Who Work From Home Due To The Coronavirus? *Forbes*. Retrieved from https://www.forbes.com/sites/tomspiggle/2020/05/21/can-employers-monitor-employees-who-work-from-home-due-to-the-coronavirus/?sh=bae29122fb78

Stacey, R. D. (1996). *Complexity and creativity in organizations*. Berrett-Koehler Publishers.

Stanford, F. C. (2020). The Importance of Diversity and Inclusion in the Healthcare Workforce. *Journal of the National Medical Association*, *112*(3), 247–249. doi:10.1016/j.jnma.2020.03.014 PMID:32336480

StarrL. M. (2020). *Leadership Definitions and Themes*. doi:10.13140/RG.2.2.13471.79527

Stewart, G. L., & Brown, K. G. (2020). *Human resource management: Linking strategy to practice* (4th ed.). Wiley.

Stobierski, T. (2021, June 21). 15 eye-opening corporate social responsibility statistics. *Harvard Business Review*. Retrieved from: https://online.hbs.edu/blog/post/corporate-social-responsibility-statistics

Stock, C., Helmer, S. M., & Heinrichs, K. (2021). COVID-19 related disruption in higher education students' health and wellbeing: Implications for university action. *Frontiers in Public Health*, *10*. https://www.frontiersin.org/articles/10.3389/fpubh.2022.1015352/full PMID:36187608

Stogdill, R. M. (1948). Personal factors associated with leadership: A survey of the literature. *The Journal of Psychology*, *25*(1), 35–71. doi:10.1080/00223980.1948.9917362 PMID:18901913

Stogdill, R. M. (1950). Leadership, membership and organization. *Psychological Bulletin*, *47*(1), 1–14. doi:10.1037/h0053857

Stogdill, R. M. (1974). *Handbook of leadership: A survey of the literature*. Free Press.

Stogdill, R. M. (1974). *Handbook of leadership: A survey of theory and research*. Free Press.

Stogdill, R. M. (1975). The Evolution of Leadership Theory. *Academy of Management Proceedings*.

Stokols, D. (1996). Translating Social Ecological Theory into Guidelines for Community Health Promotion. *American Journal of Health Promotion*, *10*(4), 282–298. doi:10.4278/0890-1171-10.4.282 PMID:10159709

Stone-Johnson, C., Hubbard, L., Resultan, B., & Steilen, K. (2023). Responsible School Leadership: Exploring Role Expansion in Crisis and Beyond. *Journal of School Leadership*, *0*(0), 472–490. Advance online publication. doi:10.1177/10526846231174149

Stordeur, S., D'Hoore, W., & Vandenberghe, C. (2001). Leadership, organizational stress, and emotional exhaustion among hospital nursing staff. *Journal of Advanced Nursing*, *35*(4), 533–542. doi:10.1046/j.1365-2648.2001.01885.x PMID:11529953

Storper, M. (1997). *The regional world: Territorial development in a global economy*. Guilford Press.

Studies, A. (2019). Is the Amish population growing? Available at: http://groups.etown.edu/ amishstudies/frequently-askedquestions/?doing_wp_cron51578415405.4935638904571533203125

Studies, A. (2020). *Population growth*. Available at: https://groups.etown.edu/amishstudies/ social-organization/population-growth/

Sull, D., & Sull, C. (2022). How to fix a toxic culture. *MIT Sloan School of Management Review*. https://sloanreview.mit.edu/article/how-to-fix-a-toxic-culture/

Sullivan, J. (2018). *The Complete Guide to Conflict Resolution in the Workplace*. AMACOM.

Sultana, U. S., Darun, M. R., & Yao, L. (2015). Transactional or transformational leadership: Which works best for now? *International Journal of Industrial Management*. https://ijim.ump.edu.my/images/pdf/4.pdf

Sun, H., Pofoura, A. K., Mensah, I. A., Li, L., & Mohsin, M. (2020). The role of environmental entrepreneurship for sustainable development: Evidence from 35 countries in Sub-Saharan Africa. *The Science of the Total Environment*, *741*, 140132. doi:10.1016/j.scitotenv.2020.140132 PMID:32886991

Sun, J., & Leithwood, K. (2017). Transformational school leadership effects on student achievement. *Leadership and Policy in Schools*, *11*(4), 418–451. doi:10.1080/15700763.2012.681001

Surratt, H., Otachi, J., Slade, E., Kern, P., King, V., Kelly, T., & DiPaola, R. (2023). Optimizing team science in an academic medical center: A qualitative examination of investigator perspectives. *Journal of Clinical and Translational Science*, *7*(1), E57. doi:10.1017/cts.2023.3 PMID:37008610

Svalina, V., & Ivic, V. (2020). Case study of a student with disabilities in a vocational school during the period of online virtual classes due to COVID-19. *World Journal of Education*, *10*(4), 115–123. doi:10.5430/wje.v10n4p115

Tableman, B. (2004). School culture and school climate. *Best Practice Briefs*, *31*, 1–10.

Tang, K. N. (2019). *Leadership and Change management*. Springer Singapore. doi:10.1007/978-981-13-8902-3

Tannenbaum, R., & Schmidt, W. H. (1958). How to choose a leadership pattern. *Harvard Business Review*, *36*, 95–101.

Tannenbaum, R., Weschler, I. R., & Massarik, F. (1961). *Leadership and Organizations*. McGraw-Hill.

Tedla, B. A., & Kilango, N. C. (2022). The role of school leadership toward improving student's achievement: A case study of secondary schools in Changchun, China. *Journal of Positive School Psychology*, *6*(4), 6744–6755.

Temples, A., Simons, D., & Atkinson, M. (2019). Strategic employee training and development in a changing world. *International Journal of Training and Development*, *23*(1), 1–10.

Tepper, B. J. (2000). Consequences of abusive supervision. *Academy of Management Journal*, *43*(2), 178–190. doi:10.2307/1556375

Terry, G., Hayfield, N., Clarke, V., & Braun, V. (2017). Thematic analysis. In C. Willig & W. S. Rogers (Eds.), *The SAGE Handbook of Qualitative Research in Psychology* (pp. 17–37). Sage. doi:10.4135/9781526405555.n2

Tett, R. P., Fox, K. E., & Wang, A. (2005). Development and validation of a self-report measure of emotional intelligence as a multidimensional trait domain. *Personality and Social Psychology Bulletin*, *31*(7), 859–878. doi:10.1177/0146167204272860 PMID:15951360

Tett, R. P., & Guterman, H. A. (2000). Situation trait relevance, trait expression, and cross-situational consistency: Testing a principle of trait activation. *Journal of Research in Personality*, *34*(4), 397–423. doi:10.1006/jrpe.2000.2292

Thanh, N. H., & Quang, N. V. (2022). Transformational, transactional, Laissez-faire leadership styles and employee engagement: Evidence from Vietnam's Public Sector. *SAGE Open*, *12*(2), 1–18. doi:10.1177/21582440221094606

Thapa, A., Cohen, J., Guffrey, S., & Higgins-D' Alessandro, A. (2013). A review of school climate research. *Review of Educational Research*, *83*(3), 357–385. doi:10.3102/0034654313483907

Thiel, P. (2014). *Zero to One: Notes on Startups, or How to Build the Future*. Crown Business.

Thomas, K. W., & Velthouse, B. A. (1990). Cognitive elements of empowerment. An "interpretative" model of intrinsic task motivation. *Academy of Management Review*, *15*(4), 666–681.

Thompson, A. A., Strickland, A. J., & Gamble, J. E. (2005). *Crafting and executing strategy: Text and reading* (14th ed.). McGraw-Hill.

Thompson, C. S. (2020). Theories and applications of transformational school leadership. *Journal of Thought*, *54*(3/4), 55–72.

Thompson, H., & Matkin, G. (2020). The Evolution of Inclusive Leadership Studies: A literature review. *Journal of Leadership Education*, *19*(3), 15–30. doi:10.12806/V19/I3/R2

Thorpe, H., Brice, J., Clark, M., & Sims, S. (2020). The transdisciplinary health research apparatus: A Baradian account of knowledge boundaries and beyond. *Health*, *26*(3), 361–384. doi:10.1177/1363459320961429 PMID:33012195

Tichy, N. M., & Devanna, M. A. (1986). *The transformational leader*. Wiley.

Tien, N. H., Anh, D. B. H., Ngoc, N. M., & Do Thi, Y. N. (2019). Sustainable social entrepreneurship in Vietnam. *International Journal of Entrepreneurship*, *23*(3), 1–12.

Tierney, P., Farmer, S. M., & Graen, G. B. (1999). An examination of leadership and employee creativity: The relevance of traits and relationships. *Personnel Psychology*, *52*(3), 591–620. doi:10.1111/j.1744-6570.1999.tb00173.x

Tilbault, L., Schweyer, A., & Whillans, A. (2018). *Winning the War for Talent: Modern Motivational Methods for Attracting and Retaining Employees*. doi:10.1177/0886368718808152

Timmons, V., & Wagner, M. (2008). *Inclusive education knowledge exchange initiative: An analysis of the statistics Canada participation and activity limitation survey*. Canadian Council on Learning.

Tkacik, M. (2022, August 16). *'A place to die': For-profit health care crisis exposed* [Video] YouTube. https://www.youtube.com/watch?v=xzaCZs_qtI4

Todnem, R. (2005). Change management: A review of current thinking. Leadership &amp. *Organization Development Journal*, *26*(3), 195–204.

Toronto, C. E., & Remington, R. (2020). *A step-by-step guide to conducting an integrative review*. https://dl.uswr.ac.ir/bitstream/Hannan/141158/1/9783030375034.pdf

Torraco, R. J. (2005). Writing Integrative Literature Reviews: Guidelines and Examples. *Human Resource Development Review*, *4*(3), 356–367. doi:10.1177/1534484305278283

Tulane University School of Public Health and Tropical Medicine. (2021). *How to improve cultural competence in health care*. Author. https://publichealth.tulane.edu/blog/cultural-competence-in-health-care/

Turban Wan Yan, D. (2016). Relationship of eudaimonia and hedonia with work outcomes. *Journal of Managerial Psychology*, *31*(6), 1006–1020. doi:10.1108/JMP-07-2015-0271

Turja, T. (2022, March). Rather sooner than later: Participatory change management associated with greater job satisfaction in Healthcare. *Journal of Advanced Nursing*. https://www.ncbi.nlm.nih.gov/pmc/articles/PMC9306817/

Turkyilmaz, A., Akman, G., Ozkan, C., & Pastuszak, Z. (2011). *Empirical study of public sector employee loyalty and satisfaction: Industrial Management & Data Systems*. Academic Press.

Turner, J. R., & Baker, R. M. (2019). Complexity theory: An overview with potential applications for the social sciences. *Systems*, *7*(1), 4. doi:10.3390ystems7010004

Tykkyläinen, S., & Ritala, P. (2021). Business model innovation in social enterprises: An activity system perspective. *Journal of Business Research*, *125*, 684–697. doi:10.1016/j.jbusres.2020.01.045

Tyler, C. F., & Erickson, A. (2007). Have you got the business to become a leaders? *Strategic Communication Management*, *11*(4), 15.

Uhl-Bien, M., & Marion, R. (2011). Complexity leadership theory. In A. Bryman, D. Collinson, K. Grint, B. Jackson & M. Uhl-Bien (Eds.), The SAGE handbook of leadership (pp. 468-482). SAGE Publications.

Uhl-Bien, M. (2021a). Complexity and COVID-19: Leadership and followership in a complex world. *Journal of Management Studies*, *58*(5), 1400–1404. doi:10.1111/joms.12696

Uhl-Bien, M. (2021b). Complexity leadership and followership: Changed leadership in a changed world. *Journal of Change Management*, *21*(2), 144–162. doi:10.1080/14697017.2021.1917490

Uhl-Bien, M., & Arena, M. (2018). Leadership for organizational adaptability: A theoretical synthesis and integrative framework. *The Leadership Quarterly*, *29*(1), 89–104. doi:10.1016/j.leaqua.2017.12.009

Uhl-Bien, M., & Marion, R. (2009). Complexity leadership in bureaucratic forms of organizing: A meso model. *The Leadership Quarterly*, *20*(4), 631–650. doi:10.1016/j.leaqua.2009.04.007

Uhl-Bien, M., & Marion, R. (Eds.). (2007). *Complexity leadership: Part 1: Conceptual foundations*. IAP.

Uhl-Bien, M., Marion, R., & McKelvey, B. (2007). Complexity leadership theory: Shifting leadership from the industrial age to the knowledge era. *The Leadership Quarterly*, *18*(4), 298–318. doi:10.1016/j.leaqua.2007.04.002

Uhl-Bien, M., Meyer, D., & Smith, J. (2020). Complexity leadership in the nursing context. *Nursing Administration Quarterly*, *44*(2), 109–116. doi:10.1097/NAQ.0000000000000407 PMID:32134869

Unger, D., Goh, S. K., Whelan, J., & Burns, P. (2019). Toxic leadership: A meta-analytic review of negative outcomes for individuals and teams. *Journal of Occupational and Organizational Psychology*, *92*(3), 577–599.

United Nations Children's Fund. (2021). *Education disrupted: The second year of the COVID-19 pandemic and school closures*. https://data.unicef.org/resources/education-disrupted/

United Nations Educational, Scientific and Cultural Organization. (2020). *COVID-19 impact on education*. https://en.unesco.org/COVID-1919/educationresponse

United Nations Educational, Scientific and Cultural Organization. (2022). *Knowledge-driven actions: Transforming higher education for global sustainability*. https://unesdoc.unesco.org/ark:/48223/pf0000380519

United Nations Educational, Scientific and Cultural Organization. (2023). *The role of higher education institutions for lifelong learning*. https://www.uil.unesco.org/en/role-higher-education-institutions-lifelong-learning

United Nations. (2020). *Policy Brief: Education during COVID-19 and beyond*. https://www.un.org/development/desa/dspd/wp-content/uploads/sites/22/2020/08/sg_policy_brief_covid-19_and_education_august_2020.pdf

University of Minnesota. (n.d.). *1.1 What is human resources?* Author. https://open.lib.umn.edu/humanresourcemanagement/chapter/1-1-what-is-human-resources/

Urio, P., Murphy, S. P., Moses, I., Chua, C., & Darkwa, I. (2021). Exploring the gendered effects of the COVID-19 pandemic on academic staff in Tanzania. *Alliance for Africa Partnership Perspectives, 1*. https://muse.jhu.edu/article/837365

Urošević, S., Karabasevic, D., Maksimovic, M., & Stanujkic, D. (2016). Impact Of Demographic Factors on Motivation and Satisfaction of Employees in The Leather and Footwear Industry. *Tekstilna Industrija,* 45-55. Available at: https://www.researchgate.net/publication/309617116

Uysal, G. (2019). 3rd Definition of SHRM: HR Systems Approach. *Management Studies*, *7*(5). Advance online publication. doi:10.17265/2328-2185/2019.05.011

Valenzuela, K. (2007). *I Want To Be A Leader*. https://ezinearticles.com/expert/Ken_Valenzuela/107414

van Droffelaar, B. (2021). Episodic memories of wilderness experiences foster sustainable leadership style transformation. *Journal of Management Development*, *40*(6), 486–502. doi:10.1108/JMD-12-2020-0393

Van Knippenberg, D., & van Ginkel, W. P. (2022). A diversity mindset perspective on inclusive leadership. *Group & Organization Management*, *47*(4), 779–797. doi:10.1177/1059601121997229

Van Knippenberg, D., van Ginkel, W. P., & Homan, A. C. (2013). Diversity mindsets and the performance of diverse teams. *Organizational Behavior and Human Decision Processes*, *121*(2), 183–193. doi:10.1016/j.obhdp.2013.03.003

Van Maanen, J. (1988). *Tales of the Field: On Writing Ethnography*. The University of Chicago Press.

van Wart, M. (2003). Public-Sector leadership theory. *Public Administration Review*, *63*(2), 214–228. doi:10.1111/1540-6210.00281

van Wilgen, B. W., & Wannenburgh, A. (2016). Co-facilitating invasive species control, water conservation and poverty relief: Achievements and challenges in South Africa's Working for Water program. *Current Opinion in Environmental Sustainability*, *19*, 7–17. doi:10.1016/j.cosust.2015.08.012

Varnham, K., Ross, T., Daltry, J., Day, M., Cooper, G., & Lindsay, K. (1998). Recovery of the Antiguan racer. *Journal of the IUCN/SSC Invasive Species Specialist Group*, *8*, 21.

Varpio, L., Paradis, E., Uijtdehaage, S., & Young, M. (2020). The distinctions between theory, theoretical framework, and conceptual framework. *Academic Medicine*, *95*(7), 989–994. doi:10.1097/ACM.0000000000003075 PMID:31725464

Vecchio, R. P. (1988). *Organizational Behavior*. The Dryden Press.

Vedenik, J., & Leber, P. (2015). Change management: The view through the prism of three different models. Management &amp. *Marketing Challenges for the Knowledge Society*, *10*(1), 5–17.

Veitch, C. R., Clout, M. N., & Towns, D. R. (Eds.). (2011). *Island Invasives: Scaling up to meet the challenge*. Occasional Paper SSC No. 62. IUCN.

Venkatesan, M. (2022). Marketing Sustainability: A Critical Consideration of Environmental Marketing Strategies. In Products for Conscious Consumers (pp. 151-166). Emerald Publishing Limited. doi:10.1108/978-1-80262-837-120221009

Vilhauer, H. (2018). *An investigation into full-range leadership and leadership development methods in public parks and recreation organizations in California* [Doctoral Dissertation]. The University of San Francisco. https://repository.usfca.edu/cgi/viewcontent.cgi?article=1423&context=diss

Villegas, A. M., & Lucas, T. (2002). Preparing culturally responsive teachers: Rethinking the curriculum. *Journal of Teacher Education*, *53*(1), 20–32. doi:10.1177/0022487102053001003

Vitello-Cicciu, J. M. (2003). Innovative leadership through emotional intelligence. *Nursing Management*, *34*(10), 28–32. doi:10.1097/00006247-200310000-00010 PMID:14557778

Vollero, A., Siano, A., Palazzo, M., & Amabile, S. (2020). Hoftsede's cultural dimensions and corporate social responsibility in online communication: Are they independent constructs? *Corporate Social Responsibility and Environmental Management*, *27*(1), 53–64. doi:10.1002/csr.1773

Vos, D., van der Westhuizen, P., Mentz, P., & Ellis, S. (2012). Educators and the quality of their work environment: An analysis of the organizational climate in primary schools. *South African Journal of Education*, *32*(1), 56–68. doi:10.15700aje.v32n1a520

Voss, B. L. (2000). The Arc of Ambition: Defining the Leadership Journey. *The Journal of Business Strategy*, *21*(2), 47–56.

Vroom, V., Porter, L., & Lawler, E. (2015). Expectancy theories. *Organizational Behavior, 1*, 94-113.

Wadhawan, S., Gupta, N., Kaur, A., & Bhardwaj, A. (2022). Transformational leadership and employee performance amid COVID-19 crisis. *Journal of Information and Optimization Sciences*, *43*(6), 1431–1441. doi:10.1080/02522667.2022.2117345

Wagler, I. (2011). *Growing up Amish: A Memoir*. Tyndale House Publishing.

Wajdi, B. N. (2017). The Differences Between Management And Leadership. *Sinergi: Jurnal Ilmiah Ilmu Manajemen*, *7*(2), 75–84.

Waldman, D. A., Siegel, D. S., & Stahl, G. K. (2020). Defining the socially responsible leader: Revisiting issues in responsible leadership. *Journal of Leadership & Organizational Studies*, *27*(1), 5–20. doi:10.1177/1548051819872201

Walker, T. B., & Lawrence, N. (2022). *Advocacy for Protected Areas in the Caribbean: A Collaborated Approach to Ecotourism in Antigua and Barbuda. CABI Books*. CABI International. doi:10.1079/9781789249033.0005

Wallen, E. (2023). The Role of Emotional Intelligence in Healthcare Leadership: A Literature Review. *Journal of Healthcare Leadership*, *15*(1), 25–35.

Waltz, C. W., & Bausell, R. B. (1981). *Nursing Research: Design, Statistics and Computer Analysis*. F.A. Davis.

Walumbwa, F., Avolio, B., Gardner, W., Wernsing, T., & Peterson, S. (2008). Authentic leadership: Development and validation of a theory-based measure. *Journal of Management*, *34*(1), 89–126. doi:10.1177/0149206307308913

Wang, C., Ghadimi, P., Lim, M. K., & Tseng, M. L. (2019). A literature review of sustainable consumption and production: A comparative analysis in developed and developing economies. *Journal of Cleaner Production*, *206*, 741–754. doi:10.1016/j.jclepro.2018.09.172

Wang, G., Oh, I.-S., Courtright, S. H., & Colbert, A. E. (2011). Transformational leadership and performance across criteria and levels: A meta-analytic review of 25 years of research. *Group & Organization Management*, *36*(2), 223–270. doi:10.1177/1059601111401017

Wang, M., & Wan, W. (2022). The Impact of Transformational Leadership on Employee Well-being during the Pandemic. *Journal of Occupational and Environmental Medicine*, *64*(5), 391–400.

Wang, S. (2019). School heads' transformational leadership and students' modernity: The multiple mediating effects of school climates. *Asia Pacific Education Review*, *20*(3), 329–341. doi:10.100712564-019-09575-3

Wasserman, I. C. (2021). Complex times: Leading with vulnerability and integrity. In B. M. Ferdman, J. Prime, & R. E. Riggio (Eds.), *Inclusive Leadership: transforming diverse lives, workplaces, and societies* (pp. 83–96). Taylor & Francis.

Waterman, H. (2011). Principles of 'servant leadership' and how they can enhance practice. *Nursing Management*, *17*(9), 24–26. doi:10.7748/nm2011.02.17.9.24.c8299 PMID:21473215

Watson, D., & Tellegen, A. (1985). Toward a consensual structure of mood. *Psychological Bulletin*, *98*(2), 219–235. doi:10.1037/0033-2909.98.2.219 PMID:3901060

Watts, G. W. (2012). The power of introspection for executive development. *The Psychologist Manager Journal*, *15*(3), 149–157. doi:10.1080/10887156.2012.701136

Watts, L. L., Steele, L. M., & Mumford, M. D. (2019). Making sense of pragmatic and charismatic leadership stories: Effects on vision formation. *The Leadership Quarterly*, *30*(2), 243–259. doi:10.1016/j.leaqua.2018.09.003

Weijters, B., Cabooter, E., & Schillewaert, N. (2010). The effect of rating scale format on response styles: The number of response categories and response category labels. *International Journal of Research in Marketing*, *27*(3), 236–247. doi:10.1016/j.ijresmar.2010.02.004

Weinberger, L. A. (2009). Emotional intelligence, leadership style, and perceived leadership effectiveness. *Advances in Developing Human Resources*, *11*(6), 747–772. doi:10.1177/1523422309360811

Weiss, M., Razinskas, S., Backmann, J., & Hoegl, M. (2018). Authentic leadership and leaders' mental well-being: An experience sampling study. *The Leadership Quarterly*, *29*(2), 309–321. doi:10.1016/j.leaqua.2017.05.007

Western, S. (2019). *Leadership: A critical text* (3rd ed.). SAGE.

Whitaker, T. (2010). *Leading school change: 9 strategies to bring everybody on board*. Eye on Education, Inc.

White, M., & Epston, D. (1990). *Narrative Means to Therapeutic Ends*. W. W. Norton & Company.

Whitmer, A., Ogden, L., Lawton, J., Sturner, P., Groffman, P. M., Schneider, L., Hart, D., Halpern, B., Schlesinger, W., Raciti, S., Bettez, N., Ortega, S., Rustad, L., Pickett, S. T. A., & Killilea, M. (2010). The engaged university: Providing a platform for research that transforms society. *Frontiers in Ecology and the Environment*, *8*(6), 314–321. doi:10.1890/090241

Widodo, A. (2017). Teacher Pedagogical Content Knowledge (PCK) and students' reasoning and wellbeing. *Journal of Physics: Conference Series*, *812*, 012119. doi:10.1088/1742-6596/812/1/012119

Williamson, P. C. (2011). *Social Impact: A Definition*. Retrieved from http://www.socialimpactcenter.com/social-impact/

Williams, R., Bertsch, B., Van Der Wiele, A., Van Iwaarden, J., & Dale, B. (2006). Self-assessment against business excellence models: A critique and perspective. *Total Quality Management & Business Excellence*, *17*(10), 1287–1300. doi:10.1080/14783360600753737

Williams, W. A. Jr, Brandon, R.-S., Hayek, M., Haden, S. P., & Atinc, G. (2017). Servant leadership and followership creativity. *Leadership and Organization Development Journal*, *38*(2), 178–193. doi:10.1108/LODJ-02-2015-0019

Wilson, K., Brookes-Kenworthy, C., Hosking, R., Huang, C. K., Montgomery, L., Neylon, C., & Ozaygen, A. (2019). *Open knowledge profile of South Africa higher education and research institutions*. https://openknowledge.community/wp-content/uploads/2020/11/South-Africa-Institutional-open-knowledge-report-2019.pdf

Wilson, K., Kiuna, A., Lamptey, R., Veldsman, S., Montgomery, L., Neylon, C., Hosking, R., Huang, C. K., & Ozaygen, A. (2020). Open access and research dissemination in Africa. *ELPUB 2020: 24th edition of the International Conference on Electronic Publishing*. 10.4000/proceedings.elpub.2020.20

Wilson, K., Montgomery, L., Neylon, C., Huang, C. K., & Handcock, R. N. (2022). The Curtin Open Knowledge Initiative: Sharing data on scholarly research performance. *LIBER Quarterly*, *32*(1), 1–22. doi:10.53377/lq.11544

Winkler, I. (2010). *Contemporary leadership theories: Enhancing the understanding of the complexity, subjectivity and dynamic of leadership*. Springer Science & Business Media.

Witmer, G.W., & Hall, P. (2011). Attempting to eradicate invasive Gambian giant pouched rats (Cricetomys gambianus) in the United States: Lessons learned. *Island invasives: Eradication and management,* 131–134.

Wonga, C.-S., & Lawb, K. S. (2002). The effects of leader and follower emotional intelligence on performance and attitude: An exploratory study. *The Leadership Quarterly*, *13*(3), 243–274. doi:10.1016/S1048-9843(02)00099-1

Wong, P. T., & Page, D. (2003). Servant leadership: An opponent-process model and the revised servant leadership profile. *Proceedings of the Servant Leadership Research Roundtable*.

Wood, G. (2009). *Body language myth: The 7%-38%-55% rule*. Retrieved from https://psycentral.wordpress.com/2009/03/03/body-language-myth-7-38-55-ruledr-gary-wood-psycholog/

Wood, J. (1999). Establishing internal communication channels that work. *Journal of Higher Education Policy and Management*, *21*(2), 135–149. doi:10.1080/1360080990210202

Woods, E. H., & Martin, B. N. (2016). What leadership behaviours were demonstrated by the principal in a high poverty, high achieving elementary school? *Cogent Education*, *3*(1), 1172935. doi:10.1080/2331186X.2016.1172935

WordSense Dictionary. (n.d.). Available at https://www.wordsense.eu/

WorkandJam. (n.d.). *Mona High*. https://www.workandjam.com/bl/education/schools/mona-high.htm

World Business Council for Sustainable Development. (2010). *Sustainability: A Global Survey of Corporate Practices*. Retrieved from https://www.wbcsd.org/web/publications/WBCSD_Survey_2010.pdf

World Economic Forum. (2021). *The COVID-19 pandemic has changed education forever. This is how*. https://www.weforum.org/agenda/2020/04/coronavirus-education-global-covid19-online-digital-learning/

World Health Organization. (2015). Retrieved from https://www.who.int/

World Health Organization. (2020). *WHO Director-General's opening remarks at the media briefing on COVID-19 – 11 March 2020.* https://www.who.int/director-general/speeches/detail/who-director-general-s-opening-remarks-at-the-media-briefing-on-covid-19---11-march-2020

World Wildlife Fund (WWF). (2018). *Living planet report 2018: Aiming Higher.* WWF International.

Woudstra, G. (2021). *Mastering The Art of Team Coaching: A comprehensive guide to unleashing the power, purpose and potential in any team.* SRA Books.

Wright, K. B., Shields, S. M., Black, K., & Waxman, H. C. (2018). The effects of teacher home visits on student behavior, student academic achievement, and parent involvement. *School Community Journal, 28*(1), 67–90.

Wright, P. M., & McMahan, G. C. (1992). Theoretical perspectives for strategic human resource management. *Journal of Management, 18*(2), 295–320. doi:10.1177/014920639201800205

Wu, L., & Norman, I. J. (2006). *An investigation of job satisfaction, organizational commitment and role conflict and ambiguity in a sample of Chinese undergraduate nursing students* (Vol. 26). Nurse Education Today. doi:10.1016/j.nedt.2005.10.011

Xiao, C., & Hu, L. (2010). Etymological archeology and modern research of the concept of education. *University Education Science, 121*(3).

Xiao, Y., & Watson, M. (2019). Guidance on conducting a systematic literature review. *Journal of Planning Education and Research, 39*(1), 93–112. doi:10.1177/0739456X17723971

Xirasagar, S. (2008). Transformational, transactional and laissez-faire leadership among physician executives. *Journal of Health Organization and Management, 22*(6), 599–613. doi:10.1108/14777260810916579 PMID:19579573

Yadav, S., & Agrawal, V. (2017). Challenges Face by Transformational leader and suggestions to solve the challenges. *International Journal of Research in IT and Management, 7*(5), 34–43.

Yanka Perkasa & Fardinal. (2021). *The Influence of Organizational Culture.* Internal Control.

Yaslioglu, M. M., & Erden, N. S. (2018). Transformational leaders in action: Theory has been there, but what about practice? *IUP Journal of Business Strategy, 15*(1), 42–53.

Yavuz, M. (2019). *Transformational Leadership and Authentic Leadership as Practical Implications of Positive Organizational Psychology.* Academic Press.

Yavuz, M. (2019). Transformational leadership and authentic leadership as practical implications of positive organizational psychology. In Handbook of Research on Positive Organizational Behavior for Improved Workplace Performance (pp. 122–139). IGI Global. ISBN 13.

Yazcayir, G., & Gurgur, H. (2021). Students with special needs in digital classrooms during the COVID-19 pandemic in Turkey. *Pedagogical Research, 6*(1), em0088. Advance online publication. doi:10.29333/pr/9356

Yin, R. K. (2017). *Case Study Research: Design and Methods* (6th ed.). Sage Publications.

Yooyanyong, P., & Muenjohn, N. (2010). Leadership styles of expatriate managers: A comparison between American and Japanese expatriates. *The Journal of American Academy of Business, Cambridge, 15*(2), 161–168.

Yost, P. R., & Plunkett, M. M. (2009). *Real time leadership development* (Vol. 7). John Wiley & Sons.

Young, J., & Donovan, W. (2020). Shifting to online learning in the COVID-19 Spring. Policy brief. Pioneer Institute for Public Policy Research.

Yousaf, S., Latif, M., Aslam, S., & Saddiqui, A. (2014). Impact of Financial and non-Financial Rewards on Employee Motivation. *Middle East Journal of Scientific Research*, *21*, 1776–1786.

Yue, C. A., Men, L. R., & Berger, B. K. (2021). Leaders as communication agents. *Current trends and issues in internal communication. Theory into Practice*, 19–38.

Yu, H., Leithwood, K., & Jantzi, D. (2002). The effects of transformational leadership on teachers' commitment to change in Hong Kong. *Journal of Educational Administration*, *40*(4), 368–389. doi:10.1108/09578230210433436

Yukl, G. (2011). Contingency theories of effective leadership. The SAGE Handbook of Leadership, 24(1), 286-298.

Yukl, G. (1981). *Leadership in Organizations*. Prentice Hall.

Yukl, G. (1989). Managerial Leadership: A Review of Theory and Research. *Journal of Management*, *15*(2), 251–289. doi:10.1177/014920638901500207

Yukl, G. (1999). An evaluation of conceptual weaknesses in transformational and charismatic leadership theories. *The Leadership Quarterly*, *10*(2), 285–305. doi:10.1016/S1048-9843(99)00013-2

Yukl, G. (2008). How leaders influence organizational effectiveness. *The Leadership Quarterly*, *19*(6), 708–722. doi:10.1016/j.leaqua.2008.09.008

Yulianti, K., Denessen, E., Droop, M., & Veerman, G. J. (2021). Transformational leadership for parental involvement: How teachers perceive the school leadership practices to promote parental involvement in children's education. *Leadership and Policy in Schools*, *20*(2), 277–292. doi:10.1080/15700763.2019.1668424

Zaccaro, S. J. (2007). Trait-based perspectives of leadership. *The American Psychologist*, *62*(1), 6–16. doi:10.1037/0003-066X.62.1.6 PMID:17209675

Zacher, H., Pearce, L. K., Rooney, D., & McKenna, B. (2014). Leaders' personal wisdom and leader–member exchange quality: The role of individualized consideration. *Journal of Business Ethics*, *121*(2), 171–187. doi:10.100710551-013-1692-4

Żadkowska, M., Dowgiałło, B., Gajewska, M., Herzberg-Kurasz, M., & Kostecka, M. (2022). The Sociological Confessional: A Reflexive Process in the Transformation From Face-To-Face to Online Interview. *International Journal of Qualitative Methods*, *21*. doi:10.1177/16094069221084785

Zavaleta, E. S., Hobbs, R. J., & Mooney, H. A. (2001). Viewing invasive species removal in a whole-ecosystem context. *Trends in Ecology & Evolution*, *16*(8), 454–459. doi:10.1016/S0169-5347(01)02194-2

Zeidner, M., Matthews, G., & Roberts, R. D. (2012). The emotional intelligence, health, and well-being nexus: What have we learned and what have we missed? *Applied Psychology. Health and Well-Being*, *4*(1), 1–30. doi:10.1111/j.1758-0854.2011.01062.x PMID:26286968

Zeleza, P. (2006, November 11). *Beyond Afro Pessimism: Historical Accounting of African universities*. Pambazuka News. http://www.pambazuka.net/en/category.php/features

Zhang, Q., Oo, B. L., & Lim, B. T. H. (2019). Drivers, motivations, and barriers to the implementation of corporate social responsibility practices by construction enterprises: A review. *Journal of Cleaner Production*, *210*, 563–584. doi:10.1016/j.jclepro.2018.11.050

Zhang, W., Liu, Y., Das, S. K., & De, P. (2008). Secure data aggregation in wireless sensor networks: A watermark based authentication supportive approach. *Pervasive and Mobile Computing*, *4*(5), 658–680. doi:10.1016/j.pmcj.2008.05.005

Zhang, W., Sun, S. L., Jiang, Y., & Zhang, W. (2019). Openness to experience and team creativity: Effects of knowledge sharing and transformational leadership. *Creativity Research Journal*, *31*(1), 62–73. doi:10.1080/10400419.2019.1577649

Zhao, S., Huang, T., & Xi, J. (2022). Understanding the evolution of regional tourism efficiency: Through the lens of evolutionary economic geography. *Sustainability (Basel)*, *14*(7), 11042. doi:10.3390u141711042

Zhou, J., & Oldham, G. R. (2001). Enhancing Creative Performance: Effects of Expected Developmental Assessment Strategies and Creative Personality. *The Journal of Creative Behavior*, *35*(3), 151–167. doi:10.1002/j.2162-6057.2001.tb01044.x

Zou, W.-C., Tian, Q., & Liu, J. (2015). Servant leadership, social exchange relationships, and follower's helping behavior: Positive reciprocity belief matters. *International Journal of Hospitality Management*, *51*, 147–156. doi:10.1016/j.ijhm.2015.08.012

# About the Contributors

**Darcia Ann Marie Roache** worked for private and public sector organizations in Jamaica in the capacity of accountant, director of administration, and acted as chief executive officer. Her work experiences also included research assistant and programme leader for organizations and universities in Csnada and America. Her passion for administrative work led to her pursuing both a master's and doctoral degree in Business Administration. She now works as research supervisor, second examiner, and adjunct faculty for the Universities of the West Indies, the Commonwealth Caribbean, Regina, Lakeland College, and the Management Institute for National Development. Dr. Roache obtained her second PhD in Educational Administration from the University of Saskatchewan. She has published several articles and book chapters on educational leadership, transformational leadership, positive leadership practices, social inequities, and manifestation of microaggression. Dr. Roache is a firm believer in the Lord Jesus, who guides and directs her pathway. Her career ambition is to become a professor.

* * *

**Ansar Abbas** earned his Ph.D. at the University of Airlangga in Surabaya, Indonesia. He teaches as an associate professor at MYU (Muslim Youth University) in Islamabad, Pakistan. He published numerous qualitative and quantitative journal articles and book chapters. Key areas of study that he pioneered include leadership theory, leadership psychology, modern slavery, the development of human capital, the study of both positive and negative psychological traits, the study of spirituality and spiritual intelligence, the development of research models and frameworks, studies of well-being and positive psychology, and the study of positive emotions. In addition, he is extending his knowledge by participating in various practical academic activities that promote the development of research, such as acting as a reviewer, editorial assistant, and editor for several national and international publications. He has worked in management, administration, higher education, and research for 15 years.

**Muhammad Junaid Ahsan** is currently engaged as a guest visiting Ph.D. at CBS (Copenhagen Business School) in Denmark. He is also actively involved in his doctoral studies, specializing in Business and Management studies, under the Department of Economics and Management at the University of Pisa, Italy. Muhammad's research interests revolve around sustainability, leadership, corporate social responsibility, and the field of organization science.

**Veysel Altunel** is a Ph.D. student and Graduate Research Assistant in Curriculum & Instruction: English Education at LSU's Lutrill & Pearl Payne School of Education. He is interested in Learner Autonomy, Data-Driven Learning, Individual Differences, and Educational Technologies. Veysel's research explores innovative approaches to enhance education, fostering personalized and technology-driven instruction.

**Lyle Beson** is an Associate Professor in the Department of Mangement and Organizations in the MacEwan School of Business. His research interests focus on holistic leadership development. These include undergraduate development leadership skills, team building skills, and negotiating skills. He is also interested in undergraduate self-confidence development in the preceding areas.

**Susana Bernardino** is an Adjunct Professor of Management at the Polytechnic of Porto - Institute of Accounting and Administration (ISCAP), S. Mamede de Infesta, Portugal, and researcher at CEOS.PP/ISCAP. She completed her under-graduation degree in Management at the Faculty of Economics of the University of Porto, where also obtained the curricular part of the master's course in Finance. She got her PhD in Management in 2014 from the Portucalense University. Her research interests focus on social entrepreneurship, entrepreneurship, social and solidarity economy, smart cities, urban and regional development. and crowdfunding.

**Timothy S. Beyak** is a history and global studies teacher with the Louis Riel School Division. His interests focus on rhizomatic learning, language and literacy, and practitioner research. In 2021, he graduated with a Master of Education in curriculum, teaching, and learning from the University of Manitoba. His thesis study explored the intra-actions of teaching and learning within a global studies classroom and the entangled ways of being/doing/becoming that involve students, teachers, community members, and other organic/inorganic, human/nonhuman, and living/nonliving agents. He supports healthy community, citizenship, and human rights goals through education and service work. Tim received the Learners' Teacher Recognition Award from the University of Manitoba Centre for the Advancement of Teaching and Learning in 2014 and the Betty A. Nicks Fellowship in Education for academic merit and service work in 2017.

**Simon A. Black** received his MSc in Conservation Biology in 2008, and in Organisational Psychology in 2017, both from the University of Kent. He previously received his Ph.D. in management from the University of Bradford in 1993, winning the 1994 EFQM European Quality Award for his doctoral thesis. After a decade in commerce and industry, he turned his focus to wildlife conservation, joining the Durrell Institute for Conservation and Ecology in 2008, and delivering its MSc in Conservation Project Management alongside wildlife research and management consultancy. He is an alumnus of the Mauritian Wildlife Foundation and works with major NGOs across the world. He is a trustee of Wildwood, the UK's leading rewilding charity. He has authored over 50 international articles and is a co-author of Species Conservation: Lessons from Islands (2018, Cambridge).

**Darrell Norman Burrell** is visiting scholar at the Samuel DeWitt Proctor Institute for Leadership, Equity, and Justice at Rutgers University. Dr. Burrell has two doctorate degrees and five graduate degrees. Dr. Burrell received his first doctoral degree in Health Education from A.T. Still University in 2010. In 2021, Dr. Burrell completed his 2nd doctorate, a Doctor of Philosophy (Ph.D.) in Cybersecurity Leadership and Organizational Behavior at Capitol Technology University, Laurel, MD. Dr. Burrell completed a Master of Arts in Interfaith Action at Claremont Lincoln University as a Global Peacemaker Fellow in 2016. He has an EdS (Education Specialist Post Master's Terminal Degree) in Higher Education Administration from The George Washington. He has two graduate degrees, one in Human Resources Management/Development and another in Organizational Management from National Louis University.

Dr. Burrell has a graduate degree in Sales and Marketing Management from Prescott College. He has over 20 years of management, teaching, and training experience in academia, government, and private industry.

**Tashieka Burris-Melville** is a lecturer in the Faculty of Education and Liberal Studies at the University of Technology, Jamaica. She currently serves as programme leader for the M.Ed. and Ph.D. in Educational Leadership and Management in the faculty. She holds a Doctor of Education specializing in Leadership and Professional Practice from Trevecca Nazarene University and a Master of Arts in Linguistics from the University of the West Indies, Mona. Dr. Burris-Melville has taught courses in academic writing, linguistics, and leadership at the undergraduate and graduate levels. Her research interests include sociolinguistics, emotional intelligence, writing in higher education, teamwork development, collaborative and inclusive leadership, transformational leadership, and online teaching and learning. Dr. Burris-Melville is a member of several professional organizations, including the American Psychological Association (APA), the Institute for Educational Administration and Leadership-Jamaica (IEAL-J), the Association of Leadership Educators (ALE), the International Leadership Association (ILA), and the National Council of Teachers of English (NCTE).

**Sharon Burton** delivers more than 25 years of experience. She earned a Ph. D. in Cybersecurity Leadership and a DBA in Quality Management: Business Process Improvement. She is recognized for exhibiting an aptitude for leading organizational change, as well as developing and managing process improvement, documenting high-impact business requirements, writing/authoring, and driving continuous improvement. Publications include more than 90 peer-reviewed and academic texts: journal articles, textbook chapters, business books, and conference proceedings. Publications - Artificial Intelligence, Cyber Security, Leadership, Andragogy, Business Process Improvement, Diversity and Inclusion, Entrepreneurship, Quality Customer Service, Engaged Scholarship and Civic Responsibility, and Mentoring & Coaching. Certifications: Master Lean Six Sigma Black Belt, Change Management, Advanced Telemedicine and Telehealth, Kaizen Leadership, Strategic Workforce Planning, and Kirkpatrick Four Levels Evaluation. Certificates: Diversity, Equity, & Inclusion, and Artificial Intelligence/Robotic Processing. Diplomas: Artificial Intelligence Computer Vision 2.0, Robotic Starter Training, and Business Analyst Training. One badge is earned in Artificial Intelligence (AI) Computer Vision. Dr. Burton serves as a dissertation chair for Capitol Technology University and an adjunct faculty member for Post University and Capitol Technology University.

**Giuseppe Umberto Cantafio** is a Senior Lecturer (Academic Development APP and TEF) teaching Business and Innovation for the MBA Programme and for the MSc in International Business and Management. Prior to my role at the University of Sunderland in London, I worked as a Lecturer and researcher on the impacts and scenarios evaluation of Autonomous and Connected Transport at the University of Greenwich. I held posts at Northeastern University in Boston, San Diego State University and the Universita Mediterranea of Reggio in Calabria, Italy, where I was a researcher for the MAPS-LED Project, exploring multi-disciplinary approaches to plan smart specialisation strategies for local Economic Development.

**Shanna Challenger** is an award-winning environmentalist who possesses over 6 years of demonstrated ability and technical expertise working in areas of high biodiversity importance, maintaining pest-free island ecosystems and creating positive environmental change with a wide variety of stakeholders across Antigua and Barbuda, and the wider Caribbean region. Through the prestigious Chevening scholarship, Shanna graduated with an MSc in Conservation Biology from the University of Kent, and she is currently employed as the Coordinator of the Offshore Islands Conservation Programme at the Environmental Awareness Group. For her environmental conservation efforts, Shanna was the 2020 recipient of the Euan P. McFarlane Award for Outstanding Environmental Leadership by the Community Foundation of the Virgin Islands, and recently accepted the Young Environmentalist Award at the 2022 Antigua & Barbuda National Youth Awards. Sparking life-changing moments between people and wildlife has always been her life's calling, and she thrives in finding compelling ways to tell stories that demonstrate the irreplaceable value of her country's biodiversity.

**Christell Chesney** is a Social Conservationist with an MSc in Conservation and Rural Development. She was also a recipient of the prestigious Chevening Scholarship (2019/20) and the Conservation Leadership in the Caribbean Fellowship (2017-2018). With over six years of experience, Christell has supported several development projects locally and has assessed the performance of conservation organizations in Africa, the USA, and across the Caribbean and Pacific islands. Her main areas of expertise include community and stakeholder engagement, socio-economic, conflict, and gender research, and project management.

**Marisa Cleveland** is adamant about supporting efforts toward the betterment of the human condition. Cleveland is the executive director for The Seymour Agency, a trustee for Hodges University Board of Trustees, and co-author of the leadership book, There Is No Box. Cleveland holds an Ed.D. in Organizational Leadership from Northeastern University, and an M.A. in Educational Administration and a B.A. in Speech Communication from George Mason University.

**Simon Cleveland** is professor of project management at Purdue University Global. Dr. Cleveland is a graduate of George Mason University with Bachelor of Science degree in Business Management, the George Washington University with a Master of Science degree in Project Management, City University of Seattle with a Master of Arts degree in Leadership, has a Ph.D. in Information Systems from Nova Southeastern University and Ed.D. in Organizational Leadership from Northeastern University. He is also certified as a project management professional (PMP), Disciplined Agile Scrum Master (DASM), Certified Scrum Master (CSM), Six Sigma Black Belt (SSBB) expert, and Information Technology Infrastructure Library (ITIL) foundations expert. Dr. Cleveland is the author of over 50 peer-reviewed publications in journals and conferences, and is a three-time recipient of the prestigious Dr. Harold Kerzner Scholarship which is awarded by the Project Management Institute Educational Foundation. Professionally, Dr. Cleveland has worked as both technology manager, program manager and PMO Director for organizations such as MD Anderson Cancer Center, Department of Homeland Security, NASA, Accenture, and AOL.

**Margie Crowe** is a retired United States Air Force lieutenant colonel, leadership & DEI consultant, published writer, higher education director and professor with broad experience in government and civilian programs, strategic planning, as well as published works focused on leadership practices affecting policies and programs in social justice, anti-racism, and DEI. She has consulted for the military, law enforcement, and private sector, as well as presented at academic and professional conferences on topics related to leadership, DEI, and digital equity and literacy. Margie holds a BA in political science, MS in international relations/national security, MA in special education, a postgraduate degree and a doctorate degree in educational leadership, and a training certificate in racial equity literacy facilitation.

**Alma Duklaska** is an accomplished entrepreneur, and educator, holding a Master's Degree in Business Administration with a major in Human Recourse Management and Leadership. Her résumé highlights her significant experience leading many teams. Working at the Ministry of Justice and being involved in numerous research studies has inspired her to make an impact in leadership and human resources theory and practice. Her expertise is on the study of leadership, particularly as it relates to the extent to which it inspires followers and advances the organisation's overall goals.

**Dian Ekowati** is a prominent academician at the Department of Management Sciences, Faculty of Economics and Business at the University of Airlangga. From QEC, Head of International Office and Partnership, Deputy Executive Director, and Head of Airlangga Global Engagement, she is now Head of the Planning and Development Board for Airlangga University. She has produced numerous book chapters, journal articles, conference papers, and social development research projects. In addition to these endeavors, Dr. Ekowati teaches and does research with many Ph.D. and master's students at the undergraduate and graduate levels. In addition, she has expertise in qualitative research and analysis, organizational theories and behavior, change management, and internationalization. She holds a Ph.D. in Management of Change and Strategies, Interorganizational Network, Organization Politics/Power, and Organizational Territoriality from the University of York, United Kingdom.

**Rakotoarisoa Fenitra** graduated from the Faculty of Economics and Business, Department of Business Administration, Universitas Airlangga, Surabaya Indonesia. His area of interest falls in Entrepreneurship, human behavior, tourism, and marketing in particular, while general interests are related to human development approaches and empirical research.

**Alessandro Ferrazza** is a Senior Lecturer in the department of International business and management at the University of Sunderland, London Campus. Prior to his role at the University of Sunderland in London, he worked worked for several years in senior management positions in global corporations.

**Ralph Gigliotti** serves as Assistant Vice President for Strategic Programs in the Office of University Strategy and Director of the Center for Organizational Leadership at Rutgers University, where he provides executive leadership for a portfolio of signature academic leadership programs, consultation services, and research initiatives. He holds part-time faculty appointments in the Department of Communication (School of Communication and Information), Ph.D. Program in Higher Education (Graduate School of Education), Department of Family Medicine and Community Health (Robert Wood Johnson Medical School), and Rutgers Business School. His research and consulting interests explore topics related to leadership, crisis, strategy, team dynamics, organizational communication, and training and development within the context of higher education.

**Suzzette Harriott** has dedicated herself to guiding individuals, groups, and leaders through their unique journeys toward success. This is evident in her extensive work that spans across several complex areas, such as Diversity, Equity, Inclusion, and Belonging (DEIB), Self-Compassion and Impostor Syndrome, Emotional Intelligence, Transformational Leadership, Cultural Communication, and Group Dynamics. Suzzette's expertise extends beyond academia and into the corporate world. She has held prominent leadership roles in respected international organizations, where she has expertly steered change, created synergies, and crafted strategies focused on organizational agility and efficiency. She brings a global perspective to her consulting work, helping organizations worldwide tailor their DEIB strategies to local contexts. This reflects her steadfast commitment to promoting universal inclusion and acceptance. At present, her research delves into the fascinating relationship between Impostor Syndrome and Self-Compassion, offering enlightening insights into the human psyche. However, Dr. Suzzette Harriott is much more than her impressive degrees and titles. She stands as a symbol of empathy, a driver of change, and a fervent supporter of transformative education. Through her work, she tirelessly advocates for diversity, kindness, and the importance of self-understanding.

**Arica Hill** is an Antiguan environmentalist presently serving as the Executive Director of the Environmental Awareness Group in her home country. A recipient of an Australian Leadership Award, Arica holds an MSc in Environmental Management (Sustainable Development) and later went on to complete a Fellowship at the United Nations Framework Convention on Climate Change. Arica has been working in the environmental field for more than a decade and championed the Plastic Bag Ban in Antigua and Barbuda. Her work presently focuses on providing people and communities with the resources they need so that conservation action can be locally led. She believes strongly that real change comes through communication, and desires to see not just the sustainable use of natural resources, but an appreciation for them as well.

**Daniel Horton**, MD, MSCE, is Assistant Professor of Pediatrics and Epidemiology, Chancellor's Scholar, and a founding faculty member in the Center for Pharmacoepidemiology and Treatment Science (PETS) at Rutgers University. Dr. Horton is a board-certified pediatric rheumatologist, clinical epidemiologist, and pharmacoepidemiologist, whose research focuses on the utilization, effectiveness, and safety of medicines in large pediatric populations; the origins and management of juvenile idiopathic arthritis and other chronic childhood conditions; and the determinants, complications of, and immunologic response to SARS-CoV-2 infection.

**Raziq Hussain** is assistant Prof. at the Department of International Relations, Muslim Youth (MY) University Islamabad.

**Natasha N. Johnson** is a Clinical Instructor of Criminal Justice and Criminology in the Andrew Young School of Policy Studies at Georgia State University. A career educator since 2001, her research focuses on critical theory, equity, and social justice leadership, particularly within the K-20 sector. Her other research areas include intersectionality, educational law, policy, and governance, and curriculum development. Dr. Johnson holds multi-state reciprocity and has previously worked as a teacher, guidance counselor, assistant dean, instructional leader, and curriculum developer domestically and abroad. She is a David L. Clark scholar, a CETLOE Faculty Teaching Fellow, and her work is published in SAGE, the Oxford Research Encyclopedia of Criminology and Criminal Justice, Taylor & Francis, the Routledge Focus series, Psychology of Violence, the popular press, and several highly acclaimed educational leadership journals.

**Hannah Keim** is a graduate student in the department of Second Language Education at McGill University, Quebec, Canada. Hannah Keim's research focuses on how language usage and acquisition can affect speakers linguistic and cultural identities.

**Carlos Lee** is an Assistant Professor of Educational Leadership within the College of Human Sciences and Education (CHSE) at Louisiana State University. In addition, Dr. Lee is Program Coordinator for the online MEd in Educational Leadership and advisor to students enrolled in this degree program. Dr. Lee brings more than 20 years of administrative and teaching experience to the CHSE. His research interests include social and fiscal forces impacting governance, management theory, and policy evaluation.

**Henderson Lewis, Jr.**, Ph.D., is an Assistant Professor of Educational Leadership within the School of Education, College of Human Sciences and Education, Louisiana State University, Baton Rouge. His research interest includes change management and governance models in school systems, leadership development for principals and superintendents, and mentorship of African-American males in education. Dr. Lewis has served as an educator in Louisiana for over 25 years with services extending across the southern region of the state. Dr. Lewis began his career as an educator in his hometown of St. Bernard Parish. He served his community in the role of a mathematics teacher, curriculum coordinator, and later as an 11-year elected school board member. Dr. Lewis continued his career journey by the assuming role of a charter school and district leader in New Orleans. His career journey afforded him the opportunity to serve the residents of East Feliciana Parish as the Superintendent of Schools. Dr. Lewis has served his last 7 years as the Superintendent of NOLA Public Schools, where he oversaw the historic 2018 unification of public schools in New Orleans with those schools run by the state of Louisiana and created the first decentralized school district in America.

**Pei-Ying Lin** is a professor at the Department of Educational Psychology and Special Education of the University of Saskatchewan, works with diverse populations of children, youth, parents, in-service and pre-service teachers, university faculty members and staff as well as testing agencies over the years. Her research interests include the use of varied research methods for studying assessment practices and policies for students with special needs and English language learners. She continues working on an array of research projects since her doctorate at the Ontario Institute for Studies in Education of the University of Toronto. See for more information about her teaching, research, and services.

**Quatavia McLester** is a PhD candidate in the Business and Industrial/Organizational Psychology program at The Chicago School of Professional Psychology – Washington, D.C. She holds a Master of Science in Industrial/Organizational Psychology from Austin Peay State University. She holds a Bachelor of Science in Psychology and a minor in Applied Statistics and Data Analysis from Kennesaw State University. She is currently serving as a Board Certified Behavior Analyst for a private mental healthcare agency. Her research interests include processes and outcomes of organizational development and change at the individual, group, and systems levels and the effects of destructive leadership within organizations.

**Kezia H. Mkwizu** is a PhD in Tourism at The Open University of Tanzania in Tanzania. She has now completed her Postdoctoral Scholar under the Directorate of Research Publication and Innovation (DRPI) at The Open University of Tanzania. She mentors PhD students locally and internationally from countries including Botswana, Ethiopia, Kenya, Liberia, Nigeria, Uganda and USA. Her research interests focus on tourism but not limited to tourism. She has attended local, international and high-level conferences. She has published articles and is a reviewer in international conferences and various international peer-reviewed journals.

**Fabio Moscoso-Duran** is a Ph.D. in International Economics of Fribourg University, Switzerland. International consultant in innovation, competitiveness, strategy, and business planning. Researcher of Economic and Social Analysis (IAES), University of Alcalá de Henares. Associate Professor UNAD University.

**Carlos Muñoz-Maya** has a PhD in Administration from the University of Celaya (Mexico), master's degree in teaching from the University of La Salle, specialist in Logistics from the EAN University, specialist in Finance Management from the Grancolombiano Polytechnic, Business Administrator from the Javeriana University, with extensive experience in teaching at the national level. Experience as a researcher and co-investigator on issues such as organizational management, competitiveness, sustainable management and corruption in micro, small and medium-sized companies and as an advisor and consultant on issues related to financial management and the formulation and evaluation of projects in both public and private companies. Director in national companies with responsibilities in planning, direction and management. Experience in the financial, logistics and commercial area in the financial and manufacturing sector.

**Ashly Nyathi** is a seasoned Human Resources Practitioner, holds an honours degree in Human Resource Management from the Midlands State University (Zimbabwe) & a Masters Degree in Business Administration from the International University of Management (Namibia).

**David Ocampo-Guzman** has a Master in Science, Universiteé Du Quebec a Chicoutimi. Máster in Organizational, Management, Universidad EAN. Business Administrator Universidad EAN. Expert in defining, aligning and addressing strategic planning and directing for companies and organizations, especially Small and Medium sized firms. (SMEs). Very competent in attending organizational restructuring requirements for both private companies as well as public entities, leading assessment and evaluation processes procuring a profound and thorough organizational diagnosis, allowing the implementation of new management models and/or the upgrade of current ones, which include designing and applying Key Performance Indicators (KPIs).

**Cynthia Onyefulu** is a Professor of Educational Assessment in the Faculty of Education and Liberal Studies at the University of Technology (UTech), Jamaica. She holds a PhD in Educational Psychology, with a specialization in psychometrics, from the University of Alberta in Canada. Her primary research interests and publications since completing the terminal degree have been focused on, among others: classroom assessment practices, teacher education, programme and policy evaluation, and research ethics and management. Professor Onyefulu has authored and co-authored several peer-reviewed journal articles and book chapters. She is also the editor of a peer-reviewed book and the author of numerous commissioned studies. She has served as a reviewer for the American Educational Research Association, the Continental Journal of Education Research, the Caribbean Education Research Journal, the Collected Essays on Learning and Teaching, and the World Education Research Association, among others. She was the Editor-in-Chief of the Journal of Arts, Science and Technology. Professor Cynthia Onyefulu is a member of the Assessment in Higher Education Network (AHE), the American Educational Research Association (AERA), the Caribbean Case Researchers' Association (CCRA), the Bioethics Society of the English Speaking Caribbean (BSESC), and the Mixed Methods International Research Association Caribbean Chapter (MMIRA-CC).

**Rafael Pérez-Uribe** is a Doctor of Business Sciences, U. Nebrija. Diploma of Advanced Studies in applied economics, U. Nebrija. Master's Degree in Organizational Management, EAN University. Maître es Sciences, University of Quebec to Chicoutimi. Specialist in Evaluation and Construction of Management Indicators for Higher Education, School of Business Administration. Postgraduate Studies as Kenkyusei (Associate Researcher) in Total Quality Control and Quality Circles, Fukushima University, Japan. Business Administrator, Universidad Jorge Tadeo Lozano. Director of the research group on the management of large, small and medium-sized enterprises (G3pymes) and Professor attached to the Management of Research of EAN University.

**Beryl Peters** is the Director of Practicum and Partnerships at the Faculty of Education, responsible for overseeing and providing leadership for the practicum components of the B. Ed. program. She is a member of the Department of Curriculum, Teaching and Learning with specialty areas in arts education, curriculum, and teacher education. She holds a Ph.D. in Inclusive Education (University of Manitoba) and a Master of Music (East Texas State University). Dr. Peters has many years of experience teaching in K-12 public schools and post-secondary from Texas to the Yukon. Prior to her appointment as Director of Practicum in August 2018, Dr. Peters was an Arts Education Consultant with the Manitoba Department of Education where she coordinated the development and implementation of curricula and resources for K-12 Arts Education. Her research focuses on arts education, multiliteracies, teacher education, and critical pedagogy. Dr. Peters holds multiple teaching and research awards including the national 2012 Arts Researchers and Teachers Society Doctoral Graduate Research Award for her doctoral research.

**William L. Quisenberry** is an Educator, Mentor, Coach, Researcher, and Consultant that seeks to use a servant approach to helping others achieve their goals. Dr. Quisenberry resides in Lexington, KY and has a diverse background that includes studying and practicing within the field of business administration, coordinating implementation projects for Fortune 500 clients, managing and overseeing vendors/suppliers, operations management, project management, marketing, research analysis, consulting, and teaching at the collegiate level. Dr. Quisenberry has collaborated and worked on projects with a variety of major organizations in the marketplace that include: Lexmark International, Halliburton, Branch Banking and Trust, The U.S. Department of Veterans Affairs, Wal-Mart, The U.S. Army Corps of Engineers, Accenture, IBM, Best Buy, Lockheed Martin, John Hancock Financial, and the World Trade Center Association. Dr. Quisenberry holds a Bachelor of Business Administration (BBA) degree in Finance, a BBA in Marketing, as well as a Master of Business Administration degree from Sullivan University's Graduate School of Business, and a Post-Graduate Certification in Forensic Accounting from Davenport

University. He also possesses a Doctor of Business Administration (DBA) degree with a specialization in Leadership from Walden University. Dr. Quisenberry's dissertation was titled, "Common Characteristics and Attributes of Self-Managed Virtual Teams." He was nominated for Walden University's Outstanding Research award and his study was also nominated for the University's Doctoral Study of the Year award. Dr. Quisenberry strives to remain active in his local community. He currently serves on the Board of Directors for Fostering Goodwill, an agency based in Lexington, KY that seeks to provide resources, training, and mentorship to young adults who have aged out of the foster care system. He serves with multiple grassroots organizations that strive to build relationships, offer training, mentorship, programs, and services to various individuals or communities facing difficult challenges, such as at-risks youth, marginalized communities, and homeless populations. He also collaborates with several international organizations on similar outreach projects and initiatives. Dr. Quisenberry's background and current efforts help to shape his teaching approach, which emphasizes servitude and transformational leadership. He views his Learners as clients who all have something to contribute to the classroom, society, and life in general. With this in mind, he seeks to create an international community of servant, transformational leaders who are willing to leverage their experiences, training, education, and research to be positive social change agents.

**Nancy E. Reichman** is a Professor of Pediatrics at Robert Wood Johnson Medical School and has maintained a Visiting Professorship in the Department of Economics at Princeton University for many years. Reichman is an economist with a broad portfolio of research focusing on linkages between socioeconomic status and health, including studies of determinants of infant and child health, effects of child health on family resources, sources of health disparities, and effects of public policies and other contexts on child and family well-being.

**Kareen Reid** is a trained educator and has been teaching for over 25 years and sees teaching as her passion; she has a Master of Education Degree in Teaching and Learning from the Saint Mary's University of Minnesota and a Doctor of Philosophy in Educational Administration from the University of Saskatchewan. She has been with the Department of Educational Administration at the University of Saskatchewan since 2016, where she obtained her Ph.D. in Educational Administration. Her research focused on The Influence of School Leadership Practices on Culturally Responsive Pedagogy for Newcomer Students. She served in different roles, such as Teacher Assistant, Research Assistant, Lecturer, and Guest Lecturer. She also volunteered as a mentor and on several committees. Kareen is a Researcher, an Educator and an Author.

**Kevin Richardson** currently serves as an Associate Professor of Business & Technology at Edward Waters University. He is a Certified Diversity Professional and a Certified Trainer. Dr. Richardson has two doctoral degrees and three graduate degrees. In 2016, he received his first doctorate degree in Operations and Quality Management Systems from The National Graduate School (Washington, DC). In 2021, Dr. Richardson received a Philosophy of Doctorate (Ph.D.) in Technology Management of Information Systems from Capitol Technology University (Laurel, MD). He completed a Master of Science in Natural Resources Economics and Corporate Sustainability at Virginia Tech University (Blacksburg, VA). Dr. Richardson has a graduate degree in Information Systems Engineering Management from Harrisburg Science & Technology University (Harrisburg, PA), and his third master's degree in Counseling Psychology from Springfield College (Charleston, SC). Dr. Richardson has over 25 years of management, teaching, and training trainer experience in academia, government, and private industries. His university teaching experience included teaching at Edward Waters University, Bethune Cookman University, Allen University, The National Graduate School of Quality Management, and Morris College.

**Alexis Rotondo** is a student in the Ernest Mario School of Pharmacy at Rutgers University. Alexis served as an intern for the New Jersey Alliance for Clinical and Translational Science in Fall 2022. Her primary focus during the internship involved the study of interdisciplinary approaches to team science in biomedical sciences and an exploration of insights related to teamwork, team dynamics, and team collaboration from professionals outside of biomedical science. She intends to build upon this research in her future interprofessional pursuits in the field of pharmacy.

**Saleria Sterling Shaffer** was born in Baton Rouge, Louisiana in 1970. She grew up attending Southern University A&M College football games with her family. Education was top priority in the Sterling household. Shaffer earned a Bachelor's and a Master's in Elementary Education from Southern University A&M College. She is currently pursuing an Educational Specialist Degree in Curriculum & Instruction from Louisiana State University with plans to enter the Louisiana State University P-12 in Educational Administration Program in the spring of 2024. While entering her twentieth year in education, she is an educator in the Zachary Community Schools. Mrs. Shaffer serves as Gifted & Talented Lead Teacher for the Gifted & Talented Department and a Gifted Resource Teacher to K-12 learners. Outside school, Mrs. Shaffer serves as Grand Organist in the Ester Grand Chapter Order of Eastern Star Prince Hall Affiliation Louisiana Jurisdiction, Worthy Matron for Pride of St. Francisville Chapter #12, and musician for Mt. Pleasant Missionary Baptist Church and God's Grace Ministries.

**Sadrag Panduleni Shihomeka** holds a PhD in Media and Communication from the Department of Media and Communication at the School of History, Culture, and Communication, Erasmus University Rotterdam. His PhD research project focused on citizen engagement: politics and digital media in Namibia. Additionally; MBA and a Bachelor of Education (Secondary). Currently, Dr Shihomeka is the Head of Department for Higher Education and Lifelong Learning as well as a Senior Lecturer for Media, Educational Technologies and Research in the same Department in the School of Education at the University of Namibia. He is a Digital Ethnographer and served in different capacities as a lecturer, undergraduate and postgraduate research supervisor, consultant, secondary school teacher and facilitator for various workshops and trainings in Namibia. His research interests are on new media and politics; inclusive/exclusive democracy and virtual spheres; digital literacy and politics, educational technologies, education and politics, digital democracy, digital divide, political participation, Digital Skilling, Digital Romance and Cyber Bullying/crime, Social Media Ethic.

**Fendy Suhariadi** is a Professor of Psychology majoring in Industrial and Organizational Psychology and Human Resources Management. Now, has a responsibility as Head of Human Resources Development Doctoral Degree in Postgraduate School in Airlangga University.

# Index

## F



## G



## H



## I



## L



## M



## N



## O



## P



## Q



## R

## S



## T



## U



## W

# 7,300+ E-BOOKS. ADVANCED RESEARCH. INCLUSIVE & AFFORDABLE.

IGI Global
PUBLISHER of TIMELY KNOWLEDGE

## IGI Global e-Book Collection

- **Flexible Purchasing Options** (Perpetual, Subscription, EBA, etc.)
- Multi-Year Agreements with **No Price Increases** Guaranteed
- **No Additional Charge** for Multi-User Licensing
- No Maintenance, Hosting, or Archiving Fees
- Continually Enhanced & Innovated **Accessibility Compliance Features** (WCAG)

**Handbook of Research on Digital Transformation, Industry Use Cases, and the Impact of Disruptive Technologies**
ISBN: 9781799877127
EISBN: 9781799877141

**Handbook of Research on New Investigations in Artificial Life, AI, and Machine Learning**
ISBN: 9781799886860
EISBN: 9781799886877

**Handbook of Research on Future of Work and Education**
ISBN: 9781799882756
EISBN: 9781799882770

**Research Anthology on Physical and Intellectual Disabilities in an Inclusive Society (4 Vols.)**
ISBN: 9781668435427
EISBN: 9781668435434

**Innovative Economic, Social, and Environmental Practices for Progressing Future Sustainability**
ISBN: 9781799895909
EISBN: 9781799895923

**Applied Guide for Event Study Research in Supply Chain Management**
ISBN: 9781799889694
EISBN: 9781799889717

**Mental Health and Wellness in Healthcare Workers**
ISBN: 9781799888130
EISBN: 9781799888147

**Clean Technologies and Sustainable Development in Civil Engineering**
ISBN: 9781799898108
EISBN: 9781799898122

*Request More Information, or Recommend the IGI Global e-Book Collection to Your Institution's Librarian*

**For More Information or to Request a Free Trial, Contact IGI Global's e-Collections Team:** eresources@igi-global.com | 1-866-342-6657 ext. 100 | 717-533-8845 ext. 100

www.ingramcontent.com/pod-product-compliance
Lightning Source LLC
LaVergne TN
LVHW080620300926
849162LV00005B/1215
* 9 7 8 1 6 6 8 4 8 8 2 2 5 *